## THE BEST, WORST & MOST UNUSUAL

# THE BEST,
# WORST
# AND
# MOST UNUSUAL

## *Noteworthy Achievements, Events, Feats and Blunders of Every Conceivable Kind*

Bruce Felton & Mark Fowler

*Galahad Books • New York*

# Contents

# PART I

*To Judy and to Jessica*

# Acknowledgments

Special thanks to Laurence Ogden Booth, Judith Felton, Jessica Kaplan, and Richard Schickel for their assistance in the writing of this book.

Information House wishes to thank the following persons for their assistance in the compilation and development of this book: Pat Fogarty, Joyce Shue, Peggy Bedoya, Sheila Arnott, Irit Spierer, Anne Columbia, Nancy Doyne, Art Springer and Buddy Skydell.

# Introduction

*It is a very sad thing that
nowadays there is so little
useless information.*

—OSCAR WILDE

Critics, by definition, are not reticent. They are paid not to be squeamish about saying precisely what they feel is wrong—or right—about a string quartet, a Broadway musical, or a new film, and rarely are they reluctant to antagonize their readers if their art demands that they do so.

But it's a rare reviewer who will go so far as to categorize a work of art as the absolute best or worst in its field. That, however, is precisely what we've been presumptuous enough to do in *Felton & Fowler's Best, Worst, and Most Unusual,* a miscellany of the outrageous in which we've assembled the opinions of experts in an improbably broad range of disciplines, from Beethoven on the best composer ever (Handel) to Dwight D. Eisenhower on the best movie ever made (*Angels in the Outfield*). Moreover, we've made incursions deep into exotic and unlikely regions—such as politics, religion, and psychology—where reviewers don't normally tread. The fact is, critics in the past have generally had the good sense to restrict their opinions to the field of the arts. Indeed, there is ample artistic criticism here, including notes on the best "Eggplant-That-Ate-Cleveland" film ever made, the worst love scene in literature, and the most unusual composer of all time.

But suppose, for just one moment, that you needed some solid, no-nonsense advice on where to find the best muktuk? Or the world's worst seafood dinner? We humbly suggest that you might check with *Felton & Fowler's Best, Worst, and Most Unusual.*

Like that seafood dinner—or the world's most unusual cheese—this book is meant to be nibbled at in moderation; not swallowed whole. And despite its chapter-by-chapter progression from one discipline to the next, feel free to flip open the book at random wherever you might happen to be—on the beach, in a stalled subway, in the bathroom—and jump haphazardly from chapter to chapter according to your mood or interest.

In the midst of this jumping, the reader will also be required to make an occasional leap of faith. While reading about the most unusual beard or the worst musical instrument, you may mumble discontentedly, "Do they really expect me to believe that?" Our answer is yes—for the most part. All the facts and anecdotes we have collected are based on published nonfiction accounts purporting to tell the unexaggerated truth. As to the veracity of our sources, *Newsweek*, Plutarch, Will Durant, and *The New York Times* aren't vouching for us, and we aren't vouching for them.

The judgments offered in this book are both subjective and objective, rational and hysterical, serious and sardonic. In assessing their validity, you should bear in mind the words of Leonardo da Vinci: "I take no more notice of the wind that comes out of the mouths of critics than of the wind expelled from their backsides."

If you find yourself standing up and cheering at things that should have been said long, long ago, fine. But if, on the other hand, the claims made here offend you or strike you as arrogant—if, in fact, you find the very idea of a book of bests, worsts, and oddests preposterous, you're in good company: Film critics Rex Reed and Robert Hatch, for example, told us that the very idea of such a book is "pretentious" (Reed) and "dumb" (Hatch).

And novelist Leon Uris was even more blunt. "It's the worst idea for a book I've ever heard," he wrote us. He's probably off. There have been other books written that are unquestionably worse than this one. You'll find them described in the literature section of *Felton & Fowler's Best, Worst, and Most Unusual.*

# Contents

# Fine Arts

**Best Art Forger:** Han van Meegeren was a good painter in his own right, but he soon discovered that painting fake Vermeers was more lucrative than painting authentic van Meegerens. Unlike hack forgers, he did not copy existing works. Instead, he painted completely new works in Vermeer's style, even inventing a nonexistent middle period. Van Meegeren's first Vermeer was *Christ at Emmaus*, which was not only accepted as an original but was even hailed as a masterpiece by the critics. It was worth $250,000 to the previously impoverished painter.

During the Nazi occupation of the Netherlands, van Meegeren painted and sold five more Vermeers of the middle period; one, *Christ and the Adulteress*, was bought by Hermann Goering. This was van Meegeren's downfall. After the war, Dutch officials began to search for the collaborators who had sold the Dutch masterpiece to the Nazis, and the trail led directly to van Meegeren. Faced with a charge of treason, van Meegeren confessed his forgery; the experts laughed. Even when he explained how he had baked the paintings in the oven to reproduce the "seventeenth-century" cracks, they doubted his claim. Finally, to convince the courts and the world that he could indeed imitate the master, he undertook to paint still another Vermeer—*Christ Amongst the Doctors*.

Faced with the emergence of a new Vermeer right before their eyes, and faced with the evidence of a new X-ray technique, which proved that van Meegeren had painted all the masterpieces he claimed, the experts had to eat crow. Van Meegeren was exonerated of treason, but was sentenced to one year in jail for forging Vermeer's signature. Exhausted from the trial, the great forger died before he could be imprisoned.

**Worst Art Collection:** Are all the great religious artists of the world dead? The question is raised because, in the summer of 1974, when the Vatican decided to establish a minimuseum of twentieth-century religious art, the best they could come up with was a 542-item collection that is, in the words of *Time* magazine art critic Robert Hughes, "an aesthetic swamp." The Botticellis, the Michelangelos, the Raphaels are not among the 250 artists included in this sampling. Instead, there are endless rows of "weak, vulgar bronzes of recent pontiffs" that have all the charm of an outsized, tarnished Lincoln-head penny. And, out of an apparent dearth of genuinely religiously motivated art, there is a strange abundance of inane landscapes whose only claim to religiosity is a church steeple tucked in the corner.

None of this is terribly surprising, however, since the Vatican has let it be known that it will cut corners wherever possible in stocking and maintaining the museum and depend primarily on the gifts of artists and collectors rather than its own purchases. Says Hughes, the collection "will probably remain more of a curiosity than a museum: an embarrassing document of religion's inability in recent years to provoke aesthetic responses."

**Worst Drawing:** *Le Remède* by Antoine Watteau depicts a reclining Venus about to receive an enema administered by her chambermaid.

**Worst Painting:** There are plentiful examples of artistic incompetence melded exquisitely with thematic ignorance. An unnamed Dutch painter depicted the sacrifice of Isaac, with Abraham holding a loaded blunderbuss to his son's head. The German painter Berlin painted a Madonna and Child, with the subjects being serenaded by a violinist. In a Last Supper scene, painted by a French artist, the table has been set with cigar lighters. Another Frenchman painted Adam and Eve in Eden, fig-leafed and innocent, with a fully dressed hunter nearby pursuing ducks with a shotgun.

**Worst Sculpture (European):** *The Fountain of Bacchino*, found in the Boboli Garden behind the Pitti Palace, in Florence, Italy. Bacchino was the court dwarf of Cosimo I, an obscure Florentine potentate in the sixteenth century who commissioned the minor sculptor Niccolo Pericoli to design the garden and create the sculpture.

Watteau, *Le Remède*

For out-and-out bad taste, the monument to Enrico Toti, the legless hero of the Austrian invasions into Italy in the nineteenth century, is a rival to *The Fountain of Bacchino.*

**Worst Sculpture (World):** A series of war dead memorials commissioned throughout the 1950s and 1960s by the American Battle Monuments Commission is, according to former *Times* art critic John Canaday, the world's worst sculpture. "If our military tactics had paralleled the absurdity with which the National Sculpture Society has memorialized our battles," he writes, "the G.I.'s would have landed on the beaches in rowboats and wearing hoop skirts. These memorials do not say 'Remember.' They do not even say 'Forget.'"

**Most Unusual Art Critic:** Paul Cezanne acquired a bright green parrot of excellent voice, which he taught to repeat one phrase over and over again: "Cezanne is a great painter!"

**Most Unusual Conceptual Art:** We could single out *one* work of conceptual art as the most unusual ever created, but as Richard Nixon might have said, it would be wrong. We'll offer several, then, and let you judge for yourself:

Californian Chris Burden had himself crucified on the roof of a

The Fountain of Bacchino

Volkswagen; real nails were used and they were driven through his palms. He's also had himself filmed crawling on his naked stomach across a Los Angeles parking lot littered with broken glass.

Austrian artist Rudolf Schwarzkogler began cutting away at his penis with a knife, piece by piece, in the name of art. (He ultimately bled to death.)

Vito Acconci, who has exhibited—in more than one sense—at the Sonnabend Gallery, in New York, masturbated under a ramp over which the visitors walked. He has also dressed his penis in doll's clothing and, in yet another opus, bit himself all over his body.

**Most Unusual Display of a Painting:** *Le Bateau,* painted by Henri Matisse, was exhibited upside down in the Museum of Modern Art, New York City, for forty-seven days in 1961. Over 100,000 people had seen the painting before anybody noticed.

**Most Unusual Painting:** After touring the Mississippi River for years and making thousands of sketches, John Banvard began

War Dead Memorials
   (Top left) Airman, Cambridge, England
   (Top right) Normandy WW II cemetery and memorial, Calvados,
   France
   (Bottom left) Honolulu WW II and Korea memorial, Honolulu, Hawaii
   (Bottom right) East Coast WW II memorial, Battery Park, New York
   City

work on the most colossal landscape ever painted. He covered nearly three miles of canvas with a panorama of some 1,200 miles of the Mississippi shoreline.

First displayed in Louisville, Kentucky, in 1845, Banvard's panorama was exhibited like a giant scroll rolled from one huge spindle to another. Soon it was drawing hundreds of spectators each day, and Banvard, who made a pretty penny on admissions, took his work on tour throughout the United States and England. From all accounts, it was not a particularly good painting, but people enjoyed watching the countryside wind by, anticipating such highlights as Cairo, Illinois, and Memphis, Tennessee.

Detractors disputed that Banvard's panorama was a full three miles long, though no one doubted that it was at least a mile in length. Upon his death, the work was cut into sections, and, for many years, parts of it were used as backdrops in South Dakota theaters.

**Most Unusual Painting Technique:** The ancient Egyptians embalmed their dead in asphaltum, a preservative which makes an excellent base for paint, especially when aged. In recent centuries, Egyptians have taken to exhuming mummies and grinding them to dust to produce the paint which is so greatly prized among discriminating artists.

**Most Unusual Photograph:** Chris Burden arranged to have himself shot by a friend with a Winchester .22 while a third participant recorded the experience in a sequence of photographs. Burden's intention had been only to be grazed but the marksman had an off-day and Burden wound up in the hospital with a nasty gunshot wound in his left arm. In any event, he sold the pictures, along with several others, to a New York art dealer for $1,750.

**Most Unusual Sculpture:** *Mierda d'Artista,* consisting, as one would suspect, of several cans of the artist's feces. The artist in this case is Piero Mangoni, of Milan.

If we stretch the word "sculpture" just a bit beyond its conventional definition, we might also include, as runner-up, the work of Swiss artist Michael Heizer. The main event of an exhibition of his works consisted of the artist using a house-wrecking machine to demolish the asphalt in front of the Berne, Switzerland, museum where the show was held.

Incidentally, ice cream magnate Louis Sherry commissioned

sculptor John Bertolini to do a bust of then President Richard Nixon in ice cream in 1970. Sherry had difficulty marketing the work and it was ultimately relegated to storage in a freezer vault in Brooklyn. And Nixon's wife Pat had her likeness done in macaroni in 1971 when she was voted Macaroni Woman of the Year by the American Macaroni Institute.

# Literature and Language

**Best Dictionary:** The Compact Edition of the *Oxford English Dictionary*, published in 1972. Through a miracle of modern-day printing technology, the thirteen volumes of the OED have been condensed into two. (The miracle part is that four pages of the original edition are reproduced on each page of the condensed version. This could make for a lot of squinting, but a high-quality reading magnifier is included with each set.) For under $100 you can purchase a dictionary that is vastly cheaper than the original, normally priced over $300, and actually easier to use. The OED's monumental ninety-one-page bibliography, citing the works of Shakespeare, Hillaire Belloc, and Sir Thomas Bastard (author of a 1598 anthology of epigrams), is reproduced in full. The real value of the OED is in the elaborate etymologies provided for each word.

**Best Library in the World:** The best library in the world, from the scholarly researcher's point of view, is the British Museum. (See also *Best Museum in the World*.) There are over six million printed volumes in the British Museum's collection and an additional sixty thousand unpublished manuscripts, including the Codex Alexandrinus and the Codex Sinaiticus, and the world's most extensive collection of Greek papyri from Egypt.

The Bibliotheque Nationale, in Paris, also stocked with six million volumes, is a similarly great library, although its holdings are not quite so varied as those of the British Museum.

**Best Mystery Writer:** Ross Macdonald. The highest praise one can bestow upon a writer of mystery novels is to call him an artist rather than a hack, and, as former *Newsweek* critic R. A. Sokolov

The Compact Edition of
the *Oxford English Dictionary*

has noted, Macdonald "has reached a breakthrough into the charmed circle of detective novelists who have been accepted as literary artists." The best of his Lew Archer novels—which *The New York Times* calls "the finest series of detective novels ever written by an American"—is probably *The Underground Man* (1971). A murder and kidnapping set against a devastating brush fire in southern California are the key elements in what may well be one of the best mystery novels ever written.

**Best Novel of All Time:** *War and Peace.* It took Leo Tolstoy six years to write *War and Peace,* less time, perhaps, than most people need to read this monolithic novel peopled with over 500 characters. It is the story of the intertwining fates of several Russian families set against the background of Napoleon's invasion of Russia from 1805–1820.

Tolstoy led a troubled life almost from birth (his family and friends nicknamed him Crybaby Leo) and he fought continually with his wife, finally leaving her at the age of eighty-two when they argued bitterly over his intention of dividing up all their property among their servants. In 1910, accompanied by his

Count Leo Tolstoy

daughter, he left home, caught pneumonia, and died in a railway station.

**Best Novel (American):** *Moby Dick.* Herman Melville was an unknown when he wrote *Moby Dick* in 1851, and he died an unknown in 1891. Those who had heard of him knew him only as the man who had lived among cannibals in the South Seas (which he had, in his earlier years, collecting material for the books that made him famous after his death. He learned a lot about whales then, enough to note in an introduction to his great novel that "the breath of the whale is frequently attended with such an insupportable smell as to bring on a disorder of the brain").

In the 1920s, Melville's ghost was reawakened and he was recognized, at long last, for the genius he was. Since then, his sprawling novel of Captain Ahab's obsessive pursuit of the great white whale "has come to be regarded as the most eminent American novel," according to Max J. Herzberg. William Rose Benét called it "one of the greatest novels . . . in the literature of the world."

Herman Melville

**Best Novel (English):** *Great Expectations*. Dickens was the favorite of many of the world's greatest writers, including Tolstoy and Dostoevsky, and Pip's story, told with peerless grace and poignancy, is easily the best of his work, free of the improbable coincidences and awkward plot contrivances that marred much of his earlier work. In 1955, sixteen of France's most noted intellectuals, including François Mauriac and André Maurois, were asked to select the twelve greatest non-French works of fiction for a special series to be published by the French state press. As the greatest novels of all time they chose *War and Peace*—and *Great Expectations*.

**Best Novel (French):** Some say Flaubert's *Madame Bovary*, others favor *The Red and the Black* by Stendhal, but it would be unfair to rate either of them higher than *Remembrance of Things Past*, the sixteen-volume novel that was the life's work of Marcel Proust and which Somerset Maugham has called "the greatest novel of the 20th century." Says Clifton Fadiman, "For some this is the greatest novel in the world. For others it is unreadable."

In any event, Proust's fame rests almost entirely on this epic of introspection, and its sixteen volumes—the most famous of which is *Swann's Way*—were brought out between 1913 and 1928. Col-

Charles Dickens

lectively, they describe through the eyes of Marcel, the first-person narrator, the lives of three families—the aristocratic Guermantes, the middle-class Swanns, and the vulgar nouveau riche Verdurins. Their fortunes are played out against a background of salons, cafes, soirees, and indiscretions, and always there is Proust's obsessive attention to detail and introspection. He spends pages on the manifold ramifications of a cup of tea.

Proust was sickly, asthmatic, and neurotic, and spent most of his waking hours in bed, swaddled in scarves, gloves, and blankets, writing frenetically, his room lined with cork to keep out noise. His windows were always tightly shut, even during the most sweltering Parisian summer days. Visitors to his room were choked with the smell of inhalants.

**Best Novel (German):** *The Magic Mountain.* Thomas Mann's masterpiece, along with those of Proust, Joyce, Tolstoy, and Melville, seems to bear out the connection between high quality and literary indigestibility. Frank Donald Hirschback wrote of it that "it bids fair to join the list of immortal works of world literature which people bring back from their summer vacations—unread." But it's worth the effort.

Written in 1927, it is the story of Hans Castorp, a young German engineer who visits a cousin recovering from tuberculosis in a sanitarium in the Swiss Alps and is himself infected and forced to take up lodging there. He remains in the diseased atmosphere of Haus Berghof for seven years, and his experience there is a comment on the root of evil in western civilization. Mann won a Nobel Prize in 1929, and later took up residence and citizenship in the United States. He died in 1955.

**Best Novel about Baseball:** *The Universal Baseball Association, J. Henry Waugh, Proprietor* by Robert Coover. We might also have chosen *The Natural*, by Bernard Malamud, or Ring Lardner's *You Know Me, Al*. In both, as in Coover's 1968 masterpiece, the game itself is of secondary importance. But we'll go with Coover, whose novel, for its originality and depth, is really without peer. J. Henry Waugh is a bank teller whose one consuming passion in life is playing—by himself—a tabletop baseball game he's invented. The meticulous record books he's kept compulsively over the years are peopled with ballplayers of his own invention, and to Waugh, they mean more than life itself. Says critic Wilfrid Sheed, *The UBA* "is the finest book to date about baseball in an admittedly thin field. But not to read it because you don't like baseball is like not reading Balzac because you don't like boarding houses."

**Best Novel About World War II:** *The Naked and the Dead.* Norman Mailer fans are split into two camps: Those who favor his later work and those who think he never did better than *The Naked and the Dead*. But few feel there has ever been a better novel of World War II. David Dempsey of *The New York Times* wrote that *The Naked and the Dead* "is undoubtedly the most ambitious novel to be written about the recent conflict," when it came out in 1948, and that "in scope and integrity it compares favorably with the best that followed World War I." C. J. Rolo of *The Atlantic* called it "by far the most impressive piece of fiction to date about Americans in the Second World War." Other novels with a World War II setting that are rated highly are *The Young Lions*, by Irwin Shaw, and James Jones's *From Here to Eternity*.

**Best Novel of Postwar America:** *Invisible Man.* Ralph Ellison's magnum opus (not to be confused with H. G. Wells's novel of the same name, which science fiction pundit John Baxter calls "the best novel ever written about invisibility"), written in 1952, was voted best novel of the postwar era in a poll of 200 noted American writers, editors, and literary critics conducted by *Book Week* magazine in 1965. It's a novel, says critic Alfred Kazin, "that has proved the most believable of the many current novels of the embattled self's journey through an American reality defined as inherently absurd." And, we think, Ellison ranks as the best of the black American novelists, outclassing James Baldwin and Richard Wright.

**Best Novel (American) of the 1970s:** *Gravity's Rainbow.* Thomas Pynchon's massive (760 pages) third novel touched off something akin to a vast, sustained universal orgasm of praise among the nation's literary critics. "If I were banished to the moon tomorrow and could take only five books along," Christopher Lehmann-Haupt of *The New York Times* rhapsodized, "this book would have to be one of them." And Bruce Allen of *The Library Journal* noted that *Rainbow* was his choice for "the most important work of fiction produced by any living writer." At the kernel of the book's labyrinthine—and at times almost impossibly intricate—plot is the development of the V-2 rocket during, and just after, World War II. But the story line takes off into distant realms far removed from, but somehow ultimately connected to, rocketry: sex, wartime London, parapsychology, obscene limericks, psychohistory, and eastern religions.

**Best Novel (American) of the Twentieth Century:** *The Sun Also Rises.* This is the novel Ernest Hemingway himself was most pleased with, the one many critics today regard even more highly than *The Great Gatsby* and *Light in August.* Written in 1926, *The Sun Also Rises* is the novel that captured better than any other work of the period the spirit of the Lost Generation, as it focuses on a group of American expatriots living in Paris. The persona is Jake Barnes, an impotent journalist hopelessly in love with Lady Brett Ashley, who eventually falls in love with a young Spanish bullfighter. The prose is spare and lean and almost parodies itself at certain points.

**Best Novel (English) of the Twentieth Century:** *Ulysses.* "With *The Magic Mountain* and *Remembrance of Things Past, Ulysses* is ranked as one of the greatest novels of the 20th century and also one of the greatest novels of all time," notes William Rose Benét, whose prose is incomparably more explicit than Joyce's: "Avowal,

*Sonnez.* I could. Rebound of garter. Not leave thee. Smack. *La cloche!* Thigh smack. Avowal Warm. Sweetheart, goodbye!

"Jingle. Bloo."

*Ulysses* is the greatest of the stream-of-consciousness novels, an epic description of a single day—June 16, 1904—in the life of three Dubliners, Leopold and Molly Bloom and Stephen Dedalus. Joyce establishes a parallel between the events in Dublin and those in Homer's *Odyssey,* with Molly the counterpart of Penelope, Bloom the counterpart of Ulysses, and Stephen the counterpart of Telemachus. He uses a variety of techniques, including newspaper headline montage, questions and answers, play dialogue, puns, parodies of literary styles, and free association. All of it is sprinkled throughout with a sufficiently heady dose of explicit language to have kept the book banned from the United States for fourteen years until 1934.

**Best Novel of the West:** *The Ox-Bow Incident,* by Walter van Tilburg Clark. A good novel if not a great one, *Ox-Bow* is the story of a lynching, and it's done with compassion and insight—qualities you rarely see in the westerns. (The movie, starring Henry Fonda and Dana Andrews, does justice to the book.) The same praise can be accorded Bret Harte's classic short story of enforced exile, *The Outcasts of Poker Flat,* which is better than any full-length western novel ever written, with the possible exception of *Ox-Bow.* Dissenting opinion: Robert Benton and David Newman call Zane Grey's *Riders of the Purple Sage* "the best of the West." Perhaps. In any event, it's certainly the best novel of *any* genre ever penned by a minor league center fielder (which Grey was. Yes, he was.).

**Best Novelist (American) of the Twentieth Century:** William Faulkner. *The Saturday Review* was "astonished," by its own admission, at the unanimity with which America's major literary spokesmen selected Faulkner as the best novelist of the century. Typical of their comments was this statement by novelist Bernard Malamud: *"The Sound and the Fury, As I Lay Dying, Light in August,* and *Absalom, Absalom!*—these four novels, written in less than ten years, are the work of a great writer, no matter how frail or frenetic the 'vessel.' "

**Best Novella:** *Metamorphosis.* If we accept E. M. Forster's dictum that anything over 50,000 words is a novel and anything shorter—but longer than a short story—is a novella, then Franz Kafka's *Metamorphosis,* written in 1916, is the best yet written, according to the sixteen-member panel who voted in France in 1955 to select the cream of non-French writing. Kafka's story tells of Gregor Samsa, the man who awoke one morning to find that he had turned into a monstrous vermin.

We might also consider *The Old Man and the Sea* which, if it is a novella and not a full-blown novel, is on a par with Kafka. Largely on the basis of this book, Hemingway won the Nobel Prize for Literature in 1954.

**Best Poet (American) of the Twentieth Century:** Robert Frost. For Alfred Kazin, it's actually a toss-up between Frost and Wallace Stevens (who sometimes jotted poetic notes to himself on his shirt cuffs while commuting to work at the Hartford Accident and Indemnity Company). While we'll stick with Frost, you might also consider stuffy old T. S. Eliot, of whom Leon Edel says, "He was the supreme case of 'a man of letters.' " There is also Ezra Pound, crazy as a hoot but brilliant beyond description. Indeed, the *best single poem of the twentieth century*—in any language—is either the collected *Cantos* of Pound, or Eliot's *The Waste Land.*

---

**Worst Book:** Ordinarily a book would have to endure the test of time and be subjected to decades of critical scorn in order to earn the epithet *the worst.* But in preparing this manuscript we have received some advance assessments suggesting that the appearance of *Felton & Fowler's Best, Worst, and Most Unusual* marks the darkest day in publishing history. For example, we contacted novelist Leon Uris as part of our research to solicit his opinions on the superior, inferior, and bizarre in literature. In his reply, Mr. Uris states emphatically, "I think your idea is disgusting. . . . This is the worst idea for a book I've ever heard."

In all modesty we suggest that you may now be reading *the* worst book, but for the final judgment we will have to await the opinions of those who, in contrast to the above-mentioned reviewers, have actually read the work.

**Worst Children's Book:** In colonial times, children were treated to a rich panoply of books, stories, and poems about the death of infants. The message was always the same: In the eyes of God, the death of a sinless child is as blessed an event as his birth. This tradition in children's literature continued to bear fruit well into the nineteenth century, and is highlighted by such titles as *A Legacy for Children; Being Some of the Last Expressions and Dying Sayings of Hannah Hill . . . Aged Eleven and Near Three Months; Christian Character Exemplified in the Life of Adeline Marble, Corresponding Secretary of the Female Juvenile Mite Society of New Haven, who Died May the 3d, 1882;* and George Headley's *A Memorial for Children, Being an Authentic Account of the Conversion, Experience and Happy Deaths of Eighteen Children.* The worst, in terms of the horror which it struck into the hearts of the young—a gauge, in those days, of its value—was *A Token for Children, being an Exact Account of the Conversion, Holy and Exemplary Lives and Joyous Deaths of Several Young Children.* Typical of its hellfire-and-brimstone admonitions were these lines: "My days will quickly end, and I must lie/Broyling in flames to All Eternity."

The American poet Julia A. Moore (see *Worst Poet [Female]*) was concerned with the moral upbringing of children. In an 1878 collection of her verse entitled *A Few Choice Words to the Public and New and Original Poems* she waxes lugubrious over the fate of Little Libbie: "While eating dinner, this dear little child/Choked on a piece of beef." Unspeakable.

As for something a bit more of this world, an early geography text, written in 1784 by Jedidiah Morse, was as stuffy and pedantic when the first of its nineteen editions was published as it would be if it were in use today. It's called *Geography Made Easy*, but the goal implied in the title is thwarted by the presence of only one map of the United States in the entire text—and that one is just a few inches square. The book is peppered with pious homilies on the virtues of learning and model dialogues for student and master (mostly student): "I am very thankful, sir, for your entertaining instruction, and I shall never forget what you have been telling me. I long, sir, for tomorrow to come that I may hear more of your information."

**Worst History Book:** *History of America in Rhyme*, written in 1882 by Major Frederick Howe. Historic events and the concept of history taken more broadly have inspired some of the world's greatest poetry (including much of Shakespeare's work). But there is a school of poets—happily limited—who have tried to bring off a systematic history of the world in verse. It doesn't work, and

Major Howe's opus is about the worst. As Walter Hart Blumenthal writes, "The Major may have been a good soldier, but as a versifier his spurs were on his tongue."

Another favorite is Adrian Hill's 381-page epic, *The Grant Poem, Containing Grant's Public Career and Private Life from the Cradle to the Grave,* published in 1886.

A third choice might be *The Tempter of Eve,* by Charles Carroll, a history of mankind from antediluvian times to 1902, the year the book was published in Saint Louis. *The Tempter of Eve* is pious, hysterical, and badly written. Carroll's main contention is that the black races, having descended from the apes (as the white races have not), are most decidedly inferior and ought to be carefully suppressed—religiously, socially, and politically.

**Worst Literary Critic:** Delia Bacon, author of *The Philosophy of the Plays of Shakespeare Unfolded.* A frustrated New England spinster, Miss Bacon became possessed by the notion that Shakespeare was a clod, and an illiterate clod at that, and that he could not possibly have written a laundry list, much less the thirty-seven plays commonly attributed to him. She thus made it her life's work to expose him and prove her thesis that the Bard's works were actually written by Sir Francis Bacon (no relation), assisted by Sir Walter Raleigh, Sir Philip Sidney, Lord Buckhurst, Lord Paget, and the Earl of Oxford.

In 1857 she published her book, which stated in 700 pages of garbled prose that the thirty-seven plays had been written over a relatively short period of time and that it had been the purpose of those involved in their writing to educate the masses. When the plays were ready to be performed, she claimed, Ben Jonson acted as public relations man, introducing them to a gullible public. Beyond the lunacy with which her views are saturated, her prose is all but indecipherable, and reading it is very much like slogging waist-deep through a sea of sludge. Says Irving Wallace in his book, *The Square Pegs,* "To be trapped in mid-page was like being caught in an armed riot."

Miss Bacon was attacked as a lunatic by her contemporaries, and to some extent they were borne out: The year after her book was published, she died in an insane asylum.

**Worst Love Scene in Literature:** In *Justine,* by the Marquis de Sade, a passionate kiss between two lovers with a penchant for the bizarre makes for what may well be the most tasteless and repulsive love scene in all literature. Before they embrace, our hero thrusts his finger down his throat as far as it will go, touching off the antiperistaltic muscles that cause him to vomit. He immediately covers his lover's mouth with his own, upchucking the semidigested contents of his stomach into *her* mouth. Our heroine, it goes without saying, immediately responds in kind, whereupon he bounces it all back at her again. Their mouths never come unglued and this alimentary tennis volley continues for a few minutes until our lover and his lass collapse exhausted in the muck.

**Worst Memoir:** *Sordid Amok!* is a 1901 work by the French madwoman Clarin de Breujere, whose prose is as incoherent as the title. In it she chronicles six months spent in a Paris insane asylum. She writes, "Human beings, looking out over the entire expanse encompassing all the marvels of the science and the Genius of Civilizations, Ancient and Modern, are still unable even to make an 'Eyelash,' which carries in itself its own inherent mystery of extension." Her motto, emblazoned on a coat-of-arms which she designed for herself, was "My Rights or I Bite."

**Worst Nonfiction Book:** *Euthanasia: The Aesthetics of Suicide* by Baron Harden-Hickey, the self-styled American founder of Trinidad. Harden-Hickey's treatise on the noble art of ending it all was published in 1894 by the Truth Seeker Company, an antireligious society and publishing house that has also offered such works as *What Would Christ Do about Syphilis?* In presenting his book to a world-weary public, the baron assembled some 400 quotations from the world's greatest thinkers, claiming only to have written the preface. (He lied: Most of the quotes were spurious.) The Baron offers some splendid methods of dispatching oneself in style—he is partial to drugs, poison, and scissors—and his book is illustrated with pen-and-ink drawings. One shows a well-dressed dandy in his throes, a drained tumbler of poison beside him. Another shows a fully dressed man sitting contemplatively on the edge of his bed, holding a pistol to his head. "May this little work contribute to the overthrow of the reign of fear!" Harden-Hickey writes. "May it nerve the faltering arm of the poor wretch to whom life is loathsome. . . . Let him calmly, without anger or joy, but with the utmost indifference, cast off the burden of existence. . . . The only radical remedy for a life of misery is death; if you are tired and weary, if you are the victim of disease or misfortune, drop the burden of life, fly away!" The baron dropped his own burden in 1898 with the aid of an overdose of morphine.

**Worst Novel of Postwar America:** *Peyton Place.* Grace Metalious's tale of love among the patios was called by Stanley Kauffmann the work of a fifth-rate talent working at peak capacity. *Esquire* called it "a novel so rotten and yet so horny that every reader stayed until the finish." Worst line: " 'Hurry,' she moaned, 'Hurry, hurry.' "

**Worst Novelist (English) of the Twentieth Century:** Eden Phillpotts. "Eden Phillpotts," wrote H. L. Mencken in a 1923 article in *Vanity Fair,* "seems to me to be the worst novelist now in practice in England." Phillpotts's interminable tales of life in Dartmoor have been compared to the Wessex novels of Thomas Hardy, but that seems altogether blasphemous and not at all fair to Hardy. Phillpotts wrote plays as well as novels and several mysteries under the pseudonym of Harrington Hext. His was a singularly versatile dullness, and he could bore you to death a dozen different ways. *The Treasures of Typhon,* a 1924 work, prompted these remarks from a New York *Tribune* reviewer: "Under the guise of conjuring up the flavor of antiquity, Mr. Phillpotts talks very much like our old friend Polonius. He not only talks very much like our old friend Polonius, but he talks very much."

**Worst Poem Ever Written:** There is an embarrassment of riches to be found in *The Stuffed Owl,* a 1930 anthology of bad verse edited by Wyndham Lewis, but the worst, the absolute schlock bottom, may well be "Catastrophe," by the nineteenth-century English poet Cornelius Whur. Whur's inspiration for these deathless lines was a young artist born without arms who supported his parents and himself through his painting:

> "Alas! Alas!" the father said,
>     "O what a dispensation!
> How can we be by mercy led,
>     In such a situation?
> Be not surprised at my alarms,
>     The dearest boy is without arms.
>
> "I have no hope, no confidence,
>     The scene around is dreary.
> How can I meet such vast expense?
>     I am by trying weary.
> You must, my dearest, plainly see
>     This armless boy will ruin me."

The works of two other nineteenth-century wordsmiths rate an honorable mention at the very least. Conceivably, you may regard them as vastly inferior to "Catastrophe" and thus more worthy of the "worst" designation. First, there is Erasmus Darwin, grandfather of Charles, and poetically obsessed with the wonders of nature as evidenced by such titles as "The Loves of the Plants" and "The Birth of $KNO_3$." Two of his individual poems bear special mention:

"Ae Fond Kiss, and Then—"

So still the Tadpole cleaves the watery vale,
With balanc'd fins and undulating tail;
New lungs and limbs proclaim his second birth,
Breathe the dry air, and bound upon the earth.
Allied to fish, the Lizard cleaves the flood,
With one-cell'd heart, and dark frigescent blood;
Half-reasoning Beavers long-unbreathing dart,
Through Eirie's waves with perforated heart;
With gills and lungs respiring lampreys steer,
Kiss the rude rocks and suck till they adhere;
With gills pulmonic breathes th' enormous Whale,
And sprouts aquatic columns to the Gale.

"The Maiden Truffle"

So the lone Truffle, lodged beneath the earth,
Shoots from paternal roots the tuberous birth.
No stamen-males ascend, and breathe above,
No seed-born offspring lives by female love.
. . . Unknown to sex the pregnant oyster swells,
And coral-insects build their radiate shells.

Robert Southey, a favorite target of Lewis Carroll and Alexander Pope, was the progenitor of some exquisitely wretched verse, of which "The Early Call" is a simply magnificent example:

By that lake whose gloomy shore
Skylark never warbles o'er,
Where the cliff hangs high and steep,
Young St. Kevin stole to sleep.
"Here at Last," he calmly said,
"Woman ne'er shall find my bed."
Oh! the good saint little knew
What the wily sex can do.
Even now while calm he sleeps

Kathleen o'er him leans and weeps.
Fearless she had tracked his feet
To this rocky wild retreat;
And when morning met his view,
Her mild glances met it too.
Ah! your Saints have cruel hearts!
Sternly from his bed he starts,
And with crude, repulsive shock,
Hurls her from the beetling rock.

**Worst Poet (American) of the Twentieth Century:**  Edgar A. Guest, the most telling criticism of whom is this anonymously penned rhymed couplet:

I'd rather fail my Wassermann Test
Than read the poems of Edgar Guest.

His work is consistently mawkish and treacly, his insights bland and repetitious. Guest's worst poem may well be "Home":

It takes a heap o' living in a house t'make it home,
A heap o' sun an' shadder, an' ye sometimes have t'roam
Afore ye really 'preciate the things ye lef' behind,
An hunger fer 'em somehow, with 'em allus on yer mind.
It don't make any difference how rich ye get t'be,
How much yer chairs an' tables cost, how great yer luxury;
It ain't home t'ye, though it be the palace of a king,
Until somehow yer soul is sort o' wrapped round everything. . . .

**Worst Poet (Female):**  Mrs. Julia A. Moore—"the Sweet Singer of Michigan" to her admirers—was partial to war and patriotism, but utterly enchanted by death and disease. In these stanzas from "The Brave Page Boys," she fused them all:

Enos Page the youngest brother—
    His age was fourteen years—
Made five sons in one family
    Went from Grand Rapids here.
In Eight Michigan Cavalry
    This boy he did enlist.
His life was almost despaired of
    On account of numerous fits.

The unutterable mediocrity of Mrs. Moore's work was equaled only by Nancy Luce, who raised chickens on her Martha's Vine-

Walt Whitman

yard farm and wrote poems about them—bad poems full of poor grammar, forced rhymes, and mawkish conceits. And on every egg that she sold, she inscribed in an elegantly cursive hand the name of the bird that produced it.

**Worst Poetry by a Great Poet:** Regardless of Walt Whitman's greater capabilities, he wrote some of the most overblown, extravagantly incoherent poetry ever to see print. Writes Walter Mermon, "That graceless, banal English of his . . . indicates a man without feeling for words, who would not shrink today from the horrible jargon of the follow-up letter of the in-reply-to-your-favor-would-say school of English composition." Contemporary critics of *Leaves of Grass*, Whitman's magnum opus, characterized it as "hexameters bubbling through sewage," and *Song of Myself*, his most famous poem, contains these lines, certainly among the worst American poetry ever published: ". . . a gigantic uvula with imperceptible gesticulations threatens the tubular downward blackness occasionally from which detaching itself bumps clumsily into the throat a meticulous vulgarity. . . ."

**Worst Review:** It was the age of discovery when Sir Thomas More's *Utopia* first appeared, and many critics were duped into believing the well-imagined communist community was a real island. One poor reviewer, a gentleman named Budaeus, went so far as to recommend that missionaries be sent to the newly discovered isle to convert the wise citizenry to Christianity.

**Worst Rhymster:** Neither Julia Moore nor Nancy Luce had a patent on bad grammar and ersatz rhymes—of if they did it was patently ignored by Rev. William Cook of Salem, Massachusetts, who wrote during the mid-1800s. "Indian Corn," which is found in a booklet of poems entitled *Talk about Indians*, which he published in 1873, has a charm all its own:

> Corn, corn, sweet Indian corn,
>     Greenly you grew long ago.
> Indian fields well to adorn,
>     And to parch or grind hah-ho!
> Where shines the summer sun,
> And plied his hoe or plough
>     Blessings to men have you not gone
> Making food of your dough?
>
> In England, in France and Germany
>     At morn, at eve, at noon
> Johnnie-cake and harmony
>     Increase the family boon.

**Worst Slip of the Tongue:** The slipperiest tongue on record belonged to the Reverend William A. Spooner (1844–1930), who was for many years dean of New College, Oxford. Reverend Spooner committed so many verbal blunders that the word "spoonerism" entered the language, meaning the unintentional interchange of the initial sounds of two or more words. For example, Spooner once explained that "It is kisstomary to cuss the bride." On another occasion he remarked that "Work is the curse of the drinking class." Spooner was capable of charging headlong into a sentence and making a half-dozen errors before it was all over. He rebuked one of his students with these immortal words: "You have hissed all my mystery lectures; I saw you fight a liar in the back quad; in fact you have tasted the whole worm." But Spooner's admirers generally agree that his finest error occurred when he referred to the good and elderly Queen Victoria as "the queer old dean."

**Worst Title:** A farce published in the seventeenth century was titled *Chrononhotonthologos, the Most Tragical Tragedy That*

*Ever Was Tragedized by Any Company of Tragedians.* The first
two lines read:

> Aldeborontiphoscophosnio!
> Where left you Chrononhotonthologos?

**Most Unusual Alphabet:** Dr. Alimamed Kurdistani of Azerbaijan,
U.S.S.R., has invented a universal alphabet, combining the characters of all the world's major languages (excluding Chinese). Dr.
Kurdistani's ABC's are now being studied by the United Nations
and other world organizations.

**Most Unusual Bibliography:** A ninety-four-page treatise on the
extermination of fleas, published in 1739 by F. E. Bruckmann,
contains the most extensive bibliography ever prepared on flea-
related literature. Bruckmann's book also features a detailed description of a newly invented "curious flea-trap for the complete
extinction of fleas," which is worn around the neck and captures
its quarry live. The author notes that the captive insects may then
be "dispatched in some way, by murder, drowning, beheading,
hanging or some similar end."

**Most Unusual Dictionary:** Lexicographers in Wales have been
working on a dictionary of the Welsh tongue for over fifty years. As
of 1970 they were up to the letter H.

**Most Unusual Epigram:** Sir William Collingborne was executed
for writing this punful little poem: "The Rat, the Cat, and Lovel
the dog,/Rule all England under the Hog." Of course, he was not
executed merely for bad puns; there was politics involved. In
1484, *Cat*esby, *Rat*cliff, and Lovel were the prime henchmen for
Richard III. Lovel was a popular name for dogs, like Spot or Fido.
And a white boar appeared on Richard's coat of arms. In a number
of productions of Shakespeare's *Richard III*, these words have
been appended and given to a character about to be executed.
(See also *Most Unusual Shakespearean Lines.*)

**Most Unusual Hack Writer:** The hack writer is a Faustian hero, a
character of great psychological complexity, a person who will do
anything for a buck. Prominent in the hack writer hall of fame
(there is no such institution, but there should be) is John Mitford.

Mitford lived in the most trying period for hack writers (1782–1831) when, no matter how versatile you were or how low you stooped, it was difficult to make ends meet and at the same time satisfy your alcoholic habit.

Between binges, John Mitford wrote for religious and pornographic publishers, as well as editing *Scourge*, the *Quizzical Gazette*, and penny-pulp journals in the poorest of taste. While composing his eminently forgettable novel, *Johnny Newcome in the Navy*, Mitford received what was probably the highest salary of his life—a shilling a day. To put his earnings to the best possible use, he slept out-of-doors for the forty-three days he was working on *Johnny Newcome*, eating only two pennies' worth of bread, an onion, and a slice of cheese each day; he spent the rest of his money on gin.

**Most Unusual Letters:** The Simon and Schuster publishing house owns the unusually brief correspondence between Victor Hugo and his publisher. To inquire how the editors liked the manuscript for *Les Miserables*, Hugo composed the following letter, quoted here in its entirety: "?". The publisher responded: "!". Such brevity is all the more remarkable when one considers that *Les Miserables* contains one of the longest sentences in the French language—823 words without a period.

**Most Unusual Library:** In the sixteenth century, a library near Cassel, Westphalia, housed "books" which had no pages and were made of wood. Each "book" was actually a book-sized box, the spine made of the bark of a specific tree and the sides made of slats of polished lumber taken from the tree. Inside the box were samples of leaves, berries, insects, moss, and fruit peculiar to that tree. All the "books" were labeled, naturally, and proportionate in size to the size of the tree which they represented.

**Most Unusual Library Collection:** The British author Delpierre noted in 1860 that there existed at the University of Cambridge library a separate shelf for books written by deranged persons and morons.

**Most Unusual Novel:** The avant-garde writer Juan Luis Castillejo, in an attack against "the tyranny of words we call literature," published a book in 1969 consisting of "several hundred pages printed randomly with the letter 'i'," according to the London

*Times.* Sales were not terribly encouraging and Castillejo did not follow through on his plans to commission several translations.

Also, in 1969, Georges Perec published his novel *La Disparition (The Disappearance)* in which the letter *e* does not appear at all. The letter *e* is the most commonly used letter in French, as it is in English.

An earlier attempt at an *e*-less novel was Ernest Vincent Wright's *Gadsby,* published in Great Britain in 1939. This literary curiosity runs some 50,000 words in length and Wright's prose is surprisingly smooth and straightforward. In fact, the e's are never missed, as one may gather from the following passage:

"Gadsby was walking back from a visit down in Branton Hills' manufacturing district on a Saturday night. A busy day's traffic had had its noisy run; and with not many folks in sight, His Honor got along without having to stop to grasp a hand, or talk; for a Mayor out of City Hall is a shining mark for any politician. And so, coming to Broadway, a booming bass drum and sounds of singing told of a small Salvation Army unit carrying on amidst Broadway's night shopping crowds. Gadsby, walking toward that group, saw a young girl, back towards him, just finishing a long, soulful oration, saying: '. . . and I can say this to you, for I know what I am talking about; for I was brought up *in a pool of liquor!*' "

**Most Unusual Novelist (English):** William Dampier, whose most famous work is *A Memoir of John Carter,* written in 1850. Dampier was a quadriplegic who not only wrote by holding a pen in his mouth but illustrated his books with pen-and-ink drawings in the same way.

**Most Unusual Poem:** "Dentologia: A Poem on the Diseases of the Teeth," written in 1840 by Solyman Brown, a New York dentist. The poem is amply footnoted with advice that is "Practical, Historical, Illustrative and Explanatory," and followed by a list of three hundred qualified dentists throughout the United States.

On a par with "Dentologia" is "Syphilis Sive Morbus Gallicus," or "Syphilis, the French Disease," a book-length poem written in Latin hexameters by the Italian Renaissance poet Girolamo Fracastoro.

Less arcane, but unique in its own right is "The Dream of a Spelling Bee," by Charles C. Bombaugh:

> Menageries where sleuth-hounds caracole,
> Where Jaguar phalanx and phlegmatic gnu

Fright ptarmigan and kestrels cheek by jowl,
  With peewit and precocious cockatoo.

Gaunt seneschals, in crotchety cockades,
  With seine net trawl for porpoise in lagoons;
While scullions gauge erratic escapades
  Of madrepores in water-logged galloons.

Flamboyant triptychs groined with gherkins green,
  In reckless fracas with coquettish bream,
Ecstatic gargoyles, with grotesque chagrin,
  Garnish the gruesome nightmare of my dream!

**Most Unusual Pornography:** On September 30, 1970, the Presidential Commission on Obscenity and Pornography issued its 646-page official report. The twelve-member panel, handpicked by President Nixon, concluded with a recommendation that all sexually explicit films, books, and magazines intended for adults be legalized (a conclusion that the president immediately condemned as morally "bankrupt").

William L. Hamling, a West Coast publisher, abridged the commission's report, added 546 immodest photographs, and distributed it for $12.50, over twice the price of the Government Printing Office's official, unillustrated edition. Within three months Hamling had sold over 100,000 copies; then the law moved in. Hamling was arrested and charged with eleven counts of "pandering to pruriency" for mailing out brochures advertising his version of the commission's finding. He was found guilty, fined $87,000, and sentenced to four years in prison.

**Most Unusual Spoken Sound:** Several tribes of South Africa, among them the Xhosa, speak languages featuring a tongue click. The word Xhosa begins with this sound *(click)ho-tza*, which occurs nowhere else in the world. In Arabic the *l* sound occurs only in the word Allah (God).

**Most Unusual Text:** A book entitled *Liber Passionis Domini Nostri Jesu Christi cum Characteribus Nulla Materia Compositis*, which once belonged to Rudolphus II of Germany, is unique. Each letter was painstakingly and beautifully scissored out of fine vellum and attached to a blue paper backing.

Another rare book, now in the Gutenberg Museum, Mainz, Germany, measures only about an eighth of an inch square. Believed to be the smallest book ever printed with movable type, it contains the Lord's Prayer in seven languages.

Finally, a library in Uppsala, Sweden, holds a translation of the Gospels printed with metal type on purple vellum. The main body of the text is in "ink" of pure silver, and the initial capitals are in gold.

**Most Unusual Translation:** In "The Jabberwock Traced to Its True Source," a paper that appeared in the February 1872 issue of *Macmillan's Magazine,* the Greek scholar Robert Scott claimed, with his tongue fixed immovably in his cheek, that Lewis Carroll's famed masterpiece of nonsense verse is no more than a competent translation of a medieval German ballad called "Der Jammerwoch." To allay suspicions that he was staging a hoax, Scott offered the complete text of the German poem.

Scott's German rendering of "Jabberwocky" is but one of several "translations" that have appeared since the 1855 publication of Carroll's poem in *Through the Looking Glass.*

**Most Unusual Word Origin:** A Mr. Daly, manager of the Dublin Theater, bet a pub pal of his that he could introduce a new word into the language within twenty-four hours. Overnight, Daly hustled around the town chalking the letters Q-U-I-Z in bathrooms and other public places. The next morning, the Dublin citizenry were all asking one another, "What does 'quiz' mean?" Daly won his bet. The probable explanation for the durability of the term is its similarity in sound and meaning to "inquisition."

# Drama

**Best Broadway Musical:** *My Fair Lady* beats out such other topdrawer musicals as *South Pacific* and *Showboat* because, apart from the music and lyrics—which are the wittiest and most tuneful we've ever heard—the book can stand on its own for dramatic value and dialogue. (After all, take away the sound of music from *The Sound of Music* and you're left with a weekday afternoon soap opera. Take away the songs from *My Fair Lady* and you still have *Pygmalion.*) *My Fair Lady*, with music by Alan Jay Lerner and lyrics by Frederick Loewe, opened in New Haven in February 1956 (where it most decidedly did not bomb) and then went on to a run of 2,717 consecutive performances in New York.

**Best Child Actor (Current):** It has been said that the only thing more insufferable than a precocious child is the mother of a precocious child. The fact is, it's a rare child who actually makes a polished or even believable actor, regardless of how talented he may be. One notable exception is Tatum O'Neal, whose single film credit to date—her performance in *Paper Moon*—qualifies her as the best child actor in the business today.

The late Brandon de Wilde was, perhaps, even a better actor, and he was never better than in the 1950 cinematization of Carson McCullers's *Member of the Wedding*, made when he was seven years old. O'Neal and de Wilde seem to be comfortable as children, and therein lies their success. They try neither to imitate adults nor to be overly precious.

For the *best child actor of all time*, it's necessary to turn back to the early years of the nineteenth century. W. H. W. Betty ("Master Betty" as he was known as a child) was born in London in 1791 and made his stage debut in Dublin in 1803. The London aristocracy fought among themselves for tickets to his S.R.O. performances and the lower classes lived for a glimpse of him as he left his dressing room to board his carriage after a matinee. The enthusiasm over his performances—he was said by many to be a better actor than Garrick himself, even in the roles that Garrick had made famous—was widespread and all but hysterical. Within three or four years of his debut, however, the cheering died away and as an adult actor, Betty had a mediocre reputation at best. He retired from the theater at the age of thirty, and died fifty-three years later, on August 24,1874.

**Best Comedy:** *The Prisoner of Second Avenue* doesn't even come close. You'll be closer—right on target, in fact,—if you choose *The Misanthrope,* by Molière. George Brandes called it "the unapproachable masterpiece of the foremost of comic dramatists." Alceste is the hero of the play, a humorless but relentlessly sincere young man desperately in love with the flighty Celimene. Molière played opposite his wife in early performances of the comedy, and there is no question that he injected much of his own passion and anger into the writing and acting of the more heated arguments between the two leads. In real life he suspected, with good cause, that Mme. Molière was unfaithful.

**Best Elizabethan (non-Shakespearean) play:** Figure it this way: Whatever it is, it's got to be something by either Ben Jonson or Christopher Marlowe. If you opt for Jonson—as we do—then it's *The Alchemist,* commonly hailed as his best play and considered by Samuel Taylor Coleridge as one of the three best plays ever written. The action takes place during the London plague of 1610, and the names of the characters—Face, Doll Common, Sir Epicure Mammon, Tribulation Wholesome, and our personal favorite, Dame Pliant—are alone worth the price of admission.

If you favor Marlowe, the choice is likely to be *Edward II,* written in 1590. According to critic Joseph Shipley, Marlowe's characterization of the young Edward III makes for "the best drawn child in the Elizabethan drama." The play was a great favorite of Havelock Ellis.

**Best Play (American) of the Nineteenth Century:** The American dramatic imagination in the nineteenth century could hardly be described as fertile, but one possibility for best play of the century is Frank Murdock's *Davy Crockett,* of which stage historian Lawrence Hutton wrote in 1891, "It is almost the best American

George Bernard Shaw

play ever written." *Davy Crockett* is in four acts of unrhymed verse and depicts a Crockett innocent, free and unspoiled by the trappings of civilization. He is illiterate, naive, a physical superman, totally honest, and in all ways the personification of Rousseau's noble savage. The play was enthusiastically received and reviewed when it opened in 1873, although there have been no major productions of it in recent memory.

**Best Playwright of the Twentieth Century:** George Bernard Shaw. Backing us up is former New York *Times* drama critic Brooks Atkinson, who rates Shaw the best if only because Shaw's "intellectually brilliant" plays—and the best of them is probably *Candida*—were the major force in world theater throughout much of the century. For *Newsday* drama critic George Oppenheimer, the choice is the Irish dramatist Sean O'Casey, whose *The Plough and the Stars* and *Juno and the Paycock* "are two of the great plays of our time." The *best American dramatist since 1900*—and perhaps the best in the world—was Eugene O'Neill. In this category the *Saturday Review* noted that *all* of the writers and critics it polled agreed that O'Neill was the best.

**Best Shakespearean Play:** *Hamlet* or *Othello.* Opinion is divided among literary critics as to which of these two was the best of Shakespeare's efforts, although one thing is certain: Of the thirty-seven plays Shakespeare wrote, there was none better than his "great tragedies": *Othello, King Lear, Macbeth,* and *Hamlet.* Many critics, Leo Tolstoy among them, have found *Lear's* greatness diminished somewhat by a lack of psychological credibility, and virtually *nobody*—with the notable exception of Abraham Lincoln—ever claimed publicly that *Macbeth* was the best single play Shakespeare ever wrote. *Hamlet* is the choice of Oscar James Campbell, who notes that the drama "possessed an inexhaustible and infinite variety." Dr. Ernest Jones, the eminent psychoanalyst and biographer of Freud, has called *Hamlet* Shakespeare's "greatest work." In an essay entitled *Hamlet and Oedipus,* he expressed great fascination with the young prince's childhood and suggested that Hamlet was motivated in thought and deed by repressed hostility towards his late father.

As for *Othello,* critic A. C. Bradley calls it "the most perfect of the tragedies in point of construction," and Samuel Taylor Coleridge wrote this of the drama: "The beauties of this play impress themselves so strongly upon the attention of the reader that they can draw no aid from critical illustration."

---

**Worst Actor:** The nineteenth-century British eccentric Ronald Coates, says Irving Wallace in his book, *The Square Pegs,* "was probably the worst actor in the history of the legitimate theatre." A Shakespearean by preference, Coates saw no objection to rewriting the Bard's great tragedies to suit his own tastes; in one memorable production of *Romeo and Juliet* in which he played the male lead, he tried to jimmy open his lover's casket with a crowbar. Costumed in a feathered hat, spangled cloak, and billowing pantaloons—an outfit he wore in public as well—he looked singularly absurd.

Coates, who proclaimed himself a second Garrick, was frequently hooted and jeered offstage for his inept, overblown performances. Quite often he had to bribe theater managers for a role in their productions and his fellow thespians, fearing violence from the audience, demanded that he provide police protection before they would consent to go on stage with him. He was slandered and laughed at throughout the British Isles and often threatened with lynchings, but he persisted in his efforts to act. At one performance, several members of the audience were violently convulsed by laughter and had to be treated by a physician. Coates was struck and killed by a carriage in 1848 at the age of seventy-four.

**Worst American Actor:** The worst actor in the history of the American stage was actually a British import—George Jones, who came to the United States from England in 1828. Known familiarly as Count Johannes, Jones became psychotically obsessed with the role of Hamlet, and played it to the exclusion of virtually everything else. As his career progressed he grew increasingly more insane, and his performances were always laughed at. Eventually, he became too mad to act any longer—too mad, in fact, to play the role of the Mad Prince, as one contemporary critic said.

Jones was also a writer of sorts. *The Original History of Ancient America, Anterior to Columbus,* which he published in 1843, claims that Tyrians and Israelites were among the first people to inhabit the Americas.

**Worst Comedy (American):** *Pleasure Man.* Mae West—yes, Mae West—was the author of this sordid little horror which opened at New York's Biltmore Theatre on October 1, 1928, and was closed by the police after two performances. Rodney Terrill, an actor, is careless with his women until the angered brother of one of his recent discards attempts to set him straight by castrating him. The brother overshoots his mark, however, and Rodney dies. It all takes place at a Broadway party attended largely by female impersonators.

While *Pleasure Man* may have been the unfunniest comedy of all, the dreariest comedy ever written came from the pen of the nineteenth-century dramatist-housewife Mrs. H. L. Bateman, and was called *Self.* Mrs. Bateman touted her work as "an original New York comedy in three acts." In Act I, a young girl, with a pile of money stashed in the mattress, dutifully hands it over to her drooling father. Mom, in the meantime, puts the son up to writing a bad check on the cash. In Act II the crime is attempted, botched, and discovered, but our heroine covers for her undeserving mother and brother by saying that *she* did it. She is thus turned out of the house in disgrace. This leaves it all up to a *deus ex machina,* in the form of a doting uncle, to set everything aright in Act III, and the play ends happily if drearily. It opened in 1856.

**Worst Play:** In 1941 an all-star cast including Jean-Paul Sartre and Simone de Beauvoir, under the direction of Albert Camus, introduced Pablo Picasso's *Désir Attrapé par la Queue* (Desire Caught by the Tail) to a Paris audience. Since that time, thankfully, it has been performed only three times, most recently in 1967 at the Festival of Free Expression in St. Tropez. With characters named Big Foot, Fat Anxiety, and Thin Anguish, *Désir* combines features of medieval morality plays with twentieth-century smut. The St. Tropez production featured a bleached blonde stripper in the role of Tart, who disrobed to the throbbing rhythms of a rock band while a chorus of go-go dancers boogalooed and slides of Picasso paintings flashed on the backdrop.

Picasso's only theatrical effort deals with elemental themes—food, money, and sex—although from the dialogue it might be difficult to figure that out: "We sprinkle the rice powder of angels on the soiled bed sheets and turn the mattresses through blackberry bushes!" Big Foot shouts at the end of the play. "And with all power the pigeon flocks dash into the rifle bullets! And in all bombed houses, the keys turn twice around in the locks!" he states categorically.

The highlight of *Désir* comes when Tart urinates on stage as a variety of disgusting sound effects play over the loudspeakers. When the mayor of St. Tropez objected to this scene, the director, Jean-Jacques Lebel, moved the play outside of the city limits. "We're not at liberty to emasculate a work of art in order to pander to bourgeois sentiment," *Time* quoted Lebel as saying.

**Worst Shakespearean Play:** *Titus Andronicus.* This was the first of Shakespeare's tragedies and, many critics feel, his worst. Set in Rome during the time of the Gothic invasions, the drama runs heavily to savagery and gore with several beheadings, dismemberments, and a rape. Possibly the most tasteless scene in the Shakespearean repertoire occurs towards the end of Act IV, when two brothers who have raped and dismembered Lavinia, daughter of Titus, are methodically mutilated by her father. After severing their heads, Titus grinds their bones to powder, which he mixes with their blood. The viscous mixture is then rolled into a thin doughy paste which is wrapped, in pie-crust fashion, around the severed heads. The dish is served to their unsuspecting mother. Marchette Chute wrote that the play "wallowed in the kind of atrocities that are still the mainstay of cheap journalism and cheap fiction." Critic J. C. Maxwell said of *Titus* that it is "the only play of Shakespeare which could have left an intelligent contemporary in some doubt whether the author's truest bent was for the stage."

Another Shakespearean lemon is *Timon of Athens,* set in ancient Greece. Says English literary critic Barrett Wendell, "In *Timon* there is such weakness of creative imagination that we can hardly realize how what goes on might really occur anywhere." And the late Mark van Doren called the play "plotless."

**Worst Theatrical Act:** When impresario Oscar Hammerstein found himself in a financial hole, he decided on a new approach. "I've been putting on the best talent and it hasn't gone over," he told reporters. "I'm going to try the worst." On November 16, 1896, he introduced Elizabeth, Effie, Jessie, and Addie Cherry to New York audiences at his Olympia Theatre. A sister act that had been treading the vaudeville boards in the Midwest for a few years, they strutted out onto the Olympia's stage garbed in red dresses, hats, and woolen mittens. Jessie kept time on a bass drum while her three partners did their opening number:

> Cherries ripe Boom-de-ay!
> Cherries red Boom-de-ay!
> The Cherry sisters
> Have come to stay!

New York audiences proved more merciful, at first, than those in the Midwest. They held off pelting the girls with garbage and overripe tomatoes at first, staring goggle-eyed in disbelief. Said the New York *World* of their premiere, "It was awful." Said *The New York Times,* "It is sincerely hoped that nothing like them will ever be seen again." One critic wrote, "A locksmith with a strong, rasping file could earn ready wages taking the kinks out of Lizzie's voice." Eventually, the Cherry sisters put up a wire screen to protect themselves from the inevitable hail of missiles showered on them by the audience, although in later years they denied that anything had ever been thrown at them. Despite their reputation as "the world's worst act," they played consistently to standing-room-only crowds, wowing their fans with such numbers as "The Modern Young Man" (a recitation), "I'm Out Upon the Mash, Boys," "Curfew Must Not Ring Tonight," and "Don't You Remember Sweet Alice Ben Bolt?"

**Most Unusual Play:** *Breath,* by Samuel Beckett, was first performed in April 1970. The play lasts thirty seconds, has no actors, and no dialogue.

**Most Unusual Shakespearean Lines:** Two popular and often-quoted lines from *Richard III* were not written by Shakespeare at all. "Off with his head; so much for Buckingham" and "Conscience avaunt, Richard's himself again!" were actually composed by Colley Cibber, an actor and frequent butt of Henry Fielding's jokes.

**Most Unusual Shakespearean Production:** Patients at the Orthodox Jewish Menorah Home and Hospital for the Aged and Infirm in New York produced and staged *Macbeth,* or a reasonable facsimile thereof, in 1964. Sample dialogue: LADY MACBETH: Did I do bad? I wanted my husband to be a somebody. MACBETH: A king I hed to be? A fifteen-room kessel vasn't good enough for you?

As alternates, you might like to consider these productions:

British playwright, Donald Howarth, journeyed to Cape Town, South Africa, to put on Shakespeare's *Othello.* He immediately ran into casting difficulties. Employing a black man to play the part of Othello in an otherwise all-white cast was ruled a violation of South Africa's apartheid laws. As the San Francisco *Chronicle* (6/19/72) reported, Howarth went ahead and produced *Othello* without Othello, writing in three new parts for white characters to replace the Moorish protagonist.

In a January 1956 production of *King Lear* at New York's City Center, Orson Welles, who had fractured his ankle in a fall, played the title role from a wheelchair.

# The Movies

===

**Best Adaptation of a Novel:** *Gone with the Wind* (as if there were any question). Margaret Mitchell, who was killed when struck by an automobile in Atlanta in 1949, admitted that she wrote *GWTW* with an eye cocked to movie rights, and had thought of Clark Gable as she created the character of Rhett Butler. Gable's use of an undeleted expletive when he leaves Scarlett ("Frankly, my dear, I don't give a damn") was unprecedented and hailed as an omen of the coming corruption of the cinema, but no matter—the film to date has grossed millions. In 1950, a poll of 200 Hollywood bigwigs voted *GWTW* the greatest movie ever.

**Best Antiwar Film:** *All Quiet on the Western Front.* And perhaps the most widely viewed film as well, just as the Erich Maria Remarque novel on which it is based is one of the best sellers of the twentieth century. The first of the antiwar movies—all war films prior to *All Quiet* glorified war and the gore of battle—it is considered by *The New York Times* to be the best ever made. Lew Ayres starred in *All Quiet,* a film in which 2,000 ex-G.I.'s were hired as extras for the battle scenes. When the movie opened in 1930, the New York *American* could not contain its enthusiasm, calling it "the mightiest war drama ever screened in the ages of history." It has also been one of the most savagely censored movies. When it played in Germany in the early 1930s—to enthusiastic audiences, incidentally—Nazi saboteurs released snakes and rats in the theaters where it was shown. During the Korean War, only heavily cut versions of the film were allowed to be shown in the United States.

**Best Children's Film:** *The Wizard of Oz.* Bosley Crowther found a place for *The Wizard of Oz* (a 1939 Victor Fleming production) on his 100-best list—the only children's film in the lot. With a cast headed by Judy Garland, Bert Lahr, Jack Haley, Ray Bolger, and Billie Burke, *Oz* counts not only as the all-time best of the children's movies but one of the greatest musicals ever made, says Pauline Kael. By the way, leave your color-adjusting dial alone when you watch *Oz* on TV—the first 18 minutes are in black and white.

**Best Comedy:** *A Night at the Opera.* The Marx Brothers were never better than in this 1935 classic, and the rudeness of Groucho, as the fly-by-night showman Otis B. Driftwood, is positively exquisite: "Waiter, the bill. . . . *Nine dollars and forty cents*—that's an outrage!" Looking up at straight woman Margaret Dumont: "If I were you I wouldn't pay it." Granted, there wasn't much to laugh at in 1935, but the controlled lunacy of Groucho, Harpo, and Chico, aided by Allan Jones, Kitty Carlisle, and Miss Dumont, had depressed (and Depressed) Americans laughing themselves silly. The stateroom scene alone is worth the price of a ticket.

**Best Documentary:** A dead heat—more or less—among these four: Marcel Ophuls's *The Sorrow and the Pity*, Antonini's *Point of Order*, and two by Robert Flaherty, *Louisiana Story* and *Nanook of the North.* The Ophuls opus, the longest of the lot and certainly the most ambitious, is also the most recent, and *Esquire's* Thomas Berger has written that it is "the finest documentary ever made."

*Louisiana Story*, however, with its splendid background score by Virgil Thomson, placed fifth on the all-time movie greats list in the 1952 British Film Institute poll.

And then there are those exquisitely delicious few moments in *Point of Order* in which Joseph Welch puts the screws to Joseph McCarthy for slandering Welch's legal assistant ("At long last, sir, have you no sense of decency? Have you no shame?")

Which brings us to *Nanook*, which scratchy, silent, and fifty-two years old, still has the edge over the others. The film is neither fiction nor fantasy, but a hard, truthful look at life in the arctic as it really was—without tears (but with tons of ice and whale blubber). The stars of this film are the Eskimo hunter-frontiersman Nanook and his family, seen struggling for survival in surroundings both beautiful and hostile. In one memorable sequence, Nanook single-handedly constructs an igloo for his family when they are caught in a storm during a hunting expedition. Working with unbelievable speed and dexterity, he cuts out bricks of ice with his whaling knife and fits them together with a watchmaker's attention to precision. Two years after this remarkable movie was made, Nanook died of starvation.

**Best of the "Eggplant-That-Ate-Cleveland" Films:** *King Kong.* We're speaking, of course, about films in which a prehistoric monster, mean, angry, and skyscraper-tall, runs amok in a large city, derailing subways, gnawing away at building foundations, chewing up little girls, and the like. The fifties were rife with such epics: *The Beast from 20,000 Fathoms, It Came from Beneath the Sea, Rodan, Godzilla,* etc. All the same, the best of them is still that 1933 masterpiece, *King Kong,* at least as far as special effects and photography are concerned. *Kong,* in recent years, has come to mean many things to many people—the Black Man enslaved, sexual frustration, the danger inherent in man's attempt to control nature. The phallic imagery of the finale, in which Kong scales the Empire State Building, is unmistakable, if unintended. David O. Selznick produced this classic and Faye Wray screamed a lot. Rod Steiger says he's seen the film twenty-three times.

**Best Film:** *Citizen Kane* (1941), produced and directed by Orson Welles. "Boy Genius" Orson Welles was twenty-four years old when he made *Citizen Kane,* a cynical cinematization of the life of newspaper magnate William Randolph Hearst. Critics raved about the movie when it opened—"It comes close to being the most sensational film ever made in Hollywood," wrote Bosley Crowther of *The New York Times* on May 2, 1941—and their enthusiasm has grown over the years. In a 1962 British Film Institute survey, seventy critics from eleven nations voted *Kane* the best film in motion-picture history, and *Kane* was the only American movie—and one of only three "talkies"—on a list of twelve all-time movie greats selected by 117 international film historians in a poll at the 1958 Brussels World's Fair. Pauline Kael of *The New Yorker* has written that *Citizen Kane* "is more fun than any great movie I can think of. . . . It is also a rare example of a movie that seems better today than when it first came out." The same might be said of *Angels in the Outfield,* Dwight D. Eisenhower's unabashed favorite. Late in his second term he confided to a *Newsweek* reporter that he had seen *Angels* fifteen times since its 1948 premiere.

Other films that rate high are Michelangelo Antonioni's early sixties' drama *L'Avventura,* Renoir's 1939 satire of prewar France

*The Rules of the Game,* and Sergei Eisenstein's silent masterpiece *Potemkin* (1925) (see *Best Historical Drama*).

**Best Film Biography:** *Ivan the Terrible.* A hazily defined category, if only because so many great films, such as *Citizen Kane* and *All the King's Men* straddle a thin line between biography and fiction. Sergei Eisenstein's two-part dramatization of the life of the Russian czar was released in 1945, the first two-thirds of a never-to-be-completed trilogy. Balked in his efforts by Soviet strictures against using montage sequences and offending Stalin, the picture seems extremely formalized today. Bosley Crowther calls *Ivan* the greatest of Eisenstein's films and the British Film Institute named it the sixth greatest movie of all time in 1952.

**Best Film in Which an Artist of Great Promise is Stricken with a Fatal Disease:** We use the term "artist" broadly, and in this case it boils down to musicians and athletes. The pickings here are slim: *Love Story, Rhapsody in Blue, The Eddy Duchin Story, Rockne of Notre Dame* (Ronald Reagan, playing George Gipp, is the hero in question), etc. The best of the genre, undoubtedly, is *The Pride of the Yankees,* the 1942 biography of New York Yankee star Lou Gehrig, starring Gary Cooper and Teresa Wright. Leonard Maltin calls it a "superb baseball biography," a movie which is "beautifully photographed and directed, tastefully written." Watch for cameo appearances by Babe Ruth, Bill Dickey, and other Yankee greats.

**Best Full-Length Cartoon:** *Pinnochio* or *Yellow Submarine.* The former is a classic of visual art and widely accepted as the best that Walt Disney ever did. The latter integrates music that has been compared favorably with the *lieder* of Schubert and a strikingly imaginative screenplay. ("Do you ever get the feeling that things are not as rosy as they appear underneath the surface?") Says Vincent Canby of *Pinnochio,* it's the film in which Disney "reached his pinnacle of creativity and technical mastery."

**Best Historical Drama:** *The Battleship Potemkin.* And, until *Citizen Kane* came along, this 1925 Sergei Eisenstein opus was widely hailed as the greatest motion picture ever made. *Potemkin* is the story of a naval uprising in Odessa harbor in 1905, and of the czarist quashing of it. One scene stands out as perhaps "the outstanding single sequence of all time," according to Bosley Crowther and a host of other critics—the massacre of the peasants by Cossack guards on the great steps of Odessa harbor. Said James Agee, it was a scene "as brilliantly organized as a movement in a Beethoven symphony." Early in the movie, a bystander is shot full in the face by a stray bullet; this scene, otherwise unremembered, was the model for a similar sequence in Arthur Penn's 1967 *Bonnie and Clyde*, in which a bank guard, likewise uninvolved, is shot during a bungled getaway attempt by the two outlaws.

**Best Horror Film:** For sheer blood-curdling repulsiveness, *The Night of the Living Dead* wins in this category. But for a more profound sort of horror spiced with greater cinematic creativity, we'll opt for *The Cabinet of Dr. Caligari*. This silent relic released in 1921 will still frighten the socks off the most hardened of filmgoers. A product of the cinematic renaissance in post-World War I Germany, it is the story of Dr. Sonnow, the maniacal proprietor of a lunatic asylum who, under the name of Dr. Caligari, performs a unique hypnotic act at a local fair with an inmate known only as Cesare.

Cesare is stored in a cabinet—*the* cabinet, naturally—and at night, when the crowds have left, Caligari commands him to murder and mutilate enemies of the good doctor. *Caligari* is just about the only horror film that ever makes it to anyone's list of all-time favorites—including those of Dwight MacDonald and the novelist Henry Miller—as well as the list of all-time bests chosen by the Brussels symposium in 1958. Robert Wiene was the producer.

**Best Monster Film:** *Frankenstein.* Boris Karloff was never better than in this 1931 John Whale classic, but the real star of the show was make-up man Jack Pierce, who labored over Karloff for nearly five hours every day during the filming: "There are six ways a surgeon can cut the skull and I figured Dr. Frankenstein, who was not a practicing surgeon, would take the easiest," he told a New York *Times* reporter in 1939. "That is, he would cut the top of the skull off straight across like a pot lid, hinge it, pop the brain in, and clamp it tight. That's the reason I decided to make the monster's head square and flat like a box and dig that big scar across his forehead and have two metal clamps hold it together. . . . The lizard eyes were made of rubber, as was his false head. I made his arms look longer by shortening the sleeves of his coat. His legs were stiffened by steel struts and two pairs of pants. . . . His fingernails were blackened with shoe polish. His face was coated with blue-green grease paint. . . ." David Zinman says that "Karloff set the standard for Hollywood horror films to come." As for Karloff—the make-up ordeal alone cost him a twenty-pound weight loss.

**Best Musical:** *Singin' in the Rain.* Gene Kelly and Stanley Donen co-directed this 1952 classic that Pauline Kael calls "just about the best Hollywood musical of all time." Set in Hollywood in the late 1920s, *Singin'* takes a wry, mirthful look at the dilemma faced by squeaky-voice matinee idols like John Gilbert as the movie industry moved from silents to talkies. Starring Kelly, Donald O'Connor, and Debbie Reynolds, *Singin'* has attracted a broad-based following in the twenty-odd years since its release, including such critics as Jay Cocks of *Time* magazine and Rex Reed, who counts himself as one of the "devoted, dyed-in-the-wool *Singin' in the Rain* fans," and John Russell Taylor, who notes that *Singin'* seems always to be first among the films "that one would take to the moon or choose to see immediately before going into solitary confinement."

**Best Mystery:** *The Maltese Falcon.* "I think *The Maltese Falcon* is the best crime picture ever made in Hollywood," says Dwight MacDonald of the 1941 thriller, and Leonard Maltin concurs: "John Huston's first fling at directing, from Dashiell Hammett's story, adds up to the greatest detective film of all time. Everyone (Humphrey Bogart, Peter Lorre, Sidney Greenstreet, Elisha Cook, Jr., Mary Astor, et al.) is great, but when Lorre calls Greenstreet a 'blundering fathead' it's sheer ecstasy." Bogart's Sam Spade is deftly faithful to Hammett's original—callous, brilliant, and wholly without fear. "But you love me!" protests Mary Astor as he prepares to turn her over to the police at movie's end. "Sure I love you, but that's beside the point," Bogart tells her. "If they hang you, I'll always remember you."

**Best Science Fiction Film:** *The Incredible Shrinking Man.* Scott Carey is sunning himself aboard his cabin cruiser one fine summer day when a cloud of insecticide passes by and engulfs him and his small craft. Six weeks later he begins mysteriously to shrink in size, losing an inch or two at first, and then half his normal height. His marriage flounders (in spite of the old saw about short men being the most virile) and he seeks comfort in a quickie affair with a circus midget, which ends when he discovers he's become even smaller than she. Dejected beyond words, he returns home and moves into a dollhouse, but is chased out by his cat, now monstrously large. Taking refuge in the cellar, he struggles for survival against starvation, tarantulas, exhaustion, and isolation. As the movie ends, he slips through a ventilator to the great outdoors—his front yard—looking up at the heavens to ponder the meaning of it all.

The special effects in this 1957 Jack Arnold production are masterfully executed, even the acting is competent, and the screenplay, based on a novel by Richard Matheson, is excellent. It's a film, says sci-fi critic John Baxter, "that for intelligence and sophistication has few equals. Arguably, it is the peak of sf film in its long history."

**Best Silent Film:** *The Gold Rush.* Or so said a twenty-six-nation poll of 117 film historians who met at the Brussels World's Fair in 1958 to compile a list of the greatest movies ever produced. Hard-pressed to come up with a single all-time best, the group placed Charlie Chaplin's 1925 silent comedy among the six greatest motion pictures of all time. *The Gold Rush* also rated highly in a poll of seventy international film critics conducted by the British Film Institute in 1962, and was named the third greatest movie of all time by a similar poll ten years later. Written, produced, directed, and partially financed by Chaplin, who starred in the movie as the Lone Prospector, the movie cost $2 million to make. Best scene: a starving Chaplin, desperate for food, cooks his shoe with the finesse and care of a cordon bleu chef, serving it up basted in its own juices and garnished with laces. He devours the meal with bittersweet gusto.

**Best Western:** *The Gunfighter* is unquestionably the greatest Hollywood western ever filmed—unless, of course, you prefer *High Noon, Shane, The Searchers,* or *The Ox-Bow Incident,* all of which rate highly and none of which has ever made it to *anyone's* ten-best-movies' list (nobody takes westerns very seriously these days, it seems). In any event, Dwight MacDonald likes *Gunfighter*—a 1950 film which Henry King directed and Gregory Peck starred in—because it shows a stock character "behaving realistically instead of in the usual terms of romantic cliche."

**Worst Comedy:** *The Big Noise.* The bubbles had just about fizzed out of Laurel and Hardy by the mid-1940s, and this 1944 dud is as depressing as it is unfunny. The action finds Stan and Ollie as detectives, hired to guard a bomb. (The French title, significantly, was *Quel Petard*—or *What a Bomb*.) Bosley Crowther wrote in *The New York Times* that the movie "has about as much humor in it as a six-foot hole in the ground." Runner-up is *The Courtship of Andy Hardy*, which film critic Leonard Maltin calls, "the most unbearable in a now-obnoxious series. If Rooney doesn't get you the Forties' slang will."

**Worst Editing of a Film:** A movie theater manager in Seoul, South Korea, decided that the running time of *The Sound of Music* was too long. He shortened it by cutting out all the songs.

**Worst Film:** An admittedly difficult choice. *New York* magazine has called Ken Russell's *The Devils* "cinematic excrement," a judgment it has yet to confer on any other film. There is also that monumental turkey of 1948, *The Babe Ruth Story*, with William Bendix. But the real winner may very well be *Myra Breckinridge*. *Time* reviewer Jay Cocks wrote of this 1970 cinematization of the Gore Vidal novel that it is "about as funny as a child molester. It is an insult to intelligence, an affront to sensibility, and an abomination to the eye." A surreal tale about a transsexual actor who undergoes sex-change surgery and emerges as a voluptuous siren bent on seducing Hollywood, the film drew universally scathing notices. *McCall's* said that "the principal horror of the film [is] its overwhelming inhumanity." And film critic Rex Reed himself, who played the presurgical Myron Breckinridge to Raquel Welch's Myra, told a nationwide television audience weeks before the opening that he had seen previews of the film and that it was "terrible." If the story intrigues you, read the book. It isn't Vidal at his best, but it's vastly better than the movie. More fun, too.

**Worst Film Biography:** Three contenders for this one. First, *The Magnificent Rebel*, a cinematic biography of Beethoven produced in Germany in 1961 by Georg Tressler. Treacly and dull, the movie, notes film historian Lotte Eisner, features a young Beethoven "with false eyelashes, played by a mediocre actor with a broad face."

Next we have *The Babe Ruth Story*, made in 1948, starring William Bendix as the Babe and Claire Trevor as his wife, which may well have been *the* worst film bio Hollywood has ever come up with. It's a casebook of sports film clichés and Bendix, who throws like a girl, is a monumental flop. The deathbed scene is even more sickening than its counterpart in *Love Story* and is to be avoided at all costs.

Finally, the *Harlow* twins. In 1965, when Joseph E. Levine announced plans to produce a film version of the life of Jean Harlow, the Hollywood screen siren, low-budget filmmaker Bill Sargeant got on his celluloid horse and decided to scoop Levine. Sargeant's cinematic mugging of Miss Harlow was filmed, spliced, edited, packaged, and in the theaters in eight days (including time out for coffee and danish and two days lost due to bad weather). Starring Carol Lynley in the title role and Ginger Rogers and Barry Sullivan as her parents, it was made of 100 percent pure plastic without a fleck of humanity or an iota of truth.

In the twilight period between the opening of Sargeant's *Harlow* and the premiere of Levine's *Harlow*, film critic Howard Thomson of *The New York Times* wrote that "Whatever the second *Harlow* picture looks and sounds like, it can't be much worse than the first." As it turned out, it was actually a little bit better.

**Worst Love Story:** *Love Story,* appropriately enough. Critics generally found this 1970 production of Erich Segal's best seller—which wasn't any better than the movie—a model of sheer pretentiousness and high-gloss plasticity, and Judith Crist's characterization of the film as *"Camille* with bullshit," was not untypical. One reviewer who differed with the majority of critics was Richard Nixon: He liked the film just fine, although he was appalled by its "excessive profanity."

**Worst Miscasting:** Connoisseurs of the incongruous recall with fondness Clark Gable's unfortunate portrayal of the title character in *Parnell,* an inept 1937 biography of the Irish revolutionary hero. Our own favorite is Charles Boyer's Napoleon in the 1938 Clarence Brown film, *Maria Valeska.* Not that Boyer is not an admirable actor, not that he doesn't put his all into the role. It's just that, as film historian Lotte Eisner has pointed out, he's too *tall* to be Napoleon and spends the entire film walking around stooped over.

**Worst Western:** *The Tall Men.* "In just 15 minutes watch three big stars sink slowly in the west," writes Leonard Maltin. The stars included Clark Gable, Robert Ryan, 1,500 Indians, 4,000 head of cattle, and Jane Russell, whose aching feet were the only point of interest in this titanic bore released in 1955. (Some nice scenes, though, including Miss Russell purring sexily in a Montana log cabin while Gable munches eagerly on a piece of mule meat. "After a long ride," he explains, "I get as hungry as a bear.")

**Most Unusual Film:** *Sleep,* the first movie ever made by America's most unusual moviemaker Andy Warhol. A 1963 opus, *Sleep* features close-ups of a naked man getting his eight hours. It is, appropriately, eight hours long.

Warhol also produced *Eat,* in which the artist Robert Indiana eats mushrooms for two hours; *Empire,* a seven and one-half hour view of the Empire State Building, shot from the top floor of the Time-Life Building; and ****, which is twenty-five hours long in the uncut version. Actually, to call it uncut is redundant, since *nothing* ever winds up on Warhol's cutting room floor. What he shoots is what you get, and that includes not just all the footage but the celluloid leaders at the ends of the film used to thread the film onto the sprockets of the spools.

**Most Unusual Film Rating:** Boston newspapers ran an advertisement in 1970 for Walt Disney's *Peter Pan* which carried an "R" rating (Children under eighteen not admitted without parent or guardian).

**Most Unusual Pornographic Movie:** At England's Chessington Zoo, officials embarked upon a revolutionary plan to perk up the chimpanzees' flagging sex life and get the apes to mate: show them skin flicks. First step in the program, before the chimps would be graduated to hard-core porn, would be a BBC documentary film showing chimpanzees cuddling. "We tried it in three cages in the ape house," said zoo spokesman Andy Bowen. "The orangutans were only interested in the projector. The gorillas became aggressive. But Cressida [an eight-year-old female chimp] was just overcome with passion."

# Music

**Best Ballet Dancer (Current):** Rudolf Nureyev. Critical acclaim for this forty-year-old Russian-born premier danseur is unanimous—from Clive Barnes to Hubert Humphrey (who once bubbled after a Nureyev performance, "Excellent, wonderful—and I don't usually cotton to that kind of dancing"). Hubert Saal, music editor of *Newsweek*, has called Nureyev "the reigning prince of dancers," and Serge Grigoriev, the noted Soviet ballet dancer, says of Nureyev that "he is every bit as good as Nijinsky." In London, Saal reports, Nureyev has become something of a latter-day matinee idol, "transforming Victorian reserve into Elizabethan enthusiasm. Covent Garden audiences are highly spiced with bobbysoxers who shower the stage with flowers and chant, 'We want Rudi, preferably in the nudi.' "

**Best Ballet Score:** *Swan Lake,* by Pëtr Ilich Tchaikovsky. It's the music we're concerned with here, not the choreography or the staging, and many critics agree that in *Swan Lake,* in his last three symphonies, and in his violin concerto Tchaikovsky reached the height of his creative powers.

Composed in 1875, *Swan Lake* was not well received at first, but is today a fixture of the standard concert repertoire—with or without dancers. (You may be interested to know that *Swan Lake,* as ballets go, is especially hard on a dancer's feet; the average ballet dancer, in a typical production of *Swan Lake,* will completely wear out four pairs of ballet shoes.)

**Best Chamber Work:** Beethoven's String Quartet no. 14 in C# Minor (opus 131). The best Beethoven is late Beethoven, and his five last string quartets, opus nos. 127, 130, 131, 132, and 135, composed in the final years of his troubled life, are commonly regarded as the pinnacle of Beethoven's aspirations and the greatest works of chamber music ever composed (as well as among the most difficult to play and appreciate). "For variety and complexity of texture—thin, transparent passages contrasted with densely woven contrapuntal ones; bristling pizzicato phrases alternating with sweeping legato themes—these quartets had never been equalled," writes Walter E. Nallin. Of the best of them, the C# Minor, Beethoven said, "Never have I written a melody that affected me so much." Says critic Martin Bookspan, the Quartet "is perhaps the most consistently 'other-worldly' and 'sublime' of Beethoven's final quartets—and probably of all music."

**Best Choral Work:** Bach's *The Passion According to St. Matthew.* Not that there aren't others that might also fill this spot—two, to be exact: Brahms's *German Requiem,* which he composed in 1868, and Handel's oratorio, *Saul,* composed in 1739, four years before the completion of *Messiah.* The Brahms and the Handel are certainly more immediately accessible than the *St. Matthew Passion,* and more *fun* at first, too. The drama of the Brahms requiem is more readily apparent and *Saul* abounds in the catchy tunes and rousing choruses that *The Passion,* on first hearing, may seem to lack. But in the final analysis, Bach's *St. Matthew Passion* may well be the most moving, human choral music ever heard. It was written in 1729.

**Best Composer:** Ludwig van Beethoven, who straddled the classical and romantic periods of music, may well be regarded as the Big One, the composer who single-handedly turned the symphony from a pleasant enough parlor diversion into a medium of artistic expression. The only other two possible choices, it would seem, would be Mozart and Johann Sebastian Bach—except that Beethoven himself once wrote that George Frederick Handel "was the greatest composer who ever lived."

**Best Composer (American):** Charles Ives or George Gershwin. Both are favorites, but Ives seems to have the edge. Leonard Bernstein, who gave Ives's monumental Second Symphony its first public hearing in 1951—it had been composed in 1897—calls Ives "our first really great composer—our Washington, Lincoln, and Jefferson of music." Ives, like the poet Wallace Stevens, was a highly successful insurance executive by trade, and never tried very hard to have his music performed publicly. Of all his com-

Ludwig van Beethoven

positions, his best are thought to be his four symphonies and the revolutionary *Concord* Sonata for piano. When it was first performed on January 20, 1939, at New York's Town Hall, Lawrence Gilman of the New York *Herald Tribune* had this to say: "The sonata is exceptionally great music—it is, indeed, the greatest music composed by an American and the most deeply and essentially American in impulses and implication. It has passion, tenderness, humor, simplicity and homeliness. It has imaginative and spiritual vastness. It has wisdom and beauty. . . ." And so on. Some of the piano chords in the *Concord* Sonata and in Ives's Fourth Symphony are so complex that they can be struck correctly only with a specially sized block of wood.

Gershwin, of course, is better known. The prevailing sentiment is that he might well have become the greatest American composer bar none, had he not been cut down at his peak: He was only thirty-nine when he died of a brain tumor. He had completed his most ambitious concert work to date, the Concerto in F for Piano and Orchestra, and was just turning his talents more fully to symphonic composition when he died.

**Best Composer of the Twentieth Century:** Igor Stravinsky. While Bela Bartok may have composed the *best single piece of orches-*

*tral music* of the twentieth century—the Concerto for Orchestra—Stravinsky is unchallenged as the century's best composer. While the composer was still living, Joseph Machlis wrote of him that "for half a century [he] has given impetus to the main currents in contemporary music." Stravinsky's best-known work, the *Rite of Spring,* may also be his best, but when it premiered in Paris in 1913, praise was scant. Fistfights broke out among the audience and some of the performers were hooted off the stage. Fortunately for Stravinsky, and for us, the work and its composer's genius were ultimately vindicated.

**Best Opera:** Mozart's *The Magic Flute.* Mozart may well have been the greatest of the operatic composers, and *The Magic Flute,* his last opera and the next-to-last work he composed before dying a pauper's death of Bright's disease at the age of thirty- five, is the ultimate synthesis of music and poetry. "That Mozart was equal to any demands of the theater, in whatever style, is shown by his triumphant treatment of the libretto," Robert Lawrence has written. Meanwhile, Alan Rich, of *New York* magazine, finds another Mozart opera—*The Marriage of Figaro*—the best opera ever composed.

But then there are the two supreme achievements of Giuseppe Verdi, *Otello* and *Falstaff,* and there are those who feel that it was Verdi, not Mozart—and *certainly* not Wagner—who brought opera to its apotheosis. "When we examine the pages of an *Otello* or a *Falstaff,*" Olin Downes says, "we come across such expressions and such admirable theater, and such a master's treatment of orchestral resources delegated to their place in relation to the stage, as neither Wagner nor any other composer of his school ever dreamed of."

**Best Opera Singer:** When Puccini heard Enrico Caruso perform *Manon Lescaut* with the New York Metropolitan Opera, the composer whispered, "He is singing like a god." While it is, of course, nearly impossible to compare modern singers with those who performed before the invention of the Victrola, we can say with confidence that Caruso was the most popular, famous, and successful opera singer of all time. It was the exceptional power displayed throughout his magnificent range that won him his highest compliments. That range is well demonstrated in an excerpt from *La Juive,* which he considered his finest recording.

All in all, his personal appeal and his treasured recordings vastly extended the audience for opera. There was scarcely ever an empty seat at one of his performances, and when he sang in Europe, tickets were auctioned off at unheard-of prices. Edouard de Reszke, an outstanding bass with the Metropolitan, described Caruso's attraction simply: "I have never heard a more beautiful voice."

**Best Performance of the 1812 Overture Ever:** Performances of Tchaikovsky's 1812 Overture have traditionally been augmented by the sounds of cannon and gunfire. In a recent working of the overture in Atlanta, conductor Robert Shaw added real explosives to the score. When he pressed the button smoke filled the concert hall and a loud blast shook the audience. The smoke set off a supersensitive fire alarm that alerted the local fire department who arrived, axes and hoses in hand. The concert ended early.

**Best Pianist (Contemporary):** Vladimir Horowitz. The lines began to form at the box office of New York's Carnegie Hall twelve hours before tickets went on sale in 1965 for Vladimir Horowitz's first piano recital in twelve years. Horowitz played to a packed house and rave reviews on that now-historic night, and Harold C. Schonberg, music critic of *The New York Times,* noted the following morning, "He still has a staggering technique—all the color and resonance in the world and a sonority that is unparalleled in the history of piano playing." A specialist in the works of the early romantics, Horowitz's *piece de resistance,* surprisingly, is a piano transcription of John Philip Sousa's *Stars and Stripes Forever,* which he introduced at a 1953 recital marking the twenty-fifth anniversary of his American debut. The performance was a tour de force, in which Horowitz's keyboard was magically transformed into a full-scale march band, complete with piccolo and sousaphone. One reviewer described Horowitz's performance as "possibly the most phenomenal pyrotechnical exhibition in the entire annals of piano playing."

**Best Piano Concerto:** Beethoven's Fourth. Beethoven wrote five concerti for piano in all, and the most famous, certainly, is his Fifth, the *Emperor,* although there are some who call it that more for its pomposity than for its grandeur. The real plum among Beethoven's piano concerti, his Fourth in G Minor, fell into obscurity during his lifetime, but was restored to popularity by Felix Mendelssohn, who played it publicly in Leipzig in 1836. "Although it does not offer virtuosos such an excellent chance to show off as the Fifth," write Wallace Brockway and Herbert Weinstock, "it is flawlessly constructed, original in detail, and inspired in melody." Beethoven accomplishes a bit of musical tradition-snubbing by opening the concerto with a statement by the unaccompanied piano and not by the orchestra.

Other possibilities are two concerti of Mozart's—his A Major (K. 414) and his C Minor (K. 491)—and Brahms's Piano Concerto no. 1 in D Minor. Don't look for the same jewellike craftsmanship in the Brahms as you'll find in the Mozart. Brahms was a troubled, brooding man writing in the turbulent idiom of romanticism, and this concerto—which he originally intended as a full-blown symphony—is overpowering in its intensity and lyrical beauty. It was used effectively as background music for the Leslie Caron film, *The L-Shaped Room,* in the early sixties.

**Best Piano Sonata:** Again, Beethoven. This time, it's his Piano Sonata no. 32 in C Minor, opus 111. Beethoven's earlier keyboard classics—the *Moonlight Sonata*, the *Appasionata*, the *Pathetique*—are all beautiful, but they've been done to death. (You'll notice, once again, that we've excluded non-Beethovian candidates. The piano sonatas of Brahms and Mozart are great music, but they lack the depth and inventiveness of Beethoven's.) Musicologists Wallace Brockway and Herbert Weinstock write that "in the realm of musical history, it is not easy to be dogmatic, but it may be affirmed positively that Beethoven here set the limits of the piano sonata. No other composer has even remotely approached it in amplitude of conception, perfection of design, vigor of movement or rightness of detail."

**Best Rock Group:** The Beatles did for rock music what Henry Ford did for the automobile and Babe Ruth did for baseball—infused it with new life and made it respectable. Their first album-long departure from rock orthodoxy—*Sergeant Pepper's Lonely Hearts Club Band,* released in 1966—maintains an almost impossibly high level of quality in every song. One critic likened the songs on that album to the art song cycles of Schubert and Mahler. Some say the Rolling Stones did as much for rock as the Beatles did, but remember, the Beatles did it first. And, we think, better.

**Best Rock Song:** *Sergeant Pepper's Lonely Hearts Club Band* is still the best rock album ever released. Appropriately, side two closes with the best song in rock history—"A Day in the Life." It's a drug induced vision of timelessness and despair, with a final chord that takes *forever* to disappear.

**Best Symphony:** Beethoven's Ninth Symphony. Of all the symphonies ever composed—and there've been thousands—the possible choices for "all-time best," it seems, boil down to just six: Beethoven's Third (the *Eroica*), his Fifth, and his Ninth (the *Choral*); and Mozart's last three—nos. 39, 40, and 41. Many critics have singled out the Mozart 40th in G Minor as being the most flawlessly constructed, the most melodic, and the most substantial of the six. But musicologist David Ewen feels that the mighty Ninth Symphony is Beethoven's "highest flight of fancy in the symphonic form—one of the most indestructible masterpieces in the entire realm of art." And T. S. Eliot wrote that Beethoven, in the last movement of the Ninth, was somehow aspiring to transcend music and reach for something almost divine.

**Best Symphony Orchestra:** The Chicago Symphony, with Georg Solti conducting. If the Philadelphia is the Cadillac of orchestras, the Chicago is a Maserati at the very least. *Esquire* calls the Chicago the best in the world, which it's clearly become since the Hungarian-born Solti took over the reins in 1969. The Chicagoans have a well-rounded repertoire, but do best with the Romantics. Their Mahler symphonies are superb.

**Best Violin Concerto:** Tchaikovsky's Violin Concerto in D Major. As fashionable as it has become to deplore the emotional excesses of romanticism, Pëtr Ilich Tchaikovsky managed to get it all together in his violin concerto—a magnificent synthesis of sensuality and substance. A virtuoso piece in the extreme, enormously difficult to play, its melodies are more engaging than those in the Beethoven Violin Concerto in D Major, and more stirring and substantial than those in the Mendelssohn E Minor concerto. Tchaikovsky, who was to die of cholera in 1893, was long troubled by feelings of artistic and creative inadequacy and freely admitted that he was "no Beethoven." But Rosa Newmarch has said that the "brightness and infectious gaiety" of the concerto's third movement "would probably have delighted Beethoven."

**Worst Avant-Garde Concert:** At the Third Annual New York Avant-Garde Music Festival in 1965, Korean composer Nam June Paik presented his lengthy *Prelude in D Minor*. Space prevents us from reviewing the performance in full, but we do feel that the highlights should be recorded for posterity. Perhaps future generations can learn from this mistake.

The composition opened with an action painting by Mr. Paik entitled "Homage to John Cage" (see also *Most Unusual Composer*); the composer applied black paint to the canvas with his hands and hair. This was followed by the demolition of an upright piano, the cracking of several eggs (amplified for the audience's benefit), and the production of various ear-splitting feedback shrieks.

The concert then moved into its second phase as nails were driven into another amplified piano. Showing intelligence that few gave him credit for, Paik proceeded to cut off his paint-soaked hair. In the *Prelude*, as in many avant-garde works, audience participation figured importantly in the performance. The composer ran out into the rather sparse crowd and squirted shaving cream on a number of appreciative music lovers. One man allowed Mr. Paik to scissor off his tie and shirt.

In the *Prelude*'s final movement, cellist Charlotte Moorman entered clad only in a *cello*phane sheath. A man dressed in black, poised motionlessly on all fours, served as her bench. For a while Miss Moorman played variations on a theme from Saint-Saens' *Le Cygne*. Then, midway through the piece, she put down her bow, ascended a six-foot ladder (assisted by Mr. Paik), and executed a "swan" dive into an oil drum filled with water. Emerging from the drum with the cellophane adhering tightly to her body, Miss Moorman finished off *Le Cygne*.

Howard Klein, a critic for *The New York Times*, termed the *Prelude in D Minor* "a study in instant ennui. Fraught with pretensions of profundity," Klein continued, "Mr. Paik's efforts lacked any spark of originality, sensitivity, or talent." Still, the *Prelude* was only the opening event of the week-long series, and Klein expressed some optimism about upcoming performances: "Maybe the festival will improve. It couldn't get worse."

**Worst Ballet Score:** *Ballet Mecanique*, by George Antheil. The French composer George Antheil—who was born in Trenton, New Jersey—conceived his *Ballet Mecanique* as a musical evocation of America, Africa, and steel. Scored for two airplane motors, eight xylophones, two octaves of musical bells, sixteen mechanical pianos, an automobile horn, a siren, two large sheets of tin and two of steel, and assorted humming and buzzing devices, alarm clocks, torpedoes, fan belts, electric screwdrivers and police whistles, the piece caused a near-riot when it premiered in 1926. Critics on both sides of the Atlantic were outraged and called Antheil's effort a monument to cacophony. And the *Times* of London had this to say about the ballet's premiere in Britain: "The concert is being organized as a benefit to Mr. Antheil and the promoters hope that the proceeds will enable the composer to remain in Europe and continue working there. In self-defense a concert should be organized on this side to enable Mr. Antheil to return to New York and pursue his studies quietly there."

**Worst Baton Technique:** During a 1975 concert in Mexico City, Uruguayan conductor José Serebrier accidentally stabbed himself through the hand with his baton. While musicians and chorus members gasped, blood gushed from the wound, staining his white tuxedo shirt and splattering his shoes. "The baton broke into pieces," the conductor later said. "One piece was sticking through my hand. Ironically, I never use a baton. But I decided to use one for this performance because I thought it would help achieve greater musical control. That was a mistake." Nonetheless, Serebrier continued conducting without missing a beat, deftly removing the wooden fragment from his hand and wrapping the wound tightly in a handkerchief during a lull in the music. He was treated at a nearby hospital following the concert and was back on the podium—sans baton—the following evening.

**Worst Beethoven Composition:** *Wellington's Victory,* or *The Battle* Symphony, opus 91. American and European music critics are all but unanimous in their choice of *Wellington's Victory* as rock-bottom in the Beethoven repertoire. Beethoven composed the work at the request of the German inventor-showman Johann Nepomuk Maelzel, the inventor of the metronome, as a demonstration piece for the "Panharmonicon." This was a Rube Goldberg-like device which Maelzel was touting as a mechanical orchestra. It consisted of an interconnected assortment of wind instruments through which a bellows blew with the notes controlled by a revolving brass cylinder with pins. Maelzel's plans foundered, but the symphony, commemorating the Duke of Wellington's 1813 victory over Napoleon at the Battle of Vitoria, in Spain, remains. Today, it is occasionally performed by a live human orchestra, augmented with all manner of muskets, cannon, and small-gage howitzers. Much of it is reminiscent of the soundtrack for a grade B western.

**Worst Composer:** "I remember meeting Max Reger in those years," Igor Stravinsky reminisced. "He and his music repulsed me in about equal measure." On other occasions Stravinsky made the unflattering comparison, ". . . as dull as Reger." In short, Max Reger is a prime candidate for honors as the worst composer.

Max Reger

No one accuses Reger of being without talent, but rarely has such technical virtuosity been put to poorer use. Working around the turn of the century, he incorporated two divergent influences into his music: the contrapuntal style of the sixteenth century and that of marching bands, of which he was inordinately fond. His compositions are generally regarded as ponderous, overworked, and cluttered with too many notes. Critic David Ewen puts it gently: ". . . he utilized formidably complex harmonic and contrapuntal structures, generally too intricate for their own good."

Of course, Reger had his good qualities: He was endowed with perfect pitch and is credited with a number of quotable, caustic aphorisms. "The life of a composer is work, hope, and bicarbonate of soda," he once said. Indeed, as a habitual drunk, Reger must have relied heavily on bicarbonate of soda. Even when he was abstaining from alcohol he still drank compulsively, downing as many as eight cups of beef bouillon at a sitting. Once he became ill from overindulging in lemonade. His physical appearance is best described as sniveling, and Paul Rosenfeld once remarked that Reger resembled "a swollen myopic beetle with thick lips and a sullen expression."

His music has been largely ignored, although he did receive some posthumous recognition when Hitler singled him out as a personal favorite. But still Max Reger is remembered as a musical reactionary who did his best to put the phony back in symphony.

**Worst Composition of the Twentieth Century:** Edgar Varese was the composer of *Ionization,* a musical representation of the action of ions with atoms. "It recalls schooldays in the chemical laboratory, where hydrogen sulfide was produced to the merriment of students and the horror of teachers," wrote the music reviewer of the Havana *Evening Telegram.*

**Worst Concert:** Tommy Dorsey brought eight members of his band to the monkey house of the Philadelphia Zoo in 1940 for a historic experiment designed to determine whether simians appreciate music. Well, you ask, did they dig it? ". . . The monkeys couldn't stand it," according to a zookeeper interviewed by the musical journal *Etude.* "The band first played some violent jazz. The chimpanzees were scared to death. They scampered all over the place, seeking the protection of their keepers and hiding under benches. . . . One chimp tried to pull the trombone away from Tommy Dorsey." The response to that number was so bad, in fact, that the band was forced to stop playing. One old chimp in particular had such a wounded and resentful look on his face that the band members couldn't bear to continue.

Then Dorsey tried a different style, launching into the mellow strains of his theme song, "I'm Getting Sentimental Over You." Almost immediately the animals began to calm down. They sat patiently on their benches, the keeper said, showing none of their previous agitation and "watching the players with interest."

**Worst Musical Instrument:** Louis XI of France commanded the Abbot of Baigne to invent a preposterous musical instrument to entertain His Majesty's friends. The Abbot good-naturedly agreed to undertake the assignment, and after a few hours at the drawing board, he gathered together a herd of hogs—ranging from nursing piglets to full-fledged swine. Under a velvet tent, he lined them up with the low-voiced porkers on the left, the middle-range sows in the middle, and the soprano piglets on the right. Then the Abbot modified an organ keyboard, attaching the keys to a complex apparatus terminating in a series of small spikes, one poised over the rump of each pig. The courtiers were gathered together and the Abbot played his keyboard, causing the spikes to prick the pigs, who naturally let out a piercing squeal, each in its own particular voice range. The tunes were actually recognizable, and the concert was adjudged a success by all.

There is another, similar story in French musical history about a fellow in the mid-1800s who trained cats to howl on command. He publicly performed a work called *Concert Miaulant* or Meowing Concert, which was also quite well received.

**Worst Opera:** *The Padlock,* a comic opera first produced at London's Drury Lane Theatre in 1768 (libretto by Isaac Bickerstaffe, music by Charles Didbin). The protagonist is Mungo, an inarticulate West Indian slave with a burning urge for self-expression, as evidenced in this aria:

> Dear heart, what a terrible life I am led!
> A dog has a better that's sheltered and fed
>   Night and day 'tis the same;
>   My pain is deir game
> Me wish to de Lord me was dead!
> Whate'er's to be done
> Poor black must run
> Mungo here, Mungo dere,
> Mungo everywhere;
> Above and below,
> Sirrah, come, sirrah, go;
> Do so, and do so.
> Oh! Oh!
> Me wish to de Lord me was dead! (and so forth)

Mungo ties one on in Act III and stays drunk until the final curtain, making himself generally obnoxious and losing whatever sympathy he may have earned for himself in Acts I and II.

**Worst Opera Singer:** Florence Foster Jenkins was involved in a taxi crash in 1943 and afterwards found that she could warble "a higher F than ever before." Yet even with her new and higher F, few would dispute that she was the worst opera singer of all time.

No one knows how many singers fail in the nation's showers, but Mrs. Jenkins dared greatly, failing in drawing rooms from Philadelphia to Newport, and ultimately on October 25, 1944, failing before a jammed house at Carnegie Hall. For a number of years, Mrs. Jenkins's career was an in-joke among cognoscenti and a few music critics, who wrote intentionally ambiguous reviews of her performances: "Her singing at its finest suggests the untram-

Florence Foster Jenkins

meled swoop of some great bird," Robert Lawrence said in the *Saturday Review*.

A wealthy and well-padded matron (pictured here as the "Angel of Inspiration"), Mrs. Jenkins bore a resemblance to Margaret Dumont, the *grand dame* of the Marx Brothers movies. It was impossible to keep the diva's true talent a secret for long. Her Carnegie Hall appearance and her recording, "The Glory of the Human Voice," (RCA LM 2599) brought her national attention. Reviewing her record, *Newsweek* opined, "In high notes, Mrs. Jenkins sounds as if she was afflicted with low, nagging backache."

Mrs. Jenkins was aware that people were laughing at her when she sang the Bell Song from *Lakmé* or her favorite arias from *Die Fledermaus*, but they also applauded energetically. She was convinced that she brought her audiences pleasure with her singing; and surely she did.

**Worst Piano Concerto:** It was Max Reger who produced the world's worst piano concerto. These remarks, by former New York *Times* music critic Olin Downes, are typical: "The Reger Piano Concerto is to our mind a most inflated, pretentious bag of wind. . . . The orchestration is . . . swollen, thick and prevailingly in bad taste. Little bits of ideas are pretentiously and noisily bunched together and they get nowhere. . . . What incredibly bad taste, and poor invention!"

**Worst Popular Singer:** Elva Miller. Mrs. Miller, as her admirers know her, has a voice about as good as your mother-in-law's, but she wasted no time hitting the charts in 1966 with a nightmarish rendition of "Downtown." Some 250,000 fans bought the Capitol Records single and later Mrs. Miller came out with an album of old favorites.

**Worst Rock Song Ever:** What makes a rock song memorably bad? Is it the mind-smothering lyrics, the non-melody, the offensiveness of the performer—or of the pimply faced blind date you first heard it with? Actually, most bad rock songs are eminently forgettable. One called "Only in America," released in 1964, still clings leechlike to our unwilling memory:

> Only in America
> Land of opportunity,
> Would a classy girl like you
> Fall for a poor boy like me.

And so forth.

**Worst String Quartet:** Critical reaction to Max Reger's String Quartet opus 109 was similar to that which greeted virtually all of his works: scandalized, sarcastic, enraged. Irving Kolodin, writing in the New York *Sun*, observed that while the piece looks like music, sounds like music, and "might even taste like music," it remains stubbornly "not music. . . . Reger might be epitomized as a composer whose name is the same either forward or backward and whose music, curiously, often displays the same characteristic."

**Worst Symphony:** Any one of the nine symphonies of Louis Spohr, a mid-nineteenth-century German composer, has a fair crack at the title, but our choice is his Symphony no. 2. Bland, yet pretentious; unmemorable, yet grating to the ears; altogether, a colossal bore. Although Spohr was in the vanguard of the German romantic revolt in music, he had little use for Beethoven's later works and didn't care a hoot about the music of Weber either. At the age of seventy-three he broke his left arm and was no longer able to play the violin. He died heartbroken two years later.

The fourth symphony of the Austro-American composer Ernst Krenek has also inspired some choice critical prose. Critic-composer Virgil Thomson called it "a pseudomasterpiece, with about as much savor to it as a paste-board turkey." Music critic John Briggs, of the New York *Post,* wrote after a performance of the work in 1947, that hearing it is like "suddenly being transported to Mars and not knowing whether to be amused or infuriated." In calling Krenek's output sterile and barren of passion, Olin Downes was considerably more generous than the Russian critic V. Gorodinsky, who said about *Jonny Spielt Auf,* Krenek's best known opera, "There is nothing in it but filth, dirt, cold cruelty and sticky frog-like sexuality, combined with the dry rationalism of a biped calculating machine."

**Worst Tone Poem:** The tone poems of Edgar Varese have inspired some of the most vitriolic criticism ever penned. New York *World* critic Samuel Chatzin wrote that *Ameriques* "seemed to depict the progress of a terrible fire in one of our larger zoos." Ernest Newman, of the New York *Evening Post* wrote that *Integrales* "Sounded like a combination of early morning in the Mott Haven freight yards, feeding time at the zoo, and a Sixth Avenue trolley rounding a curve, with an intoxicated woodpecker thrown in for good measure." And F. Brust, writing in the Berlin publication *Germania,* said that *Arcana* was reminiscent of "an insanely raging zoo . . . or a mass of men thrown into the crater of an erupting volcano in a hideous slaughter."

**Most Unusual Composer:** Harry Partch. It wasn't enough for
Harry Partch that he toss the twelve-tone scale, good enough for
the likes of Beethoven and Irving Berlin, into the dustbin and invent his own forty-three-note octave; he found it necessary to
invent and build his own musical instruments as well. They included the Whang Gun, a seventy-two-stringed surrogate cithara,
glass bells which he called "cloud chamber bowls," a strange,
marimbalike instrument called a "boo," and his most famous creation, the bloboys, consisting of three organ pipes, a bellows, and
an automobile exhaust pipe.

Partch began composing in 1923 at the age of twenty-two, but it
wasn't until the late 1960s that he made his New York debut. He
was best known in California, where a succession of grants from
the Carnegie, Fromm, and Guggenheim foundations kept him sufficiently above water to continue composing and attacking what he
called "the tyranny of the piano scale, a wholly irrational, oppressive lid on musical expression." Some of Partch's music was recorded on Columbia records, and it included such pieces as "Visions Fill the Eyes of a Defeated Basketball Team in the Shower
Room," "And on the Seventh Day Petals Fell on Petaluma,"
"Daphne of the Dunes," "Water, Water," and "U.S. Highway,"
which incorporates the conversation of hoboes on a freight train.

Equally unconventional are the compositions of John Cage. His
father was an inventor whose influence may go far toward explaining Cage's music. The foremost avant-garde composer for thirty
years, Cage proved his durability at a recent retrospective at New
York's Alice Tully Hall in honor of his sixtieth birthday; after all
these years his compositions still drew enthusiastic cheers and
heartfelt boos from the audience.

Cage's early work emphasized percussion. For example, his
*Third Construction* (1941) was scored for rattles, drums, tin cans,
claves, cowbells, a lion's roar, cymbal, ratchet, texponaxtle, quija-
das, cricket caller, and conch shell. More recently, however, he
has placed as much emphasis on the event as on the sounds. It is
interesting to note the differences between Cage and Handel; in
Cage's *Water Music* (1952), the performer repeatedly pours water
from a full container into an empty one, carefully regulating the
timing of the slosh with a stop watch; the composition also includes the riffling of playing cards and static produced by a radio.
This is what the composer calls "everyday music," derived from a
heightened awareness of the world around him. He explains it this

way: "Now I go to a cocktail party. I don't hear noise. I hear music."

Cage's compositions also show the input of Eastern philosophy. Many works are scored to include the casting of Chinese dice (the fortune-telling process of the *I-Ching*) to determine the order of the sounds to be performed; this is known as "aleatory music." On other occasions Cage relates Zen parables as a part of his performance. The Zen Buddhist fascination with silence can also be detected in his music. *Four Minutes Thirty-three Seconds* (1952) is intended for one or any number of instruments; it consists of three silent movements of 30", 2'23", and 1'40", during which the performers sit poised with their instruments without playing.

One of Cage's most remarkable works is *Theater Piece* (1963), first staged in Rome. Fusing Marx Brothers' antics with neodadaist art, the pianist enters by throwing a dead fish into his instrument. One musician walks around the stage dragging a chair loudly across the floor, while another, wearing a nightgown, hands out soggy pizzas to the audience.

John Cage is now a musical director with the Merce Cunningham dance company. He spends much of his spare time collecting and writing about mushrooms.

And while we're considering unusual composing techniques, both Schubert and Beethoven are said to have composed some of their greatest works in the bathtub.

**Most Unusual Mozart Composition:** Franz Joseph Haydn, Mozart's mentor, challenged his young pupil to write a piece for the piano that the elder composer could not play on first sight. Mozart accepted the challenge on the condition that if Haydn failed to play the composition, he would buy the champagne that night at dinner. In five minutes, Mozart finished what appeared to be a rather simple little score. Haydn launched into it confidently.

Halfway through the piece, Haydn found his left hand down at the bottom of the keyboard, his right way up at the top; astonishingly, the score called for the performer to play a solitary note right in the middle of the keyboard at the same time. Haydn broke off in disgust. "Nobody can play such music!" he said. Mozart then took the sheet music and sat down at the piano himself. He rushed through the simple first section, arriving at the part with his hands stretched wide apart. At the appropriate instant, Mozart leaned over and struck the "unplayable" note with his unusually large nose.

Haydn bought the champagne.

**Most Unusual Popular Singer:** No one knows what Alan Stivell is trying to say when he sings "Ur blank, ur blank, ar chopinad/ar chistr 'zo eit bout evet," but he is, nonetheless, having great success as a top-billed musical attraction throughout France. Stivell, who hails from Brittany and sings in Breton, is intensely nationalistic about his Celtic heritage, and his music, he says, "is an expression of outrage against French colonialism and its tools of TV and radio." Stivell accompanies himself on an electric thirty-one-string Celtic harp, or on the Cornish bagpipes, and is backed up by one of the best rock bands on the European scene.

# Pop Culture

**Best Board Game:** Monopoly, which has been around since the 1930s when $2,000 was a lot of rent to pay on a hotel on Boardwalk, still has more fantasy-based appeal than any of its imitators. There is just enough skill involved in the game to make it interesting, but not so much as to make it a tedious and taxing mental exercise. And, more than any other game, it satisfies the oral-acquisitive needs of most people.

**Best Hobby:** "Nearly every family has a favorite pet, such as a cat, dog, or parrot, to which they become attached and would like to have preserved when it dies," says Alfred Burkley. "By knowing taxidermy, and often from personal knowledge of the pet, you can preserve such specimens just as they were in life." Burkley knows whereof he speaks: He is president of the Northeastern School of Taxidermy in Omaha, Nebraska, a seventy-one-year-old correspondence school that has graduated some 450,000 satisfied bird-and-animal stuffers throughout the world.

The dimensions of taxidermy are varied. In addition to the stuffing and mounting of moose, horned toads, raccoons, and family pets, there is also "novelty taxidermy . . . a novel and fun-to-do sideline of regular taxidermy." Enjoying this amusing spin-off of the taxidermist's art takes only a good sense of humor and good aim with a rifle; the idea is to bag all the frogs, newts, rabbits, and squirrels you can find and dress their stuffed little corpses in anything from Prince Albert coats to Chicago White Sox uniforms—whatever tickles your funnybone—and arrange them in humorous real-life settings. Thus, in a NST brochure, we see a small group of coked-up frogs playing in a small jazz combo; a rabbit business executive having his hair cut by a rabbit barber while a rabbit manicurist does his nails; and a family of nattily dressed chipmunks out for a Sunday stroll.

The standard fee for stuffing a lion is $800; for stuffing a deer's head, $90. If you're good, you can earn $14,000 for stuffing an elephant. In fact, Sotheby's, the chic London gallery, recently auctioned off a stuffed great auk for $21,000.

**Best Mystery TV Series:** *Time* magazine film critic Richard Schickel chooses "Peter Gunn," which premiered back in 1958 starring Craig Stevens, Lola Albright (remember *her*?), and Herschel Bernardi. "Gunn" was infinitely more true-to-life, better written, and better acted than others of the genre.

Somehow "Alfred Hitchcock Presents" should be mentioned here, even though comparing it with "Peter Gunn" is a little like trying to add apples and oranges. Hitchcock's droll introductions and his epilogues, in which (in keeping with federal law) he punished an evildoer who may have gone scot-free during the drama itself, were sometimes as good as the rest of the show itself.

**Best Parade:** The Festival of Dionysus was always a time for luxury and revelling wherever there were Greeks. In honor of the god of wine, Ptolemy II (309–246 B.C.), Macedonian ruler of Egypt, orchestrated a splendid procession including all the animals of the Alexandria zoo—the finest in the ancient world.

The crowd gathered in the stadium in the early morning hours, as the parade was scheduled to begin at dawn and continue to dusk. One of the early features was a lavish float carrying a tremendous statue of Dionysus, attended by a host of admiring priests, priestesses, and dancing girls; the float was drawn by twenty-four straining men. There were countless men dressed as satyrs, frolicking lasciviously with women in Eastern dress, and all the while the wine flowed and flowed.

Then, according to the chronicler Athenaeus, the menagerie was led in. At the head was a tremendous elephant, the tallest ever seen, covered with trappings of gold and festooned with ivy leaves, and on top of his back was a satyr cavorting and directing the great beast. The lead elephant was followed by 24 elephant-drawn floats, 60 drawn by billy goats, 12 by lions, 6 by nanny goats, 4 by wild asses, 15 by buffalo, 8 by ostriches, and 7 by stags.

Next came the camels. Ptolemy II introduced camels to Egypt and he was particularly proud of his one- and two-humped stable. The camels drew a series of wagons, each carrying a romantic-looking tent "in the fashion of the barbarians" with an enticing woman in slave dress dancing alongside. Then came troops of Abyssinians loaded down with ivory tusks, ebony, trunks filled with jewels, and sacks of gold dust. Hunters crowded into the arena accompanied by thousands of fierce mastiffs. There were exotic birds in reed cages, flocks of sheep, a two-horned rhinoceros, more camels laden with spices and perfume, countless statues of the gods, Ptolemy, and Alexander; bevies of concubines carrying banners proclaiming the names of every Greek settlement in the world, a choir of 600 men in precious crowns, an orchestra playing richly ornamented citharas, 2,000 perfectly matched bulls, censers, potted palm trees, and, of course, vats brimming with wine. Finally, there were two colossal sculptures—one of Jupiter and one of Alexander—and a last chariot sending up clouds of incense.

**Best Stand-up Comedian:** Henny Youngman (see also *Most Unusual Stand-up Comedian* and *Worst Stand-up Comedian*).

**Best Television Documentary:** It was Edward R. Murrow of CBS who introduced the documentary to television, and by 1960 he had achieved virtual perfection in the form. "Harvest of Shame," a 1960 "CBS Reports" study of the plight of migrant farm workers in the South was as incisive as *Grapes of Wrath*, as eloquent, and in many ways more immediate.

**Best TV Quiz Show:** "The G. E. College Bowl." Why, *why* did they ever take America's favorite question-and-answer game off the air? Fast-moving, gripping, and *honest*, "College Bowl" became a national institution and was the one thing that made Sunday night, surely the most depressing time of the week, bearable. ("There's the whistle to start the first half—you're playing for a thirty-point bonus. In what Shakespearean play did an English king receive a gift of tennis balls from the Dauphin of France?") Sadly, Allen Ludden, the show's first "man with the questions," later sank to the plumbless depths of "Password" (a better parlor game than a TV show) and became, we think, the worst quizmaster/emcee in TV history. (His only evidence of talent, writes George Frazier, "would seem to be an inane grin.")

**Best TV Quiz Show Host:** Groucho Marx. That is, if you really do consider "You Bet Your Life" a quiz show—and you really do consider Groucho a host. (*Our* parents taught us that a host was always polite to his guests and Groucho was forever saying things to contestants like "You're a model? What do you model—clay?")

George Fenneman was almost as good a straight man as Margaret Dumont.

**Best TV/Radio Newscaster:** Edward R. Murrow. For nearly thirty years the greatness and mediocrity of broadcast journalists has been measured against the achievement of Edward R. Murrow, who is generally regarded as the greatest newsman in radio and television history. Murrow's "See It Now" series in the early 1950s—and in particular, the episodes in which he publicly confronted Joseph McCarthy at a time when the rest of the broadcast profession sat tight, waiting to see what move the Wisconsin demagogue would make next—are still unmatched for eloquence and courage.

Murrow died of lung cancer at his home in Pawling, New York, in 1965. ("I doubt that I could spend even half an hour without a cigarette with any ease or comfort," he said on a documentary he did on the dangers of cigarette smoking.) At the time of his death, Eric Sevareid of CBS said, "He was a shooting star and we will live in his afterglow a very long time."

**Best TV Show:** Attempting to choose the best television show ever screened is, we admit it, quite a dilemma. After all, can anyone say that Ed Murrow was better than Richard Boone—or that "Playhouse 90" was a better show than "See It Now"?

All the same, we'll make a choice. The all-time best TV show was probably the old Sid Caesar Saturday night classic "Your Show of Shows," with Imogene Coca, Howard Morris, Carl Reiner, and a staff of writers that included Woody Allen and Mel Brooks.

**Best TV Situation Comedy:** "You'll Never Get Rich," known more widely if less accurately as "The Phil Silvers Show." Silvers starred as the ever-enterprising Sergeant Ernest G. Bilko ("Line forms to the right for tickets to the Come-as-You-Were-on-the-Day-You-Were-Drafted-Dinner-Dance,") and Nat Hiken wrote most of the scripts, which still play well as reruns. An episode starring a chimpanzee who is inducted into the army was probably the high point of the series.

Dick Van Dyke made some of his earliest TV appearances on the Bilko series, and later was the star of "The Dick Van Dyke Show," thought by many critics, including *Time* film reviewer Richard Schickel, to be the funniest, most sophisticated family sitcom in television history. Produced by Sheldon Leonard and featuring a can't-lose cast—Van Dyke, Mary Tyler Moore, Rose Marie, and Morey Amsterdam—the show, say Arthur Shulman and Roger Youmans, "differed from many of its contemporaries in the situation comedy field in that it was often genuinely funny."

**Best TV Western:** "Have Gun, Will Travel." Richard Boone starred as Paladin, the first of the *thinking* cowboys, and the title of this series, as everyone must know by now, was lifted from his calling card: "Have Gun, Will Travel—Wire Paladin, Hotel Carlton, San Francisco." Paladin puffed expensive cigars; quoted Byron, and, as Arthur Shulman and Roger Youmans write, "completed his rounds with a unique combination of epicurean zest, Spartan valor and existential ennui."

Many critics, nonetheless, prefer "Gunsmoke," in which James Arness, fresh from his sensitive portrayal of "the Thing," starred as the equally formidable, if somewhat more communicative, Matt Dillon, assisted by gimpy sidekick Dennis Weaver, Amanda Blake as Miss Kitty, and Milburn Stone as Doc.

**Best True Confession Story:** In 1791, Alexander Hamilton, first Treasury secretary of the United States and co-drafter of its Constitution, found himself in a bit of a pickle. Earlier that year, he had listened sympathetically to the plight of Maria Reynolds who had come to his office in dire need of financial help since her husband had recently deserted her. Responding as much out of ardor as out of magnanimity, Hamilton agreed to do what he could, and a few nights later appeared at her home with the needed cash. Mrs. Reynolds was grateful, to say the least—so grateful, in fact, that she melted in Hamilton's arms, whereupon the great statesman, who was married and the father of five children, had his way with her.

And continued to have his way with her whenever the duties of state and family allowed him to get away. It all went quite smoothly until Mrs. Reynolds's AWOL husband reappeared on the scene and handed Hamilton an ultimatum: Pay or be exposed as an adulterer. Hamilton, of course, had no choice but to pay off Reynolds. Having satisfied his blackmailer, he continued his liaison with Mrs. Reynolds without interruption.

A year later Reynolds was convicted of shady dealings with the government and went to jail and soon after that Hamilton and Mrs. Reynolds ended their affair. But five years later, some political foes of Hamilton's falsely accused him in public of having been an intimate of Reynolds and conspiring with him to defraud the gov-

Alexander Hamilton

ernment. Hamilton's reputation was at stake and rather than be marked forever as a crook, which he was not, he told the entire story of the Maria Reynolds affair and all its sordid details in a pamphlet that had as big an audience in its day as *Forever Amber* and *Peyton Place* had in theirs. Alternately spicy and bathetic, it was the first of the great true confession stories, and it cleared Hamilton's name as a public statesman. And, happily, Mrs. Hamilton forgave him as well.

---

**Worst Board Game:** Something called Group Therapy, which came out a few years ago and is packed in a black box that's just full of mischief. The game equipment includes a stack of cards that contain such no-nonsense instructions as "Tell the person on your right a secret you've never told anyone before," and "Hold each player in a way that shows how you feel about him." If played right, the game stirs up a lot of anxieties without actually allowing the players to resolve them comfortably. A must for the masochistic.

**Worst Commercial:** Oxydol detergent ran an ad campaign in 1965 that included a TV commercial showing black women discussing their wash. This early attempt at representing the black buying public in advertising was marred by an announcer saying "When it's whiteness you're after . . ." and at the end, "Colored things come out nice, too."

**Worst Fad:** In the early 1960s, the specter of nuclear war frightened some 200,000 families throughout the United States into taking their government's advice and building concrete-reinforced fallout shelters beneath their homes. Fallout shelters, as you may recall, were drab, windowless affairs at best, stocked with drinking water, medicine supplies, food, clothing, blankets, playing cards, and anything else needed to survive a two- or three-week enforced confinement physically and psychologically intact. Many shelter-builders also kept a handgun or high-powered rifle handy against the possibility of an invasion by an unsheltered neighbor who demanded to be taken in and given protection. In fact, debating the merits of shooting your best friend between the eyes rather than letting him elbow his way into your shelter and drain off your family's oxygen supply was a favorite dinner-table/cocktail party diversion throughout the nation.

**Worst Hobby:** Annetta Del Mar of Chicago had a hobby that made members of Polar Bear clubs (who go swimming in the winter) seem like pikers. She used to freeze her entire body, except for her head, in ice. Turning professional for the New York World's Fair in 1939–1940, she had herself frozen as often as thirty or forty times a day. She attributed her remarkable ability to withstand cold temperatures to "willpower."

**Worst Record (Spoken Word):** A long-playing record of George McGovern reading from the great inaugural addresses of Washington, Lincoln, Jefferson, and Theodore Roosevelt is available from Spoken Arts, Inc.

**Worst Stand-up Comedian:** Henny Youngman (see also *Best Stand-up Comedian* and *Most Unusual Stand-up Comedian*).

**Worst TV Broadcasting Gaffe:** The Oakland Raiders were down by nine points in a crucial game against the New York Jets, broadcast live over NBC on a Sunday evening in 1968. As the Raiders made a concerted dash towards paydirt, millions of screens across the nation went blank as NBC prematurely cut short its coverage of the game and put on a regularly scheduled production of "Heidi" in its place. While the NBC switchboards were swamped with phone calls from apoplectic fans—so swamped, in fact, that the incessant ringing drained the power from the switchboard and the entire system broke down—the Raiders miraculously scored two quick touchdowns in the final seconds of play and won the game.

**Worst TV Mystery Series:** "Martin Kane, Private Eye," which premiered in 1949 and featured four different actors playing the lead in four successive seasons. (This must be a record of sorts—comparable to Joe DiMaggio's fifty-six-game hitting streak.) "Kane" was the first in the TV detective-mystery genre and in its shoot-em-up primitivism was probably the worst.

**Worst TV Quiz Show:** Maud Walker, a fifty-four-year-old Australian housewife, was a big winner on the daytime television game show "Temptation." The excitement was too much for her, and she suffered a fatal heart attack on camera. As sort of a consolation prize, a station executive offered a videotape recording of the show to the Walker family: "I'm sure they would like to see how happy she was," he explained.

To lay to rest an old rumor, Pinky Lee did not have a heart attack on his television show. Actually, it was his sinuses: His acute sinus infection brought on a convulsion.

**Worst TV Show:** Considering the hypnotic appeal they had to a large segment of the television-viewing public, "Strike It Rich," the Lever Brothers-sponsored tearjerker/giveaway show of the early 1950s, and the similarly based "Queen for a Day" probably represent television programming at its nadir. Both shows limited their contestants to those with sob stories to tell ("Mrs. Eustace's husband was fatally injured on the job last summer when he fell into a steaming vat of airplane mucilage, leaving her with nine children and a brain-damaged Lhasa apso to look after."). On one memorable "Strike It Rich" episode, a pregnant young woman, recently deserted by her husband, threatened to give up her child for adoption unless someone could come up with some cash for her—fast. Jack Gould, TV-radio reporter for *The New York Times*, called it "an example of television programming gone berserk."

**Worst TV Situation Comedy:** Lots of contenders here, but top honors, we feel, go to "I Dream of Jeannie," which came along in 1965 and still haunts the airwaves with incessant reruns. At one point in the history of this unnecessary series, NBC was badgered with letters and phone calls from irate viewers who objected to what seemed a rather tasteless episode-by-episode shrinking of Jeannie's already abbreviated attire. As it turned out, Jeannie, played by Barbara Eden, was pregnant, and grew more pregnant with each episode while the costume remained the same.

We have other favorites in this category, and had you caught us on another day, we might just as well have chosen any one of them as absolute worst: "Ozzie and Harriet," "Gidget," "Gomer Pyle," "The Beverly Hillbillies," and perhaps the most tasteless ongoing series in broadcasting history, "Hogan's Heroes."

**Worst TV Western:** "Bonanza." It was just about everyone's Sunday night favorite in the early and mid-1960s, but that doesn't make it *good*. This simpleminded series about the Cartwrights was all tears and flapdoodle with frequent doses of low comedy that were more inane than genuinely funny. Richard Schickel calls it the worst western ever.

**Most Unusual Circus Act:** In the summer of 1859, French acrobat Charles Blondin crossed a 1,300-foot rope strung across Niagara Falls. To stave off boredom, he walked some of the way with his hands and feet tied, some of the way on stilts, and some of the way with his feet in a gunnysack. Finally, he took a small stove out on the rope and fried up an omelet.

**Most Unusual Commercial:** The London *Daily Mail* noted in 1971 that a Protestant clergyman, Rev. Ronald Stephens, had been signed to endorse Blue Brand margarine in a television commercial. "I believe it is my duty to spread the Gospel at every opportunity," he told reporters, some of whom assumed that "the Gospel" was the brand of margarine he would be plugging. Sample line: "Margarine has goodness in it and the body needs the fats in margarine as the soul needs God."

**Most Unusual Dance:** In their annual snake dances, the Moqui Indians of Arizona hold rattlesnakes in their hands and mouths as they whirl around ecstatically. The rattlers are neither drugged nor defanged, yet only rarely is a dancer bitten, and even then the results are scarcely ever serious. Perhaps the dancers gradually immunize themselves with injections of venoms, or perhaps they have a secret antitoxin; it is a mystery known only to the initiates of the cult.

The ceremony in some ways resembles the services of certain Christian fundamentalist sects who test their faith by treading on serpents or holding them between their teeth. They find the justification for this unusual worship service in Mark 16: 18, in which Jesus describes the signs distinguishing true believers: "They shall take up serpents; and if they drink any deadly thing, it shall not hurt them." A Tennessee judge ordered an end to such rites after rattlers bit several worshippers, killing one, at a revival meeting in 1973.

A more lighthearted dance is the Rhathapygizein in which young Balkan misses kick their bare feet back up against their own buttocks, turning both buttocks and feet quite pink.

**Most Unusual Festival:** With the regularity of the swallows returning to San Juan Capistrano—and on the same day—hundreds of buzzards flap back from their winter homes to the dead, twisted trees of Hinckley, Ohio. Now, the citizens of Hinckley are no fools. They recognize a great and salable natural wonder when it hovers ominously over their heads, and they have honored the buzzards accordingly. Policemen in Hinckley wear a shoulder patch featuring three hungry buzzards against the background of the golden sun. And every March 15, the merchants of Hinckley sponsor a buzzard festival that attracts upwards of 20,000 tourists to welcome the migrating scavengers to their summer nesting grounds.

**Most Unusual Juggler:** Quadriplegic Matthew Buckinger (1674–1722) of Nuremburg, Germany, overcame his handicap and became a proficient musician, entertaining on the flute, bagpipes, dulcimer, and trumpet. Married four times, he supported his wives and eleven children with the money he earned as an artist and writer. But what startled Buckinger's contemporaries most of all was his considerable skill as a juggler.

**Most Unusual Parade:** In Sparta, celibacy was a crime, and the state designated the appropriate age for marriage—thirty for men and twenty for women. Men who remained bachelors beyond that time lost their right to vote, and, worse still, they were forbidden to attend the processions in which the young men and women danced and revelled in the nude. Not that the unmarried did not have their chance to march through the streets without any clothes on. According to Plutarch, the holdouts were frequently ordered

**HINCKLEY** - They did it again! The world famous Buzzards of Hinckley Ridge have returned to their roosting area in Hinckley, Ohio.

Official Buzzard Spotter, Sgt. Rod Berger, of the Metropolitan Park Rangers spotted the first buzzard near the roost area at 6:15 AM March 15th. This official sighting touched off the largest celebration of its kind anywhere in the world. The buzzards have been returning to their roosting area in Hinckley since before recorded history; every year on this date. History books have

records of this wonder of nature dating back to the early 1800eds.

This Sunday has been designated Buzzard Day in Hinckley by the Hinckley Chamber of Commerce. Crowds of visitors, from all over North America will be in Hinckley to help welcome the buzzards home. Countless others will be watching the celebration on TV news broadcasts, and listening to radio accounts of the buzzards arrival.

Winners of the popular 'Clock the Buzzards' contest conducted by WJW Radio will be announced as soon as the thousands of en-

tries have been examined. The first prize in the contest will be a vacation for two to Buzzards Bay Mass. The lucky winners will be flown there by American Airlines.

Others will be visiting Hinckley as winners of a Buzzard Poem contest being conducted by WTOD in Toledo, Ohio.

The visitors to Hinckley will eat over 1500 lbs. of sausages, and mountains of pancakes, at Hinckley Elementary School. They will listen to the barbershop sounds of the Singcopations as they sing the song 'When the

Buzzards Return to Hinckley Ridge', along with other favorites. The Buzzard lovers will see close up the three live buzzards on display through the courtesy of the Cleveland Museum of Natural History.

Many local organizations will have displays at the school for visitors to see. A ham radio station K8JAS, will be on the air from Hinckley. The station operated by Hinckleyite, Joe Purta will make contact with over 1000 other ham operators to

and award a special Buzzard Day certificate to them.

Buzzard Day is by far the largest one day event in Medina county, with the total attendance in Hinckley surpassing most professional sports events held in nearby Cleveland. It has shown an increase in attendance every year since the first Buzzard Day in 1957. Hinckleyites on vacation are instantly recognized at being from 'Americas' Best Known Township' thanks to their friends. The Buzzards of Hinckley Ridge.

# HINCKLEY REPORTER

"America's Best Known Township"

Volume 16    Number 1    Published and sponsored by Hinckley Chamber of Commerce, Inc., P.O. Box 354, Hinckley, Ohio 44233    March 16, 1973

## REPRESENTIVE BATCHELDER TO MEET WITH HINCKLEY RESIDENTS

**HINCKLEY**-An opportunity for Hinckley residents to attend an informal meeting with their State Representative has been set for Monday March 19th at 8:30 in the Hinckley Townhall.

Representative Bill Batchelder III will be present to answer your questions on issues effecting Hinckley residents on a state and local level. Mr. Batchelder will also be able to inform local residents on the status of bills now before the legislature.

The meeting was arranged by Hinckley Township Trustees, and will be conducted on an informal basis, with all attending having an opportunity to be heard.

ALL EYES ARE UP—This weekend visitors from all over the country will be in Hinckley for the annual Buzzard Day observance. Most of them will visit Buzzards Roost in the park for a first hand look at the famous Buzzards of Hinckley Ridge. photo by Dave Bibalko

## Sewer Hearing Recessed

**MEDINA**—A standing room only crowd fill the large court-room at the Medina County Courthouse to voice their opinions on the proposed sewer district and treatment plant planned for Brunswick and parts of Hinckley.

The strong opposition to the sewer system has been spearheaded by the Hinckley Environmental Protectors (HEP) They have been supported in their opposition by the Brunswick Hills - township Trustees, who have retained attorney William Batchelder II of Medina. HEP was represented before the County Commissioners by their counsel L.A. Reed.

Both groups have opposed the planned construction since it was announced over one year ago. They say that it is primarily to benefit the City of Brunswick and is not needed in other areas. They claim that sewer construction will destroy the semi-rural nature of the area, by forcing the lowering of lot sizes.

Mr. Batchelder, and Mr. Reed and others told commissioners that the promise that they made to Hinckley residents in the path of the proposed sewer not to have to tap in unless they wanted to was in violation of Health Department rules. The attorney said that according to law all landowners would have to tap in and use the sewer, if and when it is available.

The question of the availability of federal funds was also said to be in doubt, due to administration cutbacks in federal spending.

Many of those present objected to the 10:00 a.m. time of the hearing saying that it was set at that time to discourage the working man from attending to voice his opinion.

Due to the many questions raised at the hearing, the commissioners recessed the hearing until Tuesday April 10 at 8:00 p.m. at the courthouse. Commissioners said that if the attendance at that hearing was too large that it would be moved to a larger location in Medina.

## Trustees Plan Meeting On Road Constuction

**HINCKLEY**-The Hinckley Township Trustees have announced that an open meeting has been set for April 11 at 8:00 in the townhall to review the requirement regarding the use of concrete for roads in any new development in Hinckley.

The meeting was sparked by the recent request by developer James Navratil when he asked that he be allowed to use asphalt for roads in his new development off of Rt. 303, just east of River Rd. Navratil has been present at several recent trustees meeting and engaged in verbal exchanges, some of them quite heated, with township officials.

Navratil recently complained that trustees were moving too slowly in this matter, and that the

date for the meeting on the matter (April 11) was inconvient for him. Trustees replyed that the meeting was set in order to hear the remarks of experts on both sides, and not the pitch of a salesman.

Trustees Chairman, Don Maatz said that trustees have contacted several experts in the field who will be present at the meeting. Among them will be a representative of the Asphalt Institute from Columbus and Mr. James A. Shanteman, District Engineer and Representive of the Portland Cement Association.

Also present will be Jack Forman, Medina County Engineer, and one or two notable engineers in the field of road construction.

## Rubbish Pickup To Start April 21st

**HINCKLEY**—Township trustees have set another large item rubbish pickup for Hinckley. The pickup will start with the southwest portion on the township on Saturday April 21st.

Other parts of Hinckley will have collection on following Saturdays. The schedule will be announced in time for residents to be aware of it.

Trustees Chairman, Don Maatz also said that some residents were again dumping trash at the townhall. Maatz said that this practice must stop. Residents are only to bring trash to the townhall at the prescribed time on Saturdays when the truck is there. He said that those who dump can be prosecuted for littering.

### TRUSTEES WELCOME VISITORS

The Hinckley Board of Township trustees, Chairman Don Maatz, Robert Hale, and Joe Schwager, extend a big welcome to those from out of the area who are visiting Hinckley to help celebrate Buzzard Day.

The Trustees, the elected representives of the people of Hinckley, hope that your stay in Hinckley will be pleasant, and hope that you will visit us again.

THEY ARE REAL FRIENDLY-Buzzard Lady, Sandra O'Brien holds a live buzzard on her arm. Sandra and the buzzards will be at the Buzzard Day celebration March 18th.

Buzzard Day Festival, Hinckley, Ohio

to parade naked for the amusement of their fellow citizens—even in the February snows—while singing a song in which they proclaimed themselves justly punished for having flouted the marriage laws. And Plutarch records that chronic misogamists ran the risk of being attacked, scratched, kicked, and beaten by bands of furious women.

**Most Unusual Record (LP):** Staten Island, New York, speech pathologist Jerry Cammarata says his latest brainchild, a fifty-two-minute-long LP record labeled "Auditory Memory," "makes a great gift," and indeed, it does make a great gift for the man who has everything, except, perhaps, for his hearing. Both sides of the record are completely silent.

Cammarata, who occupies an unchallenged double berth in *The Guinness Book of World Records*—for sitting in a bathtub seventy-five hours straight and for singing for ninety-six hours nonstop in the New York City subway system—says that "being forced to sit and listen to nothing gives you a chance to conjure up previously learned musical experiences," which all people have, he notes, "except for imbeciles." Moreover, it provides a welcome relief from noise pollution, the tensions of everyday life, and the relentless din of rock 'n' roll which, he suggests, "is damaging to your ears."

**Most Unusual Stand-up Comedian:** Henny Youngman. "Man walks into a psychiatrist's office, says, 'Doc, nobody listens to me.' Psychiatrist says, 'Next.' "

Youngman is no skinflint when it comes to dispensing punch lines, dealing out two-liners at five a minute with brief pauses to drag his bow across his violin strings. Percentage-wise, relatively few of his jokes would make it on their own, but he hits his audience with such a carpet-bombing barrage that the sheer speed of his delivery is hilarious. In 1972 Youngman taped 230 of his best (or worst) jokes to be dispensed with candy bars from a chain of vending machines in Dallas.

**Most Unusual TV Documentary:** In 1966 the British Broadcasting Company offered on their nightly news program a five-minute docu-feature on the complexities of spaghetti-growing in Italy. "Throughout Italy millions of pasta farmers are working harder than ever before to harvest their crop before it falls prey to the pests that ravaged much of the crop last season," an even-voiced announcer told his audience. His narration was the voice-over to

BBC footage of farmers in broad-brimmed hats working their way up neatly trimmed aisles of spaghetti plants in the Italian farmlands, plucking sun-ripened strands of spaghetti from the branches and storing them in wicker baskets. "Special efforts have been taken this year to ward off the spaghetti weevil, which has been especially destructive in recent years," he said. Not a word was mentioned about levity or satire; no smiles were cracked, no giggles escaped, and millions of British viewers accepted, if with some surprise, the fact that spaghetti grew on trees.

**Most Unusual TV Show:** In 1970, thousands of viewers took seriously "The Million Mark Game," a game-show parody broadcast over West German TV. The emcee designated several "victims" who were assigned to proceed toward a specific destination and were promised a million marks if they reached it safely. In the meantime, a search party of "killers" was similarly assigned to hunt down the "victims." In a modern-day replay of Orson Welles's classic 1938 radio dramatization of "The War of the Worlds," several thousand people panicked. At the same time, several "victims" phoned in to say that for a million marks, they'd be willing to take their chances. One man, evidently fascinated by the whole thing, telephoned the TV station after the hoax was made public, and asked if he could be considered as a future victim in case the producers decided to bring the show back on a serious basis.

# *Journalism*

**Best American Daily Newspaper:** *The New York Times.* The Great Gray Lady of American newspapers has come in for a lot of criticism in recent years as being too indiscriminating in its presentation of the news, too selective in weeding out material that might embarrass the Establishment, too stodgy—and even too inaccurate. All the same, it still heads just about every list of best American newspapers, including one by *Time* magazine in 1964 and another by *The Saturday Review. Esquire* magazine says, "Let's face it. *This* is the national newspaper; all the rest are regional collections of press releases. If you still care about living in America and the world, you need it *bad.*"

There is one other candidate for all-around top-drawer professionalism and it also comes out of New York—*The Wall Street Journal.* Its thrust is largely financial, true, but you're making a mistake if you think that the only people who read it are investment bankers and drab-looking men in white shirts and wing tips. Says British journalist Henry Fairlie, it's the only American paper to have mastered "the technique of the background news story."

**Best Circulations:** The most widely read newspaper in the United States is the New York *Daily News,* with a daily circulation of 3,108,832. *Asahi Shimbun,* a Japanese daily, is the best-circulated paper in the world, with a circulation of 9,257,000. As for magazines, *Reader's Digest* leads the list with a monthly circulation of 17,586,000.

**Best Comic Strips:** The Washington *Post.* That is, if you mean the newspaper with the biggest—and presumably best—selection of comic strips of any daily in the United States, according to a survey by *Time* magazine.

As for the *best single strip,* front runner is "Peanuts," by cartoonist Charles Schulz. Rarely inane, often insightful, and almost always funny, "Peanuts" outstrips (if you'll pardon the pun) any of the other *funny* funnies, with the possible exception of Walt Kelly's "Pogo," and is heartwarming to boot, without ever being gushy. Martin Jezer notes that "Peanuts" "probably holds the distinction of being clipped out of more newspapers and posted on more bulletin boards, lockers and walls than any other of its newsprint relatives on the comics page."

The *best single line ever uttered by a comic strip character* was uttered by Pogo: "We have met the enemy and he is us."

**Best Crossword Puzzles:** Again, *The New York Times.* The best crossword puzzles are in New York—and, more specifically, some feel, in *New York* magazine. But the puzzle that graces the last page of that weekly is merely an import from the *Times* of London. So it really doesn't count.

With that dismissal we turn to *The New York Times,* which, for day-to-day consistency of quality, offers the best puzzles anywhere. Will Weng took over from Margaret Farrar as puzzle editor of the *Times* in 1968, and the puzzles have since grown a bit—but *just* a bit—easier. Nobody knows how many daily readers of the paper turn to the puzzle first, even before glancing at the first page or the obits, but chances are it's a sizable percentage of the total readership. "Some people say the puzzle is a waste of time," says Weng, a one-time reporter and copy desk editor of the *Times.* "Well, it's like the movies, concerts—they're all wasting time. Which one you choose depends on how much pleasure you get out of it." The puzzles are constructed by free-lancers, but it's editor Weng who's at the receiving end of both the praise and the invective that the puzzles often prompt. One of his favorite letters was from a faithful solver who was outraged by what he considered a below-the-belt use of numerals in one Sunday puzzle. "If I ever meet you in a restaurant and you are under four feet tall, I will be very abusive," he wrote.

The best single puzzle ever to appear anywhere—if difficulty is a measure of quality—was published in the February 1965 issue of *Esquire* magazine and touted as "the world's hardest crossword puzzle."

**Best Humor Columnist:** Russell Baker. Art Buchwald, whose thrice-weekly column is distributed by the Los Angeles *Times* syndicate to 363 United States newspapers, is the favorite of mil-

# THE WORLD'S HARDEST CROSSWORD PUZZLE

*(Answers appear on page 288.)*

## ACROSS

1 Symbol (ə) representing an unstressed central vowel sound
6 Hero of "Lalla Rookh" tale
11 Pretty : Colloq.
16 Shrill trilled sounds
17 Part of a name in Robin Hood tales
18 Character in "A Masked Ball"
20 Fawn-colored
21 One type of alcohol
22 With : Dial.
24 Its symbol is X
25 Where the Byelukha is
27 Gem of changeable color
29 Testimonial : Abbr.
31 Drumlin
33 Hero of Thackeray burlesque
35 Name in the news, June, 1958
36 Author of "Louisiana Hayride"
37 Common noun suffix
39 En —— de (as regards) : Fr.
40 Cloth of undyed wool
42 Type of church proclamation
43 Heads of vegetables, as cabbages, in Britain
45 Basically
48 Ornamental plasterwork
49 Joins together, as if by dovetails
51 Item used in drafting
52 Kind of flower or moss
53 Where Trim is
55 Till
56 Indian girl's short-sleeved bodice with very low neckline
57 Squirrel's nest
60 Cape of Smith Island, off N.C.
62 Riffian's neighbor
63 Yesterday : Lat.
64 Musical direction
67 A number : Abbr.
68 Coffee plantation in Brazil
70 Prismatic crystal
72 Paper screen serving as wall or sliding door
74 Ahead of the game
76 A hater of tobacco smoke
78 Profits for distribution : Slang
79 Part of the Empire State
80 Sea lavender
81 Famous citizen of Toledo
83 Whidah
84 Passau's waterfront
85 Twenty, in combinations
87 Wildcat akin to the jaguarundi
89 Powder used as a photographic developer
90 Roscoe's relatives
91 Make a gesture of respect
92 Cinco's neighbor
93 Europeans
95 Name in the news, 1922
98 Go haywire, in a way
101 What perennials do
105 Love song, old style
106 Aqueous solutions of gum
108 Chorus, in a way
109 Native of region S of the Hindu Kush
110 Certain prices in Wall Street
111 Oversupply
113 Skate, French style
114 Early version of the adding machine
115 Great Tom's voice
116 Gallic expostulation
119 Verthandi, for example
120 —— heredes
121 Uralic people living in Siberia
124 Combining form in many medical terms
126 One of the ologies
127 Formidable feature of the Bernese Oberland
129 Radio and signaling expression
131 Vertical grooves on the median lines of upper lips
133 Of impressively generous size
134 Certain to get
135 Nymph in Greek myth
136 Small Persian rug
137 One of a trio in baseball broadcasting
138 Greats and others

## DOWN

1 Wild sheep of Asia
2 Top, in Italy
3 Viking who ruled over what is now Normandy
4 —— right, legal term
5 Tree of the dogwood family
6 Time of repose : Abbr.
7 Substance separated unchanged from another substance
8 Tall and thin
9 Common French phrase
10 Blend by imperceptible degrees
11 Concern of shipping concerns
12 Amount by which a container of liquor falls short of being full
13 Dissimulation
14 Slight modifying quality
15 Abbreviation in medical parlance
16 A thousand years
19 Mount Cook, in New Zealand
20 Doric garment
23 African fox with outsize ears
24 Moderate reddish-orange color
26 Sentence in controversy
28 In the bag
30 Shakespearean role
32 Part of a proverb dating back to 1150
34 Entries on a flow chart : Abbr.
36 Bombay site of ancient rock-cut temple
38 One of Hawaii's symbols
40 Rossetti's —— Beatrix
41 Part of a coronation ceremony
42 Idolatry
44 Musical term
46 Third group of a certain series
47 Very high up
48 Bearing : Comb. form
50 Springs on the Yampa River
52 One cause of absenteeism in schools
54 Describing many a notion
56 Works with a bricklayer's tool
57 Loincloth worn by Hindus
58 Term in typesetting
59 Famous first name in music
61 Hebrew letter
64 First ——
65 Vest, for one
66 Results of serendipity
69 Variety of apple
71 Pour —— (for fun) : Fr.
73 Dweller on the shore of Little Minch
75 Large wildcat
77 Variety of green quartz
82 Buoyantly
86 Exclamation of impatience
88 Showy tanagers of South America
91 Language of the Vogul
94 Slangy term from 1949
95 Birds of the genus Nestor
96 Burden of a "wobblies" song
97 Have —— in
98 Severe or harsh : Dial.
99 Not *domani*
100 Famous name in turf lore
102 Relative of Vendémiaire
103 Gaelic cry of grief
104 Part of an archaic refrain
106 Chicken with black, white or buff feathers
107 Phenomenon possibly connected with increased rainfall
110 Part of O'Henry's last words
112 Start of many an Alma Mater song
115 God represented as half man and half fish
116 Wine town of S. Italy
117 Sponge, in zoology
118 Relatives of 116 Across
121 Be the author of
122 Berlin's "always"
123 Mighty, in combinations
125 Mongol of Chinese Turkestan
128 Endings for town, train, etc.
130 One type of chemistry : Abbr.
132 Places to live : Abbr.

lions, but he's completely outclassed by Russell Baker of *The New York Times*. Baker is a better writer than Buchwald, more inventive, more profound, more literate, and—most important—much funnier. Buchwald's columns, particularly in recent months, have a formularized look about them, as if they'd been stamped from a cookie cutter. Funny, yes—but they've rarely diverged from the rather outworn topic of presidential politics. Baker's subject matter is much more varied than Buchwald's and he is stylistically more versatile.

**Best Magazine:** *Encounter,* of which *Esquire* magazine has said, "probably not as good now as when it was backed by the CIA, but still the best general monthly magazine going." *Esquire* itself is responsible for what is certainly the biggest—542 pages—and probably the best single issue of any magazine ever published anywhere in the world: its October 1973 issue, marking the fortieth anniversary of the magazine. Most of the material in that issue had previously been published in *Esquire,* but with writers like Hemingway, Fitzgerald, Faulkner, and Baldwin filling its pages— who cares?

**Best News Photography:** The New York *Daily News* has been billed for umpteen years as "New York's picture newspaper," and its photography, especially in the centerfold, is probably as good as any daily photojournalism to be found anywhere in the United States, although that is a distinction of dubious worth. Better quality is found across the Atlantic. Says *Esquire* magazine, the Sunday supplement of the *Times* of London offers "the best example of photography used in support of an idea. The fusion of pictures and text is often aimed at by other magazines, but rarely accomplished."

**Best Sunday Edition of a Newspaper:** *The New York Times.* It used to be said of the mammoth old *Saturday Evening Post* that reading it in bed was a hazard; should you fall asleep, it would fall on you and crush you to death. Today the same *caveat* might apply to the Sunday *Times* which, at sixty cents, is still the biggest journalistic bargain in the United States. The average issue has 350 pages and weighs nearly three pounds. In addition to the same splendid news coverage as in the daily edition of the *Times*, there is also the *Times* magazine, which is still the best Sunday supplement in America despite a reputation in some circles for superficiality and blandness; the Sunday "Book Review," on a par with the *Times Literary Supplement* (of London) and alone worth the price of the paper; and the "News of the Week in Review," which scoops *Time* and *Newsweek* by two days and has better news coverage and in-depth analysis of current issues than either of the two major news magazines.

---

**Worst American Newspaper:** The Manchester *Union Leader*. The *Union Leader*'s fair-to-middling circulation of 64,000 is a deceptively modest indication of the paper's real sway—not only in northern New England but throughout conservative America. Its closest companion, the Nashua *Telegraph*, boasts but a third of the *Union Leader*'s circulation, and the *Union Leader* is the only daily newspaper distributed throughout the state of New Hampshire.

The editorial alter ego of right-wing blatherer William Loeb, the paper's news columns and editorials betray a narrow isolationism tinged with bigotry and ignorance that places the paper among the ten worst newspapers in the United States according to the journalistic review [*More*]. Loeb once ran a lead editorial in his paper scoring the formation of a gay students' organization at the University of New Hampshire. The headline: BOOT THE PANSIES OUT OF UNH. On another occasion, he printed a scathing indictment of Henry Kissinger under the heading: KISSINGER THE KIKE?

Another favorite of [*More*] is the New Orleans *Times-Picayune*, which, after 138 years of daily mediocrity, still boasts a circulation of well over 200,000. "This bloated, sluggish, myopic giant of the Delta morn," says [*More*], is still peppered with some eminently forgettable features: "A five-column Sears ad on the op-ed page and Jane Fonda vilified on the editorial page. . . . Ads that look like news stories. . . . News stories that read like ads. Pitiful Washington coverage. No investigative reporting at all."

**Worst Magazine in the United States:** The evils of *People*, Time-Life's drippy new nonmagazine, and the mindless outrages of *Cosmopolitan* are as nothing compared to *Kampfruf*, the official publication of the National Socialist League. Based in Los Angeles, the NSL is the official organization of Nazi homosexuals not only in twenty-five states throughout the nation but in several foreign countries as well. *Kampfruf* (which means battle-cry) is a monthly and its pages are adorned with lots of swastikas, pictures of naked men, and editorials which play up Hitler's admiration of noted gays like Frederick the Great and Richard Wagner. While its small core of subscribers are generally euphoric ("How long we have waited, we Aryan homophiles, for someone with strength and daring to wrench the wheel from those who have steered Gay Liberation hard to the left," writes one reader), others are less enthusiastic, including the National Socialist White People's Party, in Arlington, Virginia. "On the question of homosexuality," they recently editorialized in the *Nazi Bulletin,* "the position of National Socialism is crystal-clear and unequivocal: Queerism is unnatural and a sick perversion of the life instinct."

**Worst News Photo of the '70s:** A serious diplomatic rift between the governments of Japan and South Korea in September 1974, prompted thirty-two Korean demonstrators to hack off their index fingers publicly and then present them at the Japanese embassy in Seoul, South Korea, wrapped in newspaper, like the remains of a fish-and-chips dinner. The fingers were photographed for publication in the Korean *Times.* Later reporters discovered that the South Korean government had paid handsomely for this "spontaneous" act of patriotism; demonstrators received anywhere from $125 to $375 for each finger they sacrificed.

**Worst Public Opinion Poll:** The *Literary Digest* Presidential Straw Poll of 1936. The *Literary Digest* had polled nearly 2.5 million voters and by the morning of November 1, just four days before Franklin Roosevelt's bid for reelection, the news magazine made its prediction: 370 electoral votes and a resounding victory over FDR for Kansas Republican Alfred M. Landon. But by election night, Roosevelt had been swept into a second term by the most overwhelming landslide in American history, winning 523 electoral votes to Landon's eight. Red-faced and miffed, the *Digest*'s editors vowed to do better next time. They never got the chance; the magazine went bankrupt and disappeared within a year.

**Most Unusual Edition of a Newspaper:** Editor-in-chief Mickey Carlton of the Richman (British Columbia) *Review* published a special edition of his paper in 1970 "designed to please everyone and offend nobody." Excised from the *Review*'s pages for one day was anything that could be even remotely construed as beyond the bounds of good news or good taste: reports of court proceedings, crime stories, pictures of indecently clad women, and angry editorials. The lead story on page one concerned a local farmer's purchase of a $4,000 heifer, which was photographed with objectionable parts of its anatomy airbrushed out. The paper sold miserably and provoked much criticism. Carlton apologized for the lack of "lively news" in the "special pink tea issue, dedicated to the minority who prefer to view the news through rose-colored glasses."

**Most Unusual Press Conference:** During his years in the White House, John Quincy Adams liked to rise before dawn, grab a towel, and slip out unseen through the back door for a quick dip in the Potomac before taking on breakfast and his presidential duties. One day, having cavorted in the water for an hour or so, he stepped up onto the bank to dry himself and, stark naked and dripping wet, found himself face-to-face with Anne Newport Royall, a noted investigative reporter of the day, sitting on his underwear. Adams quickly stepped back into the water to cover his privates and then demanded that Miss Royall leave, but she insisted on first asking him some rather pointed questions about his pet project, the Bank of America, which she heartily opposed. For all his anger, Adams had no choice but to grant the unexpected interview. In later years, the crusading Miss Royall was tried and convicted in the court of the District of Columbia for being a "common scold."

# Sports

**Best (Baseball) Batter:** The best batter and probably the greatest all-around player in the history of the game was Tyrus Raymond "Ty" Cobb who played with the Detroit Tigers and the Philadelphia Athletics. Some of his records include:

Highest lifetime batting average .................... .367
Most lifetime hits ................................ 4,191
Most seasons leading the major leagues in batting .... 11
Most consecutive seasons batting over .300 .......... 23

But Josh Gibson of the old Negro leagues may have been the best ever. From 1930 to 1946 he hit some 800 home runs, clouting as many as 89 one season and 75 in another. In one 1934 contest he hit the only home run ever to clear the roof of Yankee Stadium.

Rogers Hornsby of the St. Louis Cardinals batted .424 in 1924, the best season's batting average recorded in modern baseball.

James F. "Tip" O'Neill, of the old American Association's St. Louis club, hit .492 in 1887, when bases on balls were counted as hits.

The longest hitting streak ever achieved was by Yankee outfielder Joe DiMaggio in 1941. DiMaggio hit safely in fifty-six consecutive games that year between May 15 and July 16, finally going hitless in a night game against Cleveland on July 17. During that period he hit 15 home runs, drove in 55 runs, and batted .408.

The home run records of Babe Ruth, Roger Maris, and Hank Aaron are common knowledge: Ruth hit 60 in a 154-game season in 1927; Maris hit 61 in a 162-game season in 1961; and Aaron's 733 home runs to date are the most ever hit in a lifetime.

Among the more arcane home run records: Stan Musial of the

St. Louis Cardinals hit five home runs in a doubleheader in 1954; Dale Long of the Pittsburgh Pirates homered in eight consecutive games in 1956; Wes Ferrell of the Cleveland Indians hit nine home runs in 1931, the most ever hit by a pitcher in a single season. He also won 22 games that year.

**Best (Baseball) Fielding Play:** Willy Mays's catch off Vic Wertz in the opening game of the 1954 World Series. In the eighth inning of that game Cleveland Indian first baseman Vic Wertz walloped a towering drive to center field. Mays ran as fast as he could—which was *fast*—and caught up with the ball 450 feet from home plate, catching it one-handed with his back to the diamond. Said Mays after the game, "I knew I had it all the way."

Al Gionfriddo, an obscure utility outfielder for the Brooklyn Dodgers, robbed Joe DiMaggio of a home run in the 1947 World Series with a running catch that many feel was greater than Mays's play in 1954. Arthur Daley of *The New York Times* called it "one of the most unbelievable catches ever seen anywhere."

**Best (Baseball) Manager:** John J. McGraw. In a 1939 poll, John McGraw was voted by sportswriters as the greatest manager ever. Hot-tempered and aggressive, McGraw was most famous as manager of the New York Giants from 1902 until poor health forced his retirement in 1932, just two years before he died. "McGraw was a scrapper who fought with umps and tongue-lashed players," according to sportswriter Ralph Hickok, but he was scrupulously honest, a brilliant tactician, and universally respected by his own players and by opponents. Under McGraw's tutelage, the Giants won ten pennants and four World Series.

The won-lost record of Connie Mack hardly compares with that of McGraw, but sheer managerial longevity may very well qualify him as McGraw's equal. From 1901–1950 he managed the Philadelphia Athletics, piloting them to nine pennants and five world championships. As brilliant a field strategist as McGraw, and as ruthlessly honest, he was otherwise McGraw's opposite. Quiet and circumspect, he dressed in street clothes when he managed and rarely if ever left the dugout to argue with an umpire. A man of boundless grace and patience, he was seldom called anything other than "Mr. Mack" by his own or opposing players.

**Best (Baseball) Pitcher:** The choice is traditionally between Walter Johnson, Christy Mathewson, and Cy Young, with the edge going to Johnson who pitched for the Washington Senators from

1907–1927, winning 416 games and turning in a 2.17 earned run average with perhaps the best fastball in the history of the game. But Satchel Paige, who played most of his career in the Negro leagues, joining Bill Veeck's Cleveland Indians in 1948 as a forty-two-year-old rookie, may well have outclassed them all. According to Dizzy Dean, who watched him pitch, and major league stars like Joe DiMaggio and Charlie Gehringer, who played against him, Paige was the best ever.

**Best (Baseball) Player (Current):** This is a category that inevitably evokes arguments. Our choice is Reggie Jackson of the Oakland A's, whom Ted Williams has called "the most natural hitter I've ever seen." In 1973 Jackson led the American League in home runs (32), runs batted in (117), runs scored (99), game-winning hits (18), and slugging percentage (.531). His .293 batting average was tenth best in the league. Jackson is fast—he does the 100-yard dash in 9.6 seconds—plays right field better than anyone in the major leagues since Carl Furillo, and is unquestionably the major force on the best team in professional baseball today.

**Best (Baseball) Runner:** James Thomas "Cool Papa" Bell. When he was voted into Baseball's Hall of Fame in 1974, baseball commissioner Bowie Kuhn called "Cool Papa" Bell "the fastest man ever to play baseball." Bell played twenty-nine years in the Negro leagues, the California Winter League, the Mexican League, the Cuban League, and in the Dominican Republic, but never in the major leagues. During a 200-game season in 1933 he stole 175 bases and in another year his remarkable speed was the major factor in a .480 batting average. Judy Johnson, a long-time friend and rival who played against Bell, says that an infielder could not afford to play at his normal depth when Bell was at bat. "If you played in your regular position," he says, "you'd never throw him out."

**Best (Baseball) Season (Individual Athlete):** Babe Ruth was baseball's greatest player and the best year he or anyone else in baseball history ever had was 1920 (and not, as you may have thought, 1927). That was the Babe's first year with the New York Yankees, as Ruth's biographer Robert W. Creamer has pointed out, and the statistics tell the story: 54 home runs, 137 runs batted in, 137 runs scored, 9 triples, 36 doubles, 14 stolen bases, and a .376 batting average. His astronomical .847 slugging average that year surely ranks among the great achievements of Western man.

**Best (Baseball) Team:** The 1927 Yankees. "The 1927 Yankee team has been called the greatest of all time more often than any other club in the annals of baseball," notes Joe Reichler, baseball editor of the *Associated Press*. Babe Ruth hit 60 home runs that year, batting a lusty .356 and driving in 164 runs. First baseman Lou Gehrig was no less impressive with 47 homers, 175 runs batted in, and a batting average of .373. Left fielder Earl Combs batted .356, center fielder Bob Meusel batted .337—with 102 r.b.i.'s—and second baseman Tony Lazzerri batted .309, hitting 18 home runs and driving in 102 runs. Yankee pitching that season was equally superb: Herb Pennock posted a 19–6 record, Waite Hoyt was 20–7, Urban Shocker 18–6, and Wilcy Moore, one of the most reliable relief pitchers of all time, 19–7. The Yankees finished 19 games ahead of the second-place Philadelphia Athletics in 1927, and won 110 games—an American League record that stood until the Cleveland Indians broke it with 111 victories in 1954. (The Indians were subsequently defeated in the World Series by the New York Giants, four games to none.) The Yankees went on to take the Pittsburgh Pirates in four straight games in the World Series. Those who were present say that Pirate morale was demolished during batting practice before the opening game; Pittsburgh players stared goggle-eyed as the Yankees' "Murderers' Row" rifled baseball after baseball into the grandstands.

**Best (Baseball) Umpire:** Bill Klem. Known as "the Old Arbiter," Klem was a National League umpire from 1905–1942. Early in his career he locked horns with John McGraw over a close call and incurred the Giant manager's unending wrath; or so it seemed. Within a remarkably short time McGraw became convinced of Klem's utter honesty—and skill—as did everyone else in the National League, and often insisted that Klem be behind the plate during crucial games for the Giants.

**Best Basketball Team (College):** The University of Kentucky Wildcats of 1948–49. This is the team, according to sportswriter Luke Walton, that is "generally acknowledged as the greatest college basketball team of all time," a tough five-man combination that worked like a well-oiled machine. After they graduated, the five—Alex Groza, Wallace "Wah-Wah" Jones, Ralph Beard, Joe Holland, and Clifford Barker (who could balance a basketball on one finger)—turned down most of the bids they'd received from the professional teams and bought their own franchise in Indianapolis instead, playing in 1949 as the Indianapolis Olympians—a

1948–49 basketball team at the University of Kentucky

team they represented not only on the court but in the front office as well, as owners and members of the board.

**Best Dive:** At Fort Lauderdale, Florida, twenty-six-year-old Mike King dove from a hovering helicopter into the water, 150 feet below. He did it, he said, to break the old high-diving record of 135 feet and it cost him two broken vertebrae.

**Best Exercise:** True believers in isometrics maintain that the best exercise is to push down on your office desk with all your strength, in an attempt to drive it through the floor. Others insist that bench-pressing 400-pound barbells is the way to get in shape. Still others have asserted that making love combines pleasure with excellent conditioning. Poppycock, says Dr. Kenneth H. Cooper, the physical fitness advisor to the Air Force and author of *Aerobics*, probably the most sensible book available on keeping fit. "I'll state my position early," he writes in *Aerobics*, "the best exercises are running, swimming, cycling, walking, stationary running, handball, basketball, and squash, and in just about that order." After carefully measuring a wide variety of exercises according to the energy it costs the body to perform, Dr. Cooper concludes that isometrics, calisthenics, and weight lifting are inferior to sustained activity. And while golf, tennis, and volleyball are better than nothing, you are fooling yourself if you think they are keeping you hale and hearty. Only exercises that make continuous

Jim Thorpe

demands on the lungs, heart, and blood system—that require a lot of oxygen over a long period of time—are sufficient to produce a significant training effect.

**Best Football Player (College):** Doak Walker. Walker played for SMU in the late 1940s and, according to sportswriter Dan Jenkins, "did more things well in football, including win—and win with a mediocre team—than just about anyone who ever played. He passed, ran, punted, caught, place-kicked, blocked and defended." O. J. Simpson, while not as versatile as Walker, was perhaps the game's *best runner*. During the late 1960s, as a running back for USC, he gained over 3,500 yards and scored 36 touchdowns in 22 games.

**Best Football Player (Professional):** Jim Thorpe. He once punted a football 70 yards and the chief distinction of that punt was that it was his shortest kick of the day. Sportswriter Walter Manning writes of Thorpe, "Anyone who ever saw him play agrees: Jim Thorpe was the best, the absolute best ever to pull on a pair of cleated shoes." A halfback who began playing professional football in 1915, Thorpe later joined the fledgling National Football League, playing with such now defunct clubs as the Oorang Indians, the Toledo Maroons, the Rock Island Independents, and the Canton Bulldogs, finishing up in 1925 with the New York Giants. But it would be unfair merely to bill Thorpe as the best football player in the history of the game; he was also the greatest and most versatile athlete in modern times—a track and field star in the 1916 Olympics, a major league first baseman, and a star at basketball, lacrosse, wrestling, and soccer.

**Best Football Punt:** In an American Football League game in 1969, New York Jets' kicker Steve O'Neal punted practically the length of the field— 98 yards—for the longest kick in the history of professional football. Said one sportswriter who was present, "It went further—literally—than a lot of home runs I've seen."

**Best Football Team:** The 1941 Chicago Bears. On December 6, 1940, as the National Football League season was drawing to a close, the Chicago Bears whipped the Washington Redskins 73–0 in a game that was not merely an embarrassment to the Redskins but a taste of things to come for the Bears. With top-seeded stars such as Clyde Turner, George McAfee, and quarterback Sid Luckman (whom coach George Halas claimed never called a wrong play), the 1941 Bears have been called the greatest team ever by *Sports Illustrated*. They capped a magnificent 10–1 season by demolishing the New York Giants 37–9 in the NFL playoff game.

**Best Golfer:** Bobby Jones. Jones was a star of the 1920s and his best year, ironically, was also his last as an active golfer—1930. That was the year he achieved the Grand Slam, or the Impregnable Quadrilateral as the pedants know it. Copping the Impregnable Quad meant winning both the American and British Open and Amateur championships, a feat that may well never be duplicated. Jones was something of a golfing Mozart, playing his first U.S. Amateur Open at the age of fourteen. He died in 1972 at the age of seventy.

**Best Physical Fitness Freak:** Alan Jones had polio when he was five years old, and when he was seventeen he was laid up with a back injury so serious that doctors told him, "You'll never be able to do any heavy lifting and you'll probably be confined to a desk job the rest of your life." Were they ever *wrong!*
   On August 17, 1974, Jones, a Marine Corps captain from Portland, Oregon, did 27,003 sit-ups in thirty hours to set a new world's record. Apart from a badly chafed bottom—which he tried to con-

trol during his sit-ups by dousing himself liberally with talcum powder—Jones suffered no ill effects from his record-breaking feat. In fact, the following morning he rose early and went on a camping trip with his wife and daughter.

Jones's reason for going after the world's sit-up record, or so he told his friends, was to make it into *The Guinness Book of World Records.* In fact, come July 4, 1976, he plans to go after another *Guinness* superlative by swimming the Mississippi River—lengthwise—in record time.

"The long-distance swimming record is 1,826 miles in 176 days," says the stockily built twenty-seven-year-old. "I know I can go farther and faster. I'll swim approximately from Minneapolis to New Orleans." Jones has also swum 100 miles down the turbulent Columbia River—in a wet suit—in thirty-five hours, and led a four-man relay team in running 310 miles nonstop across the entire state of Oregon.

"I was never all that good at traditional sports," he says of his collegiate days at the University of South Dakota, where he graduated in 1969, "so I decided to concentrate on endurance events. I want to see how far I can push myself, maybe go where no one has ever gone before."

**Best Proof That Winning Is Not Everything, It's the Only Thing:** The Incas of ancient Peru played a primitive form of basketball, the object of which was to shoot a solid rubber ball through a stone ring placed high on a wall. The winner was traditionally awarded the clothes of all spectators present. The loser was put to death.

**Best Tennis Player (Current):** Tops on the pro circuit today is twenty-two-year-old Jimmy Connors, who beat Ken Rosewall in the men's singles at Forest Hills in 1974 and whom *Sports Illustrated,* among other respected voices in the sports world, calls the best player in the business today. Connors's forte is the two-handed ground shot—and running strength that is unique. Says veteran Jack Kramer, "The kid is unconventional in that he doesn't overpower anybody with serve or volley, or even quickness. His countershots, returns and passes are what beat people."

**Best Tennis Player Ever:** Bill Tilden. The greatest courtsman of them all, Big Bill Tilden of Philadelphia made his mark, predictably, during America's Golden Age of Sports—the 1920s—turning professional in 1930 and playing well into the '40s. (He died in

1953.) Equipped with a powerful backhand and forehand and probably the best service the game has ever seen, Tilden was an early master of what came to be known in later years as "the big game"—the smashing serve followed by an aggressive rush to the net for some jaw-smashing volleying. Sportswriter Allison Danzig calls Tilden the best ever, and so did an international poll of tennis journalists in 1969.

**Best Unicyclist:** Steve McPeak has the distinction of mastering the world's tallest unicycle—a one-wheeled vehicle thirty-two feet tall. On a modest little thirteen-foot unicycle, McPeak rode from Chicago to Los Angeles in six weeks in 1968.

---

**Worst (Baseball) Batter:** New York Yankee pitching star Lefty Gomez is unofficially regarded by many sportswriters and baseball buffs as the weakest hitter in modern times. But these other, less storied names are also immortalized in the record books:

Monty Cross, a shortstop with the Philadelphia Athletics, who batted .182 in 1904, the lowest season's batting average ever recorded in the major leagues; George McBride, Washington Senator shortstop, who hit an anemic .218 in 1,652 games between 1901–1920—the lowest lifetime batting average of any modern player. McBride also compiled the lowest lifetime slugging percentage—.264; Ed Brinkman, Washington Senator infielder, who made 82 hits in 444 times at bat in 1965; Bob Buhl, Milwaukee Brave pitcher, who went 0-for-70 in 1962; Charlie Pick of the Boston Braves, who went hitless in 11 times at bat in a 26-inning game against the Brooklyn Dodgers—the longest game ever played—in 1920; and pitching star Sandy Koufax, who struck out 12 consecutive times during his rookie season with the Brooklyn Dodgers in 1955.

**Worst (Baseball) Fielder:** Outfielder Babe Herman, of the old Brooklyn Robins, is said to have been struck on the head more than once by fly balls he'd intended to catch. There is also hard-hitting New York Giant third baseman Charlie Hickman, who muffed almost two out of every ten chances in 1900 for an .836 fielding percentage—the worst ever.

Many players have pulled five errors in a nine-inning game, but second baseman Andy Leonard of the Boston Braves made *nine* errors in a game in 1876, the National League's first year. And while four errors in one inning is a record held by many players, a feat by third baseman Mike Grady of the New York Giants is still unsurpassed; in an 1895 game he made four errors *on a single ball.* It happened this way: Grady bobbled an easy grounder long enough for the batter to reach first base safely: error number one. He then fired the ball across the infield high above the first baseman's outstretched arm for error number two. The runner scampered to second base and turned toward third; the first baseman's throw reached Grady in ample time to nail the runner, but he dropped it for error number three. And finally, as the runner headed for home, Grady threw the ball to the catcher and watched it sail into the grandstand: error number four.

**Worst (Baseball) Team:** The 1962 New York Mets. Question: What has eighteen legs and lives in the cellar? Answer: the New York Mets. Or so went a popular joke of the day. Paragons of ineptitude, the Mets in their first year of existence dropped their first nine games, slipped unobtrusively into last place, and remained there for the rest of the season, mathematically eliminating themselves from the pennant race by the beginning of August. Despite help from one-time Brooklyn Dodger stalwarts Duke Snider and Gil Hodges and from home run king Frank Thomas, the Mets ended the season with a laughable 40–120 record, 60½ games behind the pennant-winning San Francisco Giants. Mound star Roger Craig led the pitching staff with a 4.51 earned run average, winning ten games and losing twenty-four; Al Jackson also starred, with a 4.40 e.r.a. and an 8–20 record. Legend has it that after an especially devastating series of losses, the Mets were rained out and celebrated with a victory party.

The 1899 Cleveland National League ball club was, in its own fashion, even worse. After winning the first game, they lost the next seven. Team members began to desert, and by midseason the manager had resigned in disgust and was succeeded by Joe Quinn, an Australian undertaker. Under his aegis the team continued to flounder, losing 40 of the last 41 games and ending the season 20–134, 80 games out of first place. A hotel cigar clerk talked Quinn into letting him pitch the last game of the season in exchange for a box of his best Corona-Coronas. Why not? Quinn figured. The cigar clerk was beaten, naturally, and by the following season Cleveland had dropped out of the league.

**Worst Exercise:** An eye infection suffered as a youth permanently damaged Aldous Huxley's vision. Later, he became a follower of

Dr. William Bates, a prominent physician who advocated a series of unusual exercises for improving eyesight. One that Huxley found especially valuable was "nose writing." If the myopic reader cares to practice a little nose writing, he should imagine that his nose, like Pinocchio's, is eight inches long. Focusing your eyes on the end of your extended nose, pretend it is a pen and move your head about as if to sign your name. "A little nose writing," Huxley says in *The Art of Seeing*, "will result in a perceptible temporary improvement of defective vision." A word of caution, though: We tried about five minutes of nose writing, scrawling such sentences as "Aldous Huxley had a prominent proboscis" in the air, without results.

**Worst Football Defeat:** The referees were kind to the Cumberland College eleven when that team locked horns with Georgia Tech in 1905. They stopped the game midway through the third quarter, with Tech leading 220–0. The Tech quarterback Leo Schlick, alone, had scored 100 points.

Cumberland's gridiron contingent that year may well have been the *worst football team ever fielded.* Actually, there hadn't been a team at the school to speak of until Tech invited Cumberland to play on Tech's home turf. The Cumberland coach scouted up enough players to make a team, and they included Gentry Dugat, who had played two games in his entire life (one in high school, the other in prep school) and had to have the meaning of "down" explained to him. On the way to play Tech, several of the players detrained at a stopover in Nashville, got lost, and missed the game.

Years later, fullback A. L. Macdonald recalled that he "had made our longest gain of the day when I lost five yards around right end." One team member is said to have fumbled the ball behind scrimmage with the massed strength of the Georgia Tech line racing toward him. "Hey, pick it up," he yelled to a teammate nearby.

"You pick it up," said the teammate. "You dropped it."

**Worst Football Strategic Blunder:** Roy Riegels, a defensive lineman for the University of California, picked up a Georgia Tech fumble in the second quarter of the 1929 Rose Bowl and galloped 65 yards in the wrong direction. He was finally tackled on USC's own two-yard line by teammate Bennie Lom. Appropriately, Riegel's error proved to be the margin of defeat for USC: On the next play Georgia Tech scored a two-point safety by tackling USC's punter in the end zone and went on to win by a score of 7–6.

Minnesota Viking lineman Jim Marshall repeated Riegels's miscue thirty-five years later in a game against the San Francisco 49ers at San Francisco. In the first quarter Marshall picked up a 49er fumble, spun around a few times à la Riegels, and then headed off toward his own goal line, crossing it unhampered and throwing the ball gleefully into the air. It was Bruce Bosley of San Francisco who broke the news to Marshall and none too gently, by throwing his arms around him and thanking him for the two-point safety he'd just scored for the 49ers. All the same, the Vikings went on to beat the 49ers 27–22 and Marshall came into demand after the season as an after-dinner speaker.

**Worst Football Tackle:** Rice University halfback Dicky Moegle was in the clear and racing toward a 95-yard touchdown run in the 1954 Cotton Bowl at Dallas. Suddenly, Alabama fullback Tommy Lewis jumped off the bench as Moegle was running past him and stopped the ball carrier with a flying tackle. Instantly horrified at his own misdeed, he crawled back to the bench cursing himself for his impulsiveness while 75,000 fans went slack-jawed with disbelief.

The referee himself picked up the ball and carried it the rest of the way to the Alabama goal line, giving Rice the touchdown that Moegle surely would have scored, and Rice went on to win 28–6. Years later, as a high school coach, Lewis watched in disbelief as one of his own players made the same mistake with his team ahead 12–7 and a minute left to play. They lost 13–12.

**Worst Football Team (Current, College):** The California Institute of Technology played its first football game in 1893, taking a 60–4 drubbing from USC, and since then they've coasted downhill all the way, compiling a record of 105 wins and over 300 losses. Most of those wins came in Cal Tech's early years; they haven't had a winning season since 1957, and today they field what many consider the nation's worst college team, a gridiron contingent so relentlessly inept that these days they dare to play only against junior varsity teams and junior colleges.

Not that it should be any different. Cal Tech is a science and engineering school, perhaps the best in the nation; it's never been known for its athletic program. ("Cal Tech is about as well known for its football team as *The Wall Street Journal* is for its sports section," says Harold Brown, the school's president.) Barely 20 percent of the team members, who average about 160 pounds in weight, come to Cal Tech with any varsity high school experience, many must learn the game from scratch. "I only have two rules," says their coach, Tom Gutman. "Don't miss practice and wear your helmet at all times." However anemic their performances, the Cal Tech eleven "play closer to their potential than most kids," Gutman argues. After a 74–28 loss to Pomona College, Gutman had nothing but praise for his charges. "At halftime we led 28–27," he said. "But since our guys had to play both offense and defense, as usual we were physically worn down in the second half."

---

**Most Unusual Archer:** Mohamet II was an avid archer who insisted on practicing his art upon moving targets. Citizens straying too near the palace were frequently found studded with arrows, and it did not take pedestrians too long to learn to stay well out of the range of their mad sultan. Understandably, Mohamet was disappointed when he discovered that his people were avoiding him. Left with no alternative, he ordered the palace guard to round up a regular supply of Istanbullians for hazardous assignment as royal prey.

At last, the terrified Turks appealed to Sheik Ul-Islam, an influential man of the cloth, who was one of the few who still dared to approach the world's most imprudent archer. After patient and tactful negotiations, the sheik persuaded Mohamet to limit his practice to eight targets a day—restricting himself to prisoners of war.

**Most Unusual Baseball Card:** According to *Esquire* magazine, the people who make the dusty pink squares of bubble gum never issued a baseball card of the immortal Solly Hemus. The object was to keep kids buying and buying, trying to get the picture of Solly that would complete their collection. The Hemus image remains untarnished by this scandalous revelation; there is no reason to suspect that Solly knew about the dastardly scheme.

**Most Unusual Baseball Contract:** In the years before the lively ball, when major league baseball was still a nickel-and-dime operation, players were often asked—and more often required—not only to room together but to share the same hotel bed as well in order to cut expenses. Rube Waddell and Ossie Schreckengost, a top-notch pitcher-catcher combo for the Philadelphia Athletics, were willing bedfellows until a nocturnal quirk of Waddell's almost severed their friendship. To prevent further friction,

Schreckengost demanded from manager Connie Mack that a clause be written into his contract forbidding Waddell from eating animal crackers in bed. His demand was met.

**Most Unusual (Baseball) Extra-Inning Game:** On May 1, 1920, the Boston Braves and the Brooklyn Robins (Remember?) played to a 1-1 deadlock before the game was called after 26 innings on account of darkness.

Fidel Castro provided a good example of situation ethics when he was pitching a baseball game in Cuba in 1964. After the last out in the last half of the ninth inning, Fidel's team still found itself behind, but the never-say-die premier decreed that the game should go into extra innings.

**Most Unusual (Baseball) Ground Rule:** At Fenway Park, home of the Boston Red Sox, the pigeon-fly rule is observed. If a batted ball strikes one of the countless pigeons that make their home in the stadium, the ball (though not necessarily the pigeon) is ruled dead.

**Most Unusual (Baseball) Home Plate:** Cliff Carroll, who played professional baseball in the late 1800s, brought his pet monkey with him to every game. When Carroll's pet caught a cold and died the Pittsburgh team held a special ceremony and buried the monkey under home plate.

**Most Unusual (Baseball) Home Run:** "Doc" Cutshaw, who played infield for a variety of National League teams in the early years of this century, hit a sizzling ground ball at Ebbets Field in Brooklyn in 1913, that struck the outfield fence and then, miraculously, rolled up the fence and into the grandstand for what was then scored as a home run.

**Most Unusual (Baseball) Ladies' Day:** To boost their flagging attendance, the Washington Senators offered freebies to the ladies one day in 1897. George "Winnie" Mercer, a dashingly handsome pitcher, was on the mound for the Senators and argued with the home plate umpire, Bill Carpenter, on virtually every pitch. The women rallied behind Mercer, of course, growing increasingly angry at Carpenter as the game progressed. Apoplectic with rage, they stormed onto the field after the last out, chasing the umpire back to the clubhouse, mauling him savagely and tearing off his clothes. Having chased their quarry to safety behind closed doors, the women rioted outside the clubhouse, hurling bottles and paving stones at the door and rampaging through the stadium, digging up the infield turf and ripping out the seats. Some time later, Carpenter escaped through a rear exit.

**Most Unusual (Baseball) Player:** Pete Gray. He lost his right arm in a car accident at age six, but remained determined to make baseball his career. In 1943, his first year in professional baseball, he played for the Three Rivers Club in the Canadian-American League, leading the league with a .381 batting average. He batted .333 and stole 68 bases the following year, and in 1945 played center field with the St. Louis Browns. His batting average slipped to .218 that year, but he did manage to hit six doubles and two triples. Playing a cautious defense, he would field a ball with his gloved hand and then tuck the glove under the stump of his right shoulder and grab the ball with his left hand to throw it into the infield, all in one fluid motion.

In 1951, St. Louis Browns owner Bill Veeck signed Eddie Gaedel, a 3'7" midget as a pinch-hitter. Before 20,299 fans, Gaedel made his first—and only—pinch-hit appearance against the Detroit Tigers. With a strike-zone of perhaps twenty inches, he walked, naturally, and was replaced by a pinch-runner, never to be seen on a major league diamond again. Two days after his controversial appearance, the baseball commissioner's office banned all midgets forever from the field of major league play.

**Most Unusual (Baseball) Stolen Base:** Germany Schaefer, an infielder for the Pittsburgh Pirates and other National League clubs from 1901–1918, once reached second base on a double and then proceeded to steal first. He did it, he later said, to confuse the pitcher.

**Most Unusual (Baseball) Team:** Our candidates for this category are the Kids and the Kubs, the two teams that comprise the Three Quarter Century Softball Club, Inc., of St. Petersburg, Florida. Strong legs and a keen eye are important, but no one gets to play unless he's at least seventy-five years old. The Kids and the Kubs lock horns three times a week from November through March, and their stars include Jim Waldie, who is eighty-eight and plays left field for the Kids with the long-legged grace—if not quite the same speed—of a Ted Williams. He bats regularly over .400 and nails runners down consistently with a rifle throwing arm. Bill Davis, a triple threat as catcher, pitcher, and second baseman, is ninety-one and refuses to take a warm bath to soothe his bad back. One of the club's youngest players, seventy-six-year-old Ed Stauffer, used to pitch for the St. Louis Browns. One season he was barred from the mound after pitching a shutout. He also led the league in hitting, with an .835 batting average and a record-breaking 30 home runs.

**Most Unusual Boat Race:** The Todd River, in Alice Springs, Australia, is the site of an annual regatta in which two-member crews, standing inside bottomless boats which they grip by the gunwales, run a foot race along a course mapped out on the dry river bed. The races were cancelled in 1973 when torrential rains flooded the Todd River, washing out the activities. The gods looked with greater favor and sunnier skies, however, on the elders of the Cowichan Bay Privy Council, of Cowichan Bay, British Columbia, and allowed them to hold their annual motorized outhouse races, one of the more popular sporting attractions in western Canada.

**Most Unusual Boxing Match:** In April 1893, Bowen and Burke fought 110 rounds to a draw for the lightweight championship of the South. Burke, a Texan, had both hands broken and was saved by the bell from a knockout count in the 48th round. Bowen, a hometown boy, kept insisting that he would put him away in just another round or two, but at midnight, according to *The Police Gazette*, the crowd began singing "Home Sweet Home" and by two in the morning much of the crowd was gone. Finally the referee called the fight, with Bowen protesting he would "send him to heaven in 111."

**Most Unusual Chess Player:** When the eccentric Austrian inventor Johann Nepomuk Maelzel decided there was no longer a market for his mechanical orchestras (see *Worst Beethoven Composition*), he purchased a mechanical chess player from the son of its late inventor, Baron von Kempellen, and went on tour with it in the United States in the 1820s. Dubbed "the Turk," the machine consisted of a massive and rather expressionless Turkish man carved of wood, turbaned, robed, bedecked with jewels, and seated behind a wooden chest, a chess-board carved into its top. The Turk, Maelzel would tell audiences up and down the East Coast, is not only the world's only mechanical chess player but more skilled at the game than any human on the face of the earth. Is there anyone among you, he would ask, who would care to challenge him?

Mechanical chess player

The inevitable volunteer would then be seated facing the automaton. Maelzel, after opening all the doors of the chest to expose a whirring clockwork of coils, springs, cogs, rods, and brass fittings—and to demonstrate that its workings were totally mechanical—cranked up the machine and let it play. The Turk's hand slowly zeroed in on its piece, moved it, and then came to rest on a velvet pillow next to the board. When the volunteer completed his move, the Turk's arm mysteriously reactivated itself and played move number three. It generally had the human opponent checkmated within an hour after the opening move.

What the audience didn't know was that despite Maelzel's candor in showing them the innards of the Turk, there really was somebody inside pulling the strings—a young Frenchwoman at first, and then a chess expert whom Maelzel had imported from Europe. The internal structure of the chest allowed his assistant to move from one compartment to another rather quickly on a series of casters and skateboards, and with Maelzel opening only one door at a time, it wasn't difficult at all to escape detection.

A down-and-out former chess-playing associate of Maelzel's blew the impresario's cover in 1837, by telling the popular French magazine *Pittoresque* the secret of the Turk's success. The Turk's popularity soon waned and the once-wealthy Maelzel went broke, drinking himself to death the following year.

**Most Unusual Combat Sport:** Popular—but against the law—in Hong Kong, cricket fighting inspires heavy betting and is not unlike cockfighting. The spectators are seated around an inverted wooden tub that serves as the ring and owners pull out their fighting insects from under their shirts. After irritating the combatants' antennae with a small brush, the festivities commence, and by the time one cricket has had its ears pinned back—or worse—much violence will have been done. Not recommended, as they say in the movie review biz, for the squeamish.

**Most Unusual Fishing Lures:** Lobsters are scared to death of octopuses. Clever fishermen in New Caledonia fasten a dead octopus to the end of a long pole and dangle it in a pool filled with spiny lobsters. The crustaceans freeze in terror, and divers can easily harvest them by hand without fear of being pinched.

Some Japanese fishermen use cormorants as hunters use falcons. The cormorant is a large, voracious sea bird, with ducky-looking feet and a pouch under its bill like a pelican. The fishermen clip their wings and send out ten or twelve cormorants from their small boats, controlling them with leashes. They also fasten iron collars around the birds' necks to keep them from swallowing their catch. Even though their stomachs are getting no satisfaction for their efforts, the cormorants cannot control their impulse to dive for fish. They dive repeatedly, only to have the fishermen pull them in and shake the catch out of their pouches.

**Most Unusual Football Coach:** In October 1965, Dr. Gustave Weber, president of Susquehanna University in Pennsylvania, accepted with reluctance the resignation of head football coach Jim Garrett and his coaching staff, with two games left to the season. In the four years that Garrett had been coach he had led his charges to a remarkable 39–4 record, but this season they had yet to win a game and Garrett, frankly, was disgusted. With two games left and no coach in sight, Weber decided to coach the team himself. After all, he'd been a nine-letter man during his undergraduate days at Wagner College and felt he could make a passable job of coaching.

Sportswriters from all over the nation descended on the Susquehanna campus to get the real story behind the college-president-turned-football-coach, and Weber announced that he had a few strategic tricks up his sleeve that might cause Susquehanna's critics to think twice about downgrading the team again.

Unfortunately, Susquehanna lost both games.

**Most Unusual Football Player (Current):** Garo Yepremian, a top-rated field-goal kicker for the Miami Dolphins, broke into professional football in October 1966. Three weeks prior to his first appearance he had never even *seen* a football game, and four months before that he had never even seen a *football*.

Cypriot-born, he had lived most of his life in London and came to the United States for the first time in June 1966 to visit a brother in Indianapolis. Yepremian was a skilled soccer player with a strong, accurate kick, and his brother suggested that he remain in the States and try for a football scholarship at a university.

He tried and it didn't work simply because he lacked a high school diploma. At his brother's suggestion, Yepremian sought tryouts with a number of professional teams and after seeing his stuff, both the Atlanta Falcons and the Detroit Lions offered him contracts. He signed with Detroit.

In his first few outings Yepremian failed dismally. Then, in a mid-November game against the Minnesota Vikings, Yepremian came into the game in the second quarter and kicked three quick field goals to bring Detroit up from behind to a 12–10 lead over the Vikings. He went on to kick a total of six field goals in that game, setting a new National Football League record, and helping Detroit to edge out Minnesota 32–31.

**Most Unusual Football Team:** Plainfield Teachers College had just trounced Ingersoll 17–0 and the New Jersey school's fast-talking PR man Jerry Croyden raced back to his office to phone in the score and highlights to *The New York Times* sports desk. It had been Plainfield's third shutout victory in as many outings that 1941 season and while the *Times* had buried its coverage of those games among the used car ads and the birth announcements, people were beginning to sit up and take notice with this third victory. In the coming weeks Plainfield extended its unbroken string of wins, chewing up teams like Scott College and Chesterton, and with each phone call the rewrite man on the *Times* kept Croyden on the phone a bit longer, drawing out more color from him, more background dope on the players, more comments from Plainfield's up-and-coming coach.

The star of the team was John Chung, a Chinese-born quarter-back who was averaging a 9.3-yard gain on each carry and had scored more than half his team's points. Sportswriter Herbert Allan wrote in the New York *Post*, just one of a number of big-city dailies in the Northeast that were covering the team, that, "if the Jerseyans don't watch out, Chung may pop up in Chiang Kai-shek's offense department one of these days." As the season wore on and Chung continued eating up the yards, Croyden let it be known that "the prowess of Chung may be due to his habit of eating rice between the halves."

Suddenly, the Plainfield eleven had the rug pulled out from under them. On November 13, Croyden's office issued this press release: "Due to flunkings in the midterm examinations, Plainfield Teachers College has been forced to call off its last two scheduled games with Appalachian Tech tomorrow and with Harmony Teachers on Thanksgiving Day. Among those thrown for a loss was John Chung, who has accounted for 69 of Plainfield's 117 points." It was a tough break for the Plainfield team; a few more victories and they would have commanded national attention for sure. The *Times* sports desk was disappointed.

As it turned out, it wasn't failing exam scores that wiped out the team. New York *Herald Tribune* reporter Cas Adams was the one who broke the real story: There *was* no Plainfield Teachers College, no team, no rice-eating Chinese quarterback. The team and its winning record were a *hoax* cooked up by Morris Newburger, a senior partner at a Wall Street brokerage house. Each Saturday he and other employees at the firm took turns posing as Jerry Croyden to phone in the mythical ball scores. After some of the embarrassment among the *Times*'s sports staff had worn off, Cas Adams of the *Tribune* penned this tribute to the Plainfield Eleven, an anthem sung to the tune of "High Above Cayuga's Waters":

> Far above New Jersey's swamplands
> Plainfield Teachers' spires
> Mark a phantom, phony college
> That got on the wires.
> Perfect record made on paper,
> Imaginary team,
> Hail to thee, our ghostly college,
> Product of a dream!

**Most Unusual Gladiators:** Thais still bet on contests between Siamese fighting fish. When a particularly courageous fighter dies, admirers hold an elaborate funeral, complete with brightly dressed mourners, music, and dancing.

**Most Unusual Physical Education Program:** When students change classes at St. Helen's School in Newbury, Ohio, the halls are crowded with unicycles. Each student is required to learn unicycle riding in gym class and encouraged to ride at every opportunity. Believing that everyone should have at least one skill that is exceedingly daffy, Steve McPeak, the unicycle-riding headmaster of St. Helen's, originated the program. (See also *Best Unicyclist.*)

**Most Unusual Rugby Rule Infraction:** Almost anything goes in rugby, but Corporal George Wright of the British Commandos carried passion a bit too far during a Devon Rugby Football Union match in which he played during the 1974 season: He bit an opposing player on the ear, an act less affectionate than it may sound. For the offense he has been suspended from the Union until 1976.

**Most Unusual Ski:** How long have downhill racers been schussing along mountainsides at nearly 100 miles per hour? Well, the Swedes found an ancient ski preserved in a peat bog that was carbon-dated at 3,000 B.C.

**Most Unusual Track Meet:** A tribe of South American Indians periodically conduct zany track meets called *bimiti*. The contestants run a long course toward a trough filled with the local brew (called *paiwari;* see also *Worst Beverage*). The runner who reaches the trough first has the honor of bathing in the intoxicating suds. Rarely, however, does anyone finish the race. Enthusiastic young girls line the sides of the course to cheer on their favorites and to throw red pepper and ashes at the others. With all the dust and pepper in the air, all the runners are soon coughing, sneezing, and rolling on the ground, much to the delight of the fans.

**Most Unusual Track Record:** Larry Lewis ran the 100-yard dash in 17.8 seconds in 1969, thereby setting a new world's record for runners in the 100-years-or-older class. Lewis was 101.

# Government

---

**Best Act of Diplomacy:** The crafty French foreign minister Talleyrand had a flair for polite diplomatic evasion. When asked whether the ailing George III had died, Talleyrand replied, "Some say that the King of England is dead; others say that he is not dead; but do you wish to know my opinion?"

"Most anxiously, Prince," the questioner said.

"Well, then, I believe neither! I mention this in confidence to you; but I rely on your discretion: The slightest imprudence on your part would compromise me seriously."

**Best Calvin Coolidge Story:** When Will Rogers told them, stories about America's most taciturn president were reprinted in newspapers all over the country. This one is typical and true: Calvin Coolidge fell asleep at his large oak desk during the middle of the work day. After dozing for some time, he awoke with a start and inquired of his chief of staff, "Is the country still here?"

**Best First Lady:** Eleanor Roosevelt—who else? Neglected by her husband in matters connubial, she played a more central role in government affairs than did any other first lady in the nation's history. Said one anti-Roosevelt columnist, "FDR is 20% mush and 80% Eleanor."

**Best Flag:** Hudson's department store in Detroit displays its famous American flag every year on Flag Day, June 14. First exhibited at the 1939 World's Fair in New York City, the Grand Old Rag measures 235 by 104 feet and weighs nearly three-quarters of a ton; each of the stars is a full five and a half feet high. By the way, "Keep your eye on the Grand Old Rag" was the original last line of George M. Cohan's famous song. He later changed it when people reacted with horror at his overfamiliarity.

**Best Imperialist:** Homely, shy, and weighing just over one hundred pounds sopping wet, William Walker (1824–1860) realized every American boy's dream and became president—first of Sonoran Mexico, and later of Nicaragua. Justifiably, he has been called "the greatest American filibuster," in the old sense of the word meaning a meddler in foreign politics.

An unsuccessful physician and journalist, Walker was lured to California by the great gold rush, but he arrived too late to stake out a profitable claim. Turning his eyes southward, he and a band of armed irregulars crossed the Mexican border into southern California and seized control of a vast stretch of desert; on January 18, 1854, Walker proclaimed himself president of an independent republic. As soon as the Mexican government recovered from the initial shock, it sent troops to cut off the crazy adventurers from their supplies and reinforcements. On the verge of starvation, Walker's men retreated back across the border, but their leader's appetite for conquest and high office had been whetted.

In 1855, at the request of a small band of Nicaraguan revolutionaries, Walker and a fifty-seven-man private army launched an expedition to Central America, and within a year they had toppled the ruling government. Walker was inaugurated president of Nicaragua in July 1856, and his regime was promptly recognized by the United States. As head of state, he planned to establish "a southern republic founded on Negro slavery" and began plans to build a sea-level canal connecting the Atlantic and Pacific oceans. But the diminutive imperialist made the fatal error of opposing Commodore Cornelius Vanderbilt, who had a stranglehold on the Central American economy. Vanderbilt financed an armed contingent from El Salvador, Honduras, Guatemala, and Costa Rica to throw out the Yankee president.

Still claiming to be the legitimate ruler of Nicaragua, Walker attempted to regain power in 1860, but was apprehended by Honduran authorities. And on September 12 he was executed by a firing squad.

**Best Orator of Modern Times:** President Franklin D. Roosevelt. The Roosevelt image has fallen on hard times over the past few years, what with disclosures by his son Eliott of his father's marital infidelities and his vacillation in the face of the German military buildup in the 1930s. Nonetheless, no one can fault FDR's or-

Thomas Jefferson

atorical skill. His voice was magnificent, his style was spellbinding. Listen to a record of any of his speeches—in particular, his Day of Infamy Address to Congress the day after Pearl Harbor and his First Inaugural.

**Best Political Leader of the Twentieth Century:** If it's beneficence and courage we're talking about then the choice is Winston Churchill, according to Jenkin Lloyd Jones, editor and publisher of the Tulsa *Tribune*. If we're talking about effectiveness, then Jones feels the choice is Josef Stalin. Our own candidate is Mahatma Gandhi, who, by demonstrating the power of passive resistance, changed the course of history not only on the Indian subcontinent but throughout the world.

**Best President (U.S.):** In a 1948 poll of fifty-five American historians and political scientists conducted by Harvard University historian Arthur Schlesinger, Sr., five past American presidents were designated "great": George Washington, Thomas Jefferson, Abraham Lincoln, Woodrow Wilson, and Franklin Delano Roosevelt. A similar poll in 1962 yielded identical results. But there is a difficulty in labeling any one president as the greatest of all time: each of the five "greats" in the two polls was marked by a Shakespearean "fatal flaw." That, anyway, is the opinion of Montana State University historian Morton Borden, who has added five other presidents to the "great" list in a study he made in 1962: John Adams, Andrew Jackson, James Knox Polk, Grover Cleveland, and Theodore Roosevelt. All things considered, Lincoln and Jefferson are probably the all-time best.

**Best Unsuccessful Presidential Candidate:** Americans don't always elect the best man. Franklin Pierce beat Winfield Scott, Warren Harding beat James Cox, Dwight D. Eisenhower beat Adlai Stevenson, and, perhaps the greatest loss the nation has ever sustained in this regard, Calvin Coolidge defeated John W. Davis, the Democratic contender, in the 1924 presidential election. Historical novelist Irving Stone calls Davis a "thoughtful liberal" who might have had the intellectual tools Coolidge lacked and who "would have listened to the experts and put a curb on wild speculation and the pyramiding of paper wealth," thus averting the Great Depression. His ability to draw the best out of men of diverse views was great, and he never lost sight of the interests of both big business and the working class. Says Stone, "John Davis would have made the kind of president of whom Thomas Jefferson would have approved."

**Worst Act of Diplomacy:** During the Middle East war of 1948, Warren Austin, the then U.S. Ambassador to the United Nations, urged the Arabs and Jews to resolve their disagreements "like good Christians."

**Worst Bureaucratic Verbal Obfuscation:** The following clarification of terms is found in the California State Code of the Division of Consumer Services, Department of Consumer Affairs: "Tenses, Gender, and Number: For the purpose of the rules and regulations contained in this chapter, the present tense includes the past and future tenses, and the future the present; the masculine gender includes the feminine and the feminine the masculine; and the singular includes the plural and the plural the singular."

**Worst Campaign Slogan:** The Whig slogan "Tippecanoe and Tyler, too," first chanted during the presidential election campaign of 1836, was an attempt to capitalize on General William

Henry Harrison's distinguished military record. The Democrats countered by ballyhooing the heroism of their vice-presidential candidate, Colonel Richard M. Johnson, who claimed to have killed the Shawnee Indian chief Tecumseh at the Battle of the Thames. Johnson's friends originated the slogan: "Rumpsey, dumpsey, Rumpsey, dumpsey/Colonel Johnson killed Tecumseh." Pulitzer Prize-winning historian Samuel Eliot Morison asserts that this couplet has never been surpassed for "electioneering imbecility."

**Worst Case of Governmental Red Tape:** *Esquire* magazine reported in 1963 that Mrs. Agnes Matlock of New Hyde Park, New York, had charged in a lawsuit that her house had burned to the ground while the two fire departments that had answered her call argued over which one had jurisdiction to put out the fire.

The town council of Winchester, Indiana, passed an antipornography law, but the editors of the town's only newspaper refused to publish it on the grounds that the statute itself was pornographic. Unfortunately, a law does not take effect in Winchester until it has been published in a newspaper.

**Worst Congressional Study:** In 1970, United States Representative Thomas P. "Tip" O'Neill, Jr., of Massachusetts, assigned a staff aide to prepare a detailed research report on the length of men's hair. "We discovered that since the time of Christ, the male species has worn long hair and beards about 90 percent of the time," the congressman reassured a hair-harried nation. "The western world turned to short hair and clean-shaven faces only after the Prussian victory over France. All the great heroes of America have worn long hair. It's nothing for Americans to get alarmed about."

**Worst Event:** Realizing full well the innumerable ghastly, base, vain, cruel, dishonorable, stupid, and vile actions perpetrated by mankind, it is with all humility that we nominate the following as a candidate for the exalted title "Worst Event of All Times."

Inez de Castro was secretly married to Don Pedro on January 1, 1347. Three years later she was assassinated by agents of Don Pedro's father, who was King of Portugal and a long-standing political foe of Inez. When Don Pedro heard of his wife's murder, he was overcome with rage and sorrow. Even when he captured the assassins and had them gruesomely tortured and executed it did his heart no good.

Not long afterward, the old king died, and Don Pedro ascended the throne as King Pedro I. His first royal act was to have Inez's body removed from the grave, carried to the palace in a magnificent procession, and placed upon a sumptuous throne. There she was crowned "Queen of Portugal." Don Pedro personally placed the orb and scepter of her office into her ghastly hands. Then, in a bizarre second funeral, Inez was returned to the grave.

Epilogue: Pedro ruled well for many years, earning the epithet Pedro the Just.

**Worst First Lady:** Mary Todd Lincoln. First ladies are supposed to stand to the side, quiet and demure, like Bess Truman, and avoid clogging up the machinery of statework—or else they should participate productively and imaginatively in their husband's administration, as did Eleanor Roosevelt. Mary Todd Lincoln followed neither route and, according to one biographer, made her husband's life "a hell on earth." In retrospect, historians and psychoanalysts agree that she was mentally disturbed and could have benefited from medical treatment. During her husband's first year as president, she overspent a congressionally approved appropriation of $20,000 for interior refurbishing of the White House by $6,700 and Lincoln hit the badly peeling ceiling. "It would stink in the nostrils of the American people to have it said that the President of the United States had approved a bill overrunning an appropriation of $20,000 for *flub dubs* for this damned old house, when the soldiers cannot even have blankets," he snorted.

**Worst Mayor of a Big City:** Richard Daley, say his supporters, gets things done in Chicago. The very thing for which he is so bitterly criticized by his opponents—his viselike grip on all facets of Cook County politics and government, which he has maintained for over twenty years—makes him a model of mayoral effectiveness.

Maybe so, but Mussolini also made the trains run on time. Chicago's police are still among the most corrupt in the nation, its public works system still among the most primitive. During the 1968 riots, Daley himself captured the essence of the situation as well as anyone: "The police," he said, "were not there to provoke disorder. They were there to maintain disorder." During uprisings in a black ghetto on Chicago's South Side, Daley issued his now-famous "shoot to maim" order, and at a city hall press conference, he once petulantly told a reporter, "Don't confuse me with the facts."

The East Coast's answer to Mayor Daley is Frank Rizzo of Philadelphia. A former chief of police, Rizzo once volunteered to take a lie-detector test in a supreme gesture of good faith. He failed. Chief executive of the nation's fourth largest city, he once telephoned the city editor of the Philadelphia *Inquirer,* one of several journalistic flies in the ointment of his political aspirations, and called him a "faggot."

**Worst Political Action Group:** The René Guyon Society, based in Alhambra, California, claims a membership of 670 conscientious parents dedicated to stopping "our kids' headlong plunge toward drugs and crime." Their novel solution to these problems—as well as suicide, divorce, alcoholism, and gambling—is to turn children on to "healthy sex." In the dispassionate words of the *Encyclopedia of Associations,* the Guyon Society serves as the voice for "those advocating child bisexuality protected with double contraceptives by age eight." This position is aptly summarized in their motto: "Sex by age eight—or else it's too late."

As a political action group, members work actively for the repeal of statutory rape laws and other legislation frustrating youthful sexual expression. The society proudly claims Freud, Wilhelm Reich, and Dr. René Guyon as its spiritual forebears. (For the uninitiated, the mysterious Dr. Guyon was a judge on the Thailand supreme court for thirty years and the author of a much-ignored volume entitled *Sexual Freedom.*)

**Worst President (U.S.):** Warren G. Harding or Ulysses S. Grant. The Schlesinger surveys drew the same conclusion in 1948 and 1962: As presidents go, Grant and Harding were the worst ever. "Both were postwar presidents who, by their moral obtuseness, promoted a low tone in official life," wrote Schlesinger, "conducting administrations riddled with shame and corruption." Schlesinger's remarks appeared in the July 29, 1962 edition of *The New York Times,* just three months before Richard Nixon swore he was leaving politics forever after being defeated by Edmund Brown for the California governorship.

**Worst Presidential Election:** Governor Samuel Tilden of New York ran against Rutherford B. Hayes in the election of 1876. Tilden, who had made a name for himself by busting up the corrupt Tweed ring, appeared to have won a clear victory from the preliminary returns. But three Southern states and Oregon submitted two sets of votes and there were reports that many Democrats had been turned away from the polls. A Congressional Investigatory Committee, composed of eight Republicans and seven Democrats,

Ulysses S. Grant

was set up to review the disputed returns. In a backroom deal, Northern Republicans apparently convinced a few Southern Democratic power brokers to accept Hayes's election in return for a promise to remove Yankee troops and to overlook violations of the Fourteenth Amendment. When the vote came, the Investigatory Committee divided on strict party lines, and the contested states were marked up in Hayes's column, giving him a 185 to 184 electoral college majority, even though Tilden received 250,000 more popular votes. In the *Oxford History of the American People,* Samuel Eliot Morison writes, "There is no longer any doubt that this election was stolen."

**Worst Public Works Proposal:** For years, sparrows and pigeons have made their nests above the main entrance of the massive marble building that houses the United States Supreme Court, carrying out frequent carpet-bombing attacks on the steps below. In 1975 the nine justices, having suffered too long in silence, unanimously requested a House appropriations subcommittee to back a $45,000 measure to "birdproof" the building. Said Justice Harry Blackmun, "You are literally in danger, in going up those steps, of having bird droppings all over you."

**Worst Senator (Current):** William Scott (D-Virginia)—according to a poll of 200 congressmen, journalists, congressional staff members, and Capitol Hill regulars conducted by *New Times* magazine. "The man is the most morally corrupt individual I've ever known," one former aide of Scott's told the Richmond *Mercury.* "There's nothing to admire. . . . He's irascible, uncooperative . . . and he chases women in the office. . . . A man like that needs a psychiatrist." Scott is the man who told the *Washingtonian* that "The only reason we need zip codes is because niggers can't read." When asked by a reporter to name the highlight of his freshman year in the Senate, he replied pensively, "Being sworn in was perhaps the highlight of the year."

**Worst Senatorial Rationale:** In 1970, Senator Richard B. Russell voted for the ABM (Anti-Ballistic Missile) because, "If we have to start over again with another Adam and Eve, then I want them to be Americans and not Russians, and I want them to be on this continent and not in Europe."

And Indiana congressman Earl Landgrebe—the man who was arrested for selling bibles to passersby on the streets of Moscow; who once snapped at reporters, "Don't confuse me with facts; I've got a closed mind"; who told a newsman on the day Richard Nixon resigned the presidency that he thought congressional favor was switching to Nixon—once explained that he had voted no on a bill to appropriate funds for cancer research because the cost was excessive and besides, discovering a cure for cancer would only change "which way you're going to go."

**Worst Unsuccessful Presidential Candidate:** William Jennings Bryan. Bryan had three stabs at the presidency—in 1896, 1900, and 1904—and had he made it any of those times the entire nation would have been crucified on a cross of cornstarch. This yammering, blathering religious fanatic was most true to form as the small-minded prosecuting attorney in the famous Scopes Monkey Trial of 1925, and psychographic studies of his words and actions indicate that he was one of two bona fide psychopaths to run for the presidency. (The other was George McClellan, Lincoln's opponent.) Campaigning against McKinley in 1900, Bryan told a crowd, "Friends, tonight my little wife will be going to sleep in a cramped hotel room on the other side of town, but come next March she'll be sleeping in the White House!" He waited for the cheers, and then someone shouted, "Well, if she does, she'll be sleeping with McKinley, because he's gonna win." Irving Stone writes of Bryan, "His mind was like a soup dish, wide and shallow; it could hold a small amount of nearly anything, but the slightest jarring spilled the soup into somebody's lap."

**Worst World Leader (Current):** When Idi Amin, the strongman president of Uganda, went on a pilgrimage to Mecca, rain fell for the first time in fifty years. It was only a few drops, but Amin interpreted the unexpected shower as divine anointment. Since then he has been insufferable.

For instance, although Big Daddy (as he likes to be known) received his military training in Israel, he has recently become a virulent anti-Semite. "Hitler was right about the Jews," Amin wrote in a cable to Kurt Waldheim. "The Israelis are not working in the interests of the people of the world, and that is why they burned the Israelis alive with gas in the soil of Germany."

A 1973 speech he delivered in Brazzaville contained one of the most absurd. statements ever uttered by a world leader, as measured against some mighty stiff competition: "Some Asians in Uganda have been painting themselves black with shoe polish. If anyone is found painting himself with black polish, disciplinary action will be taken against him." But to minorities in that African nation, Amin's policies are no joke; he deported 42,000 Asian citizens and resident aliens on just a few weeks' notice. A less malevolent but equally perverse presidential fiat established severe penalties for wearing miniskirts.

Big Daddy also has an uncanny ability to antagonize fellow heads of state. Since coming to power, he has precipitated a number of border wars with neighboring countries. And on July 4, 1973, he sent Richard Nixon a "get well card" from one statesman to another, wishing him "a speedy recovery from Watergate."

---

**Most Unusual Campaign Song:** Ferdinand Lop was a perpetual candidate for the French presidency and a much-beloved loser. A timid, leftist intellectual, he drew most of his meager support from students at the Sorbonne. Eventually his campaigns became a half-serious, half-satirical tradition, resembling the quadrennial efforts of Harold Stassen and Pat Paulsen in the United States. Lop dubbed his personal political party the "Front Lopulaire." And, according to *Horizon* magazine, his platform called for radical "Lopeotherapy," including the elimination of poverty after

10 P.M., the nationalization of brothels, and the relocation of Paris to some rural area where the air is fresher. Enthusiastic followers composed a catchy campaign song, to the melody of "The Stars and Stripes Forever": "Lop, Lop, Lop Lop Lop, Lop Lop Lop! Lop Lop Lop, Lop Lop Lop, Lop Lop LOP Lop!"

**Most Unusual Country:** The Sovereign Military Order of Malta, more commonly known by the acronym S.M.O.M., occupies a three-acre estate called the Villa de Priorato di Malta in Rome, Italy. S.M.O.M. still maintains diplomatic relations with several nations and is thus considered not only the world's tiniest country but also the most unusual. While its territorial holdings are slight, S.M.O.M. is governed under an impressive constitution ratified in 1957.

**Most Unusual Election:** In 1962, some 46,000 Connecticut voters wrote in the name of Ted Kennedy for United States Senator. Kennedy was running in neighboring Massachusetts.

**Most Unusual Emperor:** Joshua Norton was a wealthy San Francisco businessman who lost all his money and found himself living in a squalid rooming house, working in a Chinese rice factory. Depressed and idle, he began to fixate on the ills of the Union and soon came to be known among his friends as "the Emperor" for his loudly stated views on the need for an emperor to assume the reins of power. Then, having completely lost touch with reality, he dropped off this message at the offices of the San Francisco *Bulletin* on September 17, 1859:

> At the peremptory request and desire of a large majority of the citizens of these United States, I, Joshua Norton, . . . declare and proclaim myself Emperor of these United States; and in virtue of the authority thereby in me vested, do hereby order and direct the representatives of the different states of the Union to assemble in Musical Hall, of this city, on the first day of February next, then and there to make such alterations in the existing laws of the Union as may ameliorate the evils under which the country is laboring and thereby cause confidence to exist, both at home and abroad, both in our stability and in our integrity.

Thereafter, Norton assumed—in his own mind, at least—full imperial powers. He appeared in public dressed in a secondhand officer's uniform with blue and gold trim. His proclamation appeared in newspapers and was widely read.

He abolished both major political parties, dissolved the Republic, scheduled a national convention and ordered that a new constitution be drawn up. His friends and former business associates humored him completely, giving the penniless emperor everything he demanded.

Norton's fame—and the willingness of people to cater to his bizarre fancies—extended far beyond the city limits of San Francisco. He dined in the finest restaurants, announcing himself to the headwaiter and being seated at the best table in the house. He had no qualms whatsoever about chewing out a delinquent waiter or sending back an overdone steak, and, of course, he never paid for his meal. Norton rode free in buses, lived free in a dingy room in a boarding house, and issued "Bonds of the Empire" to finance his government. These were printed gratis by a friend in exchange for a promise to appoint him Chancellor of the Exchequer. They bore Emperor Norton's likeness and were worth fifty cents.

He levied taxes too—twenty-five cents on small shopkeepers, three dollars or more on industrialists. A local paper noted that he would often accost a friend and "attempt to negotiate a loan of several million dollars, and depart perfectly contented with a two- or four-bit piece."

Norton died in 1880 at the age of sixty-two, and received an elaborate funeral, paid for by his friends and worthy of a legitimate state ruler. The headline in the San Francisco *Chronicle* the following day was LE ROI EST MORT.

**Most Unusual Empress:** Without repeating any of the racier stories about her life, Catherine the Great of Russia still ranks as the most unusual female monarch. It is said that she preferred water with gooseberry syrup to any other drink. Informed sources report that she delighted in having her feet tickled and her fanny slapped. During her reign, there were many who obliged her in this respect.

**Most Unusual English Queen:** Richard I, Coeur de Lion (Lion-Hearted), took Berengaria, the beautiful daughter of Sancho VI of Navarre, to be his bride; she thus became Queen of England and Richard's other realms. Richard, of course, became a legend in his own time. For the troubadours he was the very symbol of chivalry; but he was a lousy husband. Berengaria was willing to follow her lord, even to the battlefields of Palestine, yet Richard soon left her behind. Over the remaining nine years of his life, the crusading twelfth-century king saw Berengaria only once more, for a few short weeks. While Richard pursued Odyssean adventures, the Queen endured her loneliness in Italy and later in France, earning a small place in history as the only English monarch never to set foot on the island over which she reigned.

**Most Unusual Example of Political Censorship in the Free World:** Stare at a map of North America for 30 seconds and then turn away and say the first thing that pops into your mind. If it's "Nikolai Lenin," you may have more political savvy than you give yourself credit for: In 1974, a map of the North American continent that appeared on a newscast over Turkish television looked so much like a profile of Lenin to the public prosecutor that he conducted an investigation to determine whether it constituted illegal communist propaganda.

**Most Unusual Explanation of the Watergate Affair:** Bad diet makes for bad government, says Sir Dingle Mackintosh Foot, British elder statesman: "If the Americans had a substantial breakfast of bacon and eggs," he says, "they wouldn't have these problems. A proper breakfast adds to your judgments. You can't expect to start the day on cereals, shredded wheat, muck like that."

**Most Unusual Holiday:** Each year on March 17, Bostonians celebrate Evacuation Day—the day the British troops withdrew from their city. Though the date may have a familiar ring, there are probably a lot of Bostonians who have never heard of the holiday they observe. It seems the city's Irish politicians were looking for a nonethnic way to make St. Patrick's Day a legal day off from work, and a microscopic reading of the history books uncovered E-Day—an unlikely excuse for putting on the green.

**Most Unusual King:** As best we can determine, James Jesse Strang (1813–1856) was the only monarch ever crowned within the borders of the United States. Strang was an influential Mormon elder, and following the mob murder of Joseph Smith in 1844, he sought to assume the mantle of church leadership. Although Strang produced two gold tablets covered with strange writing, purportedly proving that he was the divinely appointed successor, Brigham Young commanded the allegiance of the majority of Mormons. Strang, along with several hundred loyal followers, withdrew to Beaver Island, a desolate romantic wilderness on northern Lake Michigan.

The sect named their rugged new home "Zion." And on July 8,

1850, Strang, dressed in a flowing robe that once belonged to a Shakespearean actor, accepted a base metal crown ornamented with glass stars, and assumed the title James I, King of Zion. The new monarch instituted an early model of the welfare state, providing social security and old-age pensions, as well as legalizing polygamy. At first this little kingdom seemed too weak and far away for the government to worry over, but when the king began to intercept "enemy" lake shipping and interfere with the profitable business of smuggling whiskey to the Indians, federal and state officials sprang into action.

James I was arrested on charges of treason and brought to Detroit for trial. But the government prosecutors had not reckoned with the soaring eloquence of His Highness. Strang argued persuasively that he was "being persecuted for religion's sake," and he was acquitted by the sympathetic frontier jury.

Ironically, the downfall of James I was not to come at the instigation of a foreign power, but rather through the treachery of a few of his own subjects. For some unknown reason, Strang decreed that all the women of the sect should adopt short skirts and pantaloons, in the fashion of Amelia Bloomer. The bloomers were exceedingly unpopular with men and women alike, and two disgruntled husbands who could not tolerate the sight of their wives in pants, assassinated the first, and last, King of Zion.

**Most Unusual Political Essay:** "The Demonstration of the Fourth Part of Nothing and Something; and All; and the Quintessence taken from the Fourth Part of Nothing and its Dependencies containing the Precepts of Sanctified Magic and Devout Incantation of *Demons* in order to find the origin of the Evils of France and the Remedies for them," by Demons, a sixteenth-century French attorney. The author of a work entitled *Eccentric Literature* elucidates Demons's work thusly: "Demons said that he had determined to bring to light a classification of the shades of his timid obscurity in the quintessence which he had taken from nothing and to give an explanation of the enigma of his invention."

**Most Unusual Poll:** A Birmingham, Alabama, newspaper polled its readers on the following question: "If you had one extra place in your fallout shelter, who would you give it to?" Politicians finished last.

**Most Unusual Postal System:** In 1877 a society was formed in Belgium to promote the use of cats to make mail deliveries. The theory was that since they have a wonderful sense of direction they could be used like homing pigeons to deliver small packets of letters. To demonstrate the feasibility of the program, thirty-seven cats from Liège were tied up in a gunnysack and transported to a spot twenty miles from town. One found his way home within five hours, and all the rest returned within twenty-four. Despite this impressive performance, the authorities never adopted the idea.

**Most Unusual President (U.S.):** At 12:00 noon on March 4, 1849, Zachary Taylor was scheduled to succeed James Polk as president. But March 4 was a Sunday and Taylor was a very religious old general who refused to violate the Sabbath by taking the oath of office. Thus, under the Succession Act of 1792, Missouri Senator David Rice Atchinson, as President Pro Tempore of the Senate, automatically became president of the United States. Atchinson is said to have taken his high office very much in stride. Tongue in cheek, he appointed a number of his cronies to Cabinet positions, then he had a few drinks, and retired to bed to sleep out the remainder of his administration. On Monday at noon Taylor took over the reins of government, but Americans can look back on the Atchinson presidency as a peaceful one, untainted by even a hint of corruption.

**Most Unusual Republic:** The oldest republic and one of the smallest is Andorra, nestled in the Pyrenees Mountains. Charlemagne ceded the 190-square-mile country to a handful of mountaineers in A.D. 805 in return for the assistance they had given his armies in battling the Moors. As part of the price for independence, Andorra pays $200 in tribute.money to France and Spain biennially. They are also obligated to send the bishop of Urgel 12 capons, 12 hens, and 24 cheeses. The bishop traditionally returns the offering.

The Andorrans are careful not to develop their small but rich lead and silver deposits for fear working mines might make their powerful neighbors covetous. They have an annual defense budget of 300 pesetas—about $5—which they spend for blanks and fireworks to celebrate their independence day. Their last war was World War I, which lasted forty-four years. Andorra played such a minor part in that engagement that the Allies forgot to invite them to the Versailles Peace Conference and consequently the proud mountaineers did not formally terminate their state of belligerency against the Germans until 1958.

The Andorran economy is based on tourism and smuggling.

**Most Unusual Socialist:** Charles Fourier (1772–1837) was a utopian socialist with some sensible ideas and a lot of peculiar ones.
(His sensible ideas are no concern of this book.) Fourier advocated that the world be divided into small communities called
phalanxes in which everyone would eat seven meals a day—three
or four of them salads. Fourier loved parades almost as much as he
loved salads, so the members of a phalanx would be issued one set
of work clothes and one set of parade clothes.

Each person would pursue the trade for which he was best qualified. Since children enjoy playing in the dirt, they would be
dressed in bright uniforms and assigned to collect the garbage.
Fourier loved the moon almost as much as he loved salads and
parades, so he planned to put several new moons in the sky. Some
people consider this scheme prescient in light of the space program; others still consider it silly.

Fourier recognized that sex was a fundamental human drive, but
he felt that it interfered with more important things when people
engaged in it all the time. Thus, he would set aside one week in
the year when the phalanx could indulge in any and all sexual activities, while the rest of the year they remained celibate.

**Most Unusual State Mottoes:** The meanings of many state mottoes
are far from self-evident. For one thing, many of them are in Latin,
perhaps to disguise their insipidity. A personal favorite is the New
Mexican slogan: *Crescit Eundo*, which means "It grows as it
goes." The motto of Washington is *Alki* (Chinook Indian for "By
and By").

**Most Unusual Supreme Court Nominee:** This is Senator Roman
Hruska's (R-Nebraska) emotional tribute to Supreme Court
nominee Harold Carswell, a man who was unusually usual: "Even
if he were mediocre, there are a lot of mediocre judges and people
and lawyers, and they're entitled to a little representation, aren't
they? We can't have all Brandeises, Frankfurters, and Cardozos."

**Most Unusual Unsuccessful Presidential Candidate:** Victoria
Woodhull was a distinctive nineteenth-century hybrid of genius
and charlatan. As a young girl, she traveled with her family's medicine and fortune-telling show. Her enthusiasm for mesmerism—
healing with magnets and hypnosis—eventually brought her to
New York where she made the acquaintance of Cornelius Vanderbilt. Vanderbilt set her up as a stockbroker, and soon she was
financially independent. Ms. Woodhull began to develop an active

Cartoon of Victoria Woodhull

interest in the women's suffrage movement and founded a newspaper in which to voice her unorthodox opinions. Among the innovations she endorsed were short skirts, an end to capital punishment, legalized prostitution, birth control, free love, and vegetarianism. She was the first publisher of the "Communist Manifesto" in the United States. On April 2, 1870, Ms. Woodhull became a candidate for the presidency, running on the ticket of the National Radical Reformers. The vice-presidential nominee was Frederick Douglass, the famous black orator and abolitionist. When she showed up at the polls on election day, she was, predictably, denied the right to vote for herself. She ran for the presidency four more times, until she married a wealthy banker and emigrated to England.

She admitted to living with two men at the same time, which could have done her political ambitions no good. But there is little doubt that Victoria Woodhull was the most colorful and original presidential candidate in American history.

**Most Unusual Vice-President:** Until Spiro Agnew became a household word, there was no such thing as an unusual vice-president. Wilson's VP, Thomas Marshall, showed unusual promise when he said, "What this country needs is a good five-cent cigar!" but he never said or did anything else that anyone can remember.

Spiro Agnew made vice-presidential history when he emerged from colorless anonymity and became one of the most controversial men in America. His phrase-making alone would assure him a status even greater than Tom Marshall. Who can forget "nattering nabobs of negativism," "effete corps of impudent snobs," "fat Jap," or "If you've seen one slum, you've seen them all"?

And, finally, there was Agnew's untimely departure from office to begin a new career writing spy novels. Only one other man ever resigned from the vice-presidency—John Calhoun—and that was in a pique over states' rights.

# The Law

Best Executioner: In Thailand public executions are still fashionable, often drawing large crowds, and an aggressive law and order campaign in recent years has brought many convicted felons face-to-face with Nai Mui Juicharoen, Thailand's official executioner. Aficionados of capital punishment have admired the style and efficiency with which Nai Mui dispatches his victims, and Thai newspapers have built him into something of a folk hero. One journal featured two photographs of Nai Mui on its front page. One depicted him in the line of duty—about to blast out the brains of a condemned man—and the other showed him in a lighter moment—dandling little children on his knees.

Each execution earns Nai Mui $17.50 and business is booming. In the fashion of Wild West gunslingers, he memorializes each man he has killed with a notch in his rifle stock; at last count there were over 120 notches. But most importantly, Nai Mui seems to delight in his work and is eager to take on increased responsibilities, if necessary, to stem Thailand's rising crime rate. "I could manage to execute 100 a day if I had to," he boasts.

At least one politician wants to bring back the good old public execution in the United States. Odell McBrayer, a recent Republican candidate for governor of Texas, not only came out in favor of restoring the death penalty but he also advocated live television coverage from the death house. There was one proviso, however: "I favor televising executions only if not done offensively," he said.

Best Policeman: A headline in *The New York Times*, February 5, 1970: SAIGON POLICEMAN CITED FOR HONESTY. It seems the young officer was offered a ten-dollar bribe and turned it down.

The South Vietnamese government thought this was such an exceptional act of character that they awarded him a medal of honor.

---

**Worst Form of Disorderly Conduct:** Dick Hyman quotes the following judicial opinion in *It's Still the Law,* his comprehensive collection of peculiar old laws still on the books: "It is disorderly conduct for one man to greet another on the street by placing the end of his thumb against the tip of his nose, at the same time extending and wriggling the fingers of his hand." (*The People* v. *Gerstenfeld*, 1915, 156 New York City, 991)

**Worst Form of Revenge:** In Sicily it was once a customary act of revenge to bite off your spouse's nose if he or she was unfaithful. Nose-biting was also a bizarre part of the vendettas—or blood feuds—for which Sicily was long famous. This practice resulted in a thriving rhinoplasty business, as various medical men and quacks attempted to create replacement noses; these were the first serious experiments in plastic surgery.

**Worst Punishment:** Here is proof that Richard the Lion-Hearted was not a nice guy. Holinshed reports that Richard issued the following guidelines for punishing murderers: "Who kills a man on shipboard, shall be bound to the dead body and thrown in the sea; if a man is killed on shore, the slayer shall be bound to the dead body and buried with it." Richard is also credited with institutionalizing tar and feathering as a punishment for thievery.

When one noble miscreant appeared before Empress Anne of Russia she at least gave him a choice: death by hanging or sitting on a nest of eggs and clucking like a chicken.

**Worst Tort Suit:** When twenty-five-year-old Gloria Sykes was hit by a cable car in San Francisco, it appeared on first examination that she had merely suffered a few cuts and bruises. Only later did she discover that the accident had caused her serious psychological and neurological damage. She filed suit, claiming that because of her run-in with the cable car she became a nymphomaniac, engaging in sexual relations with nearly one hundred men. The court found in Miss Sykes's favor and awarded her $50,000 in damages.

Her lawyer, Marvin Lewis, has become something of a specialist in this odd field. In 1974 he took the case of a forty-seven-year-old mother of seven from Santa Ana, California, who was suing a health club for $1 million. The woman charged that she was trapped in a sweltering sauna for ninety minutes—a traumatic experience which compelled her to pick up twenty-four men in barrooms.

---

**Most Unusual Alibi:**  Not every revolutionary group has the police making excuses for them, but when a women's collective claimed credit for the bombing of Harvard University's Center for International Affairs, in October 1970, the Cambridge police gallantly defended them. "This was a very sophisticated bomb," a police spokesman said. "We feel that women wouldn't be capable of making such a bomb."

**Most Unusual Arsonist:**  Nine Houston firemen confessed to setting a series of fires in southeastern sections of the city to relieve their boredom. U.P.I. quoted one investigator as saying, "They liked to see the red light and hear the siren."

Martin C. Reilly of Pittsfield, Massachusetts, had an even more ironic career as an arsonist. In 1962 he burned down his eighteen-room house to avoid paying property taxes. With the home in ashes, the town of Pittsfield sought to collect back taxes nonetheless.

**Most Unusual Court Case:**  Case #7595 in the records of the District Court of western Pennsylvania is listed as *The United States v. 350 Cartons of Canned Sardines*. At issue was whether or not the cartons had been improperly marked for interstate commerce. At the conclusion of the jury's deliberation, the foreman announced, "The jury find a verdict in favor of the United States and recommends the mercy of the court." To which presiding Judge Gibson replied with equal levity, "We will take your recommendation of mercy under consideration."

**Most Unusual Defense:**  In 1821, long before the *Miranda* decision, a man named Desjardins was apprehended as an accomplice in the murder of the Duke de Berri. While in custody, he abjectly confessed to the crime. Shortly after, however, he repudiated his confession. In court, Desjardins defended himself by claiming to be a notorious liar, and he called dozens of witnesses to his bad character and complete unreliability. The court was persuaded, and Desjardins was found not guilty on the basis that no one could believe a word he said.

**Most Unusual Execution:** Two classic stories about the condemned cheating the hangman.

Joseph Samuels of Sydney, Australia, was accused of stealing a bag of gold and silver coins, killing a policeman in the process. He was duly convicted and sentenced to be hanged in September 1803. Up to the last moment, Samuels protested his innocence. The real murderer, he said, was a spectator in the crowd gathered to watch the execution—a rogue named Isaac Simmonds. Simmonds and Samuels exchanged curses, and the crowd grew uneasy, but the marshals, intent on getting the dirty business over with, slipped the noose around their prisoner's neck.

Samuels stood silently on the cart; the driver snapped his whip above the horses; the team pulled away. Samuels dropped, hung for a moment, then fell to the ground. The hangman's knot had come undone, and Samuels lay in the dust unconscious, but alive.

He was too stunned to stand again, so the marshals sat him on the end of the cart the second time. Again, the cart pulled away. This time the rope unravelled, leaving Samuels dangling with his feet barely touching the ground. Crowds at executions are not notably sentimental, but they could not stand to watch a man die the hard death of strangulation; they screamed for the marshals to cut him down.

They tried and failed a third time to hang Joseph Samuels, but the rope snapped cleanly. He was returned to jail and later released. Simmonds—the man in the crowd—was eventually implicated in the murder, brought to trial, and routinely executed. In a made-for-television movie, Samuels would have reformed and married Suzanne Pleshette, but, in fact, he remained a thieving drunk to the end of his days.

The other story is similar: Will Purvis was convicted of murder, a crime his friends said he could never commit. They tried to hang him on February 7, 1894; as in the Samuels story, the knot slipped loose. The crowd intervened and would not allow the executioners to try again. Later, when the governor refused to pardon Purvis, his friends broke him out of jail and hid him until a new governor was elected. The new governor commuted his sentence to life imprisonment, and finally he was released altogether.

Twenty-two years later another man confessed on his deathbed to the crime Will Purvis had been accused of.

**Most Unusual Felon:** A talking crow was arrested in Myzaki City, Japan, in 1972 for pecking children and using obscene language in public. Refusing to answer questions at the police station, the bird was released and appeared on Japanese television a few days later.

In 1963, a rather mulish donkey owned by Osorio Fernandez, a Brazilian farmer, was arrested and charged with the murder of a young boy whom it had kicked in the head.

**Most Unusual Hijacking:** It sounds almost too pat to be true, but police in Santa Fe, Argentina, arrested a man who boarded a city bus, drew a revolver, and demanded to be driven to Cuba.

**Most Unusual Jail Break:** While seventy prisoners and visitors watched, Mrs. Cynthia Knell removed the screws from a glass partition in a Santa Ana, California, prison. She then put the window to one side, and she and her convict-husband calmly walked out of the building.

**Most Unusual Judge:** Sir Francis Page's reputation as the most severe jurist in eighteenth-century England earned him the moniker, "the Hanging Judge." He also had a weakness for limericks and bad jokes. When he was nearly eighty and quite feeble, a friend asked him how his health was holding up. "My dear sir," Page replied, "you see I keep hanging on, hanging on."

**Most Unusual Kidnapping:** At the tender age of two, W. S. Gilbert was kidnapped from his parents in Naples, Italy. He was ransomed on a pound sterling per pound baby basis—twenty-five pounds in all. When baby Gilbert grew up and became Arthur Sullivan's famous collaborator, he made use of the kidnapping in two of his operettas.

**Most Unusual Laws:** When will society quit trying to outlaw the victimless crime? According to James Terry Taylor, Jr., there is an old law, still on the books, in Lexington, Kentucky, against carrying an ice cream cone in one's back pocket.

Paul Steiner mentions an earlier regulation imposed by Emperor Joseph of Austria forbidding nuns to wear corsets.

Still further back in history, Roman prostitutes were required by law to wear yellow hair. This piece of legislation was responsible for a fad among the amorous of the upper class. Bales of blond hair were imported from Germany and made into wigs for the rich; hairdressers made fortunes on bleach jobs. The emperor Claudius's less than faithful wife Messalina was one of the first fine ladies to set the towhead trend.

**Most Unusual Law School Textbook:** *The Criminal Prosecution and Capital Punishment of Animals,* written by E. R. Evans in 1906. Suing a giraffe for defaulting on his refrigerator payments? Want to get an exhibitionist fruit fly away from innocent women and children and behind bars where he belongs? This is your book. For the more numerically inclined, there is *The Problem of the Law of Justice Solved by Arithmetic: Statement of What Passed for Many Years Between Dr. John Dee and Some Spirits,* published in England in the eighteenth century.

**Most Unusual Lawyer:** A French lawyer, Bartholomew de Chassenie, launched his distinguished legal career in 1510 by defending the rats of the village of Autun against the charge that they had stolen the barley crop. De Chassenie was merely a court-appointed counsel (since the rats had not bothered to secure their own), but he pleaded the case with imagination and conviction.

When the case was first called, the bailiff failed to produce any rats. De Chassenie leapt to his feet; his clients, he argued vigorously, could not be tried *in absentia* unless the state could show that it had made a genuine effort to inform them of the serious charges against them and to bring them to the bar. What's more, since every rat in Autun had been named in the charges, every rat had a right to be present in the courtroom. The judge sustained the defense's objection and ordered a delay.

In a second appearance in court, de Chassenie produced a bombshell: A number of his clients (who had a right to be presumed innocent) had been attacked by vicious cats on the way to the court. Certainly the state could not expect them to appear unless it could guarantee their safety. Again, the judge was persuaded and he issued an injunction prohibiting the cats from molesting rats on their way to the trial.

Unfortunately, the records of the case that have been preserved are incomplete and do not tell us the final verdict. But it is known that Bartholomew de Chassenie, after the conclusion of this *cause célèbre,* was involved in many more animal trials, both as a defense lawyer and as a prosecutor. In fact, de Chassenie was involved in the historic cases establishing that animals are subject to anathema and excommunication by the Church as well as civil prosecution.

**Most Unusual Oath:** Since the Romans had no Bibles on which to swear, it was the custom to place one's right hand on one's testicles when swearing to tell the truth. The English word "testimony" is derived from this practice.

**Most Unusual Ordeal:** Once upon a time, the judicial process was much simpler. Instead of haggling for years over points of law and agonizing through appeals, people simply passed the question of guilt or innocence along to "the Great Judge." Trial by ordeal was for the most part a *Catch-22* proposition: You threw a suspected witch in the pond—if she floated she was guilty, if she drowned she was innocent. In contrast, the Chinese developed a comparatively sensible method of lie detection—the ordeal of chewing rice. The accused was given a handful of dry rice to eat. A guilty person, the theory went, would be so nervous that his mouth would go dry, leaving him unable to swallow; in contrast, an innocent person, theoretically, had less on his conscience and more saliva in his mouth.

**Most Unusual Racket:** An article in the June 28, 1967, issue of *The New York Times* carried the following headline: GARBAGE CARTING IN GRIP OF MAFIA.

**Most Unusual Recidivist:** When his wife ruined dinner by undercooking the roast, Noel Carriou grew livid and fumed silently. In the middle of the night he kicked her out of bed and she suffered a broken neck, dying shortly thereafter. Carriou, a Parisian night watchman, received a twelve-year prison sentence. He was released after seven years for good behavior and remarried. This time his wife burnt the roast and Carriou screamed, "You cook like a Nazi," stabbing her to death. He received an eight-year prison term.

**Most Unusual Rehabilitation Program:** In the *Ignorance Book*, Webb Garrison describes a unique rehabilitation program in the Illinois state prison system. With all the controversy over behavior modification in prisons, it is surprising that more people have not heard of Dr. John Pick's facial modification approach. Operating on the theory that a new face makes a new man, Dr. Pick has performed plastic surgery on hundreds of inmates who have requested it. Statistics show that prisoners with new mugs have a much lower recidivism rate than the prison population as a whole.

**Most Unusual Rip-off:** If you saw *The French Connection,* you have some idea what the "good guys" went through to confiscate all that heroin. The New York Police Department locked nearly $3 million worth away in its vault for use as evidence. When next they bothered to check on the contraband, they found that someone had replaced nearly $1 million worth of the potent white powder with sugar. All signs pointed to an inside job, and as of this writing the process of finding out which of the "good guys" are "bad guys" is still underway.

**Most Unusual Traffic Fine:** Run a stop-sign in Fargo, North Dakota, and it will cost you *either* a twenty-five-dollar traffic fine *or* a pint of blood. This unusual choice was offered to minor traffic violators in 1974 by municipal court judge Thomas Davies, who figured it was a good way of dealing with a long-standing blood shortage in Fargo. He was somewhat concerned, however, that the unconventional fines "would screw up the courts' bookkeeping."

**Most Unusual Traffic Violation:** In Jackson, Mississippi, in 1972, police flagged down a car that was zigzagging randomly through traffic and discovered that the driver was blind. He was being directed by a friend in the seat next to him who said he was too drunk to drive himself.

**Most Unusual Warrant:** During an archaeological dig in the ancient city of Aquila, an engraved copper plate was discovered in an antique marble vase. The first sentence on the plate (found in 1810) in Hebrew characters reads: "Sentence rendered by Pontius Pilate, acting Governor of Lower Galilee, stating that Jesus of Nazareth shall suffer death on the cross." On the back is written: "A similar plate is sent to each tribe." Exactly who had the plates engraved, or what their purpose was, is not known, but what appears to be the death warrant of Jesus is now preserved in the sacristy of the Chartem in Naples.

# The Military

**Best Weapon:** Nippon Oils and Fats Co., Inc., a Japanese firm, has developed a new explosive called Urbanite that demolishes rock, concrete, and steel with little noise and less violence. The explosive is so safe, in fact, that it can be detonated at rush hour in the middle of a busy city without threat to life or limb.

The secret, says a spokesman for the company, is Urbanite's slowness to burn. While the basic ingredient is nitroglycerin, the political terrorist's friend, several "secret ingredients" have been added to reduce its burning speed to about a fourth of dynamite's and the resultant noise to about one-third that of a jackhammer. The price, however, is about four times that of dynamite.

**Worst Court-martial:** Seabee Leon L. Louie made naval history as the first person ever to be court-martialed for pie throwing. A group of bored sailors at Port Hueneme, California, devised a slapstick plan "to boost morale," and Louie was elected to do the pitching. At the morning muster of the 700-man battalion, Louie dutifully withdrew a chocolate cream from a paper bag and squashed it in the face of Chief Warrant Officer Timothy P. Curtin.

Navy prosecutors didn't think it was funny, and in December 1974 the young Seabee was brought to trial. Louie's attorney called Soupy Sales as an expert for the defense, who testified that he has been on the receiving end of "more than 19,000 (pies) since 1950. It's the thing you can really do to relieve tension without hurting anybody."

**Most Humiliating Defeat:** It was the law in the Greek city of Amyclae to hold one's tongue. The Amyclaeans had often panicked when they heard rumors that the powerful Spartan army was coming, and to put an end to defeatism, a law was passed forbidding rumors. Violators were to be executed.

When the Spartans actually did appear, no one had the courage to report it, and the city was overcome without a fight.

**Worst Intelligence Report:** The English of King Harold's day wore their hair cut about shoulder length, and only the priests had shorter locks. Receiving reports that a party of Normans had landed on English soil, Harold sent out a spy to estimate their numbers and the potential threat they posed. When the secret agent observed a thousand close-cropped Norman soldiers, he mistakenly reported to the King that the French had sent an army of priests across the Channel to "chant masses." This miscalculation of William the Conqueror's forces was one factor contributing to Harold's defeat at Hastings.

**Worst Military Regulation:** In an effort to maintain military discipline "in and out of uniform" during the last days of the American presence in Vietnam, Major Paul M. Boseman, operations officer of the 377th Security Police Squad, issued the following order: "Salute when you recognize an officer, even though you both, officer and non-commissioned officer, are nude."

**Most Unusual Aircraft Carrier:** During World War II, Great Britain established what was commonly referred to as "the Department of Bright Ideas" to review suggestions submitted by ordinary citizens for new weapons and other schemes to aid the war effort. Most of the plans were egregiously impractical: perpetual motion machines, a design for a rubber raft the size of England that would float in the North Sea and confuse German pilots, and so on. But Project Habbakuk was different, says astronomer Patrick Moore who screened suggestions for the DBI. The idea was to carve a suitable iceberg off the North Polar cap, blast and bulldoze it into shape, tow it into the English Channel, and use it as an aircraft carrier. Should the iceberg be hit by enemy bombs, one would simply fill the holes with water which would soon freeze back into a level and usable landing strip. This giant effort at ice sculpture was never actually undertaken, but for a while, Moore says, Project Habbakuk had "the full backing of the War Cabinet."

Netherlands' army soldiers

**Most Unusual Army:** The army of the Netherlands is like no
other. Recently it became the first fully-unionized fighting force in
the world, and the aggressive young union, known as the VVDM,
has instituted some remarkable changes in military life. The union
experiments have made the Dutch army "more humane" or "a
laughing stock," depending on whom you listen to.

For one thing, the Dutch army *looks* different. There are few
crew cuts among the troops. The union insists on a soldier's being
able to wear his hair in any style he pleases; the only requirement
is that long-haired men wear hairnets when operating heavy machinery. When out on maneuvers, most recruits have shed those
nasty, heavy, combat boots in favor of sneakers.

The union also frowns on saluting—"a strange way of contact
between people"—and only on ceremonial occasions is this primitive custom observed. Other innovations include a new abbreviated twelve-month stint of service for draftees, and overtime pay
for such undesirable assignments as KP and weekend guard duty.
There is one important issue on which the union has yet to de-

velop a position: war. But since the VVDM has close ties with Dutch pacifist organizations, there is little reason to fear that the Netherlands will launch an unprovoked attack on France, Germany, or even Luxemburg.

In charge of this gentle army is the new Socialist Minister of Defense Vredeling (whose name, loosely translated, means "peacenik"). Recently a newspaper reporter spoke to him about the Netherlands's role in NATO: "Frankly I know nothing about it," he said. It seems the Minister had been promised another, more prestigious Cabinet post, and he received the job in the Defense Department as a kind of consolation prize. "And I have an allergy to uniforms," he complained.

**Most Unusual Cannon:** The *Chemical and Engineering News* recently hailed the development of a pneumatic cannon that can fire dead chickens at speeds up to 620 miles per hour. The National Research Council of Canada devised this unique piece of artillery to test airplane parts likely to be struck by birds. The cannon will accommodate either the standard four-pound chicken, for testing windshields, or the rugged eight-pound bird, for testing tail assemblies. The big gun will also fire synthetic chickens.

**Most Unusual Cannonballs:** During a naval battle between Brazil and Uruguay in the middle of the nineteenth century, the Uruguayan vessel ran out of shot. Captain Coe, the commander of the ship, ordered the cannons loaded with Dutch cheeses. "They were too old and hard to eat anyway," he reasoned. In a few minutes Coe's ship opened fire again. According to William Walsh, the first two cheeses went sailing over the mark, but finally one crashed into the mainmast of the Brazilian ship, shattering into thousands of pieces. Cheese shrapnel killed two sailors standing near the Brazilian admiral. After taking four or five more cheeses through the sails, the prudent admiral ordered his ship to retire from the engagement.

**Most Unusual Cause of a Major War:** Militantly Catholic, King Ferdinand of Bohemia vowed to crush the Reformation. But his repressiveness provoked a revolt, and in 1618, angry Protestant nobles stormed his castle in Prague and hurled two royal councillors from the window. They fell seventy feet to the ground, later claiming that they were saved only because they prayed fervently to the Virgin Mary as they plummetted earthward. However, history records that they survived the fall by landing in a pile of horse excreta. In any event, the Defenestration of Prague was the immediate cause of the Thirty Years' War.

On the minor war level: Grease was the cause of the Sepoy Rebellion, an uprising of colonial troops in India between 1857 and 1858. A rumor that some newly issued cartridges for the regulation Enfield rifles were greased with pig and cow fat touched off a mutiny among Hindu and Moslem soldiers. At that time, rifle shells had to be uncapped in one's mouth, and the mutineers believed that this was a mortal sin, since it violated their religions' dietary laws against eating pork and beef.

**Most Unusual Cavalry:** Contending they were the "ideal mounts" for the Southwestern cavalry, Jefferson Davis, as Secretary of War under President Pierce, persuaded Congress to authorize $30,000 for the purchase of eighty one-humped camels. A skeptical Lieutenant Edward F. Beale took delivery of the first thirty-four dromedaries at Indianola, Texas, in 1856.

At first the experiment did not go well; horses bolted in terror whenever they saw the strange creatures; soldiers were afraid to ride them. Worse yet, the army hired a Turkish veterinarian as its camel expert, solely on the basis of his Near Eastern ancestry. Having no experience whatsoever with camels, he once tried to cure a sick animal by tickling its nose with a chameleon's tail.

It wasn't long, however, until the camels began to demonstrate their merits. They could carry 1,000-pound loads, travel thirty or forty miles per day, and go without water for six to ten days. Lieutenant Beale was won over by their performance. "My admiration for the camels increases daily with my experience of them," he reported to the War Department. The lieutenant even learned Arabic in case the animals were homesick.

Forty-six more joined the stable in 1857, and the War Department officially declared the experiment a success, asking the Congress for permission to import an additional 1,000 camels for cavalry service. But the government was preoccupied with the threat of civil war, and the noble plan was forgotten.

**Most Unusual Cavalry Engagement:** In 1794 French General Charles Pichegru led the French revolutionary forces in their invasion of the Netherlands. It was the dead of winter when the French entered Amsterdam. There, Pichegru learned from informers that the Dutch fleet was stationed nearby, off the town of Den Helder. A cavalry brigade was sent north to report exactly on the vessels' whereabouts. Arriving in Den Helder, the French discovered the Dutch ships frozen fast in the bay; urging their horses out on the ice, the French cavalry managed to surround and capture the entire Dutch fleet.

**Most Unusual Chemical Warfare:** Abandoning their lands before the advancing armies of Pompey the Great, ancient Spaniards left behind great tubs of azalea honey. When the delighted troops discovered the sweet booty, they immediately took to eating great globs of it with their fingers. Soon most of the men were deathly ill, the victims of toxic impurities in the honey. The Spaniards, who had been waiting patiently in the hills, then swooped down on the disabled legions.

**Most Unusual Draft Dodger:** During the Civil War, Grover Cleveland hired a substitute to fight in his place. It was a common and perfectly legal practice, if something short of heroic. During the presidential campaign of 1884, however, it appeared that the charge of draft dodging might prevent him from ever occupying the White House. Cleveland was saved when it was discovered that his Republican opponent, James Blaine, had also evaded the draft by hiring a substitute.

**Most Unusual General:** General Richard S. Ewell, who fought gallantly for the Confederacy at Winchester and Gettysburg, sometimes hallucinated that he was a bird. For hours at a time he would sit in his tent softly chirping to himself, and at mealtimes he would accept only sunflower seeds or a few grains of wheat.

**Most Unusual Intelligence Operation:** In his fascinating book *Of Spies and Stratagems*, Stanley P. Lovell, the wartime director of research and development for the OSS, describes how the leaders of the intelligence community planned to wage glandular warfare against Adolf Hitler. In the midst of World War II, the OSS commissioned a wide-ranging study of the health and habits of the Führer. Among other interesting findings, the report suggested that Hitler was not so virile as he would have liked the world to believe. In fact, in Lovell's words, Hitler was "close to the male-female line. A push to the female side might make his mustache fall out and his voice become soprano." This, the OSS believed, would destroy his charismatic appeal for the German people, drive him from office, and bring a more reasonable leader to power.

To give Hitler that little push, the OSS hoped to capitalize on his well-known fondness for vegetables. They bribed his personal gardener to inject large quantities of estrogen into carrots headed for the Führer's table. But, alas, this ingenious (not to say absurd) "destabilization program" failed. Lovell speculates that either Hitler's official tasters noticed something funny in the carrots or, more likely, the gardener was a double-crosser who kept the bribe and threw away the hormones.

**Most Unusual Lieutenant Colonel:** The Portuguese army honored Anthony, its patron saint, by bestowing upon him the honorary rank of lieutenant colonel. (One wonders what Saint Anthony could have done to make major general.)

**Most Unusual Pilot:** Russian scientists were looking into the possibility of training cats to pilot air-to-air missiles in 1970. Their research was presumably based on a B. F. Skinner proposal to use pigeons as bombardiers that the noted behaviorist had offered to the United States Navy during World War II.

This isn't to suggest that the military conscription of animals was unheard of before Skinner. Earlier in the war, a Swedish scientist had developed a program for training baby seals to plant mine charges on ships. The seals fared better as frogmen than cats would later fare as airplane pilots for, as Skinner has noted, felines get airsick quite easily. Aware of this complication, the Soviet researchers have also considered using the severed brain of a cat in the pilot's seat rather than the whole animal.

**Most Unusual Siege:** Nothing was sacred to King Cambyses I of Persia. Herodotus speaks of him "opening ancient tombs and examining the dead bodies." The lowest blow of all occurred when Cambyses laid siege to the Egyptian city of Memphis in the sixth century B.C. The Persian knew that Egyptians held cats to be sacred. (Perhaps he learned this in the tombs; see also *Most Unusual Auction.*) He ordered his troops to gather up all the cats they could find, and then heave them over the walls of the city. The horrified defenders immediately surrendered rather than risk further injury to the animals.

**Most Unusual Submarine:** Leonardo da Vinci was quite willing to put aside his painting and anatomical studies and apply his genius to military engineering when called upon by the pope or his patron Ludovico Sforza. A few of his inventions may have been put to use on the battlefield, but many, including his designs for tanks, diving suits, helicopters, and parachutes never got off the drawing board even though they were technically promising.

Of all his machines of war, Leonardo was most enthusiastic about his design for a submarine. The idea was simple: He sketched a small boat propelled by a pedallike apparatus that could handle a crew of one or two. The submariners would sneak up on enemy vessels and use a large drill device to bore holes below the water line of their wooden hulls, sending the foes to Davy Jones's locker. Indications are that he was well on his way to developing a unique system for delivering air to his crew. At least he was excited enough about the process to scribble a cryptic note to himself (Da Vinci usually wrote from right to left) to "choose a simple youth" as his assistant in making a scale model—a dolt who would be unable to leak, or even comprehend, the secret.

Ultimately, however, Leonardo abandoned the project, apparently on humanitarian grounds. He was reluctant to make his design known to politicians "on account of the evil nature of men." Although Leonardo felt the submarine could morally be used against the infidel Turks, he feared that once it was in the possession of the doge of Venice or the pope they might also turn it against their European enemies. This prospect was intolerable to Leonardo, who felt that drowning was far too horrible a death to bring upon any Christian.

In order for any submarine to cruise underwater, it must carry a certain amount of ballast. In its day, the USN *Trout* transported some fabulous dead weight. It was February 1941 and the *Trout* had finished unloading its cargo of munitions and supplies on embattled Corregidor. Ordinarily the crew would have made up for lost weight by taking on gravel, but with the Japanese pressing their offensive, gravel was urgently needed for the construction of fortifications. The navy was faced with a problem.

Then someone suggested gold; compact, heavy, and easily loaded, it would make ideal ballast. The Philippine government and private mining companies were anxious to move their assets out of the country for safe keeping, and after some hasty negotiations the crew of the *Trout* began loading the hold with 583 gold bars, valued at $9 million. For additional weight, eighteen tons of silver pesos, worth over $300,000 were brought on board, as well as crates and trunks filled with negotiable securities.

Weighted down with a cargo worthy of the Spanish galleons, the *Trout* fought its way back across the Pacific and safely delivered every glittering brick to authorities in San Francisco.

**Most Unusual Uniform:** On the battlefield during the Mexican War, General Zachary Taylor wore a "hickory shirt," made of heavy twilled cotton with blue pin stripes, a civilian sack-cloth coat, and a straw hat. At the opposite extreme, and equally in violation of army regulations, was George Armstrong Custer, of last stand fame, who often wore a dandy blue velvet uniform.

**Most Unusual War:** We mention two ridiculous wars, but there are certainly others. In 1739 Captain Jenkins insisted that the members of the British Parliament examine a jar containing what he claimed was his ear. According to Jenkins, a Spanish scoundrel had removed it with a saber. While some historians have challenged Jenkins's story, there was no doubt that he *had* lost his ear somewhere, so the British fought the War of Jenkins's Ear. Fortunately, no one else could work up as much enthusiasm over the ear as Jenkins, and the war came to an early end after a few inconclusive naval battles.

One of the briefest wars on record was the skirmish between Honduras and El Salvador in 1969. The two nations had been engaged in an ongoing border dispute and had broken diplomatic relations with one another. However, the immediate cause of the war was El Salvador's 3–0 victory over Honduras in the World Cup soccer playoffs. The two sides exchanged fire for about thirty minutes before cooler heads prevailed.

**Most Unusual Weapons:** In 1972, the Committee to Re-elect the President assembled thousands of "Democracy kits" to be dropped over North Vietnam in a renewed effort at winning the hearts and minds of the people. The kits consisted of diamond pins and handsome pen-and-pencil sets—the latter decorated with the presidential seal and the signature of Richard Nixon—of the sort presented to generous political contributors. They had been left over from the campaign.

On a smaller scale, a group calling itself the Aliens of America sent postcards to all nine Supreme Court justices in 1974, concealing a tiny packet of nerve gas beneath each stamp. No injuries were reported.

Also, scientists in Great Britain have developed an antiriot device that emits sound and light waves which produce vomiting, nausea, and epileptic convulsions.

**Most Unusual Weapon (Ancient):** A man named Callimachus defended Constantinople against the naval assaults of the Saracens with a substance called "Greek fire." The mysterious concoction, probably containing naptha, sulphur, and pitch, could be extinguished only with wine or vinegar—water made it spread. Invented in the seventh century, it was extremely effective, and several times saved Constantinople for the Greeks. The ingredients were a closely guarded secret for 400 years, but finally the Mohammedans duplicated the formula. Greek fire continued in use until the advent of gunpowder.

Archimedes, the great Greek scientist and mathematician, is said to have invented a mirror that focused sunlight on the sails of the Roman fleet, causing them to burst into flames. The ingenious machine could not save the city, however, and Archimedes died in the sack of Syracuse (212 B.C.).

Finally, in a war against the Greeks in ancient times, Jewish soldiers were armed with very stale potato pancakes to hurl at enemy infantrymen.

**Most Unusual Weapon of the Future:** The navy has disappointedly abandoned its top-secret Project Aquadog. The goal of that hush-hush research had been to teach dogs to swim underwater and attack enemy frogmen. But apparently navy scientists are going ahead with experiments to establish the feasibility of using dolphins to retrieve spent torpedos that have missed their mark.

**Most Unusual Women's Corps:** Women now play an active role in the armed forces of Israel and other nations, but in the 1800s this was unthinkable. Thus the "Army of Wives" makes the rebellion of T'ien-wang all the more unusual.

T'ien-wang was a religious fanatic who believed he had a holy mission to overthrow idolatry. No ascetic holy man, he had a harem of thirty wives, and many of his followers were also polygamists. When the fighting got tough, the wives of T'ien-wang's sect were formed into a women's militia commanded by women officers. Altogether, half a million women garrisoned the city of Nanking in 1853. The Army of Wives held the city until 1864 when the uprising was finally crushed by the central government. In a cinematic conclusion, T'ien-wang committed suicide amid the flames of the palace he had usurped.

# Religion

---

**Best Grace:** Oliver Cromwell, the Puritan Lord Protector of England, often said this prayer before dinner: "Some people have food, but no appetite; some people have an appetite, but no food. I have both. The Lord be praised!"

**Best Shrine:** The Kailasantha shrine of Ellora, India, was once just an ordinary mountainside. Throughout the eighth and ninth centuries, sculptors cut away the exterior rock, leaving a beautiful temple—built from the top down. A wonder of advanced planning, the pillars, statues, ornaments, and foundation had to be anticipated practically from the first cut.

---

**Worst Church:** The All Saints Church of Sedlac, Czechoslovakia, was looted of all its fine ornaments in 1600. Undeterred, the worshippers of Sedlac set about redecorating their house of worship with human bones. They exhumed the remains of nearly 10,000 people for what is surely the most macabre interior in all of Christendom. The highlights are a bony chandelier, made predominantly of femurs, and hundreds of skulls piled in the shape of the Schwarzenberk family crest. *Fodor's Czechoslovakia* calls it a "ghastly fascination."

**Worst Crucifix:** The commercialization of Christ offers endless potential for human debasement. The worst crucifix we've ever seen is sold in Venice and features a plastic Jesus glued by his Roman captors to a cross of colored seashells. A milk chocolate cross sold at Easter time in the United States runs a very close rec-

Bone chandelier in All Saints Church, Sedlac, Czechoslovakia

ond and is our undisputed favorite as the *tastiest* crucifix ever marketed, filled to its hollow center with real chocolaty goodness—an Easter-time treat for the whole family.

**Worst Deity:** If you are smitten by the red-robed bitch goddess Shitala, the best you can do is get plenty of bed rest, pray fervently, and don't pick the scabs. The most dreaded deity in Indian mythology, Shitala is said to ride through the countryside atop a donkey, thrashing her victims with reeds until their bodies are covered with purulent, running sores. The victims all go delirious with pain and die within a few days.

Shitala is the goddess of smallpox.

**Worst Miracle:** In Bombay, India, in 1966, a Hindu yogi named Rao announced his intention to walk on water. Six hundred prominent members of Bombay society were invited to witness the spectacle, with tickets going for as high as $100 each.

Garbed in flowing robes, the snowy bearded mystic stood majestically on the side of a five-foot deep pond, prayed silently, and then stepped boldly into the void. He sank immediately to the bottom.

**Worst Pope:** Boniface VIII may have been the most impious pope. He once said that a man has about as much chance of enjoying life after death as "a roast fowl on the dining table." If his metaphysics were in error, Boniface is surely occupying the position deep in Hell that Dante assigned him.

For wickedness and incompetence, however, no pope can quite compare with John XII, a man whom Church scholar E. R. Chamberlin called "the Christian Caligula." A member of the outrageous Theophylact line, John served both as religious leader of the Western Church and temporal ruler of Rome. To maintain his power he recruited armed gangs from among the Roman mob and terrorized the honest citizenry. He was an avid gambler who constantly invoked the names of foul demons to bring him luck, and as Chamberlin documents "his sexual hunger was insatiable." He depleted the wealth of the papacy by giving away Church lands and holy relics to his favorite mistresses, and it is not an exaggeration to say that he turned the Lateran into a brothel. There may even have been truth to the charge that he was a rapist.

As a moral leader, John couldn't have been worse, and he was no better at politics. He enlisted the support of Otto I, the king of Germany, against Italy's King Berengar II; soon, however, he double-crossed Otto, and the German promptly conquered Rome, called a synod to depose John, and installed the antipope Leo VIII. In 964 John regained power only to be murdered within the year.

**Worst Shrine:** The president of Toyota Motors in Japan is planning a shrine that promises to be somewhat less than sublime. He has set aside $445,000 to erect an edifice to honor the souls of persons killed in Toyotas throughout the world.

**Worst Synod:** The Council of Constance, convened from 1414 to 1418, removed the scandalous Pope John XXIII from office and was supposed to institute a general housecleaning.

John XXIII was accused of poisoning his predecessor and then bribing his way into office. Before the council finished its investigation, they had also charged him with atheism, adultery, and incest. John was later declared an antipope, but no prelate would take his soiled title until the saintly Angelo Giuseppe Roncalli chose to be called John XXIII in 1958.

As far as the council was concerned, they were hardly in a position to cast the first stone. Gebhard Dacher, a contemporary chronicler, reported that there were 18,000 priests, 83 wine merchants, 346 clowns, dancers, and jugglers, and 700 harlots in attendance. Another source places the number of harlots at closer to 1,500.

**Worst Theological Dispute:** Whenever artists set out to depict Adam and Eve in their innocence, they run into a theological problem that has been acrimoniously debated for centuries. The subject of this ongoing controversy was "that tortuosity or complicated nodosity we usually call the Navell," as Sir Thomas Browne put it in 1646. Browne contended that since Adam and Eve were created and not born, they should be portrayed with smooth, unindented abdomens. Then, in 1752 Dr. Christian Tobias Ephraim Reinhard published the definitive work on the issue—*Untersuchung der Frage: Ob unsere ersten Uraltern, Adam und Eve, einen Nabel gehabt (Examination on the Question: Whether Our First Ancestors, Adam and Eve, Possessed a Navel).* Dr. Reinhard argues the pros and cons interminably, siding ultimately with the antinavel forces.

In actual practice, artists vacillated for many years, and an examination of Adam and Eve portraits from the Middle Ages and Early Renaissance shows some with and some without. By Reinhard's time, however, the immaculate stomach was a hopeless cause. On the Sistine ceiling Michelangelo boldly asserted the legitimacy of picturing the umbilicus and greatly influenced subsequent navel tradition. In his incomparable panel of Adam receiving the spark of life from the fingertip of Jehovah, the new creation sports an inny belly button.

The navel controversy was unexpectedly revived in 1944 by the House Military Affairs Committee. Representative Durham, a North Carolina Democrat, loudly opposed distribution of a government pamphlet entitled *The Races of Mankind* to American servicemen, ostensibly because in some of the illustrations "Adam and Eve are depicted with navels," an insult to fundamentalists everywhere. There were, however, some cynics who maintained that the congressman was really more concerned about a statistical table in the pamphlet showing that the average IQ for blacks in some Northern states was higher than the average for Southern whites.

**Most Unusual Biblical Essay:** In 1663 a noted orientalist presented to the French Academy a paper in which he concluded that Adam was 140 feet tall, Noah, 50 feet tall, Abraham, 40 feet tall, and Moses, 25.

**Most Unusual Church:** The largest active salt mine in the world is located in Zipaquirá, Colombia. Contained within the mine, 800 feet deep in the mountainside, is the great Salt Cathedral. Never has there been a place of worship so magnificent and so earthbound. The three main corridors, with ceilings arching 73 feet high, supported by columns of solid salt, took six years to excavate. The sanctuary seats nearly 5,000 people.

**Most Unusual Communion:** When Lord Strothallan, a Jacobite hero, received a mortal wound at the Battle of Culloden Field, on April 15, 1745, a priest administered the last rites and offered him a Eucharist of whiskey and oatcake, there being no bread and water available. (A less romantic source agrees that it was oatcake, but insists that Strothallan washed it down with water.)

**Most Unusual Deity:** Known as "that fat boy" among the holymen of the Upper Ganges, Guru Maharaj Ji claims to be a true avatar— a living incarnation of God. One of the sixteen-year-old perfect master's devotees is the antiwar leader Rennie Davis, who was quoted as saying, "I would cross the planet on my hands and knees to touch his toe."

Apparently even a deity must suffer the vicissitudes of modern life. His physician reports that the young guru has a duodenal ulcer, and in Detroit Maharaj Ji endured the indignity of a nonbeliever smacking him in the face with a shaving cream pie. But then there are the good things in a god's life: the $100,000 town house in London, the Telex machines, the private jets and yachts and his recent marriage to an airline stewardess, to mention just a few. Perhaps the highlight of this incarnation came at the Houston

Astrodome in the fall of 1973 when Maharaj Ji kicked off the "Millennium," billed as "the most holy and significant event in human history."

Abbie Hoffman is not so fond of the guru as his fellow Chicago Seven defendant. "If the Guru Maharaj Ji is God," he groused, "he's the kind of God America deserves."

**Most Unusual Devotional Book:** A book published in Oliver Cromwell's time bore the title: *The Spiritual Mustard Pot, To Make the Soul Sneeze with Devotion.*

**Most Unusual Exorcism:** The Hittite people of the Middle East practiced an unusual form of political exorcism. As they prepared to lay siege to a city, the warriors invited the enemy gods to come over and join the Hittite pantheon. They were not beyond a little bribery, too: The Hittites set up large vats of beer as an enticement to undecided deities and even strung red, white, and blue streamers from the city walls to show the turncoat gods the way to the free brew.

**Most Unusual Heretics:** The Ophites were an early Christian sect who felt that the temptation of Eve brought knowledge and revolt into the world, and hence was a positive rather than a sinful event. Therefore the Ophites highly revered serpents and thought the Devil was all right, too. They required that the bread of the Eucharist be licked by serpents before serving it to communicants.

Another heretical group, the Cataphiggians, were followers of a man named Montanus. While praying, they made it a habit of putting their index and middle fingers in their nostrils, as a symbolic gesture of faith.

**Most Unusual Hermit:** In the *Decline and Fall of the Roman Empire,* Gibbon recounts the life of Simeon Stylites, a Syrian shepherd who became an anchorite monk. After his novitiate, during which he repeatedly had to be rescued from "pious suicide," Simeon chained himself to the top of a column 60 feet high. There he remained for the rest of his life—through thirty summers and winters—a record that no flagpole sitter ever approached. To while away the decades, Simeon prayed a great deal and did sit-ups.

**Most Unusual Pilgrimage:** In her prayers Catherine de Medici asked a favor of the Lord, and when that favor was granted she made good on her promise to send a pilgrim to Jerusalem. But Catherine had asked for a big favor, and the pilgrimage she promised in return was not an ordinary one. She said that for every three steps forward her appointed representative would take one step backward. The man she hired did just that all the way from France to the Holy Land. For his service he was made a nobleman.

**Most Unusual Pope:** Over seventy historians of the papacy have insisted that a woman—Pope Joan—served for two and a half years after the death of Leo IV (855) and before Benedict III came to power. As a young girl, Joan fell in love with a less-than-celibate priest in Athens who tutored her in Latin and theology as well as romance. Her aptitude for these subjects was so astounding that she decided to pose as a man and make a career of her own in the Church. From Athens she moved to Rome, distinguishing herself for her learning and her ability to survive the rough and tumble Church politics of the ninth century. When Leo died, the unsuspecting synod elected her pope. Little is known about her actions in office, although it seems that at least one of her colleagues discovered that she was a woman. In 857, as she was entering the Lateran Church, Joan went into labor and died.

It is a great story, and several years ago Hollywood made an atrocious movie out of it starring Liv Ullmann. The only problem is that despite the word of seventy historians of the papacy, Pope Joan almost certainly never existed. No contemporary source mentions her reign, and the myth seems to have originated with a single monastic document written centuries later that shows the name Joan inserted with a caret between the names of Leo and Benedict in a roster of the popes. After the Reformation a number of Protestant propagandists gleefully latched onto the story, embellished it, and reported it as gospel—confounding reputable historians for several centuries.

In *The Bad Popes* E. R. Chamberlin does mention a woman who controlled the selection of the pope and influenced his decisions, although she did not wield power directly. Marozia was the lady's name and she had a reputation for sensuality and a penchant for Roman mob politics. As the most powerful figure in the house of Theophylact, she arranged for the election of her son, Pope Leo VI. With Leo as a figurehead, Marozia controlled the Church and the city of Rome for seven tumultuous months in 926. It is possible that the true stories about Marozia, exaggerated by successive generations of gossips, are one source of the Pope Joan legend.

**Most Unusual Relic:** In 1247 Emperor Baldwin II sent to Saint Louis a small vial purportedly containing a few drops of milk from the breast of the Virgin. Nearly thirty European churches have claimed to have similar relics.

**Most Unusual Religious Allegory:** The seventeenth century in England gave rise to some of the most imaginative religious writing ever produced, including such allegorical essays as "Eggs of Charity, Layed by the Chickens of the Covenant and Boiled with the Water of the Divine: Take Ye and Eat," "Spiritual Milk for Babes, drawn out of the Breasts of both Testaments for their Souls' Nourishment: A Catechism," and "High-heeled Shoes for Dwarfs in Holiness." Perhaps the most bizarre was "A Wordless Book." While devoid of words, the book is not without its message: there are eight pages, the first two of which are black, the second two red, the next two white, and the last two gold. They symbolize, in succession, the evil of man, his redemption, the purity of his soul, "washed in the blood of the Lamb," and finally, eternal bliss.

**Most Unusual Steeple:** Billy Graham and members of the Jesus movement frequently flash the "one way" sign—the right hand raised with the index finger pointed heavenward. Though the specific symbolism is new, the gesture has been a favorite as long as there have been pulpits. An especially well-liked preacher of the First Presbyterian Church in Port Gibson, Mississippi, frequently used that very gesture over 120 years ago. In 1859, the communicants of First Presbyterian erected a steeple in his memory, and on top, instead of a cross, they placed a cast hand with the index finger pointing up.

# Psychology

**Best Idiot Savant:** Tom Wiggins was a feebleminded fellow from Georgia with the uncanny ability to imitate any piano performance after hearing it only a single time. His keyboard work was identical to that of the master he copied, down to the subtleties of interpretation. Following the Civil War, Wiggins toured Europe, performing before enthusiastic crowds. Gradually, however, his talent began to fade.

A similar phenomenon was Kyoshi Yamashita, a very popular Japanese artist, who was totally unable to care for himself and depended on his government-appointed guardians. More than once, Yamashita was found half-naked in the streets, unaware of his own home or name. But his art shows no signs of his mental deficiency.

**Best Madman:** Not all lunatics are dribbling, unproductive wastrels who do nothing but talk to themselves on the subway and frighten people. Colin Martindale of the University of Maine studied the lives of fifty-two French and English poets recently and found that nearly half of them were psychotic and 15 percent were psychopaths. Percy Shelley, for example, hallucinated frequently and was haunted by visions of a man attacking him with a revolver. (The man in his fantasies could have been the equally unbalanced Lord Byron, who was a textbook paranoid and always carried a pistol with him.) John Keats often alarmed his friends with alternating fits of weeping and hysterical laughter, and the nineteenth-century French poet Édouard Joachim Corbière spent much of his time constructing scale-model ships and then destroying them.

**Most Unusual Anal Compulsive:** According to the catty Miss Gertrude Stein, the tidy French poet Guillaume Apollinaire always made love on an overstuffed chair because he did not want to mess up his ever-so-neatly-made bed.

**Most Unusual Cure for Kleptomania:** If you're a storeowner beleaguered by shoplifters, the people at Rent-a-Thief Canada, Ltd., a Toronto-based firm, may have the remedy you've been looking for. For $100 a day, they'll send over one of their carefully screened and trained free-lance thieves (who are mostly students and out-of-work actors) who will go through the motions of filching merchandise and getting caught and berated publicly while he's unceremoniously hauled off to the store office and the police are called. Says Les Cohen, general manager of Rent-a-Thief, "The whole thing is a put-up to show everyone present what's in store for shoplifters." The company is a subsidiary of College Marketing and Research, Ltd.

For the kleptomaniacs among us: Lady Cork (1746–1840) was wealthy enough to indulge her kleptomania without ever having to fear a prison sentence or a trip to Bedlam. Whenever she "shopped" at a London store, the proprietor would routinely assign a clerk to make notes of the items she swiped. When Lady Cork returned from a visit to friends, the maid went through her Ladyship's handbag and returned all the valuables she did not recognize. Once she filched a pet hedgehog from a neighbor and stowed it in the bottom of her carriage. Soon discovering that the prickly little animal made an uncomfortable traveling companion, she traded him to a baker for a sponge cake. "A hedgehog," she said, "is just what you need to rid your bakery of black beetles." The baker had no black beetles, but he was a man of principle and never turned down a hedgehog proffered by a Lady.

**Most Unusual Delusion of Grandeur:** In his prime Wilhelm Steinitz was one of the world's most brilliant chess players, but as he grew older he slowly went insane and was enslaved by the delusion that he could make telephone calls without a telephone and move chess pieces from one square to another without touching them. He possessed, he claimed, a unique ability to emit electric signals from his fingertips that could move objects.

Steinitz also claimed to be on speaking terms with God, and in one Icarian burst of *chutzpah*, he challenged God publicly to a game of chess. Worse yet, he offered Him a one-pawn handicap!

**Most Unusual Erogenous Zone:** According to Freud, the human nose contains tissue which becomes erect when sexually stimulated.

**Most Unusual Fantasy:** Apparently even those who are constantly called upon to make speeches must deal with butterflies in their stomachs. Winston Churchill found that a simple fantasy helped him to conquer his stage fright. Whenever he stood before a crowd, he tried to imagine that every man and woman he was addressing had a hole in his sock.

President Eisenhower is said to have taken his fantasies one step further and formed a mental picture of his audience sitting before him as naked as worms.

**Most Unusual Foot Fetish:** Probably the most unusual was the Chinese practice of binding girls' feet in early childhood. Bound feet became a symbol of sexual oppression.

According to a *Life* magazine article, the ancient Greeks had a gentler fetish. They considered a longer second toe aristocratic—a longer first toe, base and plebian.

**Most Unusual Phobias:** Mercifully, psychiatrists have not given names to every fear troubling mankind. Perhaps the most unusual phobia with a name of its own is amaxophobia, the fear of riding in vehicles. Other unlikely aversions include skokophobia (fear of spies) and triakaideaphobia (dread of the number 13).

Thomas Hobbes was afraid of the dark and always slept with a lighted lamp.

Degas suffered from nausea whenever he was in the presence of flowers or perfume.

Napoleon, whose name seems to pop up frequently in these pages, suffered from aelurophobia (the fear of cats). Once in the Palace of Schönbrunn his aide-de-camp heard a great ruckus in the general's chamber. He entered to find "mon commandant" half-dressed, lunging with his saber at a terrified kitten cowering behind a wall hanging. King Henry III of France was another swashbuckling political leader who felt faint at the very sight of a cat.

Erasmus, the Dutch scholar and humanist, came down with a fever anytime he smelled fish.

While perhaps not a phobia in the clinical sense, Winston Churchill's professed dislike of toilet seats was certainly a full-blown aversion. At his home in Hyde Park Gate, London, all of the toilets for house guests were equipped with seats, but Sir Winston's personal commode had none. When a plumber suggested that one be installed, Sir Winston answered testily, "I have no need of such things."

(For His Royal Highness Prince Philip, the Royal Consort, the superfluity of toilet seats is as nothing when compared to the unjustified extravagance of modern plumbing in general. "This is the biggest waste of water in the country by far," he once said. "You spend half a pint and flush two gallons.")

**Most Unusual Psychological Test:** *Link,* a weekly newspaper published in New Delhi, India, quoted color specialist Max Luscher as saying that a person may offer clues about his *real* personality and innermost feelings by the way he adjusts his color television set. If he makes the picture too red, says Luscher, he is probably too lustful; if he makes it too blue, he overeats; too yellow, he is too hopeful. A picture too dominated by magenta may indicate homosexuality.

# Health and Death

**Best Anesthetic:** You're going to have a nose job, an event for which you've been readying yourself emotionally for years, but a disagreement with your doctor threatens to mar the joy of it all. He would like you awake during the operation and thus wants to administer a local anesthetic. You, on the other hand, find the thought of hearing your own cartilage and bone being chipped, sliced, and hacked less than appetizing; you'd prefer to sleep through it all.

It's a common dilemma, and one that may be resolved in the near future by a drug called Lorazepam. Developed by anesthesiologists David Heisterkamp and Peter Cohen, of the University of Colorado Medical School, Lorazepam deadens sensation locally while the patient remains awake. However, it also induces postoperative amnesia, permanently blocking the patient from ever remembering the process.

**Best Blood Donor:** As of September 1974, sixty-one-year-old Joseph Kerkovsky, of Moline, Illinois, had donated 189 pints of blood—that's a bit under twenty-four gallons, or more than a Chevrolet gas tank will hold—since World War II, at hospitals and Red Cross chapters.

**Best Cure for Cramps:** Queen Victoria's physicians prescribed *Cannabis* (marijuana) for the relief of her menstrual pains.

**Best Cure for Hiccups:** There are scads of folk remedies for the hiccups: a sudden fright, standing on your head, breathing into a paper bag, holding your breath, drinking ten swallows of water, or inhaling and exhaling like a panting dog. In severe cases doctors may prescribe strong tranquilizers. But alas, all these sure-fire cures only work for some of the people some of the time, and thus we are pleased to report that Dr. Edgar Engleman of the University of California Medical Center in San Francisco has hit upon a highly reliable hiccup medicine—a teaspoonful of sugar swallowed dry.

Dr. Engleman first encountered this bit of folk pharmacy when the host of a party he attended recommended a dose of sugar for Engleman's hiccupping wife. Her hiccups stopped immediately. This inspired a series of carefully controlled laboratory experiments in which Dr. Engleman tested the sugar remedy on two groups of hiccuppers. The first group was composed of seventeen people who had been suffering from this dread affliction for only a few hours; upon swallowing a spoonful of sugar, fifteen immediately overcame their glottal contractions. The second sad group was made up of chronic hiccuppers who were in the midst of attacks that had lasted anywhere from eighteen hours to six weeks. Sugar provided immediate relief for twelve out of twenty-two in this group, and additional doses suppressed the hiccups of four more.

Dr. Engleman theorizes that sugar irritates the nerves at the back of the throat, counteracting the hiccup reflex. Salt, sand, or any gritty substance would be equally effective, but most people find sugar the most palatable.

**Best Dying Words:** The most comprehensive guide to dying utterances that we have seen is *Famous Last Words* compiled by Barnaby Conrad. In an introduction to this book,. Clifton Fadiman singles out his favorite, "Though I have weighed many curtain lines, the perfect one still seems to me Lady Mary Wortley Montagu's 'It has all been very interesting.' " (Lady Montagu, 1689–1762, was an English wit, letter writer, and victim of Alexander Pope's satires.)

Henry David Thoreau also died with grace. When a friend, attending him at his death bed, asked whether he believed in an afterlife, Thoreau replied, "One world at a time." Then, shortly afterward, he spoke two final, dreamy words: "Moose . . . Indian." The tombstone over his grave in Concord, Massachusetts, bears the concise epitaph, "Henry."

We mention three other notable candidates here, although there are certainly many others that are deserving.

As Gertrude Stein lay dying, she hoped for some foreknowledge of the Beyond. Over and over again she asked, "What is the answer? What is the answer?" When Alice B. Toklas and the others gathered around her remained silent, Miss Stein suddenly sat up in bed and called out, "What is the question?" then fell back dead.

Not long before his fatal collapse, Dylan Thomas sat drinking in a New York bar celebrating his thirty-ninth birthday and the success of his *Collected Poems*. A friend recalled his last boast: "I've had eighteen straight whiskeys. I think that's the record."

Finally, we mention William Palmer (1824–1856) who is far less well known, and deservedly so; he was hanged for poisoning his best friend. As he stepped out on the shaky gallows trap, he looked nervously at the executioner and asked, "Are you sure it's safe?"

---

**Worst Cure for Hiccups:** In *English Eccentrics*, Dame Edith Sitwell relates the woeful history of Squire John Mytton (1796–1834). Mytton took to drink at age ten and for many years he downed eight quarts of port a day. Because of his tremendous capacity for alcohol, his friend and biographer Nimrod dubbed him "Mango, the King of the Pickles." Constantly tipsy, Mytton was forever falling off his horse, racing his carriage recklessly through the streets, even riding on a brown bear in a mood of drunken hilarity. And like many heavy drinkers, Mytton occasionally suffered from the hiccups.

Nimrod describes one dizzy evening when Squire Mytton tried a novel but unfortunate cure. " 'Damn the hiccup,' said Mytton as he stood undressed on the floor, apparently in the act of getting into bed, 'but I'll frighten it away.' So seizing a lighted candle, he applied it to the tab of his shirt, and, it being a cotton one, he was instantly enveloped in flames." Two servants, hearing his shouts, rushed into the room, tore the fiery nightshirt from his back, and smothered the flames. Mytton was painfully burned, but before falling into bed he managed to observe that "the hiccup is gone, by God."

**Worst Disease:** The Foré tribe of New Guinea is afflicted by epidemics of kuru, a very rare disease characterized by trembling, dizziness, and a gradual decline into insanity. At one stage of the illness, the victim is subject to fits of excessive laughter, and in fact kuru is sometimes referred to as "the laughing death." As far as doctors have been able to ascertain, there is only one way that the slow virus that causes kuru can be transmitted from one person to another—by eating portions of infected brains. The Foré are one of the few tribes in New Guinea still practicing ritual cannibalism of their own dead.

**Worst Doctor:** For a mere $1,500 Dr. John R. Brinkley of Kansas would implant young goat glands in men who were feeling their age. According to Brinkley, the effects were miraculous; his patients supposedly enjoyed a return of their youthful energy and a sexual renaissance. (And there was no problem with bleating or other side effects.) It was a sore disappointment when patients discovered that goat glands were about as effective as Dr. Brinkley's own patent medicine—a mixture of blue dye and hydrochloric acid.

But quacks do not need results. Good public relations and a little help from the placebo effect has made many a charlatan rich, and Brinkley did well enough to buy his own high-powered radio station in Mexico, along with limousines, yachts, and a private plane. In fact, his popularity was so great that he ran for governor of Kansas three times, once narrowly losing to Alf Landon. True to form, Brinkley's politics were as bad as his medicine. He was the sugardaddy of the Silver Shirts, who, though better dressed, shared the philosophy of Germany's Brown Shirts.

**Worst Epitaph:** Pity the poor woman doomed to eternal sleep beneath this epitaph in an East Hartford, Connecticut cemetery:

> Hark! she bids all her friends adieu;
> An angel calls her to the spheres;
> Our eyes the radiant sun pursue
> Through liquid telescopes of tears.

However, this inscription found on a gravestone in a churchyard in Kent, England, is even worse:

> The wedding day appointed was
> And wedding clothes provided.
> But ere the day did come, alas!
> He sickened and he die did.

**Worst Hemorrhoids:** An article published in *The Wall Street Journal* on August 10, 1973, offers hindsight on the Battle of Waterloo. An overlooked factor in the French defeat was the health of Napoleon Bonaparte. According to medical historian Rudolph Marx, the emperor spent much of the day resting in his tent, laid low by an excruciating case of swollen hemorrhoids. Lack of sleep and opium administered by his physicians left him too groggy to mount his horse and take advantage of a breach in Wellington's flank.

**Worst Operation:** Japanese women are caught between two worlds. On the one hand there is the liberated life-style of the cities and universities and on the other there is the traditional, conservative sexual ethic which makes Victorianism seem like swinging sin. Many Japanese men would not consider marrying a woman who was not a virgin, but fortunately, modern medical science has come up with a way for an experienced young woman to return to the state of innocence. In only half an hour, and for the modest price of $150, Japanese plastic surgeons will create a new hymen. Thousands of *jinko shojo* (artificial virgin) operations are performed each year.

Americans need not titter: In 1973, at least 300 men and women in this country received lipectomies of the buttocks—also known as bottom lifts.

**Worst Remedy for a Sore Throat:** Repeated X-ray treatments for cancer of the larynx rendered Robert Hopkirk's throat more sensitive than if it had been trampled by a herd of elephants wearing cleated shoes. Unable to swallow easily, he now lives on seventy-two raw eggs a week—and nothing else.

Hopkirk, a retired painter from Sydney, Australia, estimated in January 1975, that he had consumed over 4,500 eggs since beginning the treatment two years earlier. "It's a bit monotonous," he said, "but I feel great."

**Worst Seasickness:** By way of excuse for Napoleon (see also *Worst Hemorrhoids*), it has been reported that Lord Nelson was seasick at the Battle of Trafalgar.

**Worst Suicide:** A forty-year-old man in Biella, Italy, set himself afire and then, experiencing a sudden change of heart, threw himself to the ground and rolled around on the grass in an attempt to extinguish the flames. Onlookers gasped as he rolled off a cliff and fell to his death.

**Worst Suture:** When Honduran Indians receive a severe wound, they close it with live soldier-parasol ants. Each ant is held up to the laceration; it bites down, drawing the edges of the flesh together. This process is repeated as many times as is necessary to stop the bleeding. Once the ants have locked their jaws, the patient breaks off their bodies. The heads remain in place and will not relax their hold until the wound is healed and the formic stitches are cut out with a knife.

**Most Unusual Autopsy:** André Bazile, a French convict from Nantes serving as a galley slave, died September 10, 1774 after complaining of violent stomach cramps. When an autopsy was performed with fifty incredulous medical students in attendance, the coroner discovered in the stomach of the deceased a knife, pewter spoons, buttons, and miscellaneous pieces of glass, iron, and wood. (In his report, the coroner concluded that "it must have been something he ate.")

**Most Unusual Birth Control Campaign:** In Budapest they control the pigeon population by mixing birth control chemicals with birdseed.

**Most Unusual Cemetery:** If one wishes to rest in peace alongside the greats, he should arrange to be buried in Père-Lachaise Cemetery. Chopin is interred in the high-class Paris boneyard and so are Wilde, Balzac, Rossini, Daumier, Corot, Molière, Sarah Bernhardt, and Bizet. But if we could express a personal preference, it would be to be buried next to Rin Tin Tin. Yes, Rinny is there beneath a stone which reads:

Ci Gît
le Bon Chien
Rin-Tin-Tin Au Cinema
Grande Vedette
Passant, Songe à la Brave Bete
Qui Fut Moins Chabot Que Plus Dieu

A loose translation: Here lies the honorable dog Rin Tin Tin, a great movie star; passerby, think about the good animal who was less of a ham than most.

**Most Unusual Contraceptive:** As late as the early years of the twentieth century it was traditional for a Muslim peasant woman in upper Egypt to terminate an unwanted pregnancy by lying face-down on the railroad tracks and allowing the next scheduled train to pass over her. Conversely, a woman who had difficulty conceiving would lie on her back on the tracks and allow the passing train to impregnate her.

It wasn't only in Egypt that the steam-driven locomotive was considered the embodiment of the male propulsive force. In India, women desirous of impregnation would rush to the tracks as a train approached, and as it passed, they would lift their skirts high in the hope of being made pregnant.

**Most Unusual Cure:** Israeli scientists reported in 1972 that freezing the big toe was one possible way of curing the common cold.

**Most Unusual Disease:** When the normally decorous seventeenth-century noblewoman the Marquise de Dampierre was seized on several occasions with an uncontrollable urge to scream obscenities in public, she became so thoroughly mortified that she lived a hermit's life for the next seventy years. Today, physicians know that the Marquise was the first recorded victim of what later came to be called the Tourette syndrome, a rare and understandably embarrassing nervous ailment.

Tourette sufferers invariably manifest their first symptoms—uncontrollable tics and twitches—during early to middle childhood. According to Dr. Arthur K. Shapiro, of New York Hospital's Payne-Whitney Clinic, the symptoms ultimately become verbal in nature as the patient finds himself hissing sharply at inappropriate moments, barking like a dog, shrieking, or echoing the words of others. Many patients, like Mme. Dampierre, find themselves swearing compulsively. Dr. Shapiro has treated some seventy cases of the Tourette syndrome and says that drug therapy has been highly effective in reducing its symptoms.

**Most Unusual Death:** Browsing pretentiously through the classics, we turned up a rare account of a politician smothered with affection, and a case history of terminal giggling:

The Athenian legislator Draco designed an early legal code that was, needless to say, draconian; he was nevertheless quite popular with his fellow citizens. In 590 B.C. there was a testimonial in his honor at the theater of Aegina. As Draco entered the open-air arena, thousands of well-wishers showered him with their hats and cloaks. Draco was smothered to death in the pile of clothing.

The most talented of the Greek soothsayers during the Trojan war was a man named Calchas. One day, as he was puttering around in his vineyards, a fellow prophet specializing in doom approached him and warned that he would never live to taste the fruit of the vines he was planting. Months later, after the grapes had been harvested and pressed and the wine had matured, Calchas invited his colleague to join him at a feast of thanksgiving. As the dinner commenced, the relieved host was about to raise his cup in a toast, when he allowed himself a moment of unprofessional gloating. "Repeat your prophecy of last summer," he ordered, and his guest obliged. Calchas began snickering, broke into an uncontrollable horselaugh, choked, spilled the contents of his cup, and died.

(Admittedly the ironist's art is detectable in both stories, but when faced with a choice of believing or disbelieving 2,000-year-old sources, why not choose the more interesting alternative?)

**Most Unusual Doctor's Fee:** Dr. Thomas Dimsdale received a $50,000 flat fee plus an annual pension of $2,500 for giving a half-dozen shots. Catherine II had summoned the famous physician to inoculate the royal family against smallpox and she expressed her gratitude with this prodigious shower of rubles. Other nobles also rewarded him handsomely for injections—one presenting him with a $15,000 ruby.

**Most Unusual Epitaph:** It has been widely reported that W. C. Fields's tombstone is inscribed "I'd rather be here than in Philadelphia," and at least one authority claims these were his last words. The original source of this quip, however, was a 1924 magazine article. *Vanity Fair*—now long deceased itself—invited fifty celebrities to compose their own epitaphs. The precise words of Fields's contribution were slightly less insulting to the City of Brotherly Love: "Here lies W. C. Fields. I would rather be living in Philadelphia."

Several others also came up with good lines:

"Ci Git: Alexander Woollcott [the reviewer and radio commentator] who died at the age of ninety-two. He never had imitation fruit in his dining room."

"Here lies the body of George Gershwin, American composer. American? Composer?"

And best of all: "Ci Git: Dorothy Parker. Excuse my dust."

**Most Unusual Funeral:** When His Most Gracious Majesty the Lord Grimsley of Katmandu died of a drug overdose in 1974, he

lay in state for three weeks on a silken bed amid opulent surroundings before being buried in a casket bedecked with 1,000
carnations. The funeral orations consisted, in part, of readings
from the poetry of Wordsworth and Shelley. At a cost of $3,600, it
was probably the most expensive funeral ever given a parrot. Lord
Grimsley was owned by David Bates, an antique dealer in London.

**Most Unusual Grave:** Hans Wilhelm von Thummel, a noted romantic poet, was laid to rest in the hollow of an oak tree March 1,
1824 in Noebdenitz, Germany. The tree still lives and it has long
since enclosed the poet's body in an organic sarcophagus.

More familiar, perhaps, is the story of Ben Jonson who once jok-
ingly told James I that he would like a square foot in Westminster
Abbey. When the poet passed away, James obligingly had him
buried standing up.

As an example of contemporary eccentricity in these matters,
Edward Faber of Mansfield, Massachusetts, was buried on the
eighteenth green he loved so well at Stowe Acres Country Club.

**Most Unusual Gravestone:** Chukche tribesmen of Siberia
decorated the graves of their dead with piles of reindeer antlers,
adding a new pair each year.

**Most Unusual Heart:** There was nothing particularly unusual
about the heart of Giuseppe De Mai except that there was another
just like it in his chest. In 1894 he signed a contract with the London Academy of Medicine, and was paid $15,000 for permission to
study his two hearts after his death.

Today, such a person exists, courtesy of Dr. Christiaan Barnard,
who surgically implanted a second heart in one of his South African patients in December 1974. This advance opens up wondrous
new possibilities; now there is nothing standing in the way of men
and women having three, four, or more organs of every description.

**Most Unusual Home Remedy:** Psalm 56:8 reads, "Put thou my
tears into thy bottle." The reason for this peculiar statement is that
throughout history tears have had a reputation for miraculous healing powers. Even today there are places in Afghanistan and Turkey where priests hand out small sponges before a funeral so that
the mourners can collect their tears. Following the burial, the
sponges are collected and the tears are wrung out and bottled.

**Most Unusual Hypochondriac:** Samuel Jessup died in 1817 at the age of sixty-five, but no one said that he should have taken better care of his health. Shortly before his decease, Jessup was summoned to appear in court to settle his accumulated apothecary's bill. Between 1791 and 1816, Mr. Jessup popped a total of 226,934 tablets and capsules. In the last five years of his life, as if in anticipation of the end, he averaged seventy-eight pills a day. His finest year was 1814 when he downed 51,590 altogether or over 140 per day. Also on Mr. Jessup's bill was a charge for 40,000 bottles of emulsions, juleps, syrups, and eluctuaries.

**Most Unusual Mortuary:** Before the energy crisis, it seemed like a promising undertaking. In 1968 Hirschel Thornton of Atlanta, Georgia, celebrated the grand opening of the world's first drive-in mortuary. Resting peacefully, the deceased was displayed behind a glass wall, while the motorists could file by and pay their last respects without ever having to leave their cars.

**Most Unusual Pain Relievers:** Dr. M. B. Greene, a New York anesthetist, made medical history in 1938. Until that year, the only known relief from the pain of abdominal cancer was injections of addictive morphine. After years in the laboratory, he discovered a nonpoisonous painkiller derived from cobra venom.

Galen, the most highly respected physician of the second century A.D., recommended that a good jolt from an electric fish was ideal for curing headaches. The learned Greek's remedy would have been dismissed as foolishness only a decade ago, but recent experiments with low amplitude electricity indicate that it *can* be useful in the treatment of migraines and chronic pain.

As long as we are on the subject of eels, we should mention a demonstration that took place at the 1939 World's Fair. A most unusual telegram was sent from the fair grounds to Eleanor Roosevelt in Washington, with electric eels providing the current for transmission.

**Most Unusual Pregnancy:** An Indonesian woman reported in 1969 that she had been pregnant for over eighteen months and that her unborn child could recite lengthy passages of the Koran from memory. She said she had tape recordings to prove her claim, but she was ultimately declared a fraud by the government.

In Sydney, Australia, that same year, a fifteen-year-old girl became pregnant after swimming in a public pool, although physicians swore that she was still a virgin. Nine months later, when she gave birth to a baby boy, the courts ruled that she had been impregnated by male sperm in the swimming pool water.

Madwoman Mary Tufts gave birth to rabbits two centuries ago—or so she claimed. In any event several pamphlets were published about the claim and the ensuing controversy. Many were bound in rabbitskin.

**Most Unusual Resurrection:** The wife of the mayor of Cologne fell victim to the Plague and was buried in 1571. As he helped with the interment in the morning, the gravedigger noticed a beautiful diamond on the lady's finger. That night he stole back to the grave and dug up the coffin. As the ghoul was removing the lid, the "dead woman" moved and groaned; it seems she had merely lapsed into a very deep coma, and the doctors, in fear of the contagion, had not checked too closely for vital signs. Delivered by a would-be graverobber, the mayor's wife lived on for many years.

**Most Unusual Suicide:** A Shrewsbury Englishman, William G. Hall, ended it all in 1971 by boring eight holes in his head with an electric power drill. There would have been an angry legislature to contend with had he been a resident of the ancient island-state of Cheos, where a person contemplating suicide had to announce his intention to the Senate. The senators would then debate the pros and cons, and either grant or deny permission to the citizen to do himself in.

**Most Unusual Syndrome:** Physicians Eulogio Rectra and Warren Litts of Lewis County General Hospital in Lowville, New York, recently ministered to a woman complaining of a tingling paralytic sensation in her hand. A neurological examination showed that she had pinched two nerves—the radial and the median—near her elbow. Significantly, she had first noticed the pain and numbness two days earlier after struggling home from the supermarket with two heavy bags of groceries. "Grocery-bag neuropathy" is what the good doctors dubbed the syndrome in an article in *The New England Journal of Medicine*. "It seems that in our present day-to-day living," they wrote, "the average shopper is faced not only with the problems of inflation but also with the weight of his purchase." They related "grocery-bag neuropathy" to such other present-day ailments as "toilet-scat neuropathy," "gunbelt neuropathy," and "ski-boot neuropathy."

**Most Unusual Tomb:** In Pompano Beach, Florida, a person with a penchant for electronic immortality can purchase a talking tombstone from the Eternal Monument Company. Before he dies—and, presumably, long before death has become an imminent possibility—a customer must make an appointment to visit the firm and have himself filmed and his voice taped for the tombstone.

**Most Unusual Undertakers:** When a Spanish king dies (of course, there has not been a monarch for decades), the members of the Espinosa family, who have been royal undertakers for many generations, perform a unique ritual. Dressed in traditional mourning costumes hundreds of years old, they head the funeral procession to the Palace of Escorial, the burial place of the royal family. They stop for the night at a place about halfway; they could make the trip all in one day, but it is traditional to stop.

The next morning, the eldest male Espinosa knocks on the coffin and asks the king if he wishes to continue. Since the answer is never no, the cortege continues on to Escorial, arriving just after dark. There they find the doors of the church securely shut, even though everyone is expecting the arrival of the procession. The Espinosas rap loudly on the doors, but the monks within refuse to admit them, crying "How do you know the king is dead?" After a ceremonial argument, the monks grudgingly admit the unusual undertakers and their charge. A high mass is performed, then the king is finally laid to rest in a beautifully carved pantheon below the church.

# Nature and Science

**Best Drinking Water in the World:** Residents of Bydgoszcz, Poland, turned on their water taps one morning in 1973 and got beer instead of water. A damaged valve in a brewery there had diverted several thousand gallons of the foaming brew into the city's water supply.

**Best Invention:** Thomas Crapper, a London-born sanitation engineer, invented the Valveless Water-Waste Preventer, the prototype of the modern flush toilet.

Crapper was a child of the Victorian age, when waste disposal was at best a primitive art. His business completed, a Victorian flushed his toilet simply by pulling a chain that sent the wastes, along with water from a cistern, sluicing into a pipe that emptied, ultimately, into the Thames. Queen Victoria, on viewing the Thames at a public ceremony, is said to have asked, "What are all those pieces of paper floating in the river?" Mustering up all the tact demanded by the age, one of her aides answered, "Your majesty, they are notices that swimming here is forbidden."

The excrement explosion brought England to a crisis point in the 1870s and the British Board of Trade spearheaded a drive to produce a solution. Crapper took up the call and came up with his valveless wonder, using the moveable metal float that is still the driving force behind many toilets today. The float greatly improved the efficiency of waste disposal, made real the miracle of indoor plumbing, and stemmed the huge outflow of water that threatened England so direly. At the 1884 Health Exhibition, Crapper proudly demonstrated the efficacy of his invention by disposing of a sponge, three wads of grease-laden paper stuck to the bowl, and ten large apples.

Flushed with victory, Crapper went on to develop several highly marketable spinoffs from his original invention, including a prison model in which the plumbing pipes were inaccessible to violence-prone convicts, and Crapper's Chainless Seat Action Automatic Flush. (A lift of the seat and the toilet is flushed. Chain optional.) In later years, as president and owner of T. Crapper & Co., Chelsea, he was commissioned to install toilet facilities in the country home of King Edward II at Sandringham.

**Best Meteor Shower:** Skywatchers say the most interesting meteor shower occurs annually on December 13, when the Geminids burn themselves out in the earth's atmosphere at a rate of about fifty per hour. Every thirty-three years or so, however, those who bother to look up on mid-November evenings witness heaven's most spectacular fireworks. An estimated 300,000 shooting stars per hour fell in the Leonids showers of 1799 and 1833, and on November 17, 1966 some 2,500 meteors per minute spilled out of the constellation Leo and blazed across the northern Arizona sky.

The largest known meteorite also fell on northern Arizona, near Winslow, about 27,000 years ago. The iron-nickle fireball struck the earth with the force of a thirty-four megaton atomic bomb and blasted a crater 4,150 feet across. But probably the most unusual meteorite is the Black Stone of the Ka'ba—the most sacred shrine of Islam. Western scientists have never had an opportunity to examine it, since nonbelievers are forbidden to enter Mecca under penalty of death, yet descriptions suggest to some that it is three shattered pieces of burnt-out space scrap. The legend is more romantic. The Angel Gabriel is said to have presented the stone to Abraham, and centuries later Mohammed ascended into heaven from it. According to tradition the rock was originally pure white, but it has turned black as it absorbed the sins shed by pilgrims to the Ka'ba.

Thomas Jefferson was one of many who preferred the legends about shooting stars to the facts. When informed in 1807 that astronomer Benjamin Silliman had established that meteors do indeed come from outer space, the president replied, "I would rather believe that a Yankee professor would lie than believe that stones fall from heaven."

**Best Method of Preserving Documents:** Pepsodent may purge the yellow from your teeth, but a similarly effective agent to prevent newsprint from yellowing and ultimately crumbling into nothingness has only recently been discovered, and its main ingredient, surprisingly, is good old club soda.

Richard Smith, an assistant professor of librarianship at the University of Washington, offers this recipe for preserving newsprint for generations yet unborn: Dissolve one milk of magnesia tablet in a quart of bottled club soda, mix well, and let the stuff chill for eight hours or so in a refrigerator.

Next, pour it out into a shallow pan and soak your document—or documents—in it for an hour. Remove the papers and pat them dry as well as you can before allowing them to dry more fully. The effect of this soaking, says Smith, is to counteract the processes which eat away at the cellulose fibers of the paper, causing it to turn yellow and brittle with age. Having timeproofed them with your favorite brand of bottled club soda, you'll be able to keep your documents intact and readable for as long as 300 years—not bad when you consider that the normal lifespan for a page of untreated newsprint is no more than a century. However, you must remember to have the papers resoaked every fifty years.

**Best Star:** The brightest event ever seen in the heavens appeared on the morning of July 4, 1054 A.D. The great nova, as Oriental astronomers describe it, was six times brighter than Venus and was only outshone by the sun and moon. For twenty-three days the nova could be observed in broad daylight.

---

**Worst Cold Wave:** At Verkhoyansk in eastern Siberia the temperature occasionally plunges to 90° below zero. If a traveler ventures out without a mask or an air-warming apparatus, his breath freezes in the air and falls to the ground with a soft crackling or whispering sound. Should he inhale, his lungs will immediately be coated with frost.

**Worst Comet:** "It may well be the comet of the century," Harvard astronomer Fred Whipple predicted. Other experts forecast that by January 1974, when Comet Kahoutek was to make its closest approach to the sun, it would be by far the brightest object in the sky. Its fifty-million-mile long tail would stretch one sixth of the way across the sky and its vaporized head would have five times the luminosity of the full moon. Kahoutek, everyone agreed, would be the kind of comet that caused the people of the Middle Ages to start saying their prayers and swelled the ranks of monasteries. Telescope and binocular sales boomed as would-be comet watchers prepared to get a good look.

But when Kahoutek kept its appointed rendezvous with the sun, it turned out to be, in *Time* magazine's words, "a faint smudge." Diehard fans in their Kahoutek sweatshirts stared in vain at the southwestern horizon, still hoping to catch a glimpse of the celestial disappointment, but few could pick it out with the naked eye. Venus and Jupiter far outshone it. As for the experts, they went skulking back to their observatories, like weathermen wearing raincoats on a sunny day.

So Halley's retains the unchallenged title of best comet. It is not the brightest ever seen, but it has the virtue of reliability. The earliest recorded sighting was in 467 B.C., and it has appeared regularly every seventy-six years since then. The superstitious say it was an omen of the destruction of the temple of Jerusalem, Attila's invasion of Western Europe, and the Norman conquest of England. You can wager confidently that it will appear in the sky at 9:30 P.M. (GMT) on February 9, 1986.

**Worst Drinking Water in the United States:** The nation's worst drinking water is in Lawrenceville, Illinois, and unless you've got relatives there or have a weakness for oil refineries, your chances of avoiding this south-central Illinois town are better than even. Large quantities of sulfur have evidently found their way into the city's water supply, because the filmy gonk that comes out of the water taps there has a decidedly eggy taste. Residents of Lawrenceville have inured themselves to the daily indignities of brushing their teeth, but short-term visitors invariably make do with bottled water, Coca-Cola, or gin.

*Living Wilderness* magazine recently carried a story about a barge containing 264,000 bottles of Scotch that foundered and sunk to the bottom of the Detroit River. A salvage crew had no difficulty raising the vessel and every bottle was recovered undamaged. But as soon as the liquor was brought to shore the Food and Drug Administration impounded it, spilled out the Scotch, crushed the bottles, and buried it all in a landfill. The owners were outraged. Why did the government destroy their perfectly good, unopened spirits? An FDA spokesman replied firmly, "Anything that has been submerged in the Detroit River is contaminated."

**Worst Interplanetary Communications System:** Astronomers are convinced that somebody is out there. When radio telescopes first picked up mysteriously regular signals from deep space, a number of sober scientists entertained the idea that intelligent beings from some distant civilization might be trying to communicate with us.

As it turned out, pulsars—those strange, gigantic collapsing stars—were the source of the unusual radio patterns. But the odds, they say, are overwhelmingly in favor of life somewhere else in the universe and recently earthlings made their first serious attempt to contact aliens.

On the side of the Pioneer 10 spacecraft, which sent back the first close-up pictures of Jupiter and will become the first man-made object to leave our solar system, NASA scientists engraved a stylized picture of a man and woman with their right hands raised in a gesture of peace and greeting. (At least they hope that's the way the gesture will be interpreted.) And should extraterrestrial beings happen on the NASA probe, engraved symbols will tell them where we are so they can write back or pay us a visit.

While admittedly this method is about as crude as putting a message in a bottle and throwing it in the ocean, at least it is friendly, whereas the mode of communication proposed by Frenchman Charles Cros in the 1870s could have led to a terrible misunderstanding with the Martians.

Cros spent years trying to persuade the French government to construct a colossal magnifying glass that would focus the sun's rays on the Martian desert. The lens might then be manipulated slightly, burning letters and words into the planet's surface. Patrick Moore describes this scheme in *Can You Speak Venusian?*, a book about eccentric astonomers, and he poses an excellent rhetorical question: "I wonder what words Cros proposed to write?"

**Worst Invention:** The files of the United States Patent Office are filled with descriptions of inventions that might just as well have been left uninvented. One example is patent #560,351, held by Martin Goetz, "A Device for Producing Dimples." In the muddy prose of patent applications, this is how it works:

"The apparatus consists principally of two revolving arms which are pivoted and hinged together after the manner of a pair of compasses, the upper part being connected to a brace.

"When it is desired to use the device for the production of dimples, the knob of the arm must be set on the selected spot on the body, the extension put in position, then while holding the knob with the hand, the brace must be made to revolve on its axis."

**Worst Science:** The torture of political prisoners is no longer the primitive, hit-or-miss operation it was up until the last century. According to a recent article in *New Scientist,* the prestigious British publication, the systematic torture of individuals for political purposes is a growing technology that incorporates the latest advances in electronics, physics, behavioral psychology, biochemistry, and pharmacology. In fact, the governments of some thirty nations have hired specially trained scientists specifically to establish and carry out torture programs.

In Brazil, for example, scientists have perfected the *piquada*, which resembles a hatpin, packs an electric shock strong enough to cripple a horse, and is inserted beneath the fingernails. Also popular in Brazil these days is the Mitrioni vest, rumored to have been invented by a United States AID administrator. The vest is inflatable and is wrapped tightly around the victim's midsection and then pumped, blood-pressure-machine style, until the subject cries uncle. If he doesn't the vest can easily crush him to death.

Perhaps the worst of the "new wave" of torture methods, and certainly one of the most novel, is Aminazin, a drug that causes its victim to grow intensely hyperactive and uncontrollably restless. It has been used with great success to interrogate enemies of the state in the Soviet Union.

**Worst Scientific Project:** *Esquire* magazine reports that Dr. R. J. White of Cleveland expressed the following aspiration for his profession at a meeting of organ transplant specialists in Fiuggi, Italy: "We must, we want to think of transplanting the head."

Another gentleman who dares dream great dreams for science is J. V. Walker, a public health officer in England. He has suggested that researchers develop a pill that will postpone puberty until after students complete college.

**Worst Smell:** Ethyl mercoptan ($C_2H_5SH$) is one of the most powerful of smells and, to most noses, the worst. The odor is said to resemble that of rotting cabbage or sewer gas, except that it is somewhat purer and more revolting.

**Worst Substance:** The researcher who discovered it knew it was good for something. After all, you could shape it, stretch it, snap it, or roll it into a ball and bounce it. Later, it was accidentally discovered that you could flatten it and take an impression of newsprint. But what was it? Why, it was Silly Putty, of course.

Kids loved it and parents hated it. Mom and dad soon found that the original Silly Putty formula had a delightful way of fusing with the fibers of the living room carpet when left out of its container overnight, making it as difficult to remove as old chewing gum. Though this quality was later corrected, the original formula is still regarded with loathing by thousands of unforgiving parents.

Like the Blob, Silly Putty oozed inexorably over the nation. Some 32 million plastic eggs filled with the devil's goo were sold in the first five years of production, and its success inspired the invention of at least one other despicable substance—Flubber.

**Worst Theory of Evolution:** Kiss Maerth, the Yugoslavian-born author of *The Beginning Was the End: Man Came Into Being Through Cannibalism—Intelligence Can Be Eaten,* accepts Charles Darwin's premise that our ancestors were apes, but that is about the *only* similarity between his theory of evolution and that of the great nineteenth-century naturalist.

According to Maerth, the apes fed primarily on each other's brains. Since brains are an aphrodisiac, the apes' dinner-table preferences increased their sex drive, an effect which in turn whetted their appetite for more brains.

The major result of this gluttonous ingestion of the brains of their contemporaries was to swell the size of their own brains and make the apes more intelligent. However, this enlargement of their brains took place at a faster rate than the enlargement of their skulls, producing (a) presumably, some pretty fierce headaches and (b), for the apes, an inflated sense of their own importance in the universe. And that, Maerth suggests, is why we're in the mess we're in today.

**Worst Valley:** In the high Andes between Peru and Chile there is a valley through which people only dare pass in the daylight. Thousands of people who have tried the crossing at night have fallen victim to what is now known as Carrión's disease—a fatal anemia. Only those who have survived the illness and developed an immunity venture to live in the deadly valley.

A Peruvian medical student named Carrión first identified the disease which is carried by a sandfly so small that it slips through mosquito netting. The insects have an aversion to light, but millions swarm out of their hiding places after sundown. Chileans had done most of the research on the disease, but the War of the Pacific had just ended and the chauvinist Carrión wanted the medical credit to go to Peru. To make a positive identification of the anemia's source, he injected himself with serum from the sandflies; the injection proved his point but also caused his death.

**Worst Weather in the United States:** Among American cities, Bismarck, North Dakota, is the least tolerable—in the winter months, that is. According to records kept by the National Climatic Center of the United States Department of Commerce, the average daily temperature range for Bismarck in January is between 20° and −0°F. (They've recorded temperatures there as low as −43°.)

The most infernal town on the map—during the summer—is Phoenix, Arizona, where daily temperatures in July generally hit 105°F. In all fairness, however, Phoenix did have 219 clear days in 1973, the most of any United States city.

---

**Most Unusual Almanac:** The oldest known almanac dates back to 1200 B.C. Written in red ink on a papyrus scroll, it offers the standard daily advice based on astrological parameters, including such wisdom as "Do nothing at all this day."

A famous English almanac was published by Francis Moore. According to William Walsh, Moore would dictate his weather predictions off the top of his head—snow, sleet, rain, dry, cloudy, cold, and so on—as fast as his secretary could write them down. One unusual prediction secured Moore's reputation for accuracy. He was sleeping one afternoon when his secretary foolishly woke him up to inquire, "What weather shall I put for Derby Day [June 3] 1867?" Half asleep, Moore replied irritably, "Cold and snow, damn it!" As it turned out, it did snow on June 3, 1867. From then on, no matter how many times Moore was wrong, people would forgive his saying, "Ah, but remember Derby Day!"

**Most Unusual Fire:** Throughout the first half of this century a fire burned in a coal mine near Straitsville, Ohio. Smoldering underground for fifty-two years, the fire was finally put out only after it had caused $50,000 worth of damage and threatened hundreds of homes in the area.

**Most Unusual Foundation:** Roger Ward Babson was a stock market tycoon and a friend of Thomas Edison. One day the inventor said off-handedly, "Babson, you should look into gravity," or something of the sort, and Roger took up the challenge with a passion. He established and endowed the Gravity Research Foundation which now "serves as a free clearinghouse for everyone seriously interested in the causes and possibilities of gravity."

The *Anti*-Gravity Foundation might be a more accurate name, since most of the organization's efforts and funds have gone toward researching and developing a functional flying carpet. Specifically, the foundation sponsors an annual essay contest, offering $1,000 for the best paper of approximately 1,500 words on 1) a gravity insulator or reflecting device; 2) an alloy whose atoms are agitated by gravity, thereby offering a means of propulsion; or 3) any other means of harnessing the power of gravity. In recent years, Babson's followers have devoted most of their efforts to discrediting the theory of relativity, which, if correct, would make a gravity reflector or propulsion device an impossibility.

It is perhaps noteworthy that the foundation maintains an exhibit of 5,000 birds originally collected by Thomas Edison.

**Most Unusual Glacier:** In the Beartooth Mountains of Montana there is a glacier imbedded with millions of grasshoppers. Two centuries ago the immense swarm made a forced landing on the ice and was quick-frozen by a snowstorm. Today the grasshoppers are still excellently preserved, and when the glacial surface melts birds and bears gather to feed on the two-hundred-year-old insects. A vivid description of the Grasshopper Glacier appears in James L. Dyson's *The World of Ice:* "So numerous have these insects been at times that the odor of their putrefaction has been detected a quarter of a mile away."

A similar grasshopper graveyard has been reported at 16,000 feet on Mount Kenya in Africa.

**Most Unusual Heat Wave:** A freak heat wave hit the central coast of Portugal on July 6, 1949, sending the temperature up to 158°F for a period of two minutes. Moments later the mercury slid back down to the mid-120s. No satisfactory explanation for this fleeting swelter has ever been put forward.

**Most Unusual Laser Beam Application:** The greatest advance since the knife: A physicist at the University of Maryland has developed a technique for opening oysters with a laser beam.

**Most Unusual Mountains:** Consult a topographical map of Alaska and you can locate a pair of twin mountains officially known as the Jane Russell Peaks. In the same spirit, people in the South of France are now using a melodious adjective to describe a rolling, knobby landscape: (Gina) *lollobrigidienne*. In truth, this metaphor is as old as the hills. According to *A Dictionary of Americanisms,* the word Teton, as in "Grand Tetons," is derived from the French word téton, meaning a woman's breast.

**Most Unusual Rain:** About nine o'clock in the evening on July 25, 1872, a dark cloud appeared over Bucharest, Rumania. Moments later it began to rain. The ladies and gentlemen in their evening clothes were surprised not only by a shower of water but also by thousands and thousands of black worms, about the size of honey bees, that fell from the sky.

Frequently, red and green rains have been reported, apparently caused by algae or other small plants somehow caught up in a cloud. Animal storms are less frequent, but there are a number on record. For example, Padeborn, Germany, experienced a storm of snails in August 1892; their shells shattered all over the streets from the velocity of their fall.

**Most Unusual River:** The comingling of two tributary streams in Algeria forms a river of ink: One brook contains iron; the other, which drains from a peat swamp, contains gallic acid. Swirled together, the chemicals unite to form a true black ink. (Black Brook in upstate New York is formed by a similar chemical blend.)

**Most Unusual Science:** Among the rarer "ologies" are argyrothecology, the branch of learning devoted to money boxes, and dendrochronology, the science of determining how old a tree is by its rings. The time-honored science of beer-making is known as tegestology. And finally, this book is an example of morology—the study of foolishness.

**Most Unusual Smell:** To a sizeable portion of the male population in America, there is one fragrance that is more pleasing to the nose than roses or lilacs or orchids—the smell of a new automobile. Now, the chemists of Frank Orlandi Company in Long Island City, New York, have done our olfactories a great service. They have synthesized "new car smell," making that delightful odor available to dealers selling foul and musty used cars.

**Most Unusual Substance:** Ordinary atoms are composed of electrons whirling around protons and neutrons. Recently physicists have discovered a complete set of antiparticles, so that, theoretically at least, there can be "looking-glass atoms" with electrical charges that are completely reversed. Separated from regular matter, this "antimatter" would be perfectly stable. But if matter and antimatter were brought together, each substance would annihilate the other in a tremendous, total-energy explosion. Some cosmologists speculate that for every particle in the universe there may be a corresponding antiparticle. In other words, somewhere there may exist antiworlds populated by antibeings—in an entire antiuniverse.

**Most Unusual Value for Pi:** According to R. Horwink's *Odd Book of Data*, a nineteenth-century Danish schoolmaster calculated the value of $\pi$ out to 800 decimal places, an effort that stretched over his entire lifetime. A computer programmed to perform the same task took just a few hours to check his figures—and he was right. But to the Kansas Legislature of an earlier year, it was all wasted effort. Kansas once passed a law rounding off the value of pi from 3.14159265 . . . (and so on) to an even 3.

**Most Unusual Volcano:** At 19,344 feet above sea level, Mount Cotopaxi near Quito, Equador, is one of the highest active volcanoes in the world. When it blew its snow-capped top in 1877, there was only a modest lava flow, but the accompanying heat melted the nearby glaciers and caused flooding throughout the area. The flooding, in turn, created a tremendous mud flow that spilled down the mountainsides at speeds up to fifty miles per hour and devastated villages over 150 miles away. Even the writers for Hollywood catastrophe movies would have difficulty imagining a more freakish natural disaster.

**Most Unusual Water:** Lithium is a light metallic salt used in the treatment of manic depressives. Recently, Dr. Earl Lawson, a biochemist from the University of Texas, discovered that there is enough natural lithium in the water supply of El Paso, Texas, to keep the entire city happy and a little high. In the same way that natural fluorides prevent tooth decay, Dr. Lawson believes that lithium in the water supply is a factor in the city's low incidence of mental illness.

**Most Unusual Waterfall:** In the Koolau Mountains of Oahu, Hawaii, waterfalls spill over the high cliffs; the waters are caught by powerful updrafts, evaporated into a soupy mist, and blown back up over the cliffside. From a distance the waterfall appears to flow upward.

**Most Unusual Weather Forecaster:** Mrs. Fanny Shields of Baltimore, Maryland, owned a cat named Napoleon back in the 1930s who could predict the weather with an accuracy that was deadly.

During an especially severe dry spell that gripped Baltimore in 1930, when human meteorologists were offering no hope for relief, Mrs. Shields phoned the Baltimore newspapers and told them that rain would fall within twenty-four hours. How could she be so sure? the papers asked. Easy, she told them. She had just seen her cat Napoleon sitting with his front paws extended before him and his head on the ground, his own way of indicating that it was going to rain. The papers, needless to say, took her for a madwoman.

The following day, it rained.

In the ensuing months, the papers published Napoleon's forecasts regularly. They were accurate more often than not.

# Plants and Animals

**Best Insect Repellent:** According to the Canadian national parks service, the most effective insect repellents are those containing diethyltoluamide, a pungent chemical that disgusts mosquitoes, blackflies, and ticks. A superpotent repellent containing a similar polysyllabic ingredient was developed by the U.S. Army to repel Vietnamese bugs; it also works well on domestic varieties and is now available at many army surplus stores. Caught without your diethyltoluamide, you might try rubbing orange or lemon peel on your skin for temporary protection. Garlic is also an effective repellent if you can stand it yourself. In fact, garlic juice can be lethal to mosquitoes and scientists are investigating its usefulness as a biodegradable substitute for DDT.

**Best Parents:** The temperature during the long Antarctic night may plunge to −80°F. Under these inclement conditions it is only through a heroic combination of patience and acrobatics that emperor penguins manage to hatch their eggs. Two-thirds feathers, the emperors are magnificent birds, standing nearly four feet tall. The female lays a single egg in midwinter and immediately departs on a long fishing trip, leaving her mate with the responsibility for incubation. In the bitter cold the egg would freeze almost immediately if it touched the ground. To protect it, the male stands for sixty days on one foot, holding the egg next to his warm underbelly with the other. Occasionally he switches feet, but throughout this period he eats nothing at all. Finally, when the chick is about ready to hatch, the female returns to take over the child-rearing tasks, and the famished male waddles off to the ocean for some fishing of his own.

179

Emperor penguin holding chick on its feet

**Best Pet:** A number of New York City pet stores are importing gecko lizards from the South Pacific for sale to apartment dwellers. The gecko, which comes in a number of attractive pastel colors, makes an excellent pet. During the day he sleeps peacefully behind the refrigerator or stove, but at night he prowls the kitchen in search of his favorite prey—cockroaches. The shy and soft-skinned lizard is voracious, consuming hundreds of roaches a week; once a pet gecko has devoured all the insects in the house, he makes a wonderful gift for a neighbor with a vermin problem. Geckos are clean, quiet, and require no grooming, although they have been known to shed their tails when frightened.

The gecko played a role in a complex ecological crisis in Malaysia leading up to the world's most unusual airlift. In its efforts to control disease-carrying mosquitoes, the Malaysian government sprayed infested areas with DDT. The poisoned mosquitoes were devoured by roaches, which in turn fell prey to geckos. The residual poison was not enough to kill the hardy lizards, but it did affect their central nervous system, slowing them down and making them easier targets for hungry cats. The cats, however, were more vulnerable to DDT, and they began dying by the hundreds. With the cat population dwindling, the number of rats skyrocketed;

Gecko lizard

parts of Malaysia were thus threatened with a serious rodent problem.

At this point, the World Health Organization stepped in and recommended an end to the use of DDT. Then, to restore the ecological balance, they airdropped whole planeloads of cats into remote areas where rats roamed fearlessly.

---

**Worst Animal:** Don't invite a sloth to your next dinner party or get
stuck sitting next to one on an airplane. Apart from their maddening laziness, sloths are unquestionably the biggest bores of the
animal kingdom.

Biologists Theodore Bullock and James Toole, fascinated by the
sloth's inborn gift for doing nothing for hours on end—and doing it
at a snail's pace—studied the animal's physiology in depth to determine what makes it tick. Or, more precisely, what makes it not
tick.

Three-toed sloth

For one thing, they found that its nervous system is depressingly sluggish and its reflexes all but nonexistent. Sloths will not so much as flinch, much less jump, at a sudden noise, and if a sloth is dropped from a height, it will remain in the position in which it lands and sag to the ground like a sack of flour, rather than set itself aright.

Moreover, only female sloths can maintain constant body temperatures, and they do that only when they're pregnant. Sloths can turn their breathing off and on at will without suffering any physical damage, and ingested food takes a good two weeks to make its way from one end of the alimentary tract to the other.

Indeed, ennui oozes from the sloth's very pores. In the words of the seventeenth-century naturalist Nehemiah Grew, the sloth is "an animal of so slow a motion, that he will be three or four days, at least, in climbing up and down a tree."

**Worst Flower:** There was a great deal of excitement at the New York Botanical Gardens on June 8, 1937; at long last, the giant Sumatran calla lily (*Amorphophallus titanium*) had burst into blossom. Its flower was the largest ever recorded, measuring eight and a half feet in height, four feet in diameter, and twelve feet in circumference. More precisely, the huge stalk was inflores-

Giant Sumatran calla lily

cent containing thousands of small flowers. Regrettably, however, the distinctive fragrance somewhat dampened public enthusiasm for the calla lily; it smelled like rotten meat. Indonesians call it the "corpse flower."

**Worst Insect Repellent:** The Canadian national park service is the source of this invaluable warning: "If you eat bananas, your skin will exude an odor which is very attractive to mosquitoes."

**Worst Pet:** While visiting in Tunis, Alexander Dumas, author of *The Three Musketeers* and *The Count of Monte Cristo*, was very much taken with "a superb vulture, a bird without fault." Jurgutha was the bird's name, and his Tunisian owner was anxious to sell since it devoured "everyone and everything that came near," most recently the tail of a pet dog that strayed too close. Dumas was satisfied with the price, and after having a muzzle made for the powerful beak, he arranged to have Jurgutha shipped back to France. Under Dumas's care the animal became quite tame, frequently offering its bald head to be scratched. The eccentric author's only dissatisfaction with his new pet was that, despite diligent efforts, he could not teach it to say "Scratch pretty Polly's head." On the Champs Elysées in Paris, Dumas occasionally terrified poodles and pedestrians as he strolled along with Jurgutha hopping in tow on a silver leash.

On the subject of pets, *Newsweek* magazine reported in 1974 a growing market in tarantulas in the United States. Pet shop owner Doris Mahalek of Detroit said that she had sold several hundred of the venomous creatures over the past three years and that "everybody—longhaired kids, doctors and attorneys—is buying them."

**Worst Toad:** The *Bufo marinus* is an especially ravenous species of toad which Australia imported from South America in the 1930s to eradicate the cane beetles that were ravaging crops in Queensland. The Aussies had undersold the toads' voraciousness, however, because after the beetles were gone, the toads, now grown to as much as eight inches in length, reproduced wildly and took to devouring garbage, Ping Pong balls, dogs, cats, and cattle, killing their prey with a poisonous glandular secretion. By the early 1970s the *Bufo* explosion had become something of a biological nightmare in Australia. The National Wildlife Department was offering a $30 reward for each toad brought in. "Wanted: Dead or Alive" posters proliferated throughout the continent, and, as a public service, at least one radio station was broadcasting tape-recorded mating calls of male *Bufos* in an attempt to lure love-starved females to destruction.

There is also a variety of clawed frog from Africa that is especially dangerous. A bunch of them escaped from a biology laboratory at the University of California at Davis recently and threatened to upset the ecological balance in the area by devouring the fish in nearby Putah Creek.

**Most Unusual Animal:** No book of wonders would be complete without a tribute to the duckbilled platypus. When the first speci-

Duckbilled platypus

men was brought to England from Tasmania in 1880 the zoologists were perplexed. Its two-foot-long body was covered with thick gray-brown hair (definitely mammalian); it had a broad, flat tail (not unlike a beaver); it had webbed feet and a wide rubbery bill (ducky); the brain was a single hemisphere (positively reptilian); behind the rear ankles were two spurs that secrete poison (like a snake). Most improbably of all, this freakish animal was reported to lay eggs. Most zoologists agreed there was only one explanation: *Ornithorhynchus anatinus* was a hoax!

Soon, however, the hoax theory had to be discarded when a

team of scientists discovered a whole pond full of platypi in New South Wales, and they turned out to be even more marvelous than a preserved specimen could suggest. They growl like dogs; they live most of their lives in the water, but are also able tree climbers; they dine mostly on worms, which they store in pouches at the sides of their mouths like chipmunks. The females do indeed lay eggs—two at a time—and they also give milk. Lacking true nipples, the milk is simply secreted from the mammaries through primitive slits; babies lap the milk from their mother's hair.

Ultimately zoologists defined a completely new order, Monotremata, (most primitive living mammals) in which to classify the platypus. Recent studies of the way its spinal cord is attached to its brain have offered new evidence that the platypus is, in effect, the missing link between reptiles and mammals.

**Most Unusual Arboriculturist:** John D. Rockefeller and Kubla Khan shared a passionate fondness for trees. Whenever either of the great men saw a particularly nice specimen, he would buy it, have it pulled up, roots and all, and transplant it in the grounds of his own estate.

**Most Unusual Bedfellow:** There is an old nursery rhyme that begins, "Barber, barber, shave a pig." It sounds like nonsense, but pig-shaving was once a common practice in parts of northern China. On winter nights rural Chinese would bring pigs to bed with them for warmth, and they soon discovered that a porker makes a more pleasant bedfellow when its sharp and muddy bristles have been shaved off.

**Most Unusual Conversations:** The French philosopher Descartes once speculated that monkeys and apes actually have the ability to speak but keep silent to avoid being put to work. As it turns out that may not have been so far from the truth. Consider these unusual conversationalists:

A chimpanzee named Gua, raised by Winthrop and Luella Kellogg during the 1930s, could understand over 100 words though it never learned to speak. The first chimp ever to utter human words was Vicki, trained by Keith and Cathy Hayes; she could say and correctly apply the words "momma" and "poppa" (referring to the Hayeses) and "cup" as well as comprehend many more expressions.

The mouth, tongue, teeth, and central nervous system of chimps are apparently not well designed for handling human language and that seems to be the main obstacle standing in the way of their becoming politicians (or orators of another kind). But when Allen and Beatrice Carter taught American sign language to a chimp named Washoe, he immediately became quite talkative. Washoe uses his naturally dexterous fingers to signal out complete sentences. He can understand and form 140 different words and his favorite expression is "Give me fruit juice." In an even more unsettling development, Bruno and Booee, two chimps at the University of Oklahoma, have also mastered sign language and now use it *to converse with each other.* Oklahoma scientists are particularly anxious to discover whether Bruno and Booee will try to teach sign language to their children.

And finally, Lana, a chimp at the University of Georgia, uses a computer keyboard with one hundred symbols to communicate with *Homo sapiens.* There is no doubt among scientists that Lana is capable of using language abstractly and forming syntactically correct sentences. As yet she has not said anything much more profound than "Lana wants a tickle." But then, as Descartes suggested long ago, she may just be holding out on us.

**Most Unusual Corsage:** On his first voyage to the New World, Christopher Columbus was intrigued by the corsagelike ornaments worn widely by both men and women in the West Indies. They were made of popcorn.

**Most Unusual Dog Fancier:** Francis Henry Egerton, the Eighth Earl of Bridgewater (1756–1829) was one of the most eccentric dog fanciers of all times. He dressed all of his high-class canines in well-made leather boots, and each night he hosted a favored dozen at his own dinner table. While the dogs sat in armchairs with napkins primly tied around their necks, butlers in formal dress dished out the food from sterling serving pieces. But the earl would not tolerate a breach of good manners. A sloppy eater would be dismissed from the table and sent to dine alone in disgrace.

Queen Victoria kept as many as eighty-three dogs at one time in Buckingham Palace, and could call them all by name. In *Useless Facts of History,* Paul Steiner records that after her coronation Victoria's first royal act was to wash her favorite dog.

**Most Unusual Dog Story:** Charles Burden of Missouri had a black and tan hunting dog named Old Drum whom he loved with a passion that bordered on the unnatural. On the morning of October

29, 1869, after a sleepless night waiting for Old Drum to return home from a day of romping in the woods, he found his canine cohort lying in a creek quite dead, his belly full of buckshot. Old Drum, it appeared, had been the victim of a gangland execution.

Burden suspected his neighbor and brother-in-law, Leonidas Hornsby, of the misdeed. Hornsby, a short, foul-tempered man with bad breath and a congenital scowl, denied the accusation vehemently. Nonetheless, it was well known that his dimwitted nephew, Dick Ferguson, had a standing order to shoot to kill any dogs who trespassed on his uncle's land, and that in the past, he had done a lot of shooting to kill.

Burden decided to sue. He hauled Hornsby before a jury who voted in his favor. Hornsby, however, had the decision reversed on appeal, but Burden claimed he had found some new evidence, and so the case went to a third court, and finally a fourth.

It was this fourth and final trial—the longest, most dramatic, and most skillfully argued of all—that decided the case, and a nation of dog lovers, legal buffs, and sensation-seekers followed it avidly.

Representing the plaintiff was the noted attorney George Graham Vest, who later became a United States senator. Representing the defendant was yet another senator-to-be, Francis Marion Cockrell, assisted by Thomas T. Crittenden, a future governor of Missouri.

Oratory flew like shrapnel across the courtroom, and Vest's summation was the height of wretched excess. ("Gentlemen of the jury, a man's dog . . . will sleep on the cold ground where the wintry winds blow . . . if only he may be near his master's side. . . . He guards the sleep of his pauper master as if he were a prince. . . . When riches take wings and reputation falls to pieces, he is as constant in his love as the sun in its journey through the heavens. . . .") As bathetic as it was, it was just such oratory that saved the day for Burden and the court ordered Hornsby to pay damages of fifty dollars to the appellant. A great moral victory had been won and a grateful nation rejoiced.

In the ensuing years, songs and sonnets were written about Old Drum, a mythology based on his life and untimely death arose, and he was memorialized by dog lovers everywhere. On the wall of the Warrensburg, Missouri, courthouse where the trial was held, there is a bronze plaque commemorating Burden's—and Old Drum's—victory. There is a monument to him on the banks of Big Creek, where he met his end, made from stone sent from most of the states of the nation, the Great Wall of China, the White Cliffs of Dover, France, Germany, Mexico, Jamaica, South Africa, the

West Indies, and Guatemala. Yet another memorial—this one a statue created by the noted sculptor Reno Gastaldi—was unveiled in Warrensburg in 1958. The attorney-general of Missouri and Captain Will Judy, editor of *Dog World*, dedicated the work.

**Most Unusual Elephant:** Pink elephants exist. Pachyderms are fond of taking dust baths, and in some areas of Africa, where the soil is rich in iron, the dust caked on their skin gives them a bright pink color.

**Most Unusual Exterminator:** If you can judge the quality of exterminators by the quality of their clientele, then the Messrs. Tiffin and Son of London were topnotch. In 1851 they were appointed "Bug Destroyers to Her Majesty and the Royal Family." Robert Mayhew's *London Labor and the London Poor* includes a candid interview with the elder Mr. Tiffin, who described what it was like plying his trade in Princess Charlotte's bedroom: "Just at that moment I did happen to catch one, and upon that she [the young princess] sprang upon the bed, and put her hand on my shoulder, to look at it. . . . She said, 'Oh, the nasty thing! That's what tormented me last night; don't let him escape.' I think he looked all the better for having tasted royal blood."

**Most Unusual Insect:** The aweto (*Hipialis vivescens*), found in New Zealand, behaves like a cross between a caterpillar and a vegetable. Found at the foot of a large myrtle tree, the aweto buries itself among the roots a few inches below the ground and lives there peacefully until it is full grown. Then it undergoes a strange metamorphosis: The spore of a vegetable fungus fastens itself to the aweto's neck, and from the spore grows an eight-inch high stalk resembling a cattail. Gradually the vegetable takes over the living aweto, filling up all the space within its skin, but leaving the external body unchanged. When the vegetable has completely replaced the caterpillar, both become hard and dry, then die. Dried awetoes are gathered and burned to produce a dark pigment. In its curious life cycle, it is not fully understood how, when, (or why) the aweto reproduces itself.

Another interesting bug story: It is a little known fact that bedbugs bark enthusiastically when they smell human flesh. With this in mind, United States Army scientists devised a scheme to conscript the tiny *Cimex lectularius* for service in Vietnam. Their plan was to pack bedbugs in capsules rigged with miniature radio transmitters. The capsules were to be dropped on suspected Viet

Cong hideouts; if a radio man overheard their hungry barks, the brass would order in the jets and artillery.

American participation in the war ended before the bugs could see active duty, but, as *Newsweek* magazine reports, scientists continue to find *Cimex* an interesting study. It seems that the little critters have an amazingly high sex drive and are polymorphously perverse in the extreme. When a male sees other bedbugs copulating, he becomes very excited and immediately joins in the affair with a partner of either sex. Moreover, according to Jacques Carazon of the National Museum of Natural History in Paris, a male bedbug no longer deposits his sperm in the female's reproductive tract. Whereas ancient bedbugs found preserved in the Pyramids made love in the conventional way, today's swinging *Cimex* punctures the female's abdomen for insemination. Miraculously, the female, in what by evolutionary standards is a very short time, has developed a special tube which carries the sperm from her stomach to her ovaries.

*Xylocoris maculipennis* is a cousin of the *Cimex* which also has peculiar sexual habits. Males of this species often copulate with other males, and their sperm becomes intermingled. When a male has sexual relations with a female, the sperm he transmits is a combination of his own and that of his male partners. This remarkable sex life would seem to frustrate the process of natural selection, leaving the paternity of young bedbugs almost wholly to chance.

**Most Unusual Mermaids:** The dugong is a relative of the manatee living in the Indian Ocean and Australian waters. Both species are members of the order *Sirenia,* so named because at a distance they vaguely resemble women floating with their heads and shoulders out of the water, giving rise to the myths about sirens and mermaids. Of the two, the grayish dugong is the more womanly; the female's breasts are placed high on its torso, like a woman, and she has a habit of holding her young to her breast in a very human posture. A Madagascar fisherman must perform an elaborate religious rite before selling a dugong; among other obligations, he must take an oath that he has not had unnatural relations with his strange and gentle captive.

Like men and elephants, the dugong cries, shedding real tears, when it is in pain or distress. A dugong on exhibit in a Ceylon zoo cried almost daily for years, as if pining for its freedom. Zookeepers collected the tears and sold them as a love potion.

Hunted for their hides, tusks, oil, and palatable flesh, dugongs are now rarely seen.

**Most Unusual Mule:** A mule is by definition the sterile hybrid of a jackass and a mare, as distinguished from a hinny, which is the offspring of a stallion and a jenny. Old Beck, a she-mule owned by Texas A & M University, was an exception. Displaying the legendary stubbornness of her breed, Old Beck defied convention and gave birth to two baby mules—one by a jack and one by a stallion.

**Most Unusual Pet:** An article in *American Horseman* reports that kings and millionaires have discovered a new house pet: midget horses. The foremost breeder of these miniatures is Julio César Fallabella who operates a ranch fifty miles south of Buenos Aires. Forty generations of selective breeding have produced what looks like a throwback to the eohippus—a full-grown pony smaller than a German shepherd. His smallest *enano* or dwarf measures only fifteen inches from ground to withers and weighs twenty-six pounds. The average is more like twenty inches in height; the price—$1,000 and up.

**Most Unusual Protozoan:** The Swedish botanist Linnaeus must have thought he had been peering through his microscope too long. But when a second squint confirmed what he had seen before, Linnaeus realized that he was in the presence of an animal like no other; he named his discovery *Chaos chaos*. In 1975 we celebrate the two hundredth anniversary of the discovery of *Chaos*, which scientists have recognized only about fifty times since Linnaeus first made its acquaintance.

As this freakish organism is the terror of the one-celled world, it must be a comfort to other tiny animals that *Chaos* is so rare. Fifty times the size of an average paramecium, it hunts in vicious packs of three, completely surrounding entire schools of smaller protozoa and devouring them without mercy. Moreover, unlike any other one-celled creature, *Chaos* has three distinct nuclei; when it gets lonely it simply wrinkles and divides into three separate animals exactly like itself. Because of its tripartite personality, the *Chaos* is often handicapped by indecisiveness. Each nucleus sets out in its own direction, stretching out a long streamer of protoplasm. An internal tug-of-war follows. Eventually, one nucleus overpowers the others, forcing them to slither along after it.

Some biologists believe *Chaos chaos* or other organisms like it may have been the link between single and multicelled animals.

**Most Unusual Retriever:** English sportsmen used to train hunting pigs to fetch their game.

**Most Unusual State Insect:** That a state would bother to honor an insect is the unusual part. Once that decision has been made, California's choice of the dog-faced butterfly seems a fine one.

**Most Unusual Stuffed Animal:** Tufts University's P. T. Barnum Museum houses Jumbo, who was once the world's largest elephant; now he is not even the world's largest stuffed elephant, since the Smithsonian Museum acquired an even more elephantine specimen. Nonetheless, Jumbo remains the most unusual stuffed elephant because, as anyone who ever saw him perform will attest to, he had personality.

# Business and Finance

**Best (Lowest) Cost of Living in the World:** If money means everything to you, you'll find Montevideo, Uruguay, to be just about the most inexpensive major city in the world in which to live, according to a study done by the United Nations Statistical Office in 1973. The study arbitrarily assigned New York City a cost-of-living index of 100 and gauged the indices of other cities in relation to it, taking into account standard prices on some 120 different consumer items. Montevideo's index is 52.

**Best Entrepreneur:** Phineas Taylor Barnum first gained fame with his American Museum in New York, where he exhibited Tom Thumb—the world's smallest man—and other freaks. Perhaps his greatest triumph was the discovery and publicity of the woman he called George Washington's wet nurse.

Joyce Heth, an elderly black woman, was already making the rounds of the sideshows as "the living mummy" when P. T. first encountered her. Though she was toothless and nearly blind, Barnum saw something in her carriage and manner that suggested gentility and greatness. He immediately signed her up for his museum, billing her as the 161-year-old woman who had mothered the father of our country. She was an immediate success. Thousands of weeping suckers came to hear her relate memories of little George and firsthand anecdotes about the Revolutionary War.

Gradually, however, the crowds began to decline. Barnum responded with another brainstorm. Under a pseudonym, he contributed a series of muckraking columns to a local newspaper claiming that Joyce Heth was not a woman at all, but actually a sophisticated automaton. The crowds came back for a second look,

# FOR ONE DAY ONLY!!!
# JOICE HETH,

Now on her return to the SOUTH, where she must arrive before cold weather, will, (at the urgent requests of many ladies and gentlemen) be seen at

# CONCERT HALL
# ☞FOR ONE DAY ONLY.☜

This is positively the LAST OPPORTUNITY, which can ever be afforded to the citizens of New England, of seeing this most wonderful woman.

JOICE HETH is unquestionably the most astonishing and interesting curiosity in the World! She was the slave of Augustine Washington, (the father of Gen. Washington,) and was the first person who put clothes on the unconscious infant who in after days led our heroic fathers on to glory, to victory and freedom. To use her own language when speaking of the illustrious Father of his country, "she raised him." JOICE HETH was born in the Island of Madagascar, on the Coast of Africa, in the year 1674 and has consequently now arrived at the astonishing

# Age of 161 Years !

She weighs but *forty-six pounds*, and yet is very cheerful and interesting. She retains her faculties in an unparalleled degree, converses freely, sings numerous hymns, relates many interesting anecdotes of *the boy* Washington, the red coats, &c. and often laughs heartily at her own remarks, or those of the spectators. Her health is perfectly good, and her appearance very neat. She was baptized in the Potomac river and received into the Baptist Church 116 years ago, and takes great pleasure in conversing with Ministers and religious persons. The appearance of this marvellous relic of antiquity strikes the beholder with amazement, and convinces him that his eyes are resting on the oldest specimen of mortality they ever before beheld. Original, authentic and indisputable documents prove however astonishing the fact may appear, JOICE HETH is in every respect the person she is represented.

The most eminent physicians and intelligent men in Cincinnati, Philadelphia, New-York, Boston and many other places have examined this *living skeleton* and the documents accompanying her, and all *invariably* pronounce her to be as represented 161 *years of age*! Indeed it is impossible for any person, however incredulous, to visit her without astonishment and the most perfect satisfaction that she is as old as represented.

☞ A female is in continual attendance, and will give every attention to the ladies who visit this relic of by gone ages.

She was visited at Niblo's Garden New York, by *ten thousand persons* in two weeks.——Hours of exhibition from 9 A. M to 1 P. M. and from 3 to 6 and from 7 to 9 P. M.—Admittance 25 cents—Children 12½ cents.

☞For further particulars, see newspapers of the day.     ☞Over

Advertisement for P. T. Barnum's Joyce Heth. (Chicago Historical Society)

and Barnum offered undeniable proof that this wonderful old lady was, in fact, a living, breathing human being.

The controversy over Joyce Heth continued even after her death. Doctors who performed the autopsy estimated that the venerable performer was only eighty-four years old. Barnum, of course, vigorously denied this charge, maintaining that they had operated on the wrong woman.

Much of Barnum's career is now legend: the founding of his

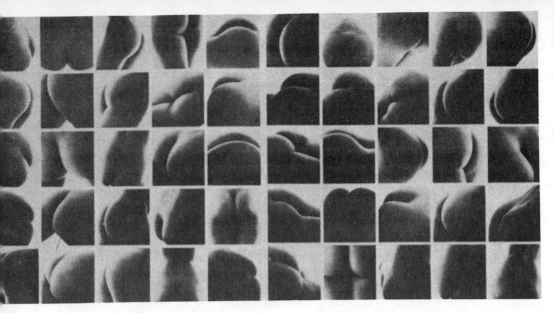

Furniture ad, first run in *Paris-Match*

circus "The Greatest Show on Earth"; importing Jumbo, the first white elephant Americans had seen; purportedly observing, "There is a sucker born every minute." He continued to float outrageous schemes throughout his life. In a gesture typical of his taste and sensitivity, one of Barnum's last acts was to telegraph the great Sarah Bernhardt when he heard that her leg might have to be amputated. Phineas offered her a flat fee of $1,000 for the severed limb. Miss Bernhardt never bothered to reply.

**Best Way to Face the Specter of Spiralling Inflation:** Secretary of Agriculture Earl Butz was seen at a Capitol Hill Club party pilfering food from the buffet table and wrapping it in napkins to take home.

**Worst Advertisement:** In Mexico, no one puts down Emiliano Zapata and gets away with it. In 1970, a magazine advertisement for Elgin watches made note of Zapata's notorious watch-stealing campaign and his much-bandied threat to kill any railroad conductor who tried to pull a fast one on the revolutionary hero by wearing an inferior timepiece. Said the ad, "It's a good thing Zapata's gone. He'd be stealing Elgins as fast as we could make them."

Sociologist José de Fonseca of Mexico City saw the advertisement and bridled, doubly piqued by the crass commercialism of an offer to readers of a "handsome Zapata poster" for one dollar

He retaliated by producing a poster ad for a mythical "Darkie Beer" that was deliberately and consummately tasteless. Under the heading WASHINGTON EN ONDA CON LAS NEGRAS ("Washington Swung with the Darkies") was a crumpled dollar bill and this legend: "George Washington, United States secessionist, had an excessive fondness for black slaves, according to legend. He used to sneak out of his home silently at night and head for the slave quarters, where he would abuse them.

"For us, Darkie is not a person, but a beer. We know you'll enjoy it."

Across the Atlantic, European journalism really touched bottom in 1969 when *Paris-Match* ran a furniture ad featuring fifty bare derrieres covering a 'two-page spread. The copy: "Yes, that's where it's at. We agree with Madame de Sevigne, who wrote, 'Most of our troubles come from having our asses squarely in the saddle . . .' Our job is to sit you down anatomically, socially, and somewhat philosophically."

**Worst (Highest) Cost of Living in the World:** Predictably, it's Tokyo, Japan, where gasoline goes for as much as two dollars a gallon and, at a coffee-shop counter, a Coke can run you a dollar or more. The Japanese industrial boom has inflated the city's cost-of-living index to 117.

**Worst Horatio Alger Story:** The worst Horatio Alger story is the story of Horatio Alger himself, the man who made a fortune writing 119 books on the rags-to-riches theme. Alger was a notorious spendthrift and he died totally destitute.

**Worst Monetary System:** Postwar inflation diminished the value of the Hungarian pengo in 1946 to 1/828 octillionth of what it had been before the inflation spiral began.

**Worst Status Symbol:** Bracelets worn by high-ranking Suka tribesmen in Ethiopia are purposely made so tight that they almost stop the flow of blood. The hands of the rich often become shrunken, withered, and virtually useless. To the Suka, withered hands are a status symbol, and the more atrophied their hands become the prouder the aristocrats are of them.

**Most Unusual Advertisement:** One memorable evening in 1952, Parisians craned their necks and saw the most spectacular display advertisement ever conceived. On the low, overhanging clouds the name of a commercial airline appeared in gigantic illuminated letters. The innovation, which promised to be as momentous in the history of publicity as the appearance of the first sandwich man, was made possible through a complicated system of spotlights and huge color transparencies.

The next day, "skylighting" was the talk of the town. The newspapers predicted that soon the names of wines, cheeses, soaps, underclothing, and movie stars would be flashing on the firmament. But the city council had other ideas. They insisted that the skies of "the City of Light" should remain forever dark, and the projection of brand names on clouds was outlawed.

**Most Unusual Auction:** In 1970, a London collector auctioned off several Napoleonic relics including the emperor's death mask and a generous portion of his body hair, all for an estimated total of $72,000. *Punch* reported on what was "undoubtedly the saddest news item in a long time: The fact that Napoleon's penis was withdrawn (sorry, that's the auctioneer's word, not ours) from a sale at Christie's because no one was willing to pay more than $40,000 for it." The item, described in the auction catalog as a "small, dried-up object," was placed back in its box and then taken back by its American owner.

In March of 1890, Leventon and Company of Liverpool, England, auctioned off 180,000 mummified cat bodies from an Egyptian burial ground near Beni Hassan. While Leventon felt they might command a higher price as a novelty gift item, the cats went for a little less than ten dollars per ton.

According to Herodotus (Book I, 196), the Babylonians ran an unusual marriage auction. All the young women of marriageable age were brought to the central market place. The attractive girls naturally commanded high prices, and the money raised from their sale was put toward dowries for the homely ones (with the ugliest receiving the largest endowment). There was only one concession to romance: If either party was dissatisfied with the transaction, the monies were refunded to the general pool and the marriage annulled.

On March 28, 193 A.D. the Roman Empire was put up for auction by the Praetorian Guards. In *The Decline and Fall of the Roman Empire* Gibbon tells how a wealthy senator named Didius Julianus bought most of Europe and the Mediterranean for a donation of 6,250 drachmas to each guard. Didius ruled for only two months before he was assassinated.

**Most Unusual Billion:** In the United States as well as in France, a billion is a thousand millions. But in Great Britain a billion is defined as a *million* millions. To check this, just ask yourself how many British billionaires you have met.

**Most Unusual Business Enterprise:** A group of Venezuelan businessmen announced in 1972 their intention to breed cats and market the bodies. The paws would be sold as good-luck keychains, the fur would be sold for brush bristles, and the insides would be sold as surgical gut—and, presumably, violin strings.

**Most Unusual Checks:** Artist Marc Chagall pays for even his smallest purchases—toothpaste and cigarettes—with personal checks. Years ago he discovered that most merchants would not cash them, figuring that Chagall's signature makes the checks valuable collector's items. As a result, Chagall easily maintains a healthy balance in his account.

**Most Unusual Convention:** "Pretzels in a Changing World" was the theme of the 1974 annual convention of the United States Pretzel Manufacturers' Association. Equally unusual was a convention of Pakistani eunuchs who gathered in Sukkur in 1970 to discuss common problems.

**Most Unusual Counterfeiter:** As a youth, Diogenes the Cynic, who spent his life searching for an honest man, was forced to leave the town of Sinope when he and his father were convicted of counterfeiting. Much later an adversary attacked the philosopher for his unsavory past, and Diogenes replied "Such as I was, so you are now; such as I am, you will never be," which was more sophisticated than saying "Sticks and stones may break my bones."

A nonsequitur: Before his death Diogenes requested to be buried with his head pointed straight down because he believed that the world would soon be topsy-turvy.

For the *most unusual case of counterfeiting:* Six men were arrested by police in Florence, Italy, in 1974. The charge: trafficking in counterfeit blue jeans. Eight thousand pairs of the contraband slacks were seized in the bust.

**Most Unusual Millionaire:** At the time of her death, Hetty Green (1834–1916), known as "the Witch of Wall Street," was reckoned the richest woman in the world with a fortune totaling nearly $100

Hetty Green

million. She inherited $6 million from her father and accumulated the rest through a long series of spectacular investments in the stock market. But despite her uncanny talent for making money, she was utterly mad.

For years she wore the same dress which was originally black but turned green and then brown with age. For undergarments she used old newspapers collected from trash baskets in Central Park. Her home was an unheated tenement in the Chelsea section of Manhattan and her diet consisted almost entirely of onions, eggs, and dry oatmeal, since preparing hot food would have added precious pennies to her fuel bill.

Perhaps the saddest instance of Hetty Green's stinginess involved her son Edward who at age nine was run over by a wagon drawn by a St. Bernard dog. Although his leg was seriously injured, his mother refused to call a doctor, taking him instead to a number of free clinics. Eventually Edward's leg had to be amputated, an operation that might not have been necessary if he had received the medical attention that his mother could certainly afford.

**Most Unusual Miser:** Sheik Shakhbut, the former leader of Abu Dhabi, was one of many Arab potentates who made a killing in oil revenues. But while Shakhbut was crafty at making money, he was no great shakes at spending it. Eventually, a lot of people in Abu Dhabi began wondering why, with all the oil being pumped out of their land, they weren't seeing any income, and Shakhbut was deposed. An inspection of the royal bedroom provided at least a partial solution to the mystery of the disappearing treasury. It seems the sheik had been hording a tremendous fortune right in his chambers, stuffing currency in his mattress and dresser and hiding it under his bed and in his closet. It was impossible to determine precisely how much Shakhbut had socked away because at least $2 million in paper money had been devoured by rats.

**Most Unusual Money:** Yap Islanders in the South Pacific used to measure their wealth in giant stone wheels that measure six to twelve feet in diameter and weigh over a ton. Such stones do not occur naturally on the island; they were brought there over a century ago by an Irish trader.

On the island of Santa Cruz in the West Indies, the original Indian tribes used chains of beautiful feathers for currency. At the opposite extreme are the Amazon rainforest tribes who use curare poison (in which they dip the tips of blowgun darts) as a medium of exchange.

Traders from Connecticut used strings of onions for currency on voyages to the West Indies and South America; they were strung in standard lengths with a standard trade value.

Finally, the Incas never used money and had no word for it in their language. Yet their treasures of gold, jewelry and art, stolen by the Spaniards, enabled Spain to put the world on the gold standard.

**Most Unusual Philanthropy:** For years a national glass firm has had a standing offer to fix windows broken by sandlot baseball players for free; on the average they replace 3,000 per year.

**Most Unusual Receipt:** The French philosopher Voltaire once composed a biting epigram about his patron Frederick the Great of Prussia. Frederick was a tolerant man, but he could not permit such impertinence from a mere author living off the royal bounty. To teach the wit a lesson he ordered him flogged and instructed the flogger to demand a receipt for his services. Voltaire complied with the following voucher:

"Received from the right hand of Conrad Bochhoffer thirty lashes on my bare back, being *in full* for an epigram on Frederick II, King of Prussia, *Vive le Roi*. [Signed] Arouet de Voltaire."

**Most Unusual Salary:** Of course, it is chicken feed by today's standards, but in 1930 Babe Ruth's salary of $80,000 a year looked pretty good. When someone asked whether it was fair that he was receiving more than President Hoover, the Babe remarked, "Well, I had a better year."

**Most Unusual Speculative Boom:** In 1906 someone started a rumor that the mint accidentally mixed gold with the copper in 1902 pennies. Soon throughout Virginia and North and South Carolina speculators were buying up 1902 pennies at incredible prices; in some places pennies were going for as much as twelve cents apiece. Within a week, however, the government discredited the rumor, and the penny market crashed.

At the risk of starting a new speculative boom in pennies, as of this writing, the copper in pennies is valued at slightly more than one cent.

**Most Unusual Status Symbol:** According to Hall's law, there is a statistical correlation between the number of initials in an Englishman's name and his social class. Members of the upper class have significantly more than three names and/or initials, while members of the lower class average 2.6.

**Most Unusual Tax:** Rhode Island State Representative Bernard C. Gladstone decided his constituents would not stand for a state income tax. As an alternative source of revenue, he introduced a bill calling for a two-dollar tax on each act of sexual intercourse.

**Most Unusual Tax Deductions:** W. C. Fields once claimed deductions for charitable contributions to churches in the Solomon Islands and depreciation on his lawnmower.

**Most Unusual Union:** In 1968 a convention of beggars in Dacca, India, passed a resolution demanding that "the minimum amount of alms be fixed at 15 paisa [three cents]." The convention also demanded that the interval between when a person hears a knock at his front door and when he offers alms should not exceed 45 seconds.

# Consumer Products

**Best Airline:** Once *Newsweek* could say, Freelandia is "America's newest and freakiest airline." Now Freelandia is no more, but it was great while it lasted. On board, the stewardesses served organic peanut butter and honey sandwiches, while the carrot juice flowed like wine, and the rock bands blared. It was an airborne party. And best of all, Freelandia was technically operated as an air-travel club, which kept the fares incredibly low: New York to Geneva for $100 as an example.

Painted bright banana yellow, with a hand waving by-by on the tail assembly, the Freelandia jet was unmistakable. It will be missed.

**Best Airship:** To detractors the early dirigibles were known as "sick whales," and their miserable safety record proved that they were worthy of such abuse. All three candidates for the best airship lived in fame and went down in flame. The queen of the airships was the *Hindenburg,* which exploded so spectacularly in Lakehurst, New Jersey, on May 6, 1937; she featured staterooms for seventy-two passengers, showers, a grand piano, and a cargo capacity of over fifty tons. The airship *Akron,* built for the United States Navy, was outfitted with a retractable runway in her underbelly capable of launching and landing five sparrow hawk fighter planes. After the *Akron* met disaster in 1933, her sister ship *Macon* inherited the sparrow hawks. In addition to being the world's only flying aircraft carrier, the *Macon* was the fastest dirigible ever built, with a top speed of eighty-five knots, as well as the first flying machine with a dial telephone system. One especially popular device on the *Macon* was a "sub-cloud car," which allowed an observer to be lowered down through the clouds, like a bucket down a well.

Airship *Akron* in hangar at Akron, Ohio

Out of hometown chauvinism we mention that the *Macon* and the *Akron* were both constructed at the Goodyear Airship hangar in Akron, Ohio, the largest building in the world without internal supports, enclosing over 55 million cubic feet of Akron air. Sudden temperature changes often cause clouds to form in the top of that mammoth structure, resulting in brief indoor showers.

The word blimp, by the way, has a curious etymology; it was inadvertently coined in December 1915 by Lieutenant A. D. Cunningham during an inspection tour of the British air station at Capel. While Cunningham was examining His Majesty's airship *SS-12*, he could not resist tweaking the gasbag with his thumb and forefinger. The inflated fabric responded with a deep rubbery echo. Amused by the odd noise, Cunningham tried to imitate it: "Blimp!" he said experimentally, then straightened his face and continued with the formal inspection. Officers accompanying him spread the story, and since that date nonrigid airships have been called blimps.

**Best Automaton:** Archytas, a craftsman of Tarentum, Greece, is said to have assembled a mechanical pigeon that could actually fly in 400 B.C. This intriguing but unlikely claim aside, a Monsieur Vaucanson exhibited what was probably the most unusual automaton ever constructed. His windup flute player, displayed in Paris in 1738, would put a miniature flute to its lips, finger the valves, and blow a real tune.

**Best Bottle:** A bottle blown in Leith, Scotland, in 1751, is believed to be the largest ever produced by human lungs. It reportedly measured forty by forty-two inches and held nearly two hogsheads (126 gallons).

According to *Gourmet* magazine, the largest standard bottle for champagne is the Nebuchadnezzar, containing five gallons of bubbly.

**Best Light Bulb:** Clarence Whited screwed a 150-watt light bulb into a ceiling socket in his home in Raven, West Virginia, over thirty years ago and has been using it ever since.

**Best Mirror:** Looking into mirrors can be fun again, thanks to Milton Doolittle, inventor, industrial engineer, and "friend of the overweight." Doolittle has invented a mirror, which he calls "Select-a-Size," that reflects favorably on overweight persons by making them look thinner. How much thinner? That depends on the user: A special control knob alters the curvature of the glass, so that the mirror-gazer's girth will wax or wane before his or her very eyes. In fact, thin people can fatten up without stuffing themselves with chocolate malteds and Drake's Ring-Dings simply by adjusting the control knob appropriately.

Aside from flattery addicts, who will buy the Select-a-Size? In the two years since it was put on the market, its buyers have included health spas, fashion designers and, most significantly, doctors and therapists who have used it as an aid in helping obese patients slim down.

**Best Pen:** For $400, Randy Meyer, of Lexington, Kentucky, purchased a set of steel-belted tires touted to be impervious to bullets, bombs and spikes. Perhaps. Shortly after they were installed, Meyer ran over a sharp object and had a blow-out. The sharp object was a ballpoint pen. "It still wrote," he said.

**Best Protection Against Obscene Phone Calls:** An electronics company called Telident, Inc., has come up with a device that strips the obscene phone caller of his anonymity and makes it a snap to trace calls. It consists, essentially, of a box that attaches to the receiving telephone and provides a digital read-out of the caller's phone number and area code, even if he is calling from a pay phone or from a private phone with an unlisted number. Telident says that the device also provides protection against telephoned bomb threats and ransom demands as well as salesmen offering real estate deals in the Poconos. Makes a wonderful gift for the insecure.

**Best Toilet:** Imagine a flush toilet that uses no water, no energy to speak of, produces no odor, and turns all wastes deposited therein, along with kitchen scraps, into rich, usable compost. Such a device does, in fact, exist, and the Swedes have a name for it—which is only natural, since they invented it. It's called a Multrum.

The Multrum is hardly a new invention—it's actually been around since the mid-1940s—but its price—$1,500—still keeps it beyond the means of all but the very rich or the very fastidious. There are about 1,000 Multrums in use today throughout Scandinavia and Germany as well as in the New Hampshire and Massachusetts homes of Abby Aldrich Rockefeller, daughter of Chase Manhattan Bank President David Rockefeller. Miss Rockefeller read about the Multrum in a gardening magazine not long ago and was so impressed that she purchased American rights to it, founding a company called Clivus Multrum USA Inc., and named herself president.

**Best Toilet Paper:** Top honors go neither to Scott, Charmin, or an old Sears-Roebuck catalog, but rather to the neck of a well-downed goose, according to Gargantua, the gargantuan protagonist of Rabelais's *Gargantua and Pantagruel*. At the age of five, Gargantua experiments with all manner of materials—feathered bonnets, a lady's neckerchief, an adult cat, gourd leaves, cabbages, beets, a pillow, a slipper, a hat, a lawyer's briefcase, and then several varieties of fauna, including a hen, a chicken, a rabbit, a pigeon, an otter, and a cormorant, before settling on a goose's neck. "Do not imagine that the felicity of the heroes and demigods in the Elysian Fields arises from their asphodel, their ambrosia, or their nectar, as those ancients say," he tells his doting father. "It comes, in my opinion, from their wiping their arses with the neck of a goose, and that is the opinion of Master Duns Scotus too."

**Worst Ashtray:** Our mind is aswim with early memories of ghastly ashtrays shaped like grotesque faces with the laughing mouth serving as the bowl, ashtrays shaped like half-shut eyes, and one model in the shape of an unshod foot, embossed with the legend, "I get a kick out of Rhode Island." The worst, however, is most likely a toilet-shaped number imprinted with an image of the Basilica of St. Anthony and sold at a gift shop across the street from the Basilica in Padua, Italy.

**Worst Picture Postcard:** A Dallas picture postcard magnate turned out a souvenir postcard of the assassination of President Kennedy early in 1964. The card shows an aerial view of the scene of the shooting, pinpointing the Texas Schoolbook Depository, the grassy knoll, and the motorcade route. A smiling inset of the late president looks down at the scene from the upper righthand corner.

A series of twelve postcards depicting the high points of the life of Napoleon I also represent some sort of peak in conceptual stupidity and historical inaccuracy.

**Worst Toilet Paper:** An unnamed Swabian shoemaker published a pamphlet two centuries ago in which he attributed the moral decay of mankind to the use of indoor plumbing and toilet paper. The solution to man's woes, he said, lay in man's tending to his needs in the "great outdoors," using leaves and moss instead of paper. In so doing, the poisons that defiled his body and soul would be released into the surrounding air and he would undergo a complete physical and spiritual purification. Love among men would be enhanced, people would be humbler and more diligent, and the Kingdom of God on Earth would be brought much closer to realization.

**Worst Toy:** In 1968 a Japanese firm introduced a toy atomic bomb that flashes, bangs, and emits a cloud of real smoke.

**Worst Vehicle:** "So get your girl and take her tandem down the street/Don't you know you're an asphalt athlete. . . . Grab your board and go sidewalk surfing with me." Jan and Dean sang about it, the *Quarterly Skateboarder* wrote about it, and millions of kids all over the world did it.

The skateboard was an outlet for all those would-be surfers

stranded in Des Moines or Cincinnati, hundreds of miles from the nearest salt water wave. It was a unique vehicle that offered the combined thrills of surfing, skiing, and soapbox derby racing, along with the economy of roller-skating. The skateboard required the balance of gymnastics and the grace of the dance. Also, the skateboard was a menace.

As one California company was turning out 100,000 boards a day, hospitals were admitting countless young people with broken arms, broken legs, and severe concussions. A number of deaths were reported as reckless hoedaddies rode that imaginary perfect wave down their driveways into oncoming traffic. But what caused the greatest concern were those scabs. "Wiping out" in the warm Pacific is undoubtably preferable to wiping out on macadam, asphalt, or cement. And it was probably the sight of all those grisly scabs, and not the more serious injuries, that caused many communities to outlaw skateboards.

---

**Most Unusual Bed:** Khumarawayh, the Mohammedan caliph of Egypt from 884–895, was a man who enjoyed the good things in life. For example, he believed that a man's castle is his home, so he covered the palace walls with his favorite metal—gold. But in the twentieth century Khumarawayh should be remembered fondly as the man who invented an early prototype of the waterbed. In *The Age of Faith* Will Durant informs us that Khumarawayh "taxed his people to provide himself with a pool of quicksilver on which his bed of inflated leather cushions might gently float to win him sleep."

During the last six weeks of his life, Cardinal Armand Jean du Plessis de Richelieu, Louis XIII's powerful and devious minister, occupied another extraordinary bed. Sorely afflicted with headaches, hemorrhoids, boils, and a disease of the bladder, Richelieu slept and worked in a vast litter transported by twenty-four bodyguards, in this way managing to continue with his diplomatic duties. In addition to his bed, the Cardinal's magnificent litter contained a chair, a table, and his private secretary who penned Richelieu's letters and made notes of his conversations. When the traveling bed proved too large to enter through the doors of any building Richelieu proposed to occupy, he commanded his bodyguards to batter down the walls.

**Most Unusual Bell:** Cast in 1733, the gigantic Moscow Bell, also known as the Czar Kolokol Bell, weighs 440,000 pounds and measures twenty-two feet eight inches in diameter. It fell when work-men attempted to hang it, and a twelve-ton "chip" broke off the lip. For a while it was used as a small chapel; now it rests atop a platform in front of the Kremlin.

**Most Unusual Cigar:** Cigars shaped like matzohs, the flat, unlea-vened breads eaten by Jews during Passover, are manufactured and sold by the Nat Sherman Company, a New York tobacconeer. The Sherman company also markets a corkscrew-shaped cigar known to the public as the Sherman Twist.

**Most Unusual Clocks:** Nicholas Grollier de Serviere invented a clock in 1679 that consisted of a small lizard climbing a post on which the hours and minutes were marked. The lizard's snout, Grollier claimed, always pointed directly at the correct time. He also devised a similar clock which featured a mouse crawling along a calibrated horizontal block.

In A.D. 807, the emperor Charlemagne was presented with a more elaborate timepiece by Caliph Haroun-al Raschid. It was round, as were most clocks of the day, and powered by water. In place of twelve numbers on the dial there were twelve doors. At six o'clock, for example, the sixth hour door would open and six brass balls would be dropped out in succession and strike a bell. All the doors would remain open until twelve o'clock, when figurines of mounted horsemen appeared from each of the holes and paraded around the dial.

A bicycle clock was constructed by Frenchman Alphonse Du-hamel. Twelve feet high, the works, the dial, the ornament, and every other detail are all made out of bicycle parts. It strikes the hours and quarters on a bicycle bell and reputedly keeps very good time.

A clock in Worsley Hall, Lancashire, England, always struck 13 o'clock instead of one. The Duke of Bridgewater, who was once master of Worsley, was constantly complaining that his workmen returned late from their lunch hour. The workers explained that they did not notice when the clock struck only a single time—the signal for them to go back to work. Consequently, the Duke had the mechanism adjusted so that it struck a loud, insistent thirteen times.

**Most Unusual Cup:** It was a classical custom to take impressions of beautiful bosoms to serve as molds for golden drinking vessels. Marc Antony, for instance, used to drink from a goblet shaped around the breast of Cleopatra; a cup in the antique fashion,

Chicken Doodle

molded on the breast of Marie Antoinette is still on display in the porcelain factory of Sèvres.

**Most Unusual Fuel:** In the grip of the Great Fuel Panic of '73, a Belvedere, California, outfit calling itself "Captain Calculus and the Normal Street Mechanics Institute" published a booklet offering detailed instructions on how to run an automobile on chicken excreta. The major step in the Great Conversion is to build a special cauldron in which the wastes are heated to produce methane gas. Entitled "Chicken Doodle," the guide sells for $1.25.

In addition, Harold Bate, an English inventor, has devised the ideal rural vehicle for times of energy crisis—an automobile that runs on pig manure. To the relief of antiodor pollutionists, there is an intermediate step between pig and tank, in which manure is distilled into methane gas.

**Most Unusual Lock** (and no doubt the best): At the French Crystal Palace in the eighteenth century, a combination lock was exhibited which required 3,674,385 turns of the dial to open and close it. It reportedly took one man 120 nights to lock and another man an additional 120 nights to unlock.

**Most Unusual Oil Spill:** According to the *Smithsonian* magazine, a storage tank in Allen Park, Michigan, developed a leak and spilled nearly 10,000 gallons of oil into the Rouge River during the winter of 1973. Since the river was frozen, much of the oil collected in a huge, slippery puddle on top of the ice. When ecologists analyzed the puddle they were surprised to find that it was 100 percent pure vegetable oil. The tank, it seems, was the property of the Frito-Lay Company and it contained the oil they used to fry potato chips. In fact, the oil had been oozing its way across Frito-Lay's executive parking lot in a one-inch slick for several weeks. Walking to and from their cars, the oblivious potato chip execs splashed through the oil twice a day without complaint.

**Most Unusual Picture Postcard:** When the United States took possession of the Philippines after the Spanish-American War, there was a rumor that an army patrol exploring the interior of Luzon had discovered an isolated tribe of headhunters, called the Ingorot, with long, prehensile tails. According to the rumor, the government was trying to hush up the Ingorot story to protect the tailed people from harassment. Still, the evidence was undeniable. Several soldiers returning from the Pacific swore they had seen men with tails. In Manila someone produced a photo of an Ingorot, complete with tail; the photo was reproduced as a picture postcard and thousands were mailed all over the world.

Needless to say, the rumor was totally false. Anthropologists at the Smithsonian Institute discovered the original photo of the Ingorot man, and he had a very ordinary posterior; the postcard was a fake. Apparently the rumor got started because, like many tribes, the Ingorot dressed up in animal costumes, sometimes wearing horns and tails for their religious ceremonies.

This is just the most recent yarn about the existence of tailed men. Such stories, always tinged with racism, have been around since man first noticed that he was lacking what most mammals had. Marco Polo told of a tailed race on the island of Lambri: "In this kingdom are found men with tails, a span in length, like those of a dog, but not covered with hair." For centuries it was the half-believed gossip of the Continent that Englishmen had tails in their britches.

**Most Unusual Radio:** The world's most unusual radio, when it's perfected, will be worn in the vagina and send out electronic signals to the doctor's office when the wearer ovulates. It is still in the drawingboard stage at the Tyler Clinic in California.

**Most Unusual Ropes:** According to Bishop Charles Henry Fowler, a Methodist missionary who visited Japan in 1888, all the women of a northern province cut their hair and wove it into three tremendous ropes, the largest measuring ten inches in circumference and 2,600 feet in length. The half-mile-long braids were used in the construction of a magnificent wooden shrine.

**Most Unusual Silk:** A large Mediterranean clam secretes milky strands up to twelve inches long from its foot. The fibers of this "beard" were gathered by the ancients and woven into a beautiful golden silk. Pulitzer-prizewinning science writer Thomas R. Henry has speculated that this remarkable fabric may have been the Golden Fleece sought by Jason and his Argonauts. Small quantities of golden silk are still being produced in Italy, and a glove made of this rare material is on display in the Smithsonian Institution.

**Most Unusual Toilet Paper:** During the mid-1960s, when the Indonesian rupiah was valued at 325 to the dollar, travelers throughout the Indonesian archipelago discovered that the cheap, porous paper used in the printing of one-sen notes, worth $1/100$ of a rupiah, made a more-than-satisfactory toilet tissue and was vastly less expensive than commercially marketed tissue since 32,500 one-sen notes could be obtained in most banks for one dollar.

**Most Unusual Toothpaste:** Doggy-dent is a beef-flavored toothpaste for dogs developed and patented by Ursula Dietrich, a California dentist.

**Most Unusual Vehicle:** When future archaeologists are digging through the ruins of our civilization, one find they will have difficulty in comprehending is a strange stick with a metal spring at one end to which two pedals are fastened. The pogo stick, which originated somewhere in France, infected England and America in 1921. There was international rivalry over who would perfect the pogo: "American pogo sticks are in every way superior to ours," complained the British magazine *Punch*. And there were pogo stick competitions, like the hula hoop competitions a generation later. A young lad won the first New York *Daily News* pogo contest in 1921 by hopping 1,600 times in fifteen minutes and traversing 600 yards in eight minutes.

Recently a Los Angeles firm introduced a motorized pogo stick, powered by a single-cylinder, two-cycle engine. It gets 30,000 hops per gallon of gas.

**Most Unusual Vending Machine:** A major breakthrough in the vending machine industry is the Liquormatic, patented by a man named Billy Utz in 1970. The would-be buyer inserts a special plastic ID in a slot to establish that he is of legal age. Then he is required to pass a simple mechanical test to demonstrate his sobriety. (For many drunks, getting the coins in the slot would be test enough.) Only then will the machine sell the customer his bottle of J & B.

**Most Unusual Wallpaper:** In the Crystal Palace at the Great Exhibition in London, held in 1851, a wallpaper pattern was displayed, which depicted a hunting scene in a lush forest. Twelve thousand separate blocks were used in the printing.

# Food

**Best Advice Handed Down to Us by the Ancients:** "Avoid beans as you would matricide." (Pythagoras in *Golden Verses*)

**Best Banquet:** *Larousse Gastronomique* describes a banquet that François I hosted for Catherine de Medici (1519–1589) in Paris. It was one of the most sumptuous ever staged: "30 peacocks, 33 pheasants, 21 swans, 9 cranes, 33 ducks, 33 ibises, 33 egrets, 33 young herons, 30 young goats, 99 young pigeons, 99 turtle doves, 13 partridges, 33 goslings, 3 young bustards, 13 young capons, 90 quails, 66 boiling chickens, 66 Indian chickens, 30 capons, 90 spring chickens in vinegar, 66 chickens 'cooked as grouse,' were served at the banquet. There were a great number of other dishes from which butcher's meat was excluded, being considered too ordinary, which, however, did not prevent the organizer of this monster banquet from serving to his guests many young piglets, rabbits, and a vast quantity of vegetables such as asparagus, broad beans, peas, and artichokes."

**Best Barbecue:** A folksier feast was staged by John Calloway when he became governor of Oklahoma in the 1930s. Nearly 100,000 Sooners were served at a barbecue that sounds like a Texas joke come true. The cooking was done in giant trenches; coffee was brewed in a 10,000-gallon vat; and the victuals included beef, pork, mutton, chicken, goose, duck, buffalo, bear, antelope, squirrel, 'possum, 'coon, rabbit, and reindeer.

**Best Beer:** If you doubt that beer is a serious subject, just consider how it changed the course of American history. In *The Pilgrim Journal* New England's first colonists tell why they decided to put to shore at Plymouth Rock instead of sailing south toward a warmer site. "We could not now take time for further consideration, our victuals being spent and especially our beer."

The definition of a snob is a person who insists that European beers outclass American brew. Actually, a panel of tasters assembled by the Consumers' Union in 1969 judged two American products, Coors and Miller High Life, to be among the very best. They were ranked well above Löwenbrau, Wurzburger, and other prestigious European brands, although it must be remembered that the imports may deteriorate with the long shipping delays. For our money, the best beer of all is Labatt's, a rich, middle-bodied beer produced in New London, Ontario. Labatt's is widely available in the Midwest at competitive prices.

**Best Candy:** In Kuala Lumpur, Malaysia, in 1969, police impounded a cache of chocolates containing large doses of sexual stimulants which, they said, had been smuggled into the country from Thailand and Japan. The candy came in six or seven varieties.

**Best Chicken:** For unsurpassed tenderness, try Chicken a la Toulouse-Lautrec. The great, grotesquely formed painter of Paris low-life scenes was also a gourmet chef, and a number of his favorite recipes have been collected in a beautifully illustrated book entitled *The Art of Cuisine*. Toulouse-Lautrec reveals that the secret of delectable chicken is in the killing. "In order to make chickens immediately edible," he writes, "take them out of the hen run, pursue them into open country, and when you have made them run, kill them with a gun loaded with very small shot. The meat of the chicken, gripped with fright, will become tender."

But suppose some night you are too tired for the chase, where can you find the best carry-out fried chicken? Several authorities recommend Colonel Sanders' Original Kentucky Fried Chicken. In a recent full-length profile of Harland Sanders, *The New Yorker* said, "His fast frying process produces fried chicken of a quality unknown in New York restaurants and rare even in Southern restaurants." An editor of *The Ladies' Home Journal*, who surveyed 153 fast food restaurants was even more enthusiastic. "Kentucky Fried Chicken is terrific," he said, "and I don't care who knows. I cannot resist the stuff."

But when picking up your chicken, it might be wise to resist the mashed potatoes and gravy. The gravy has been the Colonel's pet peeve ever since he sold his recipe and franchises to a Mc-

Donald's-like supercorporation. After sampling the gravy that the corporation substituted for his own, the colonel sputtered, "How do you serve this goddamned slop? With a straw?" A corporation executive interviewed by *The New Yorker* was apologetic. "Let's face it," he explained, "the Colonel's gravy is fantastic, but you have to be a Rhodes scholar to cook it."

Colonel Sanders now spends most of his time at the hotel and restaurant he operates in Shelbyville, Kentucky. In the Louisville–Lexington area he is an honored citizen, and on slow news days the local papers often send a reporter around to solicit his views on world affairs. Once a reporter asked him what he thought about hippies. The colonel smiled benevolently and said, "They eats chicken, don't they?"

**Best Diet:** The weight loss regimen offered by Weight Watchers, Inc.—an adaptation, really, of a diet that's been available at the New York City Board of Health's obesity clinic for years— provides dieters with the most filling, varied menus, the most sensible approach to eating, and the best track record of any diet now being popularly touted. The Weight Watchers' program, with its frequent snacks, ingenious recipes (Weight Watchers Moussaka; Weight Watchers Blue Cheese Dressing; Weight Watchers Veal Parmigiana) and filling meals does not merely keep you full and pacified. You will actually feel uneasy about eating as much as you are required to on the diet, and then be amazed when the excess pounds come off so easily.

**Best Hamburgers:** The best hamburgers in the United States are at Winstead's Drive-In in Kansas City, says food expert Calvin Trillin, and the *best chopped chicken liver* is at the Parkway, a kosher restaurant at 163 Allen Street on New York City's Lower East Side. For the *best fish chowder*, he claims, it's Glady's Canteen, in Lunenberg, Nova Scotia.

**Best Ice Cream:** Vala's hand-packed ice cream, sold in Chicago, wins out over Breyers' hand-packed, Basset's ice cream, made in Philadelphia, and Häagen-Dazs. All four are marked by a smooth texture and a purity of flavor. Chocolate marshmallow is the flavor to try if you're sampling Vala's for the first time. Breyers' vanilla fudge and the chocolate of both Basset's and Häagen-Dazs are also superb.

**Best Pizza:** While pizzas of all shapes and varieties are served in restaurants and trattorias throughout Italy, the true birthplace of this delicacy is the United States. Thus, while Italians who visit American shores are often critical of the quality of Italian cuisine in the States—even the food served in the finest Italian restaurants rarely meets their standards—they cannot afford to be so uppity when it comes to pizza. The fact is, the best is found right here.

Most pizzas we've sampled are good, a few are very good (most notably the unconventional offerings of Goldberg's pizzerias in New York City). The best, however, is in Chicago, and is made by Due's. Visitors to the Windy City often pick up a pie or two, or as many as they can stuff into their baggage, and bring them home frozen. It makes sense; even frozen, Due's pizzas are better than anything else we've tasted fresh. The crust is as thick as a bagel; you can literally get lost in the cheese; and there is enough chopped meat in a single pie to keep a McDonald's freak happy for days. There is also something indescribably *different* about Due's pies, a level of quality that transcends the bounds of conventional pizzadom, breaking through into the sphere of the godlike. It's still the best food bargain in Chicago.

**Best Restaurant in the United States:** As a crusty old restaurateur who ran a charming little Polynesian bistro in Honolulu told us some years ago: "One man's meat is another man's poi, son." The fact is, there is no accounting for taste, and there is even less accounting for taste in matters gastronomical. Nonetheless, we'll side with food expert Calvin Trillin who calls Kansas City "the best eating town in the world," and Arthur Bryant's Barbecue there, "the single best restaurant in the whole world." The specialty of the house is hickory smoked meat baked in a brick oven. The tables are covered with yellow oil cloth.

A more conventional choice for best restaurant in the United States—one that would sit better with connoisseurs—is Lutèce, in New York City. The cuisine is French and the appetizers are superb, particularly the mouseline of pike with lobster sauce. A party of ten can share, as an appetizer, an escallop of salmon served on a three-foot-long wooden platter. If you go for dinner, expect to pay at least sixty dollars for two. The 1974 Mobil Travel Guide gives Lutèce five stars—its top rating—along with only five other restaurants in the country: La Grenouille in New York City, La Maisonette in Cincinnati, la Dome in Fort Lauderdale, Florida, and the Mandarin in San Francisco. Oddly, Mobil makes no mention at all of New York's Chinatown, which, viewed as one sprawling, multistreet restaurant, might well be the best single place to eat in the whole country.

Lutèce

**Best Soft Drink:** Vernor's Ginger Ale, produced and marketed in Detroit, Michigan. Even the canned stuff is better than the bottled brew of most other brands. The secret, says *Esquire* magazine, is in the aging process. Vernor's lets its extract mellow for four years.

---

**Worst Alcoholic Beverage:** In 1974, police in Pocatello, Idaho, arrested two women on charges of manufacturing and selling an ersatz brandy which was distilled from water, vodka, and urine. Meanwhile, a whisky distillery in Calcutta, India, proudly proclaims on its labels: "Excellent whiskey made from high-quality Scotch grapes."

Insecticide was the secret ingredient in one particular batch of *guajiro lina*, a rumlike brew distilled from sugar cane and sold widely in Nicaragua. A tavern keeper there made the mistake of decanting a supply into some empty insecticide cans and the unfortunate mixture killed eleven customers. His own end came when he defiantly quaffed a pint of the stuff to discredit public accusations that his liquor was poisoned. He died within minutes.

**Worst Beer:** The advertisements exclaim: "Oh, my gosh, it's Frothingslosh!" Old Frothingslosh beer, bottled only around the Christmas holiday season by Iron City Brewing, is billed as the "pale, stale ale with the foam on the bottom." It is not a breakthrough in brewing, however, which enables them to make this revolutionary claim; they simply paste the label on upside down.

The worst beer according to a Consumers Union tasting panel was Tudor, the A & P store brand. Most tasters concluded that Tudor was excessively sweet, lacking in bitterness, and low in carbonation; several remarked that "Tudor tasted more like apple cider than beer." The CU test was conducted before the introduction of Hop 'n Gator, which was without doubt the saddest event in the history of brewing. Hop 'n Gator, as the name makes insipidly plain, combines the flavors of beer and citrus juice. It is an abomination.

**Worst Beverage:** The Uape Indians of the upper Amazon cremate their dead. To absorb the admirable qualities of the deceased, his ashes are mixed with *casiri,* the local alcoholic beverage, and drunk by all the members of the family with great reverence and fond memories.

Masai tribesmen from East Africa mix blood drawn from their cattle with sweet milk. Blood is an indispensable part of their diet because it provides salt, which is very scarce in the Masai territories.

*Paiwari,* another slightly alcoholic drink from the Amazon, is made by scorching meal from the cassava plant. The Indian women chew this preparation, then expectorate it into a vat to ferment. The *paiwari* chewers are a highly professional group who have their lips specially tatooed to ward off evil spirits that might enter their saliva.

**Worst Candy:** Next time you sink your choppers into a Three Musketeers or a Mary Jane, try not to think about the 200,000 bars and 7,100 boxes of factory-fresh candy that were found by the Federal Food and Drug Administration in 1971 to be riddled with rat pellets and dead bugs. Unfortunately, the FDA released its findings after most of the candy had been sold.

**Worst Chicken:** *Atlas* magazine reported in 1971 that the Japanese had begun breeding and marketing a new type of chicken, called the *buroira* (a mispronunciation of *broiler*). The chicken is cooped up in a cage so small that it can neither walk, scratch around, or flap its wings, and growth is artificially accelerated by twenty-four-hour lighting and a diet that includes cyclamates, tranquilizers, antibiotics, hormones, a heady dose of miscellaneous nutritional acids, and laxatives. The main objection to the new product was the hormones, which reportedly could produce enlarged breasts in men.

**Worst Cookbook:** *The Joys of Jell-O*, published in 1964.

**Worst Diet:** The Doctor's Quick Weight Loss Diet, more commonly known as the Stillman Diet, with its monastic adherence to meat, cottage cheese, and tap water, drains all the charm and pleasure from the eating experience and turns it into a purely biological function. And the quick-loss variation diets that Dr. Stillman has devised—his Baked Potato and Buttermilk Diet, his Yogurt Only Diet, and his Bananas and Milk Diet ("By considering a banana as one meal, and a glass of skim milk as another meal . . . you can eat nine . . . 'meals' a day and still total only 900 calories") are as laughable as they are unsatisfying, and less unsatisfying than they are nutritionally unsound.

The sacrifice-all-for-the-sake-of-your-body type of regimen has proved that when the calories go down, emotional tension goes up. Doctors in Jerusalem's Hebrew University Medical School recently studied the emotional effects of massive weight loss on ten people who had dieted off between 110 and 240 pounds apiece. One of them committed suicide; all the others required in-hospital psychiatric care. However, when they stopped dieting, lifted the ban on Hostess Twinkies, and regained the lost poundage, their depression vanished and all was bright and rosy again.

**Worst Diet Book:** *Calories Don't Count*, by Dr. Herman Taller. Oh, but they do, *they do!* the Federal Trade Commission countered in an injunction that barred Dr. Taller, in 1963, from continuing to distribute his book. By that time, he had been catapulted to fame and fortune on a wave of Hershey Kisses and Hostess Snowballs, exhorting millions of adipose Americans to consume as much as 5,000 guilt-free calories a day. ("Extra slices of chicken? Ridiculous! I eat extra chickens.") Dr. Taller's prescription for losing unsightly pounds was to eat as much as you wanted so long as you took care to maintain a balance of two-thirds fats, one-third proteins, and practically no carbohydrates. Low carbohydrate diets, of course, are nothing new, and while doctors debate their safety, it is true that some people lose weight on them. What made Dr. Taller's diet unique, however, were the miraculous CDC tablets that one took while following this regimen; the pills, he said, were the key to maintaining your health while shedding weight. Moreover, CDC pills purportedly decreased cholesterol, prevented heartburn, fought colds, and increased sexual potency.

A month's supply of CDC tablets ran as high as $600, a hefty sum by any standards. But when the Food and Drug Administration found that the tablets were not only ineffective but contained nothing but safflower oil, they pressed charges. Investigators discovered that Taller and the pharmaceutical company had a little deal arranged whereby Taller was getting a percentage on all the CDC tablets sold, and together they were getting fat off the overweight. The company and Taller were both convicted of mail fraud and violations of the Food, Drug and Cosmetics Act.

Taller's spiritual ancestor in dietary folly was the French writer Gleizes, who wrote some ten books on vegetarianism, all of which endlessly repeated the same theme: Meat is godless, vegetables are holy. Gleizes is said to have deserted his wife because she refused to stop eating beef.

**Worst Food Faddist:** Horace Fletcher (1849–1919) is believed to have composed the motto: "Nature will castigate those who don't masticate," and certainly it is the finest statement of his firmly held conviction that we chew too little and, therefore, do not get the full nutritional value out of our food. It is basic Fletcher dogma, still defended by many grandmothers, that one should chew each morsel thirty-two times, once for each tooth. Furthermore, soup and milk should be sloshed around in the mouth for a full fifteen or twenty seconds until the saliva has had ample opportunity to do its work.

Fletcherism was good for Fletcher. On his fiftieth birthday he bicycled two hundred miles in a single day; and in 1903 he tested the endurance of his legs on Yale's ergometer, raising three hundred pounds 350 times, twice the record of Yale's most formidable athlete. His meals, consisting primarily of milk, maple sugar, and prepared cereals, cost him an average of eleven cents a day, and once as an experiment he lived on potatoes alone for fifty-eight days.

Horace Fletcher

John D. Rockefeller and Upton Sinclair were among the millions of Fletcher faddists in the early 1900s who were determined to chew their way to good health and long life. Novelist Henry James publicly declared, "Horace Fletcher saved my life, and, what is more, he improved my disposition." Gradually, however, the chewing craze faded, in part because it made for incredibly long and boring meals, and in part because it conflicted with another favorite maxim of grandmothers: "Eat your food before it gets cold."

**Worst Fruit:** The durian. It's about the size of a bowling ball, covered with sharp, stiff, spiny points, and grows on trees throughout southeast Asia, most predominantly in Malaysia, Thailand, and Indonesia. The business end of a durian, which is the inside, is mucuslike in consistency, and the unique flavor is reminiscent of garlic, smoked ham, and rancid cheese. Durians, known throughout the orient as the "king of fruits," are prohibitively expensive when not in season—a medium-sized fruit may go for five or six dollars—and potentially lethal in the hands and stomachs of the unanointed. (One danger is in their weight. Unwitting foreigners have been known to be struck fatally on the head by durians falling from trees. Others have made the mistake of washing down a durian dessert with a quart of beer. The resultant gas has blasted their insides to smithereens.) Walk through the vegetable stalls in Singapore or Bangkok during durian season and you'll swear the city's sewage disposal system is on the blink. English novelist Anthony Burgess, in fact, has said that dining on durian is a lot like eating vanilla custard in a latrine.

**Worst Ice Cream:** A few new flavors released and mercifully retracted in recent years have been especially offensive to our palates: bubblegum (a Baskin and Robbins' specialty), fig, and licorice. If you're dieting, take special care to avoid Weight Watchers' vanilla or strawberry "frozen dessert" (the chocolate is passable). The taste of the strawberry is virtually indistinguishable from that of the carton in which it is packed (try it if you don't believe us) and the vanilla is the chalkiest, most indigestible substance we've seen short of the barium mixtures they make you swallow in preparation for gastrointestinal X rays.

**Worst Meal:** In 1971, Hans and Erna W., a Swiss couple vacationing in Hong Kong stopped to eat at a Chinese restaurant there and asked the headwaiter to take their pet poodle, Rosa, into the kitchen and find it something to eat. The waiter misunderstood their request, however, and the couple was aghast when Rosa was brought to their table done to a turn in a round-bottomed frying pan, marinated in sweet-and-sour sauce, and garnished with Chinese vegetables. The meal was left uneaten and the couple were treated for shock.

**Worst News for Health Food Addicts:** Dr. Alice Chase, who wrote *Nutrition for Health* and other books on the science of proper eating, died recently of malnutrition.

**Worst Peanut Butter:** Just what are those chunks in Hoody Chunky Style Peanut Butter? A 1972 Oregon health department investigation disclosed that some were peanuts, some were rodent hairs, and some were rat pellets. The investigators also found that some of the peanuts used in Hoody were contaminated with rodent urine.

Hoody executives were sentenced to serve ten days in prison for health code violations. It was not, as you might think, the mere presence of rat hairs that got the Hoody executives in trouble; it was the presence of an unconscionable number. In an effort to crack down on unsanitary conditions at food processing plants, the United States Food and Drug Administration issued strict new guidelines in 1972 on the amount of foreign matter permissible in packaged foods. They make very depressing reading: 1) no more than an average of 50 insect fragments or two rodent hairs per 100 grams of peanut butter will be acceptable; 2) no more than ten fruit fly eggs or two larvae will be allowed in 100 grams of tomato juice; 3) no more than 150 insect fragments are acceptable in an eight ounce sample of chocolate.

Bon appétit!

**Worst Recipe:**  Here it is, the recipe that *The Joy of Cooking* dared not print, *Homme Rôti avec Patate*. The method of preparation we present was the favorite among cannibals in the Fiji Islands, although the Irish, the Picts, the Congolese, the Aztecs, and the eleventh-century Danes also enjoyed interesting variations of this dish.

Most anthropophagists agree that selecting the right brand and cut is very important, and on the island of New Britain, human meat was sold in butcher shops, greatly simplifying this problem. A number of cultures, notably the Fuegians, distinctly preferred females, ranking their flesh even higher than a good dog (which "tastes of otter"). In the Solomon Islands, women were fattened for roasting like pigs. Some connoisseurs favored white meat, including a Tahitian chief who explained that "The white man, when well roasted, tastes like a ripe banana." But the Fijians generally found other Polynesians more delectable; Europeans were "too salty."

For the details of a Fijian feast, we are indebted to anthropologist A. P. Rice, who published this eye-witness account in a 1910 issue of *The American Antiquarian and Oriental Journal:* The first step is to eviscerate the carcass and wash it thoroughly in salt water. Next, "the carver, with his huge implements of split bamboo, cuts off several members of the body, joint by joint. His assistants then folded them separately in (plantain) leaves and carefully place them in an oven, a simple contrivance of a hole in the ground, lined with hot stones." Roasting time is approximately the same as for pork—forty minutes per pound—and the meat is served with baskets of yams. "The heart, thighs, and arms above the elbow are termed dainties by skilled epicureans," Rice notes.

**Worst Sandwich:** The Hubert Humphrey Special. "My favorite sandwich," says the senior senator from Minnesota, "is peanut butter, bologna, cheddar cheese, lettuce, and mayonnaise on toasted bread with lots of catsup on the side. Another favorite is toasted peanut butter, cheese and bacon, or, if I am in a hurry, just peanut butter and jelly."

**Worst Seafood Dinner:** In 1974 fishermen from Cebu Province, in the Philippines, landed an eighteen-foot-long hammerhead shark weighing over a ton and brought it to market in Manila where they prepared to cut it up before the very eyes of a throng of eager customers-to-be. The customers lost their appetite for fish, however— and, presumably, for anything else—when the severed head of a woman slid embarrassingly out of the fish's stomach. Those who hung around for more watched the fishermen cut deeper into the shark's innards and exhume several human limbs as well as the remains of a dog.

**Worst Soft Drink:** Two soft drinks, Squirt (bottled in the United States) and Pshitt (French) vie for dishonors as the worst name for a beverage; no one knows how many customers decide not to buy these products rather than going through the embarrassment of asking, "Do you have Squirt?"

A small Ohio pop company, now defunct, adopted the brand name Norka. In their radio and billboard advertisements they hammered in the slogan, "And remember, Norka spelled backwards is Akron."

But the more significant question is which soft drink *tastes* the worst, and in the course of our research a clear choice emerged: Diet Moxie, vintage 1962. Moxie is a New England concoction, first developed in 1884, with a flavor that compares unfavorably with horehound drops. The brand name has entered the American language as a colloquial noun meaning "vigor" or "spunk," perhaps because it takes a good deal of spunk to swallow the stuff.

In the late 1960s Frank Armstrong, the president of Moxie Industries, contemplated introducing Old Moxie to the Old South. He hired a crack research organization to find out whether Southerners liked the taste. "It had the worst ratings they ever recorded," Armstrong confessed to *Forbes* magazine. "Nine out of ten said they wouldn't buy it again."

Moreover, back in 1962, soda manufacturers were still a long way from perfecting the technique of artificial sweetening. Moxie and bitter saccharine combined to form a flavor that defies description, although one who dared try it volunteered the adjective "painful."

**Worst Source of Nutrition:** If one is really down on his luck and starving, he might consider licking some cancelled or uncancelled postage stamps. The glue is a mixture of eassava (the source of tapioca) and corn—starchy but nutritious.

**Worst Vegetable:** The rabage. In 1924 a Soviet geneticist named Karpenchenko successfully crossed a cabbage and a radish, producing an entirely new vegetable—the *Rephanobrassica* or rabage. (An unfortunate name, but clearly rabage is preferable to cadish.) Rabages in turn could produce little rabages, and there was great hope for a plant with a plump, edible root and a delectable, leafy head. Much to the world's misfortune, despite determined efforts at selective breeding, the rabage yielded only the straggly greens of a radish and the small, useless roots of a cabbage.

This suggests another brief disputed story about selective breeding. Isadora Duncan sat next to George Bernard Shaw at a dinner party one evening in London. Miss Duncan had recently read a book on eugenics, and she was much impressed with the idea that people of ability had an obligation to find each other and produce talented offspring. Confidently, she suggested to the playwright that theirs would be the eugenically ideal marriage—the most graceful and beautiful woman in the world and the wittiest, most talented writer. "Yes, Miss Duncan," Shaw replied politely. "But what if the child should have my body and your brains?"

**Worst Wine:** Two-hundred seventeen Italian wine merchants were arrested in 1969 for producing and attempting to market nearly three million gallons of a mysterious brew which consisted, in part, of ox blood, ammonia, and banana skins and contained not a single grape.

---

**Most Unusual Appetizer:** Muktuk is an Eskimo delicacy consisting of whale skin and a layer of whale blubber, often served as an appetizer before dinner. The best is found in Nome, Alaska, probably at the Nugget Inn No. 3. First-time tasters of the dish find it a bit like cod-liver oil in solid form.

**Most Unusual Bread:** A Cairo museum displays a loaf of bread found in one of the Pyramids. Archaeologists say it is 4,500 years old and very stale.

**Most Unusual Cake:** In June of 1730, Frederick William, King of Prussia, invited his entire army—30,000 guests in all—to a picnic dinner. To top off the meal the King ordered a team of eight horses to draw in the most colossal cake of all time: eighteen yards long, eight yards wide, and one-half yard thick. The cake was made from thirty-six bushels of flour, 200 gallons of milk, one ton of butter, one ton of yeast, and over 5,000 eggs. Frederick's army was too full to finish the dessert, so slices were distributed to civilians in nearby villages and towns.

**Most Unusual Cheese:** It is mind expanding to contemplate that there are more microbes in a two-and-a-half-pound wedge of cheese than there are people on this earth. Imagine, then, how many tiny organisms lived in the 34,591-pound cheddar made by the Wisconsin Cheese Foundation in 1964. Well over 10,000 thoroughbred Guernsey and Holstein cows contributed to the project, which was displayed at the New York World's Fair.

**Most Unusual Cocktail:** Pliny the Elder foisted thirty-seven volumes of hearsay on the world, which it took scholars fourteen centuries to correct, and he is the source of this tidbit. Nevertheless, there is sufficient scientific substance to the following story to make it somewhat credible.

Cleopatra, Pliny says, once made a wager with Marc Antony that she could spend over three million dollars on an evening's entertainment. There were dancers garbed in specially made costumes of gold and rare feathers; there were jugglers and performing elephants; there were a thousand maid servants attending to the couple's every need; and there was a seemingly never-ending banquet of indescribable splendor. At the end of the evening, Cleopatra proposed to toast her lover with a vessel of vinegar. But first she dropped her exquisite pearl earrings into the cup, each worth a small kingdom, and watched them dissolve. Then she raised the sour cocktail of untold value to her lips and drank it down.

Pearls, it is true, are largely carbonate and will dissolve in a mild acid solution such as vinegar. Complete dissolution, however, would probably take several hours in vinegar too potent to quaff with a smile. But if Cleopatra crushed her pearls first, the powder would have melted immediately with a gentle effer vescence in a solution that one could drink without severe gastrointestinal distress. So perhaps, just perhaps, Pliny was telling the truth about this grandly romantic and profligate gesture.

This story leads us to a discussion of *aurum potabile* or liquid gold, which was considered the greatest wonder drug of them all during the Middle Ages. Even in the Renaissance a cocktail of gold was occasionally prescribed for patients who could afford it. Court records show that Louis XI took an emulsion containing ninety-six gold coins for treatment of his epilepsy. Usually the gold was mixed with borage, balm, sugar, cinnamon, and other exotic ingredients to make it more healthful and more palatable. Gold therapy was believed to be especially effective for smallpox and warts and was also considered an excellent enema.

**Most Unusual Coffee:** Frederick the Great of Prussia is said to have preferred his coffee brewed with champagne rather than water.

**Most Unusual Cookies:** First prize in the 1972 Susquehanna Valley Science Engineering Fair went to high school student Velma Anstadt, of Turbatville, Pennsylvania, who whipped up a batch of cookies made with earthworms. She told the judges that they were "an excellent source of protein."

**Most Unusual Dessert:** A favorite in Tanzania is white-ant pie made by mixing sweet white ants with banana flour. The taste is a little like honey nougat.

**Most Unusual Food:** Manna is first mentioned in Exodus when the Lord promises to "rain bread from heaven" for Moses and the children of Israel starving in the desert. This is the description found in Exodus 16: 14–15: "And when the dew that lay was gone up, behold, upon the face of the wilderness there lay a small round thing, as small as the hoarfrost on the ground. And when the children of Israel saw it, they said one to another, 'It is manna': for they wist not what it was."

Now, however, we do "wit" with some certainty what it was. Manna is a sweet, granular substance secreted by two varieties of scale insects that live on tamarisk shrubs. In the Sinai region through which the Israelites passed in their flight from Pharoah, manna accumulates only during the month of June; sometimes it is plentiful, sometimes it is scarce. As Marston Bates reports in *Gluttons and Libertines: Human Problems of Being Natural*, the

Sylvester Graham

Arabs still collect this substance, which they call *man-es-simma* (bread from the sky). And in Iraq nearly sixty thousand pounds of scale secretions are gathered each year and sold in the bazaars of Baghdad. Manna is mixed with eggs and almonds to make candy, which is perfectly in keeping with the Biblical description: ". . . it was like coriander seed, white; and the taste of it was like wafers made with honey."

Moving from the sublime to the ridiculous, we note that cereal magnate C. W. Post introduced a brand of corn flakes in 1904 which he called "Elijah's Manna." Fundamentalists everywhere were incensed by the desecration of the prophet's name and the vulgar reference to the bread of heaven. England refused to register the trademark. Under fire, Post changed the name to Post Toasties.

**Most Unusual Food Faddist:** Sylvester Graham (1794–1851) was a temperance lecturer who became convinced that a purely vegetable diet would depress the appetite for demon rum. His thought found full flower in the classic work *Bread and Bread Making* in which he developed the idea that whole wheat bread is more healthful than white. In 1847 his advocacy of this position caused a riot of Boston bakers intent on lynching the "mad enthusiast." The police were unable to control the crowd, and the disturbance was quelled only when Graham's followers shoveled slaked lime on the mob from the second-story windows of the lecture hall.

Graham survived to espouse other visionary reforms: taking cold showers, sleeping on hard mattresses with the windows open, eating rough cereals, wearing looser and lighter clothing, and practicing cheerfulness at meals. He had many enthusiastic adherents, among them Horace Greeley, some of whom lived and ate together in Graham boarding houses. Emerson called him "the poet of bran bread and pumpkins." Now, alas, Sylvester Graham is virtually forgotten, but his spirit lives on in the cracker bearing his name.

**Most Unusual Ice Cream:** Long before Dolly Madison and all that, the emperor Nero had ice imported from distant snow-capped mountains for frozen deserts.

**Most Unusual Meat:** In 1896 a woolly mammoth was found frozen in a Siberian glacier, his flesh perfectly preserved by the long deep freeze. What meat could be rescued from the wolves was canned and shipped back to Moscow, where Czar Nicholas II and a select group of scientists are said to have dined on the prehistoric fare. Several other mammoths have been found in the Siberian permafrost over the last century; those who claim to have tried it say the flesh is black in color and tastes like a cross between bear and whale.

As far back as the first century, mammoth steaks were reported to have graced royal tables. During a Roman meat shortage, Herod Agrippa I, governor of Judea, served glacier-preserved Pachydermata from the Caucasus at a dinner party for the emperor Caligula.

Archaeologists say the ancient Greeks almost surely must have stumbled on a number of mammoth skulls, which are common throughout the Mediterranean area. The most impressive thing about a mammoth skull is its large nasal cavity. Since few Greeks had ever seen a living elephant, they may have mistaken a mammoth skull for the head of a gigantic one-eyed man, giving rise to the story of Polyphemus in the *Odyssey*. As late as the fifteenth century mammoth skulls were occasionally identified as the crania of Cyclops.

**Most Unusual Milk:** Dehydrated milk is not new; the warriors of Genghis Khan dried mares' milk in the sun until it became a fine powder which could be stored indefinitely. To reconstitute it, they would mix the old-fashioned Samalac with water in a leather pouch and tie it to a horse. A day's galloping homogenized it into a thin, white soup.

**Most Unusual Mug:** The glass-bottomed tankard enabled a drinker to hoist a few beers and still keep an eye on potential cutthroats. This common drinking vessel (with an uncommon history) is said to have occasioned the friendly admonition: "Here's looking at you."

**Most Unusual Pie:** Born in 1619 in Oakham, England, Jeffery Hudson was only seven years old and eighteen inches tall when he entered the service of the Duke of Buckingham. One evening, as a merry entertainment, the Duke decided to serve Jeffery in a cold pie to his guests, Charles I and Queen Henrietta Maria. The Queen was so pleased with this little practical joke that she convinced the young dwarf to join her own retinue.

**Most Unusual Poison:** Tomatoes were widely thought to be poisonous in the American colonies until 1733 when a Virginia physician named Dr. Siccary demonstrated that not only were they not poisonous but they were delicious and healthful. Dr. Siccary was so enamored of the lowly tomato, known in those days as the "love apple," however, that he went to his grave sincerely believing that "a person who should eat a sufficient abundance of these apples would never die."

**Most Unusual Restaurant:** In this vast and wondrous land of ours there is, happily, only one restaurant catering exclusively to dogs and cats, and it is the Animal Gourmet, on Manhattan's Upper East Side. For the "pet owner who cares," there is a menu that compares favorably to the bills-of-fare offered at New York's finest biped restaurants, and it includes shrimp cocktail, liver paté, beef bourguignon, steak and kidney ragout, braised chicken livers, poached fish filet, and beef Wellington.

"We sell about three hundred meals a week," says Bill Poulin who, with Joe Mitseifer, owns and operates the restaurant. "The food we serve our customers is bought in the same places you and I buy our own food."

Poulin's and Mitseifer's love for animals—and good food—has turned an aversion to. feeding animals canned pet foods into a profitable enterprise. As the sign above the entrance proclaims,

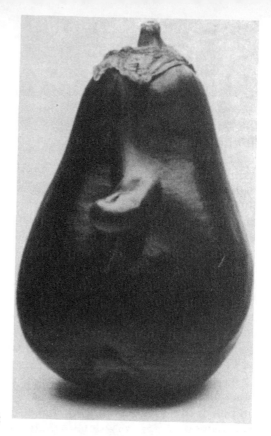

Richard Nixon eggplant

"We do not prepare dog and cat food. We prepare food for dogs and cats." Meals are served at small tables with white table cloths; the beverage of the day, every day, is water. Animal Gourmet also caters birthday parties for animals and with advance notice they'll provide flowers, favors, and a birthday cake made of dog meal, liver, whipped powdered milk and cream.

"I'm a Pennsylvania hick and Bill once worked as a lumberjack," says co-owner Mitseifer, "and we have had the Duchess of Windsor here to feed her two pugs. And we have the lady from the Bronx who takes a bus and subway and lugs a forty-pound metal crate with her alley cat in it. She feeds it here with a little silver spoon. Just think how lonely she'd be without her cat."

**Most Unusual Steak:** A ten-pound steak arriving in Circle City, Alaska, during the gold rush was sold for a price that seemed unbelievably inflationary until recently. At first there was open bidding for the meat, with offers soaring as high as thirty-five dollars per pound. When fist fights broke out among the bidders, it was decided to raffle off the steak instead. Over $480 worth of tickets were sold with each of the winners receiving one slice.

One of the most highly honored pieces of meat in history was served to Charles II of England who exclaimed, "For its merit it should be knighted, and henceforth called Sir-Loin." Some authorities have claimed that this was the origin of the butcher's term, but the Oxford English Dictionary cites earlier mentions of sirloin. Rather than coining a new word, they credit Charles with making a bad pun.

**Most Unusual Vegetable:** *New York* magazine reported in 1973 that an eggplant bearing a startling resemblance to the beleaguered President Nixon had been purchased by a Manhattan housewife in a midtown supermarket.

# Life-Styles

**Best Life-Style:** The Kalapalo Indians who live on the savannas of central Brazil have the world's most relaxed society, spending well over half their lives in their hammocks. Adults average twelve hours of sleep a night and catch two or three naps during daylight hours as well. At most the men work two or three short days a week fishing for picuda in the tributaries of the Amazon. And though wild game abounds, they are too peaceable to hunt.

Simplicity characterizes all aspects of their lives. In addition to fish, they dine mainly on manioc, lice, and butterflies. The men wear only a belt of beads around their waists; married women wear a string of shiny wedding bells. Although women often have several lovers and a fish occasionally disappears from its owner's pot, the Kalapalo are not troubled with problems such as infidelity or theft. To accuse a neighbor of theft or a mate of infidelity is considered far more dishonorable than the acts themselves. But the most distinctive aspect of Kalapalo life is leisure, and in their abundant spare time they enjoy gathering together and improvising melodies on wooden flutes.

**Best Proof That Californians Are Not Like the Rest of Us:** California is currently the scene of a mushrooming "gluers" movement spearheaded by people who like to glue things—small things, preferably, like costume jewelry, rubber mice, teeth, baby beads, tennis balls, bottle caps, plastic salt shakers—to bigger things, like cars and buildings. Dickens Bascom, a noted northern California gluer, looks forward to the day when he can join other gluers and purchase a large office building and decorate it in their fashion. "I'm determined to do it," he says. "I think it's something people need."

**Best Streakers:** Most college administrators were very tolerant of the mercifully short-lived fad of streaking; few suspensions or expulsions were recorded, and it is apparent that deans and policemen would rather see students running around in nothing but their tennis shoes than engaging in sit-ins or occupying buildings. In short, most streakers had nothing to lose. In this permissive climate, two dozen West Point cadets emerge as the best streakers and the only heroes. With their clothes off and their military careers on the line, they raced across the campus of the United States Military Academy, pursued, Keystone-cops style, by a platoon of apoplectic officers—and they got away with it.

---

**Worst Gift:** Victor Emmanuel II (1820–1878) was the first king to rule over a united Italy, and he might therefore be a prominent figure in history even if he hadn't won immortality as the giver of one of the most vulgar gifts imaginable. For some unfathomable reason of his own, the monarch allowed the nail of his big toe to go untrimmed for one whole year at a time. Each New Year's Day was the occasion for the annual paring ceremony, and by that time the nail had grown to be a full half-inch long, or even longer in good years.

The royal clipping was then passed on to the king's jeweler, who took the unpromising "gem," polished it, shaped it, edged it with gold, and encrusted it in diamonds. In the hands of the skilled craftsman, the nail was transformed into a presentable and quite valuable bauble. Victor Emmanuel made it a custom of turning over this little piece of himself to his favorite mistress of the moment. The most stunning collection of *ongles de roi* was accumulated by the Countess Mirafiori, whom the king ultimately married.

**Worst Life-Style:** The Yanomamo tribesmen who inhabit the dense rainforests near the Brazil-Venezuela frontier are male chauvinists unexcelled in viciousness. They beat their wives savagely at the least provocation, real or imagined, and nearly all Yanomamo women are covered with scars and ugly welts—tokens of their husbands' affection. A common punishment for a misbehaving wife is to rip the bamboo earrings right out of her pierced lobes.

But the women also contribute to the incomparable cruelty of Yanomamo society, most notably by murdering their female infants (strangulation with vines is the preferred method) until they deliver a son. And once they have borne a male heir, the women are permitted to kill all unwanted children, regardless of sex.

The two principal pastimes of Yanomamo males are drug-taking and war. A man and his brother-in-law tend to be the closest companions in Yanomamo society, and they spend much of their days lying together in a hammock blowing the hallucinogenic powder *ebene* into each other's nostrils. Under the influence of this powerful substance, as anthropologist Marvin Harris has recounted, they experience incredible illusions, walk around on all fours growling, and chat with demons. At war, the Yanomamo are notoriously dirty fighters. Whenever possible, they sneak into enemy villages at night and club in the skulls of unsuspecting sleepers.

Nor is it safe to be a Yanomamo's friend. When one village invites another over for a friendly feast, it is understood that there will also be "competitions." The favorite sport is a chest-pounding duel in which one man takes a rock into his hand and slams it against the chest of the other competitor as hard as he can. The opponent, if he is able, then returns the blow, and they exchange wallops until one or the other sinks to his knees. Those who prefer more aggressive play take turns smashing each other over the head with bamboo poles. The Yanomamo are proud of the gashes they receive in these games and they shave their heads and paint the wounds bright red to exaggerate them.

A dinner guest is fortunate if he comes away with just a few scars on his head and chest. Not infrequently one village invites another to dinner only to massacre all the men and gang-rape the women. Well aware of this tradition, the guests are always on their guard and may come with the intention of striking first and slaughtering their hosts.

**Worst Singles Party:** For weeks in advance newspaper advertisements in Chicago and Toronto inquired naughtily, "Can singles parties lead the way to a better understanding of international affairs?" Those answering yes were invited to what the promoters billed as "the largest, highest, and longest singles party in the history of Western civilization." The original, grandiose plan called for 2,000 Canadians to fly to Chicago where they would join 8,000 Americans at the Regency Hyatt O'Hare Hotel for an amorous November (1973) weekend. There, among North America's most eligible unmarrieds, they would enjoy an ultrahip fashion show, seven big-name rock bands, "the biggest, most sumptuous buffet ever presented," and of course the pleasures of companionship.

To their credit, only 200 Canadians invested $130 to join the gathering, but swarms of local young people more than made up for the poor Canadian turnout. The festivities began well enough: The sexes were about evenly represented; the rock bands were loud, if not well known; the dancing was spirited; there was the usual amount of disrobing and tossing of the fully dressed into the heated swimming pool. The first sign of trouble came when the buffet was opened. The ravenous socializers were disappointed to see only cold cuts, pickles, and rye bread, and even that was soon devoured. Then, as the crowd continued to swell and incidents of gate-crashing began to occur, the hotel management grew nervous and they decided to close the bars. Starved, thirsty, and suspecting a rip-off, the crowd turned nasty. There was a lot of littering, some property destruction, and a false alarm that brought a hook and ladder and a lot of firemen to the party.

George Russell, writing in *The New York Times* described the event as "an ugly form of social Darwinism," which promoted the "survival of the swingingest, of the least sensitive." Well, that may have been the reason for the party's failure, but more likely it was the shortage of booze.

**Worst Streakers:** The worst streak, as far as consequences for the participants, occurred when two naked students parachuted from a rented Cessna 182 over the University of Georgia campus. Blown off target, one landed in the playground of a married students housing complex and the other touched down in a cesspool. This was followed the next day by the most disingenuous streak when the two parachutists performed the whole scene over again for photographers.

**Most Unusual Aphrodisiac:** In 1929 an incomplete skull of Peking Man was discovered—one of the most important archaeological finds of all time. Also that year, the Japanese were readying for their invasion of China. Hurriedly, Peking Man's remains were packaged for transport out of China to safety, but when the trunk containing the priceless skull arrived in Shanghai, it was empty. No one is certain what became of Peking Man, but one report maintains that the bones were stolen by local blackmarketeers, ground into a fine powder, and sold as an aphrodisiac.

**Most Unusual Aryans:** In 1938 a rising Nazi journalist faced a stumbling block in his career. Although three of his grandparents were of indisputable Teutonic blood, his maternal grandmother was a full-blooded Sioux Indian. The Chamber of the Press consulted with National anthropologists, who huddled, referred to their books, and concluded that the young man had no problem: The Sioux, it turns out, are Aryans. Some of the same anthropologists probably worked on the tremendous scholarly effort of 1941–1942, assembling evidence that the Japanese allies were also of solid Aryan stock.

**Most Unusual Bastard:** Perhaps the most talented illegitimate of all time was Leonardo da Vinci, although those other bastards, Richard Wagner, Napoleon, and Boccaccio, might argue the claim.

Grover Cleveland (see also *Most Unusual Draft Dodger*) fathered an illegitimate son; he publicly admitted the fact and made a generous provision for the boy's welfare. Much to the credit of the electorate, they forgave him his indiscretion and twice elected him president—the only chief executive to serve two nonconsecutive terms.

**Most Unusual Beauty Contest:** Ivan the Terrible was among several Russian czars who chose their brides in a nationwide beauty contest. As many as 2,000 eligible young ladies and their parents, the pick of the provinces, were brought to Moscow for the long and rigorous selection process. After weeks of interviews and fancy balls, the czar and his advisors would single out the woman with the most pleasing figure, manners, and wit to become the czarina.

Not surprisingly, this relatively democratic procedure was popular with the proletarian parents of pretty daughters, who aspired to become in-laws to the most powerful man in all of Russia. By the time of Alexis Romanov, the beauty contest was such a well established tradition, that it posed an obstacle to his extraordinary plan to marry a woman he loved. To avoid disappointing hundreds of families, Alexis staged a contest, as usual, but rigged it so that beautiful Nathalie Narychkine, his beloved, would emerge the winner. Nathalie and Alexis were the parents of Peter the Great.

**Most Unusual College:** In Morogoro, a suburb of Dar es Salaam, Tanzania, a "sex college" was established—next door to the town's busiest bar, according to a news item in *Baraza*, a local paper. The school's *raison d'etre*, according to a promotional brochure, "is to teach girls new and modern ways of welcoming rich men." Only the cream of the area's secondary school dropouts are eligible for admission and classes are held for four hours a day. The degree offered is the mysterious D.W.D.

**Most Unusual Courtesy:** A number of practices that are now codified as "good manners" are the outcome of the old practice of emptying chamber pots in the streets. A common expression in Elizabethan London was *Gardez, l'eau*—or look out below—the polite scream before you dumped your chamber pot out of an upper story window. The streets had open sewers, which presented a constant hazard to pedestrians as coaches sloshed by near the curb. To protect a lady and her garments from an unexpected splash of sewage, gentlemanly escorts took to walking between the lady and the dangers of the street.

The hero in this brief history is Sir John Harrington, who was one of the men who invented the flush toilet—a device that has been invented and reinvented several times in history. According to one disputed derivation, it is in his honor that the privy is known as the john or jakes. (See also *Best Invention.*)

**Most Unusual Curse Words:** The ancient Arabs used to invoke the awesome laxative powers of the fig when swearing. Similarly, the Greeks often uttered a phrase that loosely translated means, "Rhodesian cabbage!" (Rhodesian cabbage was highly valued as a hangover cure, but that hardly explains why it became a swear word.)

Louis IX of France had a very low tolerance for swearing, which is one of the reasons why he became known as Saint Louis. He became very upset when he heard people say *pardieu* (by God) or *cordieu* (God's heart) and finally he decreed that cussers should have their tongues branded with a hot iron. To protect their tongues, the courtiers began to swear by the king's dog Bleu, hence the curses *parbleu* and the ever popular *sacrebleu*, which have come down to the Frenchman of today.

**Most Unusual Duel:** Two gentlemen of equally high merit, one German and one Spanish, sought the hand of Helene Acharfequinn, the daughter of Maximilian II. In their ardor, the suitors proposed to fight a duel over who should have the privilege of marrying the beautiful Helene. But their prospective father-in-law would not allow them to risk their noble blood, and instead he proposed an unusual contest: Whichever gentleman could put his rival in a gunnysack would become his son-in-law.

The rivals wrestled with skill and vigor for more than an hour until the German, Baron von Talbert, succeeded in bagging his opponent. Talbert hoisted the bag, carried it across the room, and placed it at the feet of Helene, proposing then and there.

**Most Unusual Euphemism:** During World War II, overly demure members of the French Resistance announced their need to use the toilet by saying, *"Je vais telephoner à Hitler."*

**Most Unusual Greeting:** It is the custom among some tribes in New Guinea to greet a woman with a kiss on her bare left breast. A fine how-do-you-do.

**Most Unusual Life-Style:** A very subjective judgment: In 1971 a Philippine government official made contact with the Tasaday people of Minanao Island. The most isolated and primitive tribe yet known to anthropologists, they are true stone-age men who have never seen metal tools. The concept of war is unknown to them, and in fact they have no word for it in their language. Most of their goods are held in common, and the lush rainforest provides them with all the food they can eat. Most of the families live together in one central cave. When asked if they had any wants or needs, one bachelor asked for a wife. But except for the shortage of women in the tribe, they appear to be perfectly content with life as it was lived 10,000 years ago.

Sadly, we must report, all that is changing. A recent article asserts that since establishing contact with the outside world, the Tasaday have taken to smoking commercial menthol cigarettes.

**Most Unusual Manifestation of the Victorian Ethic:** *Lady Gough's Book of Etiquette* notes that arranging books on shelves must be done with the utmost discretion so that a book written by a male author is not placed adjacent to one by a female author to whom he is not married.

**Most Unusual Marriage Proposal:** In January 1964 a Masai chieftain offered to buy the blonde actress Carroll Baker for 150 cows, 200 goats, and $750 cash. As a measure of how highly he thought of Ms. Baker, a Masai warrior usually spends about $200 and 12 cows for a wife.

It is of economic and sociological interest to note that in the *Odyssey* the slave girl Euryclea was purchased by Laertes for twenty oxen. So the price has remained relatively constant.

**Most Unusual Masher:** Enrico Caruso was once arrested for making a pass at an attractive young woman in the monkey house of the Central Park Zoo.

**Most Unusual Sexologist:** In 1776 the Temple of Hymen, established by the eccentric Dr. James Graham, opened its doors and began teaching "the art of preventing barrenness, and propagating a much more strong, beautiful, active, healthy, wise, and virtuous race of human beings than the present puny, insignificant, foolish, peevish, and nonsensical race of Christians, who quarrel, fight, bite, devour, and cut each other's throats about they know not what." Graham furnished his pleasure dome with erotic paintings and statuary, as well as providing the most tasteful vocal and instrumental music. The overhead was tremendous, and from the first it was a losing proposition, but Graham continued to support the operation for several years with money out of his own pocket.

Dr. Graham was a strict vegetarian and drank nothing but cold water. From his point of view, the prime attraction of the Temple of Hymen was his "Eccentric Lecture on Generation," which was a mishmash of puerile eugenics and sexual "how-to" all presented in the chastest of words. From his audience's point of view, the prime attractions were the handsome females—among them Lady Hamilton and other daring ladies of the upper crust—who appeared naked, in the interest of science.

**Most Unusual Sexual Ethics:** Not surprisingly the Toda language has no word for adultery. The Todas of Southern India expect a woman to have at least one lover in addition to as many as six husbands. Todas are of the opinion that if a girl is still a virgin at her wedding, her maternal uncle will be taken ill and die. Fortunately, if the doomed uncle discovers the bride's shameful innocence in time, he can save himself by shaving off her hair.

If a Toda woman dies without having acquired a lover, the elders of the village are forced to appoint one because the grieving lover plays an important role in the funeral service.

**Most Unusual Streakers:** The most unusual streaks were the so-called "reverse-streaks." At a number of nudist camps, residents raced across the grounds fully clothed in defiance of camp regulations.

**Most Unusual Waiters:** In 1973 Jack Cione's night club in Honolulu introduced the bottomless waiter. Business has been booming ever since with a predominantly female clientele.

**Most Unusual Wedding:** In the Marquesas Islands a bridegroom walks to his father-in-law's house on a human street formed by the prone wedding guests. He steps from back to back at a stately pace. (If there are too few people to pave the entire route, the people at the back race up to the front of the line to be stepped on again.) At the altar the groom eats a raw fish that has been fileted and diced on a human body. Presents are distributed and there is a great feast, and finally at the end of the festivities, the street of bodies is formed again for the groom's return home.

# People

---

**Best Anti-intellectual:** History's most effective anti-intellectual was Shih Huang Ti (259–210 B.C.). Shih was the complete man of action who rose to the throne of the small state of Ch'in at the age of twelve and waged constant warfare for twenty years until he had unified the countless squabbling states of China into a single nation; the effort cost some 1,500,000 lives. Having "pacified in turn the four ends of the earth," he became China's first emperor and turned his attention to the problems of administration. He standardized the written language, devised a harsh penal code, built long straight roads, and began construction of the Great Wall of China.

Scholars were an irritation to Shih; they constantly compared his actions to the standards for a good ruler set down in the Confucian texts—and found him wanting. When a few dared to criticize his cruelties outrightly, the emperor decided to remove them. He summoned the 460 most prominent wise men to his palace and put them on trial. But when it became clear that distinguishing the innocent from the guilty would be a long and difficult process, Shih simply ordered that all 460 be buried alive.

The books were next to go. One copy of each book (actually huge bamboo scrolls) was brought to the Imperial Library and every other manuscript in the country was ordered destroyed. Those caught concealing books were gruesomely tortured and executed, but many book-lovers learned the Confucian works by heart in order to preserve them. Poetry, philosophy, and history fed the huge bonfires that lit up the night sky of China.

Shih's motives for the conflagration were threefold. First, he did not wish to be bound to the code of conduct and ancient rites set down in the Confucian texts. He also felt that literary freedom was divisive and hindered the cultural unification of his country. And finally he reasoned that if all the old history books were destroyed, recorded history would begin with the reign of Shih.

**Best Gambler:** A consistent winner at the tables is highly unusual. Therefore, it is indeed noteworthy that Charles Wells broke the bank at the Monte Carlo roulette table fifteen times in 1890. Understandably encouraged by his success, he returned in 1891 and broke the bank five more times.

**Best Linguist:** Cardinal Mezzofanti of Bologna, Italy, taught Cockney slang to Lord Byron. It was merely one of over 100 languages and dialects the cardinal could speak and understand. Reliable sources insist that he was fluent in at least fifty tongues, including Walachian, Guzarati, Algonquin, and Pegu. He could chat a little in Frissian, Chippewa, Lettish, Quechua, Tonquinese, and many others. He found Chinese to be the most difficult language to master, requiring approximately four months of study. Perhaps the most cosmopolitan speaker of all time, Cardinal Mezzofanti never traveled outside of Italy.

**Worst Alchemist:** Heinrich Kurschildgen was no less successful than the alchemists of old, but he merits the title "the worst" because he was the most recent flop in this great tradition of failure. Kurschildgen was a dye worker who managed to convince a gullible university professor that he had discovered mysterious rays that made all matter radioactive. With a little tinkering, he promised, a device could be developed which would split the atom and make gold.

The professor described the plan to some of his right-wing friends, among them Herr Hugenberg, an important industrialist and newspaper publisher. Patriotic businessmen were interested not only because it was a chance to make huge personal fortunes but also because they saw alchemy as a way to pay off the Weimar Republic's debts under the Treaty of Versailles. As Kurschildgen embellished his claims, asserting that the rays might also cure cancer and purify steel, eager investors sunk tens of thousands of marks into the scheme. Soon, word got around of this promising enterprise and before Kurschildgen was exposed as a fraud, inquiries about the process were coming in from America, Britain, and Switzerland.

There is a persistent rumor that Hitler employed a number of alchemists who worked full-time throughout the war trying to turn lead into gold. While we could find no evidence of this, perhaps the Kurschildgen story is the source of the Hitler rumor.

**Worst Job in the Court:** During the reign of François I, 1515 to 1547, the exalted position of chair-bearer was introduced to the French court for the first time. It was surely the worst job any courtier ever brown-nosed to earn, and yet because it provided a rare opportunity to be with the king in the most intimate of circumstances, the office was much coveted. The chair-bearer, you see, was charged with carrying around His Majesty's portable toilet and attending to his royal needs thereon.

Following François's initiative, Catherine de Medici also acquired a "chair," appointed chair-bearers, and dressed them in elaborate uniforms. Ordinarily Catherine's chair was outfitted with seat cushions of red and blue velvet, but for one year following her husband's death, Catherine, in her grief, substituted a black velvet seat as a symbol of mourning.

The toilet, portable and stationary, continued to play an important role in French politics for years to come. Louis XIV, for example, announced his marriage to Madame de Maintenon while astride his *chaise d'affaires* (business seat) as he delicately called it. Hopefully for such momentous public occasions he observed the custom of earlier monarchs, who sweetened the fragrance of their chairs with tansy and other mild herbs.

Louis XV boasted of a remarkable toilet decorated with Japanese landscapes and birds worked in gold and brightly colored relief, inlaid mother-of-pearl borders, bronze fittings made in China, a merry red lacquer interior, and a padded seat of green velour. An inventory conducted at the Versailles Palace shortly before the French Revolution noted the presence of nearly three hundred toilets. From that you may draw your own conclusions.

**Worst Reformer:** Carrie Nation (1846–1911), America's most extraordinary temperance agitator, stood six feet tall and had the arms and shoulders of a professional wrestler. When she stormed into a saloon, swinging her legendary hatchet, few dared to oppose her. She was jailed more than thirty times in her crusading career and there is little doubt that in her time she was, in the words of writer Ishbel Ross, "by all odds the most meddlesome woman in the country."

Carrie had fanaticism in her blood. Her mother was absolutely

Cartoon of Carrie Nation

convinced that she was Queen Victoria and always wore the long purple velvet gowns and crystal crown that befitted a monarch. Early in life Carrie began to develop fixed ideas of her own and her first marriage to Dr. Charles Gloyd gave direction to her eccentricity. It is not unfair to say that the meek doctor was driven to drink by his overbearing wife. Eventually he fled his spouse, took refuge in the Masonic Lodge (where women were not admitted), and drank himself to death. From then on Carrie was a confirmed foe of drink and the Masons.

Her second husband was a preacher, the Reverend David Nation, who also found Carrie more than a little intimidating. During his sermons she used to sit in the front pew and embarrass him by loudly correcting his grammatical mistakes; when he announced a hymn, she would overrule him and insist on singing one of her own favorites. Probably the reverend was relieved when his wife deserted him to take up her "divinely appointed" career of "hatchetation," as she put it.

Mrs. Nation's first triumphs were in Topeka, Kansas, where she organized ministers, college students, and the teetotalers of the Women's Christian Temperance Union into a holy mob bent on destroying every saloon in town. They marched through the streets arm-in-arm singing "Onward Christian Soldiers" or chanting "Smash, smash, for Jesus' sake, smash!" When they came to a gin mill, all hell broke loose. Following Carrie's lead, the marchers threw rocks through the mirrors, destroyed all the glassware, and chopped up the bar, furniture, walls, and floors with their inevitable hatchets. Carrie's favorite feat was to rake an entire counter of good booze onto the floor with a single sweep of her hatchet. The place in ruins, she would shout with the fury of a prophet, "Praise God, another joint gone."

Soon she developed a nationwide reputation and formed the National Hatchet Brigade, which published a periodical called *The Smasher's Mail*. She took on national figures, such as Teddy Roosevelt, whom she characterized as "that blood-thirsty, reckless, and cigarette smoking rummy." No saloon in the country was safe. Once she stormed into John L. Sullivan's drinking establishment in New York City, and tradition has it that the bare knuckles champ fled in terror. Toward the end of her career her zeal extended to other reforms besides temperance. She took to knocking cigarettes out of men's mouths as they walked down the street, hatcheting paintings of nudes, and covering nude statuary with her own cape.

Could one expect less of Victoria's daughter?

**Most Unusual Explorer:** In 1823 Captain John Cleves Symmes, a hero of the War of 1812, brought his case to Congress. For several years he had been researching and documenting his marvelous and sincerely held beliefs about the interior of the world: "I declare the earth is hollow and habitable within, containing a number of solid concentric spheres, and that it is open at the poles twelve or sixteen degrees," he wrote in a circular addressed "To All the World." All he desired was a ship and a few brave scientists to accompany him in the descent through the "Symmes Hole" at the North Pole into the "warm rich land, stocked with thrifty vegetables and animals, if not men" that they would surely find within.

Captain Symmes was a popular figure on the lecture circuit and thousands of Americans, moved by his arguments, petitioned Congress to support an expedition to "Symmezonia," as they called it. Representative Richard M. Johnson of Kentucky (who later became vice-president) championed Symmes's cause on the House floor and finally forced the question to a vote. Symmes' proposal was defeated, but twenty-five congressmen did vote in favor of a "journey to the center of the earth." Circumventing the un-

John Cleves Symmes

imaginative Congress, John J. Reynolds, a Symmes disciple, persuaded the secretaries of the Navy and the Treasury under President John Quincy Adams to outfit three ships for a voyage to the interior; before the adventurers could set sail, however, Andrew Jackson came into office and quashed the plan.

Captain Symmes died in 1829, but his vacuous theory survived him, inspiring a short story by Edgar Allen Poe ("Ms. Found in a Bottle") and Jules Verne's novel about the subterranean world. In 1878 the captain's son, Americus Vespucius Symmes, edited his father's collected works, which continued to interest unconventional thinkers until Robert Peary reached 90°N in 1909 and found no hole.

**Most Unusual Hero:** We shy away from calling Paul Revere the worst hero, because he made many unheralded contributions to the Revolution. But the "Midnight Ride," so highly touted by Longfellow, was not all it was cracked up to be.

First of all, according to an article in the *Smithsonian* magazine, Revere was not alone on that April night in 1775. Two other colonials, William Dawes and Dr. Samuel Prescott, rode with him, and they had not gotten to many Middlesex villages and farms before they were approached by a British patrol. Both Dawes and Prescott escaped, but Paul Revere was captured. The British put a loaded pistol to his temple and ordered him to talk. Showing discretionary valor, the famous Boston silversmith told them everything they wanted to know about where he had been and why. And another thing Longfellow forgot to tell us: Revere was riding as a mercenary that night; the Boston patriots paid him five shillings for his efforts.

**Most Unusual Hypnotist:** Franz Mesmer (1734–1815) believed that there is an invisible magnetic fluid coursing through the body that controls a person's physical and mental health. To heal, he reasoned, it was necessary to control the flow of this fluid. Mesmer began conducting experiments in which he waved magnets slowly back and forth in front of his patients; on other occasions he immersed them in tubs filled with warm water and iron filings. All this soaking and waving sent some of his clients into a deep trance. Mesmer was jubilant: They were magnetized!

Later, Mesmer found that he could induce a trance without the tubs and magnets, simply by waving his hands in front of the subject. But instead of discarding the magnetism theory, he concluded that there was a strange "animal magnetism" in his hands. Moreover, iron and people were not the only things he was convinced he could magnetize. "I have rendered paper, bread, wool, silk, stones, leather, glass, wood, men, and dogs—in short, everything I touched—magnetic to a degree," he wrote.

Mesmer's penetrating eyes, entrancing gestures, and long purple robes, set in the soothing environment of his office with a pianoforte playing softly in the background, combined to make Mesmer a competent, though theoretically naive, hypnotist. In fact, "mesmerism" appears to have had a genuinely therapeutic effect on some people, particularly those suffering from hysteria. A few exceptional cures and the public's eternal enthusiasm for miracle healers made Mesmer immensely popular in Paris. But establishment physicians and the French government were less enthusiastic about his methods. A board of inquiry (of which Benjamin Franklin was a member) was set up to investigate whether Mesmer was a quack, fake, or medical hero. The verdict was quack, with a measure of fake, and Mesmer was forced to retire to Switzerland, where his popularity declined.

**Most Unusual Mathematician:** There are numerous accounts of people who have performed incredible feats of calculation instantaneously. Karl Gauss, a pioneer in non-Euclidean geometry, had this ability. Another well-documented case of a man with a mind swifter than a pocket calculator is the story of George Bidder, who won the mathematics prize at Edinburgh University in 1822. Bidder was once asked to figure how far a pendulum that swings 9¾ inches in one second would travel in 7 years, 14 days, 2 hours, 1 minute, and 56 seconds—taking the year to be 365 days, 5 hours, 40 minutes, and 50 seconds long. After meditating for a little less than a minute Bidder replied, "2,165,625,744¾ inches!" (Check it yourself.) George Bidder went on to become an accomplished civil engineer.

**Most Unusual Name:** Boxing buff Brian Brown, of Wolverhampton, Great Britain, named his daughter, born in 1974, after all twenty-five world heavyweight champions. Brown told newspaper reporters that he planned to take the child—Maria Sullivan Corbett Fitzsimmons Jeffries Hart Burns Johnson Willard Dempsey Tunney Schmeling Sharkey Carnera Baer Braddock Louis Charles Walcott Marciano Patterson Johanssen Liston Clay Frazier Foreman Brown—to see her first professional boxing match "when she is three or four months old, so that she can soak up the atmosphere." That would prepare her, he said, for a career in "promotion or management or something similar." Brown explained that he had been hoping for a boy.

At her christening in 1883, Arthur Pepper named his daughter Anna Bertha Cecilia Diana Emily Fanny Gertrude Hypatia Inez Jane Kate Louisa Maud Nora Ophelia Quince Rebecca Sarah Teresa Ulysses Venus Winifred Xenophon Yetty Zeus Pepper— one name for every letter in the alphabet with P for Pepper displaced to the end.

**Most Unusual Occupational Hazard:** For schoolteachers, sportscasters, even telephone operators, sore throats and laryngitis are all in a day's work. Rock 'n' roll singers, however, frequently are prey to a much more serious and longer-lasting deterioration of the vocal cords. In fact, many rock stars, in the pursuit of their careers, literally scream their lungs out.

Recently, Dr. Eugene M. Batza of Cleveland Clinic's Department of Otolaryngology, examined a five-member rock combo and found that all of them suffered from chronic, aggravated laryngitis, as well as nodules and inflammation of the vocal cords. The symptoms were so serious, in fact, that the group was forced to call off a long string of engagements and undergo medical treatment. "The risk of permanent degenerative change is always present," says Dr. Batza, who has since taken a closer look into the hazards of singing rock 'n' roll for a living.

What makes the rock singer's plight so much worse than the operatic soprano's or the folk singer's is, more often than not, a hectic schedule that has him singing three or four hours perhaps four or five nights a week for several months at a stretch in addition to rehearsals and recording sessions. Moreover, rock singing puts an intolerable strain on the voice. Nonetheless, rock singers are generally unwilling to take the care needed to avoid permanent damage to the larynx.

"They fear that a radical change in their vocal style will lead to oblivion as artists," the doctor says. "They rely on their youthful resiliency to carry them through, but they would do well to remember that singing is a physical activity. Abuse of the pitching arm, particularly after fatigue has noticeably set in, can be catastrophic to the serious athlete."

Contemporary orchestral music is as hard on the nerves of its performers as rock music is on their vocal cords. After studying 208 orchestral musicians, two West German psychiatrists concluded that musicians who frequently play present-day compositions are often beset by a broad range of symptoms, including chronic nervousness and irritability, insomnia, earaches, and impotency.

**Most Unusual Old Man:** R. S. Kirby, author of *Kirby's Curious and Eccentric Museum,* recounts the story of Old John Weeks of New London, Connecticut, who married his tenth wife when he was 106. (The blushing bride was sixteen.) Kirby also insists that after Weeks lost all his gray hair, he began growing a new head of brunette locks. In 1798, he died—at the age of 114. A few hours before his passing, Weeks dined on three pounds of pork, two pounds of bread, and nearly a pint of wine.

**Most Unusual Part-time Job:** Serving working-class families who could not afford an alarm clock, Mrs. Mary Ann Smith of London ran a thriving business. For a few pennies a month, she would shoot a volley of peas against their windows to awaken them at the specified hour.

**Most Unusual Philosopher:** Historians would have us remember Jeremy Bentham as the founding father of utilitarian philosophy, passing over his other, more remarkable accomplishments. For example, Bentham invented scores of neologisms, including the words "maximize" and "minimize." He also devised a round prison called the "panopticon," which permitted a single jailer to sit in the center and watch over a full house of convicts. All in all, he lived a full, happy, eccentric life, organizing all of Western thought into a single system, and doting on his beloved teapot (named Dickey) and his cat (named Reverend Dr. John Langborne).

In his last will and testament, Jeremy Bentham left a large fortune to University College in London on the condition that his preserved body be displayed annually at the board of directors' meeting. Dr. Southward Smith, Bentham's physician and the executor of his will, has described the exhaustive effort invested in carrying out the philosopher's wishes. "I endeavored to preserve the head, untouched," the doctor wrote, "merely drawing away the fluids by placing under it . . . sulphuric acid, but 'twas without expression. Seeing this would not do for exhibition, I had a model made in wax by a distinguished French artist. I then had the skeleton stuffed out to fit Bentham's own clothes and this wax likeness fitted to the trunk. The whole was then enclosed in a mahogany case with folding glass doors, seated in his armchair and holding in his hand his favorite walking stick."

The body was dutifully displayed at every board meeting until 1924, when it was relegated to an exhibit area. During the London blitz in World War II, University College was heavily bombed, and the wing that housed Jeremy Bentham's body was almost completely destroyed. Miraculously his remains came through unscathed.

**Most Unusual Shepherds:** Much of the rich pasturage of the Landes district of France is partially covered with water. If they had to slosh through the bogs and shallow pools on foot, the Landesmen would never be able to keep up with their roaming flocks. To solve this problem, the Landes shepherds wear tall stilts. Each man also carries a long walking stick, which he uses to keep his balance on rough terrain. When he wants to rest, the shepherd uses this third pole as a seat, forming a high and steady tripod. If a Landesman has some spare time, he knits while seated atop his tripod—a rare sight indeed.

**Most Unusual Wet Nurses:** In many primitive societies, an unweaned baby whose mother has died is fed directly from the teats of cows or milk goats. And among some reindeer herding tribes, even adults commonly take nourishment directly from their does. Conversely, anthropologists have reported that in some African and South Seas cultures women think nothing at all of nursing orphaned baby animals right along with their own children.

Yet, in industrial societies, most people find something strange and unsettling about drinking anything but pasteurized cows' milk poured from bottles or cartons. For example, men and women lunching along the Bois de Boulogne in Paris used to marvel at and cheer the daily ritual of Monsieur Le Comte, the father of Toulouse-Lautrec. Each morning Le Comte rode a brood mare to his favorite cafe. There, he would invariably order a sherry, return to the hitching post, and milk his steed right into the glass.

This leads us to a delightfully Oedipal story about John D. Rockefeller: As he passed his ninetieth birthday, the withered millionaire was troubled by the absence of teeth and a shattered digestion. The only food that he could keep down was pure mother's milk. Reportedly, several wet nurses on his domestic staff were kept busy lactating his meals. (We searched in vain for a written version of this anecdote, but we offer it here on the authority of writer Gore Vidal, who recounted it on David Susskind's television show.)

# Fashion and Grooming

**Best Bath:** The Baths of Caracalla, in Rome, Italy, constructed during the reign of the Roman emperor Marcus Aurelius, were a mile in circumference. They offered hot and cold running water and a lot more: theaters, temples, a festival hall, and complete facilities for nearly 30,000 bathers.

While he could not compete with Marcus Aurelius, George Blumenthal of New York City owned the top of the line in the personal tub. He floated his rubber duck in a $50,000 bath carved from a single block of Italian marble.

**Worst Color:** It caused a sensation in the French court when the young Dauphin, son of Marie Antoinette, publicly displayed his ignorance of toilet training. The delightfully uninhibited boy inspired the fashion designers to create a whole line of clothes in a new color, *Caca Dauphin.*

**Worst Cufflinks:** In 1969 Dino Drops, Inc. introduced a matching cufflink and tie-pin set made out of petrified dinosaur dung.

**Worst Fashion:** English nankeen was quite the fashion in France during the abbreviated reign of Louis XVI. Because this fad was undercutting the market for French fabrics and unfavorably affecting the balance of trade, the monarch decided to take drastic action. He decreed that executioners wear only nankeen. Given this macabre endorsement, the nankeen fashion soon died.

In 1793, of course, Louis XVI went to the guillotine himself. Louis's death considerably unnerved Czar Paul I of Russia and

Lenin in vest

every other king and queen. Paul believed that the clothes make the man, and thus he attributed the French Revolution, in part, to recent radical innovations in men's clothing, particularly the popularity of the vest. To prevent any revolutionary nonsense in Russia, he ordered that any man caught wearing a vest should be executed. If you think Paul was a fool, take a look at this picture of Lenin.

**Worst Oppression of Females:** Until quite recently, a Bulgarian woman was permitted only one bath in her lifetime—on the day prior to her wedding. And in South Sclavonia, females could bathe only rarely during childhood and not at all as adults.

**Most Unusual Bald Pates:** Samuel Johnson mentions a theory current in the eighteenth century, "That the cause of baldness in men

is dryness of the brain, and its shrinking from the skull." Whatever
the cause, baldness has been throughout the ages the bane of men,
both great and small.

Suetonius records that Julius Caesar was extremely self-con-
scious about his receding hairline. When the most exotic massages
and hair tonics failed to produce new follicles, like so many others, he resorted to combing his hair forward to cover the bare
spots. Suetonius notes wryly that of all the honors conferred upon
him by the Senate, Caesar most treasured the laurel wreath because wearing it helped to disguise his baldness.

The chronicler Claudius Aelianus asserts that the death of the
Greek playwright Aeschylus was indirectly attributable to hair
loss. Forewarned by a soothsayer that he might die from the impact of a falling object, Aeschylus left the cities, with all their hazards, and retired to the countryside with its safe, wide-open fields.
Alas, his precautions were in vain. One afternoon as Aeschylus
was walking through a meadow, an eagle, carrying a tortoise in its
talons, spied the dramatist's bald pate and mistook it for a rock. Intending to crack open its dinner, the bird released the tortoise
from a height of one hundred feet; it struck Aeschylus squarely on
the skull, killing him instantly.

**Most Unusual Bathtub:** The *National Geographic* recently described a solid gold bathtub weighing 313½ pounds that is a popular feature in a Japanese hotel. The management charges two dollars a minute for a dip and hints that bathing in the tub ensures
long life.

Less regal but more imaginative was the "bag bath," which was
first invented by a Doctor Sanctorius of Padua (d. 1636), only to be
forgotten and reinvented several other times in lavatory history.
The bather crawled into a large leather (later, rubber) sack, took
off his clothes within, and had the top of the bag sealed around his
neck like a collar. Hot water was then poured in through a funnel
at the bather's shoulder; it washed over his body and down towards his feet where it drained out of a long spout. If the bather
preferred a leisurely soak, the spout could be plugged. And certain models had watertight arms and gloves, like oversized space-
suits, enabling one to read or write while enjoying the continuous
cleansing flow. But Dr. Sanctorius believed that the principal advantage of his bag bath was that it allowed the bather to receive
visitors in all modesty and decency.

Water is definitely the preferred fluid for bathing, but milk has
also enjoyed some popularity. In the Roman era, bathing in milk

was a rather common luxury, and Nero's wife, Poppeia, insisted on something a little better, she-asses' milk. More recently, Beau Brummell (1778–1840), the wealthy English fop, made a habit of bathing in ordinary cow's milk.

**Most Unusual Beads:** In some coastal areas of Italy, squid eyes are strung and used for necklaces and bracelets.

**Most Unusual Beard:** Banary Bhat, a farmer in South India, was dismayed over the commonly held belief that bee-keeping is dangerous, and ventured to prove otherwise. He found that by placing a queen bee on his cheek, he would soon attract a huge swarm of her followers and that they would cling beardlike to his face. According to an item in the *Asia Magazine,* a Sunday newspaper supplement that circulates throughout the Far East, Bhat's wife ran screaming from the house the first time she saw her husband in his beard. However, he eventually reassured her by showing that he could eat dinner, smoke, play cards, and do just about anything else, without bodily risk.

During Abraham Lincoln's campaign for the presidency, a dyed-in-the-wool Democrat named Valentine Tapley from Pike County, Missouri, swore that he would never shave again if Abe were elected. Tapley kept his word and his chin whiskers went unshorn from November 1860 until he died in 1910, attaining a length of twelve feet six inches. In his declining years Tapley developed an obsessive fear that someone might rob his grave to get at his remarkable beard, and in his will he was careful to set aside a large sum of money for a double-strength tomb.

For a while Frederic Chopin, the composer and pianist, wore a beard on only one side of his face. "It does not matter," he explained. "My audience sees only my right side."

Presumably Chopin would have been required to pay only one-half of the standard beard tax had he lived in eighteenth-century Russia. Czar Peter the Great aspired to Europeanize his nation in every conceivable way, and since beards were the exception in Europe, Peter wanted his own subjects to be clean-shaven. An ill-conceived attempt to outlaw chin whiskers nearly touched off an armed rebellion, so in 1705 the czar resorted to a more moderate strategy—taxation. Bearded men were required to pay the tax collector fifty rubles a year. Excepted were poor peasants who were permitted to wear their beards tax free in their own villages; but on entering or leaving a town, unshaven peasants had to remit one kopek.

**Most Unusual Cosmetic:** In the court of King Louis XV, many of the women took to wearing false eyebrows made of moleskin. And in Greenland a few centuries ago, wealthy women dyed their faces blue and yellow.

In 1969 Mr. Kenneth, one of America's foremost cosmetologists, brought out a line of creams, rouges, and special applicator brushes for bosom makeup.

**Most Unusual Earmuffs:** Work elephants near the Bangkok, Thailand, airport were constantly disturbed from their labors by sonic booms and other loud noises, so the considerate Thai government is supplying them with elephant ear protectors.

**Most Unusual Eye Makeup:** To continue in this scientific vein, researchers have found that men are more attracted to women with dilated pupils. This comes as a justification of the practice of women in Renaissance Italy who enlarged their pupils by applying drops of belladonna. (Note that belladonna means beautiful woman.)

**Most Unusual Fashion:** Marie Antoinette was the Jacqueline Kennedy of the eighteenth century. If the queen styled her wig in a particular fashion, all the ladies of the court were soon wearing their hair the same way. And when the First Lady of Louis XVI became pregnant, the best-dressed of Paris and Versailles wore cushions under their gowns in imitation. For nine months they inserted larger and larger cushions, to keep pace with Marie's expansion. Then suddenly, with the birth of the Dauphin, cushions became passé.

**Most Unusual Hair:** Because of the overdevelopment of his scalp muscles, a nineteenth-century Frenchman, Pierre Messie, was able to make his hair stand on end at will. For variety, Messie could even make one patch of his hair stand up while the rest lay flat.

**Most Unusual Haircut:** The Athenian orator Demosthenes had difficulty disciplining himself to tend to his studies instead of going out on the town. His solution was to shave one side of his head, leaving the hair long on the other; he looked so ridiculous that he was ashamed to be seen in public.

**Most Unusual Hair Dressing:** The Warraus of the Orinoco Delta in Venezuela pomade their hair with honey and shiny colorful fish scales.

**Most Unusual Hair Restorer:** Balding Peter Biggs of England reported in 1973 that he had gotten good results from horse manure rubbed into his head.

**Most Unusual Hat:** The three qualities one looks for in a hat are style, comfort, and durability. For generations New Guineans have been wearing a headdress that embodies all three virtues: a close-fitting turban made from spider webs.

**Most Unusual Jump Suit:** Rock singer-guitarist Dan Hartman does his performing these days garbed in a $5,000 silverized jump suit that is music's answer to pantyhose. It's called the Guitar Suit, simply enough, and it's made of Laurex, a stretchy synthetic. The guitar fits into a pelvic pouch fitted with electrodes that transmit the signal through wires sewn into the lining of the suit into a small but powerful transmitter in the thigh. To adjust tone and volume, the singer presses a button on his left sleeve.

"It's a dynamite way to perform," says Hartman of the suit, which he designed in collaboration with Los Angeles fashion stylist Bill Witten. "I can feel the vibrations in my body. I know what an expectant mother must feel like. I am the music."

**Most Unusual Mustache:** Elizabethan gentlemen perfumed and tinted their mustaches; the favored colors were bright red, orange and purple. Shakespeare pokes fun at this practice in several of his comedies: In *A Midsummer Night's Dream,* for instance, a character speaks derisively of "your straw colour beard," which presumably did not match the rest of the hair in view.

**Most Unusual Ornament:** Certain tribesmen of New Guinea deserve mention. They wear the tusks of wild boars inserted through gradually enlarged slits in their nostrils.

**Most Unusual Pearl:** The Pearl of Allah is neither round nor especially beautiful, but it has the virtue of weighing over fourteen pounds. Currently owned by Wilburn Cobb of California, its value is estimated at about $4 million. As any spectacular ornament should, the Pearl of Allah has a deadly curse connected with it:

The first diver who tried to harvest it had his hand trapped in the giant Tridacna clam which produced the gem and was held underwater until he drowned.

The Tridacna clam of the East Indian Ocean is itself a wonder. When mature, it measures up to four feet in diameter and weighs nearly six hundred pounds, shell included. The slippery animal living inside can grow as large as twenty pounds—enough to make 150 gallons of clam chowder.

**Most Unusual Perfume:** Scientists have established that certain perfumes have a real physiological effect on males. It is amazing, however, what people think smells good. For instance, Plutarch noted that Spartan ladies perfumed themselves with butter. The emperor Augustus, on the other hand, believed in mixing scents, applying mint to his arms, palm oil to his royal chest, and essence of ivy to his knees.

**Most Unusual Purse:** Who says you can't make a silk purse out of a sow's ear? Arthur D. Little, a pioneer in synthetics, took the old Shakespearean adage as a personal challenge. He boiled down hundreds of sows' ears into a milky fluid, and then, through an elaborate spinning and drying process, reduced the juice to a long, continuous strand of synthetic silk. A purse woven from this silk is on display in the Smithsonian Institute.

**Most Unusual Shaving Cream:** A Barry Goldwater nostrum: "If you don't mind smelling like a peanut for two or three days," says the Arizona Republican, "peanut butter is a darn good shaving cream."

**Most Unusual Tattoo:** Even though it is almost surely legend, the story of lightning prints is worth repeating simply because it is so bizarre. Various venerable and unreliable sources claim that when people are struck by lightning or are very near a place where lightning hits, through some process that is a cross between tattooing and photography they may be imprinted with images of nearby objects. The most believable story took place in 1830 at the Chateau Benatonière in Levandee, France. A young woman was seated in a chair with an ornately carved back when lightning struck the castle. She felt a painful burning and when she stood up, her host noticed that her dress and back had been imprinted with the design of the chair.

Most of the stories, however, are more like this: A man was

hanging up a horseshoe in the middle of a storm, when lightning hit the good luck charm. Through the mysterious process of lightning printing he received a horseshoe-shaped scar on his neck.

**Most Unusual Zipper:** In 1964 an intrepid inventor patented the "Forget-Me-Not." The device attaches to a little boy's zipper and causes an alarm bell to ring if his fly comes open.

# Places

Best (Safest) City in the United States: Lakewood, Ohio. And Lakewood is not only safe from crime but from fire as well, with an all but obsessively enforced municipal program for inspecting homes and businesses for fire-code violations.

David Franke, author of *America's 50 Safest Cities*, combed through the crime statistics of the 396 cities in the United States with populations over 50,000, fed them into a computer, and found this bedroom suburb of Cleveland to have the lowest crime rate of all. Lakewood is an old city, with a top-grade police force, excellent radium-arc street lighting, and a predominantly middle- to upper-middle-class population that evidently is comfortable living cheek-to-jowl with Cleveland, one of the nation's less endearing cities and hardly a paragon of urban tranquility itself.

On a smaller scale, Coal Township, Pennsylvania, (population 12,000) is even more halcyon. In 1973, according to statistics released by the F.B.I., Coal Township reported no murders, no rapes, and no cases of grand larceny. It was, in fact, the largest of only nine towns in the country with populations in excess of 10,000 to have no incidence of major crime.

Best City in the United States if for No Other Reason Than: The Chicago city council outlawed pay toilets in the Windy City by a 37–8 vote in 1974, a direct response, evidently, to the efforts of the Committee to End Pay Toilets in America. "You can have a fifty-dollar bill," the committee's nineteen-year-old president, Michael Gessel, told newsmen as he kicked off a national crusade against coin-operated commodes, "but if you don't have a dime, that small metal box is between you and relief."

**Best Country to Visit:**  New Zealand. Our authority is J. Hart Rosdail, of Elmhurst, Illinois, who is enshrined ungrammatically in
*The Guinness Book of World Records* as "the man who has probably visited more countries than anybody." More precisely, Rosdail
has set foot in all but five of the world's 225 countries, and New
Zealand, he says, offers the finest combination of scenic
wonders—including breathtaking mountain-and-fjord coastal
country—native hospitality, and general ambience. The cost of living is still reasonable there and the quality of living in major cities
like Wellington and Christchurch far outshines urban life throughout the United States and most of Europe. One discouraging note,
however: according to a study conducted by the New Zealand
Cancer Society, two out of three New Zealand children smoke cigarettes before they are seven years old.

**Best Museum in the World:**  If you have even the remotest interest in ancient civilizations, then it's London's British Museum
where you can spend a rainy afternoon or two trying to decipher
the Rosetta Stone.

The Stone, they say, is to the British Museum what the Spirit of
Saint Louis is to Washington, D.C.'s Smithsonian Institute—
unquestionably the greatest non-art museum in the world. (Clas-
sifying it more specifically than that would be impossible. Millions know it as "America's attic.") Running a close second in the
non-art category is Chicago's Museum of Science and Industry.

The world's best art museum—if we can exclude the British
Museum—is the Louvre, in Paris, which is not only the world's
largest museum but architecturally its most beautiful. The best art
museum in the United States is New York City's Metropolitan
Museum of Art, which has the best temporary exhibits anywhere
in the nation.

**Best Place to Hitchhike:**  It is probably easier—and more fun—to
hitchhike in Australia than it is anywhere else in the world, according to free-lance writer Jourdan Houston, writing in *Saturday
Review World*. Hitchhiking-related crimes are rare there, he says.
Cars with willing drivers are available, and hitchhiking is not only
commonplace but supported by the government. Tourist bureaus,
in fact, are only too happy to provide you, on request, with inside
tips for hitching in the outback, where you'll need all the help you
can get. (Towns in the outback are tiny for the most part and
spaced hundreds of miles apart, with nothing but sagebrush and
billabongs in between.)

Native hospitality also makes for easy, pleasant hitchhiking in Japan. Thumb a ride there and you may also find yourself invited to dinner and an overnight stay. In Poland, tourists and natives alike pay a registration fee to enroll in a government-administered hitchhiking plan. Thumb-riders are given a block of coupons which are used as "carfare" to be paid to drivers who pick them up. Drivers with the most coupons are eligible for prizes.

**Best Rest Spot in the World:** If it's absolute peace and quiet you're after, visit the territory staked out by the Mabaan tribe in the Sudan. Religious dogma among the Mabaans forbids noise of any kind, and the only sounds ever heard in Boing, their main town, are the patter of raindrops and the occasional lowing of a cow. Background noise, in fact, has been judged to be about one-tenth as loud as a refrigerator's hum. Incidentally, don't try whispering secrets in the area. The Mabaans, nurtured on years of silence, can pick up conversational tones at 100 yards, and your average seventy-five-year-old Mabaan hears as well as twenty-five-year-olds.

**Best Zoo in the United States:** For millions of wilderness-loving urbanites, New York, with its magnificent zoological gardens in the Bronx and Central Park, used to be known as Zoo City. (There are plenty of people who still call it that, but for different reasons.) Today, however, the best zoos in the United States are in San Diego, Chicago and St. Louis, Mo. The Saint Louis Zoo, the best of them all, has been redesigned in recent years to allow its animals to roam about with a greater degree of freedom in the closest duplication possible of their natural environment. (The Bronx Zoo, which does run a close second, has also done this.) The result is a unique and nontraditional experience for the zoo-going public.

---

**Worst Air of any United States City:** New York City and Chicago are probably the worst places in the United States to breathe, according to statistics issued by the Environmental Protection Agency. Automobile emissions, as well as fumes from fuel burning, incineration, manufacturing, and other sources give the air in both cities their characteristic bouquet.

As for water, Cleveland's Cuyahoga River is probably the *nation's foulest waterway.* At its dirtiest points the river is more than

50 percent acid and industrial wastes. It has even caught fire on several occasions.

**Worst City (United States):** Edward A. Hanna thinks that Utica, New York (population 91,000) is "A lousy place to live," and that its young people would do well to leave the place as soon as they can. Hanna should know: He's the mayor of Utica.

The spectacle of a mayor publicly holding his own town up to ridicule is a rare one, indeed, but then Utica's sorry economic state, its skyrocketing unemployment figures, its all-around urban decrepitude are singular. As Hanna sees it, it's the business interests, the banks, and what he calls "the chamber of no commerce" that have sucked the life-blood from the scraggly neck of this wheezing, underfed chicken of a metropolis. Because of the business establishment's efforts at keeping new business out of the city, Hanna said in a city hall press conference, "Progress is our least important product."

In July 1974, the banks, by turning down his repeated requests for a mortgage, throttled a builder's plans to put up a hotel on a lot that had been vacant and unused for fourteen years. For Hanna, it was the last straw. He responded by withdrawing all of the public funds—several million dollars—from the banks and storing it out of the city.

**Worst City (World):** Calcutta. Sir George Otto Trevelyan wrote in 1863: " . . find, if you can, a more uninviting spot than Calcutta. . . . The place is so bad by nature that human efforts could do little to make it worse; but that little has been done faithfully and assiduously." That judgment is still accurate today.

A creation of the British colonists, Calcutta is by nature plagued by sultry summers and stifling humidity. Mark Twain complained that the weather is "enough to make a brass doorknob mushy." Today, perhaps as many as 10,000,000 people are crowded into the metropolitan area; the population density is appalling—102,000 per square mile, as compared with 27,900 per square mile in New York City. Visitors are invariably shaken by the awful and inescapable beggary, and they find it difficult to reconcile it with the fact that Calcutta is the richest and most heavily industrialized city in India. Thousands sleep in the streets at night; 35,000–40,000 lepers live as outcasts within the general misery. Calcuttans live a nightmare spawned by colonialism and the Industrial Revolution. Yet Winston Churchill said he was glad to have seen it once, "so I will never have to see it again."

**Worst College Campus:** Imagine 1,400 well-scrubbed youngsters carrying biology textbooks and hymnals, scurrying in and out of the abandoned hulls of an old "World of Tomorrow" exhibit at Disneyland or the '64 New York World's Fair, and you'll have a fair picture of the plastic-and-aluminum wonderland that is Oral Roberts University, in Tulsa, Oklahoma. Tulsans like to tell tourists that "unless you've seen ORU, you haven't seen Tulsa," unaware, evidently, that not seeing Tulsa does have its benefits. Just the same, the $50-million campus is worth looking at if you are in the area, especially for the 200-foot-high "Prayer Tower," which looks like nothing so much as an upended vibrating dildo girdled with an inner tube. It may well be America's ugliest religious structure.

**Worst Country to Visit:** The Union of Soviet Socialist Republics, says Rosdail. It isn't that the country lacks for scenic wonders, cultural diversity, or native hospitality. It's just that "the Russian secret police, combined with the stifling governmental bureaucracy make it all but impossible for the traveler to move freely from place to place. Traveling in the Soviet Union," says Rosdail, "is more frustrating than it is anything else."

**Worst Crime Rate in the United States:** Compton, California, a suburb of Los Angeles. Its proximity to Los Angeles means, of course, that if the muggers don't get you, the smog will. Compton heads Franke's "most dangerous" list, followed by Newark, New Jersey, and then Detroit. Interestingly, neither New York, Saint Louis, Los Angeles itself, Chicago, nor Philadelphia appear among the top ten.

**Worst Family Entertainment:** Hong Kong's Tiger Balm Gardens. Tiger Balm itself is a godsend—a eucalyptus salve sold commercially throughout the Far East and used to treat everything from chigger bites to hangover. It's the closest thing we know of to an all-purpose drugcounter nostrum that works. But the Gardens are another story! Designed by Tiger Balm industrialist Aw Boon Haw, the Gardens are a concrete-and-plaster Disneyland of the Vulgar, consisting largely of loudly colored murals and friezes that depict graphically the sadistic torture and mutilation of the prisoners and enemies of mythical Chinese kings. One memorable series of relief-painted panels shows the poor wretches being disemboweled, dismembered, crushed by steamrollers, having their eyes plucked out by hot irons and their organs gnawed by beasts.

Wilbur Glenn Voliva

There's fun for the family to be had in your nearest nuclear bomb test area as well. Former Atomic Energy Commissioner James Schlesinger took his family to view the controversial Amchitka Island atomic bomb test in 1972 and told reporters, "My wife is delighted to get away and it's fun for the kids."

**Worst Geographer:** During the Apollo moon flight of Christmas 1968, Astronaut Frank Borman looked back on the old globular earth and wondered aloud whether their historic flight would influence the thinking of Samuel Shenton—the organizer of the International Flat Earth Society. It didn't. Nor would it have shaken Wilbur Glenn Voliva, the Christopher Columbus of flat earthology and the worst geographer of the twentieth century.

Voliva was a millionaire fundamentalist who for many years had complete ecclesiastical and secular control over the small theocratic community of Zion City, Illinois. Taking the Bible as his sole authority on all questions, Voliva was absolutely convinced that the earth is as flat as the proverbial pancake—circular, yes, but certainly not spherical. At the center of the pancake is the North

Pole and the edges are surrounded by a vast wall of ice, which we mistakenly call the South Pole. We can praise God that this ice wall exists, Voliva said, because it prevented Antarctic explorers like Sir James Ross from sailing right off the edge of the world. As for Magellan and others who claimed to have circumnavigated the globe, they merely sailed all the way around the outside edge of the disc; it was an extraordinary achievement, but it did not prove the earth was round.

Voliva also had fixed ideas about the firmament. The sun, he said, is only three thousand miles away and it moves in a continuous circle above the disc. The sky is exactly what it appears to be, a great blue-black vault to which the stars are fastened. And the moon, like the sun, spirals freely above us at a constant height.

Wilbur Glenn Voliva had confidence in the validity of his beliefs: "I can whip to smithereens any man in the world in a mental battle," he said. "I have never met any professor or student who knew as much on any subject as I do." Every year he ran an advertisement in the Chicago and Milwaukee papers offering $5,000 to anyone who could convince him that the world was not flat. No one ever could.

**Worst Museum:**  The Syphilis Museum in Liverpool, England. The museum has long since gone the way of the dodo, but when it was in business, fathers took their progeny there to gaze in horror at an endless display of the withered organs, diseased tissue, and shriveled corpses of men and women who had flirted with Sin and thus met the grisliest of ends. Douglas Day describes the museum in his 1973 biography of English novelist Malcolm Lowry who was taken on several rather traumatic visits there during his boyhood.

**Worst Park:**  To Western visitors one of the most peculiar aspects of Hinduism has always been cow worship. But orthodox Hindus hold *all* animal life in high esteem and there are sects devoted to the worship of snakes, monkeys—and rats. In the city of Bilaner, in Rajasthan, there is a temple consecrated to rat worship; thousands of the ravenous rodents gather there to be fed and pampered. On the main street in Calcutta, Hindus of similar persuasion maintain what is surely the most repellent public recreation facility in the world, rat park. As William Drummond, a reporter for the Los Angeles *Times*, describes it, "dozens of the fat brown creatures play and cavort in broad daylight while human pedestrians pass nonchalantly by." As a footnote: Rats and mice in India consume an estimated 2.4 million tons of grain a year.

**Worst Place to Hitchhike:** Hitching is illegal in Mexico and generally to be avoided. Violators are often summarily deported unless they can show that they've got sufficient funds to support themselves. In Afghanistan hitching is an exceptionally dangerous activity, as it is in Uganda, where several hitchers in recent years have reported being shot at.

In the United States thumb your rides with discretion, or not at all, in Maine and Nevada, where the talmudic proscriptions against hitchhiking are strictly enforced. This does not necessarily mean that violators are thrown in the slammer for a day or two. We know of a few people who, while trying to flag down a ride on a state highway in Nevada, were picked up by troopers, driven some distance (in air-conditioned comfort, of course) and dropped off in the middle of nowhere.

**Worst Taxi Drivers:** As a group, the rudest, most opinionated taxi drivers in the world are in New York City. Naturally exceptions exist, hundreds of them no doubt, but the major impression one forms after trafficking in New York's taxi system for any length of time is the greed and thickheadedness of its drivers. In 1974, one unknown driver charged an unsuspecting French tourist fifty-two dollars for the ride from Kennedy International Airport to midtown Manhattan, about five times over the going rate; another took a $168 fare from a Guatemalan family of three for a similar half-hour drive. Anomalies? Perhaps. Just as likely to happen outside New York? Hardly.

Similarly, taxi drivers in Bangkok, Thailand, can make getting there considerably less than half the fun. Most cabs in the Thai capital are equipped with meters that no doubt work, but it's a rare driver there who won't tell you that his meter is broken and then set a fixed price for the ride in advance. Go along with his offer and you'll most probably pay a higher fare than what you'd have to pay on the meter. As for reckless drivers, the world's worst are in Paris, France, and Taipei, Taiwan.

**Worst Tourist Attractions:** Visit the Indianapolis Speedway on an off-day, and for twenty-five cents you can ride around the two and one-half-mile track in a small touring bus operated by a driver who doubles as a tour guide with a penchant for the grotesque. "We're coming around the first half-mile bend," he says. "This is where Bill Vukovich slammed into the retaining wall in the 1973 Memorial Day race and died instantly. . . . There's the third turn. Eddie Sachs's car blew up here in 1966 and he died on the way to the hospital. . . . In 1972, a car crashed through the fence crippling the driver and incinerating several spectators in the first few rows." The tour takes about twelve minutes. Refreshments are available at a small souvenir stand near the departure point.

The Reversing Rapids in Saint John, New Brunswick, is another attraction that the tourist can pass up. We began seeing signs for the rapids as soon as we crossed over the Maine border into Canada. On arriving in Saint John (which prides itself as the Loyalist City—a haven for British sympathizers during the Revolutionary War), we made directly for the tourist office in the new city hall. There we received a complicated set of schedules and the advice that "to fully appreciate the Reversing Rapids, they must be seen at high, high slack, and low slack tides." Most spectacular of all, according to our advisor, was low slack, when the mighty Saint John River, the largest on the Eastern seaboard, suddenly ceases its swift white water plummet from the interior highlands to the Bay of Fundy. The reason: The treacherous tides of Fundy, ranging up to fifty feet in height, overpower the Saint John at that moment and send it rushing and spilling over itself back up toward the mountains. The Mic Mac Indians believed it was a miracle.

We were in luck. Low slack was only fifty minutes away. So we hurried to Reversing Rapids Park, where we joined about fifty other people from all over Canada and the United States. The Saint John itself wasn't as we'd pictured it. It was wide, and muddy brown, and rather tired looking. Across from the park, there was a large factory that was churning out great quantities of white, and rather polluted-looking foam, which drifted casually downstream. "Well," we thought, "isn't it a crime how they've ruined this great natural wonder! It's like the American side of Niagara Falls." Still, we had visions of the wild, clean tides of Fundy surging in—a tremendous wall of sea water driving the Saint John back toward its source—so we positioned ourselves as close as we dared to the river, fearful that the powerful waters might engulf us there.

Everyone checked his watch. It was 5:35. The foam wasn't sliding downstream quite so rapidly now. Then it was the appointed moment: 5:37 ADT. The foam and current came to an exceedingly gradual halt. Everyone looked seaward, expecting the deluge. Nothing. Then, imperceptibly at first, the white foam began moving again, regurgitating dully back toward the factory. After another few minutes someone in the crowd asked, "Is that it?" That was it.

If the recent war has not thrown the schedule off, a new hotel called Lot opened in the town of Sodom late in 1973. Israeli officials say the Lot is just one of several new hotels that have gone up in recent years due to the extraordinary tourist boom in Sodom. Incidently, the discovery of gas wells in the area has led some geologists to speculate that a natural gas explosion might have caused the destruction of the sinning cities. The effect of such massive combustion, they argue, would resemble the description in Genesis 19: "The Lord rained upon Sodom and upon Gomorrah brimstone and fire from the Lord out of heaven."

Another place that is attracting a lot of tourists these days is Alcatraz Island. The government recently opened the abandoned maximum security prison to visitors. There is now a regular ferry, and a number of ex-convicts have landed jobs as tour guides.

**Worst-zoned Neighborhood:**  For years the Carioto family of Pittsburgh has lived next door to a tombstone workshop, across the street from a cemetery, and just a few houses away from yet another tombstone workshop. But when an entrepreneur applied to the local zoning board for permission to put up a crematorium within smelling distance of the Cariotos' kitchen, the family begged the zoners for mercy.

"We've managed to adjust to living with graveyards and tombstone factories in our midst, but the prospect of a crematorium twenty-five feet from the kitchen window is too much to bear," Mr. Carioto told the zoning board. "It's already changed our lives."

Said Mrs. Carioto, "If someone says something like 'You burned the chicken,' I fall apart. The children's friends will say something like 'What did you do with this meal, cremate it?' and we push our plates away. I just can't take the jokes."

---

**Most Unusual City:**  With a population of 500,000, Brasilia is the largest "new" city in the world and certainly the strangest. Laid out in the shape of a swept-wing jet, Brazil's new capital rises above a stark and treeless plain. Chief architect Oscar Niemeyer pledged at the beginning of the staggeringly expensive project "Never to fall into the hitherto customary banal style of building." True to his promise, Niemeyer's concrete, glass, marble, and steel designs are unique and disturbingly surreal. The streets are the widest in the world; the central avenue, for instance, is 370 yards wide—five times the width of the Champs Elysées.

Poet Elizabeth Bishop, who has lived in Brazil for many years,

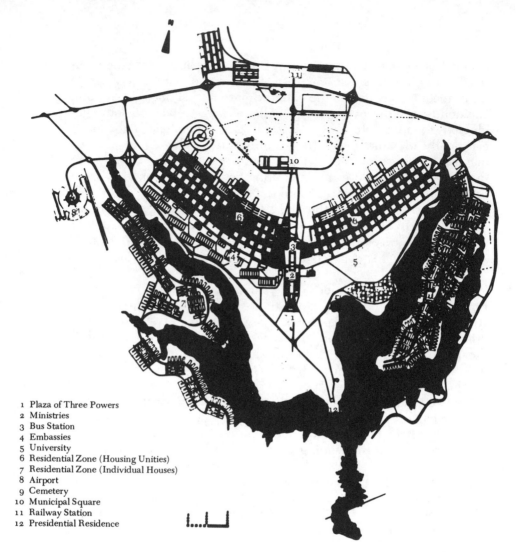

1 Plaza of Three Powers
2 Ministries
3 Bus Station
4 Embassies
5 University
6 Residential Zone (Housing Unities)
7 Residential Zone (Individual Houses)
8 Airport
9 Cemetery
10 Municipal Square
11 Railway Station
12 Presidential Residence

Plan for Brasilia, the federal capital of Brazil

believes the new capital is a stunning experiment and yet a failure: "Individual buildings are very beautiful . . . but there is
little feeling of scale; the buildings are lost in the surrounding
vastness, and even within the city limits the sensation of being on
another planet—as everyone puts it—is overwhelming." John Dos
Passos has called it "an inverted Pompeii," rising from the bleak
landscape in an eerie way that is reminiscent of the Roman resort
excavated from the lava flats.

Pakistan is also building a new capital from scratch. It remains
to be seen whether Islamabad will be what Brasilia was meant to
be, the world's best-designed, most comfortable, and most human
environment.

**Most Unusual Island:** Santorini, also known as Thera, is a small
island in the Aegean Sea not far from the coast of Greece. Actually
what was once a single island is now three small islands due to
the cataclysmic volcanic eruptions that periodically rearrange the
geography. The hills of Santorini were last shaken in 1866 when
an underwater volcano shot flames and brimstone up through the
ocean and thirty feet into the air.

But this rare and spectacular display must have been insignificant compared to the tremendous explosion that shattered the volcanic cone of Santorini in the fifteenth century B.C. The mammoth
tidal wave which resulted wiped out the flourishing coastal cities
of Crete, hundreds of miles away. Moreover, several archaeologists have speculated that the Minoan colony on Santorini, which
was heaved into the sea and covered with a thick layer of black
ash, may have inspired the myths about the lost city of Atlantis.

# Architecture

---

**Best Building in the United States:** The Chicago Civic Center. Not just another pretty place, the Chicago Civic Center made it with ease to *Fortune* magazine's 1966 list of the ten best buildings in the United States. Here is what architect Douglas Haskell has written about the 465,000-square-foot skyscraper, completed in the mid-1960s with public financing from an $87 million bond issue: "In Chicago the random viewer slowly begins to understand that the big new Civic Center . . . has a reason for looking so wonderfully light on its feet. There are just four full-height columns across that entire wide front, and the eight seven-foot spans of the horizontal trusses between them are Bunyanesque. But all is carried with casual grace and charm. Nobody standing outside would guess that there are several theatre-sized courtrooms on some upper floors inside . . ." Visually, the most striking feature of the building is the steel itself, which has begun to turn a "fiery red" as it rusts, and, says Haskell, will eventually turn to "a dark whiskey tone, flattered by adjoining windows of amber-colored glass."

**Best Hotel in the United States:** The Plaza, in New York City. When the Plaza opened its doors on a crisp fall day in 1907, hundreds of New Yorkers lined the streets to watch the hoopla and to see the Alfred Gwynne Vanderbilts arrive by limousine to check in as the hotel's first guests. It was billed then as "the world's greatest hotel" and its magnificence has never waned. The Plaza is best known for the efficiency of its staff, and *Esquire* Travel Editor Richard Joseph who, by his own count, has checked into well over 1,300 hotel rooms over the years, numbers the Plaza, along with the Mauna Kea Beach Hotel on Hawaii's Kona Coast, among the three greatest hotels in the world.

The Mauna Kea, incidentally, is Joseph's choice for best resort hotel in the world. Built in 1966 at a cost of $15 million, the hotel sits in the shadow of the 13,800-foot volcano after which it is named, comfortably isolated from the plasticized commercialism of Waikiki on what may well be the most beautiful stretch of beach in the entire island chain. Every one of the 154 guest rooms has its own *lanai* (porch), and is decorated with bedspreads and upholstery material handwoven under the direction of a Siamese princess. Says Joseph, "Walking through it is like strolling through an open-air museum and art gallery—past Hawaiian quilts hung as tapestries, bronze ceremonial drums and red-and-gold scroll boxes from Thailand . . . Japanese and Chinese scrolls and paintings, New Guinea carvings and masks, brass candelabra from Hindu temples, an antique wood and brass chest from Zanzibar . . . Buddhist figures from all over the Orient."

**Best Hotel in the World:** The Gritti, in Venice. Again, the considered opinion of Richard Joseph—and of Ernest Hemingway, journalist John Gunther, French mystery writer Georges Simenon, Somerset Maugham, and Elizabeth Taylor, all of whom have been regular guests at the Gritti. Built as a Doge's palace in the sixteenth century, it was converted into a hotel only recently—1948, in fact—but, as Joseph writes, "You'd be willing to swear that you read about Keats staying at the Gritti, or about something happening there to Henry James." With almost no staff turnover at all from year to year, even the one-time guest is remembered when he returns to the Gritti, and his preferences—for idiosyncratic drinks, for flowers in his room, for overdone steak smothered in tomato ketchup—are accommodated without his asking.

**Best (Most Beautiful) Structure in the World:** The Taj Mahal. When Arjumand Banu Begum, the wife of the seventeenth-century Mogul emperor Shah Johan, died in childbirth, the Shah knew that your standard garden variety funeral and burial plot simply wouldn't do. For twelve years, beginning in 1632, 20,000 laborers toiled at his behest to complete the Taj Mahal, and when the Shah himself died some sixteen years later, he was interred there as well in a separate casket next to his matchless wife. Located in Agra, India, about 110 miles south of New Delhi, this paragon of architectural symmetry is best viewed on a clear night with a full moon, although its magnificence remains undimmed even if you view it with a bad hangover in a heavy drizzle. Architect H. R. Nevill wrote that the Taj Mahal "is within more measurable distance of perfection than any other work of man." Even if you've never seen it—never been to India, in fact, or even east of Philadelphia—call it "the Taj." Your friends will be impressed.

There is a nameless but awesome beauty to Stonehenge, located on Salisbury Plain in England, that is as sobering as it is thrilling, and Chicago architect Laurence Ogden Booth calls this ancient monolith the world's most beautiful structure. It was built, most likely, by the Druids, probably around 3,600 years ago, and appears to have been a temple of sky worship, although no one knows for sure. The symmetry and perfection of the Taj are absent, of course, and so is the comforting feeling that you know what you're looking at. Stonehenge is at its best at sunset.

---

**Worst (Ugliest) Hotel:** An affront to any tourist's eye is the Marlborough-Blenheim Hotel, on the boardwalk at Atlantic City, New Jersey. Occupying five acres of choice real estate, its architecture borrows from the Spanish, Moorish, and Queen Ann styles. Or so they say. All the same, for the benefit of its guests the Marlborough-Blenheim makes up in creature comforts what it lacks in outward beauty, and is probably the only hotel in the world to offer hot and cold running salt water in each room.

**Worst House:** Mrs. Sarah Winchester was the superstitious heiress to the Winchester rifle fortune. In 1880 she consulted a medium who confirmed what she already suspected; her house was haunted. It's the restless souls of those murdered with Winchester rifles, the medium told her. The only way to ward them off was to build a house with endless rooms. If the house were ever completed, the medium warned, the angry ghosts would carry Mrs. Winchester off with them into the other world.

Mrs. Winchester took this advice quite seriously. For thirty-eight years she kept nearly fifty carpenters working full-time until her Victorian mansion in San Jose, California, sprawled to an incredible 160 rooms. Only a fear of the supernatural could explain the totally absurd construction. There are stairs leading nowhere; hallways come to a dead end; a window opens to a wall; a door leads to another blank wall; towers have been completely closed off so there is no entrance. To further confuse any intruding spirits, Mrs. Winchester planted a mammoth hedge that completely conceals the house from the road. But few of the carpenters or gardeners ever met the lady of the house. She walked

Marlborough-Blenheim hotel, Atlantic City, New Jersey

quietly around the grotesque structure in a long black veil, and only the butler, who served her meals on the $30,000 gold dinner set, ever saw her face.

You can now visit Winchester House. But we wouldn't advise it if you suffer from the willies.

**Worst Monument in the United States:** Squat and sinister, and designed with a mysterious dearth of windows, the Lyndon Baines Johnson Library, on the campus of the University of Texas in Austin, reminds one of a malevolent flat-headed fish resting on the ocean floor. The storage bin for some 31 million documents that Johnson collected during his thirty-two-year political career, it is not simply a memorial to a president, but a monument to anal retentiveness. As *Time* magazine architecture critic Robert Hughes says, "It may be that no politician has ever been so gripped by the indiscriminate urge to retain everything he produced, initialed, touched, or was sent." Stored in the library are still-classified documents on the Vietnam War. There is also a 1951 covering letter which Richard Nixon sent Johnson along with

Victor Emmanuel monument

a three-pound box of jumbo deluxe dried California figs, courtesy of the California Fig Institute.

**Worst Monument in the World:** The Victor Emmanuel Monument, in Rome. A competition was held throughout Italy in 1884 to determine who would have the honor of designing a monument to Victor Emmanuel II. The winner was the architect Count Giuseppe Sarconi, and construction began under his direction in 1885. Sarconi died, however, long before the monument could be completed, and so it bears the thumbprints of a half-dozen mediocre architects. The monument is huge and grotesque, suggestive of a retarded giant dressed up in Sunday finery. Architectural historian Henry-Russell Hitchcock calls it "the most pretentious of all nineteenth century monuments."

**Worst Office Building:** The world's worst office building was also, until recently, the tallest—the twin towers of New York City's World Trade Center, 110 stories of steel-and-concrete mediocrity on Manhattan's nether tip. Besides blighting the skyline and affronting the eye, the World Trade Center is also a wretched place to work. "When I approach the building, I just don't want to go in there," says one employee. Says another, "Sometimes I just walk out, intending to get out for an hour for lunch, and can't make myself come back."

The Center's horrors are many—inexplicably sealed mail chutes, hopelessly snarled telephone lines, centrally controlled office lighting that can be controlled after hours only by means of a written request submitted at least a day in advance—but the building's denizens reserve a special place in their spleens for the elevators. Plummeting downward so fast that their walls shake audibly, they break down frequently, spilling over with humanity during rush hours. "Sometimes I feel like a lemming—or a salmon swimming upstream," says a New York State employee who works in the building. "If I can't leave at 4:45 I wait until a quarter past five or I walk down stairs rather than be squeezed into the elevator." A woman whose office is on the eighty-second floor describes the noontime trip to the cafeteria: "I have to take a local elevator to the seventy-eighth floor, then an express to the first floor, then an express to the forty-fourth, then an escalator to the forty-third, where I get a lousy meal."

Many workers have complained of psychosomatic ailments that are directly traceable to the Center—one Manhattan physician has treated five such patients. Leonard Levin, a staff member of the New York Racing Board, whose office is in the Center, says, "There *is* one wonderful thing about the World Trade Center. It feels sooooooooo good when you get home at night!"

**Most Unusual Apartment Building:** The Spanish architect Antonin Gaudi designed Casa Milá in Barcelona, one of the most singular living spaces in the world. Albert B. Brown of S.U.N.Y. at Buffalo has paid tribute to it as one of Gaudi's "highly imaginative and dramatic experiments" that gain their effects through "bizarre form and ornament." There are very few straight lines in the entire building, and even the rooms themselves take on organic shapes rather than the traditional Western cube. The front of the building, far from being flat, is a series of gentle swells, suggesting waves. Overall the effect is one of curves and swirls, like a natural object formed by the wind or the sea. Casa Milá is universally recognized as one of the very finest examples of "art nouveau" architecture.

**Most Unusual Bridge:** Ever since it was erected in 1831, London Bridge had been sinking into the muddy bottom of the Thames at a rate of one-eighth-inch per year. Thus in 1967 Queen Elizabeth sadly announced that the venerable span designed by John Rennie would have to be torn down and replaced before it fell down once and for all, as promised in the children's song. The old bridge was put up for sale and the highest bidder was Robert McCulloch, an oil and chainsaw tycoon, who offered a cool $2,460,000 for the ten thousand tons of granite slabs.

Piece by piece, the famous structure was dismantled, numbered, and shipped by boat and truck to Lake Havasu City, Arizona. The total moving bill amounted to $5,600,000. McCulloch built an artificial island in Lake Havasu, and London Bridge was reassembled across the narrow channel between island and mainland. Appropriately McCulloch has named the channel the Little Thames.

The Lord Mayor of London joined 40,000 celebrants for the rededication in October 1971. To mark the event, skydivers dove, skywriters wrote, and balloons and doves were released while a recording of Big Ben tolled sonorously over the loudspeakers. In its first year among the palm trees, pubs, and fish-and-chips joints of Lake Havasu's three-acre English Village, London Bridge attracted over a million tourists.

**Most Unusual Campsite:** Wesley Hurley, President of Hi-Rise Campsites, Inc., believes that most weekend backpackers don't want to sacrifice the comforts of city living in order to go camping. Acting on that belief, Hurley's firm plans to build the world's first hi-rise campground, in downtown New Orleans.

The twenty-story building, to be constructed at a cost of $4 million, "will be unique," Hurley claims. "It is designed for today's different brand of camping. People don't want the woodsy bit now; they want to camp in comfort near the city." Campers will park their cars on the eight lower floors of the building and then take the elevator up to one of 240 individual campsites on the upper twelve stories, all of which will be equipped with electrical connections and carpeted with astroturf.

**Most Unusual Drawbridge:** One of the smallest achievements in civil engineering is Somerset Bridge at Ely's Harbor, Bermuda. It opens just wide enough to let a sailboat mast slip through.

"Le Manneken Pis"

**Most Unusual Fountain:** Brussels is the home of one of the world's most beloved fountains: Le Manneken-Pis. The innocent brass boy with the protruding belly has been passing water from his inexhaustible bladder into the pool below since 1619; the people of Brussels refer to him now as "our oldest citizen." Designed by sculptor François Duquesnoy, the little boy has received medals, swords, honors, and offers of clothing from three and a half centuries of distinguished visitors including Louis XV and Napoleon Bonaparte.

**Most Unusual Hotel in the World:** La Parra, located 49 feet below water off the coast of Spain near Malaga. Getting there is half the fun, since there are no boats or other craft that serve the hotel. Thus, guests must swim there, with their gear sealed in a watertight rucksack.

The Parra, which can accommodate twelve guests at a time, is the brainchild of underwater explorer Dr. Hans Hass and Austrian businessman Theodor Soucek. Its "rooms" are a complex of glass bubbles (a social area bubble, a kitchen bubble, a dormitory bubble, etc.) and accommodations are quite comfortable. At present the major attraction at La Parra is its nightly underwater concerts in which the audience lolls about on the floor of the sea while music is piped through speakers in the surrounding gardens. Says Hass, "The music comes from all sides and you can feel it all over your body. It's as if you're right in the middle of the orchestra."

For the mountain-climbing public, a hotel was opened for business in December 1970, 12,800 feet up the side of Mr. Everest in Nepal. You can fly to. your room directly from Katmandu Airport, or go it on foot, a twelve-day trek. The rooms all have views of the world's fifteen highest mountains and the beds are equipped with optional oxygen tents.

The most unusual hotel, architecturally, is shaped like an elephant drinking from a trough and called, reasonably enough, The Elephant House, located in Margate City, New Jersey. The building is 75 feet long and 85 feet tall and topped by a howdah which serves as an observation deck offering a splendid view of the Atlantic. It was designed by architect James V. Lafferty in 1883, who built another elephantine edifice that same year in Coney Island, New York. One hundred twenty-two feet tall, it was bigger than its New Jersey cousin, housing a cigar store in one foreleg, an elevator shaft in the other, and staircases in both hindlegs. Patrons could rent rooms in whatever part of the animal's anatomy they desired. The Coney Island hotel burned down in 1896.

**Most Unusual House:** In tropical Africa, several tribes hollow out the baobab tree and set up housekeeping inside. The trunk can reach a thickness of 30 feet, for tree house living that is both spacious and gracious.

The baobab has such a peculiar shape that an Arabian legend maintains that the devil must have pulled it up and replanted the tree with its branches underground and its roots in the air.

**Most Unusual Igloo:** A Toronto architect is manufacturing pre-fab igloos. Already he has sold a number of the structures, made of fiberboard and covered with frosty-looking polyurethane foam, to Eskimos in the vicinity of Hudson Bay.

**Most Unusual Mortar:** How often mortar is taken for granted! Truly memorable mortar was used in the construction of the Alexander Column in Leningrad. Erected in 1834 during the bitter Russian winter, workmen mixed the lime and sand with vodka instead of water to prevent the goo from freezing.

Baobab tree

The Koutoubia, a holy tower in Marrakech, Morocco, is nearly 800 years old, and a sweet scent still lingers around it. The sultan who built the Koutoubia ordered 960 bags of musk mixed with the mortar.

**Most Unusual Motel Chain:** There's free parking for guests and all major credit cards are accepted (including Heed-thy-Master Charge and BankAmericat) at American Pet Motels, Inc., a one-million-dollar nationwide motel chain enterprise based in Chicago. Dogs and cats sleep in brass beds in private rooms that are carpeted with wall-to-wall astroturf.

St. John's Animal Inn, in Cockeysville, Maryland, provides essentially the same accommodations to dogs and cats, but on a smaller scale. All rooms have piped-in music and hotel staff members are available around the clock to console homesick guests.

Going one step further, at Margaretsville, New York, dog-lover Ron de Strulle directs Campo Lindo, America's only summer camp for dogs. De Strulle offers his charges a well-balanced diet and a full program of summer-fun activities including counselor supervised treasure hunts for hidden dog biscuits and after-dark campfires, where the dogs sit around a fire all toasty-warm and the counselors strum their guitars and sing. Sometimes, the dogs join in.

One of the nicest things about Campo Lindo is that the dogs are allowed to do their own thing to a refreshingly large extent, at least where eating is concerned. One animal, for instance, has a passion for Fruit Loops and skimmed milk, another for barbecued chicken; both are catered to without question. There is also a legally blind Bedlington terrier who is accompanied everywhere by her own seeing-eye dog.

In deference to the inevitable anxiety that the dogs' owners will experience during the separation from their pets, de Strulle sees to it that "progress reports" on the animals, signed in ink with the animal's pawprint, are sent regularly. "It's like getting a postcard from your dog," he explains.

**Most Unusual Pyramid:** "Coin" Harvey was a self-taught economist and journalist who wrote a fuzzy-minded yet influential book entitled *Coin's Financial School.* Harvey was an advisor to William Jennings Bryan during each of his three campaigns for the presidency, and many of the theories set down in *Coin's Financial School* became part and parcel of the populist ideology. Yet it is not so much Harvey's economics as his ambitious plan to attain immortality that interests us here. For Coin Harvey dreamed of becoming the American Tutankhamen.

Egypt has magnificent pyramids, as does Mexico, but there are no noteworthy pyramids in the Ozarks, and Coin Harvey set out to remedy that oversight. The Harvey Pyramid was to be less ostentatious than Cheops; the blueprints called for a 60-foot square base, with the apex rising 130 feet into the air. The architects decided to use concrete rather than limestone blocks in the construction and the tip was to be crowned with stainless steel. Harvey selected an isolated valley near Monte Ne, Arkansas, as the site. He anticipated that over the centuries the valley would fill with soil eroded down from the surrounding mountainsides, covering and preserving the pyramid. Thousands of years hence, archaeologists would rediscover the Harvey Pyramid and open it to find the treasures and memorabilia of our age—including, of course, a copy of *Coin's Financial School.*

At first the fund-raising went very well, and soon there was enough money to sink a shaft into the bedrock and begin a foundation. Then, tragically, the depression hit and the flow of contributions dried up. As a last hope, a crowd of supporters gathered at the Monte Ne excavation site in 1931 to nominate "Old Coin," the people's economist, for the presidency. If Harvey had been elected could he have gotten the economy back on its feet? That remains one of history's big "ifs." In his last hurrah, Coin Harvey received 800 votes to Franklin Delano Roosevelt's 22,829,501.

# *The Unexpected*

**Best News for Bartenders:** The California Board of Equalization once ruled that bartenders cannot be held culpable for misjudging the age of midgets.

A boon to bartenders of an earlier age was the ancient Greek law which made it a crime *not* to get drunk during the annual festival of Dionysus. Sobriety was considered an affront to the god.

**Worst Kiss:** In Pontoise, France, recently, a girl was attacked on the street by a masher who tried to kiss her. In self-defense she bit off his tongue.

**Worst Luck:** Caesar Beltram of Lyons, France, was struck by lightning five times. He died of pneumonia.

**Worst Noise:** When the volcano on Krakatoa Island erupted, the sound of the tremendous explosion was heard on Rodriguez Island in the Pacific 3,000 miles away.

**Most Unusual Augury:** When Julia, the daughter of Caesar Augustus, was curious about the sex of her unborn child she consulted a trustworthy oracle. The wise man advised her to carry a fertile chicken egg between her breasts. After twenty-one days she hatched a healthy rooster. And sure enough, Julia presented Augustus with a grandson.

**Most Unusual Disappearance:** Out of many candidates, probably the most romantic of all unsolved disappearances is the story of the Roanoke Island Colony off the coast of North Carolina. Roanoke was the birthplace of the first child of English parentage in the New World, Virginia Dare (born August 18, 1587).

After the initial exploration of the island, most of the settlers returned to England for the winter, leaving only fifteen men to maintain the settlement. When a subsequent party arrived, the fifteen had disappeared.

A new colony of 100 settlers was established before the ship again returned to England. The next visitors to Roanoke found that all the members of the colony had vanished. There were no signs of violence and no graves or bodies to suggest illness. In fact, all they found was the word "Croatoan" carved on one tree and "Cro" carved on another. An extensive search turned up nothing.

While there have been many legends—the existence of a blue-eyed tribe of Indians in the vicinity, and so on—no satisfactory explanation has ever been brought forward.

**Most Unusual Escape:** A modern Jonah: In February of 1891 James Bartley, a British harpooner for the whaling ship *The Star of the East*, fell overboard near the Falkland Islands and was swallowed by a wounded sperm whale. Several hours later the whale was captured. While it was being rendered, Bartley was discovered in the gigantic stomach, still alive. After a three-week bout with insanity, Bartley recovered and told about his incredible adventure. (It was easy to breathe, he said, but the heat and the humidity were terrible.) Bartley suffered no lasting injury, although his hair and skin were permanently bleached white.

# ANSWERS TO WORLD'S HARDEST CROSSWORD PUZZLE

| | | S | C | H | W | A | | S | E | L | I | M | | Q | U | I | T | E | |
|---|---|---|---|---|---|---|---|---|---|---|---|---|---|---|---|---|---|---|---|
| | C | H | I | R | R | S | | A | D | A | L | E | | U | L | R | I | C | A |
| | C | H | A | M | O | I | S | | B | U | T | Y | L | | A | L | O | N | G | O | F |
| C | H | I | | A | L | T | A | I | | C | H | A | T | O | Y | A | N | T | | R | E | F |
| H | I | L | L | | F | O | G | A | R | T | Y | | N | A | G | Y | | K | A | N | E |
| I | T | I | O | N | | F | A | I | T | | B | E | I | G | E | | B | A | N | N | S |
| L | O | A | V | E | S | | I | N | E | S | S | E | N | C | E | | P | A | R | G | E | T |
| I | N | D | E | N | T | S | | T | S | Q | U | A | R | E | | C | H | A | L | I | C | E |
| | | M | E | A | T | H | | U | P | T | O | | C | H | O | L | I |
| D | R | A | Y | | F | E | A | R | | A | R | A | B | | H | E | R | I | | F | F | F |
| H | U | N | D | | F | A | Z | E | N | D | A | | I | R | I | S | | S | H | O | J | I |
| O | N | T | O | P | | M | I | S | O | C | A | P | N | I | S | T | | M | E | L | O | N |
| T | I | O | G | A | | B | E | H | N | | E | L | G | R | E | C | O | | B | I | R | D |
| I | N | N | | I | C | O | S | | E | Y | R | A | | E | L | O | N | | R | O | D | S |
| | | U | N | H | A | T | | S | E | I | S | | S | L | A | V | I |
| K | I | N | G | T | U | T | | R | U | N | A | M | O | K | | D | I | E | D | O | W | N |
| A | M | O | R | E | T | | M | U | C | I | L | A | G | E | S | | R | E | E | C | H | O |
| K | A | F | I | R | | H | I | G | H | S | | G | L | U | T | | P | A | T | I | N |
| A | B | A | C | | D | O | N | G | | M | A | I | S | N | O | N | | N | O | R | N |
| S | U | I | | S | A | M | O | Y | E | D | E | S | | O | S | T | E | O | | B | R | Y |
| | M | T | E | I | G | E | R | | W | I | L | C | O | | P | H | I | L | T | R | A |
| | | H | E | R | O | I | C | | I | N | F | O | R | | O | E | N | O | N | E |
| | | S | E | N | N | A | | G | O | I | N | G | | T | E | S | T | S |

# PART II

# Acknowledgments

Special thanks to Sheila LaLima, Judith Felton, Barbara Dziorney, Ed Levy, Jody Sheff, Donna Gould, Mary Greene, Edward Kagen, Jessica Kaplan, Richard Mittenthal, and Buddy Skydell in the writing of this book.

# Contents

# Introduction

―――――――――――――――――――――

> *"Please,   sir,   I   want   some more."*
>
> —OLIVER TWIST

When music critic Paul Hume of the Washington *Post* panned a recital given by Margaret Truman, he incurred the wrath of an influential and protective father. "I have just read your lousy review," Harry Truman wrote him. "You sound like a frustrated old man who never made a success, an eight-ulcer man on a four-ulcer job, and all four ulcers working. I have never met you, but if I do you'll need a new nose and plenty of beefsteak and perhaps a supporter below."

What did Paul Hume do in the face of this unprecedented Presidential scorn? He continued writing perceptive and incisive criticism.

The original *Felton & Fowler's Best, Worst and Most Unusual,* to which this volume is a companion piece, did not evoke an Executive censure or threats of bodily injury. But a few critics and readers, including at least one state representative, have challenged some of our selections, in print or in person, and raised some compelling questions about our taste, our intelligence, and our sanity. Faced with such challenges, we stand firm on our judgments—as firm as Gibraltar, as firm as Paul Hume, and eager to sail forth over new waters.

The fact is once you've trafficked in the business of assigning best, worst, and most unusual honors to all that is classifiable in this world, as we did in our first book, it's just not that easy to quit. Dwight Eisenhower's five-star sleepwear (*Best Pajamas*), "The Battle Hymn of Lieutenant Calley" (*Worst Record*), Adolf Hitler's halitosis (*Most Unusual*

*Cause of World War II*)—these are the stuff of endless pleasures and sinful delights. The sheer demonic *addictiveness* of bests, worsts, and oddests is one reason we chose to write a second volume.

Not that *More Best, Worst and Most Unusual* is merely more of the same, like the reheated remnants of last night's veal roast, or a second helping of clams casino. We're not concerned here with repeating or even updating any of the material that appeared in volume I.

Nonetheless, the overwhelming question remains: Is this book really necessary? Surely, nothing in this world is more accountable for its existence than a sequel. Does this book justify the massive expenditure of wood pulp, ink, and binder's glue that went into its making? Does it offer anything genuinely new to a jaded public?

We think so. In volume I we made much of our reliance on the views of experts and opinion leaders in the various fields. We quoted Stravinsky on the worst composer (Max Reger) and Pauline Kael on the best movie (*Citizen Kane*). With *More Best, Worst,* however, we have dispensed, to a large extent, with the opinions of others, trusting more readily our own instincts. In fact, as you leaf through the twenty-one chapters, it will soon become apparent that we don't presume to hand down aesthetic pronouncements or break new critical ground. Our intent, rather, is to raise a few eyebrows and to perpetrate the occasional outrage. As in this volume's progenitor, we've relied, in all cases, on published nonfiction accounts purporting to tell the unexaggerated truth.

Jacques Vaché, the immoderate Dadaist, once clambered onto the stage of a Paris theater, and brandishing a loaded pistol, threatened to shoot anyone who applauded a play he disliked. We are more tolerant. We hardly expect you to agree with all of our selections; we don't always agree with each other. But hopefully these mini-entries will serve to acquaint you with some of the personalities, events, achievements and fiascoes that struck us as curious.

# Fine Arts

**Best Painting Technique:** In his eighties and partially bedridden, Henri Matisse continued to sketch portraits from a reclining position, employing a four-foot-long stick with a brush or piece of charcoal attached to the end.

Less well known to Western museum-goers is Huang Erh-nan, a distinguished Chinese artist of the 1920s. Huang's technique was to fill his mouth with black ink and paint delicate strokes on fine silk paper with his tongue. His favorite subjects were butterflies and lotus flowers.

**Best Sculpture:** Qualitatively, it remains to be seen whether Korczak Ziolkowski's nude sculpture of Chief Crazy Horse will surpass *Winged Victory*, the *Venus de Milo*, or Rodin's *Gates of Hell*. But quantitatively, Ziolkowski's work promises to dwarf Mount Rushmore.

About thirty years ago, the ambitious sculptor picked out Thunderbird Mountain in South Dakota as a suitable piece of granite to carve, and after some complicated dealings with the federal government he managed to buy the site. Working with only a jeep, a jackhammer, and a crowbar, he began roughing out the contours of his masterpiece. Then, about ten years ago, Ziolkowski raised enough money to purchase a bulldozer with a fifteen-foot blade that has considerably facilitated work on the sculpture.

Thus far, visitors have to use their imagination to see the enormous profile of a mounted Indian chief facing westward across the Black Hills, but when the sculpture is completed it will be hard to miss. The monument will measure 641 feet in length and 563 feet from top to bottom. A house could fit in the horse's left nostril and four thousand men could stand on the chief's arm. Tourists are already beginning to flock in for a sneak preview, and Ziolkowski is ready for them. He has constructed a one thousand-car parking lot alongside his home, plus a few conveniences like a post office, a museum, hot dog and souvenir stands, and an observation terrace where a twenty-foot, sixteen-ton model of the Crazy Horse monument is on display. There is an admission charge of three dollars per car, which goes to the nonprofit Crazy Horse Foundation.

If work continues at its present rate, the sculptor should be putting the finishing touches on the Chief in about twenty years.

---

**Worst Aesthetic School:** William L. Shirer in *The Rise and Fall of the Third Reich* describes the formal opening of Munich's "House of German Art," in 1937: "In this first exhibition of Nazi art were crammed some nine hundred works, selected from fifteen thousand submitted, of the worst junk this writer has ever seen in any country. Hitler himself made the final selection." And he did it with great gusto. At one point "he became so incensed at some of the paintings accepted by the Nazi jury presided over by Adolph Ziegler . . . that he had not only ordered them thrown out but had kicked holes with his jack boot through several of them. 'I was always determined,' he said in a long speech inaugurating the exhibition, 'if fate ever gave us the power, not to discuss these matters but to make decisions.' "

Ordinarily, Hitler and Adolph Ziegler saw eye to eye on matters of taste. A fourth-rate technician specializing in sexually obsessed paintings of icy "Aryan" women, Ziegler once did a nude portrait of Geli Raubal, Hitler's onetime girlfriend. The Führer was ecstatic and hung it over his desk in the chancellery office in Berlin.

The favorite subject of Nazi artists, however, was the artists' favorite Nazi. Fritz Erler painted a portrait of Hitler in 1939 which, in the words of critic Harold Rosenberg, made him look like "an apocalyptic chauffeur—someplace between Valhalla and Munich." Herman O. Hoyer went one step further in his adoration and entitled his canvas of Hitler addressing a Nazi rally, "In the Beginning was the Word." And the decadence was not confined to Germany. In 1940 Ferruccio Vecchi executed a sculpture of Mussolini standing on top of himself; *Il Duce*, nude, with sword upraised, is mounted on an enormous bust of his own head.

**Worst Painting:** The most famous work of the Greek painter Zeuxis, a picture of Helen of Troy, was hailed as a masterpiece by his contemporaries. Less successful was his last painting, a portrait of an elderly woman. According to the chronicler Festus, when the portrait was completed in 397 B.C., Zeuxis found the brushwork so abominably bad that he began chuckling uncontrollably and in a matter of minutes laughed himself to death.

---

**Most Unusual Art Collection:** The Hans Prinzhorn collection in the Heidelberg psychiatric hospital is comprised of five thousand paintings, drawings, and sculptures by over four hundred fifty professional and amateur artists—all certifiably mad.

A certain amount of insanity is tolerated and even demanded from artists, but there are limits. At the age of twenty-six, Richard Dadd, a noted nineteenth-century English artist as well as a homicidal maniac, killed his father and fled to the Continent intending to assassinate the emperor of Austria. He was arrested, brought back to London, and committed to Bedlam Hospital where he was encouraged to continue with his painting. In Dadd's case, the onset of insanity was accompanied by a strange and marvelous improvement in his work. His *Oberon and Titania* is one of the greatest, albeit weirdest, paintings of the Victorian era.

**Most Unusual Conceptual Art:** Here is an update on recent triumphs of this school:

Walter De Maria, a forty-year-old Californian, filled three rooms of a Munich gallery with three feet of dirt . . . Iain Baxter urinated in a field just the other side of the Arctic Circle in the name of art.

Conceptualist Rafael Ferrer dragged hundreds of pounds of ice onto the loading ramp of New York's Whitney Museum and let it melt.

Dennis Oppenheim persuaded a farmer in Whitewater, Wisconsin, to lend him 1,200 bales of hay and several wagonloads of corn. With the help of twenty-five art students from Wisconsin State, Oppenheim piled the hay in an intricate geometric maze, dumped the corn in the center, and drove a herd of cattle up to the perimeter of the construction. This avant-garde sculpture, aptly entitled "Hay Maze," lasted only until the Holsteins reached the corn.

**Most Unusual Form of Body Painting:** Body painting has long been an important ritual among the peasants of Iraq, but the bodies painted are those of farm animals, not the peasants themselves. Each spring, as the cycle of nature begins anew, the farmers pull out their brushes and poster paints to appease the gods and fend off hostile spirits by painting their animals in a variety of color schemes dictated by ancient tradition: green for newly hatched chicks, magenta for the faces of calves. The udders of full-grown cows are redone in red, the teats in green. Most colorful of all are cattle bred for meat: since their fertility and reproductive prowess must be jealously protected, only their genitals are painted, and those a brilliant blue.

**Most Unusual Fountain:** In our previous volume, we singled out "Le Manneken Pis" in Brussels as the world's most unusual fountain. We might also have mentioned the grotesque mask at the Villa D'Este in Tivoli, Italy, that spews a continuous torrent of water from its nostrils or the female sphinx, also in the Villa D'Este, that squirts a fine liquid jet from each nipple. But now we have found a still more remarkable though evanescent fountain: artist Bruce Nauman himself. The only shortcoming of his "Portrait of the Artist as a Fountain" is that it doesn't accommodate wishing pennies.

**Most Unusual Gallery:** A controversial new art gallery was established by Terry Fugate, of Kalamazoo, Michigan. Posters went up all over New York City advertising the grand opening of the Jean Freeman Gallery located at 26 West 57th Street in Manhattan. Announcements appeared in modish art magazines that Justine Dane would be showing her work. Wine and cheese would be served.

Art aficionados who showed up for the gala event were disappointed to discover that neither the gallery nor the artist nor the West 57th Street address existed. *The New York Times* called it a "non-gallery of no-art," but Mr. Fugate preferred to think of his hoax as an authentic work of conceptual art.

Perhaps it was. As critic Jack Burnham once observed in *Artforum,* "The ultimate medium of conceptual art" would seem to be "mental telepathy."

**Most Unusual Mural:** The Rockefeller family selected the Mexican artist Diego Rivera to paint the enormous mural which was to dominate the main lobby in Rockefeller Center. As the magnificent work neared completion in 1938, someone noticed a familiar bearded face in the foreground of a group of workers. Yes, Rivera acknowledged, that was Lenin leading the proletarian masses to victory, and that deformed little syphilitic girl in the corner symbolized "life under capitalism." Although over $21,500 had already been invested in the mural, young Nelson Rockefeller, who was in charge of interior decorating, ordered that it be chipped away, piece by piece.

"Portrait of the Artist as a Fountain"

**Most Unusual Still Life:** Paul Cézanne was an exceptionally slow and meticulous worker at the easel—so slow, in fact, that when he set out to paint a bowl of apples and oranges, the fruit would often rot before the canvas was completed. As a result, Cézanne used wax fruit as models for many of his still lifes.

# Literature and Language

**Best Book:** W. H. Auden once said that if he were marooned on a desert island and could have only one book to read over and over, he would choose the *Oxford English Dictionary* since it contains the components of all the great books in the language.

The question, "What in your opinion is the best book you have ever read?" often evokes clichés, but can also elicit some very revealing replies. In 1890 an enterprising publisher presented a long list of highly respected books to the leading cultural figures of his day and asked them to select the ones that meant the most to them. The results were published in a pamphlet entitled "The Best Hundred Books." Carlyle picked Homer, Plato, Hume, and Adam Smith in that order. Swinburne recommended Shakespeare, Aeschylus, the Bible, Homer, and Sophocles, while William Morris opted for the Hebrew Bible, Homer, and Hesiod. John Ruskin wrote back, "The idea that any well-conducted mortal life could find leisure enough to read a hundred books should have kept me wholly silent on the matter," but after some additional prodding, he put Edward Lear, the great limerick writer and nonsense poet, at the top of his list. Oscar Wilde was also reluctant to choose one hundred "best books." "I fear it would be impossible," he said, "because I have written only five."

The Bible, Shakespeare, and Homer were the overwhelming favorites of men of letters during the nineteenth century, and the honor roll would remain essentially unchanged today. A few modern works that might turn up near the head of our own "Top One Hundred" include the novels of Tolstoy and Dickens and Freud's *General Introduction to Psychoanalysis*.

**Best Hack Writer:** Don't ask us how—or why—he did it, but Indian mystic Sri Chinmoy set some sort of record in 1975 by composing 843 poems in twenty-four hours. That same year he also made headlines in the art world—that's "art" with a decidedly lowercase "a," mind you—by turning out 16,031 paintings in a single day. Chinmoy, who has authored over 260 spiritual books, attributes his enormous creative energy to meditation and an ascetic life.

**Best Language:** One way of arriving at a selection in this category is to apply a modified version of the ontological argument. Since God, by definition, is perfect in every respect, it follows that He should speak in the perfect language. Admittedly, the Deity has been known to say a few words in every language, with a flawless accent, but for many centuries theologians have debated what tongue comes most naturally to Him.

If you guessed Hebrew, you are wrong. According to Andrew Kempe, a leading Christian scholar of the seventeenth century, God first spoke to Adam and Eve in Swedish; Adam replied in Dutch; and the Serpent tempted Eve in French—but of course! An ancient Iranian legend agrees that three languages were spoken in the Garden of Eden but offers a different opinion on which ones. Adam and Eve conversed in Persian, the most poetic language; the Serpent seduced Eve in Arabic, the most persuasive language; and the angel Gabriel told the fallen couple to clear out in Turkish, the most menacing language.

Ezra Pound was ignorant of Persian, but of the dozen written languages he knew he singled out Chinese as the most poetic, due in part to its ideographic rather than alphabetical characters. The most melodious languages, said Pound, are ancient Greek and Provencal.

Hebrew is the purest language, morally speaking, and modern-day Israelis constantly have to borrow swearwords from Arabic to express otherwise ineffable emotions. It has been said that Gaelic is the best language for approaching God because it has no single word expressing a simple, straightforward "no."

English, contrary to what schoolteachers used to say, is one of the easiest languages to learn because it is uninflected and avoids the whole issue of gender. Mark Twain observed that "a gifted person ought to learn English in thirty hours, French in thirty days, and German . . ." well, German "ought to be gently and reverently set aside among the dead languages, for only the dead have time to learn it." But Charles V may have outlined the definitive hierarchy of languages when he declared, "I speak Spanish to God, Italian to ladies, French to men, German to soldiers, English to geese, Hungarian to horses, and Bohemian to the Devil."

Big Bill Thompson, the Anglophobe mayor of Chicago, had a similarly low opinion of English. At his urging, the Illinois State Legislature passed a bill in 1935 declaring, "The official language of the State of Illinois shall be known hereafter as the American language." Speaking English was expressly forbidden (*Illinois Revised Statutes* [1935], Chapter 127, Paragraph 177.)

**Best Poem (American):** Out of the chorus of great American poets— Dickinson, Eliot, Robinson, Frost, Stevens, Pound, Lowell, and Roethke, to name a few—only two have achieved undisputed literary immortality: Edgar Allan Poe, who sired the French symbolist movement, and gray-bearded Walt Whitman, the most exuberant and original voice of his generation. Whitman's "I Saw in Louisiana a Live-Oak Growing," "The Dalliance of Eagles," and "I Sing the Body Electric" are among the most brilliant lyrics in the language, and his "Song of Myself," with its panoramic vision, its "untamed and untranslatable" diction, and its sweeping Biblical prosody, is the best poem written in the New World:

> I celebrate myself, and sing myself,
> And what I assume you shall assume,
> For every atom belonging to me as good belongs to you.
>
> I loafe and invite my soul,
> I lean and loafe at my ease observing a spear of summer grass.
>
> My tongue, every atom of my blood, form'd from this soil, this air,
> Born here of parents born here from parents the same, and their parents the same,
> I, now thirty-seven years old in perfect health begin,
> Hoping to cease not till death.
>
> Creeds and schools in abeyance,
> Retiring back a while sufficed at what they are, but never forgotten,
> I harbor for good or bad, I permit to speak at every hazard,
> Nature without check with original energy.

There are dissenting opinions. The distinguished president of a major university published an anthology of his favorite poems, omitting Whitman altogether; instead, Columbia's Dwight Eisenhower chose Oliver Wendell Holmes's "Old Ironsides," Samuel Woodworth's "The Old Oaken Bucket," and the plaintive English pastoral "Little Boy Blue."

**Best Poet:** T. S. Eliot once said, "Shakespeare and Dante divide the world, there is no third." We feel, however, that Goethe and Homer also deserve consideration in any discussion of poetic perfection. A recent computerized study revealed that of all Western writers Goethe and Shakespeare possessed the largest vocabularies and the most extensive command of words. And when mad, mellifluous Ezra Pound was asked if there was a single poet from whom one can learn as much about poetry as one learns about music from Bach, Pound replied no, but added that Homer is the poetic figure most nearly comparable in stature to Bach. And if pressed to name the best of the best, *we* would choose blind Homer.

It is instructive to note that Rod McKuen has netted more royalties from his sentimental verse than Eliot, Pound, Frost, and Yeats earned together in their entire literary careers. But it does not follow that profitable poetry must be wretched poetry. The highest-paid and most prolific poet of all time was Abul Qāsim Mansur, who wrote under the pen name Firdausī. He was the author of the *Shah-nama* or *Book of Shahs,* the most influential of Persian poems, a work that has been called "the bulwark of the Persian soul."

Firdausī presented the first cantos of the *Shah-nama* to Sultan Mahmud in the year A.D. 999. Mahmud, incidentally, may have been poetry's greatest patron; the chroniclers assure us that he had "four hundred poets in constant attendance." And the sultan liked Firdausī's rhymes best of all; he gave the poet plush quarters in the palace and reams of ancient documents to incorporate into the epic, which was to be a complete history of the Persian kings from 700 B.C. to A.D. 700. For each couplet of the finished poem, the sultan promised Firdausī one gold dinar (worth approximately $4.70).

In the year 1010, Firdausī delivered his beautiful but interminable song of 60,000 couplets—the longest poetic work ever composed by a single individual. The price tag: a bargain at $282,000. But Mahmud's philistine advisers claimed the fee was exorbitant, and persuaded the sultan to send Firdausī a mere 60,000 silver dirhems ($30,000) instead. In a supreme gesture of artistic scorn, the poet divided the fee, giving half to his bath attendant and half to a sherbet salesman. Following this insult to the sultan, Firdausī was forced to flee the royal court. He took refuge in a bookseller's loft and later found a new patron, Prince Shariyar of Tabaristan.

Ten years afterwards, Sultan Mahmud was particularly struck by the beauty of a couplet quoted by a visiting troubadour. He asked the author's name. "Firdausī," was the reply. Mahmud was moved and repented his miserliness. He immediately sent a camel caravan laden with 60,000 gold dinars' worth of indigo to Firdausī along with a letter of apology. (As Will Durant comments, "If we may believe these figures, and our equivalents, poetry was one of the most lucrative professions of medieval Persia.") Ironically, the caravan arrived in the village of Tus just as a funeral procession bearing Firdausī's body to the grave was passing through the streets.

**Best Reader:** It took twenty moving men three days to haul away all the books found in Joseph Feldman's four-room apartment. Over 15,000 volumes, or roughly seven truckloads, were piled from floor to ceiling, stacked on the stove, and overflowing the sinks and bathtub.

This extraordinary library, worthy of a small university, was accidentally discovered when firemen entered Feldman's home on an inspection tour after putting out a blaze on a lower floor of the Greenwich Village building. They entered through a two-foot-wide path between the mountains of books; otherwise every available space was crammed with tomes on art and philosophy, contemporary novels, histories, biographies, and even a Chinese dictionary—most of them belonging to the New York Public Library.

When Feldman, a fifty-eight-year-old attorney, was asked why he had hoarded so many books, he replied, "I like to read." And when it came out that he did not even have a valid library card, an associate wondered aloud how he had gotten all those volumes out of the library. "In large quantities," Feldman said.

**Best Word:** James Joyce once offered the opinion that "cuspidor" is the most beautiful word in the English language. In French the most euphonious entry in the lexicon is *"les hemorroïdes"* (no translation necessary), or at least that was the choice of the poet Charles Baudelaire.

---

**Worst Acronym:** The editors of *Science News* have uncovered the most unspeakable of all acronyms in the pages of a Hughes Aircraft publication. The word is PUMCODOXPURSACOMLOPAR and it's short for pulse-modulated coherent Doppler-effect X-band pulse-repetition synthetic-array pulse compression side lobe planar array.

**Worst Binding:** We encountered this macabre item while leafing through a copy of *The American Funeral Director*, the leading morticians' journal: "Eugene Sue (1804–1857), the French novelist, inherited a fortune and became the talk of Paris because of his high-flying ways. His mistress had an equal eye for the sensational—in her will she directed that a set of his books be bound with her skin." Foyle's, the internationally famous London bookshop, sold a very special edition of

Sue's *Vignettes: les Mystères de Paris* to an elderly spinster in 1951. The cover was made from skin taken from the shoulders of the author's long-dead mistress. The appraised value was twenty-nine dollars.

**Worst Chance for Hitting the Best-Seller List:** Australian writer William Gold has penned fifteen books over the past eighteen years and not one has been sold to a publisher. Armed with a resilience that would put a bocci ball to shame, Gold is well along on yet another book—a sixty-thousand-word satire on, predictably enough, the publishing industry.

Consistency demands that we mention, if only in passing, another book that hardly threatens to run away with the National Book Award, in this or any other year: *A Guard Within*, by Sarah Ferguson. It's described by the publisher, Pantheon Books, as "an account of Miss Ferguson's painful adjustment to the sudden death of her psychiatrist."

**Worst Essay Contest:** In honor of America's Bicentennial, the National Football League sponsored a $10,000 prize essay contest. Ranging from 500 to 750 words in length, the essays were to explore "The Role of the National Football League in American History."

**Worst Journalist:** To research an article on the evils of prostitution, a nineteenth-century British newspaper reporter named W. T. Stead purchased the services of a thirteen-year-old girl for ten pounds and kept her in a London brothel. He was ultimately arrested and sent to jail.

**Worst Magazine:** The excesses of *Kampfruf,* the official organ of Nazi homosexuals in the United States (see *Felton & Fowler's Best, Worst and Most Unusual,* page 83), are bland fare compared to *Soldier of Fortune,* a new quarterly also known by its subtitle of "The Journal of Professional Adventurers." As *New Times* magazine bluntly puts it, "It deals with killing people."

*Soldier,* edited and published by Robert Brown, a forty-two-year-old ex-Green Beret, has a mailing list of four thousand and offers, among other features, shopping tips on hand grenades and high-powered sniper rifles. The lead story in one issue told of three thousand unpaid volunteer soldiers who attempted to land in Vietnam and wipe out Vietcong strongholds singlehandedly. "There are a lot of veterans in this country who have tasted the excitement of combat and can't adjust to humdrum civilian life again," says Brown. The magazine, he says, "is anti-dope, pro-military, pro-Israel, pro-guns, and pro-cops."

**Worst Misprint:** One evening in 1915, President Woodrow Wilson escorted his fiancée, Edith Galt, to the theater, prompting a reporter for the Washington *Post* to note that rather than watch the play, "The President spent most of his time entertaining Mrs. Galt." Unfortunately, perhaps insidiously, the word "entertaining" was misprinted as "entering."

**Worst Poet:** "The most startling incident in my life," wrote the great William McGonagall, "is the time I discovered myself to Be a poet, was in the year of 1877 . . . in the bright and balmy month of June when trees, and flowers, Were in full bloom. [sic]" Until that calamitous day, McGonagall had been a weaver, but at the age of fifty-two he abandoned his loom and embarked on one of the most prolific and preposterous careers in literary annals.

Like Vachel Lindsay, he traveled from house to house declaiming his verse and selling his manuscripts for a few pennies or a bite to eat. But unlike Lindsay, McGonagall was supremely untalented. His verse was characterized by spastic cadences, sour rhymes, grammatical atrocities, and bad spelling. At first, audiences who came to hear McGonagall in Dundee, Edinburgh, New York, and London sat silent and slack-jawed in disbelief. Later, as his notoriety spread, the literati came to his readings armed with rotten vegetables and pelted him with tomatoes and eggplants as he recited passages from "The Famous Tay Whale," "The Attempted Assassination of the Queen," and our personal favorite, "The Battle of Abu Klea":

> Oh, it was an exciting and terrible sight,
> To see Colonel Burnaby engaged in the fight;
> With sword in hand, fighting with might and main,
> Until killed by a spear thrust in the jugular vein.

But small excerpts cannot do McGonagall's poetry justice; he could be outrageously bad at epic lengths. By way of example, we quote a portion of his temperance ode, "The Demon Drink":

> Oh, thou demon Drink, thou fell destroyer;
> Thou curse of society, and its greatest annoyer,
> What has thou done to society, let me think?
> I answer thou hast caused the most of ills,
>     thou demon Drink.
>
> Thou causeth the mother to neglect her child,
> Also the father to act as he were wild,
> So that he neglects his loving wife and family dear,
> By spending his earnings foolishly on whiskey, rum, and beer.

William McGonagall

And after spending his earnings foolishly he beats his wife—
The man that promised to protect her during life—
And so the man would if there was no drink in society,
For seldom a man beats his wife in a state of sobriety.

And if he does, perhaps he finds his wife fou',
Then that causes, no doubt, a great hullaballoo;
When he finds his wife drunk he begins to frown,
And in a fury of passion he knocks her down.

And in the knock down she fractures her head,
And perhaps the poor wife is killed dead,
Whereas, if there was not strong drink to be got,
To be killed wouldn't have been the poor wife's lot.

Then the unfortunate husband is arrested and cast into jail,
And sadly his fate he does bewail;
And he curses the hour that ever he was born,
And paces his cell up and down very forlorn.

And when the day of his trial draws near,
No doubt for the murdering of his wife he drops a tear,
And he exclaims, "Oh, thous demon Drink, through thee I must die."
And on the scaffold he warns the people from drink to fly . . .

And that's not the half of it.

McGonagall was absolutely convinced of his own greatness although he failed to persuade anyone else. McGonagall's selected poems are now available from the Stephen Greene Press and in a perceptive introduction to that volume, James L. Smith, Ph.D., pays tribute to the Dundee poetaster as "unquestionably the great master of Illiterature in the language."

**Worst Poetry:** They used to say that if you locked a dozen chimpanzees in a room equipped with typewriters for a thousand years, one of them would accidentally type out *King Lear*. Today that process has been refined and accelerated through the use of sophisticated high-speed computers. A programmer can now feed a basic vocabulary into a machine's memory (including an ample assortment of "o'ers," "opes," "e'ens" and other poeticisms), add some basic rules about sentence structure, and, *voilà*, the machine creates instant poetry. A human editor need only select the best lines and assemble them in some suitable order.

Will the Dantes of tomorrow forsake the garret, don lab coats, and enroll in computer programming school? Here are some early cybernetic verses by which to judge:

> Under a lamp the nude is vain.
> Broccoli is often blind.
>
> Life reached evilly through empty faces
> Space flowed slowly o'er idle bodies.

A computer at the Cambridge Language Research Institute was programmed to compose haikus:

> All white in the buds
> I flash snowpeaks in the Spring.
> Bang the sun has fogged.

And in the most advanced experiment to date, Edwin Morgan has programmed computers to write "code poems." One lyric reads: "TEYZA PRQTP ZSNSX OSRMY VCFBO . . ." and so on for another sixty-seven words.

**Worst Reference Book:** In neglecting to check the veracity of the material sent in by their correspondents, the editors of *Appleton's Cyclopaedia of American Biography* were leaving themselves wide open to pranksters. In 1919 a wary librarian did a bit of investigative research and found that fourteen of the biographies in the most recent edition were of nonexistent people and that they'd been continually reprinted since 1886. The disclosure embarrassed the *Appleton's* people no end and prompted them to institute a more exhaustive check of their own which turned up an additional seventy counterfeit biographies.

**Worst Words:** An August 1946 poll of the National Association of Teachers of Speech generated a list of the ten most unpleasant sounding words in the English language. They were, in no particular order: phlegmatic, crunch, flatulent, cacophony, treachery, sap, jazz, plutocrat, gripe, and plump.

Moving from phonology to semantics, we recently found that the most potent and popular of English obscenities was not always so disreputable. The "f word" first appeared in print in "Ane Brash of Wowing" ("A Bout of Wooing") by the Scottish poet and one-time Franciscan monk William Dunbar. No attempt was made to suppress this shocking stanza when it was published in 1503:

> He clappit fast, he kist, and chukkit
> As with the glaikis [1] he were ouirgane; [2]
> Yit be his feiris [3] he would have fukkit;
> Ye brek my hart, my bony one!
>
> 1) feeling   2) overcome   3) manner

The term also appeared liberally in the verses of the earl of Rochester and other poems of the period up until 1600 when publishers banned it from the printed page. "Fuck" even disappeared from dictionaries, including lexicons of slang, for nearly three centuries, and to this day none of the major dictionaries—Webster's, Oxford, or Random House—have dared to define it for fear of incurring a buyers' boycott. (Boswell notes that when a prudish lady congratulated Dr. Johnson for omitting objectionable four-letter words from his dictionary, he arched his eyebrows and replied, "So you have been looking for them, madam?")

---

**Most Unusual Dictionary:** The G. & C. Merriam Company, publishers of the Merriam-Webster dictionaries, owns title to the definitions of several million English words and expressions, every one of which is on file, spelled *backwards*, at their offices in Springfield, Massachusetts.

The file was begun as a lark by a former Merriam editor, but it is still tended carefully and updated regularly because of its usefulness to lexicographers and linguists studying word structures and suffixes. As Dr. Frederick Mish, a Merriam editorial director, notes, a student desiring a readout of all English words ending in the suffix "-tion" need only reverse the letters and look under "noit" (as in noitacav, noitaton, noitatigiditserp, and so on and os htrof). No published dictionary has yet resulted from the backwards file, but it does seem a possibility for the future.

**Most Unusual Home-Study Language Course:** How do you say "Please don't squeeze the Charmin" in German? A West German company manufactures toilet paper containing a twenty-six-lesson course in English on each "silky and resistant" roll. Says the advertising copy, "Learn English whenever you want in a quiet corner."

**Most Unusual Language:** Esperanto speakers wear little green stars on their lapels when traveling so they can identify each other. Think back now, how many green lapel pins have you seen in the last five years?

Actually the self-advertised "second language of the world" has far more speakers than we would have guessed—nearly eight million according to one estimate. Nineteen radio stations, most of them in polyglot Eastern Europe, offer some Esperanto programs, and a complete bibliography of Esperanto publications would include over thirty thousand books and ninety-seven periodicals. The works of Shakespeare, Agatha Christie, Mao Tse-tung, Norman Mailer, and hundreds of other writers have been translated by zealous Esperantists, and there are even Esperanto volumes in Braille.

If French is the language of love, Esperanto is the language of idealism. Inventor Ludovic Zamenhof (1859–1917) borrowed elements from all the major European tongues to produce a streamlined language that he hoped would break down the communication barriers dividing mankind. The grammar Zamenhof devised is so exquisitely simple that it can be described on a single page. All nouns end in -o, all adjectives end in -a, stress invariably falls on the next to last syllable, and verbs undergo no changes for person or number. The meanings of unfamiliar words can be quickly grasped: *"Bela,"* for instance, means "beautiful"; *"mal-"* is a prefix meaning "opposite"; hence, *"malbela"* means "ugly." People who know at least one foreign language are often able to decipher a certain amount of Esperanto with no instruction at all.

> En la komenco Dio kreis la ĉielon kaj la teron. Kaj la tero estis senforma kaj dezerta, kaj mallumo estis super la abismo; kaj la spirito de Dio ŝvebis super la akvo. Kaj Dio diris: Estu lumo; kaj fariĝis lumo.
>
> (Gen. 1: 1–3)

Studies have shown that a novice can learn Esperanto in one-tenth to one-twentieth the time it takes to master a national language.

**Most Unusual Library:** A 1973 issue of the *Special Libraries Association Bulletin* described the marvels of the Playboy Enterprises reference library in Chicago, Illinois. The opulent décor features dark walnut paneling adorned with some of the original artwork that has appeared in *Playboy* over the years. On the shelves are some eight thousand volumes and three hundred periodicals, including many that you will never see at your neighborhood public library. Needless to say, the entire contents of each issue of *Playboy*, including the centerfolds, has been meticulously cross-referenced and indexed. A professional librarian and three assistants are there to serve cocktails and to see that no one clips out the pictures. And the *SLA Bulletin* notes in passing that at least one assistant librarian was herself the subject of a centerfold.

One of the more unusual holdings of the library is a complete set of *Playboy* back issues in Braille. To pirate an old Woody Allen joke, we wonder whether Braille readers really bother with the articles or just turn to the centerfold and rub the good parts.

For readers on the East Coast who can't commute to Chicago, we direct you to the most titillating item in the New York Public Library. It is call number *Z 1891, a microfilm entitled *Die Erotik Der Antike in Kleinkunst und Keramic*. There, in superminiature, are all the sexiest coins and pottery from the Classical period. Culled from very private collections in Germany and Italy, these illustrations depict the great art works that may never be on exhibit in the Metropolitan, the Louvre, or the Vatican Museum.

**Most Unusual Literary Prize:** For twenty-six years Hart, Schaffner, and Marx, the men's clothing manufacturer, gave out lucrative annual literary awards. Now, alas, that line has been discontinued and we are left with the Pulitzer prizes, the National Book awards, and the Loubat Prize. The Loubat Prize, for the benefit of greedy but uninformed young authors, is a juicy $1,200 tidbit, awarded every five years for "the best book on 'Numismatics of North America'." Or, if coin collecting fails to fire your imagination, you might try for the biennial Watmull Prize—$500 presented by the American Historical Association for the best history of India originally published in the United States.

James Michener, who lives in Bucks County, Pennsylvania, has never won the Athenaeum Literary Award. That honor goes to the best book on any subject written by a man or woman "living within thirty miles of Philadelphia City Hall." Unluckily, Michener lives forty-two miles from paydirt.

Perhaps the most serendipitous literary award of all: Russian novelist Alexandr Solzhenitsyn was the recipient of two thousand Bic ballpoint pens, courtesy of Robert P. Adler, president of the Bic Pen Corporation.

**Most Unusual Manuscript:** Beat generation prophet Jack Kerouac (*On the Road, Big Sur*), of whose work Truman Capote once said, "That's not writing, it's typing," pounded out many of his works on one continuous roll of paper.

**Most Unusual Name:** See "Music," *Most Unusual Conductor.*

**Most Unusual Newspaper Editorial:** According to Theo Lippman, Jr., H. L. Mencken once ran a full-page editorial in the Baltimore *Evening Sun* entitled "Object Lesson." It consisted of one million dots and a brief note stating that each dot stood for a federal government job-holder.

**Most Unusual Private Edition:** Thomas Wirgman spent over $200,000 privately printing a series of books of which no more than six copies were ever sold. His most sizeable work, *The Grammar of Six Senses*, is complete gibberish, and yet the author insisted that if his ideas were only put into practice the world would enjoy "perpetual peace and harmony." Each page in his volumes was printed on a different color stock, and Wirgman fussed over the rainbow of pages continually to get the sequence of colors exactly right. The arrangement of the pages within the covers was determined by the "ideal procession of hues" rather than the syntax or the sense of the manuscript.

Another color-conscious writer was Alexander Dumas *père,* author of *The Three Musketeers* and *The Count of Monte Cristo.* Dumas always composed his novels on blue paper, his poetry on yellow paper, and his nonfiction on rose paper. To do otherwise, he said, was "unspeakable."

**Most Unusual Tongue Twister:** Take a deep breath and see if you can read aloud the following entry from the Health, Education and Welfare Department's "Interstate Certified Shellfish Shippers List": "RS-Reshipper—Shippers who transship shucked stock . . . or shell-stock from certified shellfish shippers. . . . (Reshippers are not authorized to shuck or repack shellfish.) RP-Repacker—Shippers, other than the original shucker, who pack shucked shellfish. . . . A repacker may shuck shellfish or act as a shell-stock shipper. . . ."

**Most Unusual Translation:** "*Ecce Eduardus Ursus scalis nunc tump-tump-tump occipite gradus pulsante post Christophorum Robinum descendens.*" Or in other words, "Here is Edward Bear, coming downstairs

now, bump, bump, bump on the back of his head, behind Christopher Robin."

The passage is taken from *Winnie ille Pu*, a Latin translation of A. A. Milne's children's classic published by E. P. Dutton & Co. just before Christmas in 1960. A European physician named Alexander Leonard spent three painstaking years preparing the manuscript. Alas, it seems unlikely that many parents bothered to read the 126-page Roman-revival text to their children. In fact, the only people who took the book seriously were curmudgeonly classicists, who generally reviewed the book in the accusative case. Nevertheless, as a three-dollar conversation piece, *Winnie ille Pu* enjoyed considerable success; over 60,000 copies were sold.

All the familiar Milne characters were present and accounted for; Piglet was renamed Porcellus, Rabbit became Lepus, but Heffalump is Heffalump in any language. Here is another excerpt for rusty Latinists to puzzle out: *"Suspiria duxerunt et consurrexerunt . . . deinde spinis nonnullis vepris e natibus evulsis ad mutua dicta reddenda conoodorunt."*

# The Performing Arts

---

**Best Actor:** Chuck Connors is the choice of film and TV buff Leonid Brezhnev, but we will opt instead for Sir Laurence Olivier, who has been widely acclaimed as the ablest living actor on the English-speaking stage. And deservedly so. Olivier is an intellectual actor; by that we mean he has the experience, creativity, and intelligence to play a standard role and to bring to it a fresh and provocative interpretation of his own devising. He also has that rare ability to adapt himself so convincingly to a part that the audience forgets they are watching Laurence Olivier. There's no mistaking Richard Burton, and Orson Welles is always Orson Welles, but Olivier *becomes* Richard III or Hamlet or the hero of a Noel Coward comedy.

Three shades vie for honors as the greatest English tragic actor of all time. Probably the foremost claimant is David Garrick (1717–1779) who revolutionized the theater by substituting a natural, unstudied acting style for the fustian and pompous French manner. Alexander Pope, viewing his first Garrick performance, raved, "That young man never had his equal as an actor, and he will never have a rival." The alcoholic, megalomaniacal Edmund Kean (1787–1833) might have challenged that assessment with a flashing sabre. Kean was the theater's most magnificent villain, interpreting Shylock and Macbeth with a combination of humanity and brilliant malevolence; but he was dreadful in romantic parts and his Romeo was a laughingstock. Sir Henry Irving (1838–1905) is the third member of this illustrious triumvirate; audiences never tired of his Iago.

Edwin Forrest and Edwin Booth were America's finest players; the latter was considered Kean's only serious contemporary rival.

**Best Cinematic Special Effects:** The El Rey Theater, in Manteca, California, burst into flames shortly after a showing of *The Towering Inferno*.

The fire, of undetermined origin, gutted the theater before firemen could put it out.

**Best Conductorless Orchestra:** In a crescendo of revolutionary zeal, the Pervyi Simfonicheskyi Ensemble made its Moscow debut in February 1922. It was a creditable concert, and will be remembered throughout musical history as the first performance of a major world orchestra without a conductor. The idea of a conductor—a single musical dictator controlling every tremolo and pizzicato—seemed contrary to the egalitarian ideals of the Russian Revolution. And so the radical musicians began an intriguing experiment to see if they could orchestrate their own music and keep time for themselves.

The musicians performed together for four harmonious seasons, inspiring the formation of conductorless ensembles in Paris, Berlin, and New York. Then, about 1926, the group began to be troubled by dissension and internal discord. Some orchestra members charged that the first violinist was acting as a *de facto* leader because he set the tempo at the beginning of each piece, and kept time by nodding his head. Others challenged the propriety of such class distinctions as "first" and "second" bassoonist. Increasingly, rehearsal time was consumed by frustrating ideological squabbles. And in 1928 the Pervyi Ensemble was dissolved.

**Best Kettledrum:** The University of Texas Longhorn Band owns a kettledrum that is twenty-five feet in circumference. When used, it has to be pulled by a tractor.

**Best Opera House:** Writing in *Horizon,* Joseph Wechsberg has singled out Milan's La Scala as the best place, in terms of talent and ambience, to hear great opera. The building itself, built in 1776, can accommodate more than three thousand spectators, and the lobby is graced with statues of Rossini, Bellini, Donizetti, and Verdi, whose works were first presented at La Scala. Acoustically the auditorium is perfect, although if you listen very carefully, you may hear faint echoes of Caruso, Chaliapin, Melba, and other immortal voices from the past.

Wechsberg applauds La Scala as a theater where people still express their feelings openly. Arguments within the audience are a common occurrence, fist fights still break out in the gallery, shoes and other tokens of disapproval are occasionally hurled onstage, and, more likely than not, the man sitting next to you will hum the familiar arias right along with the great tenors.

No other opera house could possibly compare with La Scala, but if you are ever in Vienna the Staatsoper is a good second choice. Far less

La Scala, Milan

impressive is the Paris Opera, which owes most of its fame to Lon Chaney's movie *Phantom of the Opera*. Wechsberg dismisses it as a "pompous mausoleum with an apathetic orchestra and second-rate singers." Of the world's major opera houses, it is the worst.

**Best Record Album Bargain:** RCA Records has released the longest playing LP record ever—a 69½-minute album featuring pianist Tedd Joselson and the Philadelphia Orchestra, conducted by Eugene Ormandy, in performances of the Tchaikovsky Piano Concerto no. 1 and the Prokofiev Piano Concerto no. 2. However, recording technicians say that while it is possible to cram as much as thirty-six minutes of music on one side of a record, sound quality begins going sour after thirty minutes.

**Best Violinist:** Although connoisseurs generally concur that modern violin technique is superior to nineteenth-century fiddling, Nicolò Paganini (1782–1840) is still recognized as the king of the strings. Contemporary performers find many passages in Paganini's own flamboyant compositions difficult, even unplayable.

Like Franz Liszt, Paganini lived a wildly romantic life. A cult of hero worshipers dressed as he dressed, dined where he dined, and followed him from concert hall to concert hall all over Europe. He was an irrepressible ham who could not resist making "embellishments and improvements" on the masterpieces of Mozart and Beethoven, and often he was guilty of vain displays of virtuosity. On August 25, 1805, Paganini gave a command performance for Napoleon on a one-stringed instrument. Later he began composing original one- and two-stringed pieces as a challenge to other violinists and to show off his own deftness and speed. On other occasions, he played with frayed strings, hoping that one or more would break so that he could triumphantly overcome this handicap.

Paganini was also a compulsive gambler who once lost his violin at the gaming tables. He made a tremendous fortune from his concert tours and squandered it all on roulette.

**Best Wildlife Recordings:** Every year the British Wildlife Recording Society holds a competition to select the finest natural soundtracks in a variety of categories. For example, in 1972, Ray Goodwin of Gloucestershire won the coveted award for "most unusual entry" with his tape of "a Roman snail eating a lettuce leaf." One reporter described the piece as a series of booming, ear-shattering crunches lasting about two minutes. It was Goodwin's second major triumph in two years. His 1971 recording of a dung beetle at work and play copped the grand prize that year.

Eavesdropping on wildlife can be a fascinating and challenging hobby. One must learn to overcome the animals' natural shyness and suspicions and, at the same time, solve the complex technical problems of transporting sensitive microphones and equipment to bogs, swamps, and treetops. It is not enough to sit in the comfort of your living room, taping private conversations in your ant farm. The Society requires that "All recordings must be of creatures wild and free."

There are 170 dedicated members of the Wildlife Sound Recording Society, the only organization of its kind in the world. As you would expect, the Society owns a wonderful collection of recorded twitters, shrieks, snarls, grunts, whistles, howls, and buzzes—including the very first birdsong recording, made in 1898 by Ludwig Koch—the Father of Wildlife Sound Recording—on an old Edison cylindrical Gramophone record.

One final note: The winner of the "mammal division" in 1972 was Arthur Acland, a seventy-year-old retired underwear salesman from Kent. His winning entry: "A humorous recording of a hedgehog barking to warn off other spiny members of his tribe as he sipped a bowl of milk."

**Worst Hollywood Musical:** Diva Geraldine Farrar of New York's Metropolitan Opera Company filmed a silent movie version of *Carmen* in 1915.

**Worst Musical School:** In his seminal *Art of Noise,* published just prior to World War I, composer Luigi Russolo set down the dogma of the Futurist movement in music: "We derive much greater pleasure from ideally combining the noises of streetcars, internal combustion engines, automobiles, and busy crowds, than from rehearsing the *Eroica* or the *Pastorale.*" As this declaration suggests, the compositions of Russolo and his compatriots were far ahead of their time—and often out of time, as well. These dedicated practitioners of cacophony anticipated the work of our avant-garde contemporaries and scored hisses, grunts, farts, snorts, laughs, and splashes into their music.

The public was hostile and unreceptive. So, in preparation for a Futurist concert scheduled for April 1914 in Paris, Russolo and his fellow musicians underwent intensive instruction in boxing. It served them well. In the midst of a strident, raucous rendition of the *Fourth Network of Noise,* the audience rose to assault the performers. Acting on a well-rehearsed contingency plan, the embattled Futurists broke into two groups. One cadre continued to produce offensive sounds, while the others, still dressed in their tuxedos, successfully defended the stage. Eleven members of the audience were hospitalized with concussions and fractured bones. The Futurists escaped with minor cuts and bruises.

**Worst National Anthem:** Periodically a bill is introduced in Congress to replace "The Star-Spangled Banner" with a more singable melody, such as "America the Beautiful." Whatever its poetic virtues—and they too are highly questionable—the United States national anthem has long been regarded as among the world's worst, and the Cleveland *Press* recently urged in an editorial that the anthem be packed away "with due and becoming affection." Nobody, it claimed, "except an especially courageous and flexible operatic soloist can negotiate it without fudging on the high notes."

Perhaps a more fitting national anthem would be the work of an obscure Boston composer named Greeler. According to *Music World,* Greeler set the entire United States Constitution, including the Bill of Rights, to music in 1874. "The performance did not last less than six hours. The preamble of the Constitution forms a broad and majestic recitative, well sustained by altos and double basses . . . the Constitutional Amendments are treated as fugues." The passages on states' rights were in a minor key for bass and tenor. *Music World* states that the Constitution was performed numerous times before enthusiastic audiences, but now, apparently, the score has been lost.

**Worst Opera Performance:** Maria Jeritza and Enrico Caruso once appeared together in a memorable production of *Carmen* at New York's Metropolitan Opera House. As part of the elaborate staging, real horses were used to draw the coach of Carmen and Escamillo onstage in the final act. Faced with the bright footlights and the large audience, one of the horses making his Metropolitan debut became very fidgety. Finally, the stallion expressed his stage fright in a highly unsanitary fashion right on center stage.

Soon after, during the climactic scene when Caruso was called upon to stab Jeritza, the diva refused to fall and die. Caruso stabbed her a second time and shouted "Die! Fall, will you!" Madame Jeritza screamed back, "I'll die if you can find me a clean place."

**Worst Record:** Worse than "Santa Jaws," more ghastly than the plague of teen-age death songs, was "The Battle Hymn of William Calley," a country and western apologia for a misunderstood war hero. It sold 1.5 million copies.

Alternatively, you might pick up a copy of "Lie" (ESP 2003) and play it at your next party. "Lie" is the first and only album recorded by Charles Manson. One of the more interesting cuts is "Garbage Dump," a folk-rock variation on the basic melody of "O Christmas Tree," with Charlie's own inimitable lyrics:

> You could feed the world with my garbage dump.
> That sums it up in one big lump . . .
> When you're livin' on the road
> And you think sometimes you're starvin'
> Get on off that trip my friend
> Just get in them cans and start carvin' . . .
> There's a market basket and an A & P,
> I don't care if the boxboy's starin' at me,
> I don't even care who wins the war,
> I'll be in them cans behind my favorite store.

Manson sings some of his compositions *a cappella*, and on others the famed Manson girls provide a creditable choral back-up; the small strident voice of Squeaky Fromme is nowhere to be heard. The instrumental accompaniment includes Manson's own guitar-pickin', plus French horns, a sitar, tambourines, and an occasional yelp from one of the Manson Family babies who was present in the recording studio.

Less inventive than "Lie" but infinitely more utilitarian, is "Vegetation Conversation: Music and Thoughts for Things in Pots," an album designed for the modern houseplant owner who would like to sing his geraniums to sleep but simply hasn't the time. The album, released by Funny Forum, an Indianapolis company, includes such nitrogen-rich numbers as "Lament to a Plant," "Oh, the Coleus," and "No Matter How Fertile, There's No Place Like Loam."

**Worst State Song:** State songs must be inspired by the same muse who elicits high-school alma maters and bubble-gum rock-and-roll. The music is eminently forgettable; the lyrics are an interstate disgrace. Take, for example, the Oklahoma anthem, composed by Mrs. Harriet Parker Camden in 1905:

> We have often sung her praises,
> But we have not told the half
> So I give you "Oklahoma"
> 'Tis a toast we all can quaff.

And if that rhyme isn't enough to make you choke on your beer, consider the fact that for decades no law-abiding Oklahoman could possibly quaff a toast to his great state. Oklahoma was bone dry until 1959.

The Commonwealth of Massachusetts has no song, probably because of the difficulty in finding a word to rhyme with the state's name. Mississippi also lacks an anthem, although she is blessed with a necrophilic state ode:

> Here my life, ebb thou away;
> Here, my bones, turn back to clay—
> I love thee Mississippi.

The poetic dregs, however, are the Alabama state song, written by Julia S. Tutwiler:

> Broad the Stream whose name thou bearest,
> Grand thy Bigbee rolls along;
> Fair thy Coosa—Tallapoosa
> Bold thy Warrior, dark and strong,
> Goodlier than the land that Moses
> Climbed lone Nebo's Mount to see,
> Alabama, Alabama,
> We will aye be true to thee.

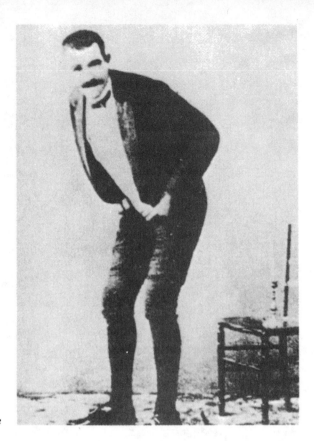

*Le Petomane*

**Worst Theatrical Prop:** At the battle of Carrhae (53 B.C.), Marcus Crassus, one of the richest men in republican Rome, distinguished himself as one of history's most inept commanders. Humiliated by a vastly inferior Parthian army, the Roman legions were, nonetheless, retreating in good order when Crassus accepted a gentlemanly offer to dine with the triumphant Parthian general. In the Parthian camp, even before dinner was served, Crassus was attacked, treacherously slain, and gruesomely beheaded. The unsportsmanlike general personally filled his old enemy's mouth with molten gold and sent the severed head to the Parthian court, where it was used to represent the dismembered Pentheus in a performance of Euripides' *Bacchae*.

**Worst Vaudeville Act:** Jadji Ali, billed as "the Amazing Regurgitator," was one of the most popular vaudeville performers at the turn of the century. His act consisted of swallowing a variety of unlikely objects and spitting them up at will. For openers, Ali regurgitated a series of watermelon seeds, imitation jewels, coins, and rings; it wasn't much to write home about. But his grand finale brought the house down every night. His assistant would set up a tiny metal castle on stage while Ali drank down a gallon of water and a pint of kerosene. To the accompaniment of a suspenseful drum roll, he would spit out the kerosene in a six-foot arc across the stage, setting the castle on fire. Then, with the flames shooting high into the air, Ali would upchuck the gallon of water and extinguish all traces of the fire.

French audiences were captivated by an even more outrageous act. In the *City of God,* Book XIV, Saint Augustine assures us, "There are individuals who can make musical notes issue from the rear of their anatomy, so that you would think they were singing." Vaudevillian Joseph Pujol (1851–1945), otherwise known as *Le Petomane,* was one soul blessed with this Rabelaisian talent, and he made it pay off handsomely. From 1892 to 1914, Pujol was a headliner at the famous Moulin Rouge, where he drew gates as large as 20,000 francs, while the Divine Sarah Bernhardt only managed to pull 8,000 francs. With his well-tempered derrière, he performed a series of phenomenal stunts—rendering flatulent impressions of famous opera singers, playing the ocarina through a rubber tube, and blowing out a candle from a distance of one foot. For an encore *Le Petomane* would solemnly ask his audience to stand while he farted the "Marseillaise."

**Most Unusual Ballet:** In 1971 jazz composer Roger Kellaway wrote a modern ballet, acronymically entitled *PAMTGG.* The work premiered at Lincoln Center featuring the capable footwork of the New York City Ballet, and as soon as the audience heard the opening bars, they got the joke.

The basic theme for the twenty-two-minute score was borrowed from the overplayed television jingle "Pan Am Makes the Going Great," and the exuberant choreography by George Balanchine included impressionistic renderings of takeoff, landing, and the postflight baggage scramble. Reviewing the performance for *Time,* critic John T. Elson said, "Somehow Balanchine can create grace out of tackiness and art of kitsch. If nothing else, *PAMTGG* leads one to wonder what kind of magic he might work if his fancy were caught by a roller derby or a pro-football game."

**Most Unusual Composing Technique:** A favorite exercise of the unorthodox composer Joseph Schillinger was to play a polyphonic composition on the piano, then challenge his audience to identify the composer. The familiar three-part counterpoint invention usually evoked the names of Handel, Bach, or Purcell. At that point, Schillinger would gleefully

Symphonic conductor Jullien

reveal that the melodies were derived from the financial page of *The New York Times*.

Schillinger's unique method of composition is described in *A Thing or Two about Music* by Nicolas Slonimsky: On a sheet of ordinary graph paper, he plotted the price fluctuations of various wholesale commodities, such as Chicago wheat, Kansas hogs, and Georgia sugar cane. He then assigned a proportionate value in musical intervals to each square on the graph; after that it was a simple matter to write a melody corresponding to the three curves. The resulting pieces were generally adjudged to be equal to the minor works of the great Baroque composers.

**Most Unusual Conductor:** In the musically arid world of Victorian England, one standout was the symphonic conductor Jullien, who used only his family name because his full name—Louis Georges Maurice Adolphe Roch Albert Abel Antonio Alexandre Noel Jean Lucien Daniel Eugene Joseph-le-Byrun Joseph-Bareme Thomas Thomas-Thomas Pierre Carbon Pierre-Maurel Barthelmi Artus Alphonse Bertrand Dieudonne Emanuel Josue Vinvent Luc Michel Jules-de-la-Plane Jules Bazin Julio-Cesar Jullien—was a bit cumbersome for concert programs. When Jullien was born in 1812, his father, a prominent bandmaster, named him after his colleagues at the Susteron Philharmonic Society.

But Jullien's name was the least of his eccentricities. Like a golfer with a well-stocked bag of irons, wedges, and drivers, he conducted different concert pieces with different batons, favoring gilt batons for Mozart compositions, silver ones for Mendelssohn, and wooden ones for dance music. For works by Beethoven, Jullien wore white gloves and conducted with a jewel-encrusted model valued at over a thousand dollars.

Incidentally, Pëtr Ilich Tchaikovsky, who became pathologically morose in his declining years and died from drinking cholera-infested tap water in 1893, is reported by some of his contemporaries to have conducted with only one hand, using the other hand to prop up his head, which he feared was in danger of falling off.

**Most Unusual Jazz Band:** Daisy Hilton played a mean alto sax, alternately sinuous and whining; her sister Violet accompanied her on the piano. Together, they boasted to reporters in the 1930s, "we are our own jazz band."

And quite an odd-looking jazz band they were too, since the British-born Hiltons were Siamese twins, joined at the hip. While they had no innate gift for music, they migrated to the United States in 1908 at age eight, determined to earn their living on the stage, and broke into vaudeville in the mid-1920s. With less than 190 pounds of playing weight between them, the sisters grew rich on their performances up and down the East Coast.

Offstage they were an amiable pair who respected each other's individuality and privacy, training themselves to "get rid of each other mentally," from time to time. Violet once explained that when Daisy had a date, "I sometimes quit paying attention and did not know what was going on. Sometimes I read and sometimes I just took a nap."

The sisters led a busy social life and received a number of marriage proposals, although some twenty states turned down their applications for marriage licenses. Violet succeeded, however, in wedding stage dancer James Moore in 1936, although the marriage was annulled a few months later. In 1941, Daisy married Harold Step.

The twins lived out their final years in relative obscurity in Charlotte, North Carolina, where they had jobs weighing fruit and vegetables in a local supermarket. They died of influenza in 1960.

**Most Unusual National Anthem:** Not all national anthems are written out of spontaneous patriotic zeal. In 1853, with envoys from Great Britain and the United States on the way, the new revolutionary junta of Costa Rica discovered to their embarrassment that their nation had no

The Hilton Sisters

anthem. The red carpet was all ready, but there was nothing appropriate for the military band to play as the distinguished guests disembarked. The president summoned Manuel Maria Gutiérrez, Costa Rica's best-known musician, to the palace where he shook his hand, called him a fine fellow, and explained that he had been selected to compose the Costa Rican national anthem—in five days or less. When Gutiérrez protested that he always played by ear and had never written down a single note of music, the president grew impatient and had the musician thrown in prison. After four days in a dungeon cell, Gutiérrez managed to set down a lively march tune, which was played for the envoys and remains Costa Rica's national anthem to this day.

Australia, which for many years had been making do with "God Save the Queen," recently sponsored a contest to select a more truly national national anthem. A prize of $20,000 was to go to the winning composer. As of this writing, no suitable song has been agreed upon, and the general quality of the entries has been so dismal that there is a growing inclination to adopt good old "Waltzing Matilda" and be done with it.

**Most Unusual Opera:** A new opera entitled *The Prophet* was the rage of Europe in 1849. Composed by Giacomo Meyerbeer, the work opened to a packed house in Paris, and later had long and successful runs in Berlin, Vienna, Milan, Rome, and London.

What particularly delighted audiences was the athletic roller-skating scene, which featured a busty diva and a portly baritone breathlessly attempting a duet while cutting figure eights on the stage. The rumble of the wheels on the wood floor was deafening.

Count Skavronsky would have enjoyed the novelty. A noted nineteenth-century Russian musician, he was the most devoted opera buff we know of. Skavronsky insisted that his wife, servants, and children address him and each other in recitative at all times.

**Most Unusual Performance of the 1812 Overture:** Tchaikovsky's 1812 Overture may be the most pyrotechnic piece of music ever composed, and during the explosive finale, even seasoned concert hall veterans have been known to lose their nerve and dive for cover. The Eastman School of Music in Rochester, New York, presented a memorable performance of this popular work in 1960. The orchestra was magnificent during the powerful strains of the czarist hymn, "God the All-Terrible," surging forward like the Russian army toward the ultimate percussion—a volley of real cannon fire. The cymbals crashed and the climactic moment arrived. The conductor electronically touched off the black powder; the thunderous roar of artillery was heard. And from the roof of the concert hall came a flurry of white duck feathers.

**Most Unusual Score:** Whim is a major element in any performance of Karlheinz Stockhausen's *Nr. 7 Klavierstück XI*. The score consists of nineteen musical fragments scattered haphazardly across the page; the pianist plays them, or doesn't play them, in any order he chooses.

As Stockhausen describes it, "The performer looks at random at the sheet of music and begins with any group, the first that catches his eye; this he plays, choosing for himself the tempo, dynamic level, and type of attack." Fortunately, the composer provides guidelines for determining when the piece is over; otherwise it might continue forever. "When a group is arrived at for the third time, one possible realization of the piece is completed."

Since some fragments may be played only once, and others not at all, perhaps the best possible rendition of the *Klavierstück* is to select the shortest segment and play it three times prestissimo.

**Most Unusual Special Effect:** The film was *The Scent of Mystery*, produced by Mike Todd, Jr., in 1960. Critics called it "the first movie that stinks on purpose." And, thankfully, it was the only film ever to employ the glorious "Smell-O-Vision" process.

The vehicle was a mediocre detective yarn that provided far more scent than mystery. Adequate performances by Denholm Elliott and Peter Lorre were disguised by cheap perfumery. When, for example, Lorre poured himself a snifter of fine cognac, an odor vaguely resembling brandy came spewing out of the small "scent vents" located behind every seat in the theater. And when the lame plot took Lorre to the Festival of the Bulls in Pamplona, Spain, the audience could actually smell . . . well, it was overwhelming.

The Smell-O-Vision process was developed, if not perfected, by "osmologist" Hans Laube. And it *was* superior to a competitive technique, "amazing Aroma-Rama," used in *Behind the Great Wall*, which appeared about the same time. Aroma-Rama relied on the theater's conventional ventilation system to deliver the odors to the audience, and soon the room was swirling with clouds of contending fragrances.

In *The Scent of Mystery*, Laube dispensed a total of fifty-two different essences, including apples, peaches, wine, pipe tobacco, shoe polish, incense, peppermint, roses, and garlic. But, as Bosley Crowther wrote in *The New York Times*, "If there is anything of lasting value to be learned from Michael Todd, Jr.'s *Scent of Mystery*, it is that motion pictures and synthetic smells don't mix. . . . The odor squirters are mildly and randomly used, and patrons sit there sniffing and snuffling like a lot of bird dogs trying to catch the scent." The smells were often tardy in arriving, and Crowther concluded that the vents would be better used "to squirt laughing gas at the audience."

Curiously enough, there was a precedent to Smell-O-Vision in vaudeville days. Sadakichi Hartman, billed as a Japanese-German inventor, once tried to present a "perfume concert" at the old New York Theater. He set up fans on stage and proposed to blow perfumed smokes toward the audience, each odor representing a different country. He managed to get through England (roses) and Germany (violets) before hecklers drove him from the stage.

**Most Unusual Vaudeville Act:** One of Oscar Hammerstein's rarer finds was "Sober Sue," whom he introduced to audiences at New York's Victoria Theater in 1908. During intermissions, Sue would appear on stage and Hammerstein would offer $1,000 to anyone who could make her laugh. There were lots of takers, but no one succeeded: Sue's jaws were set more immovably than if they had been encrusted in portland cement.

Hammerstein's ten-minute diversion achieved instant fame, and Broadway's top comedians came to shower Sue with their best material. Meanwhile, Hammerstein was reaping the benefit of countless thousands of dollars worth of free talent, because no one could get Sue to release so much as a smirk. Only he and her agent knew that she *couldn't* laugh. Her facial muscles were paralyzed.

# Pop Culture

**Best Board Game:** The rules of the game are the same as those of conventional chess, but the playing equipment is somewhat different: in the words of one chess historian, "alcoholic chess is played on a large board on which, instead of pieces, stand glasses or bottles of strong drink; and if you capture a piece you must drink up its contents." According to writer Patrick Ryan, Emmanuel Lasker (1868–1941), the German grandmaster, once won a game of alcoholic chess by sacrificing his queen early in the game. The queen, in this case, was a quarter-litre bottle of cognac which Lasker's opponent was duty-bound to polish off before making his next move. With his vision blurred and his mind turned to soup, he played sloppy chess and Lasker won handily.

Another famous match is said to have been played in Hungary in 1898 on an outsized board drawn on a billiard table. The kings were bottles of champagne, the queens liebfraumilch, the rooks, knights, and bishops tokay, and the pawns inexpensive table wine. As the story has it, the game started well, but quickly degenerated into chaos. By midgame both players were under the table.

**Best Chess Game:** In a memorable contest between Frank Marshall and Stephan Levitsky at Breslau, Poland, in 1912, Marshall made what aficionados have described as "one of the most brilliant moves in chess history"—a timely queen sacrifice. Levitsky took a few seconds to ponder his position, then resigned. Suddenly, the quiet, reserved chess audience burst into wild cheers and applause, and in a spontaneous outpouring of enthusiasm, they showered the board with gold coins.

But perhaps the boldest move of all was executed during a 1937 championship game between Alexander Alekhine and Max Euwe. On the sixth move, Euwe offered an unprecedented knight sacrifice. The great

## FRENCH DEFENSE

*White:* S. Lewitzky    *Black:* F. J. Marshall

| | | | | | |
|---|---|---|---|---|---|
| 1 P-Q4 | P-K3 | 9 PxP | B-K3 | 17 Q-K2 | BxN |
| 2 P-K4 | P-Q4 | 10 N-Q4 | BxP | 18 PxB | QxP |
| 3 N-QB3 | P-QB4 | 11 NxB | PxN | 19 RxP | N-Q5 |
| 4 N-B3 | N-QB3 | 12 B-N4 | Q-Q3 | 20 Q-R5 | QR-KB1 |
| 5 KPxP | KPxP | 13 B-R3 | QR-K1 | 21 R-K5 | R-R3 |
| 6 B-K2 | N-B3 | 14 Q-Q2 | B-N5 | 22 Q-N5 | RxB |
| 7 0-0 | B-K2 | 15 BxN | RxB | 23 R-QB5 | Q-KN6! |
| 8 B-KN5 | 0-0 | 16 QR-Q1 | Q-B4 | Resigns | |

If 24 RPxQ, N-K7 mate. If 24 BPxQ, N-K7ch, etc. If 24 QxQ, N-K7ch, 25 K-R1, NxQch, 26 K-N1, NxR wins easily.

The Marshall-Levitsky chess match

Alekhine spent over an hour considering the countless ramifications of the move. In the end, he did not accept the sacrifice, but was so demoralized that he could not continue the play. "What a daring and imaginative move, and what a startling departure from orthodoxy," exclaimed one in the chorus of enthusiastic chess writers. (Since then, grand masters have played and replayed that knight sacrifice thousands of times; the current consensus is that Alekhine should have accepted the challenge and taken the knight.)

**Best Contest Entry:** The U.S. Army Materiel Command in 1974 ran a "Name-the-New-National-Headquarters-Building-and-Win-$100" contest. The AMC's Contest Committee sifted through some five hundred entries, finally settling on one submitted by civilian Frank Sikorski: "The AMC Building."

**Best Days:** Thanks to *Chase's Calendar of Annual Events,* there is always cause to celebrate. This comprehensive listing of holidays, feasts, anniversaries, and memorials proves that every day is a red-letter day. We mention just a few of the hundreds of important occasions that you may have neglected to observe in the past.

To begin with, the second week in January is "Save the Pun Week." And April 5 is "National Tomb Sweeping Day" in Formosa, followed soon after by "National Panic Week" (April 8–15) and "National Hostility Week" (April 15–22), when the humor societies of America conduct their National Hostility Championships. April 23 through May 6 marks "Write a Love Poem Fortnight," during which all Americans are encouraged to read and write romantic verse.

There are many festivals sponsored by corporations, including Doctor Scholl's "Give Your Feet a Treat Month," better known as May. In a more serious vein, June has been designated "Fight the Filthy Fly Month," "to make the public aware of the dangers of tolerating the typhoid flies." (You have been warned.)

"National Fink Week" is celebrated during the last week of June. Its purpose is "to restore dignity to the honorable surname of Fink," and on June 26 Finks from all over the country converge on the small town of Fink, Texas, to strike a blow against ridicule. In answer to Mother's Day and Father's Day, Zero Population Growth groups have proclaimed August 1 "National Non-Parent Day."

You might also circle on your calendar September 2, "Mustache Day"; October 21–27, "International Whale Watching Week"; and November 8, "Dunce Day," the supposed birthday of Duns Scotus, the unfortunate eleventh-century theologian from whose name the word "dunce" is derived. In addition, there is an almost endless series of food commemorations, including "National Peanut Month" (March), "National Artichoke Week" (April 18–27), "National Macaroni Week" (October 9–18)—some of these are long weeks—and best of all, "International Pickle Week" (May 22–31) "to give recognition to the world's most humorous vegetable."

After all that, it is a relief to discover that January 16 is "National Nothing Day," providing Americans "with one national day when they can just sit without celebrating, observing, or honoring anything." "National Nothing Day" is sponsored by the National Nothing Foundation based in Capitola, California.

**Best Do-It-Yourself Project:** If you are good with your hands, here's a way to occupy yourself on those long winter nights. Instead of wiring together a Heathkit FM tuner or a new amplifier, why not make your own A-bomb? It's fun and it's simple. In fact, according to nuclear physicist Theodore Taylor, "any reasonably intelligent person can build his own nuclear bomb."

The Public Television network hired a twenty-year-old MIT student to test Dr. Taylor's thesis. Said the young do-it-yourselfer, "I was really quite surprised at how easy the bomb was to design." He spent five weeks reading in the MIT library and made one trip to Washington to inspect unclassified Manhattan Project documents before sitting down to draw up his blueprints. "I estimate it would cost about $10,000 to actually build, weigh about 800 pounds, and require about fifteen pounds of plutonium," he said. The resulting explosion would be equivalent to

1,000 tons of TNT, sufficiently powerful to do in about 100,000 people. (The student asked the news media not to divulge his name for fear a terrorist organization might attempt to kidnap him.)

Producers of the science series "Nova" took the student's plans to United States weapons experts who refused to speculate on whether the homemade device could be detonated, but Dr. Jan Prawitz, a physicist with the Swedish Ministry of Defense, said there was a fifty-fifty chance it could go off.

**Best Parachute Jump:** By now just about everyone knows of Philippe Petit's legendary tightrope stroll in the summer of '74 between the twin towers of New York City's World Trade Center—the second tallest and worst-designed office building in the world. (See *Felton & Fowler's Best, Worst and Most Unusual*, p. 278.) Almost a year later to the day, an exhibitionist skydiver from Queens, New York, made his way past security guards to the roof of the Center's North Tower, where he surveyed the city 1,300 feet below. He then took off the construction worker's garb with which he had disguised himself, changed into sweatshirt, shorts, and silver helmet, donned a twenty-six-foot army surplus parachute, and jumped.

It took Owen J. Quinn two minutes to fall the 110 stories to the ground, and during that time he was buffeted by winds that flung him against the building, bruising his leg. He also had a scare: after free-falling 600 feet, he pulled the rip cord, but the parachute failed to open. "I knew that might happen on a jump from that altitude, because you don't have a lot of speed built up," he later said. "It was a bit of a shock, but I just sort of looked at it and at that instant it opened."

Parachute jumps from skyscrapers are not common, essentially because no man-made building is high enough to assure jumpers they'll have enough time for their chutes to open. FAA regulations prohibit skydiving from a plane flying lower than 2,500 feet, and Lee Levinson, manager of the Lakewood, New Jersey, Parachuting Center, said that Quinn's feat "was extremely dangerous and not too bright. It violates all the safety rules of parachuting and common sense."

Indeed, it did, but Quinn, a veteran of 850 jumps, seemed unruffled by the monumental risk he took. Quinn had done hard-hat work on the Tower in the earliest stages of construction, and said, "When I first saw the designs and found out there was going to be a straight vertical drop of 1,350 feet, I said, 'Boy, that would be a nice place to jump.' "

Shortly after landing, setting himself aright, and limping away from the point of impact, he was arrested by police who handcuffed him, put him in a wheelchair, and took him directly to Beekman Downtown Hospital in Manhattan, where psychiatrists deemed him mentally competent. While at the hospital he told physicians and newspaper reporters that his jump, while inspired by Petit's tightrope act, was less a lark than a political statement: "If people decided not to eat once a month," he said, "and to send the money to the needy poor, then it would help the situation." Quinn also told reporters that he had no objection—none, whatsoever—to being questioned by a psychiatrist.

"No," he told them, "I expected it. Why not? You just don't go and jump off a building."

**Best Slot Machine:** In the lobby of the MGM Grand Hotel in Las Vegas in 1975, a twenty-five-year-old gambler bagged the highest payoff ever made by a slot machine—$152,683. An official of the hotel said that the jackpot had been accumulating in the machine ever since the hotel opened for business in 1973.

**Best Soporific:** Calvin Coolidge kept a copy of Milton's *Paradise Lost* by his bed and used to read a few pages every night to help put him to sleep. (See "Health and Death," *Best Night's Rest.*)

Like many Victorians, Charles Dickens kept the head of his bed aligned precisely with the North Pole so that the earth's magnetic field would pass longitudinally through his body, ensuring him of a refreshing night's rest. Using similar logic, some Islamic worshipers point their beds toward Mecca.

Millionaire Cornelius Vanderbilt was an insomniac and a believer in the occult. He was never able to fall asleep unless the four legs of his bed were planted in dishes filled with salt, which kept malevolent spirits from attacking him.

**Best Television Performance Before a Congressional Investigating Committee:** Testifying before a televised session of the House Un-American Activities Committee in 1955, actor Zero Mostel declined to give information about alleged Communist involvement in the entertainment industry. After invoking the Fifth Amendment several times, Mostel answered repetitious questions by raising his right hand and wiggling five fingers. When asked, "What studio were you with?" he replied, "Eighteenth Century-Fox." Impatiently, the chairman demanded, "Do you want that statement to stand?" Mostel pondered for a moment, then said, "No, make that Nineteenth Century-Fox." At the end of the session the witness rose and said, "I want to thank the Committee for making it possible for me to be on TV because I've been blacklisted from it for five years."

**Best Television Show:** While we are not about to abdicate the position we took in *Felton and Fowler I*—namely, that the old Sid Caesar comedy series, "Your Show of Shows," was the best TV show ever—we are more than willing to give equal air time to dissenting views from responsible parties. Thus, we'd like to report that in a poll of three thousand TV industry executives conducted in 1975 by the Broadcast Information Bureau, "Show" came in second. First place went to "Perry Mason."

"Mason," you'll recall, premiered on network TV in 1957, scored high ratings, and ran nine years before being farmed out to local syndicates. Today, Raymond Burr's anachronistically skinny neckties are visible on seventy-nine local channels throughout the United States.

A memorable series, certainly, but was it the best? To be sure, the three thousand pollees listed no fewer than 302 different series as their all-time favorites. Those who didn't choose "Perry Mason" opted for "The Defenders." Or "Omnibus." Or "The Milton Berle Show." Or "Captain Video." Or . . . "Mason" just got more votes than any other program.

Nonetheless, the five top-seeded series in the survey—"Mason," "Your Show of Shows," "Star Trek," "Playhouse 90," and "The Mary Tyler Moore Show," in that order—had one thing in common, according to Willard Block, vice-president of MCA: "The writers are or were given more time to provide good scripts than the average show." An advertising agency vice-president who took part in the poll added, "Courtroom dramas have always had tremendous appeal in every medium, especially with strong casts like 'Perry Mason.' "

Perhaps. We liked "Perry Mason" a lot. But "The Defenders" was even better. And the best TV has ever offered is still "Your Show of Shows."

---

**Worst Amusement Park:** If you are ever nostalgic for Khe Sanh, if you miss the deafening roar of incoming artillery shells, simply head for Cape Canaveral, Florida, home of America's most outlandish amusement park.

"It's a Fantasyland type of thing," explains Giles Pace, the director of "New Vietnam." Construction of this model Vietnamese hamlet began in August 1975, and the details are frightfully authentic, right down to the last punji stake. The rice paddies will be tilled by barefoot men and women, dressed in the familiar pajama garb; water buffalo are being imported from Southeast Asia; irrigation dikes crisscross the three hundred-acre site; and hundreds of banana and palm trees are being planted in the area. Soon, sampan rides will be offered on the nearby Banana River.

Already nearly sixty Vietnamese refugees have joined the park staff; they will form the core of an artisan community that will turn out hand-woven rugs, ceramic elephants, and other souvenirs. Others will join them to man the restaurants and fast-food stands that will dish out tempting Saigon specialties.

But New Vietnam is more than boiled rice and bamboo shoots. This is Vietnam as it used to be in the heyday of the American presence. Alongside the sixteen thatched native huts will be a simulated U.S. Special Forces barracks, fortified with trenches, moats, sandbag walls, and miles of barbed wire. And here is where the real fun begins: "After a tour gets inside the camp, we'll have a recording broadcast a firefight, mortars exploding, bullets flying, Vietnamese screaming," says Pace. Actors in surplus army fatigues will fire blanks at the fanatical enemy hidden in the underbrush, and the kids can help out, too, taking a turn at the trigger of a model machine gun.

New Vietnam is the brainchild of the Reverend Carl McIntyre, the fundamentalist New Jersey preacher who organized the Victory Marches on Washington during the 1960s. "Tourists are just going to love this," he promises.

**Worst Board Game:** The Ideal Toy Corporation has marketed a new board game called Titanic, based on the 1912 sea disaster of the same name. It's billed as "the game you play as the ship goes down."

**Worst Chess Set:** *Soviet Life* ran a feature article on Nikolai Syadristy, a craftsman from Uzhgorod, who hand-carved a set of chess figures so small that they can only be distinguished when magnified two thousand times with a microscope. Syadristy has also forged horseshoes for fleas.

**Worst Christmas Cards:** During the 1969 Yuletide season, the Palestinian terrorist organization, El Fatah, issued a series of colorful Christmas cards depicting a group of gentle, wide-eyed children—one with a submachine gun slung over his shoulder. Sales of the cards in Lebanon and abroad netted El Fatah $100,000 in revenues, which went toward the purchase of arms.

The official Black Panther Party Christmas cards, also distributed in 1969, were filled with irreverent (one is tempted to say black) humor.

One greeting featured a white Santa Claus emerging from the fireplace to find a warm welcome awaiting him. A black father pokes a loaded carbine right in the old bowl-full-of-jelly, while a little boy prepares to cave in the jolly intruder's skull with the trunk of a small Christmas tree.

**Worst Crossword Puzzle:** Stumped by an especially tough puzzle, a crossword addict in West Germany stuck with it through the night, repeatedly waking her sleeping husband for assistance. The fourth time she woke him, he became violently enraged and strangled her. The court acquitted him on grounds of temporary insanity.

**Worst Hoax:** Nearly two centuries after it was perpetrated, the Berners Street Hoax of 1809 seems a wonderful jape, the mirthful brainchild of a comic genius at his inventive best. Hearing of it for the first time, moviegoers think immediately of the now-classic stateroom scene in the Marx Brothers' *A Night at the Opera.* In truth, the hoax was something less than funny. It was a day-long nightmare for everyone concerned.

It began with Theodore Hook, a notorious practical joker, strolling down Berners Street, a residential avenue on the outskirts of London. For no special reason the house at 54 Berners Street, a nondescript affair set back from the pavement like all the other row-houses up and down the street, struck his fancy. Hook boasted to his companion, a man named Higginson, that he could make the house, unprepossessing as it was, the most famous spot in London. He invited Higginson to bet that he couldn't do it and his friend accepted the wager.

Within a few days, Hook had ascertained that the sole inhabitant of the house was an elderly widow named Mrs. Tottingham. Over the course of the next two weeks he sent out more than a thousand letters over Mrs. Tottingham's forged signature, each one filled with mischief.

Early one morning, with Hook watching the action from a well-chosen hiding place across the street, a dozen chimney sweeps converged at Mrs. Tottingham's front door and announced, logically enough, that they were there to sweep the chimney. Mrs. Tottingham was perplexed. She hadn't contracted any chimney sweeps and despite her apparently honest confusion, the sweeps, some of whom had traveled from the opposite end of the city, were up in arms. While she haggled with them, several men drew up to the front door, each with a cart bearing a ton of coal, "as per your esteemed order." Of course, Mrs. Tottingham had ordered no coal. Nor had she ordered the truckload of furniture—miscellaneous tables, chairs and endpieces—that soon arrived, nor the shipment of tap beer, the mammoth organ, the several bushels of potatoes, nor the hearse, which were brought to her home within a few minutes.

Confectioners arrived too with their wares, along with other merchants—wigmakers, hairdressers, butchers, machinists, jewelers, grocers, furriers, seamstresses, repairmen, and opticians. Two physicians also arrived, as well as a dentist, each intent upon examining Mrs. Tottingham for the ills she had described in her letters.

While all this was taking place, Berners Street was hopelessly congested with deliverymen, carts, and onlookers. The police also came to restore order but proved ineffectual. Then the Duke of York, Commander-in-Chief of the Army, arrived. He had been written that one of his men lay moribund at 54 Berners Street and desperately needed to see him at once. Following on the Duke's heels were the Archbishop of Canterbury, the Lord Chief Justice, the Governor of the Bank of England, and the Lord Mayor of London.

It was the last who put an end to all this knavery. He, it seems, had been victimized himself in much the same way, and had reason to suspect Hook as the perpetrator of the fraud. Additional cadres of police officers were called out, and soon peace and order were restored. As for Hook, he won his bet and maintained his anonymity. However, he made a point of not being seen publicly in London for quite some time.

**Worst Hobby:** Warning: *The Practitioner*, a leading British medical journal, has determined that bird-watching may be hazardous to your health. The magazine, in fact, has officially designated bird-watching a "hazardous hobby," after documenting the death of a weekend bird-watcher who became so immersed in his subject that he grew oblivious to his surroundings and consequently was eaten alive by a crocodile.

**Worst Lottery Prize:** In Australia, one is better off avoiding lotteries and playing the kangaroos instead. Herbert Chun of New South Wales purchased a lottery ticket and won $70,000. When told the good news, he became so excited that he suffered a fatal heart attack. . . . William Lane and Harold Richards both died after winning nearly $250,000 apiece in lottery prizes. . . . And by the time lottery officials got to Annie Harris with the news that she'd bagged the $20,000 prize, she was also dead, her body slumped in her easy chair.

**Worst News for Bicentennial Buffs:** Father of his country or not, George Washington may well have been *sterile*. Or so claims a Virginia urologist, Dr. M. J. V. Smith, of the Medical College of Virginia. Washington fathered no children, Smith points out, and he suffered from a variety of debilitating diseases, including smallpox, rotten teeth, consumption, amoebic dysentery, pleurisy, malaria, and a genetic impairment called Kleinfelter's syndrome, that could well have rendered him sterile. And not much fun to be with, either.

**Worst News for Nostalgia Buffs:** *The New York Times* reported that on the old "You Bet Your Life" TV quiz show, Groucho Marx used idiot cards.

**Worst News Photo:** A team of ten photographers employed high-powered speedboats, skin-diving gear, waterproof camera equipment, and extremely powerful telephoto lenses to snap candid pictures of Jacqueline Kennedy Onassis sunbathing in the nude on a remote private beach. (See also "Fashion and Grooming," *Best Dressed.*) Although it took fifteen months to get the blurry, but recognizable, full-frontal shots, the effort paid off handsomely. The Italian magazine *Playmen* bought the first rights to the photographs for $75,000, and the pictures were later reproduced in *Rolling Stone* and other publications throughout the world. Columnist Jack Anderson wrote that Mrs. Onassis was furious when her husband Aristotle refused to finance a suit against the photographers for invasion of privacy.

**Worst Picnic:** The Jaycees and the Yakima, Washington, Police Department got together to sponsor a picnic for eight hundred fifth and sixth graders from Yakima Valley School in May 1975. The main attraction: a loaded .50 caliber machine gun lent for the day by the Marine Corps Reserve. According to Gunnery Sgt. Richard Cecil of the Marines, the children fired off some three thousand rounds of blank ammunition during the day's festivities. Afterwards, they all went to the movies to see, improbable as it sounds, *The Gang That Couldn't Shoot Straight.*

**Worst Publicity Stunt:** Herostatus burned down the temple of the goddess Diana at Ephesus in the fourth century B.C. for the sole purpose of ensuring that his name would live forever in history books.

**Worst Show-off:** In an unannounced departure from her script, Chris Chubbuck, a Sarasota, Florida, newswoman shot herself through the head during a local evening newscast in 1974.

That same year a twenty-two-year-old Oregon disc jockey of more subtle inclinations quietly strangled himself on the air with a telephone wire to the strains of "Softly as I Leave You."

**Worst Stunt:** For sheer idiocy (combined with a strong death wish), no human endeavor can quite compare with high-altitude jumping, which was in vogue during the 1800s. The fad was originated by Samuel Patch of Pawtucket, Rhode Island, the Evel Knievel of his day. In 1827 Patch announced his intention of diving off the Paterson Bridge. The authorities tried to arrest him for his own protection, but he eluded them and plunged ninety feet into the swirling Passaic River. When he bobbed to the surface, alive, Samuel Patch was a national hero.

His next challenge was Niagara Falls. Patch selected a high precipice on Goat Island as his point of departure. He jumped feet first, fell half the height of the falls into the river, and survived. But Patch's thirst for danger had still not been satisfied, and he turned his attentions to the treacherous Genesee Falls. With a large crowd to cheer him on, he made a running leap fom the banks of the Genesee "into the abyss below, a distance of 125 feet." Patch jumped on November 13, 1829. They did not find his body until March 17.

Samuel Patch was dead, but Steve Brodie, a foolhardy newsboy from New York City, took up the torch. On July 23, 1886, he jumped from the Brooklyn Bridge into the East River and lived to tell the tale. Acclaimed as "the man who took a chance," Brodie toured variety halls and theaters re-creating his famous leap. With a cry of "I'll save the girl" he would hop six feet from a cardboard bridge down onto the stage, while the propman provided a splash of confetti. Brodie might have been forgotten had he not risked his life one more time. On September 7, 1889, wearing an India rubber suit, Brodie allegedly jumped the full height of Niagara Falls—165 feet—and swam to shore uninjured. Few witnesses were present, and there were some who said that the jump was nothing but an elaborate hoax. Understandably, Brodie was reluctant to do it again. Regardless of what happened that day, his name became a part of the American language; Webster's defines a "brodie" as "a suicidal leap, hence a fall or flop."

Richard Nixon, Adlai Stevenson, J. Robert Oppenheimer, Judge Learned Hand, and other celebrities have done a little jumping of their own, albeit from less exalted levels. For his *Jump Book,* published by Simon & Schuster in 1960, photographer Philippe Halsman persuaded fifty famous people to kick up their heels, while he captured their capers on film. It is one of the oddest picture books ever compiled.

**Worst Television Comedy Show:** In King's Lynn, England, a fifty-year-old bricklayer suffered a fatal heart attack after laughing uncontrollably for nearly an hour at "The Goodies," a prime-time television comedy show. His wife told reporters that she planned to write to the show's producers to thank them "for making my husband's last minutes so happy."

**Worst Television Sportscasting:** The TV producers and not the quarter-backs were calling the signals at the 1975 Blue-Gray all-star football game. Unbeknownst to the coaches or players, executives of Mizlou, the independent network covering the contest, had arranged to shorten the first quarter from fifteen to twelve minutes so that it would fit neatly into its scheduled time slot. Later, as the tempo of play picked up, Mizlou was afraid the game would end too early, and word went out to the timekeeper to slow the game down. The North mounted a dramatic last-minute drive and the last minute seemed to last forever. As the clock stood still, the Blue scored on a fifty-one-yard pass, then with three seconds remaining kicked the extra point to win, 14–13—long after regulation time should have expired.

**Worst Way to Swallow a Sword:** Any sword swallower worth his throat lozenges knows that trying to swallow a thirty-six-inch Toledo when you're angry or upset is folly. "When you're upset, tight spots develop in your throat," explains Lady Estelline Pike, a free-lance swallower based in New York. "If you try swallowing then, you'll get in trouble." Lady Estelline, who first plied her trade in Kansas in the 1920s, says she suffered her first on-the-job injury in 1958 when she tried downing a World War I bayonet after an argument with her boss. "I bled internally and saw a doctor," she remembers, "but there was nothing to do but take antibiotics, drink fruit juices, and just wait for it to heal." These days Lady Estelline performs regularly in a small theater in midtown Manhattan; her impressive fourteen-blade arsenal is a far cry from the spoons and barbecue forks she worked with in her heyday. She claims she never has sore throats.

**Worst Wedding:** While performing a marriage ceremony in Madison, Wisconsin, Reverend Joseph Mueller fell dead of a heart attack.

"It was the most beautiful thing I've ever seen," said Mueller's assistant, Reverend James Kaczmarek, who immediately took up where the stricken Mueller had left off, and completed the Wedding Mass. "It seems fitting that a man who devoted his life to God should die on the altar, and it's as if my whole purpose in being there was just to give him the last rites. Too few people are lucky enough to have that kind of death."

---

**Most Unusual Bicentennial Pageant:** The Boom Boom Room of Miami Beach's Fontainebleau Hotel has an adult Bicentennial revue featuring a topless Betsy Ross and, for the finale, a nude Statue of Liberty.

**Most Unusual Card Shuffler:** For big-time blackjack dealers in the gambling dens of Las Vegas, card shuffling is one of those nuisance chores, like dental-flossing your teeth at bedtime or brushing out the loose hair from your cat. Now a professor of hotel administration at the University of Nevada in Las Vegas has come up with a way to end the bother of card shuffling once and for all: the professional card shuffler. According to the professor, the shuffler would be hired by the casino to do nothing but roam the tables shuffling the cards for dealers, who will then have as much as 25 percent more time to place bets—and hopefully, win more money for the house.

**Most Unusual Censor:** Marty Snyder, a sixty-year-old Republican committeeman, was appointed to the Clarkstown, New York, censorship board in 1973. Snyder, who is blind, told reporters that his handicap would not interfere with his work on the board, which reviews X-rated movies. "Pornography isn't a case of seeing," he said, "it's a case of feeling." Although Snyder denied that he was a stuffed shirt, he did express some nostalgia for the movies of the twenties and thirties, "when at least a girl had a thing across her back."

England's best-known censor was Thomas Bowdler (1754–1825) who excised every bawdy passage and suggestive pun in Shakespeare's thirty-seven plays. Bowdler even went so far as to eliminate characters whom he judged lacking in redeeming social value, among them Doll Tearsheet in *Henry IV, Part Two*. It is a tribute to Bowdler's acute sensitivity in matters of decency that many high school texts still follow his expurgations word for word. Another landmark volume in the war on smut was the 1833 bowdlerized edition of the Bible, edited by that well-known lexicographer Noah Webster. The following is a tempting sample of what you *won't* find in Webster's Bible:

> Thy navel is like a round goblet, which wanteth not liquor; thy belly is like an heap of wheat set about with lillies. Thy two breasts are like two young roes that are twins.
>
> (Song of Sol. 7: 2–3)

**Most Unusual Cocktail Party:** Several hundred guests attended a bizarre cocktail reception at the Paris Zoo in 1817, held inside the iron-and-wood framework of a giant stuffed elephant. Less bizarre, but more ambitious, was a monumental bash hosted by the Roman emperor Justinian in A.D. 537 to mark the completion of the Hagia Sophia, the great church of Constantinople. Roasted, served, and consumed at the feast were 6,000 sheep, 1,000 oxen, 1,000 pigs, 1,000 chickens, and 500 deer.

**Most Unusual Collection:** "The most unusual collection of what?" you may ask. Well, over a period of forty years, Homer and Langley Collyer accumulated a colossal stockpile of almost everything imaginable.

People always knew there was something odd about the Collyer brothers. Both men were college graduates; Homer was a Columbia-educated lawyer. For decades they lived a totally isolated existence in the New York City home they had inherited from their gynecologist father. As far as anyone could recall, they never received any friends or visitors. In fact, they had done everything in their power to make their home uninviting; the doors were padlocked, the windows were boarded up, and the gas, water, and electricity had long ago been disconnected. But no one fully appreciated just how peculiar they were until March 21, 1947, when an anonymous tipster told the police, "There's a man dead at 2078 Fifth Avenue"—the Collyer residence in Harlem.

Squad cars rushed to the scene. When knocking and shouting brought no answer, the police decided to break down the door; they couldn't. According to the official report, their way was blocked by a huge "wall of newspapers, folding chairs, broken boxes, part of a wine press, half a sewing machine, folding beds, parts of a rocking chair, and innumerable other pieces of junk." Instead they were forced to enter through a second-story window.

After a lengthy search through the surrealistic pile of debris, Homer Collyer was discovered lying in his bed, dead of heart disease or starvation. In his hand was a copy of the *Jewish Morning Journal* dated February 22, 1920. To add to the macabre mystery, it was discovered that Homer couldn't possibly have been reading the *Morning Journal* since he was blind. The owner of a local vegetable market testified that the dead man used to eat a hundred oranges a week in hopes of regaining his sight. And, as Langley had once explained it, Homer's blindness was the reason for gathering the Everest of old newspapers: "I'm saving them for when Homer regains his sight. He can catch up on his reading."

There was no sign at all of Langley, but everyone expected that he would materialize for his brother's funeral. He didn't. And so a massive excavation was begun. Police investigators removed one hundred tons of American and foreign newspapers, thousands of cardboard boxes, countless rags, a forest of furniture, spare automobile parts, five violins, seventeen pianos, and much, much more. In all, over 140 tons of oddments were carted away.

Nineteen days later Langley's body was finally uncovered less than six feet away from where his brother had been found—buried underneath bundles of newspapers, a suitcase packed with metal scraps, a sewing

An end to the Most Unusual Collection: the body of Homer Collyer is lowered from the second story of his house.

machine, and three breadboxes. He had been killed by one of the many booby traps he had installed to protect his fabulous collection.

**Most Unusual Jukebox:** Grimes Poznikov is his real name, but he is better known to his public as "the Automatic Human Jukebox." A Midwesterner transplanted to San Francisco, Poznikov spends his days inside a fiberboard crate where he plays tolerable trumpet solos selected by passersby. On the surface, he runs his operation much like any standard jukebox: the customer drops his coin in the slot, then presses the

The Automatic
Human Jukebox

button next to the song of his choice. "Failure to pick a tune within fifteen seconds," warns a prominently posted sign, "will result in a forty-percent reduction in quality of operation or erratic performance."

Like other street vendors and artists, Poznikov plies his trade without a license, and on occasion has run afoul of the law. Once he had two municipal departments trying to determine whether he was to be classified as a street artist or a building.

**Most Unusual Pornography:** Eighteen members of the House of Representatives have been censured since that august body was first called into session in 1789. The last to receive an official reprimand was Representative Thomas Blanton of Texas, who was both censured and censored in October 1921. Officially, Blanton was charged with inserting a piece of correspondence into the *Congressional Record* that was so obscene it would make even a politician blush.

The Speaker of the House lectured Blanton with holy indignation: "Foul and obscene matter, which you know you could not have spoken on the floor, and that disgusting matter, which could not have been circulated through the mails in any other publication without violating the law, was transmitted as part of the proceedings of this house to thousands of homes and libraries throughout the country, to be read by men and women and worst of all by children whose prurient curiosity it would excite and corrupt."

We would not hesitate to excite your prurient interests with a ribald excerpt from the *Record*, but, unhappily, the smutty passage was discovered and deleted from the text before the permanent bound copies were released. Only the loose copies contained Blanton's bawdry, and most, if not all, of those have been destroyed.

Apparently Blanton's constituency was not terribly offended by his indiscretion. They reelected him the next year and continued to return him to Washington until 1937. And in 1922, just one year after he was censured, Blanton introduced a landmark reform bill abolishing free baths and shaves in the House.

**Most Unusual Television Documentary:** In 1969, Anthony Armstrong-Jones, Lord Snowdon, produced a BBC documentary in which he displayed a young chick purportedly hatched from an egg placed between the breasts of a sixty-year-old woman. A storm of controversy ensued. "Was it really possible?" the public demanded to know. By way of a precedent, Lord Snowdon produced a copy of Thomas Hardy's *Jude the Obscure* and quoted the passage where Arabella Donn tells the hero to keep his roving hands off because she is hatching a Cochin's egg. In an angry rebuttal, a knight and poultry farmer from the Isle of Anglesey characterized Snowdon and Hardy as a pair of birdbrains and stated, "It takes twenty-one days at 104 degrees F to hatch an egg and from my experience of ladies' bosoms this is rarely attainable." Britain's National Institute of Poultry Husbandry then came to Snowdon's defense. "If you tried to hatch eggs at 104 degrees you would cook them," a spokesman said. The ideal incubating temperature is 99 degrees, virtually the temperature of the human body.

**Most Unusual Television Ratings:** Here's an experience familiar to everyone at one time or another. Midway through an especially engrossing TV show, your kidneys begin to remind you, with mounting urgency, that they've been under a strain for quite a while now and you'd better do something about it in a hurry. Finally, the screen action breaks and, as the commercial comes on, you bolt for the bathroom hoping to make it back before the program resumes.

There is a lesson to be learned here about the correlation between TV programming and toilet use. Namely, that a good show with wide popular appeal will prompt vast numbers of viewers to hold off, so to speak, till the commercial, when they will race to their respective bathrooms in unison and participate in a mass flush, dramatically lowering the city's water pressure. Right? Right. Using this hypothesis, the Waterworks Department of Lafayette, Louisiana, came up with its own answer to the Nielsen ratings by monitoring the dips and rises in the city's water pressure during a prime-time screening of the movie *Airport*. Their report: "At approximately 8:30, a bomb exploded in the airplane, and from then until nine P.M., when the pilot landed safely and the movie ended, almost nobody left his television set to do anything—then there was a twenty-six-pound drop in water pressure."

A twenty-six-pound drop, brought on by twenty thousand viewers flushing away eight thousand gallons in chorus, is nothing for TV programmers to sneeze at. In fact, it is an excellent indication of just how popular *Airport* is. As for comparative figures: *Patton,* starring George C. Scott, produced a twenty-two-pound drop when it was aired on TV for the first time, while *The Good, the Bad, and the Ugly* was credited with nineteen pounds.

# Sports

**Best Acrobatic Act:** A bus carrying a team of seven Japanese acrobats plunged from a cliff near Tokyo in 1933. Death seemed inevitable as the vehicle careened violently down the mountainside, overturning several times. A few hundred feet down, however, the bus's progress was stemmed for a split second when it struck a rock. In that instant, the seven men hurled themselves through open windows and landed in the branches of a tree, bruised and dazed—but alive.

**Best Alternative to Fox-Hunting:** London businessman Walter Gilbey (of the Gilbey's Gin millions) has contrived a humanitarian, if somewhat sloppy, alternative to fox-hunting that is sure to win the blessing of animal lovers everywhere: people-hunting.

Every weekend, Gilbey flies to the wide open spaces of the Isle of Man, where he sets his bloodhounds on the trail of their quarry—a fun-loving human volunteer. No matter how fleet-footed and resourceful, the quarry eventually falls exhausted to the ground and the dogs move in for the final attack—a violent, no-holds-barred, head-to-toe licking.

"I feel just a bit frightened," nineteen-year-old volunteer "fox" Judy Matthews told London news reporters before one recent outing. "But the bloodhounds are trained just to lick the quarry when they catch up." And Gilbey added, "It is both an exciting and harmless sport, and much the thing of the future."

**Best Athlete:** In 1950, the Associated Press asked a panel of sportswriters to name the greatest athletes of the first fifty years of the twentieth century. The overwhelming first choice was Jim Thorpe.

Thorpe, who stood six feet tall and weighed 190 pounds, scored twenty-five touchdowns and 198 points for the Carlisle Institute football squad in 1912, and in both 1911 and 1912 he was selected halfback on the Walter Camp All-American team. But Thorpe was more than a grid-iron hero; he was the greatest all-around athlete of modern times. At the 1912 Olympic Games in Stockholm, he copped gold medals in the pentathlon and decathlon—the only man ever to sweep both events. (When King Gustav of Sweden presented the medals at a special reception, Thorpe hailed him with the classic greeting, "Hi, King.")

As a professional baseball player, he batted .327 for the Boston Braves in 1919. But he is best remembered as a superlative, though erratic, halfback with the old Canton Bulldogs during the growing years of professional football. He ran with the same confidence, agility, and swivel hips that Red Grange was later to display.

Thorpe died in 1953, but those who saw him play will never forget him. In his honor, the towns of Mauch Chunk and East Mauch Chunk, Pennsylvania, were joined together and named Jim Thorpe.

Other great athletes on the AP list were, in order: (2) Babe Ruth, (3) Jack Dempsey, (4) Ty Cobb, (5) Bobby Jones, (6) Joe Lewis, (7) Red Grange, (8) Jesse Owens, (9) Lou Gehrig, (10) Bronko Nagurski, (11) Jackie Robinson, and (12) Bob Mathias.

In the category of "Best Female Athlete" there was no contest. Babe Didrikson Zaharias (1914–1956) dominated women's sports for over twenty-five years. She first attracted national attention when she was named an All-American basketball player in 1930. Over the next several years, she won national championships in nine women's track-and-field events, setting numerous records, and in 1932 she earned Olympic gold medals in the javelin throw and the 80-meter hurdles. Abandoning the cinder oval in favor of the fairways, Mrs. Zaharias captured seventeen consecutive golf championships in 1947. She went on to win every major women's tournament at least once, including the 1954 U.S. National Open and the All-American Open.

Finally, as the greatest sporting event of the previous five decades, the AP writers selected the heroic comeback of "the Manassa Mauler," Jack Dempsey, in his 1923 fight against Luis Firpo in New York City.

**Best (Baseball) Catch:** In July 1931, Joe "Mule" Sprinz of the Cleveland Indians caught a baseball tossed from a blimp hovering 800 feet in the air. Sprinz handled the ball flawlessly, receiving it in an overstuffed catcher's mitt, but the impact sent a shock wave through his body that broke his jaw.

**Best (Baseball) Trade:** The Shawnee Hawks, a Class D Sooner League team, once traded Lindy Chappoten, an unpromising pitcher, to the Texarkana Bears, in exchange for twenty uniforms.

Ralph DePalma at the 1912 Indianapolis 500

**Best Billiards Performance:** The great 1920s billiards master, Henry Lewis, once sank forty-six balls in a row using his nose as a cue stick. His achievement is eclipsed only by that of George Henry Sutton, a native of Toledo, Ohio, who won national billiards honors and once chalked up a 3,000-ball run despite the fact that he had no arms.

**Best Bowling Alley:** Chances are you won't have to wait long for an alley at Tokyo World Lanes Bowling Center, the largest bowling establishment in the world. It has 252 lanes.

**Best Brick Smasher:** Tom Slaven, a thirty-five-year-old black belt karate instructor from Sydney, Australia, barehandedly smashed 4,487 bricks in one hour in 1975 to set a world's record.

**Best College Try:** Ralph DePalma took an early lead in the 1912 Indianapolis 500, but in the 199th lap, with victory just inches away, he blew a connecting rod in his Mercedes and stalled out. With no time to lose, DePalma hopped out and, aided by his mechanic, pushed the disabled vehicle across the finish line to complete the 199th lap.

And did this bit of last-minute resourcefulness win DePalma first place? Unfortunately not. Since racing rules provide that a car must finish an event under its own power in order to win DePalma was credited with completing only 198 laps and was ranked eleventh in the final standings, behind all the remaining competitors.

**Best Dive:** Forget Mike King (see *Felton & Fowler I*, page 90) and turn your thoughts to Alex Wickham of the Solomon Islands, who survived a 205-foot dive from a cliff in Australia in 1918. However, he blacked out in mid-fall and the impact of the water's surface tore off his bathing suit.

**Best Execution of the Adage "Winning Isn't Everything, It's the Only Thing":** "The important thing in the Olympics is not so much winning as taking part," or so reads the official slogan of the quadrennial Games. But Japanese marathon runner Kokichi Tsuburaya was an all-or-nothing man of the Vince Lombardi mold.

An able long-distance runner, he was his country's last hope for a gold medal in the 1964 Olympics. He turned in a courageous performance in the grueling marathon event, but could manage only a third-place finish and bronze medal.

Friends reported that Tsuburaya was desolated, and after the Games were over he sank into a long and profound depression. Two years later he committed hara-kiri, leaving behind a suicide note apologizing for having failed his country.

**Best Fan:** A Denver, Colorado, football fan, despondent over the Broncos' 33–14 loss to the Chicago Bears during the 1973 season, shot himself in the head with a revolver. Before pulling the trigger, he composed a brief note which read, "I have been a Broncos fan since the Broncos were first organized and I can't take their fumbling anymore." True to the form of his favorite team, the man failed in his suicide attempt. His name was withheld by police.

**Best Fishing Catch:** The captain of a Greek fishing boat, plying the Aegean waters off the island of Chios, laid out his nets for what he thought was a shark and bagged a Turkish submarine instead.

Spotting the periscope, he ordered his crew to sever the ropes and retreat, leaving the enmeshed sub to fend for itself. Eventually, a cruising Turkish destroyer arrived to disentangle the discarded catch.

**Best Golf Shot:** Astronaut Alan B. Shepard, who smuggled a six-iron and a package of balls on board his Apollo XIV spacecraft, became the first golfer on the moon in February 1971. Despite a busy work schedule and his cumbersome space suit, Shepard was able to get in a few minutes of practice during an extra-vehicular walk. His worst shot in the airless, low-gravity environment traveled about four hundred yards on

Astronaut Alan B. Shepard, Jr. tees off on the moon

the fly, bounced once or twice, and settled down in the fine lunar dust. "Not bad for a six-iron," Shepard remarked. And as he later explained to Vice President Spiro Agnew, "No matter how badly you hit the balls they'll go straight."

**Best Heckler:** Every player in both leagues knew Pete Adelis. You couldn't miss him, sitting there in his box behind home plate; he was six feet tall, weighed 260 pounds, and wore a size fifty-two suit. Known as "Leather Lung Pete" or "the Iron Lung," he was baseball's first and (as far as we know) only "professional" heckler.

Adelis began his abusive career as a fan of the Philadelphia Athletics. He was no ordinary boo-bird, hurling clichéd insults at the umpire; on the contrary, he was a "scientific heckler" who knew each player's personal sensitivities the way a pitcher remembers a weakness for a slow curve. The management was duly impressed with his booming voice and his ability to rattle visiting batters. Soon the club was picking up his expenses so he could travel to away-games and deflate the Athletics' opponents on their home grounds. This arrangement continued until the 1950s when the Yankees hired Adelis away from the National League to dissect the egos of their perennial rivals for the pennant, the Cleveland Indians.

The following example is typical of his strident methods: Adelis was in a box right behind home plate at Ebbets Field one day when Billy Herman came to bat. Adelis had been riding Herman hard, and the latter was already upset by the recent drowning of his friend and fellow Dodger Arkie Vaughn. When Herman took a called third strike right over the center of the plate, Adelis bellowed, "Herman—the wrong guy got drowned!" Herman dropped his bat, leaped over the fence into the stands, and chased his loud-mouthed antagonist, intent on murder. Adelis survived the assault, but was thenceforth banned from Ebbets Field.

**Best Knockout Punch:** In a match in Lewiston, Maine, on September 29, 1946, prizefighter Ralph Walton was still setting his rubber mouthpiece in place when the bell rang for the first round. His opponent, Al Couture, darted across the ring and floored him with one devastating punch. The fight lasted ten and one-half seconds including a full ten-second count.

Lewiston was also the site of the celebrated Liston-Clay fight in 1965. Many fans were still looking for their $50 seats at the heavyweight championship bout when Clay (who had not yet changed his name to Muhammad Ali) laid out Liston with the much-debated "mystery punch." Total elapsed time in the first-round KO, 1 minute 57 seconds.

**Best Pipe Smoker:** Johnny Pearce, a seventeen-year-old North Carolinian, swam two and one-half miles in 1930 while holding a lit pipe in his mouth.

A magnificent feat of endurance and natatorial skill, certainly—but acrobatics of that sort cut little ice with the purists who compete in the World Championship Pipe Smoking Contest, sponsored annually since 1949 by the International Association of Pipe Smoker's Clubs, Inc., at Overland Park, Kansas. As of this writing, the best pipe smoker ever, according to I.A.P.S.C. standards, is Bill Vargo, a forty-six-year-old automobile machinist who kept 3.3 grams of tobacco lit for two hours, six minutes, and 39 seconds in the 1975 contest, breaking Max Igree's 1954 world's record of 2:5:7.

A Finnish tobaccophile, Yrje Pentikainen, claims to have kept 3.3 grams of tobacco burning nonstop for over four hours, but I.A.S.P.C. members discount his achievement since (a) he smoked a water-hookah rather than a regulation briar pipe, (b) he used stringy tobacco rather than the harder-to-light cube-cut variety allowed in I.A.P.S.C. competitions, and (c) he added tobacco to the bowl bit by bit throughout the smoking, rather than lighting it up all at once. In other words, says the I.A.P.S.C., he cheated.

The men who converge upon the Glenwood Manor Motor Hotel in Overland Park each summer to show off their pipe puffing prowess take

27th ANNUAL CONVENTION

# INTERNATIONAL ASSOCIATION

OF

# PIPE SMOKER'S CLUBS, INC.

FEATURING
World's Champion
Pipe Smoking Contest

FEATURING
World's Champion
Pipe Smoking Contest

Announcement of the World Championship Pipe Smoking Contest

their smoking seriously, and play by a code of sharply limned rules: once the starter yells "Gentlemen, light your pipes," the competitors have sixty seconds to light the 3.3 grams of cube-cut barley tobacco they have packed into the bowl. Each is allowed a limit of two matches, and once the sixty-second starting period elapses, the nonlighters are eliminated and all unused matches and tobacco crumbs are cleared away.

Some players ignite only a small part of the tobacco, hoping that the flame will spread slowly to the rest of the bowl and thus keep the pipe going for a long burn; others go for an even burn on the top surface and try to get the heat to percolate downward. Says champion Vargo, "Some people pack their tobacco too hard and it goes out. A person should learn to pack tobacco to his own draw."

Win, lose, or—the pun is unfortunate, we admit—draw, those who participate in the annual rite evince an enthusiasm for the pipe smoker's art that borders on religious ardor. "Pipes have been a symbol of peace ever since the Indians," said one four-time champion Paul Spaniola, of Flint, Michigan. "If everybody smoked a pipe, we feel there would never be wars. You'll notice in the newspapers or on TV, or in the movies, you never see a hardened violent criminal smoking a pipe."

**Best Slow Bicyclist:** Slow-bicycling has not been drawing the crowds it used to—not since Japanese slow-cycling star Tsugunobo Mitsuishi discouraged all challengers by remaining upright and stationary on a bicycle for five hours, twenty-five minutes in 1965.

**Best Soccer Penalty:** In 1964, an accident left Janos Pek paralyzed, mute, and confined for the rest of his days to a hospital bed in Kapsovar, Hungary. However, the accident did not quench the flames of his passion for soccer. One day in 1975, Pek was listening to a radio account of an important soccer match when a forward was fouled in front of his own goal line. Before he realized what he was doing, Pek shouted, "Penalty!" It was the first time in eleven years that he had uttered a single human sound.

Pek's physicians explained that his muteness had been the result of severe psychological trauma, and that it had been cured by intense excitement. Pek's team went on to win the game and, while he remains paralyzed, he has been speaking normally ever since.

**Best State Sport:** Making a choice in this category was comparatively simple. In 1962 Governor J. Millard Tawes signed a bill recognizing jousting as the state sport of Maryland. Maryland is the first and only state so to honor a sport.

We were surprised to discover that the oldest continuously held sporting event in America is the annual jousting tournament conducted in Mount Solon, Virginia; it dates back to 1821. There is also a National Championship Jousting Tournament held every October on the grounds of the Washington Monument. The rules have changed a bit since Henry VIII buckled on his 150-pound suit of armor. Now the object is spearpoint accuracy rather than to dismount or maim one's opponent. A modern jouster, with his seven-foot lance in hand, gallops along an eighty-yard course and attempts to spear three small steel rings within a time limit of nine seconds. Competition begins with rings that are 1¾ inches in diameter, and the size is gradually decreased to one-quarter of an inch or until a champion is determined.

**Best Tennis Racket:** A tennis racket with a hitting area 50 percent larger than that of conventional rackets has been marketed by the Prince Manufacturing Company, of Princeton, New Jersey.

**Best Tennis Volley:** Howard Kinsey and Mrs. R. Roark batted a tennis ball back and forth 2,001 consecutive times during a game in San Francisco. They ended the volley after an hour and eighteen minutes because Mrs. Roark was scheduled to give a tennis lesson.

**Best Touchdown:** The Oklahoma Sooners and Oklahoma State Aggies clashed for the first time on the neutral turf of Guthrie, Oklahoma. It was a cold and stormy autumn day, November 6, 1904. In the opening minutes of the game, things were going badly for the Aggies from Stillwater; the brawny Sooner defense had thrown them for three consecutive losses, and with fourth down coming up, the ball was nestled just six inches from their own goal line. State's captain dropped back to punt and was confronted with a fearsome rush. His hurried kick went straight up, where it was at the mercy of the gale force winds.

According to the rules in those days, a loose punt belonged to whichever team recovered it, no matter where in the state of Oklahoma the ball might fall—inside or outside the end zone. The sky-high punt drifted backwards about fifteen yards, took a Sooner bounce, and splashed into the swollen Cottonwood Creek, which ran just twenty yards behind the line of scrimmage. In hot pursuit, five players from both squads plunged into the icy water. The ball bobbed up and down elusively; several players got slippery hands on it before the Sooners' left halfback, Ed Cook, finally gained possession. After swimming furiously upstream for ten yards, Cook emerged on the bank, his pads and moleskin knickers dripping, and touched the ball down for a five-point score (at the time TDs counted for five rather than six points).

Cook's heroic play set the tone for the remainder of the game. Oklahoma won, 75–0.

**Best Training:** Dr. Craig Sharp, the trainer for Britain's 1972 Olympic canoeing team, believes that vigorous sexual activity prior to athletic competition can significantly improve an athlete's performance. Specifically, Dr. Sharp cites the case of an Olympic middle-distance runner who set a world's record less than one hour after engaging in sexual intercourse, and the experience of a British miler who broke four minutes for the first time only an hour and a half after making love. Eastern European coaches are inclined to agree with Dr. Sharp; several recommend having sex on the eve of competition and report that athletes who include romantic activities as part of their warm-up feel especially loose and relaxed. They warn against sexual intercourse immediately after an event, however, cautioning that it could put a dangerous strain on the heart when an athlete is exhausted.

Spiritual counseling can be just as important as calisthenics to athletic success. (See "Sports," *Most Unusual Hurdler.*) Shariff Abubakar Omar, Kenya's most distinguished witch doctor, offered his services as a trainer to England's World Cup soccer team in 1973. In a letter to Sir Alf Ramsey, the British coach, Dr. Omar said, "I am interested in signing a one-to two-year contract with you with a view to improving England's chances of winning the world trophy." Sir Alf politely declined the doctor's metaphysical intervention and England was quickly eliminated in the preliminary rounds of World Cup competition.

---

**Worst Attendance:** On November 12, 1955 at Pullman, Washington, San Jose State and Washington State colleges played their football game as scheduled, despite high winds and a temperature of 0°F. The total paid attendance was one.

**Worst (Baseball) Manager:** While Jimmie Dykes was no pushover as a hitter, he was considerably less formidable as a manager. Between 1934 and 1961, Dykes managed six different major league teams—the Chicago White Sox, the Philadelphia Phillies, the Baltimore Orioles, the Cincinnati Reds, the Detroit Tigers, and the Cleveland Indians—and never won a pennant with any of them. That twenty-one-year managerial dry spell is the longest in baseball history.

**Worst (Baseball) Record:** Boston Red Sox catcher Carlton Fisk was struck in the groin by baseballs six times in 1975.

Another distinction of questionable worth belongs to Ed Rommel who, in a game in Washington, D.C., between the Senators and the New York Yankees on April 16, 1956, became the first major league umpire ever to wear glasses.

**Worst Bowling Alley:** Don't try to go bowling in the Soviet Union. If you've got a free evening on your hands, eat *blini*, go to the ballet, read Pushkin—but don't go bowling. It just isn't worth the trouble. The country's only public bowling alley, located at Gorky Park in Moscow, has sixteen alleys, but at last count only *three* were working, and those not too well. According to an Associated Press dispatch in 1975, the alley has been riddled with mechanical breakdowns since it opened in October 1974, and spare parts are available only from the United States.

**Worst Contact Sport:** "Purring" enjoys moderate popularity in Wales. Here are the rules: two opponents stand face to face, grasping each other firmly by the shoulders. At the starting signal, they begin kicking each other in the shins with shoes reinforced with metal toeplates. The first man to release his grip on his opponent's shoulders is declared the loser.

Or consider face-slapping, which was in vogue in Russia during the early 1930s. Nothing much to it—just two men slapping each other open-handedly until one or the other cried uncle. The most celebrated match took place in Kiev between Wasyl Bezbordny and Michalko Goniusz in 1931. They were at it for thirty hours until spectators intervened and separated the bloody-faced competitors.

There *is* one form of athletic competition potentially more violent than either of the above: Grenade-throwing is an official sporting event in the People's Republic of China.

**Worst Fans:** A true fan is one who remains loyal whether his team is winning or losing. The diehards who sat in San Diego Stadium every Sunday during the 1975 season were true fans. They cheered every fumble and every interception in the Chargers' unsuccessful bid to become the first NFL team to lose fourteen consecutive games in a single season.

On the other hand, you have the four owners of season tickets who sued the Philadelphia Eagles in 1972 for being "inept, amateurish in effort, and falling below the level of professional football competence expected of a National Football League team." The soreheads filed a breach of contract complaint, demanding a cash refund on their tickets to the season's remaining games.

**Worst Football Team:** No other football team in history—and we include prep school junior varsity squads, dental school elevens, scrub teams from the Lucasville State Home for Unwed Mothers—has ever chalked up a record as dismal as that of Bethel (Ohio) High School. In 1974, a typical season, Bethel's opponents scored 544 points against them, while Bethel scored not once. Game scores were 40–0, 53–0, 92–0, 89–0, 50–0, 33–0, 36–0, 46–0, and 49–0. In one contest, five of Bethel's eleven punts were blocked. They averaged slightly under four yards per kick.

In the opening weeks of the 1975 season, Bethel showed that it had lost no steam over the summer, getting trounced, 89–0, in two successive outings. The school's athletic director, Truman Godbey, said, "We're going to have a big celebration when we score."

**Worst Golfer:** A woman playing in the 1912 Shawnee Golf Invitational for Ladies stepped up to the tee at the sixteenth hole and sliced the ball into the Binniekill River. Following it one and a half miles downstream, in a rowboat paddled by her husband, she lashed out at the ball with boundless passion. She finally connected and the ball sailed landward and into an impenetrably dense thicket. By the time she worked herself out of the woods, onto the green, and into the cup, she had racked up 166 strokes.

**Worst Knockout Punch:** Ex-prizefighter Peter O'Toole (not to be confused with the actor of the same name) of Chester, England, capped an argument with his friend John O'Dea by biting off his nose. The severed snout was surgically refitted on O'Dea's face.

**Worst Prizefight:** In what was touted, presumably in good faith, as the fight of the century, English boxing champion Jim Mace and his American counterpart Joe Coburn danced around each other for three hours and forty-eight minutes without landing a single punch. The nonfight took place in New Orleans in 1870.

**Worst Sport:** Playing-field masochists with a love for the great outdoors—or, more precisely, for the great upstairs—can try their hands at tree-sitting, a popular amusement in Cohocton, New York, where annual tournaments have taken place since 1968. The rules are simple: each player climbs a tree in a predesignated maple grove and stays up as long as he or she can. The last player left aloft after all the others have fallen out or climbed down is declared the winner, a distinction of dubious value. "It's cold and miserable and lonely up there," says Valerie Townsley, the 1974 women's division champ, who held out for 26 hours and 32 minutes. "And if you even think about why you're up in a tree in the middle of the night, you're sunk." But the winner does receive a $100 United States savings bond, although that alone does not account for the contestants' willingness to live among the squirrels and sparrows for a day and a half.

There are various techniques that make for success in tree-sitting. Some participants dress warmly against the threat of subfreezing temperatures, always a possibility since the contest is customarily run in mid-autumn. Others dress lightly and suffer the consequences willingly since ties can be broken by penalizing the most heavily clad player. Some, like Ms. Townsley, find themselves a tolerably comfortable perch and sit stoically erect, remaining awake for the duration; others rig hammocks and try to get some sleep, a risky practice since dozing contestants have occasionally fallen from their perches.

Total allowable time in the trees is 48 hours, although few make it that far. If there are two or more contestants left, the elapsed time spent on the ground—for bathroom visits or snacks, for example—is deducted from their total. For that reason, serious competitors don't eat immediately before or during the event, thus avoiding hunger pangs. And, notes Ms. Townsley, "If you don't eat or drink anything, you won't have to go to the bathroom."

**Worst Sportsmanship:** It was May 15, 1894—a game between the world champion Baltimore Orioles and the spunky Beaneaters at Boston. The Orioles were coming to bat in the last of the third (the tradition of the visiting team batting first had not yet been established), when Baltimore's legendary third baseman John McGraw became embroiled in a fist fight with a Boston third baseman named Tucker. The benches emptied as players from both sides exuberantly joined in the ruckus, and in the stands partisans among the 3,500 spectators began trading punches.

In the midst of this melee, the fans sitting peacefully in the twenty-five-cent bleachers began to feel an unaccustomed warmth beneath them. They jumped from their seats, discovering to their amazement that pro-Boston arsonists had set fire to the stadium. On the field, some semblance of order had been restored, but the flames, shouts, and general commotion again interrupted play. Diehards in other parts of the ball park shouted impatiently, "Play ball . . . play ball!" By the time firemen managed to extinguish the blaze, 170 buildings had been destroyed, $300,000 worth of property damage had been done, and 2,000 had been left homeless.

John McGraw never forgave the Boston fans for their spontaneous, combustive behavior, and when the New York Giants—managed by McGraw—won the National League pennant in 1904, the team steadfastly refused to play in the World Series against the American League champion Red Sox.

**Worst Sports Promotion:** It started with Ladies' Day. Then there was Ball Day, Cap Day, and Nickel Beer Night. Finally, in a desperate effort to get fans to come to the ball park, the hapless Washington Senators staged a Panty Hose Night, distributing free panty hose to every woman who purchased a ticket. It was the ultimate degradation of the national pastime; had he lived to see it, Walter Johnson would have retched. Even Bill Veeck, the flamboyant general manager (and now owner) who introduced Bat Day, thought a Panty Hose Night was disgusting. "I wouldn't have something like that because that's like having Deodorant Night," Veeck said. "You embarrass people who need large ones. It's also, I think, in bad taste. And anyway you can't have all sizes."

As a general rule, a team's promotional efforts grow more absurd as their success on the field declines. Several years ago, the Milwaukee Brewers constructed a miniature Bavarian chalet above what was billed as "the world's largest beer barrel." A man dressed as Bernie Brewer,

The World's Largest Beer Barrel

the team mascot, sat in the chalet nervously watching each game. After every Brewer home run, victory trumpets and sirens would blare, a carnival of lights would flash on, hundreds of balloons were released, and Bernie Brewer would jump up and down like a maniac, slide down a long chute, and plunge, fanny-first, into the giant beer barrel with a big, crowd-pleasing splash. (Bernie Brewer stayed high and dry throughout most of the season.)

**Worst Wrestler:** Normally a skilled wrestler, Stanley Pinto accidentally entangled himself in the ropes during a match in Providence, Rhode Island. In struggling free, he pinned his own shoulders to the mat for three seconds, unaided by his opponent, who was declared the winner.

**Most Unusual Athletic Competition:** At the Olive Dell Ranch in California, they have recaptured the uninhibited spirit of the original Olympic games. Like the ancient Greeks, athletes at Olive Dell run the hurdles, put the shot, and hurl the discus totally in the nude.

The annual Nudist Olympics were originated in 1965. And in the early years there were teams from nudist camps all over the country with as many as five hundred naked spectators in the stands. Competition included the marathon, triple jump, and most other traditional events. Both sexes took part, and only in the high jump were trunks permitted—to guard against injuries on the crossbar.

Dawn Fraser, the Australian (clothed) Olympic swimming champion, has more or less endorsed the Olive Dell concept in her autobiography: "A nude Olympics," she says, "would provide an imaginative return to the days of the ancient Games and would certainly lead to a rewriting of the swim record book." We trust the new edition would have pictures.

Unhappily, however, the Nudist Olympics have fallen upon hard times. There has been a steady decline in entries; Olive Dell members and their children are practically the only contestants these days. But the thrill is still there. "I like the feeling of the air on me," said one young sprinter. Winners of individual events receive ribbons, and the overall champion is awarded a fifty-dollar savings bond—a bonus that may threaten his or her amateur standing.

**Most Unusual (Baseball) Bat:** Heinie Groh, who played third base for the New York Giants in the 1920s, customarily used a bat shaped like a wine bottle.

**Most Unusual (Baseball) Fielding Play:** In 1961, Cleveland Indian pitcher Herb Score was struck in the eye and nearly blinded by a screaming line drive from the bat of New York Yankee hitter Gil McDougald. The ball rebounded off Score's head and rolled towards first base, where the Cleveland first baseman scooped it up and made the put-out. Score was thus credited with an assist on the play.

**Most Unusual (Baseball) Foul Ball:** With two runners on base in a 1940 minor league game against the Jersey City Giants at Jersey City, a batter for the Montreal Royals bunted towards third base. While the ball trickled slowly down the base line and both runners crossed home plate, the Jersey City third baseman, Bert Hass, waited to see if the bunt would roll foul. It didn't—not of its own accord, anyway. When it was just about to stop, approximately an inch from the foul line, Haas lay down on the infield grass, put his mouth next to the ball, and blew it into foul territory. It was ruled foul and the runners had to return to their bases.

**Most Unusual (Baseball) Game:** Texarkana and Corsicana of the old Texas League locked horns on the sultry afternoon of June 15, 1902. Final score: Corsicana 51, Texarkana 3. The stars of the game were Corsicana slugger Nig Clarke, who walloped eight home runs in as many times at bat, and the Texarkana pitcher, C. B. DeWitt, who started the game and went the distance, giving up all 51 runs. DeWitt never made it to the majors, incidentally, but Clarke did. He played for various teams from 1905 through 1920, and hit six home runs in 1,536 times at bat.

However, the Texarkana-Corsicana slugfest was not the most lopsided game ever played. In 1865, a professional team calling itself the Philadelphia Athletics, scored 261 runs in a single day, first walloping a team from Williamsport, Pennsylvania, 101–8, and then taking the Danville nine, 160–11.

While we're on the subject of baseball at its most surreal, we should mention an annual ritual observed at Fairbanks, Alaska—a baseball game played on June 21, the longest day of the year. It begins at midnight and no artificial lighting is ever used.

**Most Unusual (Baseball) Home Run:** Hod Lisenbee, who pitched for the Washington Senators in the 1920s, claims that Babe Ruth once hit a screaming line drive off him that passed between his legs and soared over the centerfield fence.

**Most Unusual (Baseball) Pitcher:** Hurling for the Cleveland Nationals against Philadelphia, Hugh Daily pitched a no-hit, no-run game in 1883. On July 7 of the following year, Daily, playing with the Chicago Unions, became the second man in baseball history to strike out nineteen batters in a nine-inning game (Charles Sweeney was the first)—a major-league record since equaled several times, but never surpassed. The hapless Boston Beaneaters could manage only a single infield hit as they went down, 5–0.

What made these two performances especially impressive was that Daily was a one-armed player. His left hand and forearm had been blown off years before in an explosion. Because he pitched in an era when mitts were not required, Daily was not handicapped in the least, and on the strength of his good right arm he became one of the most successful and popular hurlers of his day.

Another exceptional pitcher was fireballing Steve Dalkowski. In 1960, playing for the Stockton Ports, Dalkowski was blinding batters in the Class C California League and scaring them to death. The righthander struck (not struck out) 665 batters, walked 726, threw as many as six wild pitches in a row, broke one batter's arm, and tore off another's ear lobe in the course of a wild, wild career spanning four seasons. South Dakota fans will never forget the day in 1958 when Dalkowski pitched a one-hitter against Aberdeen and lost, 9–8. And once in a game for Kings-port, Tennessee, he struck out twenty-four batters before being lifted in the ninth inning.

**Most Unusual Contest:** The National Tobacco Spitting Contest annually attracts two thousand spectators and several dozen expectorators to the sleepy town of Raleigh, Mississippi (population: 614). The politicians come to shake hands, the chewing tobacco manufacturers come to woo customers, but men like Don Snyder come to spit.

Snyder is a three-time spitting champion, and in 1975 he set a new world's distance record by propelling a glob of sputum-drenched tobacco thirty-one feet, one inch. To prepare for the finals, he spits two hours every day for a month before the competition. But Snyder, the greatest active spitter, stands in slack-jawed awe of George Craft, the man known to his fellow plug-chewers as the Babe Ruth of Tobacco Spitting. Before retiring at age seventy-five, Craft captured fourteen consecutive long-distance titles.

Craft, who still claims he "can hit a lizard at five paces," says he owes his spitting prowess to his mother, who taught him how to chew and spit "and could hit the fireplace from any spot in the room and never got a dab on the floor." He says he got his lips, tongue, and jaws in shape simply by eating a lot.

Out in Beaver, Oklahoma, folks are pretty proud of their World's Championship Cow Chip Throwing Contest, and rightfully so. Why, in 1971 alone, the Chamber of Commerce boxed and sold over $1,000 worth of souvenir chips. There are four classes of competition: open, men's, women's, and politicians (who are considered professionals in this sport). The four basic rules are strictly enforced: 1) No gloves allowed, 2) reinforcing or weighting the chips is prohibited, 3) only genuine dung chips may be used—no mud, and 4) if a chip breaks in mid-air, the piece that goes the farthest counts. Most people prefer to fling their chips like a discus although in recent years Frisbee-style has gained in popularity. Several years ago, former Governor Dewey Bartlett set a politician's record by slinging his chip an Olympian 138 feet; some say that mark will stand forever. A Bicentennial variation on the Cow Chip Throwing Contest was held on Oklahoma's Cherokee Indian Reservation in November 1975. Two home-pastured buffalo worked all year to produce ammunition for what sponsors called the first annual "Chiparama."

Towns all over America host other outlandish contests: New Orleans has its Tabasco Drinking Competition; Stuttgart, Arkansas, has held its World Duck Calling Championships for over forty years; Greenville, South Carolina, runs the "Crawdad 300" crayfish races. If we had to choose the most offensive of all these crank contests, it would be Central City's (Colorado) Spittin', Belchin', and Cussin' Contest; in 1974 the belchin' division featured the sounds of "the Wounded Whale," "the Dying Rhino," and "the Drunken Buffalo."

**Most Unusual (Football) Ground Rule:** There is a lot of talk in sports about the home-field advantage. At the University of Arizona that advantage has been legislated and institutionalized. An ordinance duly passed by the city council of Tucson reads in part, "It shall be unlawful for any visiting football team or player to carry, convey, tote, kick, throw, pass, or otherwise transport or propel any inflated pigskin across the University of Arizona goal line or score a safety within the confines of the City of Tucson, County of Pima, State of Arizona." Violators who dare trespass on the Arizona Wildcats' end zone face a $300 fine and a minimum sentence of three months in jail, if convicted.

Another example of governmental intervention on the gridiron comes from the small south Texas town of Premont. With less than two minutes remaining in the 1972 contest between Premont High and archrival Los Fresnos, hometown Premont was trailing, 14–12. Tempers flared and a fist fight broke out among the players. A Premont policeman rushed onto the field to help the referees separate the combatants and restore order. Whipping out a can of Mace, the officer disabled seven Los Fresnos players with a few quick squirts in the face. The boys screamed, fell to the turf, and clutched their eyes; they had to be led back to their bench for treatment by the trainer.

Meanwhile, play had resumed and Premont capitalized on the temporary incapacity of the Los Fresnos first string by completing a fifty-five-yard pass. Then, a last-second field goal brought the home team a hard-fought 15–14 victory.

They take high school football rather seriously in south Texas, and the Los Fresnos eleven was understandably upset. Premont school officials sent the town of Los Fresnos a bill for $1,200 in damages after the visitors tried with some success to tear down the locker room.

**Most Unusual Hike:** Stuntman Johann Huslinger walked on his hands from Vienna, Austria, to Paris, France—a distance of 871 miles—in 1900. It took him 55 days. Several years later Anton Haislan spent 22 months pushing his wife and daughter in a carriage a total of 15,000 miles through the streets of Paris.

**Most Unusual Hurdler:** At the 1908 London Olympics, Forrest Smithson ran and won the 110-meter hurdles while carrying a Bible in his left hand for inspiration.

Bible-toting Forrest Smithson at the 1908 London Olympics

**Most Unusual Muscleman:** Using his open palm as a hammer, strong-man Joe Greenstein can drive a nail through a metal plate with the ease of a judge rapping his gavel. He can also bend steel in his bare hands, and break free after being bound with iron chains. Incredibly, Green-stein, who lives in Brooklyn, New York, is ninety-four.

Born in Poland in 1882, Greenstein migrated to the United States at eighteen, and was variously employed as a professional wrestler, weight lifter, and circus strongman. An ardent Democrat, Greenstein consoled himself over Herbert Hoover's election in 1928 by performing a feat he'd been doing successfully for years—hammering a nail into metal with his open palm swathed in handkerchiefs. So distraught was he by the Republican's victory, however, that he accidentally held the nail upside down and drove it through his hand.

**Most Unusual Olympic Events:** When, after a two-thousand-year layoff, the Olympics were revived in 1896, the tug-of-war, standing broad jump, and one-handed weightlift were listed on the official program right alongside the classic events. And at the 1904 games in St. Louis, there were two featured events lacking in the usual Olympian dignity: The barrel jump was an absurd obstacle course littered with old wine casks that athletes clambered over and leaped through, like lions leaping through a flaming hoop. Less slapstick but equally strange was the fifty-six-pound rock throw, won by a Canadian policeman—Etienne Desmarteau—with a manly heave of 34 feet, 4 inches.

**Most Unusual Soccer Penalty:** Soccer player Dave Lovatt, of Derby, England, was slapped with a ten-shilling fine—that's about $1.20—for smiling at the referee.

**Most Unusual Soccer Play:** There is now a plaque at Rugby School in Warwickshire, England, commemorating the day when William Webb Ellis, in a moment of pique, took the rules of soccer into his own hands. But on that fateful afternoon in 1823, Ellis' unorthodox play was considered a dark disgrace and a very bad show.

Ellis was taking part in an intramural soccer match. His team was losing by an embarrassingly uneven score, and his teammates were muddling, mucking about, and generally failing to move the ball. Finally, out of supreme frustration, Ellis picked up the ball and began running madly in the direction of the opposing goal. The spectators were aghast. Use of the hands was forbidden, and many fans thought the boy intended to steal the ball. Then Ellis drop-kicked the ball past the bewildered goalie into the net for a completely illegal score.

It was shocking behavior for a college boy. The team captain apologized to the officials, the opponents, and the crowd for Ellis' unsportsmanlike conduct. And Ellis was suspended from the team.

This gross infraction of the rules was not soon forgotten. "That play at Rugby" was widely discussed and joked about at other schools throughout England. Eventually, in 1839, Arthur Pell, a star center-forward on the Cambridge soccer team, decided to add new spark to the old game by drawing up an alternative set of rules. The most important changes Pell made were to legalize holding, throwing, and running with the ball. He named the wide-open new sport after the school Ellis had attended. And that, boys and girls, is the true story of how rugby was born—the direct forerunner of American football.

Incidentally, the word pigskin is a quaint Victorian euphemism. The original rugby balls were made of inflated pig bladders. There was no standard size; it depended on the capacity of the unlucky pig.

**Most Unusual Sports Scandal:** Bad news for amphiphiles: the winning entry in the New World International Turtle Track Commission's 1974 competition was a *fraud.* "I am past words," a visibly shaken Cutler Jissom, chairman of the British-based NWITTC, told newsmen upon

Maracanã Stadium in Rio de Janeiro

learning that the prize-winning tortoise in the nine-nation, two-hundred entry race had been illegally mounted on the chassis of a toy car and mechanically propelled. "This year turtle racing stood on the verge of being a mass sport," he said. "Now attendances are bound to fall off."

**Most Unusual Stadium:** In the United States, domed stadiums, Astroturf, and other luxuries are becoming increasingly common. But the 200,000-seat Maracanã Stadium in Rio de Janeiro, the largest in the world, has a feature that no other stadium has yet installed—a moat. A nine-foot-wide, nine-foot-deep channel encircles the playing field to protect the referees and visiting teams from enraged sports fans. Unfortunately, it doesn't always do the job; after an especially unpopular call, fanatical partisans have been known to swim the moat.

**Most Unusual Track Event:** On March 4, 1928, a field of 199 men toed a starting line in Los Angeles, California. The starter's pistol sounded, and in a cloud of dust they were off on the first leg of the longest marathon race ever run—3,422 miles to Madison Square Garden in New York City.

The runners, including Olympians and rank amateurs, put up an entry fee of $100 for the privilege of participating in the "Bunion Derby," as sportswriters soon dubbed the event. But they were not running out of love for the great outdoors; there was a purse of $48,500 waiting at the finish line, with a cool $25,000 to go to the winner. Added to that was the potential for endorsements of footpowder, running shoes, jock straps, liniments, and bandages.

The derby was conducted like the nine-day bicycle races in Europe. The runners traversed a given distance each day, their times were recorded, and the runner with the lowest accumulated time was declared the winner. A total of 76 out of the 199 starters dropped out on the first day, after completing fewer than sixteen miles. The survivors followed an arduous route which took them across New Mexico and Arizona, up through the Texas Panhandle to Oklahoma, Missouri, and Illinois. One contestant was eliminated from the race by a hit-and-run driver; and by the time the road show reached Ohio, the field was down to fifty-five.

The winner was Andy Payne, a durable nineteen-year-old farmboy, whom the newspapers described as "part Cherokee and all heart." He covered the distance in just 573 hours, 4 minutes, and 34 seconds, finishing a full 15 hours ahead of John Salo of Passaic, New Jersey.

Another extraordinary track event is the all-women's Pancake Race, run simultaneously each year in Olney, England, and Liberal, Kansas. Dressed in regulation skirts, aprons, and head scarves, housewives sprint a 415-yard course while carrying an iron skillet in one hand. At three different points during the race, contestants are required to flip their pancakes; a fumbled flapjack does not result in disqualification, but the runner must retrieve it from the dust before continuing.

Tradition has it that the first pancake race occurred five centuries ago when an Olney woman discovered she was late for church and absent-mindedly dashed off to services with a frying pan in her hand. Accordingly, the finish line of the pancake race is the front door of the local church. The current record is 59.1 seconds, set by Kathleen West of Kansas in 1970.

**Most Unusual Track-and-Field Record:** Noah Young did the mile in 8 minutes and 30 seconds in a special competition in Melbourne, Australia, in 1915. He carried a 150-pound man on his back.

**Most Unusual World Record:** Gunning for the world's record in watermelon bursting, Dana Rowley released a fifteen-pound watermelon from the roof of a seven-story building in California. The fruit exploded impressively on impact, one chunk travelling 155 feet, seven inches.

# Government

**Best Executive Privilege:** Lyndon Johnson ordered that special taps dispensing ice-cold Fresca be installed in White House sinks.

**Best Foreign Policy:** Founded in A.D. 301 and occupying only twenty-four square miles of territory in the Appenines of north-central Italy, San Marino is the world's oldest and smallest republic. The tiny nation has outlasted the Roman Empire, the Renaissance wars, the Napoleonic era, and the unification of Italy by being cagey and inconspicuous. Today, nearly 30 percent of the national income is derived from the sale of brightly colored, often triangular, postage stamps to collectors around the world.

Approaching its eighteenth century of independence, San Marino, population 20,000, has just established full consular relations with the People's Republic of China, population 700 million. Further, the San Marinese have agreed to the United Nations treaty outlawing the military exploitation of outer space, and they have set a moral example for other nations by pledging that their one hundred eighty-man army will not develop or acquire nuclear weapons.

**Best Hope for New York:** In the throes of the worst and most celebrated financial crisis in its history, the New York City government surely paid insufficient attention to an offer made in 1975 by the Tigua Indians, an obscure Texas tribe, to buy back the city from the white man for twenty-four dollars in assorted trinkets. The Tiguas stipulated that the city's inhabitants would have to clear out, however, and remove all buildings from the site.

Another offer of help came from a civic-minded mystic, Joyce Luciano, who wrote New York's Mayor Abraham Beame, offering to cast a "prosperity spell" on the city. In 1974, she claimed she had saved Paterson, New Jersey, from financial ruin by getting one half of that city's population to burn green candles and the other half to burn gold ones. "Since that time it looks as though Paterson may be a model city and a prosperous one," she said.

While neither plan had any takers in New York, a state representative in Massachusetts thought that selling his state back to the Indians—*any* Indians—made eminently good sense. The legislator, Michael J. Connolly, introduced a bill that would put the entire Bay State on the auction block on January 3, 1977. The sale would take place at Plymouth Rock, he proposed, and it would be open to native American Indians *only*.

**Best National Emblem:** Ever since the Revolution of 1848, "Marianne," a young woman in a chaste Greek costume and Phrygian hat, has been the symbol of the French Republic. Finally, in 1971, Anslan, a Prix-de-Rome winning sculptor, undertook to update and reinterpret Marianne's classic style. His striking creation had a pouting mouth and ample bosom that looked very familiar; Anslan's Marianne was the spittin' image of Brigitte Bardot. "To me," Anslan said, "[Brigitte Bardot] represents femininity and womanhood. She is truly a symbol of France." French mayors apparently agree; hundreds have used public funds to purchase copies of the new Marianne for display in their offices. Author André Malraux has one and so does Radical Party headquarters in Paris. Said a radical leader, "We should be proud of her, of Roquefort cheese, and Bordeaux wine."

**Best of the Richard Nixon Watergate Tapes:** In the wake of the Watergate muddle, a tape cassette company in Paris named Peerless Enterprises came up with a nifty little package: a recording of Richard Nixon's resignation speech accompanied by printed transcripts in French and English. But the address was short and didn't come close to filling the cassette, so the tape was padded with several poems of John Keats.

**Best Presidential Bathtub:** At 325 pounds, William Howard Taft was by far the most corpulent Chief Executive in the nation's history. After getting stuck in the White House bathtub several times, he finally had a new one installed, roomy enough to accommodate four average-sized men. (Not that it ever did, to our knowledge.)

Taft was also known for his passion for cows, and kept a pet Holstein named Pauline in a pasture near the Executive Mansion. But his bovine fetish may be easier to explain than Andrew Johnson's love of mice. Johnson once told a foreign ambassador that he had come upon several white mice in the White House basement, and that rather than summon the exterminator, he provided them with a basket and fed them water and flour nightly.

**Best Protest:** To protest discrimination against Jews in the Soviet Union, the Anti-Defamation leagues of Philadelphia and Newark encouraged their members to mail boxes of matzos to the Russian embassy in Washington over the Passover holidays in 1972. The response was overwhelming. In a matter of days the embassy was buried under an avalanche of unleavened bread, and the Russian ambassador refused to accept any more suspicious-looking packages.

That left the U.S. Postal Service with a problem. An estimated ten tons of matzos inundated four local post offices, completely paralyzing normal operations. Eventually, postal officials ordered the wafers carted off to the city dump and burned.

A livid Anti-Defamation League spokesman complained that the Postal Service's action was not kosher. Under post office regulations, all packages marked with a legible return address should have been mailed back to the senders, he said.

**Best State Flag:** Walter Angst, an expert on heraldry at the Smithsonian Institution, has praised the official banner of Maryland as "our one example of a perfect state flag." The Maryland flag is derived from the coat of arms of the Calvert family, the original English proprietors of the colony. The first and fourth quadrants are emblazoned with a brilliant yellow and black skewed checkerboard design, while the second and third quadrants display a red and white "cross botonée." "This flag shouts at you with its blazing colors, 'Hey, look at me! I am Maryland,'" Angst says. He also has kind words for the flags of Colorado, Hawaii, New Mexico, and the District of Columbia.

**Best State Legislature:** The California Senate and House of Representatives were described as the nation's best in a 1971 report by the Citizens' Conference on State Legislatures. Of all the fifty states, California had the highest-paid legislators (over $19,000 a year), the best research staff, and the longest sessions. After California came New York, Illinois, Florida, and Wisconsin in descending order of excellence.

The $200,000 study ranked the legislatures according to their ability to "function effectively, account to the public for their actions, gather and use information, avoid undue influence, and represent the interests of their people." The political character of the laws enacted—progressive or conservative—was not a criterion in the ranking.

In the 1860s Judge Gideon J. Tucker of New York said, "No man's life, liberty, or property are safe while the legislature is in session." And the Citizens' Conference found that Judge Tucker's observation still applies in all too many cases. Finishing at the very bottom in the study were Delaware, Wyoming, and—dead last—Alabama. The researchers noted that in 1971 the Alabama representatives met for only thirty-six days, and they were given no office space in which to work. The legislature divided itself into fifty-two committees where little was accomplished. And worst of all, the votes in committee meetings were kept strictly secret, making it nearly impossible for the folks back home to hold their representative accountable, or even find out what he had been doing down in Montgomery. (In fairness, we should mention that there have been a few tentative signs of reform in Alabama since the study was issued.)

New Hampshire lawmakers might be candidates for welfare; according to the study, their salary was just $100 a year, the lowest in the nation.

---

**Worst Birth Control Program:** The Office of Economic Opportunity sponsored a project aimed at promoting the use of condoms among teenage boys in the ghettos of Cleveland and Philadelphia. When the program was finally scuttled after two years, government accountants did some adding and dividing and found that the feds had been purchasing the condoms used in the program at the rate of $400 a dozen.

It started in 1971, when the OEO contracted Population Services, Inc., of North Carolina, to run the program. PSI contacted social casework agencies in Cleveland and Philadelphia and came up with the names of probably promiscuous boys, fourteen years of age and older; they obtained additional names of likely prospects by purchasing mailing lists from a children's specialty company and pulling out all the kids whose zip codes indicated that they lived in ghettos. Each youngster, and there were 43,000 in all, received a direct mail advertisement which included basic sex information and redeemable condom stamps marked "Condom Information Service: worth one dollar on purchase of one dozen condoms. Write name here." Since only 254 boys cashed in their stamps for the rubbery protectives, and the feds wound up paying over $100,000 for the project, that means the condoms went for $400 per dozen.

**Worst Budgetary Cutback:** The tiny republic of Luxembourg recently opted not to send a delegation to the European Security Conference, a special parley sponsored by the Soviet Union, and arranged instead to have the Netherlands delegation handle its affairs.

When the delegates convened to vote on how the conference should be financed, the Dutch delegate moved to the hitherto unoccupied table of the Luxembourg delegation, from whence he expressed, in French, Luxembourg's position that the conference be underwritten by the United Nations. Finishing that oration, he returned to his own table and attacked Luxembourg's position—in English—exhorting all members of the conference to provide their own financial support.

**Worst Civic Improvement Project:** The city of Castro, California, is the artichoke capital of the world, and in commemoration of this distinction the city council in 1972 commissioned the casting of gigantic plastic artichokes. Lined with leafy green monuments, the streets of Castro look like the rows of some surrealistic garden.

**Worst Congressional Floor Fight:** The first brawl in the halls of Congress dates back to 1789 when Representative Roger Griswold of Connecticut called Representative Matthew Lyon of Vermont an unspeakable coward. Lyon replied by spitting in Griswold's face and attacking him with the cast-iron tongs from the House fireplace. That incident set the tone for two hundred years of unstatesmanlike temper tantrums.

By the year 1835, the threat of violence during Congressional sessions was so tangible that Martin Van Buren, as Vice President presiding over the Senate, felt compelled to wear a brace of pistols to defend himself. And as late as 1880, Speaker of the House Warren Keifer of Ohio carried a revolver in his pocket to ward off assaults on the chair.

The most vicious assault in Congressional history occurred in 1856 when Preston Brooks, a Representative from South Carolina, invaded the Senate chamber and attacked Massachusetts abolitionist Charles Sumner with a cane. Sumner fell to the floor unconscious and was injured so seriously that he was unable to reclaim his seat until three years later.

The incidence of "floor fighting" has declined in the twentieth century, but it has not altogether disappeared. In the late 1930s, Senator Kenneth McKellar of Tennessee drew a Bowie knife and took a swipe at Senator Royal Copeland of New York; he missed. More recently, Strom Thurmond of South Carolina and Ralph Yarborough of Texas wrestled for ten minutes on the floor of a corridor outside a Senate hearing room in a dispute over the 1964 Civil Rights Bill. Both men were sixty-one years old at the time, but Thurmond, who is a physical fitness enthusiast married to a woman forty years his junior, demonstrated a clear superiority in the martial arts and pinned Yarborough at least twice. Then in 1971, Edward Mitchell, a Republican from Indiana, took umbrage at certain criticisms that Democratic floor leader Hale Boggs was making about Richard Nixon during the annual Gridiron Club dinner. When Boggs, elegantly dressed in a black tie and tails, retired momentarily to the men's room, Mitchell, age sixty, followed and knocked him to the floor with one punch. It was later revealed that Mitchell had been a college champion boxer, and had once gone three rounds with Max Schmeling.

**Worst Dirty Trick:** The most familiar dirty trick of recent times occurred during the 1960 presidential campaign, when candidate Richard Nixon was making an old-fashioned whistle-stop tour of California. Disguised as a railway engineer, Democratic prankster Dick Tuck waved the train out of the station while Nixon, on the caboose, was in the middle of a speech. That incident, and the sabotage and dirty tricks of 1972, though reprehensible, are mild stuff compared with the tactics of earlier campaigns. The Tilden-Hayes election of 1876 was blatantly stolen by the Republicans. The Jackson-John Quincy Adams contest "really smelled," in the phrase of one historian. And, in fact, vicious pranks date all the way back to 1800 when Thomas Jefferson opposed John Adams.

Adams was called a tyrant and a closet Tory in the Republican press. Jefferson was assailed in Federalist newspapers as an atheist, a revolutionist, a Jacobin, an embezzler, and "a progenitor of Negro children." But there was one more charge against Jefferson, potentially more damaging than all the rest: Thomas Jefferson was dead.

The story was first planted in the pro-Jefferson Baltimore *American* on June 30, 1800, just when the presidential campaign was beginning to heat up: "It was last evening reported that the Man in whom is centered the feelings and happiness of the American people, Thomas Jefferson, is no more." And the next afternoon the Philadelphia *True American* also printed a tentative obituary: "A report was, last evening, in general circulation that Mr. Jefferson had died suddenly at his seat in Virginia. We took some pains to ascertain the source of this report and found that it was received by a gentleman direct from Fredericktown. We saw the gentleman, and were informed by him, that, being at Fredericktown Friday last, two respectable inhabitants of the place arrived there from the neighborhood of Mr. Jefferson's seat with an account of his having died in a sudden manner . . ."

Reports of the death of the Vice President elicited no statements of sympathy, no words of grief from President Adams, vice presidential candidate Charles Cotesworth Pinckney, or any other prominent Federalist politician, which is a measure of the bitterness of the campaign. On the other hand, Jefferson's friends spent July 4 in somber mourning. News traveled slowly in that era, and reports of Jefferson's death did not reach some outlying areas until the middle of July. And the truth followed about one week behind, first appearing in *The Gazette of the United States:* "It is reported that an old Negro slave called Thomas Jefferson, being dead at Monticello, gave rise to the report of the demise of the Vice President—the slave having borne the name of his master."

But it was no innocent misunderstanding; the rumors and reports were cleverly calculated to underscore Jefferson's slave-owning status, and the gossip about his affairs with black women. Had the timing been better, it might have influenced the election. But then again, it might not have. (See "Government," *Most Unusual City Council Member.*)

**Worst Election:** When Lib Tufarolo ran for mayor of Clyde Hill, Washington, in 1975, he netted 576 votes. So did his opponent Miles Nelson.

"The law says that in case of a tie you decide the election by lot," said Ralph Dillon, superintendent of elections for Clyde Hill. "The usual procedure has been to flip a coin."

Coin-flipping is not commonly regarded as the ultimate embodiment of democracy in action, and candidate Tufarolo said, "It's just ridiculous. I don't think that's how the people would want it done." Opponent Nelson, whose campaign costs totaled five dollars—five dollars more than Tufarolo's—said, "I guess it's the least offensive method of settling it." In the end it was Tufarolo who survived the coin-flipping and succeeded to the $400-a-year position. The Associated Press observed, "The community of 3,200 appears indifferent."

**Worst Emperor:** A conventional choice would be either Caligula or Nero. (The former slept with his sister and named his horse to the position of proconsul. The latter fancied himself a singer, poet, and actor and gave horrendous amateur theatrical performances that the Roman senators were required to attend; anyone caught dozing, yawning, or leaving early was put to death.) But we defiantly choose the emperor Heliogabulus as the supreme symbol of the degradation that was Rome.

Like the Guru Maharaj Ji, Heliogabulus was proclaimed a god at the tender age of fourteen. He became a member in good standing of the pantheon of Baal and had many loyal worshipers in Syria, his homeland. In A.D. 219, thanks to the scheming and bribery of his mother, Heliogabulus entered Rome as emperor, his chariot drawn by fifty naked slaves.

Heliogabulus always loved a practical joke and he is credited with inventing an early prototype of the whoopee cushion. He placed inflated animal bladders under the cushions of his guests' chairs; when the guest sat down, the bladders deflated with a loud splatting sound. Another of the emperor's favorite tricks was to ply his friends with wine until they passed out. Servants would then transport the sleepers to a menagerie inside the palace, where they would awake surrounded by toothless leopards, bears, and lions.

A spendthrift and a gourmand, Heliogabulus never gave a banquet that cost less than 100,000 sesterces ($10,000), and often he invested as much as 3,000,000 sesterces. On such lavish occasions the emperor ordered the cooks to mix gold pieces with the peas, onyx with the lentils, pearls with the rice, and ambers with the beans. Once he had six hundred ostriches killed to make ostrich brain pies for a single meal. His particular delight was the succulent flesh of conger eels. Tubs of them were kept in the palace kitchen and they were fattened with the flesh of Christians killed in the Colosseum.

But Heliogabulus was first and foremost a religious man. He retired Venus, Jupiter, Mars, and the other antique Roman deities. In their place he substituted emperor worship and ecstatic Eastern cults. He erected a giant stone phallus in the Forum and commanded all Romans to pray to it.

Soothsayers told Heliogabulus he was destined to die by violent hands. To forestall the realization of that unpleasant prophecy, he prepared for a noble suicide by stocking the palace with ropes of purple silk (for hanging), golden swords, and fast-acting poisons encased in sapphires and emeralds. It was all to no avail, as historian Will Durant records. The emperor Heliogabulus was slain in his latrine.

**Worst Government:** During its 150 years of independence, Honduras has had the world's most unstable government. To date, the archetypical banana republic has gone through no fewer than 138 revolutions. On the bright side, many of the Honduran dictators have held power so briefly they didn't have time to oppress the people.

Oppressive regimes are the rule and not the exception, and among the most savage, one would certainly have to mention Hitler's Germany and Stalin's Russia. But for cruelty combined with madness and incompetence, no leadership can quite compare with the Persian sultans of the seventeenth century. We base this conclusion on a study called "The Grand Seraglio," by writer and historian Mary Cable.

A good place to begin the grisly chronicle is with the accession of Mohammed III to the throne in 1595. His first royal act was to order the death of his nineteen younger brothers, all of whom were under eleven years of age and uncircumcised. According to orthodox Moslem tradition, no male with a prepuce could enter heaven, and so, out of compassion for their immortal souls, each of the nineteen underwent the rite of circumcision immediately before being dispatched. It makes the crime seem no less ghastly to discover that Mohammed III was simply carrying out the tried and true Law of Fratricide, which was designed to eliminate continuous plotting and civil war instigated by princes eager to assume power.

Ahmed I, the son and heir of Mohammed III, was the first to violate the Law of Fratricide. Because the Koran speaks of Allah's special love for the weak and feeble-minded, Ahmed refused to murder his moronic brother Mustafa, and simply locked him away in a part of the palace known as the Cage. Ahmed died in 1617. Mustafa became the next sultan and immediately proved that the rumors of his idiocy had not been overstated. He was led, drooling, back to the Cage, and Ahmed's fourteen-year-old son was installed in his place. This ignited a six-year civil war between traditionalists, who backed Mustafa despite his faults, and pragmatists who supported Ahmed's son. The issue was resolved when both pretenders were slain, bringing Sultan Murad IV to power.

By this time, the reader may be ready for a gentle philosopher-king. So were the people of Persia. But instead they had Murad—who, for sport, used to slice a horse in two with a single stroke of his sword. He also enjoyed pouring molten lead down the throats of men convicted for drinking alcoholic beverages. Murad waived the Law of Fratricide, a serious mistake in this instance, and allowed his kid brother Ibrahim to live a miserable, fearful existence in the Cage.

When Murad died in 1640, Ibrahim succeeded him, and Ibrahim was crazy even by sultanic standards. As a child, he had been haunted by dreams of eunuchs attacking him in the night with silk bowstrings, and when the viziers came to crown him sultan, Ibrahim barricaded himself in the Cage—certain that the eunuchs had come for him at last. When he was finally persuaded to emerge, Ibrahim turned out to be a reckless spendthrift and a homicidal maniac. He constructed a new summerhouse in the Grand Seraglio and covered the walls and floors with sable; he festooned his beard with strings of pearls and rubies. He made his favorite bath attendant commander-in-chief of the army. Even Evliya

Effendi, his best friend and closest adviser, was forced to admit that Ibrahim "was not very intelligent." He is best remembered, perhaps, as a stern and ill-tempered husband. One day, in a black mood, he had the three hundred wives in his harem tied up in gunnysacks and drowned in the Sea of Marmara.

An uninterrupted line of psychopaths ruled the Persian Empire for almost a century. One notable sultan spent fifty lonely years in the Cage before coming to the throne; at his coronation, the viziers discovered he had forgotten how to speak.

**Worst Legislative Bill:** As proof that some legislatures could use a little shaking up (see "Government," *Best State Legislature*), the Texas House of Representatives unanimously passed a bill in 1971 commending one Albert De Salvo for meritorious service to "his country, his state, and his community. This compassionate gentleman's dedication and devotion to his work has enabled the weak and lonely throughout the nation to achieve a new degree of concern for their future. He has been officially recognized by the state of Massachusetts for his noted activities and unconventional techniques involving population control and applied psychology." The late Mr. De Salvo, as you may remember, was the man accused of being "the Boston Strangler," who allegedly murdered thirteen women. Representative Tom Moore, Jr., of Waco, introduced the resolution to demonstrate how easy it is to pass so-called "special bills."

**Worst Political Demonstration:** In the early 1960s, Saul Alinsky, the late populist political organizer, visited Rochester, New York, to help organize black factory workers there. In his book, *Rules for Radicals*, Alinsky describes a plan to embarrass the Rochester social establishment: "I suggested that we might buy one hundred seats for one of Rochester's symphony concerts," he writes. "We could select a concert in which the music was relatively quiet. The hundred blacks who would be given the tickets would first be treated to a three-hour pre-concert dinner in the community, in which they would be fed nothing but baked beans, and lots of them; then the people would go to the symphony hall—with obvious consequences. Imagine the scene when the action began! The concert would be over before the first movement!" As Alinsky notes, the system would be virtually powerless to deal with such a rearguard attack.

Yet another, equally resourceful, method of biological warfare was devised by the Radical Vegetarian League, a student group at the University of Michigan. Twenty-five members stormed a newly opened McDonald's stand in Ann Arbor during the noontime rush, downed ample

Adolf Hitler postage stamp—
a philatelic coup

quantities of mustard powder and water, and proceeded to stage history's first recorded puke-in. Said Phil Cushway, a member of the RVL, "We hope this demonstration leads people to question the nature of McDonald's and other corporations that foist plastic food on the public."

**Worst Postage Stamps:** Adolf Hitler was a far from wealthy man when he came to power, but the philatelic coup of Martin Bormann soon eliminated the Führer's financial anxieties. In his memoirs, *Inside the Third Reich*, Albert Speer tells how Hitler's personal photographer, the director of the German post office, and Bormann "decided that Hitler had rights to the reproduction of his picture on postage stamps and was therefore entitled to payments . . . . Since the Führer's head appeared on all stamps (issued between 1933 and 1945) millions flowed into the privy purse."

**Worst United States Senator:** Senator William Scott, cited by *New Times* magazine as the worst United States senator, has been giving his all in the effort to sustain his image. In 1975 the Virginia Republican visited several Middle Eastern nations on a three-week "fact-finding" tour which one unnamed State Department official called "a diplomat's nightmare." While on a tour of the Suez Canal, Scott reputedly remarked to Egyptian premier Anwar el-Sadat, "This is beautiful. I've always wanted to see the Persian Gulf." Sadat politely refrained from revealing to his guest that the Gulf was 925 miles away. Scott also balked at entering a mosque on the grounds that it "isn't a Christian building"; asked Israeli Prime Minister Yitzhak Rabin, "What's all this Gaza stuff?"; and, says the State Department official, "managed to insult almost every country—especially Israel." Total cost of the junket was $15,787, which covered, among other amenities, a healthy supply of Kellogg's Country Morning, Scott's favorite breakfast food. Senator Scott, himself, denies having made these statements.

---

**Most Unusual Campaign Strategy:** If it seemed that William G. Sesler was campaigning hard enough for two men, he was—two men, that is. As the Pennsylvania Democratic candidate for the Senate in 1970, Sesler attracted the attention of reporters when he delivered speeches at precisely the same hour in both Pittsburgh and Philadelphia, 250 miles apart.

Confronted with this amazing coincidence, Sesler admitted having arranged for his identical twin brother Tom to stand in for him at the Pittsburgh rally, and on other occasions during the campaign. Most people agreed that Tom was a better speechmaker than candidate William, but it was all academic anyway. Sesler—both of him—lost the election.

**Most Unusual City Council Member:** Philadelphia voters reelected Francis O'Donnell to the city council in 1975 although he had been dead of a heart attack for nearly a week. "It seemed appropriate to remove his name from the ballot," a member of the Democratic City Committee afterwards said, "but there just wasn't enough time to change all the voting machines."

**Most Unusual Election:** During the Middle Ages, mayors of the Swedish town of Hurdenburg were elected thusly: all the candidates sat around a table, bending forward so that their beards rested on the table's surface. A single louse would then be placed at the table's center. The man into whose beard the unsheltered mite crawled would be mayor of Hurdenburg for the following year.

**Most Unusual International Incident:** When Dr. Waldo Waldron-Ramsey's pet Alsatian hound ran amok and bit eight people in Pelham, New York, in 1975, police threatened to shoot it. Waldron-Ramsey, who was Barbados' permanent delegate to the United Nations, indignantly wrote to Henry Kissinger, the Attorney General, and several other highly placed officials, and spoke darkly of "possible international consequences" should the police actually carry out their threat.

To forestall an embarrassing ambassadorial tiff with the United States, Waldron-Ramsey was immediately summoned home by his country's Ministry of External Affairs "to discuss matters arising out of the widely publicized reports." Several weeks later he was dismissed.

In Tokyo, the existence of *two* Turkish embassies also caused some ambassadorial unpleasantness. One of the embassies—the real one—reported a succession of misplaced telephone calls from people who wanted to know what the "prices" were and whether those prices included the services of attractive hostesses.

The calls, it turned out, were meant for the other embassy—a bath house/massage parlor called The Turkish Embassy, which agreed to change its name to Kojo (Japanese for Red Castle).

An historical note: A dispute over the rights to large reserves of Peruvian bat guano, used for fertilizer, almost brought diplomatic relations between the United States and that South American republic to an abrupt halt in 1851. Peace was made only when United States President Millard Fillmore intervened and helped strike a compromise between the Peruvian government and United States business interests vying for the treasured droppings.

**Most Unusual Legislative Initiative:** For most of his tenure as United States Representative from Tennessee during the 1830s, Davy Crockett dozed quietly in his chair and kept his mouth shut. But there was one issue he felt so passionately about that he was compelled to speak out—the prohibition on whiskey sales inside the Capitol building. In a memorable speech in the House, Crockett declared that whiskey in Congress should not only be legal but it should also be free. "Congress allows lemonade to members and it is charged under the head of stationery," he said. "I move that whiskey be allowed under the item of fuel."

**Most Unusual Liberation Movement:** The Doukhobors were a communistic religious sect in Russia that actively opposed the czar's conscription law of 1887. Oppressed and persecuted, they were finally forced into exile in 1898. With the aid of Leo Tolstoy and Prince Kropotkin, the anarchist theoretician, they found a new home in the Canadian province of Saskatchewan.

The word "Doukhobor" means "spirit wrestler," and the sect aggressively opposes any government interference in what they regard as strictly spiritual affairs. They refuse to register births, deaths, and marriages, and they have stubbornly resisted state pressure to send their children to public schools.

Moreover, an extremist Doukhobor faction known as the Sons of Freedom have engaged in determined anarchist agitation for over fifty years. Nude parades are this radical fringe group's principal means of political self-expression. On numerous occasions as many as six hundred to seven hundred goose-pimpled protestors have marched on govern-

The Sons of Freedom stage a protest.

ment offices and engaged in civil disobedience in Regina, Saskatoon, and other chilly Canadian prairie towns. Some fanatical members of the group also dabble in arson, terrorist bombings, and the "liberation of cattle." (The Royal Canadian Mounted Police call it "rustling.") All these actions are in keeping with their belief that "the destruction of material things may save the spiritual life."

Among the material things the "mad brothers" have destroyed over the years are forty-four schools, eight churches of rival denominations, one hospital, fifty-four sections of railroad track along with a number of passenger trains, four railway stations, twenty-two entire Doukhobor villages including hundreds of private homes, four post offices, three theaters, assorted grain elevators, stores, and factories, twenty-nine sawmills, a radio tower, and a Greyhound bus station. In addition, they have set eight major forest fires and dynamited the tomb of Peter Verigin, a conservative Doukhobor leader, eleven times.

Of the nearly twenty thousand Doukhobors currently living in Canada, officials estimate that about twenty-five hundred belong to the Sons of Freedom.

**Most Unusual Mayor:** The Reuters news service recently reported that "a controversy is raging because a foot powder named Pulvapies was elected mayor of a town of 4,100."

The coastal town of Picoaza, Ecuador, was in the midst of a listless election campaign when a foot deodorant manufacturer came out with the slogan "Vote for any candidate, but if you want well-being and hygiene, vote for Pulvapies." Then on the eve of the voting, a leaflet reading "For Mayor: Honorable Pulvapies" was widely distributed.

In one of the great embarrassments of democracy, the voters of Picoaza elected the foot powder by a clear majority; Pulvapies also ran well in outlying districts.

**Most Unusual Presidential Candidate:** Emil Matalik announced his candidacy for the presidency in the summer of 1975, but noted that his politics transcended narrow nationalism. "I'm really interested in being president of the world," he told press people. "The problems around the world are building up to an explosive point. The only solution is a world president."

Among those problems, said Matalik, is an "excess of animals and plant life. Especially trees." Under the Matalik administration, each family will be permitted a maximum of one child, one animal, and one tree.

Matalik, a former boy scout and air force officer, says that his farm in Bennett, Wisconsin, will be world capital if he is elected.

**Most Unusual Public Assistance Program:** In towns throughout nineteenth-century New England, the lame, the halt, the poor and the feeble-minded were auctioned off at town meetings much as black slaves were in the South, although the practice continued long after Lincoln's Emancipation Proclamation and the Thirteenth Amendment. One reason these "vendues of the poor," as they were called, may have been allowed to continue is that they did not come under the jurisdiction of antislavery statutes because they were not really auctions in the true sense. People bid not to *buy* the enfeebled adults and children placed on the block, but to adopt them, the winning bidder being the one who asked the smallest stipend from the town council for feeding and upkeep.

If you underbid your competitors and came away with a reasonably strong young man, let's say, he was yours to work as you pleased. You could have him cut crabgrass or catch mice or do other odd jobs, as long as you were not unreasonable in your demands. On the other hand, you might also bid for some helpless aged cripple, with an eye to making a profit on the allowance you would receive from the state. In Pennsylvania in 1894, an elderly woman named Elmira Quick, offered a low bid of $1.25 a week—and thereby purchased herself.

While vendues of the poor were basically humanitarian in impulse, abolitionists and reformers attacked them as cosmeticized slave auctions; and ultimately they died out, giving way to orphanages, public workhouses, and welfare systems of the sort known today.

**Most Unusual Scare Tactics:** Calvin Coolidge used to hide in the White House shrubbery, then jump out and scare unsuspecting Secret Service agents.

**Most Unusual Tribute to an Emperor:** The feared Spanish inquisitor Torquemada once wrote that during Montezuma's reign over the Aztecs, the emperor's son, Alonzo de Ojeda, was intrigued by a pile of bulging sacks stored in an inconspicuous corner of the palace. Alonzo undid one of the bags, assuming the contests to be gold dust, and found it contained *lice* instead.

When the boy questioned the royal advisers, he was told that the poorest of Montezuma's subjects, the landless Aztec peasants, had no gold to offer their king, and so made a habit of collecting the lice they removed from their bodies and setting them aside. When they had enough to make a respectable offering, they filled a bag with them and laid it before their beloved emperor.

**Most Unusual Welfare Program:** All residents of Lexington, Kentucky, regardless of income, are eligible to receive free pigeons from the municipal sanitation department in an innovative program aimed at ridding the city of the bothersome birds and keeping Lexington clean. The pigeons can be eaten, stuffed, trained or baked in a pie. People who've sampled the meat say it's delicious, and those who have strolled the streets of downtown Lexington say the walking's a lot less hazardous these days.

# The Law

<hr>

**Best Argument for Liberalizing our Divorce Laws:** In 1973, five successive husbands of the same Indonesian woman all died of anemia less than a month after their wedding days. While we can snicker about the probable cause of their rapid debilitation, the parents of the unlucky bride consulted a witch doctor who attributed the deaths to a vampire that had inhabited the woman's body and sucked her husbands' blood.

**Best Art Theft:** Nobody noticed anything strange about two paintings— a Breughel and a Van Dyke—that hung in an art museum in Danzig, Poland, in 1972, until the Breughel mysteriously fell off the wall one day. It turned out to be not the original, but a reproduction scissored from a cheap news magazine. The Van Dyke was similarly faked, but no one has any idea when the originals were stolen.

**Best Assault with a Deadly Weapon:** Robert Goines was a gas station owner in Indianapolis with a thief on his hands. Over the years he had lost an estimated twenty-five dollars to his undependable soda machine. One day in 1969, after giving refunds to two disappointed customers, Goines lost his own fifteen cents to the armless bandit.

Well, Goines was understandably furious. As he testified in municipal court, "I shook the machine. Then I walked over to the desk drawer, got my .22 caliber revolver, and I went over and shot the machine dead! After I fired the shot, I looked at the machine and said, 'That's the last time you're going to cheat anyone.'"

Now a jury of twelve men good and true would surely have ruled it a clear case of justifiable "machinocide." But the judge saw it differently. Goines was fined $160 and sentenced to ten days in jail for disorderly conduct and firing a gun within the city limits.

Charles E. Boles, better known as "Black Bart"

**Best Bandit:** Charles E. Boles, better known as "Black Bart," was a daring and unconventional outlaw who operated in the Sierra Nevada foothills and along the Sonoma Coast of California. Between 1875 and 1883, he robbed at least twenty-nine stagecoaches, and only once did he fail to escape with the strongbox. Unfortunately, those were hard times for California highwaymen: the Mother Lode region was pretty well played out by the 1870s, and gold was hard to come by. As a result, Black Bart's income was less than he might have made selling insurance; Wells Fargo estimated that he netted no more than $18,000 from all his spectacular holdups.

Although Bart was not the highest-paid desperado of his era, he definitely had the most original style. He robbed alone, wore a derby instead of a Stetson, and traveled to and from all his jobs on foot—"shanks mare" as he called it—since Black Bart hated horses.

His very first robbery, on July 26, 1875, was a typical example of his *modus operandi*. A man named John Shine was at the reins of the Wells Fargo stagecoach en route from Shasta to Fort Ross. Suddenly Bart ran out into the middle of the dusty road. He was wearing an old flour sack as a mask and pointed a menacing twelve-gage at the driver. "Please throw down the box," he said politely. However, when Shine hesitated, Bart shouted gruffly, "If he dares to shoot, give him a solid volley, boys." Only then did the driver notice a half-dozen rifles bristling out of a nearby chaparral, all aimed in his direction. Outnumbered seven to one, he nervously threw down the cashbox. Bart opened it, helped himself, and hurried off on foot into the underbrush. Shine breathed a deep sigh of relief, then, with a start, he realized that there were still six rifles trained on his heart. For fifteen minutes he sat there quivering in his boots before finally becoming suspicious. Ever so cautiously, he climbed down from the cab and walked slowly toward the gang of cutthroats. To his astonishment, he discovered that the threatening weapons were only wooden poles that the solitary highwayman had fastened in place to create the illusion of a band of confederates. And for the record, Bart's shotgun was not even loaded; it never was.

Soon Bart added another artistic touch to his repertoire of crime. He began composing poetry, just a single clumsy stanza at first, which he left with his incredulous victims. By his fifth robbery, in July 1878, he was up to three perfectly metrical, rhymed stanzas:

> Here I lay me down to sleep
> To await the coming morrow
> Perhaps success, perhaps defeat
> And everlasting sorrow.

> I've labored long and hard for bred [*sic*]
> For honor and for riches
> But on my corns too long you've tred
> You fine-haired Sons of Bitches.

> Let come what will, I'll try it on
> My condition can't be worse
> And if there's money in that box
> 'Tis munny in my purse.

He signed his compositions, "Black Bart, the Po-8."

Bart was finally apprehended on November 3, 1883. Convicted of only one holdup, he was sentenced to ten years in San Quentin. There he wore number 11046 (it should be retired) and was a model prisoner, serving as druggist for the prison doctor. On January 21, 1888, he was released, his sentence being shortened for good behavior. Black Bart went straight to Vancouver, British Columbia, booked passage aboard the *Empress of China* bound for Japan, and disappeared from the pages of history.

**Best Bribery Ritual:** The bribing of government officials is a highly developed art in Thailand. It works like this: the briber drops a wallet in the presence of the bribee and then picks it up and offers it to the official, explaining, "You must have dropped this." If the official is satisfied with the size of the bribe, he accepts the wallet and thanks his patron for his honesty. If he would like the pot sweetened, he returns it, saying, "Sorry, but it isn't mine." The briber is then free to try again with a more handsome offer.

**Best Counterfeiter:** In 1865, William E. Brockway printed a bogus $100 so perfect that the Treasury Department's only recourse was to withdraw all authentic $100 bills from circulation.

**Best Death Penalty:** While campaigning for reelection to Parliament, Jonathan Guinness, of Lincoln, England, injected a note of compassion into his appeal to reinstate the death penalty in Britain. Guinness suggested that the cells of condemned prisoners be furnished with razor blades, thus offering them the option of a do-it-yourself execution since, as he told newspaper reporters, "Hanging is sadistic." But when one reporter pointed out that death by razor would surely be slower, chancier, and more painful than the hangman's noose, Guinness backed off. "Well, perhaps a pill or revolver," he said. "I haven't thought this out very carefully."

**Best Form of Assault and Battery:** Montreal Judge Pierre Decary imposed a $650 fine on a man who had slapped a woman during an argument over a game of golf. Said the judge, "You must not strike a woman except with a flower." (When handing down that *obiter dictum,* Judge

Decary may have been thinking of an annual midsummer rite in Nice, France, known as the Battle of Flowers, in which both the spectators and the participants in a lavish carnival parade spiritedly pelt each other with rose petals.)

**Best Jailbreak:** A prisoner in a German jail literally chewed his way to freedom in 1907. The prisoner was Hans Schaarschmidt, serving a six-year sentence for robbery. The prison was a decaying fortress in Gera whose windows were barred not with steel but with pairs of crossed heavy wooden beams. Each day Schaarschmidt chewed away as much of them as his much-abused incisors could stand; then, to avoid suspicion, he filled in the hole with a rubbery paste made from the black bread he was fed. After three months, Schaarschmidt was able to remove the bread putty and squeeze through to freedom.

Unfortunately, with the police on his heels, Schaarschmidt was hunted down and captured within three weeks. This time he was put behind iron bars.

**Best Juvenile Delinquent:** In Buenos Aires, Argentina, police nabbed an eight-year-old boy and charged him with grand larceny in the theft of a school bus. The boy had maneuvered the bus down three levels of an indoor parking garage and into traffic when a guard spotted him. He explained that he had arranged to sell the vehicle for thirteen dollars.

**Best Law:** Dogs are prohibited from barking after six P.M. in Little Rock, Arkansas. And in Paulding, Ohio, a peace officer has the right to subdue a barking canine by biting him.

**Best Pickpocket:** General Winfield Scott, a hero of the Mexican War and an unsuccessful presidential candidate, had a wallet containing eight hundred dollars in cash stolen from his pocket while attending a White House dinner.

**Best Proof That Honesty Is Not the Best Policy:** On the application he filled out to join the police force, a Houston, Texas, resident was asked if he had ever had a police record. The applicant could not tell a lie. No, he answered, but he had once knocked over a liquor store, without being caught.

He didn't get the job. Worse yet, for his candor he was arrested and jailed for armed robbery—and for illegal possession of a .32 caliber revolver which detectives found when they frisked him at the station house.

**Best Shoplifter:** Like macrame and classical guitar, shoplifting is an art that takes time and practice to perfect. (See "Education," *Most Unusual School.*) Consider these masters: a woman working a supermarket in Nuremberg, West Germany, collapsed at the checkout counter. When passersby tried to revive her, they found a frozen chicken concealed under her hat. . . . Another woman walked into a London boutique clad only in a light summer shift, and walked out wearing 10 brassieres, 20 pairs of pants, 15 dresses, and a summer coat. . . . Also in England—in Stevenage, to be precise—a man accused of stealing purses in a shop claimed that he had become inexplicably confused; actually, he had thought he was in a library filching books.

**Best Theft:** In Argentina some years ago, a band of thieves dismantled and absconded with an iron bridge spanning the Rio Paraná. The nocturnal heist was discovered the following morning when rush-hour traffic became uncustomarily congested on the approaches to the bridge.

Argentinian police were able to trace the bridge to a local scrap merchant who had purchased it from the thieves. The criminals themselves were never caught.

**Worst Bank Robber:** An unemployed shoe salesman walked into a Queens, New York, branch of the First National City Bank and handed a teller a note demanding "all your tens, twenties, and thirties." He was arrested fifteen minutes later by a bank officer who trailed him on foot to a motel a block away.

**Worst Car Thieves:** Two thieves working a Detroit parking lot jimmied open the door of a parked minibus and began poking around for valuables. Thus occupied, they failed to notice two plainclothesmen sitting in the front seat. The officers quietly put the car in gear and drove to the police station.

**Worst Game Law:** Poachers, beware: Under British law it is now illegal to molest the Loch Ness Monster.

The very existence of "Nessie," as both the monster's loyalists and nay-sayers have come to call it, is a moot point, of course. But at a press conference in London in December 1975, a pair of ardent Loch Nessians—Robert Rines and Sir Peter Scott—offered three purportedly genuine photographs of the monster to *Nature,* the British science journal.

They also gave Nessie a scientific name as well—*Nessiteras Rhombopteryx*, which in Greek means "diamond-finned Ness monster."

Scott, a British naturalist, claimed that the pictures were "genuine photographs of what looks like an animal," in spite of one reporter's contention that the animal in question "might be a dead swan lying on its side," and another's that it looked like "a sunken Viking ship."

Yet another critic asked Rines and Scott to explain, among other things, why no remains of deceased Loch Ness monsters had ever been seen. Sir Peter suggested that Loch Ness monsters are cannibals who devour their dead, or that the Loch Ness monster instinctively swallows a bellyful of small stones when he senses death is nigh, and then sinks peacefully to the bottom of the lake to die. He had no comment when Scottish Parliament member Nicholas Fairbairn rearranged the letters of *Nessiteras Rhombopteryx* to form an interesting anagram: "Monster hoax by Sir Peter S."

**Worst Heist:** According to the *Times* of London, thieves who ransacked the offices of *Games and Puzzles*, a British publication, bagged several hundred thousand pounds in cold cash. All of it, however, was in Monopoly money.

**Worst Judge:** A municipal court judge in Los Angeles was stripped of her duties in 1975 after being charged with some twenty-four different—and all equally inventive—procedural violations.

California Supreme Court justices charged that she had "maligned" her office by habitually wearing miniskirts in court, keeping a pet poodle on her lap while she heard cases, and frequently losing her temper in court. They claimed that she capriciously threw attorneys and public defenders into the slammer if they made her angry. Worse yet, she kept a mechanical canary with a particularly irritating chirp in her pink-painted chambers. The most imaginative of her offenses was her threat to give a ".38 caliber vasectomy" to a police officer who remonstrated her for blowing her automobile horn too much.

**Worst Judge's Bench:** In his journals, Hugh Latimer, the sixteenth-century English Protestant martyr, noted that in ancient Persia, judges often conducted their business while seated on cushions upholstered with the skins of their dishonest predecessors in office.

**Worst Lynching:** A circus elephant named Mary ran amok and killed a man in Erwin, Tennessee, on September 13, 1916. Demanding justice, the enraged townspeople dragged the pachyderm to a railroad derrick, bent on hanging her. Before a crowd of five thousand curiosity seekers, the mob spent two hours stringing their victim up, only to have her fall to the ground when the steel cable holding her snapped. On their second attempt, however, the cable held and the prisoner was hanged.

To be sure, Mary was not the first quadruped to receive the death penalty, nor are courtroom trials of law-breaking animals as uncommon as one might suppose (see *Felton & Fowler I*, page 129). In fact, there is at least one textbook on the subject of animals and the law: E. R. Evans' 1906 classic, *The Criminal Prosecution and Capital Punishment of Animals*. That year, a dog accused of aiding a man in an armed robbery was sentenced to death by a Swiss court.

---

**Worst Missing Persons Search:** On an October morning in 1971, Sir Peregrine Henniker-Heaton, an official in the British Intelligence Service, disappeared after telling his wife he was going out for his daily constitutional. Scotland Yard authorities searched for Sir Peregrine for three years, but could find no trace of him. They finally located his body in an unused room of his own home, where it had been all the time.

We're also fond of this quote from a corporal in the Royal Canadian Mounted Police, who was participating in a search for a missing child in Pender Harbor, Vancouver: "We have checked the area thoroughly," he told the Vancouver *Sun*, "and there is nothing to indicate that the child is actually lost, other than the fact that she is missing."

**Worst Plaintiff:** When Lorenzo Castelli was struck and killed by a train not long ago, the nationally owned Italian railroad sued him on charges of delaying rail schedules for as much as twenty-nine minutes by "incautiously crossing the tracks and being hit by a train."

**Worst Rapist:** A twenty-five-year-old man broke into the Bronx, New York, apartment of a young mother, raped her, then proceeded to fall blissfully asleep on her bed. Police were summoned and awoke the snoring intruder with a pitcher of ice water.

Not to be outdone, a Cincinnati judge fell asleep during a rape trial. A mistrial was declared.

**Worst Will:** When the executors disclosed the contents of the will of the late Francis H. Lord, of Sydney, Australia, his wife learned that she had

Ulysses S. Grant, arrested three times for speeding

been bequeathed "one shilling for tram fare so she can go somewhere and drown herself."

Bridget Filson of Bournemouth, England, treated her widower less tightfistedly, but instructed her sister to personally deliver her husband's inheritance "to the nearest pub, where he will be found drinking to my absence."

**Most Unusual Arrest:** Only two incumbent United States Presidents have ever been arrested. None has ever been tried, convicted, or jailed, although more than one deserved to be.

On a pitch black night in 1853, Franklin Pierce was returning on horseback from the home of William Morgan in southeast Washington. With his mind swimming with the affairs of state, the President accidentally ran down an old lady crossing the street—a Mrs. Nathan Lewis. A policeman named Stanley Edelin dutifully busted the Chief Executive, presumably for reckless horsemanship. According to the police blotter, the President simply said, "I am Mr. Pierce," and he was released. The woman suffered minor cuts and bruises.

Twice in 1866 Ulysses S. Grant, while still Commander of the Army of the Potomac, was arrested for speeding—once on April 11 and again on

July 1. On both occasions he was fined five dollars in precinct court. So he was no stranger to the police when he was arrested once more on a speeding charge during his first term of office. Grant was racing his buggy west on M Street between 11th and 12th avenues, when a constable named William H. West stepped out into the road and courageously grabbed the horse's bridle. The carriage dragged him fifty feet before it stopped. Officer West, a Union veteran, immediately recognized Grant and began to apologize. But the President reportedly said, "Officer, do your duty."

The horse and rig were taken to the precinct headquarters and briefly impounded, but no charges were pressed and no trial was held because of the confusion as to whether a sitting President may be indicted without first being impeached.

**Most Unusual Bigamist:** At age thirty-two the Czech Siamese twins Josepha and Rosa Blazek entered the hospital. Although the sisters were joined at the sacrum and spinal column, Rosa gave birth to a healthy, normal baby boy. But even though the father admitted paternity and was eager to make an honest woman of his Rosa, the child was officially listed as illegitimate on the hospital records. The Czech police warned the prospective bridegroom that as soon as he pronounced his vows, he would be arrested and charged with bigamy.

**Most Unusual Case of Sex Discrimination:** Not long ago, Connecticut's Canine Control Office puckishly issued dog-license tags shaped like fireplugs. Several women immediately telephoned the office to protest that the tags symbolized only male dogs.

**Most Unusual Form of Racial Discrimination:** A family of mixed blood in South Africa, where the term "colored," incidentally, is still in use, was balked in its efforts to install a memorial plaque for their deceased dog in an all-white pet cemetery. Apparently, it is not only bipeds who are subject to South African apartheid.

**Most Unusual Jailbreak:** How's this for a high-cholesterol escape? A convict escaped from his cell in a maximum security prison in Connecticut by smearing himself from head to foot with butter and squeezing through the bars. (Which reminds us of an accident-prone rhinoceros named Rhadha who got her head caught in the bars of her cage at the Los Angeles Zoo. Firemen rescued her by lubricating her head with vaseline.)

The very term jailbreak, incidentally, implies an escape *from* a penal

Connecticut's fire hydrant dog tag

institution of some sort. But in 1975 someone broke *into* Faribault County Jail in Walters, Minnesota, and ran off with an antique pot-bellied stove.

**Most Unusual Police Force:** The Chastity Police, established by Austrian Queen Maria Theresa, was no ordinary vice squad. In their tireless efforts to uphold marital fidelity and sexual orthodoxy, the Queen's intimate storm troopers peered through keyholes and burst into bedrooms. No illicit lovers were safe from detection.

Uniformed guards were stationed in every theater and ballroom to prevent the indelicate display of ankles or hot-blooded clutching on the dance floor. All baggage and mail, even diplomatic pouches, were inspected at the border for dirty books and drawings. And any woman walking the streets alone was subject to arrest; convicted prostitutes were transported out of the cities to an all-female rehabilitation village in southern Hungary. The adaptable harlots in Vienna soon learned to walk demurely in pairs, fingering a rosary as they made their contacts.

Gossips charged that the Queen instituted the Chastity Police because she was frustrated by the philandering of her own mate, Franz I. Whatever the reason, she made life miserable for even the most discreet libertines. Once, Casanova visited Vienna with a mistress, whom he identified as his sister. The day after their arrival, just as they were sitting down to breakfast, the Chastity Police broke down the lovers' door. Under intensive interrogation, their story was proved to be false, and the two were forced to move into separate quarters. As Casanova noted in his diary, "There was plenty of money, and plenty of luxury in Vienna, but the bigotry of the Empress made Cytherean pleasures extremely difficult." Later, we are sad to relate, Casanova worked as a paid informer for the Chastity Police, and for the Inquisition in Venice, providing them with a bibliography of pornographic and antireligious works found in private libraries.

**Most Unusual Sentences:** In 1972, a Los Angeles Superior Court judge sentenced a pickpocket to a short jail term for swiping $15.11 from a woman's pocketbook. Noting the defendant's record of twenty previous arrests, the judge also ordered the man to wear enormous eight-ounce woolen mittens whenever he appeared in public for the next two years. The prospect of digital confinement was apparently more than the accused could bear; he skipped bail and hasn't been heard of since.

Unusual, if not cruel, punishments are becoming increasingly common, it seems, and they are not restricted to felonies. On the theory that he would not feel the sting of a large fine, a wealthy Californian who ran a red light was sentenced to catch, clean, and deliver fifty pounds of fresh fish to the Salvation Army. And Pierre Morganti, the mayor of Oliastro on the island of Corsica, announced in the summer of 1975 that any nudist caught lounging on Avrone Beach would be painted blue; at least three persons have learned that Morganti means what he says. Meanwhile, in nearby Linguizetta, the town council, adopting the example of Lady Godiva, requires skinny-dippers to ride naked through the streets on a donkey.

**Most Unusual "Smuggler":** In Fascist Italy, jazz was officially condemned as a decadent art form and record dealers were prohibited from importing what Benito Mussolini called "the musical expression of an inferior race." One young jazz buff who defied the ban was Romano Mussolini, the dictator's son; he smuggled the sounds of Louis Armstrong and Fats Waller right into *Il Duce*'s palace. Romano, now in his fifties, went on to become a professional jazz pianist, playing music which is, by his own description, a "cross between California and Eastern hard bop." He also plays the harmonica and guitar, and is a popular performer on the Italian night club circuit. But despite his musical progressivism, Romano remains loyal to the old faith. "I would be a Fascist now or at any time in the past. I'm a Fascist in logic and conviction as well as sentiment," he says.

**Most Unusual Theft:** A native of Fergus, Ontario, was busted by police for stealing four and a half quarts of bull semen. He told reporters, "I am not what they call a kinky."

**Most Unusual Traffic Cops:** A municipal park in Napa, California, abounds with stop signs and other similarly conventional traffic control devices, but many accidents still occurred until City Park Superintendent Bob Pelusi hired eighty-five chickens as traffic directors. Now the parks are safe again.

The chickens, of course, do nothing but strut about at the park's entrance, blithely oblivious to entering and exiting cars, but their very presence has helped reduce accidents—without the expense of installing traffic bumps or hiring human traffic cops.

"The traffic moves with caution, now," Pelusi explains. "Only occasionally does an errant driver charge through the flock." In the poultry patrol's first nine months, only nine chickens were killed in the line of duty—a reasonable price to pay, Pelusi says, for traffic safety.

**Most Unusual Vagrant:** In 1904 a trained African elephant swam from Brooklyn's Coney Island amusement park across the Verrazano Narrows to Staten Island, where peace officers picked him up and jailed him in the police stables for vagrancy.

**Most Unusual Will:** The annals of testate law are filled with eccentric wills. There was, for instance, a recent case in which a wealthy California widow left her entire fortune to God. A court challenge was brought by disappointed relatives, but before the will could be settled, a man whose house had been struck by lightning sued God's estate for damages. He failed to collect.

Here are a few alternative candidates. Madama de la Bresse, a noted French prude, directed that her life savings of 125,000 francs be used to buy clothing for naked Paris snowmen. In 1876 the courts upheld the validity of her bequest, making French snowmen the best dressed in the world. In a similar vein, Francesca Nortyega, a well-known European reformer, willed her estate to a niece on the condition that she keep the family goldfish outfitted in pants. Less generous was Varillas, a French romantic historian of the eighteenth century, who disinherited his nephew because the blockhead never learned to spell properly.

The central clause in the last will and testament of the German poet Heinrich Heine read, "I leave my entire estate to my wife on the condition that she remarry; then there will be at least one man to regret my death." (Here it might be worth recalling Heine's famous last words. When a visitor at the poet's bedside saw that death was near, he asked if he should summon a priest. *"Non,"* Heine replied in French, *"Dieu me pardonnera, c'est son metier,"*—God will pardon me, that's His line of work.)

**Most Unusual Witness:** During a 1973 murder trial in Haiti, the accused was granted an adjournment to give him the opportunity to resurrect, through a vodoo ritual, the victim, whom he wished to call as a defense witness. When the dead man failed to appear in court, the defendant was convicted.

# The Military

<hr>

**Best Argument for Disarmament:** At the Constitutional Convention of 1787, Elbridge Gerry (Founding Father, Governor of Massachusetts, and later Vice President of the United States from 1813 to 1814) argued vociferously for restricting the United States Army to three hundred men in peacetime. Said Gerry, "A standing army is like a standing member. It's an excellent assurance of domestic tranquility, but a dangerous temptation to foreign adventure."

**Best Combat Rations:** Caviar was issued as a daily ration to British soldiers in the Crimean War. Many, however, preferred chicken eggs to sturgeon eggs and wrote home complaining that they were sick of eating "black fish jam."

Caviar has been priced out of reach during recent wars, but now there is new hope for the gourmet G.I. Five Russian scientists have obtained U.S. Patent #3,589,910 for "synthetic granular caviar" which closely resembles natural sturgeon roe in texture and flavor. Derived from petro-chemicals, synthetic caviar gets its characteristic dark gray color from a superb solution of ferric lactate.

**Best Effort to Limit Defense Spending:** Standing just five feet, four inches tall, James Madison was America's shortest Chief Executive. Some Federalists insisted that he was not of presidential stature, physically or mentally, but, in our book, Madison proved his worth when war with Great Britain seemed imminent. The nation's insignificant fleet clearly needed to be enlarged and modernized, but Madison proposed that instead of building up a navy from scratch, it would be cheaper and simpler to rent Portugal's.

The Krummlauf: it fires around corners

**Best Fight Songs:** "Over There" was the most widely played American "victory song" during World War I, but there were others with considerably more pizzaz. Some, like "We're Going to Show the Kaiser the Way to Cut Up Sauerkraut," were full of malicious mischief; others were guilty of chauvinistic puns, including "We'll Yank the Kaiser's Mustache Down," and "When the Yanks Yank the Germ Out of Germany." Also worthy of note was the most repulsive love song ever crooned by a schmaltzy tenor, "I'll Kill the Kaiser for You." Our personal favorite, however, was a stirring fight song, liberally punctuated with clashing cymbals: "We Don't Want the Bacon."

> We don't want the bacon,
> We don't want the bacon;
> What we want is a piece of the Rhine.
> We'll hit Bill the Kaiser
> On the head and make him wiser,
> We'll have a wonderful time.

The fight songs of World War II were less ingenuous and more sentimental and were lacking in the bravura and xenophobia of the 1918 hit parade. One exception was "The Japs Won't Have a Chinaman's Chance," which was eventually banned from the airwaves when someone pointed out that our ally Chiang Kai-shek might be offended.

Another lampooning song in the old style called "Even Hitler Had a Mother" enjoyed brief popularity on the London stage until Prime Minister Neville Chamberlain, in an act of musical appeasement just prior to the invasion of the Rhineland, prohibited its performance.

**Best Gun:** For house-to-house fighting in urban centers, the German munitions manufacturers developed a deadly rifle that could shoot around corners. Called the Krummlauf, the gun had a curved barrel attachment and a mirror sight that enabled a soldier, while remaining hidden, to spray the street with bullets. The barrel could be quickly adjusted to fire either to the left or to the right. Curved-bore rifles were patented as far back as the American Civil War, but the Krummlauf, used during the street fighting in Stalingrad, was the first round-the-corner firearm ever issued for actual combat.

**Best Military Rule of Thumb:** Just before the 1967 Tet Offensive, General William Westmoreland appeared for the first time on "the Ten Best-Dressed List." (See also "Fashion and Grooming," *Best Dressed.*) According to military historians Roger Beaumont and Bernard J. James, the Pentagon could have anticipated imminent disaster.

Beaumont and James have isolated what they call the Sukhomlinov Effect, stipulating that "in war, victory goes to those armies whose leaders' uniforms are the least impressive." The phenomenon is named after General V. A. Sukhomlinov, commander of the Czar's armies in World War I. Sukhomlinov went to the front bedecked with a galaxy of military decorations, splendid epaulets, yards of gold braid, and an assortment of costly trappings burnished with gallons of spit and polish. He was also a military cretin who orchestrated the debacles that knocked Russia out of the war and brought on the Revolution.

Beaumont and James insist that, impartially applied, the Sukhomlinov Effect has predicted the winners and losers of the twenty-five major wars since the American Revolution, with the possible exceptions of the Spanish Civil War and the Russo-Finnish War (over which reasonable, fashion-conscious men could differ).

This important new tool tells us that the Israelis should continue their military superiority over the Arabs unless they change tailors. And, while the United States has little to fear from the dandy Soviets, we should be on our guard against the Chinese in their drab, gray Mao jackets.

**Best Propaganda:** Pharaoh Ramses II was soundly defeated by the Hittites at the Battle of Kadesh in 1294 B.C. Undaunted, the Egyptian ruler erected a memorial to commemorate his magnificent "victory." The monument endured, the Hittites died out, and generation upon generation of historians paid tribute to Ramses' military triumph. Only recently have archaeologists unearthed the truth about the Battle of Kadesh, exposing Ramses' 3,300-year-old "big lie."

**Best Solace of the Atomic Age:** It just goes to prove that every mushroom-shaped cloud has a silver lining.

While debate was raging about the disastrous effects that the inert propellants released from spray-on deodorants and other aerosols could have on the ozone layer, we read this reassuring report in *The New York Times:* "The Defense Department estimates that an all-out nuclear war would significantly deplete the protective layer of ozone in the stratosphere," but that it "wouldn't cut it to the point of endangering all life."

The earth depends on its ozone layer to absorb some of the deadly, high-intensity ultraviolet light coming from the sun. But the best guesses of the Pentagon experts are that World War III would reduce the amount of ozone over the temperate regions by only 50 to 75 percent—not enough to cause all plants and animals to fry to a crisp.

**Worst Amphibious Vehicle:** The very least a $14,000 truck, touted as amphibious, should be is *buoyant*. Even if it can't perform any useful function in the water, it should be able to stay afloat long enough for a tugboat to arrive and tow it to safety.

Unfortunately, the 14,000 reputedly amphibious "Gamma Goat" trucks purchased recently by the United States Army for $200 million can't even do that. More often than not they sink like a rock; even on dry land, they frequently break down.

**Worst Combat Rations:** During the Indochina war, a government paymaster made the mistake of dropping in empty-handed on a unit of battle-weary Cambodian army regulars, encamped near Pnompenh, who had gone unpaid for over four months. When the soldiers' demand for their back wages was rebuffed, they shot the paymaster and ate him.

Actually, the flesh of one's adversaries has been considered tasty fare by Cambodian warriors for centuries, and an enemy's internal organs—the liver in particular—are considered a fertile source of strength and fighting prowess. The soldiers who feasted on fillet of payless paymaster afterwards told Associated Press reporters that while fighting at Kompong Seila, eighty miles southwest of the Cambodian capital, they had hungrily devoured the bodies of several Khmer Rouge insurgents slain in battle.

**Worst General:** Ambrose Everett Burnside, U.S.A. In a fascinating book entitled *Jaws of Victory*, Charles Fair has skillfully chronicled the dismal history of military bungling. He concludes that the American Civil War produced an embarrassment of incompetent leaders, and "of all the wrack of terrible commanders which that conflict cast up, Burnside . . . deserves the highest mention."

General Ambrose Burnside

A West Pointer and a Mexican War veteran, Burnside certainly looked the part of a general. He was handsome, a dashing dresser, and famous for his crop of carefully cultivated whiskers. The distinctive style was named burnsides in his honor and later transposed to "sideburns."

Burnside enjoyed his finest hour at the Battle of the Crater, in the midst of Grant's Wilderness Campaign. Carrying out an inventive strategy (that was not his own), Burnside ordered his men to tunnel a distance of 510 feet under no-man's-land to the site of the enemy headquarters. There, six feet underground, the soldiers planted four tons of dynamite. When the charge exploded, there was "a muffled roar as from a volcano," and an enormous hole opened up in the ground. The Confederates were caught off guard, and for a moment the plan looked like a stroke of genius.

Then, acting with uncharacteristic alacrity, Burnside ordered his troops forward down into the crater. It was an unbelievably chowderheaded tactic, aggravated by the fact that two division commanders were drunk in the trenches. The leaderless Union soldiers stumbled down the steep sides of the pit and found it nearly impossible to climb out again. In the meantime, Confederate reinforcements moved into place, surrounded the crater, and casually picked off the Yankees trapped inside. The casualty figures showed 4,000 Union dead to 1,000 Confederates slain. Grant termed the action "a stupendous failure . . .

a positive benefit to the enemy." And when Lincoln heard about the Battle of the Crater he said, "Only Burnside could have managed such a coup, wringing one last spectacular defeat from the jaws of victory."

Years later, running on his war record, Burnside was twice elected United States senator from Rhode Island.

**Worst Military Fraternity:** Military heroes in Uganda who win favor with Idi "Big Daddy" Amin are appointed to the honorary Order of the Mosquito. Amin selected the malaria-carrying insect as the official emblem of the Order in recognition of the mosquito's important role in discouraging European settlement of Uganda.

**Worst New Weapon:** United States Army scientists have developed a supersensitive "Smell-O-Meter," originally designed to sniff out the odor of *"nuoc mam,"* a pungent fish oil sauce that both North and South Vietnamese soldiers ate with their rice. Hundreds of these delicate sensors were air-dropped along the Ho Chi Minh Trail in hopes of keeping tabs on Communist troop movements. With impressive ingenuity, the Vietcong quickly devised a strategy to neutralize the Smell-O-Meters. The troops hung buckets of urine on trees along the infiltration route, and the devices were unable to distinguish the urine from *nuoc mam.* Officially, the Pentagon discontinued use of the Smell-O-Meters because they had "a too-broad spectrum."

**Most Unusual Army:** The Greeks believed that love between two men was love in its highest form. Consequently, the armies of the Greek city-states did not discourage homosexual love affairs among the troops; in fact, many commanders openly encouraged them. For example, the Sacred Band of Thebes—that city's elite corps of shock troops—was composed entirely of homosexual pairs. The presumption was that a man would rather die than be disgraced or appear guilty of cowardice in his lover's eyes.

Similarly, in the Spartan army, the best disciplined fighting force in the ancient world, each young recruit was assigned a mature male lover who served as his instructor in martial and romantic arts. The Spartans considered it an excellent tactic to have such couples fight side by side in the field.

At about the time of Christ, the guerrilla leader John of Gischala employed a transvestite strategy. In *The Wars of the Jews,* the chronicler Josephus speaks disapprovingly of the unorthodox uniforms worn by John's men: "While they decked their hair and put on women's garments, and were besmeared with ointments: and that they might appear very comely they had paint under their eyes, and imitated not only the ornaments but the lusts of women . . . while their faces looked like the faces of women, they killed with their right hands; and when their gait was effeminate, they presently attacked men and became warriors . . . and drew their swords from under their finely dyed cloaks, and killed everyone whom they came upon."

**Most Unusual Blitzkrieg:** Students of the OSS, America's wartime counterpart to the CIA, may know of its thwarted efforts to sneak estrogen into Hitler's salads, thus turning him into a squeaky-voiced eunuch. (See *Felton & Fowler I,* page 138.) That, however, was not the only OSS attempt to play havoc with the Führer's emotional stability. During the early days of the war, an OSS staff psychologist theorized that, despite the dictator's now well-known deviant sexual predilections, Hitler was unwilling to admit to himself that pornography was rampant throughout Germany, and that if a heady dose of Aryan lewdness were to be pushed in his face, he would suffer a mental breakdown and the leaderless Germans would lose the war. The plan, then: arm a squadron of RAF fliers with several tons of the ripest pornographic art and literature available in Germany, and have them drop it on Hitler's home.

Unfortunately, the plan fell apart, essentially because the RAF fliers, ordinarily willing to carry out the orders of their government, refused to risk life and limb carpet-bombing Adolf Hitler with photographs of women copulating with Shetland ponies. The war, they said, would have to be won through less inventive means.

**Most Unusual Cause of World War II:** The Second World War may have been caused by Adolf Hitler's bad breath.

This intelligence comes from Birger Dahlerus, a Swedish industrialist who strove valiantly to keep the peace in Europe during the German military renascence of the 1930s. On September 1, 1939, Dahlerus met with the Führer in a last-minute attempt to dissuade him from invading Poland. Hitler, whose armies were to march across the Rhine and into Poland the very next day, was adamant and ranted hysterically. Said Dahlerus some time later, "His breath was so foul that it was all I could do not to step back."

**Most Unusual Draft Dodger:** At age ninety, Peter Mustafic of Hutovo, Yugoslavia, suddenly began speaking again after a silence of forty years. The Yugoslavian news agency quoted Mustafic as saying, "I just didn't want to do military service, so I stopped speaking in 1920; then I got used to it."

**Most Unusual Explosives:** Rabbits were used as deadly weapons by Khmer Rouge insurgents during the Indochina war, or so claimed former Cambodian Premier Lon Nol. Addressing the nation over state radio, Lon Nol warned of dire penalties for anyone caught marketing in contraband hares, noting that the Communists used them to carry plastic explosives into enemy encampments, where they would then explode.

**Most Unusual Gas Mask Filters:** Kleenex tissues were originally manufactured for use as gas mask filters during World War I.

**Most Unusual Military Tactic:** During the Battle of Rancagua on October 1 and 2, 1814, the Chilean patriot Bernardo O'Higgins commanded a badly outnumbered army. The revolutionaries were surrounded by Spanish troops and running low on ammunition; O'Higgins himself was seriously wounded in the intense exchange of fire. There seemed to be no hope of fighting their way out of a desperate situation.

Then, O'Higgins, who was bleeding profusely, ordered his men to round up every animal in the village—horses, burros, cows, sheep, pigs, dogs, even ducks and chickens. With their remaining ammunition, the troops scared the animals into a frantic stampede. Mooing, braying, squealing, and barking, the motley menagerie charged toward the enemy lines, scattering the terrified Spaniards in all directions. O'Higgins and his men took advantage of the confusion to ride through the breach and escape.

Four years later, Bernardo O'Higgins was installed as the first president of an independent Chile.

**Most Unusual Surrender:** As correspondents David Burrington and Don North were filming an Israeli advance on the Golan Heights during the 1973 Yom Kippur War, seven Syrian soldiers, cut off from their own lines, surged forward and surrendered to the astonished news team. Burrington filmed the surrender and NBC broadcast it a few nights later.

Another unexpected capitulation occurred when the American cruiser *Charleston* attacked the Spanish colony on Guam shortly after Congress declared war in 1898. The ship steamed into the island's harbor and opened fire, not very accurately, on Fort Santa Cruz. There was no return fire; no Spanish garrison could be seen; in fact, nothing happened at all until a small boat finally approached the warship and three uniformed officers, including the colony's governor and military commander, clambered on board. "You will pardon us for not returning your salute," the governor apologized, "but we are not used to receiving salutes here and are not supplied with proper guns for returning." The locals, who had been out of contact with Spain for months, did not know the two countries were at war. When the captain of the *Charleston* brought them up to date, they cheerfully surrendered and went along as prisoners of war, presenting the United States with a territory it governs to this day.

**Most Unusual War:** The War of Jenkins' Ear (see *Felton & Fowler I*, p. 141) was but a family spat compared to the War of the Whiskers, fought sporadically between England and France for three centuries.

When King Louis VII of France returned home from the Crusades without his beard, his wife, Eleanor of Aquitaine, mocked him savagely and demanded that he regrow his whiskers as she found him ugly without them. Louis refused and Eleanor sued for divorce. Shortly thereafter she married King Henry II of England, and demanded of her former husband that he return the ancestral acreage in southern France that had been given him as a dowry. Louis refused and England and France went to war in 1152; a stable peace was not concluded until 1453.

**Most Unusual Weapon:** The yo-yo is depicted on ancient Greek vase paintings dating back as far as the eighth century B.C. Yo-yoing was a favorite pastime of the nobility in the seventeenth and eighteenth centuries, and during the Reign of Terror in revolutionary France, the condemned aristocrats reportedly yo-yoed while awaiting their turn at the guillotine. Soon afterwards, the gadgets trickled down to the proletariat, and Napoleon's soldiers amused themselves with yo-yos as they marched toward Moscow. But according to the Duncan Corporation, which manufactures some 10 million yo-yos a year, the yo-yo came to the United States not from Europe, but from the Philippines.

For centuries Filipinos used carved stone spools attached to long strings as weapons. Hunters could climb out on low overhanging tree limbs and wait for small game to pass below. When an unsuspecting rabbit came within range, the hunter spun down his yo-yo in an effort to whack the animal on the head and stun it. The method was no more accurate than throwing stones, but if the hunter missed, he could simply snap the spool up again, instead of clambering back down the tree to gather more ammunition.

By the time Admiral Dewey captured Manila in the Spanish-American War, the stone spindle had become a popular children's toy. Kids called the device a yo-yo, which means "come-come" in the Tagalog language.

The largest yo-yo on record was designed by students of mechanical engineer James H. Williams, Jr., as a special project during MIT's January 1973 Independent Activities Period. The string was 265 feet of braided nylon cord; the spool was fabricated from two twenty-six-inch bicycle wheels joined by a steel shaft; and thirty pounds of ballast were added to the circumference bringing the total weight up to thirty-five pounds. An electric motor provided the timely "twitch of the wrist" needed to retrieve the spinner.

In a private test, Professor Williams claims, the contraption worked perfectly, unwinding down the side of a twenty-four-story building, then winding its way back up to the roof. But at the official unveiling, with a crowd of students and reporters on hand, the electrical wrist iced up, there was no twitch, and the yo-yo stalled out only 160 feet up the building on the retrieval.

# Education

Best Entrance Examination: Since A.D. 970, students of philosophy, Islamic law, history, and Arabic have gathered at Al Azhar, the beautiful and distinguished university in Cairo's old city. For many years it was the largest college in the world. Candidates for admission have traditionally faced a more challenging qualifying exam than any the Educational Testing Service has ever devised; entering freshmen are required to recite the entire Koran from memory. The text is nearly as long as the New Testament, and it requires three days to repeat, yet every one of the twenty thousand students enrolled has accomplished the task.

Best IQ: Testing experts at Stanford University have determined that both John Stuart Mill (who could read and write ancient Greek at the age of three), and Johann Wolfgang von Goethe had intelligence quotients in the vicinity of 210. Voltaire and Newton would probably have scored a respectable 190, Galileo, 185, Da Vinci and Descartes, 180, Lincoln 150, and Napoleon, 145. A figure of 150 is considered genius level.

As for the living: Testers have only been able to estimate Kim Ung-Yong's intelligence quotient, and their estimates have invariably exceeded 200. Born in Seoul, South Korea, on March 7, 1963, Ung-Yong was fluent in Japanese, Korean, German, and English by his fourth birthday; at the age of four years, eight months, he solved intricate problems in integral calculus on Japanese TV. Today he is considered by many to be the most brilliant person alive.

One factor that may—or may not—be related to Ung-Yong's limitless intellectual capabilities is the fact that both his parents, who are university professors, were born at precisely the same moment—eleven o'clock on the morning of May 23, 1934.

**Worst High School Reunion:** The Associated Press reported in 1975 that a thief broke into the home of an eighty-one-year-old Cleveland woman and, after a brief scuffle, realized she had been his schoolteacher years before. He kissed her gently on the cheek and told her, "You were always good to me." He then ran off with $210 and a television set.

**Worst Tax-Deductible Contribution to the College of One's Choice:** In Toulouse, France, in 1976, an unidentified seventy-seven-year-old man entered the medical department of a local university and made this announcement: "Two years ago I agreed to donate my body to science. Now I don't want to wait any longer. I've come here to finish myself off so that my body will be available immediately." He thereupon drew a revolver from his pocket and blew his brains out. The trustees of the university elected to accept the body.

**Most Unusual Campus Fad:** United States college students are reproducing wildly, according to recent reports. Since 1974, photostating of bodily organs and extremities has become fashionable on several East Coast college campuses, and at Princeton's Firestone Library, one undergraduate couple had themselves illicitly photostated by a coin-operated Xerox machine while they made love. Copies of the "pornostats" sold for fifteen dollars each.

**Most Unusual College Homecoming Queen:** Some years ago, the student body of the University of New Mexico elected a male student homecoming queen.

**Most Unusual Driving School:** If you are sufficiently well heeled to be riding around in a chauffeured limousine, you run a better-than-average chance of being kidnapped. So goes the rationale behind a three-day course offered to corporate chauffeurs at the Bob Bondurant School of High Performance Driving in suburban San Francisco. For a $412 tuition fee, drivers are taught how to control sudden skids, simulate accidents, drive without lights after dark, escape pursuers in high-speed chases, control a car on oil-coated skidways, and perfect the 180-degree turn in reverse.

Bondurant, a former Grand Prix racing driver, says the school originally taught police officers and Hollywood stunt drivers, but that he'd been asked by a major oil corporation "if we could put together a curriculum to train its drivers in antiterrorist procedures."

**Most Unusual Educator:** Oliver D. Birnbaum was named one of the nation's outstanding educators in 1975 by the editors of an annual educators' directory. Oliver D. Birnbaum is a sixty-pound poodle.

He was nominated for the honor by his owner, Robert Birnbaum, who is the chancellor of the University of Wisconsin at Oshkosh. Soon after he submitted an application form to the publishers of the directory, the Fuller and Dees Marketing Group of Montgomery, Alabama, his dog received a congratulatory letter. "We salute you on being nominated for this distinguished volume," it said. "Only a select number of men and women are nominated by their school officials to be included in the awards program each year." When the dog was asked for biographical material, Chancellor Birnbaum obliged with a capsule summary of Oliver's doctoral thesis in animal husbandry, and noted the candidate's authorship of several published papers in the field. By the time Fuller and Dees learned of the hoax, they had already included Oliver's name among the elite, and sold his sponsor a twelve-dollar award plaque.

A spokeswoman for the firm said that it was "degrading for the field of education that someone would sink this low." Meanwhile, Birnbaum *père* seized the opportunity to speak out against a proposal requiring that dogs on the Oshkosh campus be leashed at all times. "Consider carefully," he warned, "the effects on academic freedom of leashing an outstanding educator."

**Most Unusual Scholarship Fund:** Montreal's Sir George Williams University has established the world's first college scholarship earmarked exclusively for homosexuals. It's an annual stipend of $200 for which gay students of either sex are eligible. Academic excellence is the principal criterion, but the application form must bear the signature of the student's parent, attesting to the homosexuality of the candidate.

**Most Unusual School:** In California, a "school for shoplifters" teaches its charges, among other skills, "how to steal up to five women's suits at a time while talking to a salesclerk." The tuition is $1,500, payable in advance.

# Religion

**Best Proof of a Life After Death:** By placing the beds of dying patients on scales and noting their weight immediately before and after expiration, Nils-Olof Jacobson, a Swedish physician, concluded that the human soul weighs twenty-one grams.

**Best Way to Roust the Devil:** On April 29, 1974, when the movie version of *The Exorcist* was horrifying audiences from coast to coast, pollster Louis Harris posed the question, "Do you believe in the existence of the Devil, or not?" The results were unsettling to say the least: 12 percent of those polled were undecided, another 12 percent quibbled over the definition of "devil," and a doubting 30 percent denied Satan's existence. But the clear majority of Americans, 53 percent, answered yes—they believed the Devil is quite real and capable of influencing their lives.

If the Devil does indeed exist, it would be useful to know how to get rid of him, especially since powders and sprays are generally ineffective. The recognized Protestant authority on evicting the Devil was none other than Martin Luther. Satan pestered Luther with frequent visits and even showered him with hickory nuts on one occasion. In retaliation, Luther once threw his inkpot at the Devil—one of the most celebrated events in Church history. But the militant leader of the Reformation had even more forcible means of dealing with Evil Incarnate. Sometimes he charmed the Devil by playing hymns on his flute. In other encounters, Luther threw dung in the poor Devil's face or broke wind at him. And on at least one instance, as we learn in *The Table Talk of Martin Luther*, the pious father of Protestantism said to the Devil, "Lick my ass!" In his diary that night, Luther noted that "he [the Devil] said no more—a good way of getting rid of him."

**Worst Baptism:** When a two-headed baby was born in Buenos Aires, Argentina, the attending Roman Catholic priest, Fr. Emilio Andres Parado, was faced with a theological dilemma no less complex than the question of whether Adam and Eve had navels: should the child be baptized with one name or two? After much soul-searching and some long talks with his immediate ecclesiastical superior, Fr. Parado opted for the doubleheader approach, christening one head Carlos Alberto and the other Arturo. When the child died a few days later, the salvation of its soul(s) was insured.

**Worst Christmas Tree:** When a pre-Christmas sanitation strike turned New York City into a winter wonderland of decaying garbage in 1975, two women responded by creating a sidewalk Christmas tree from thirty plastic bags of garbage, courtesy of Joe Jr.'s Restaurant in Greenwich Village.

"To keep in the spirit," one of the women, Mrs. Michael Moriarity, said, "we decided the decorations should all be garbage themselves. First I stole some orange crates and cut them into stars tied together with red yarn. Then I cut up some orange-juice containers into bells and topped it off with an apple—half eaten."

The tree prompted a broad range of comments from passersby. One man said, "It's happy garbage, nice garbage for the season." Another called the endeavor a waste of time. "I have no ulterior motive," said Nancy Reardon, Mrs. Moriarity's collaborator. "Except that maybe New Yorkers can rise above the garbage."

**Worst Crucifixion:** On nationwide television in Santo Domingo, Dominican Republic, a mystic named Patrice Tamao had himself nailed to a cross "as a sacrifice for world peace and understanding." An unforeseen snag developed when Tamao's foot became infected the following day and physicians ordered him pried loose and taken down. His wife Marita then volunteered to be hammered up in his place.

**Worst Religion:** During the 1960s there was a local election on the island of New Hanover near New Guinea. When the ballots were tabulated, Lyndon Johnson won by a landslide. Informed by local officials that Johnson, then President of the United States, would be unable to serve, the islanders began raising money to buy him. They were willing to pay any reasonable price because Lyndon Johnson knew the occult secret of obtaining cargo.

Unquestionably the most bizarre religion in the world, the Cargo Cult is based on a fundamental misunderstanding. The cult dates back to 1893 when the first shipments of advanced Western goods began arriving from Europe. The Sepik people of New Guinea had never seen a factory—to this day there are very few factories on the island—and they naturally assumed that the wheels, steel axes, and fancy mirrors had been given to the white men by the gods. It proved impossible to explain such alien concepts as capital and mass production to a people who had always relied entirely on the deities to provide the fish, fruits, and vegetables, and other things of value in their society.

The stone age tribes were disappointed when none of the exotic cargo was ever delivered to them. Their priests concluded that the Sepik people had somehow offended the gods. If they could only expiate that sin, the dead would be reborn, the bird of paradise (now nearly extinct) would flourish and multiply, the white tyrants would be destroyed, and tempting shipments of cargo would begin arriving regularly.

The cult peaked during World War II, when valuable cargo did indeed arrive from out of nowhere. Air-dropped supplies were blown off-target, landing in the dense rain forest. Japanese, British, and American planes fell from the sky. Goods from torpedoed vessels washed up on shore. In hopes of attracting still more of the richly laden aircraft, cult members built phantom airstrips in the high mountains. They erected replicas of radio towers (without electricity) to communicate with the gods of cargo.

Whenever a powerful foreign visitor comes to the island, cult members pray he will reveal the mysteries of cargo to them. The Duke of Edinburgh let them down in 1971, and invitations to Pope Paul and Queen Elizabeth brought no results. So, recently, devotees have placed their hopes in a few cult leaders who have volunteered to be crucified or beheaded. They believe that a Christlike martyr can rid the Sepik of sin, be raised from the dead, and bring back five hundred jet transports loaded with refrigerators, clock radios, and other modern appliances.

A tribesman named Yeliwan offered himself up for sacrifice in 1972 and raised $20,000 in subscription fees from believers who wanted to witness the great event. At the last moment, the Australian government persuaded Yeliwan to give up the plan, and the money will now go toward the construction of a memorial in the Australian capital of Canberra.

**Worst Saint:** Saint Wilgefortis, who like Saint Patrick has recently fallen into disfavor with Church authorities, was one of nine sisters born to an infidel king of Portugal. At an early age, Wilgefortis was converted to

Christianity and took a vow of virginity, in spite of which her father betrothed her to the king of Sicily. The young girl prayed fervently for deliverance from the amorous clutches of the Sicilian, and miraculously, on the day of her wedding, she sprouted a full black beard and a mustache. Her fiancé lost interest. Her father, in a rage, had her crucified.

Saint Wilgefortis is traditionally invoked in the prayers of maidens who wish to be rid of unwanted suitors. In England, she is known as Saint Uncumber, prayed to by women who wish to "unencumber" themselves of husbands they do not love.

---

**Most Unusual Communion:** Roman Catholic priest Victor Salandini was ordered suspended from his clerical duties in 1971. Justifying the decision, the presiding bishop noted that Father Salandini often wore a sarape instead of the traditional vestments and that he occasionally dispensed corn tortillas instead of wheat cakes when administering the Eucharist to members of Cesar Chavez's United Farm Workers union.

**Most Unusual Dietary Laws:** Ancient Egyptians swore off three species of seafood—the lepidotus, the pike, and the sea bream—because myth had it that the fish had conspired to eat the penis of Osiris, their paramount deity, when his body was thrown in the Nile.

We might also note that, among the Jews of ancient Palestine, there was a specific dietary proscription against mousemeat.

**Most Unusual Religion:** "Golf," says Rev. Seiki Sakiyama, "is a miniature of life. We can learn about ourselves through golf. Our teachings say that in life, anger, worry and sorrow destroy success, just as in golf." Rev. Sakiyama's reverence for golf comes straight from the heart: he is the chief minister in North America of the Church of Perfect Liberty, a mysterious sect whose devotees strive for salvation and inner peace by playing golf as often as possible.

Founded in Japan by Tokchika Miki, the church is based in Osaka and claims three million adherents. New initiates, says Miki, invariably improve their golf scores by three or four strokes soon after entering the sect.

The church owns and operates some ten ritual golf courses in Japan, and others in Brazil, France, and England. However, the church fathers ran into opposition from West Coast environmentalist groups when they announced plans to build an eighteen-hole course, complete with a 250-

foot-high man-made waterfall, clubhouse, swimming pool, and church buildings, on a choice piece of acreage in California's Malibu Mountains.

**Most Unusual Witch:** In 1881, itinerant showman Jules Warner came to Athens, Tennessee, with his wonder horse Henny, touted to be the world's only clairvoyant stallion. Setting up shop in the middle of the town square, Warner invited his audience to pick a number from one to ten. Henny would then mysteriously guess the correct number and tap it out with her hoof.

It was a good show, one that had paid well for Warner in all the towns he stopped in. In Athens, however, some Bible-belting ruffians accused the horse of being possessed by the Devil. The accusation gained momentum, and soon the townspeople were blaming Henny for everything from shaving nicks to stillbirths. One day someone threw a rock at Henny's head and killed her. The body was burned to purge it of the Devil.

**Most Unusual Yarmulke:** Yarmulkes for dogs are available from Du-Say's, a New Orleans specialty shop, for $2.98. The canine skullcaps are white, with a blue Star of David, and are fitted with chinstraps. (Du-Say's also offers flannel pajamas, sunglasses, strawhats, and terrycloth bathrobes for dogs.)

**Most Unusual Yogi:** Dr. K. N. Udupa, director of the medical institute of Benares Hindu University, has trained six field rats to assume the yoga position of *sirasana*—or standing on their heads—for one to two hours a day. Dr. Udupa has wired the rodents' heads to a battery of monitoring devices, such as electrocardiogram machines, and found that, after first jolting the rats with electric shocks to make them tense, an hour of *sirasana* calmed them down and returned their vital signs to normal.

# *Behavior*

**Best Case History of Nostalgie de la Boue:** About three-quarters of a mile from the opulent palace of Versailles, in the woods beyond the carefully manicured flower beds and the 1,400 splashing fountains, Queen Marie Antoinette ordered the construction of ten humble thatched cottages. There she housed a few simple farming families, a miller, and a shepherd, and there Marie and her elegant ladies in waiting used to retire to "play at being peasants." The Queen took decadent delight in wearing homespun, milking the cows, churning her own butter, and tending a small flock of sheep. She found rural poverty a refreshing change from the cloying luxuries of the Petit Trianon or the Grand Apartments.

Members of the super-rich Vanderbilt and Morgan clans also enjoyed a little slumming; they were fond of staging "poverty socials" in the stately marble mansions of Newport. Guests arrived dressed in foul-smelling rags, ate scraps from wooden plates with their fingers, and sipped beer from rusty tin cans. This form of entertainment was particularly common during the administration of our fattest president, three hundred-pound William Howard Taft.

**Best Imposter:** A Russian janitor named David Chakhvashvili disappeared after his arrest by Soviet police in 1974. The charge: impersonating a science professor. For years the clever but unschooled Chakhvashvili had supplemented his janitor's income by lecturing university classes on "The Technological Revolution," "The Atom," "Modern Medicine," and similarly arcane topics.

Alternatively, in 1975, nineteen-year-old Roberto Coppola of Rome was arrested for impersonating a priest. Over the course of two years, Coppola had performed weddings, heard confessions, and celebrated several hundred masses. "It's a pity," he told municipal police officers who arrested him. "I liked it."

**Best Laugh:** The Italian astronomer Damascene published an influential study in 1662 linking the phonology of laughter with the humours of the human body. A laugh with a pronounced "I" vowel sound (tee-hee, for example) denotes a morose, melancholic disposition. The "E" sound, as in heh-heh, is symptomatic of a bilious character and acute indigestion, while the "A" sound, ha-ha, suggests a cool, composed, phlegmatic temperament. Most desirable is the deep throaty "O" laugh (ho-ho) emitted by cheerful, confident, sanguine individuals.

**Best Lovers:** In the Orgasm Olympics, it's the Russians who take first place. Yes, the Russians. At least that's what a Russian sexologist, A. M. Syvadoshch, would have the world believe. And who's to say he's wrong?

According to Syvadoshch, in *Female Sexual Problems,* the first sex manual ever published in the Soviet Union, 85 percent of all Russian women have had orgasms at one time or another, while only 60 percent of French women and 59 percent of British women have had them. And, he claims, not one of the Russian men he tested had ever failed to achieve an orgasm.

**Best Orgy:** The swamps of Sungei Siput, Malaysia, were the site of a mammoth love-in involving over ten thousand turned-on frogs in 1970. For an entire week, commencing on the night of November 7, the frogs copulated with bestial abandon, thrashing about in ecstasy and splitting the air with their orgasmic croaking. In fact, midway through the revel, the frogs appeared to be going through the throes of mass insanity, their croaks turned to screeches, many tearing themselves and their mates apart. The first scientific observers on the scene were baffled by what they saw and figured it to be some sort of all-out frog war. As it turned out, the first rains of the November monsoon had just fallen, and the drought-stricken creatures had, en masse, gone berserk with glee and plunged headlong into group sex.

**Best Pacifier:** Can one-month-old infants suffer from nostalgia? "Definitely," answers Dr. Hajime Murooka, a renowned Japanese obstetrician. Whenever a new baby cries, according to Dr. Murooka, the parents should first check to see if the little pipsqueak is hungry, wet, or ill. If none of these is the problem, the chances are the baby is homesick for its mother's womb.

"I spent a long time looking for a 'natural' method to put a newborn baby to sleep . . . [then] it occurred to me that a recording of a mother's body beat could serve a useful function." As Thomas Wolfe has taught us, you can never go home again, but Dr. Murooka has come up with the next best thing to being there. By implanting a tiny eight-millimeter microphone in the womb of a pregnant woman, he has successfully recorded the sounds an unborn child hears day in and day out. The recording has a good, though somewhat monotonous, beat, a liquid lub-dub, lub-dub repeated over and over again. As *Newsweek* reported, "When Dr. Murooka played the amplified sounds to screaming infants, almost every one stopped crying."

The recording works most effectively on children under two months of age. A Florida hospital recently began piping the womb song into its maternity ward with impressive results; the babies were significantly quieter, and the mothers and staff also reported feeling rather drowsy. For somewhat older children, Dr. Murooka has combined the natural maternal percussion with a soporific string accompaniment. The recordings are available from Capitol Records on either stereo discs (ST-11421) or four-track tapes.

In a related development, Dr. A. M. Grossman, writing in the *Medical Tribune*, stated that the music of Brahms's First Symphony "closely resembles the pulsations found in the intrauterine environment of the foetus."

**Best Roué:** Two farmers in Earlville, Iowa, sued neighbor Henry Bockenstedt for letting his bull break loose and wander through their pastures where, they claim, it impregnated forty-three purebred Holstein heifers in a single afternoon.

**Best Smiles:** Ray Birdwhistell, a leading researcher in the field of kinesics or body language, has determined that the best, broadest, and most infectious grins are found south of the Mason-Dixon line. Birdwhistell designates the region from Virginia to Florida and west to the Mississippi River as America's "high smile area."

Residents of the Great Lakes region, in contrast, are grim and straight-faced. In Buffalo, Rochester, or Erie, Pennsylvania, "a person smiling with an ease perfectly proper in the South might well find himself challenged to explain what he finds so funny." Traveling in the New England states, you are likely to notice "more smiling among familiars and less with strangers." Midwesterners, though, are endowed with "an extraordinary propensity to smile," Birdwhistell says.

**Best Wedding Gift:** The French Ministry of Education presented five free books to every couple married between April 29 and December 31, 1972, in an experiment designed to encourage reading. The bride and groom had their choice of two different sets of French classics. Romance played only a minor role in the giveaway plan, which was prompted by a survey showing that 57 percent of all adult French men and women have not read a book since childhood.

---

**Worst Alternative to Warts and Blindness:** Writing in the twelfth edition of *Spermatorrhea*, published in 1887, J. L. Milton cautioned growing boys against the perils of masturbation and described a newly patented invention guaranteed to work where self-discipline didn't. Based on the principles of telegraphy, it consisted of a device which, when clipped to the bedsheets, rang an alarm in the parents' room if the boy had an erection.

**Worst Aphrodisiac:** The Spanish fly is commonly thought to be a potent aphrodisiac. And so it is. The wing sheaths of this bright green Mediterranean beetle, when ground into a fine powder and taken internally, can bring on an erection within seconds. They can also cause diarrhea, urogenital inflammations, convulsive vomiting, depression, and bloody stools. Clearly, a Mantovani record and a bottle of wine are preferable stimulants.

Whatever its dangers, Spanish fly is nonetheless an *honest* aphrodisiac. A few years back an Italian men's magazine offered its readers a special bonus insert—a packet of red powder touted as a potent "tropical aphrodisiac" that would generate sexual pleasures of the most fantastic sort. Since the legality of sending sex aids through the mail was questionable, police ran lab tests on the mysterious substance and found it to be ordinary red pepper.

**Worst Courtship:** While stranded on a five-foot-long life raft for three days in the stormy Caribbean, with no water and nothing to eat but raw seagull meat and a few raisins, Anthony Pike, a Singapore schooner captain, and Jennifer Fairfax-Ross, a fashion model from Sydney, Australia, pledged their troth. They were rescued near Haiti on June 23, 1975 and married on dry land two weeks later.

**Worst Cure for Stammering:** A nineteenth-century Indiana folk remedy: to cure a child of stammering, slap his face smartly with a piece of raw liver.

**Worst Defenestration:** Distraught over her husband's infidelities, a woman in Prague, Czechoslovakia, threw herself from a third-floor window, accidentally landing on her husband who was entering the building. He died instantly; she survived.

Equally desperate, fifty-six-year-old Heinz Isecke, of Hanover, West Germany, jumped to his death from the window of his hospital room after two years of continual hiccupping. Reuters reported that complications arising from stomach surgery in November 1973 caused Isecke to hiccup thirty-six million times before he decided he couldn't stand it any longer.

**Worst Example of Social Climbing:** When a bus skidded into a river just outside New Delhi, all seventy-eight passengers drowned because they belonged to two separate castes and refused to share the same rope to climb ashore to safety.

**Worst Foreplay:** A woman in Hamburg, West Germany, somehow came by the notion that a good scare will excite a man more effectively than any aphrodisiac. So, according to police reports, she hid in the bedroom and greeted her husband with a blood-curdling shriek as he walked in the door after work. The startled spouse bolted through the locked bedroom door, tripped over a chair, and plunged through a window. He was hospitalized for a week.

**Worst Oppression of Women:** Liechtenstein, a tiny nation of twenty-three thousand tucked between Austria and Switzerland, is the only European nation that denies women the right to vote.

It also boasts the world's second largest false teeth factory.

**Worst Phobia:** Indonesian men occasionally fall prey to an obsessive fear that their penis is withdrawing into the body and that, if they do not take the matter into their own hands, so to speak, the process will ultimately kill them. The prescribed treatment, then, is simply to grasp the disappearing organ and hold on for dear life until it stops receding.

Since a typical siege of *koro*, as the malady is called, can last for hours or even days, the embarrassed victim must often ask friends, wife, witch doctor, and others to spell him in holding on to the vanishing member while he rests. He may also try to stem its inward progress with the aid of a small, specially designed notched box. The disease is purely psychological, of course, but the "treatment" frequently leaves its victims exhausted, temporarily impotent, and black and blue about the privates. Sometimes powdered rhinoceros horn, considered a potent male aphrodisiac by many in the Far East, is administered as a treatment.

**Worst Position for Intercourse:** British chemists have created a novel insecticide called hexamethylmelamide which does its work by underhandedly disrupting the sex life of Mediterranean flour moths. It's the male of the species that takes the brunt of the punishment: once exposed to the chemical, he finds that he cannot free himself after coupling with the female, who proceeds about her normal business dragging the helpless male along with her. Eventually, the permanently copulating couple are devoured by predators or die of exhaustion.

Intercourse between consenting anglerfish is limited to only one position—but what a position it is. The male, considerably smaller and weaker than the female, bites his mate above the eyes and hangs on for dear life—forever. Meanwhile, the rest of his body atrophies from disuse and by the time he dies, he has turned into nothing but a set of disembodied sex organs, his fins, body, and lower organs having withered away long before. Says MIT biologist Robert Bender, "He's essentially a male wart on the female's forehead."

**Worst Spoilsport:** At an open-air concert in Juazeiro Do Norte, Brazil, singer Waldick Soriano was singing "I Am Not a Dog," when a dog trotted onstage wearing a sign reading, "I Am Not Waldick Soriano." Angered by the prank, Soriano stopped singing and began insulting the audience. A free-for-all ensued and Soriano was forced off the stage and chased back to his hotel room.

**Worst Vice:** The worst vice is decidedly not drinking, smoking, cussing, gambling, drug taking, or fornication. Over the centuries, except for a few permissive psychologists in our own time, social critics have almost unanimously proclaimed masturbation as the vilest behavior known to mankind.

Dr. William Alcott, founder of the American Physiological Society, termed solitary licentiousness "the lowest, I may say the most destructive of practices." In *A Young Man's Guide* (1840), he describes how masturbation makes a man "tottering, wrinkling, and hoary." It leads inevitably to "insanity, St. Vitus' dance, epilepsy, palsy, blindness, apoplexy, hypochondria, consumption . . . and a sensation of ants crawling from the head down to the spine." And Dr. Alcott, an uncle of Louisa

Mae Alcott, advises that "unless the abominable practice which produced all this mischief is abandoned, death follows."

The philosopher Jean Jacques Rousseau seems to know whereof he speaks when he describes the extensive precautions a parent must take to prevent masturbation: "Therefore watch carefully over the young man; he can protect himself from all other foes, but it is for you to protect him against himself. Never leave him night or day, or at least share his room; never let him go to bed till he is sleepy, and let him rise as soon as he wakes. . . . If once he acquires this dangerous habit, he is ruined. From that time forward, body and soul will be enervated; he will carry to the grave the sad effects of this habit, the most fatal which a young man can acquire."

In the 1800s jewelers designed miniature handcuffs to restrain children from indulging themselves. There was also an adolescent boy's equivalent of the chastity belt—a small wire cage that locked over the genitals. The father was instructed to keep the key on his person at all times (See also "Behavior," *Worst Alternative to Warts and Blindness.*)

The People's Republic of China is deeply concerned about this perennial problem. A recent government sex manual for teen-agers warns that masturbation results in dizziness, insomnia, and "the erosion of revolutionary will." As a deterrent, hot-blooded youngsters are advised to get sufficient physical exercise, wear loose-fitting underclothes, and engage in "hard study of the works of Marx, Lenin, and Chairman Mao."

In marked contrast, there have been a number of cultures that respected and ritually practiced solitary sex. The Egyptians thought it was a holy act; they believed that the god Aton-Re spewed forth the universe as the climax to a session of divine masturbation. The great rivers of the ancient world—the Nile, Euphrates, and Ganges—were thought to have their source at Aton-Re's erect lingam.

**Worst Way to Engage an Anthropologist in Polite Conversation:** Talk about sex. That's what sex researchers Masters and Johnson discovered in 1961 when they tried discussing sexual dysfunctions and—horrors!—showing clinical films at a meeting of anthropologists in New York. The female anthropologists reacted to the presentation with clench-toothed impassivity, and would not comment or ask questions. The men masked their discomfort by joking.

But that was fifteen years ago, and times have changed: a grassroots sexual revolution has swept the country and anthropologists today are much more receptive to the discussion of sexual matters. Right? Wrong. Marian K. Slater, a professor at Queens College of the City University of New York, recently read through a massive collection of papers and seminar proceedings in an effort to see how anthropologists' attitudes towards sex had changed. Sex, she found out, is still not discussed by anthropologists, who apparently are afraid of being thought of as pornographers. Few scholarly anthropological papers deal openly with anything relating to sexual behavior, and she learned of many field researchers who refused to ask interview subjects questions about sex lest they be questioned themselves.

**Worst Way to Say "I Love You":** When his wife Carmelina died in 1959, Dr. Katsuabruo Miyamoto of Japan embalmed her body and then slept next to it in their conjugal bed for ten years. When police discovered that he had covered up his wife's death, the good doctor was fined three thousand dollars, which he paid by selling his house.

---

**Most Unusual Brothel:** At the Reading Room, a one-of-a-kind literary massage parlor in St. Louis, customers pay twelve dollars to be closeted for twenty minutes with a scantily clad hostess who sits in a chair and offers readings from the world's great literature—including *Incestuous Teacher*, *The Whorehouse*, and *Photographer's Passion*. Touching is a no-no, but nude readings are available for an extra charge. Says the establishment's manager, "The men don't seem to mind not touching. Judging by return customers, they must find it stimulating to have a pretty girl read them erotic literature."

Patrons, needless to say, are welcome to bring their own reading materials. If *Fanny Hill* and *Justine* leave them cold, Reading Room lovelies will accommodate them with *The Wall Street Journal*, *The Joys of Jello-O*, *Silas Marner*, or any other work of their choosing.

For the less literately inclined, there is Just Filmz Inc., a verbal massage parlor in downtown Chicago. If you're male, fifteen dollars buys you twenty minutes of nonstop dirty talk from the hostess of your choice; for an additional five dollars, she'll do her spiel topless. Jason Irwin, the owner of Just Filmz, says most of the women who work for him are ex-telephone operators. "They're naturals," he claims.

Incidentally, police in Marseilles, France, raided a brothel for the elderly not long ago. Two prostitutes, both in their late fifties, and eight customers, ranging from sixty to seventy-seven years old, were jailed. And in Sardinia, a fifty-year-old housewife received a two-year jail sentence for indulging her passion for citrus fruits by bartering her favors to local teen-age boys in exchange for oranges. Police were led to the woman after questioning several youths who had been spotted pinching oranges from local groves.

**Most Unusual Caress:** In his pioneering studies of South Sea island cultures, ethnographer Bronislav Malinowski remarked, "I have not seen one boy or girl in the Trobriands with the long lashes to which they are entitled by nature." Trobriand lovers never kiss, but in the height of passion they bite off each other's eyelashes.

**Most Unusual Chastity Belt:** Some female snakes wear chastity belts. To cap the mating process, the male garter snake secretes a rubbery "stopper" that plugs into the female's cloaca—the dual purpose vaginal-rectal opening found in many lower animals—and prevents other males from copulating with her.

According to Michael C. Devine, University of Michigan zoologist, the stopper may simply be nature's way of insuring conception by preventing a second male from contaminating the sperm of the first.

Real chastity belts—the metal-and-leather variety, first used by humans in the Middle Ages—were manufactured and sold by at least four separate companies in Paris in the early years of this century, and as recently as 1934, a baker named Henri Littiere was arrested and tried there for forcing his wife to wear one. His belt, however, was not store-bought, but a custom-made model of velvet and silver, fashioned for him by an orthopedist copying a prototypical chastity belt on display at the Cluny Museum. Littiere received a suspended sentence for his chauvinistic excesses, and was fined fifty francs.

**Most Unusual Concession to Modesty:** The earliest Christians believed that the Virgin Mary was impregnated through her ear and that other women as well had used their ears as reproductive organs. For that reason, an exposed female ear was considered no less an outrage than an exposed thigh, and a woman would not appear in public unless clad in a tight-fitting wimple.

**Most Unusual Epidemic:** Over the course of several weeks in 1963 some nine hundred persons in the neighboring villages of Mbale and Kigezi, Uganda, were seized en masse by a maddening compulsion to run wildly through the streets clutching chickens and screaming until they fell from exhaustion. Local natives attributed the running mania to the will of departed village chieftains. However, scientists and psychologists diagnosed it as a case of mass hysteria, comparable to a laughing epidemic which had overrun the town of Bukoba, Tanganyika, the previous year.

One of the earliest recorded cases of mass hysteria was that of the "biting nuns." At a convent in Germany in the fifteenth century, several nuns mysteriously began nipping at each other. Soon this undiagnosed "nun-biting" spread to other convents in Germany, and ultimately to Holland and Italy. (See also "Plants and Animals," *Most Unusual Meowing.*)

**Most Unusual Erogenous Zone:** In her monthly advice column in *Penthouse* magazine, "Happy Hooker" Xaviera Hollander has observed, "Armpits seem to be the most sexually neglected area of the human body, and yet they are important erogenous zones." Ms. Hollander will be gratified to learn that, at long last, the axillae are now beginning to receive the sexual attention they deserve, thanks to a 1975 article by psychologist Benjamin Brody published in the journal *Psychiatry.*

For openers, Dr. Brody presents some astonishing case histories illustrating the myriad romantic utilizations of armpits. He also provides a restrospective on the armpit in art, literature, and mythology, singling out instances of axillary eroticism in the poems of Catullus and in the paintings of Matisse and Titian. Then he turns his attention to the armpit in other cultures. Perhaps you didn't know that Ganda tribeswomen in Africa tickle their husbands' underarms to produce sexual arousal, or that Marquesas Islanders believe that the gods were born from the armpit of the Divine Mother. And Dr. Brody also mentions that girls in rural Austria used to squeeze apple slices under their arms while dancing, probably as a natural perfume; and at the end of the evening their gallant partners were expected to eat the slices.

Fascination with the armpit is most obvious among the Abkhasians, the Caucasian mountain people who are noted for "their longevity, serenity, and relative freedom from heart attacks." The Abkhasians consider a woman's armpits prime erogenous zones that must never be exposed in public.

**Most Unusual Flagellator:** A mechanical flagellator, capable of satisfying up to forty persons at a time, was invented in England in the early 1700s. Flagellation, mechanically or otherwise induced, was quite the rage in Europe in the early eighteenth century. Others who capitalized on its popularity included the author of *A Treatise on the Use of Flogging* (1718) and a prominent English madam named Mrs. Berkeley, who ran a highly profitable brothel specializing in beatings.

**Most Unusual Foreplay:** Planning to romance an alligator? A word of counsel: be gentle and loving and above all, don't rush her (him). Zoologists Leslie D. Garrick and Jeffrey Lang spent several months watching alligators copulate at Gatorama, an alligator preserve in south-central Florida. An alligator, they discovered, begins the lovemaking ritual not by amorously nibbling on the mate's ear or by wooing with flowers and wine. Instead, the two spend considerable time slamming their heads against the surface of the water and indulging in some "unbelievably primal bellowing." They then blow bubbles with great enthusiasm, take turns riding piggyback on each other, and suck up water and blow it out through their nostrils, all the while chortling in ecstasy. (Or doing whatever passes in alligator parlance for chortling. Actually, it sounds more like "chumpf-chumpf.") A pair of alligators, say Garrick and Lang, may dally in this manner for several hours before proceeding to actual copulation.

**Most Unusual Form of Behavior Modification:** The sleeve buttons on men's suit jackets have no known function other than to come loose and fall off, but their original purpose was coldly pragmatic. Roughcast bronze buttons first appeared on the uniform sleeves of Prussian soldiers at the order of Frederick the Great, to break them of the habit of wiping their noses on their sleeves.

**Most Unusual Form of Exhibitionism:** Shall chickens be allowed to run around naked? That's the question of the day among poultry experts, although their concern has more to do with diet than decorum. Ever since University of California biologist Ursula Abbott bred the world's first featherless—or nude—chickens in the mid-1950s, scientists have weighed the merits of preplucked birds against the drawbacks.

On the plus side, for the same amount of feed, you get more meat and no feathers, which are of dubious value to anyone other than Indian chiefs and the chickens themselves. Moreover, no feathers means no feather follicles, which are normally supported by a layer of fat. The absence of this fat makes for less shrinkage during cooking, so that bald chickens are about sixteen percent meatier than their feathered counterparts. In addition, the bother and expense of plucking the chickens is dispensed with.

On the debit side, bald chickens are vulnerable to cold, so that it costs more to keep them warm. They also eat about twice as much feed as the average chicken, and their exposed juiciness frequently invites cannibalistic attacks from other chickens. Worse yet, since feathers are normally a stabilizing influence for chickens, the bald species have trouble keeping their balance and are unable to mate. Thus, the only way to keep the species alive is through human surveillance and artificial insemination.

**Most Unusual Form of Impregnation:** Mating octopi never allow their genitals to touch. Instead, the male octopus catches his ejaculate in one of his tentacles and then deposits it manually in the female's sex organ.

**Most Unusual Form of Incest:** For the pyemotis, a mite that feeds on caterpillars, there is no such things as latency or pre-adolescence: the sex drive begins at the moment of birth. In fact, once born, the male pyemotis does nothing but hang around his mother's genital duct, nourishing himself with deep draughts of her vital fluids and waiting for a sister to be born. When a newborn female does appear, he mounts her immediately and the two copulate furiously.

**Most Unusual Hallucinogen:** "Angel's dust" is a recently developed hallucinogen that renders its users tiny—or so they imagine—according to British physician Donald Teare. Patients who ingest the drug feel they can hide in cracks in walls, he says, and several users have been injured trying to pass through keyholes.

**Most Unusual Homosexuals:** Are fruit flies lesbians? At the risk of libeling an already much-maligned insect minority, the answer is yes, some are. Robert Cook, a noted French geneticist, has observed enthusiastic courting and foreplay between mutually consenting female *drosophilia melanogaster*. However, he adds, their passion invariably fell short of actual intercourse.

**Most Unusual Prude:** A computer at the University of Akron, in Ohio, was programmed to reject instructions couched in profane language, and to print out a demand that the operator apologize.

**Most Unusual Psychotherapy:** Psychoanalysis for afghan hounds? Therapists at the Canine Behavior Institute in Santa Monica, California, frequently treat emotionally troubled dogs and their owners in joint sessions. Former patients include Tony Franciosa's beagle, Ronald Reagan's collie, and Kirk Douglas' poodle.

Yet another mental health clinic for animals has been established by a couple of behavioral psychologists at Ohio State University. "Behavior therapy can save troublesome pets a trip to the pound," say Drs. David S. Tuber and David Hothersall. "People are usually at their wits' end when they bring their pets to us. Sometimes pets have burdens that most of us would consider unbearable. Phobic human beings are difficult to live with, but phobic pets are impossible."

Some insight into just what makes animals go bonkers in the first place comes from Tokyo, Japan, where zoos are kept closed two days out of every month in accordance with municipal law. The reason is that prior to the monthly shutdowns, an alarmingly high number of beasts at the Tokyo zoos had been having nervous breakdowns which were attributed to overexposure to *people.*

**Most Unusual Resolution of the Oedipal Conflict:** James Garfield, twentieth president of the United States, lived with his mother in the White House. After the President had been gunned down by a spurned office seeker, Mrs. Garfield asked reporters, "How could anyone be so cold-hearted as to want to kill my baby?"

**Most Unusual Sex Aid:** Good news for impotence sufferers! A Houston urologist, Dr. F. Brantley Scott, has patented a device that will turn the most reluctant of penises erect, willing and able in seconds. The device consists of a pair of silicone rubber cylinders surgically inserted in the penis, and two rubber bulbs implanted in the scrotum. Squeezing bulb A will force fluid, from a reserve stored in the pelvic area, into the penis and make it erect. Squeezing bulb B will release the fluid and cause the penis to detumesce. Thus, for those willing in spirit but flaccid of flesh, love-making becomes as simple an operation as honking a bicycle horn.

**Most Unusual Sex Manual:** A pair of Italian writers, Norberto Valentini and Clara di Megli, figured that a cheap source of solid, no-nonsense sex counseling for use in their upcoming sex primer would be the confessional. So, they traveled around the country armed with a tiny tape recorder and a repertoire of confessions of imaginary sexual excesses to try out on hundreds of unsuspecting priests whose comments they taped. The book, called *Sex and Confession,* sold well, but an angry Pope Paul later charged that sneaking a tape machine into a confessional was an excommunicable offense.

**Most Unusual Skinflint:** When the Whig party nominated Zachary Taylor for the presidency in 1848, he took several days to respond. The reason for the delay was his reluctance to pay the ten cents postage due on the official letter of notification.

**Most Unusual Surrogate Mother:** There is no record of the ASPCA coming to the aid of a Eureka, California, woman who was summarily jailed not long ago for disrobing in a grocery store and sitting on some pheasant eggs in an effort to hatch them.

**Most Unusual Wedding Band:** Newlyweds are entitled by tradition to exchange handsome gold rings, but what about the newly divorced? Well, now there is a ring for them as well. New York jewelry designer Peter Lindeman has come up with what he calls the "separation band." It's a gold band patterned after conventional wedding rings, but with a difference—a break in the ring to signify the divorce. Priced at around $350, it can easily be welded whole again should the wearer remarry.

# Health and Death

---

**Best Cause of Bronchitis:** Some physicians believe that excessive use of marijuana can cause bronchitis. On the other hand, Donald Tashkin, a research scientist at UCLA, has found that marijuana is sometimes effective in treating asthmatics.

**Best Cure for Tapeworm:** Evicting a tapeworm that has taken a three-year lease on your lower intestinal tract is no mean feat: it requires cunning, self-confidence, and above all, a potent purgative. In the 1870s, a Dr. Dowler removed a 135-foot-long tapeworm from a patient by administering daily doses of elm bark, to be chewed and swallowed dutifully in moderate quantities. Yet another tapeworm specialist, Dr. H. S. Patterson, got good results from pumpkin seeds. But the most novel cure of all was a tapeworm *trap* invented in 1854 by Dr. Alpheus Meyers, of Logansport, Indiana. The device was a tiny metal cylinder, tied to a string and baited with food, which the patient swallowed after fasting long enough to work up the worm's appetite. The worm would naturally poke its head into one end of the cylinder where it would be caught by a metal spring strong enough to hold it tight, but not so strong as to decapitate it. With the quarry thus trapped, the attending physician would grasp the end of the string hanging from the patient's mouth and haul up the trap, parasite and all.

**Best Fertility Aid:** Coffee makes you fertile. According to doctors at New York University Medical School, the caffeine in coffee prolongs the lifespan of male sperm and keeps them moving—two factors which will enhance their chances of fertilizing an ovum. (If that's so, New York City should be more fertile than the Nile River Delta. Its population consumes six million cups of coffee a day.)

We may as well dispel the notion here, with the help of Tom Burnam, author of *The Dictionary of Misinformation*, that oysters have anything to do with virility. They don't. In fact, says Burnam, "they're a pretty poor source of energy in any sense. A half-dozen raw ones of the kind commonly grown along the Atlantic coast add up to only some sixty calories."

**Best Funeral Urn:** A California psychiatrist and author of *Frisbee* has requested that on his death he be cremated and his ashes mixed with raw industrial polyethylene, then molded into twenty-five professional-model Frisbees. "As I think toward the future, and envision that scene, and the hours, perhaps even years, [during] which my remains will waft through the air between the hands of those whom I have loved so much, my heart, even now, rises in expectation," he wrote in a letter to Forest Lawn Memorial Parks and Mortuaries. But it remains uncertain whether his wishes will be carried out. A Forest Lawn spokesman has informed him that "While we could, of course, conduct a cremation, we are not in a position to carry out the additional arrangements which you describe in your letter."

**Best Hospital:** If your adenoids are acting up or if you are about to have that bothersome bunion removed, may we suggest that you check into the modern, one hundred fifty-bed hospital in County Clare, Ireland, operated by the Sisters of Charity of the Incarnate Word. As far as we know, the Sisters operate the first and only medical institution with a well-stocked bar for the patients' refreshment and enjoyment.

Prices are strictly controlled so rich and poor alike can afford to hoist a pint of foamy Guinness, a mug of effervescent Harp, or a good stiff shot of Irish whiskey. Sister Theophane Collins, God bless her, originated the hospital pub "to relate conditions to . . . outside life as close as possible."

**Best Kept Secret:** Since John S. Pemberton invented Coca-Cola in 1886, only seven men have known the complete, bubbly formula, and currently only two men are privy to this information. The two never write the precious recipe down, nor do they travel on the same airplane. In short, the Coca-Cola secret is guarded more jealously than the details of the Manhattan Project.

But, after all, the Coca-Cola formula is well worth protecting. It is the most successful patent medicine ever concocted. Pemberton, an Atlanta druggist, originally marketed the sweet syrup as a cure for headaches and hangovers, and in the early days Coke certainly packed a wallop. As the advertisements said, it combined "the tonic properties of the wonderful coca plant and the famous cola nut." Cola is a mild stimulant; the coca in Coke was originally the narcotic cocaine. Now, however, the company uses "a nonnarcotic extract from de-cocainized coca leaves."

Over 90 million Cokes are guzzled daily in 158 countries, but these days the soft drink contains virtually no coca or cola. In 1916 they tried to eliminate the eponymous ingredients entirely, but the Supreme Court ruled that trace amounts must stay in the beverage if the company was to retain its famous trademark. Currently, as Pepsi and RC know very well, Coca-Cola is 99 percent sugar, water, and caffeine, with minimal amounts of caramel, cinnamon, nutmeg, vanilla, lavender, lime juice, citrus oils, glycerine, and a mystery substance known as "7X." Coca and cola amount to less than $1/100$ of one percent of the fluid we drink.

When caffeine was in short supply during World War II, Coke's chemists considered adding another mystery ingredient—extract of bat guano. Droppings, they found, could be synthetically converted into caffeine. But Coke executives rejected the idea, terrified at what would happen if the public ever found out what they were drinking.

**Best News for Knuckle Crackers:** A report in *The Wall Street Journal* notes that a survey of fifty-six inveterate knuckle crackers recently revealed "no unusual incidence of knuckle arthritis."

**Best Night's Rest:** Calvin Coolidge, twenty-ninth president of the United States, averaged ten hours sleep a night. (See also "The Performing Arts," *Best Soporific.*)

**Best Obstetrical Procedure:** Natural childbirth with a keyboard accompaniment is practiced at Halmstad Hospital, in Sweden. Expectant mothers seeking to minimize labor pain and remain awake during delivery are instructed to practice breathing exercises to a recording of Mozart's C Major Piano Concerto. Then, when the labor contractions begin, the music is turned on and is kept playing through the delivery. According to an article in the *American Family Physician*, there are far fewer fatalities among newborn infants at Halmstad than at other hospitals as a result of this technique.

**Best Vitamins:** Gevrabon, manufactured by a pharmaceutical company in Rockland, New York, is the world's first thirty-six proof dietary supplement. It contains fourteen vitamins and minerals in a base of moder-

A 1906 ad for Coca-Cola *

ately strong sherry wine, bottled, appropriately enough, in a pint-sized hip flask, with a screw-on jigger cap. The recommended daily dosage is one ounce, taken before dinner.

Gevrabon is aimed primarily at the elderly, who may find the wine-and-vitamin mixture an appetite stimulant and a mild relaxant. It may also ease body aches and pains.

---

**Worst Addiction:** It isn't unheard of for a patient being treated with heavy doses of morphine to develop an addiction for the drug that long outlasts his hospitalization. Now British physician J. A. Coterill of Leeds, has noted another treatment-induced addiction—bandages. Some patients, he has observed, continue wearing bandages, changing them when necessary, long after their injuries heal; one addict wore them for twenty-two years. Dr. Coterill even described instances of gauze addicts bribing nurses and doctors to indulge their unnatural lust for sterile dressings.

**Worst Allergy:** Some women are allergic to male sperm. In a report in *Annals of Allergy*, Mayo Clinic allergist Edwin J. Mikkelson told of a thirty-year-old woman who developed allergic symptoms whenever she made love. The symptoms ranged from vaginal itching and swelling of the eyes to blotches and hives and shortness of breath, and worse yet, appeared regardless of whom she had sexual relations with.

**Worst Anesthetist:** In south-central Illinois they still talk darkly about "the phantom anesthetist of Mattoon," who first reared his improbable head on September 1, 1944. On that evening, a woman called the Mattoon police department to report that a man had pried open the window of her bedroom and sprayed her with a "sickish, sweet-smelling gas" that had paralyzed her legs and caused her to vomit. The following evening a second woman phoned in a similar report. Over the next twelve days, a total of twenty-four attacks were reported by Mattoon townswomen, some of whom described the assailant quite graphically, down to the odor of the fumes and the pumping sound of his gas gun. The police spread their nets far and wide to track down the molester. Scouring the area, they turned up nothing and eventually made known their feelings that there was no "phantom anesthetist" at all. A few years later, psychologists investigating the affair diagnosed it as a case of mass hysteria.

**Worst Brains:** Dr. J. A. Nicholas Corsellis collects brains the way some people collect matchbooks or theater programs. To date he has amassed about thirty, fifteen of which were removed from the much-abused crania of dead British prizefighters who had fought sometime between 1900 and 1940. The remaining fifteen are of nonprizefighting men and women who died at the same time as the boxers and at approximately the same ages. All are stored in display vials of formaldehyde with the care of an Indiana farmwife putting up jars of gooseberry jam for the winter.

Now Dr. Corsellis' preoccupation with pickled gray matter is no mere evenings'-and-weekends' diversion. As head of a crack team of neurologists and researchers at Runwell Hospital in Wickford, England, Dr. Corsellis has studied boxers' brains with an eye towards proving—or disproving—the notion that the brain of one who earns his keep in the boxing ring deteriorates with wear. Or, in other words, that there really is such a thing as punch-drunk.

As it turns out, there is. In contrast to the brains of their more peaceable contemporaries, the boxers' brains showed signs of massive deterioration: loss of nerve cells, a tearing of the septum separating the brain's two halves, and a general wearing away of brain tissue.

**Worst Form of Circumcision:** Circumcision, whether it's done for medical, sexual, or religious purposes, is a routine surgical procedure involving the removal of the foreskin from the tip of the penis. But male members of the Tihama tribes in the highlands of Saudi Arabia used to volunteer themselves for a bizarre variation of circumcision designed principally to demonstrate their courage and virility (and probably to smother it forever).

Rather than merely peel away the unwanted foreskin, the ritual surgeon would make a horizontal incision in the topmost layer of skin across the stomach just below the navel, then another incision bisecting that one, extending downward over the belly, across the penis and scrotum, and down to the thighs. There would now be two flaps of skin which could be opened like the doors of a cabinet and removed, along with the skin of the scrotal sack, groin, inner thighs—and the foreskin as well.

**Worst Cure:** In February 1685, King Charles II of England died of a stroke, or so his biographers aver. In truth, it may well have been the treatment for the stroke—costly, diligent treatment, at that, performed by the finest physicians of the day—that did him in.

On the morning of the stroke, twelve physicians were summoned to the royal chambers, and they immediately embarked upon an exhaustive treatment designed to purge all poisons from the king's body. First they relieved him of nearly a quart of blood; they also fed him massive doses of emetics to make him vomit up the toxins, and everything else in his stomach, and they purged his intestines with a jolting fourteen-ingredient enema. The king's sickness, however, persisted.

Over the next few days, the doctors shaved Charles' scalp and singed it with red-hot irons, filled his nose with sneezing powder, blanketed him with hot plasters which they then tore off (much to his displeasure) and administered another series of potent enemas, one of which bore fruit, so to speak, sixteen times in one night. Still, no progress. Charles complained of a sore throat and various body aches, and he suffered cold sweats, for which the medics daubed his feet with an improbable emollient of resin and pigeon feces.

The treatment produced no results and Charles sank quickly. Frantically, the doctors carpet-bombed the ailing monarch with bleedings, trepannings, and repeated doses of purgatives, cathartics, and rock-shivering enemas in a last-ditch effort to scour his insides clean as a whistle. They fed him mysterious potions learned from ancient books— pearls dissolved in ammonia, powdered skull. Nothing worked. On the fifth day, apologizing for taking so long to die, Charles breathed his last.

**Worst Cure for the Common Cold:** Sniffles got you down? One way to unclog a stuffed head, according to a nineteenth-century Indiana folk remedy, is to inhale deeply nine times from a dirty sock. (Incidentally, catching a weasel and barehandedly squeezing it to death was considered a sure cure for arthritis of the fingers.)

**Worst Doctor:** In our previous edition we discussed the medical high jinks of Dr. John Brinkley, the Kansas physician who made a fortune during the 1930s by transplanting pairs of goat glands into elderly men to renew their sexual vigor. Poring through the annals of quackery, we have since discovered that Brinkley did not originate the gland transplant; that distinction belongs to a Russian emigré surgeon, Dr. Serge Voronoff. Preferring monkey to goat glands, Dr. Voronoff and his imitators performed thousands of operations throughout Europe and caused the price of young male monkeys to skyrocket.

Bacteriologist Edward Bach was one of those who opposed monkey gland transplants, not on the legitimate grounds that the human body soon rejected the foreign tissues, but because the operations "might instill vicious apelike qualities" in the recipients.

George Bernard Shaw, in a reply addressed to Dr. Bach, offered an impassioned defense of simian character: "Has any ape ever torn the glands from a living man to graft them upon another ape for the sake of a brief and unnatural extension of that ape's life?" Shaw asked. "Was Torquemada an ape? Were the Inquisition and Star Chamber monkey houses? Has it been necessary to found a Society for the protection of ape children, as it has been for the protection of human children? Was the late war a war of apes or of men? Was poison gas a simian or human invention? How does Dr. Bach mention the word cruelty in the presence of an ape without blushing? Man remains what he has always been: the cruelest of all the animals and the most elaborately and fiendishly sensual."

**Worst Execution:** Suicide was, paradoxically, a capital offense in Britain in the nineteenth century: if you survived your own attempt at killing yourself, the state would finish the job for you. Around 1860, according to Nicholas Ogarev, a Russian expatriate living in London, a man who had slashed his throat was taken to the gallows to be hanged for his crime. But physicians warned the executioner that hanging the man would be impossible: the pull of the rope would open the wound in his neck and enable him to breathe. Paying the doctors no heed, they hanged him anyway, writes Ogarev, "and the wound in the neck immediately opened and the man came back to life again although he was hanged. It took time to convoke the aldermen to decide the question of what was to be done. At length the aldermen assembled and bound up the neck below the wound *until he died.*"

**Worst Health Hazard:** Tight underwear is no joke, as anyone with that discomfort knows. But now word comes from two dermatologists at the University of Pennsylvania Medical School that ill-fitting skivvies can cause more than headaches and compulsive squirming. According to Drs. Otto H. Mills and Albert Ligman, 15 percent of their subjects broke out with acne shortly after wearing various tight-fitting undergarments, including undershorts and brassieres, as well as a variety of such outer apparel as turtleneck sweaters, knee socks, and football helmets.

And that's not the worst of it. In 1974 a special research unit was established at Edinburgh General Hospital to "investigate the possibility that infertility in men may be caused by tight underpants," according to the Manchester *Guardian.* Early findings: it is possible that sperm deficiencies are more common in male *Homo sapiens* than in male gorillas because men wear underwear and apes do not. To check the validity of this theory, the unit proposed to study sperm samples from two nonunderwear-clad social groups—a primitive tribe in east Africa and a regiment of Scottish soldiers, who reputedly wear nothing under their kilts.

**Worst News for Health Addicts:** In *Felton & Fowler I* we eulogized nutritionist Alice Chase, recently dead of malnutrition. Now more disheartening news: British health faddist Basil Brown died in 1975 from drinking a gallon of carrot juice a day.

**Worst Orthopedic Treatment:** A thirty-six-year-old aboriginal woman in the Australian outback was buried neck-deep in sand by her witch doctor-husband as treatment for a hip injury sustained in a fall. It didn't work. Moreover, after a month of being thus interred, she was scooped out and flown to Cairns Base Hospital, 1400 miles away, suffering from dehydration and a stroke as well.

**Worst Pregnancy:** In Teruel, Spain, in 1975, a seventy-six-year-old woman plagued with severe stomach cramps was examined by physicians who discovered that she had been pregnant since 1935.

On questioning the woman, the doctors learned that the fetus had died in her eighth month of pregnancy, but that she had not delivered the stillborn child for lack of proper medical facilities. Instead, the woman explained, her attending doctors had advised her to retain the embryo, assuming it would eventually dissolve. Soon thereafter menstruation resumed, and she suffered no ill effects other than the abdominal pains which drove her to seek medical help at age seventy-six. However, she declined to allow doctors to remove the middle-aged, calcified fetus.

**Worst Ulcer Remedy:** Here's one drugstore nostrum that may be a lot worse than the ailment it treats: "Ulcer RX," with unprocessed cow dung.

A wheezing man, redolent of barns and covered with brown dust, showed up at the emergency room of Tuscaloosa Hospital in Alabama in 1975, telling physicians that he worked in the Ulcer RX manufacturing plant in nearby Browns. The plant turned out to be an unventilated concrete blockhouse where he spent his workdays filling vials with powdered manure stored in large sacks. The operation was ordered shut down by the Alabama attorney general.

**Worst Undertaker:** An undertaker in Kuala Lumpur, Malaysia, was arrested and fined twelve dollars for trying to drum up business by selling coffins to terminally ill patients in a hospital.

**Worst Way to Promote Bowel Regularity:** A police officer in Brooklyn, New York, accidentally shot himself in the leg after dropping his pants and gunbelt in the station house men's room.

His peer in marksmanship was a New York City housing patrolman who was drummed from the force and charged with attempting to murder his girlfriend. Luckily for her, the bullet ricocheted off a bobbypin in her hair and wounded the patrolman in the leg.

---

**Most Unusual Addiction:** Don't touch that dial! The Society for Rational Psychology, based in Munich, Germany, has found that the sudden withdrawl of television from a regular viewer can cause "moodiness, child spanking, wife beating, extramarital affairs, and/or decreased interest in sex and fewer orgasms."

The Society asked 184 habitual television watchers to go cold turkey in 1971. As an incentive, they were paid approximately one dollar for every day they abstained from watching TV. Several volunteers were climbing the walls after only two days of deprivation, and not a single participant in the study lasted more than five months. The most alarming withdrawal symptom was a sharp eight percent rise in the incidence of child slapping, when parents were denied their pacifying game shows and situation comedies.

Fortunately, the antisocial behavior is reversible. When the tube was switched back on, husbands and wives reported greater satisfaction with each other, domestic tranquility was restored, and the kids were safe once more.

**Most Unusual Allergy:** A sophisticated computer at the Novosibirsk Computing Center in Siberia continually gave right answers to men and wrong or absurd answers to women. According to Tass, the official Soviet news agency, the machine was allergic to women's clothing. "Synthetic fibers produced an electric field which affected the computer's performance," a repairman said.

**Most Unusual Brain Waves:** A Canadian neurologist ran an electroencephalogram test on a serving of lime Jell-O in 1976 and found the shimmering dessert to be bristling with brain waves, which are normally accepted as evidence of life.

The physician, Adrian R. M. Upton, who conducted the unconventional EEG test by attaching electrodes to the Jell-O in the intensive care unit of McMaster University Hospital, in Hamilton, Ontario, was at

Peter Stuyvesant

pains to point out that the experiment was designed not to verify whether powdered gelatin can be trained to perform simple but useful acts or even whether it has feelings. Rather, he said, the presence of unmistakable brain waves in an EEG reading taken on an unquestionably lifeless dish of Jell-O is evidence of the basic faultiness of EEG readings in general.

"Even in the presence of brain death," Dr. Upton explained, "it's extremely difficult to get a flat EEG, because of artifacts." Artifacts are stray electrical impulses emitted by nearby surgical equipment, paging systems, etc., which are picked up by the EEG machine and recorded as brain waves. "However," he said, "a good technologist is well aware of them."

**Most Unusual Burial:** While battling the Spanish in the Caribbean, Dutch colonist Peter Stuyvesant suffered a badly mangled leg. He was rushed to nearby Curaçao for medical treatment where the shattered leg was amputated and accorded a Christian burial with full military honors!

Oddly, in the years following Stuyvesant's death in 1672, no one could remember whether it had been his right or left leg that had been severed. In some paintings it's Stuyvesant's left leg that's missing; in others it's the right. About seventy years ago his body was exhumed and the dispute was settled forever: Stuyvesant's right leg was the one he lacked.

**Most Unusual Cemetery:** São Paulo, Brazil, boasts the world's first high-rise cemetery. Conceived by architect Fernando Martins Gomes, the structure is the last word in convenience. It houses a morgue, autopsy facilities, funeral parlors, a bar, indoor parking, and meeting rooms for bereaved visitors—all under one roof. Also in São Paulo, architect Dylardo Silva e Souza has carried the city-of-the-dead concept one step further. He has designed a thirty-nine-story, $14.5 million graveyard, outfitted with 21,000 tombs and room for 147,000 cremated residents in perpetuity. The building also features a heliport, an eight-story parking garage, two churches, and twenty-one chapels.

But should the dream of Robert C. W. Ettinger come true, such structures would become obsolete, as would death itself. Ettinger is the founder of the widely publicized Cryonics movement. Cryonicians believe that the technology now exists to fast-freeze corpses immediately after death, preserve them at temperatures far below zero, and defrost them at some future date without serious tissue damage. At that time, presumably, doctors will have found the cure for cancer, heart disease, old age, elephantiasis, or whatever the cause of death may have been. And like Dr. Frankenstein, the physicians will have learned how to restore the long-deceased patient to life. Obviously it will not do to wrap your loved ones in plastic bags and pack them away next to the brussel sprouts and sherbert in your Amana freezer. A sophisticated Thermos bottle filled with liquid nitrogen serves as the frigid (but hopefully not final) resting place.

Currently, Cryonics is only for the well-to-do. Freezing, storage, and an indefinite period of care cost about twenty thousand dollars. In his book *Prospect for Immortality*, Ettinger anticipates that freezing and thawing will "no doubt be handled at first by individuals, then by private companies, and perhaps later by the Social Security System."

Over one thousand men and women now belong to Cryonics associations and subscribe to newsletters with names like *Cryonic Reports*, *Cryonics Review*, and *Immortality*. "Never Say Die" is the catchy motto of the New York Cryonics Society, one of the largest in the country; their emblem is the immortal phoenix. But what about "future shock" or the Rip Van Winkle effect? Will individuals awakened after the big sleep be able to adjust to the world of the twenty-first or twenty-second century? Cryo-Span, another cryonics organization, takes care of that problem, too, promising "postsuspension counseling on future developments."

**Most Unusual Circumcision Method:** At age twelve or thereabouts, boys of the Singh-Hur tribes of northern Bangla Desh are initiated into manhood in a two-day ritual culminating in circumcision. The instrument used is the sharpened beak of a live duck.

Why a duck? No one knows for sure, but the Singh-Hurs have been circumcising their young men that way for centuries. When a boy is deemed ripe for initiation, he is taken from his parents and isolated for two days without food in a tent several miles from his village. During that time the boy is taught the facts of life by the village elders.

When the elders have adjudged their charge sufficiently knowledgeable in such matters, they daub the boy from head to foot with brightly colored paints, and then, in the presence of the high priests, bring out the Sacred Duck, whose beak has been honed as sharp as a razor for the occasion. While the surgeon snips away the foreskin, the youth is expected to remain stoically calm. If he does, he will be desirable to women for all his years. Should he betray his pain with so much as a peep, he will be a sexual washout. In fact, the Singh-Hurs have a word—*garahumaraddakarnapo*—that is roughly equivalent to "Casanova." It translates as "one whose sexual agility has been insured by the Duck God."

**Most Unusual Doctor's Prescription:** Adam Thompson invented the modern bathtub in 1842, but his brainchild did not catch on quickly. In 1843 the Philadelphia municipal government outlawed tub bathing between November 1 and March 15. And in Boston two years later, the city fathers ruled that no one could take a bath in a tub without a doctor's prescription.

**Most Unusual Drowning:** Does washing dishes give you raw, dishpan hands? Stop complaining and count your blessings: Anton Gayer, of Esslingen, West Germany, *drowned* in his kitchen sink. According to police investigators, Gayer, a forty-two-year-old bachelor, blacked out momentarily while washing his dinner dishes, fell forward into the dishwater, and suffocated.

**Most Unusual Dying Breath:** When Thomas Edison died in 1931, his friend Henry Ford trapped the inventor's dying breath in a bottle, counting it among his most prized possessions until his own death in 1947.

**Most Unusual Dying Words:** On his deathbed at his Buffalo, New York home, on March 8, 1874, former U.S. President Millard Fillmore accepted a spoonful of broth from the attending physician and said, "The nourishment is palatable." Then he died.

**Most Unusual Funeral:** Under Rome's Second Triumvirate—Octavius, Lepidus, and Marc Antony—the lands of the idle rich were nationalized and distributed to war veterans as payment for their service. There was one loophole, however; family cemetery plots and mausoleums were exempted from confiscation.

The poet Vergil, prosperous author of the *Aeneid*, was anxious to protect his fine manor on fashionable Esquiline Hill, and he conceived a ploy so outrageous that it worked. He staged an elaborate funeral for a common housefly, claiming it was his beloved pet. Musicians and mourners were hired. Illustrious members of the artistic community delivered solemn eulogies praising the insect's loyalty and obedience. Vergil himself composed some sentimental verses for the occasion.

The total bill for the ceremony came to 800,000 sesterces, or over $100,000, but it accomplished Vergil's purpose. His mansion was officially recognized as a mausoleum and saved from expropriation.

**Most Unusual Halitosis:** The breath of newborn infants occasionally smells of garlic. The reason is that garlic eaten by the mother will work its way from her bloodstream through the placenta into the baby's system.

**Most Unusual Hiccups:** The Brazilian hiccup fish is so named because it produces loud hiccups, or a reasonable facsimile thereof, by gulping lungfuls of air and then expelling them. Hiccup fish often grow to a length of twelve feet and, under water, their hiccups can be heard a mile away.

**Most Unusual Operation:** New hope for sufferers of castration anxiety: A Filipino surgeon has accomplished the first successful graft of a totally severed male reproductive organ. Dr. Ernesto A. Palanca, the attending physician, presented a full report on the unique case before the 1975 Joint Congress of the Pacific and Asian Medical Federations at the Philippine Heart Center in Manila.

According to the Manila *Times Journal* of December 10, 1975, the patient was a thirty-six-year-old Filipino man whose genital organ was deliberately amputated at the base by his wife. The man arrived at the hospital ten hours after the incident whereupon "a surgical team immediately cooled the stump in special solutions to keep the tissues germ-free and alive. Then the severed organ itself was squeezed of blood and repairs were made on its blood vessels (artery and vein) through a very delicate technique of surgery called 'microsurgery,' using magnifiers and tiny sutures."

Following a series of seven operations in five months, the organ was again capable of "normal urination and satisfactory sexual function," Dr. Palanca said. He would not reveal whether the patient continued to live with his wife after the attack or why she had cut off the organ in the first place.

**Most Unusual Rescue:** One of P. T. Barnum's regulars was Anna H. Swan, a seven-foot, ten-inch giantess from Nova Scotia whom the showman billed as "the tallest woman in the world." On July 13, 1865, Barnum's museum in New York burned to the ground, and Miss Swan was saved from a fiery death only through the quick thinking of her sideshow comrades. Here is the New York *Tribune*'s account of the rescue: "The giant girl, Anna Swan, was only rescued with the utmost difficulty. There was not a door through which her bulky frame could obtain a passage. It was likewise feared that the stairs would break down, even if she should reach them. Her best friend, 'the living skeleton,' stood by her as long as she dared, but then deserted her as the heat grew in intensity. At length, as a last resort, the employees of the place procured a lofty derrick which fortunately happened to be standing near, and erected it alongside the Museum. A portion of the wall was then broken off on each side of the window, the strong cable was got in readiness, the tall woman was made fast to one end and swung over the heads of the people in the street, with eighteen men grasping the other extremity of the line, and lowered down from the third story amid enthusiastic applause."

**Most Unusual Personal Effects:** When King Farouk I of Egypt was deposed in 1952, he fled the royal palace in Cairo, leaving behind the following personal effects, according to the editors of *Would You Believe It?:* several pocket geiger counters, each inscribed, "Measure nuclear energy yourself;" a large collection of American comic books; six bedside telephones; fifty walking sticks; seventy-five pairs of binoculars; 1,000 neckties, many with five-inch monograms; and several photographs of copulating elephants.

**Most Unusual Suicide:** In Port Elizabeth, South Africa, a man bent on quick self-extinction found himself exasperated and still alive after shooting himself through the head, slashing his wrists with a razor, hanging himself, and swallowing a jarful of sleeping pills. With his patience all but exhausted, he finally put a stop to this nonsense by drinking hydrochloric acid.

**Most Unusual Tombstone:** Joseph Coveney was Buchanan's (Michigan) most respected businessman, civic leader, and philanthropist, and his application for permission to erect a memorial stone in the public cemetery was granted immediately by the town fathers. Coveney began construction on the monument in the early 1870s, spending several thousand dollars on materials, design and labor. But on the day of its unveiling in 1874, the pious burghers of Buchanan were shocked beyond belief: the monument they had long awaited, whose beauty they could only speculate on, was an anti-Christian abomination, a four-sided cenotaph inscribed with Satanic profanities.

On its east face was the inscription: "JOSEPH COVENEY—He died as he had lived, a disbeliever in the Bible, God, and the Christian religion. . . ." On the north face was "FREE RELIGION: The more Priests, the more Poverty. Nature is the true God, Science is the true religion. . . ." The insciption on the west face read: "FREE SPEECH: The more Religion, the more Lying. The Christian religion begins with a dream and ends with a murder. . . ." And on the west side: "FREE PRESS: The more Saints, the more Hypocrites."

When the monument was exposed, and with it, the respected Coveney's anti-Christian sentiments, the stone was quickly desecrated by vandals and graffitists who broke off its small ornaments and spat tobacco juice at the inscriptions. While newspapers as far away as Chicago attacked Coveney for his sacrilege, his closest friends and the more responsible members of the Buchanan town council poo-poohed the monument and cautioned the public not to forget the great contributions Coveney had made to the well-being of the town.

Eventually the brouhaha subsided. Coveney died in 1897 and was buried, amid little fanfare, beneath the tombstone. Today, according to *American Heritage*, the monument still stands, "but Conveney's radical sentiments have been largely obliterated by time and the elements."

**Most Unusual Treatment for Cancer:** Wilhelm Reich, the noted post-Freudian psychoanalyst, said that masturbation can be used to treat cancer.

# Nature and Science

**Best Application of Good Old American Know-How:** Dr. Harold T. Meryman of the Naval Medical Research Institute at Bethesda, Maryland, has pioneered an exciting new process called "freeze-dry taxidermy." Using the same technology that enabled Maxwell House to give us richer instant coffee, Dr. Meryman freezes likely specimens in a bath of liquid nitrogen, then sucks the ice away in a special vacuum chamber. Messy disembowelling is no longer necessary, since the new methodology preserves the animal's internal organs intact. What's more, the liver or pancreas can be reconstituted for study simply by adding water.

Meryman believes his discovery may also have important applications in the field of embalming. "What I really need is volunteers," he says. (See also "Plants and Animals," *Best Taxidermist.*)

**Best Aviators:** Without belittling the achievements of Lindbergh, Wrong Way Corrigan, or the Wright Brothers, we insist that the greatest adventurers in aviation history were four men named de Rozier, d'Arlandes, Blanchard, and Jeffries.

In the eighteenth century, no one was quite certain how far up the earth's atmosphere went, or whether the air at high altitudes was fit to breathe. So on November 21, 1783, when François Philatre de Rozier and the Marquis d'Arlandes cut the ropes restraining their hot air balloon in Paris and became the first men to fly, there were many spectators who expected them to be asphyxiated or poisoned, if they didn't break their fool necks first. Actually, the moment of greatest physical danger came after the pilots had landed in a Paris suburb. In their eagerness to grab a souvenir of the historic event, frenzied peasants destroyed the balloon and tore de Rozier's redingote to shreds.

De Rozier and D'Arlandes were the first, but the attempt to cross the

The first crossing of the English Channel by balloon, 1785

English Channel in January 1785 was an even more heroic voyage. Jean-Pierre Blanchard designed the odd-looking craft, with funds donated by Dr. John Jeffries, an American physician. Takeoff from Dover, England, was delayed when Blanchard, hungry for personal glory, refused to let his patron into the gondola; only after an impassioned appeal from the local mayor was Jeffries allowed on board.

When they were no more than half a mile from the English shore, the squabbling aviators discovered the first of several leaks in the air bag. Blanchard had outfitted the ship with sophisticated navigational equipment—sails, propellers, rudders, and "air-oars," with which he hoped to row against the wind current—all of which proved totally ineffectual; there was no way to turn and no turning back.

Midway across the Channel, Blanchard and Jeffries began to lose altitude steadily. They jettisoned their ballast, then began casting their accessories overboard. The air-oars and rudder were the first to go, followed by the anchor and their brightly colored banners. With deep regret, they threw away the bottle of fine brandy they had brought to toast their success, and soon they also shed their winter coats. Shivering in the icy winds, they were still sinking fast when the coast of France finally came into view. Blanchard removed his trousers and dropped them into the waves.

Suddenly an updraft carried them several hundred feet higher, and they found themselves drifting over land, but not out of danger. It seemed certain that they would crash into the dense forest below. In desperation, Dr. Jeffries suggested that they relieve themselves of critical ounces of ballast by emptying their bladders. This they did and, narrowly missing the treetops, the heroes landed, frostbitten and half-naked but alive, in a narrow clearing twelve miles inland from Calais. Afterwards, Dr. Jeffries soberly reported, "I have reason to believe this [urination] was a real utility to us, in our then situation."

**Best Invention:** The legend that the doughnut hole originated when a Yarmouth Indian shot an arrow through a Pilgrim mother's fried cake is purely apocryphal. Actually, Captain Hanson Crockett Gregory of Rockport, Maine, deserves full credit for inventing America's favorite void.

The breakthrough came one day in 1847 when Gregory was just fifteen years old, long before he became a famous captain of Yankee merchant vessels. For a factual account of the first hole we are indebted to a *Smithsonian* magazine interview with Fred Crockett, a descendant of the doughnut pioneer: "Young Hanson was in the kitchen of his home watching his mother make fried cakes. He asked her why the centers were so soggy. She said that for some reason they never got cooked. Then the boy decided to poke out the center of some uncooked cakes with a fork. His mother cooked them. They were the first ring doughnuts, and I've been told they were quite delicious."

Today Americans consume over $750 million worth of doughnuts annually. And, fittingly, there is now a plaque on the Gregory house in Rockport commemorating the day that Hanson discovered nothingness. It reads: "This is the birthplace of Captain Hanson Gregory who first invented the hole in the doughnut in 1847. Erected by his friends, November 2, 1947."

**Best Number:** John Fransham (1730–1810) was a wealthy English writer and freethinker. For one thing, he thought that daily bedmaking was a waste of time and "the height of effeminacy." Throughout his life, he campaigned for Parliamentary legislation forbidding people from making their beds more than once a week. Let's face it—Fransham was a little peculiar. Once when guests came for tea, he burned his prized £200 oboe in order to boil his kettle.

But John Fransham should be remembered not for his follies, but for successfully undertaking what was, in his own estimation, "the most exalted and sublime act a man could hope to accomplish." He played "bilbo catch" obsessively for twenty years. (A "bilbo catch" is a child's toy also known as a "cup and ball." A cup is mounted on a handle and a small ball is attached to it with a string. The object is to flip the ball into the cup.) Ultimately, Fransham flipped the ball into the cup 666,666 times, then gave up the sport forever.

According to the ancient numerologists and mystics, 666,666 is the perfect number. Unfortunately, Fransham did not manage to flip the wooden ball in 666,666 times in a row; he was never able to catch it more than two hundred times in succession.

**Best Rainmaker:** When the city of Los Angeles was thirsting for relief from the prolonged drought of 1905, the city fathers put their trust in God and Charles M. Hatfield (1876–1958), America's leading rainmaker. Between January and April, Hatfield "produced" a drenching eighteen inches of precipitation, raised the water level of Lake Helmet Reservoir by twenty-two feet, and collected a respectable four thousand dollar fee for his services.

But the stormiest period of Hatfield's long career came a decade later when he contracted with the San Diego City Council to end the parching dry spell in Southern California and to fill the Morena and Otay reservoirs. By a vote of four to one, the Council agreed to pay the self-proclaimed "Moisture Accelerator" ten thousand dollars if he succeeded within one year, but declined to pay one cent if he failed. Within a matter of days, Hatfield and his brother Paul had fenced off a nearby hilltop and erected a twenty-foot tower so they could conduct their experiments nearer to the clouds. Then on New Year's Day, 1916, Hatfield made his noxious offerings to the heavens. An acrid column of hydrogen and zinc smoke billowed into the sky, accompanied by a series of thunderous explosions.

Some say they felt a sprinkle that very day, and there was no question that on January 9, San Diego experienced its first real downpour in over a year. In the lakes, streams, and reservoirs, the water level began to rise steadily, and by January 19, the Morena Reservoir was filled to its eighteen billion-gallon capacity for the first time since its construction. Water began to spill over the top of the dam; highway bridges and railroad tracks were washed out; telephone and telegraph communications were disrupted; the Colorado and San Diego rivers overflowed their banks. Thousands of people had to be evacuated from flooded areas of San Diego—and from Yuma, Long Beach, Los Angeles, and San Pedro, as well.

Hatfield was surprised by his own success. "This was a phenomenon that I was never able to repeat . . . the most potent that I ever made," he said later. Traveling incognito to avoid emotional confrontations with the flooded residents, the Hatfield brothers returned to San Diego to pick up their ten thousand dollar check. But before the transferal of funds could be arranged, another severe storm hit the city. On January 26, gale winds of up to fifty-four miles per hour were reported, and a record 2.41 inches of rain descended on the area in the first twenty-four hours. Morena and Otay dams ruptured, at least twelve people were killed in the deluge, and property damage in the millions of dollars was recorded.

Vigilantes searched for Hatfield in every hotel and boarding house, intent on hanging him from his infernal weather tower. Fortunately, he had registered under an alias, as a precaution against just such a spontanous outpouring of ingratitude. But the reaction of the City Council was totally unexpected and far more disappointing. The councilmen stubbornly refused to pay Hatfield the fee they had agreed upon, even though he had filled the dams and then some. They had hired him to save the city, they said, and not to submerge it.

**Best Telescope:** A 236.2-inch refracting telescope—the world's largest—located in Russia's Caucasus Mountains, can pick up a flickering candle at fifteen thousand miles. Built in 1970, the mammoth telescope is eighty feet long and weighs 935 tons.

**Best UFO:** When was the last time you saw a flying saucer really worth writing home about? In December 1975, several police officers in three separate counties in northeast Florida reported seeing a spectacular, technicolor UFO three stories high and at least as long as three football fields. While the Federal Aviation Administration could come up with no explanation for the mysterious rainbow-colored spacecraft, several witnesses insisted they saw it land in a wooded area and then take off again. Nonetheless, at least one observer, a staff member of the Flagler

County sheriff's office, remained skeptical. "I believe in UFO's," he said, "but you know, this is a small place and UFO's just wouldn't land in this area. They'd go to New York or Chicago or some place like that."

---

**Worst Cosmology:** One day in 1870 the truth came to Cyrus Teed in a vision: Myopic scientists and explorers had it all wrong; the world we live in is not an oblate sphere; it is not even flat like a pancake; the earth was in the beginning, is now, and ever shall be, concave. Rejecting—or, rather, reinterpreting—the discoveries of Copernicus, Galileo, Newton, and Magellan, Teed concluded that what we call our "planet" is actually a small, globular bubble, an imperfection, in an infinite universe of solid rock.

The ramifications of this viewpoint are mind-boggling. The sun, moon, and stars, said Teed, float in a dark blue cloud at the center of the bubble, and the continents and oceans are distributed on the concave surface encompassing them. Night and day are produced by the rotation of the sun, which alternately displays its light and dark side to us. And as for gravity, it is simply centrifugal force produced by the slow, steady turning of the rocky universe.

The skeptical reader may raise certain objections; what about the apparent rising and setting of the sun and moon, for instance? Rest assured, this misleading phenomenon, as well as the "illusion" of the horizon and the twinkling of the stars, is explained by the laws of "Koreshan Optics." The fundamental assumption of Koreshan Optics is that light travels in a tight circle, turning back on itself. This explains, or at least it did to Teed's satisfaction, why people in San Francisco cannot look up and see Tokyo through the blue ether. On the power of his ideas, Teed recruited several thousand followers throughout the United States, whom he organized into the Koreshan Unity commune in Estero, Florida—a quasi-religious, quasi-scientific fellowship. One of the commune's projects was to measure the earth with T-squares. The results were predictable enough: Teed mapped out the incurvature of the earth, proving that we live on the inside of a bubble that never bursts.

Incredibly, Teed's heresy survived his death in 1909 and the dispersal of his disciples; it was resurrected for a time by the German Admiralty and Adolf Hitler himself. In Germany, Teed's imaginative cosmology was known as the *Hohlwetlehre*, the Hollow World Theory, and the Nazi navy found it particularly enthralling for its military applications. According to Koreshan optics, different wavelengths of light curve at different rates. Thus, theoretically, one could use sophisticated infrared sighting devices to peer over the horizon and locate the British fleet moored in British ports. This bizarre line of reasoning led Hitler to approve a strange scientific experiment described by G. P. Kuiper in *Popular Astronomy* (June 1946): "A party of about ten men under the scientific leadership of Dr. Heinz Fischer, an infrared expert, was sent out from Berlin to the isle of Rügen (in the Baltic Sea) to photograph the British fleet with infrared equipment at an upward angle of some forty-five degrees." The mission failed.

**Worst Rain:** Dick Edwards, of Fort Lauderdale, Florida, says his house has been periodically showered with an unpleasant substance from above that most certainly is *not* rain, manna, or pennies from heaven. Since he lives directly under an airport flight path, he thinks it's toilet wastes jettisoned by overhead jetliners coming in to land. When he complained, the Federal Aviation Administration suggested that he watch the offending aircraft and take down their registration numbers, but Edwards refused. "If they think I'm going to stand outside with my face to the sky, they're nuts," he said.

**Worst Rations for a Space Flight:** The Western Regional Research Laboratory of the U.S. Department of Agriculture has conducted an investigation of what foods are appropriate and inappropriate for astronauts to eat on prolonged space flights. As part of their exhaustive research, the scientists developed the first reliable quantitative measure of "the flatus-producing effects" of various rations. Onions and beans finished near the top of the flatus scale and, consequently, have been banned from the menus of all future space expeditions.

**Worst Research Project:** In separate studies in 1975, the National Institute on Alcohol Abuse and Alcoholism studied both the intoxicating effects of hard liquor on sunfish and the process by which laboratory rats rendered neurotic become alcoholics.

The studies, funded by the federal government to the tune of nearly $200,000, raised the hackles of Wisconsin Senator William Proxmire, who said that "over the years the NIAAA has spent millions of dollars in hundreds of experiments to turn normal rats into rodent 'lushes' with little or no success."

Proxmire has, in fact, made a habit of blowing the whistle on research boondoggles wherever he's spotted them. He was especially distressed at a $121,000 investigation into the effects of marijuana on men who had been sexually excited by watching pornographic movies. He called the two-year study, sponsored by the National Institute on Drug Abuse, "one of the most shocking examples of a federal love machine I have seen." Less shocking, but more arcane was a $275,000 study of precisely what happens to people in North Yemen when they chew the cat leaf.

**Worst Science:** It seems curious today that phrenology was once regarded as a respectable and progressive movement, espoused by such eminent figures as Karl Marx, Charles Baudelaire, George Eliot, Honoré de Balzac, and Queen Victoria. The most outspoken criticism came from the Church; reading cranial bumps was finally banned in Vienna, not because it was pseudo-scientific nonsense, but because it was a religious heresy contradicting the doctrine of free will.

The basic theory of phrenology was first advanced around 1800 by the Austrian anatomist Franz Joseph Gall. In essence, Gall maintained that human personality consists of a number of inborn "faculties," each of which is localized in a specific area of the brain. The larger the region of the brain, the more pronounced the faculty controlled by that region; for instance, a good-sized lump at the base of the brain, reflected in the contours of the skull, denoted a well-developed faculty of "philoprogenitiveness," the urge to produce children. By making a careful examination of the skull's hills and dales, a skilled phrenologist could, theoretically, determine a person's character and abilities.

Phrenology was enthusiastically received in the United States. Clara Barton entered nursing and Bernard Baruch went into finance on the advice of their phrenologists. General George McClelland recruited spies for the Union Army on the basis of their phrenological profiles, insisting on a prominent secretiveness faculty. Horace Greeley, the editor of the New York *Tribune*, seriously suggested that accidents might be reduced if railroad engineers were selected by the shape of their heads. Presidents James Garfield and John Tyler had their heads examined, and Ulysses Grant met so frequently with his phrenologist during his eight years in office that Democrats charged that the doctor was dictating his domestic policy. Walt Whitman often used phrenological terms in his poems and was so proud of a chart showing him to be well developed in *all* faculties that he published it on no less than five occasions.

A logical outgrowth of this illogical science was the practice, common in the south of France, of binding the heads of young children with tight bandages to squeeze their brains into desirable shapes. The object was not cosmetic, as it was among certain African and American Indian tribes, but rather the parents hoped to influence the growth of certain phrenological faculties and thereby make their children more successful, more talented, or more personable in later life.

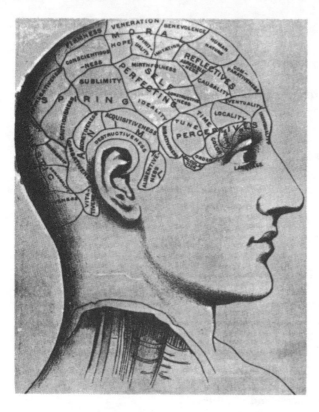

A phrenological map of the head

Epilogue: When Franz Gall died in Paris, in 1828, a postmortem revealed that his skull was twice as thick as that of the average person.

**Worst Scientific Project:** In *Felton & Fowler I* we wrote somewhat disparagingly of the great dream of Dr. Robert J. White: "We must begin to think of transplanting the head." In all fairness, we should state here that Dr. White, a Cleveland neurosurgeon, is as much a doer as a talker, and to date has successfully performed ten head transplants on monkeys. Some of the transplants continued functioning for as long as thirty-six hours, and in his later efforts Dr. White was able to keep the relocated head seeing, smelling, hearing, and responding to stimuli.

**Worst Snow:** On Christmas night of 1969, snow began falling over a seven thousand-square-mile area of southeastern Sweden. That would hardly be a remarkable occurrence, if this were not a snow of a different color—pitch black. By the morning of December 26, several inches of black snow had entirely covered the previous deep white base; when deer walked through the sable drifts they left white footprints behind them. The Center for Short-Lived Phenomena in Cambridge, Massachusetts, noted that the snow was "oily and slick, and resisted removal even with detergents." The cause of the dark precipitation was never determined, although a chemical analysis did turn up traces of DDT and PCB insecticides in the snowflakes.

**Worst State Mineral:** The Mississippi state senate recently voted down legislation that would have designated the black widow as the state spider, the earthworm as the state worm, the wharf rat as the state rat, and the vampire as the state bat. On the positive side of the legislative box score, the senators did enact an amendment making iron pyrites, better known as fool's gold, the official state mineral.

As a matter of fact, iron pyrites might be an excellent choice for a national mineral since it was the first ore mined in the colonies that later became the United States. At the Jamestown settlement in Virginia, some gullible prospector discovered a bank of yellow dirt, and, after that, as Captain John Smith laments in his diary, "There was no thought, no discourse, no hope, and no work but to dig gold, wash gold, refine gold, and load gold." Captain Newport carried a glittering cargo, optimistically valued in the millions, across the Atlantic, delivered it to the London Company to be weighed and assayed, and learned to his disappointment that it was totally worthless.

**Worst Weather:** A sign posted along the slopes of New Hampshire's Mount Washington advises climbers: "STOP. The area ahead has the worst weather in America. Many have died there from exposure. Even in the summer. Turn back *now* if the weather is bad." But "bad" is a loaded word, since even at best the winds and temperatures atop Mount Washington are hardly a picnicker's delight. On April 24, 1934, the wind there gusted to 231 miles per hour for 1.17 seconds. That's the fastest wind ever recorded.

Faster, even, than any breeze ever clocked in Fargo, North Dakota, which is surprisingly the windiest city in the United States. Winds in Fargo average 14.4 miles per hour; in Chicago, the Windy City, the average is 10.6 mph. Actually, chill winds have nothing to do with Chicago's nickname. New York *Sun* journalist Charles Dana coined the moniker in 1893 after hearing Chicago residents brag just a little too much about their world's fair that year.

**Worse Weatherman:** In 1964, the Director of the Provincial Weather Bureau in Formosa confidently predicted that Hurricane Gloria would bypass the island at a comfortable distance. The next day Gloria struck with full force. When the final toll was calculated, 239 people were dead, 89 were listed as missing, and over $17.5 million worth of property damage was attributed to the storm.

The overly optimistic weatherman was arrested at his home and charged with criminally negligent forecasting. Facing a stiff fine and a maximum sentence of ten years in prison, the meteorologist pleaded in court that he had done his best. As evidence he produced weather maps and expert testimony on how fickle hurricanes can be. The judge ruled that the prosecution had failed to prove criminal intent, and the case was adjourned indefinitely.

As a footnote, a survey of weather forecasts in the United States and England revealed that predictions made twenty-four hours in advance prove accurate about 75 percent of the time.

---

**Most Unusual Astronauts:** The Japanese are raising pigs to be astronauts. According to the British weekly, *New Scientist,* the Japan Livestock Research Institute has developed an unusually small breed of swine to be used in space flights by the National Aeronautics and Space Administration.

Meanwhile, earthbound porkers will reap whatever benefits result from a five-year study now underway at the Agricultural Research Council, in Cambridge, England, on what makes pigs bored, what keeps them happy, and how to help them sleep well. The test subjects are being housed in air conditioned, sound-proofed subterranean bunkers during the study.

**Most Unusual Counting System:** The Yuki Indians of California avoided the embarrassment of being seen furtively counting on their fingers by counting on the spaces between their fingers instead.

**Most Unusual Farm:** University of Connecticut scientists have set up an indoor vegetable factory that spits out one hundred eight-ounce heads of lettuce a day. Agricultural engineer Ralph Prince says that the scientists have been able to accelerate the growth processes of vegetables artificially by pumping a solution of nutrients through the soilbeds and bathing the plants in ersatz sunlight. The only thing missing is assembly-line conveyor belts, and those, he says, may be added in the future.

"We started with lettuce because it's an easy crop to grow," he notes. "Eventually we hope to add the makings of a whole salad—radishes, tomatoes, and even strawberries."

**Most Unusual Fertilizer:** A British physician, S. L. Henderson Smith, believes that burial and cremation are inefficient and frequently unhygienic methods of disposing of the dead. The alternative he suggests is to grind up the bodies and mix them with sewage, to produce a usable fertilizer.

**Most Unusual Form of Pollution:** Students at the State University of New York at Buffalo who threatened to throw an effigy of Richard Nixon over the Falls and into the Niagara River in 1973 were warned by police that they would be arrested for polluting. They withdrew the threat.

**Most Unusual Hailstones:** Hailstones as large as walnuts, kumquats, and even volleyballs have been recorded, but all are pallid fare compared to some man-sized beauties that fell on Germany in 1930. Five glider pilots ran into bad weather high above the mountains, and were forced to bail out. But instead of free-falling, they were *lifted* by a violent updraft to the top of a cloud where they acquired a thick coating of ice. Then, like hailstones, they plunged earthward, the ice-layer alternately melting and refreezing—and growing larger with each cycle—as they passed through successive layers of warm and cold air. All the chutes opened, and one of the men survived. But the others hit the ground frozen to death, as human hailstones.

**Most Unusual Interplanetary Communications System:** Karl Friedrich Gauss (1777–1855), one of the most innovative mathematicians of all time, proposed that hundreds of square miles in the Siberian steppes be planted with long lines of pine trees symbolically representing the Pythagorean theorem. This distinctive pattern, Gauss believed, would communicate to observers on other planets the fact that the earth is inhabited by creatures intelligent enough to know geometry—and therefore worthy of a visit.

But what should mankind's reaction be when extraterrestrial beings land on earth and make themselves known? That question was discussed by the distinguished astronomer Dr. Antony Hewish, the discoverer of the first pulsar, during a recent meeting of the International Astronomical Union in Britain. Dr. Hewish recommends that on that fateful day, "We should call a special meeting of the Royal Society and inform the politicians. Then the world would be told and a suitable reply to the aliens would be drafted."

**Most Unusual Minority Group:** Shellfish apparently have it tough in Baltimore, Maryland, which is why a law there—still standing—makes it illegal to mistreat an oyster. In her book, *You Can't Eat Peanuts in Church and Other Little-Known Laws*, Barbara Seuling also notes other statutes designed to protect the interests of animals: Fish-lassoing is outlawed in Knoxville, Tennessee. . . . In Arizona, kicking a mule is a punishable offense. . . . So is deliberately worrying a squirrel in Topeka, Kansas. . . . In California you are breaking the law if you pluck the feathers from a live goose.

The overwhelming question raised by such absurd statutes is whether they are ever actually enforced. Apparently so. In Goulburn, Australia, a man got a seven-day jail sentence for swearing in the presence of a beagle. The ill-mannered lout—John Williams Gibson—pleaded guilty, but with an explanation. After tying one on in a local pub, he said, he stepped outside and began abusing a passing dog. When the animal reprimanded him with a bark, Gibson swore at it violently.

A vegetarian postscript: Vegetables have feelings too, and since 1971, the Society for Prevention of Cruelty to Mushrooms (SPCM) has zealously guarded not only the interests of mushrooms—both edible and poisonous varieties—but also those of "other neglected or mistreated forms of life, regardless of age, race, sex, religion, or other stereotypical attributes," according to its national president, Brad Brown. Based in Bloomfield Hills, Michigan, the SPCM claims over three hundred members nationwide.

**Most Unusual Mountain:** Word comes from a Smithsonian Institution geophysicist, Dr. E. Michael Gaposchkin, that Mount Everest is not the world's tallest mountain. What is, then? Mount Chimborazo, in the Ecuadorian Andes, at a height of 20,946,233 feet.

Some explanation is in order. Dr. Gaposchkin compared the height of the two peaks by measuring from the earth's center rather than from sea level. The earth, he points out, has a prominent equatorial bulge, and Chimborazo is situated right on the top of that bulge, while Everest is located on a relatively flat part of the globe. As a result, Everest's height, measured from the earth's center, falls 7,058 feet short of Chimborazo's.

**Most Unusual Pilot:** According to Cleveland Amory, Ken Smith of Tarzana, California, has taught his dog to pilot an airplane. Sitting in a specially built harness, the sixteen-year-old German shepherd flies regularly with her master, and has over three hundred flying hours under her belt (or ninety-day flea collar).

Says Amory, "The plane has dual controls and when she sees one wing go down, she yelps, turns the wheel, and makes the wing go up until it is even again with the other wing." The dog's name, appropriately, is Radar.

**Most Unusual Rain:** Nice weather for ducks? No, not when the ducks themselves are the weather. At their Valparaiso, Nebraska, farm, Ermin Bennes and his two sons reported that thirteen dead mallard ducks fell on them from the sky.

They had been struck by lightning in midflight.

# Plants and Animals

**Best Canine Tree Climber:** Tree climbing is not a highly developed skill among dogs, but Jenny, a combination German shepherd and husky owned by George Gebracht of San Francisco, can shinny up a Dutch elm with the ease of a squirrel—which is no wonder, since she was taught to scale trees by a pet squirrel she met in her puppyhood at Golden Gate Park.

In fact, when a police officer spotted Jenny scampering about on a tree limb forty feet above ground, he informed her owner that he'd have to get her a special tree-climbing permit from the city park department.

**Best Chicken Feed:** Celeste Maspero and his sister Rosina were puzzled and not a little disturbed when police invaded their farm in Como, Italy, sealed if off, and methodically uprooted three thousand marijuana plants, the seeds of which they had been feeding to their chickens.

"They make a wonderful food for my hens," Maspero said. Oddly, police reported that the Masperos were apparently ignorant of the narcotizing effects of the plants on humans, assuming chicken feed to be the only thing they were good for.

**Best Cow:** For the overweight, a cow that gives skim milk.

Actually, any cow can be made to yield fat-free beef and milk, a discovery made by researchers at the University of California at Davis. The secret is in a specially coated low-fat grain that is fed to the cow in place of her normal grassy fare. The protein coating protects the food from being broken down by bacteria in the cow's first stomach and turned into fats. In the fourth stomach the fats are released, digested, and rendered harmless. The end product: milk and meat that will not make you fat or cause artery-clogging cholesterol deposits.

Of course, the obvious question is what does milk that is skimmed even before it leaves the cow taste like? The answer: poor to passable, depending on the batch. Most people who sampled the milk felt it was a bit too thick in texture and tasted faintly of sunflower seeds. Fat-free ice cream and beef, however, got exceptionally high marks.

**Best Dog House:** When the Collins spinsters, Rene and Sybil, died in 1973, they left behind six dogs—Yorkshire terriers and chihuahuas—that would need looking after. Sparing no cost, the sisters set up their charges in a $40,000 home with a splendid view of the village square of Caddington, a sleepy hamlet in central England. Since then, the dogs have been going it on their own.

"Sybil and Rene wanted the dogs to have the house. I promised I would look after them," said their surviving sister, Mrs. Evlene Agar, who sees to the feeding of the dogs each day but otherwise leaves them to their own devices. "They did not want them put in a home."

According to a representative of the local district council, "The rates are being paid. There have been no complaints, and there is nothing we can do about it."

**Best Fungus:** A French Minister of Agriculture was once quoted as saying, "There is still as much mystery about how a truffle grows as there is about life on the moon." And since the Apollo moon landings, there are people who believe that the life-style of the truffle may be the most baffling mystery we have left.

The philosopher Theophrastus believed truffles were the product of thunder; in the Middle Ages they were thought to spring from witches' spit. Whatever their source, the ugly fungi grow in porous soil from three to twelve inches beneath the roots of oak and beech trees. And their slightly pungent taste is incomparable. Madame de Pompadour fed them to Louis XV as an aphrodisiac; and Napoleon fathered his only legitimate son after eating truffled turkey. Current market price in the United States is about six dollars per ounce, making good truffles even more expensive than Russian black caviar. One reason truffles are so expensive is that they are hard to find. The French traditionally train hogs to sniff them out; the Italians use hounds.

Anthelme Brillat-Savarin, author of *The Physiology of Taste*, called truffles "the diamonds of gastronomy." Far and away the most precious is the black truffle (*Tuber melanosporum*) with a full, earthy flavor that is sublime. The Quercy-Périgord region near Bordeaux and the Vauchise-Gard area north of Marseilles yield the perfect fungi; overall French production is about one hundred tons per year, and steadily declining.

Trained hogs sniff out truffles.

The Italians make wild, irresponsible claims on behalf of their inferior white truffles, but do not be taken in. The proof of black superiority is that many unscrupulous merchants dye their white truffles black.

As a general rule of thumb, a bad year for wine is an excellent year for truffles. The finest truffles in recent memory were produced in 1969 when torrential rains ruined much of the French grape harvest.

**Best Pet Cemeteries:** The grassy knolls of Hartsdale Memorial Park, located in New York, the nation's oldest pet cemetery, are dotted with granite doghouses and the gravesites are strewn with catnip mice and toy bones. Reverent epitaphs carved in stone pay final tribute to departed friends: "Groffen: Will wag her loving self into Paradise."

It's a sad business being a small animal mortician, but it is not without its rewards. As of 1973, an average plot at Hartsdale cost $100, a fox terrier-sized casket $80, a carved headstone $85, plus $20 for the sexton's labor, and $5 annually for "perpetual care." Of course, more elaborate memorials are available: In Chicago's Hinsdale Animal Cemetery stands a life-size statue of Flower Pot, a pet skunk, whose tomb cost its master $1700—a small price to pay for so many pungent memories. Besides, as Vernon Lowrey, a trustee of Houston's Garden of Evergreens Pet Cemetery, declares, "It's presumptuous to flatly state that a dog (or any other pet, for that matter) doesn't have a soul." Incidentally, ancient Egyptians thought that cats were dieties, and whenever the household feline died the entire family shaved off their eyebrows as a sign of mourning.

No dogs are buried at Arlington National Cemetery, but that doesn't mean that the military ignores its fallen animal heroes. Several years ago at Hillside Acres Cemetery in Methuen, Massachusetts, a marine mascot named Sergeant was buried with full military honors; a Catholic priest conducted the obsequies, a bugler played taps, and Sergeant was lowered into the ground while two busloads of tearful leathernecks looked on. And at Hartsdale there is a tomb for the Unknown K-9, bedecked with a bronze canteen and helmet and bearing the inscription, "Valiant services rendered in the World War."

**Best Taxidermist:** After a sound night's sleep on a bare wooden floor, Squire Charles Waterton (1782–1864) customarily rose each morning at three o'clock and spent at least four hours stuffing birds before breakfast. Author of the classic *Original Instructions for the Perfect Preservation of Birds, etc., for Cabinets of Natural History,* Waterton enjoyed an international reputation as a leading naturalist and one of the most talented men ever to open a can of formaldehyde.

A visit to the Waterton estate was an odyssey in eccentricity. A new guest was often surprised to discover the master of the manor crouched on all fours behind the beautiful tapestries, and even more surprised when Waterton bared his teeth, growled like a dog, and sunk his teeth into the stranger's leg. It was just his way of getting acquainted. Among his other quirks, Waterton always went barefoot . . . kept a pet chimpanzee, which he habitually kissed goodnight . . . shared his bed with a live sloth . . . and sponsored an annual picnic for one hundred local lunatics.

His curiosity was unbounded, and he was especially fascinated by predatory animals. On an expedition to South America, Waterton slept with his toes exposed at night in hopes that a vampire bat would come and suck his blood; he was disappointed. He engaged in an acrimonious debate with John James Audubon on the subject of whether vultures locate dead carcasses by sight alone (Audubon's position) or by a combination of sight and smell (Waterton's position). And on his own grounds, he established the world's most repulsive wildlife sanctuary, devoted entirely to carrion crows, buzzards, and magpies. Other preserves practiced *de facto* discrimination against scavengers, he explained.

Waterton's revolutionary taxidermal technique involved soaking the entire skin of the specimen in a solution of alcohol and perchloride of mercury. This enabled him to shape and model the little animal from the inside. After the solution dried, the skin hardened into a permanent

Squire Charles Waterton

trophy without the need for internal stuffing. Once, when a shipment of rare animals from South America was held up by a dull-witted customs official, Waterton taxidermized a howler monkey, stretched its face to resemble the offending magistrate, dressed it in a miniature customs uniform, and displayed it in a social club frequented by the official.

For readers interested in seeing other outstanding examples of animal preservation, we recommend a visit to Potter's Museum of Taxidermy near Palace Pier in Brighton, England—the finest gallery of its kind. There you will enjoy such masterpieces as "The Death and Burial of Cock Robin"—a ghastly tableau featuring one hundred species of British birds—and "The Guinea Pigs' Cricket Match," which includes two fully uniformed teams, a brass band with tiny instruments, and bleachers packed with guinea-pig spectators guzzling bottles of ale. In all, over five thousand taxidermy pieces are on display, along with assorted curiosities such as a lamb with two heads and a duck with four legs.

**Best Toad:** Yellow-bellied toads are rare in West Germany—so rare, in fact, that when two dozen of them occupied a construction site in Hildesheim, West Germany, the town council directed the builders to redesign the plans for the fifty-house development to avoid disturbing the animals. Planners estimated that the cost of relocating would be about $122,000.

**Best Watchdog:** The Sterling Works, a San Francisco jewelry store, rents a five-year-old tarantula for ten dollars a month to guard the premises. The spider, along with an imposing sign in the display window noting that "This area is patrolled by a tarantula," has resulted in a dramatic decline in break-ins.

An Indianapolis guns-and-ammo emporium called The Bullet Hole Sport Shop warns away mischief makers with a one hundred-pound African lion named Beau, who stalks the building at night.

A seven-foot-long boa constrictor guards the entrance of an amusement arcade in Gaevle, Sweden.

---

**Worst Bees:** In the 1950s, a geneticist named Warrick Kerr imported seventy lethal African bees to his laboratory in São Paulo, Brazil, with an eye towards studying their breeding habits and learning how they might be safely crossbred with homegrown bees to beef up Brazilian honey reserves. However, Professor Kerr's bees had crossbreeding plans of their own. When twenty-six of them escaped from his labs in 1956, they immediately took to copulating with the local talent and within a few months there were several million offspring, each one every bit as aggressive and deadly as its progenitors.

Drifting northward en masse at a rate of 200 miles a year, the bees to date have passed through Bolivia, Paraguay, Peru, and Venezuela, swarming down upon cattle and humans alike without the slightest provocation. Since the first recorded human fatality in southern Brazil in 1966, the bees have disrupted weddings, garden parties, and even funeral processions. Once they plagued inmates in a jail cell so relentlessly that the prisoners assumed they were being tortured by the authorities and screamed out their confessions.

What can be done? One possibility is to take the sting out of their sting, so to speak, by mating the African killer bees with large numbers of their gentle Italian cousins. Another is wholesale extermination. Yet a third possibility is the establishment of a defensive barrier, sort of an entomological Maginot Line—across Central America. In the meantime, however, several United States congressmen, most notably Senator Robert Dole of Kansas, have called for the United States to establish joint defense measures with Canada, Mexico, and the countries of Central America.

**Worst Fish:** Back in 1969, normally sane and sober Floridians were reporting that their pet dogs had been attacked and, according to some reports, killed by catfish. The incidents occurred not while the dogs were swimming but while they were resting peacefully on their own front lawns. It was true; the walking catfish, *Clarias batrachas*, was on the prowl.

Native to Asia, the walking catfish ordinarily lives in shallow pools and streams that sometimes evaporate entirely during the dry season. Over the aeons, the fish have adapted and developed the ability to crawl across dry land with the aid of their pectoral fins. Several species of *Clarias* no longer depend exclusively on their gills to process oxygen and can survive out of water for periods up to twelve hours or more.

The walking catfish, thriving now in the fresh and brackish waters of the southern United States, are all descended from a few specimens that strolled away from a tropical fish dealer's pond. As the poodles of Florida can attest, Asian catfish are extremely aggressive. Wildlife experts say they are driving the more attractive game fish out of the lakes. In Florida and other states, *Clarias batrachas* and *Albino clarias*, the snow-white walking catfish, have been designated as dangerous species.

If they value their lives, however, the walking catfish will stay far away from the laboratory shared by Jean Caul and Lilia Maligalig of Kansas State University. The two nutritionists have noticed that home-grown midwestern catfish sometimes develop a muddy taste by scrounging for their food on mucky lake bottoms. Looking for a method of improving the flavor of catfish *in vivo*, professors Caul and Maligalig added saccharine, anise, onion juice, garlic powder, and hickory smoke to tanks at the Tuttle Creek Fisheries Research Laboratory. After a few weeks in this environment, the fish came out tasting distinctly of saccharine, licorice, onion, garlic, and smoke. Next, Dr. Caul plans to add butter and lemon flavors to the tanks in hopes that the catfish "would taste like hollandaise sauce."

**Worst Infringement on Animals' Rights:** Uniformed members of the New York City Fire Department are forbidden by law to administer mouth-to-mouth resuscitation to animals.

**Worst Ornithologist:** In the early 1890s, philanthropist Eugene Scheif-flin decided that a novel way of honoring Shakespeare would be to import into the United States at least one of every species of bird mentioned throughout the Bard's thirty-seven plays. A harmless if inventive whim on the face of it, except that the eighty European starlings released by Scheifflin in New York City's Central Park on March 6, 1890 multiplied wildly and, since the early years of this century, the bird has been a major health threat throughout the nation. Starlings roosting en masse in trees and on rooftops have showered the nation's byways with

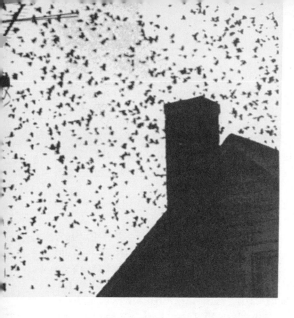

A swarm of health-threatening starlings

their droppings, from which disease-bearing bacteria are frequently transmitted to people and animals. Flocks of the winged pests have been known to decimate wheatfields and cornfields in a frighteningly short time, and in chorus, their screeching is often unbearable. In 1975, the United States Army announced plans to move in on especially large roosts of starlings around Fort Campbell, Kentucky, and spray them with Tergitol, a potent detergent that would wash away the protective coating of oil that keeps the birds from freezing to death.

**Worst Parakeet:** Argentinian gray-breasted parakeets are known as monkims to ornithologists and as winged garbage cans to those who have seen them in action. When allowed to fly loose, they devour wheat, rice, maize, and fruit crops and have cost South American farmers hundreds of thousands of dollars in ruined harvests. Worst yet, they don't talk and are not especially cute.

Nonetheless, Argentinian entrepreneurs tried exporting monkims as house pets to the United States a few years ago. The birds reproduced wildly, much as the *bufo marinus* toads did in Australia (see *Felton & Fowler I*, page 184) and became particularly obnoxious in New York, New Jersey, Michigan, Illinois, and Virginia.

**Worst Thing You Can Do to a Chicken:** In *Felton & Fowler I* we speculated on the possibility of running an automobile on chicken excreta. Now scientists at the United States Department of Agriculture say it may be possible to run a *chicken* on chicken excreta.

While feeding a chicken its own droppings may seem a foul trick, the

USDA researchers feel otherwise. They say they have been feeding their experimental subjects a delicate blend of conventional feed and reprocessed droppings and that it's been a big hit with the unsuspecting chickens. In fact, they have tried feeding cattle a similar concoction (70 percent cattle feed, 30 percent chicken feces). "It's nutritious stuff," says a USDA nutritionist, "but the cows hate the taste." Maybe some tarragon would help.

Feeding cows chicken excrement? What will scientists think of next?

Glad you asked. Feeding cows *human* excrement—and they've *already* thought of it. Or at least one scientist has, anyway—Dr. Rodney Kromann, of Washington State University, who says that freeze-dried human sewage, once it's been deodorized and sterilized, will make a tasty dish to set before a cow, although he admits that "no one likes the idea of biting into a shit-fed steak." In a paper published in *Nutrition Reports International*, Kromann reported that he had compared the chemical composition of human wastes with that of alfalfa, and found the former to be the richer of the two in nitrogen, ether extract, cellulose, and crude fiber. In fact, says Dr. Kromann, a city of thirty thousand could keep one thousand cows healthy, growing and content on nothing but the population's feces.

**Worst Zoo:** Ever since the price of oil went through the roof in 1974, tiny Middle Eastern sheikdoms and sultanates such as Qatar and Abu Dhabi have come into more money than, apparently, they know what to do with. According to a dispatch in *The Wall Street Journal*, Sheikh Zaid of Abu Dhabi recently built a zoo at the Buirami Oasis, located in the middle of the Arabian Desert and ninety miles from the nearest town. Run by German-trained zoologists, the zoo is stocked with one hundred fifty animals and an elaborate aquarium. Water is brought in from the Persian Gulf. Lines to get into the zoo are not long, it goes without saying, and foreign journalists are mystified by the sheikh's zeal in building a zoo that no one visits. A spokesman for the leader says that it has "improved the quality of life for his subjects."

---

**Most Unusual Birdcall:** The call of the South American bullbird—*cephalopterus ornatus*—sounds unmistakably like a cow's moo. Meanwhile, the world's *most boring* birdcall is that of the red-eyed vireo, a North American songbird. Vireos are endowed with perfect pitch and demonstrate that gift by unimaginatively repeating the same call as much as twenty-two thousand times a day, without even a hint of variation.

**Most Unusual Goats:** While browsing through the *Journal of Nervous and Mental Diseases*, we noticed an article on a strain of skittish goats that live only in a few areas of Tennessee and Mississippi. They are perhaps the most cowardly of all animals. Whenever they are startled by a thunderclap, a tractor starting up, or even the clatter of a feed bucket, they immediately collapse in a dead faint. From a distance, it appears that they have given up the goat, but on closer examination one finds that the animals have lapsed into a rigid catatonic state. Moments later, the goats recover their senses and return to their grazing, apparently none the worse for their experience.

This faint-hearted breed first attracted the attention of veterinarians in 1904, and recently, neurologists and geneticists have become interested in the goats' uncommon behavior, which seems to be the result of a hereditary nervous disorder. Doctors say the ailment is akin to myotonia congenita, a disorder that causes involuntary spasms in human beings.

W. S. Howard of Millington, Tennessee, is one farmer who still raises swooning goats. "They are not good for anything," he says. "But they are pretty weird."

**Most Unusual Hybrid:** A Saskatchewan cattle breeder named Roy Carlson decided to cross a cow with a Tibetan yak not long ago, hoping that the resultant offspring—call it a yow, if you will, or even a cak—would combine the grace of a heifer with the durability of a yak, and provide leaner meat and richer milk to boot.

Carlson's first step was to purchase two male yaks from a local game farm. He placed them among his one hundred twenty cows, and waited for That Special Spark. Nothing happened. The yaks, named Royal Yak I and Royal Yak II, and the cows wanted no part of each other.

Carlson then abandoned his plan to play matchmaker between yak and cow, and turned his thoughts instead to artificial insemination. But the market for yak semen is bullish these days, and Carlson had to delay that plan until he could scrape up enough cash to artificially impregnate his cows. Meanwhile, Royal Yak II broke loose from the untended feedlot where he had been kept and rampaged through the surrounding countryside, killing a dog and demolishing a parked automobile. Finally, he plunged into the South Saskatchewan River and swam to a refuge on an uninhabited island. As of this writing, Carlson was still searching for the fugitive yak, and hoping to collect the $200,000 he estimated he would need to provide enough yak semen, along with other amenities, to impregnate his cattle.

**Most Unusual Lizard:** The horned toad is armed and travels under an alias. Actually, it is not a toad at all, but a lizard—a kissing cousin of the iguana. You can recognize the horned toad by its spiny armor and bloodshot eyes, or rather its eyes which shoot blood.

Whenever this singular reptile is under the stress of great fright or anger, it constricts a muscle in its neck, closing off its jugular vein. The blood is prevented from returning to the heart; instead, it wells up in the animal's head, causing it to swell. Its eyes bulge as if they are about to pop out, and finally the pressure becomes so intense that a very fine stream of blood is discharged from an agglomeration of blood vessels at the corner of each eye. The effective squirting range is about six feet. Mixed with the blood is an irritant substance that further discourages any predator craving a horned toad for dinner.

This sanguine talent is unique in the animal kingdom.

**Most Unusual Meowing:** In the 1830s, in a classic case of mass hysteria, the nuns at a prominent French convent took to gathering together daily over a period of several weeks and meowing loudly like cats for several hours on end.

**Most Unusual Reproductive Organs:** The penis of the male flatworm is nature's answer to the Swiss army knife: apart from its copulative and excretory functions, the penis, which protrudes from the mouth, is rigged with spiky protuberances and poison-secreting glands, making it an excellent device for catching prey.

**Most Unusual Snail:** The slipper-shell snail, known also as *c. fornicata,* comes into the world totally exposed to life's indignities, and spends its formative years growing a protective shell. When the shell is complete, thus signaling the *fornicata*'s coming of age, the snail settles upon a rock and waits for Mr. Right to come along. When he does, he climbs atop his enamored's back and the two indulge in a session of subdued love-play that is necessarily homosexual since all slipper-shell snails are born male and then turn female at a certain age.

While snails one and two are thus engaged, yet a third comes along, and piles on, then a fourth and a fifth. The process continues until the vertical orgy reaches a height of eight or ten snails, some male, others female, and none particularly concerned about the sex of those adjacent to it. The snails remain stacked in this position until they die.

**Most Unusual State Animal:** As of 1975, Connecticut had no official state animal, a lack that many of the Nutmeg State's citizenry found too painful to bear. (After all, Connecticut has the distinction of being the only state in the union with a law specifically giving beavers the right to build dams.) The matter was introduced to the floor of the State House of Representatives and Senator Denardis immediately nominated the sperm whale. Senator Page was partial to squirrels, however, and challenged Denardis on one crucial point: there were no whales, sperm or otherwise, in Connecticut. Whereupon Senator Cutillo took the floor to declaim, "We have living proof that all squirrels aren't in trees."

A fourth colleague introduced the white-tailed deer, and that appealed to a lot of people until someone else pointed out that the white-tailed deer is more commonly known as the Virginia deer—clearly an inappropriate choice as Connecticut's state animal. Yet another senator, inspired by the shining pate of one of his colleagues, proposed the bald eagle. That proposal too was tabled.

It was Senator Neidtz who proposed *Homo sapiens*, and the motion was carried by a 21–13 vote. However, the vote was postponed and the matter bottled up in committee. Connecticut still doesn't have a state animal.

Nor does Mississippi have a state spider, in spite of recent legislative efforts to accord the black widow spider that honor. Comparable bills were introduced to make the earthworm the official state worm, the vampire the state bat, and the wharf rat the state rat. All were defeated. However, Governor Milton Shapp of Pennsylvania did sign into law in 1974 a bill making the firefly the official insect of that state.

**Most Unusual Variation of the Jack-and-the-Beanstalk Story:** To make the grass grow greener, Mr. and Mrs. Charles O'Neall of Tavares, Florida, fertilized their lawn with three tons of raw, fudgelike sewage. While the grass showed no special improvement, forty thousand tomato plants cropped up unexpectedly. Said Mr. O'Neall, "I don't quite know how you say it politely, but they came from people. Tomato seeds aren't digested."

**Most Unusual Worms:** Probably the best educated worms in captivity live in the laboratory of Dr. James V. McConnell of the University of Michigan. With infinite patience, Dr. McConnell has taught planarians, the common flatworms found in streams and ponds, to crawl through a series of complex mazes. Then he ruthlessly cut his educated worms in half. As worms will do, the head section grew a new tail and the tail section grew a new head; and both regenerated worms retained the maze-running skills of the original undivided specimen.

Next, McConnell took trained worms, diced them into bite-sized morsels, and fed them to uneducated worms. Placed in the same maze that the "victims" had learned to run, the cannibal worms exhibited an uncanny sense of direction. Apparently, by devouring the trained worms they had also ingested their memories and maze-running ability.

Should the reader care to conduct his own worm-running experiments, or scrounge up some good fishing bait, may we recommend the tried-and-true technique of "worm fiddling" or "worm grunting." Simply pound a four-foot hardwood stake into the ground and rub a piece of flat iron vigorously across the top; this creates intense vibrations and a god-awful noise that drives every worm within thirty feet to the surface. Worm fiddling can be tremendously effective, as they demonstrate each year at the International Worm Fiddling Championship in Caryville, Florida. In 1972 one virtuoso fiddled up seventy-four worms in thirty minutes. There is one restriction, however: To fiddle for worms in a national park, you must apply for an official United States Worm Gathering License.

**Most Unusual Zoo:** If you're bored with the tepid fare offered by most American zoos—caged zebras, smart-aleck chimpanzees that spit, smirking parrots, the inevitable array of water buffalo, geese, and trained seals—there is one place in Washington, D.C., where you will be able to glimpse zoological oddities that boggle the mind. And it isn't the Senate cloak room.

"When space explorers reach the outermost fringes of the universe, I think they will find that truth is stranger than fiction," says Alexis Doster, the curator of an exhibit of twenty-seven paintings of bizarre but altogether imaginable animals at the Smithsonian Institution's Air and Space Museum. The animals include the Squish, a cross between a shark and a squid; the Great Filter Bat, a 150-pound winged rodent that swoops through the atmosphere snatching insects in midflight; and the elephantine—and presumably frumious—Bandersnatch, best described as a 10,000-pound centipede.

"While we don't know for a fact that such creatures actually exist," says Doster, "the exhibit is not in the least science fiction." Says John Glendenning, a technologist who helped design the exhibit, "What the animals look like depends entirely on the evolution of the individual planet—how old it is, how hot or cold, how strong its gravity, and the oxygen content of the atmosphere."

# Business and Finance

**Best Advertising Medium:** What kind of man reads *Playboy?* Father Joseph F. Lupo, vocations director for the Order of the Most Holy Trinity, placed a $10,000 advertisement in the January 1971 issue of *Playboy* in an effort to recruit new priests. The ad pulled over six hundred inquiries. Father Lupo called the response "most gratifying" and noted that in terms of replies per advertising dollar spent, it was the most successful advertisement the Order had ever run.

**Best Currency:** While rubber checks are no less worthless than they ever were, rubber prophylactics are in such supply in certain parts of southeast Asia, according to *Forbes* magazine, that they are accepted as tokens on buses.

**Best Dunning Letter:** Patients who are tardy in paying their bills at the Charleston, West Virginia, General Hospital receive this form letter: "Hello there, I am the hospital's computer. As yet, no one but me knows that you have not been making regular payments on this account. However, if I have not processed a payment from you within ten days, I will tell a human, who will resort to other means of collection."

**Best Insurance Policy:** A University of Arizona undergraduate, Stan Mazanek, took an insurance company up on its direct-mail offer of cut-rate prices for students by taking out a six-month policy on a sixty-cent guppy, at a premium of one dollar. He didn't note on the application form that the insured was a fish, but then no one asked. Nevertheless, he did answer all questions accurately, supplying the height of the insured (three centimeters), and its age (six months). Mazanek received a bona fide insurance policy, with himself as beneficiary. When the guppy expired, Mazanek filed his claim and was promptly turned down—whereupon he threatened the insurers with a lawsuit. Much chagrined, the company came up with a $650 out-of-court settlement.

**Best Management:** The American Institute of Management performs the vital service of ranking major industries in terms of management performance. In 1956, the AIM evaluated the Roman Catholic Church, awarding Pope Pius XII and his mitered executives 8,800 points out of a possible 10,000. Four years later, under Pope John XXIII, the "management excellence rating" climbed to 9,010 points. Pope John's team scored significant gains in the categories of "Trustee Analysis" and "Administrative Evaluation." (We were unable to locate a rating for Pope Paul.)

With a 9,000-plus rating, the Church ranks among the best-managed institutions in the world, in an exalted class with the Aluminum Company of America, AT & T, Kodak, du Pont, GE, GM, 3M, National Cash Register, Proctor & Gamble, and Standard Oil.

**Best Nickels:** Joshua Tatum, a nineteenth-century counterfeiter, was deaf, but he wasn't dumb. With a jeweler's aid he made a small fortune turning several thousand nickels into five-dollar gold coins. When the law caught up with him, which did not take very long, there were no grounds whatsoever on which to penalize him.

It happened in 1883. Noticing that the Roman numeral "V" on five-cent pieces did not specify cents, dollars, pfennigs or corn plasters, Tatum hired a jeweler to plate several thousand coins with gold and mill the edges so that they looked like five-dollar pieces. Tatum then went from store to store making five-cent purchases with his newly minted coins. Stone deaf, he accepted the $4.95 in change pushed across the counter at him without a word. It wasn't long before he had amassed a pile of five-cent goods and a tidy bankroll.

At the inevitable court trial, the merchants he'd bilked came by the wagonload to point an angry finger at Tatum, but in the end he was acquitted. The reason was that he had never actually purchased more than five cents worth of merchandise with any of the coins, and as for the $4.95 in change—well, he never *asked* for it, did he?

In spite of the acquittal, the United States mint soon made it clear that a nickel was worth five *cents.* And defacing, marring, or otherwise altering United States currency became a federal crime.

**Best Philanthropist:** In 1974, a woman stationed herself on a midtown Manhattan street corner and began handing out money—real, legal tender United States currency in singles, fives, tens, and twenties—to any and all who passed her way. By the time police arrested her, she had given away $1,563; she still had another $1,400 in her possession. The charge? There was none. The woman was given the standard psychiatric once-over at Bellevue Hospital, found sane, and released. Police said she had violated no laws, other than those of human nature.

**Best Status Symbol:** Instead of purchasing a Porsche or a refrigerator that dispenses ice cubes and cold water right through the door, why not impress the neighbors by building your own private tower? For homeowners in the small Italian town of San Gimignano during the fourteenth century, a lofty tower was the ultimate status symbol. The first turret was probably constructed for protection against the incessant street fighting between the Guelphs and Ghibellines. But soon, for reasons of prestige, other lords began building towers of their own, each trying to outdo his rivals. In a matter of a few years, seventy-two spires sprang up; fourteen survive to this day giving San Gimignano its nickname, "the Manhattan of Tuscany."

**Best Tax:** In Hungary these days, the earnings of hack writers and other purveyors of kitsch in its various forms are subject to a special "trash tax" levied by the Ministry of Culture, and put in a special "Culture Fund" used to endow nobler artistic endeavors.

Of course, the differentiation of trash from art is no mean challenge, but nonetheless it's one which Budapest's culture czars, along with the authors of this book, embrace eagerly. Trash, by their definition, is anything that panders to popular tastes. Walter Keane's paintings of saucer-eyed children are considered trash and taxed heavily because of their huge sales; so are Jacqueline Susann's novels—every last one of them—along with plastic flowers, ugly furniture, and Muzak.

But it isn't only the merely tasteless that is subject to the trash tax. Any novel or film, for example, that stands to make a huge profit, regardless of its redeeming social or aesthetic merit, is taxed. Thus, the mysteries of Agatha Christie and the comedies of Neil Simon, both tremendously popular in Hungary, are fertile sources of Culture Fund revenue—not because they are artistically worthless, but because they are infinitely profitable.

**Best Tax Deduction:** Have you been paying off your philosophy professor to give you passing marks in Introductory Ethics? Write it off your taxes.

The Internal Revenue Service's 1971 official taxpayer's guide advises,

San Gimignano, the "Manhattan of Tuscany"

"Bribes and kickbacks to nongovernmental officials are deductible unless the individual has been convicted of making the bribe or has entered a plea of guilty or *nolo contendere*."

**Best Way to Face the Specter of Spiraling Inflation:** There'll be pfennigs from heaven for you, me, and anyone else willing to try his hand at panhandling in Düsseldorf, West Germany. In that city's nightlife district, a thirty-six-year-old man boasted upon his arrest in October 1975 of having amassed over $30,000 in handouts over a twelve-year period. Oddly, he was arrested not simply for begging, but for doing it dishonestly: he had cadged money from passersby by telling them he had just been released from prison and was down on his luck. Apparently the people of Düsseldorf are an easy mark.

This isn't to say, of course, that generosity to beggars is an exclusively Teutonic trait. That same year, Gene Weingarten, a reporter for the New York *Post*, stationed himself on one of midtown Manhattan's busier street corners and spent eight hours cadging small change from pedestrians. By day's end he had collected $48.96. Extrapolate that amount to a full working year—allowing time off for vacations and paid holidays—and you have a net annual income of $12,729, which, Weingarten pointed out, is equivalent to a gross salary of over $17,000. (One possible reason that panhandlers do as well as they do is that they are not afraid to think big. The Wall Street brokerage firm of Spencer, Trask, and Co., studied panhandling trends in New York recently and found that the average request for change has increased two and a half times in recent years. Brother, can you spare a quarter?)

If mere begging strikes you as a rather uninventive method of earning extra cash, you might take a lead from John and Stephanie Bates, of Conway, Arkansas, who figured there was a good living to be made in TV game shows. The Bateses quit Conway, moved to Hollywood, and racked up nearly $42,000 in cash and prizes in less than eighteen months. "The job market is so bad that we just decided the game shows were a good way to make a lot of money fast," said Mr. Bates.

Equally enterprising was Toshio Shimizu, a Tokyo welder who continually showed up uninvited at weddings, posing as a relative of the bride, and then deftly made off with one or more of the gifts. By the time police closed in on him, Shimizu had amassed over $13,000 worth of merchandise. Regrettably, he was arrested, jailed, and, unlike the Bateses, forced to return the booty. However, a 28-year-old jobless ex-G.I. in Minneapolis has proven that crashing *funerals* can be fun, profitable, and risk-free. According to *Harper's Weekly*, the nameless veteran appeared at funerals for several months and ate better than ever. "The next of kin have no way of knowing if you're a friend of the deceased," he explained. "After the service they invite everyone to the reception. The meals are generally excellent." A freeloader? Perhaps. But, he adds, "You have to admit one thing. I didn't go on welfare."

---

**Worst Advertising Jingle:** The copywriters on the Beecham's Pills account—Beecham's being a popular British laxative—have not ared well in their recent invocations to the muse. Most of their ad copy is dull, pedestrian stuff, suggesting the predictable link between clogged pipes and sluggish ways: "If sometimes you feel dull, out of sorts, less than your best," says one typically uninspired advertisement, "the cause could easily be constipation." Hardly the pinnacle of English prose.

In more florid times, Beecham's ad writers were able to fuse Christian theology and the mechanics of bowel evacuation to come up with this Christmastime jingle:

> Hark! the herald angels sing,
> Beecham's Pills are just the thing.
> Peace on earth and mercy mild,
> Two for man and one for child.

**Worst Bargain:** While literature is rife with stories of Faustian strivers who barter their soul to the devil for a few years of power and happiness, a man in Stockholm actually did make such a deal in 1840, although not with Satan, but with the Royal Swedish Institute of Anatomy. Out of work and in need of cash, the man sold the Institute the rights to claim his body on his death for use in the dissection labs.

Unexpectedly, however, the man was kissed with fortune, and twenty years later he was wealthy enough to buy back the rights to his corpse from the Institute. The Institute, however, refused to cooperate, so the man took his case to court, where he lost. Worst of all, the court required him to reimburse the trustees of the Institute for two permanent teeth that he had had extracted without their approval.

In any event, our hero might have done better had he lived in today's inflated times: as recently as 1970, the total market value of the human body, including fat, protein, ash, minerals, muscle tissue, eyebrows, pus pimples, and assorted fluids, was $2.10. But by 1975, the price had climbed 167 percent to a respectable $5.60, according to Northwestern University biochemist Donald Forman. That's based on a body weight of 150 pounds.

Moreover, human milk now goes for $25.60 per gallon, blood for as much as $50 a pint, and a full head of hair for $150 and more. The market is also bullish for semen, placentas, and teeth—and human skeletons fetch between $250 and $500, depending on quality and size.

**Worst Creditor:** Yosjiyuki Yonei, a salesman working for a Tokyo tool company, was arrested for telephoning a delinquent customer 4,190 times—340 times in a single day—to collect on an unpaid bill. The customer said the calls caused his wife to have a nervous breakdown.

**Worst Investment:** Tulips were first introduced to Europe in 1559 by Conrad Gesner, who brought back specimens from the royal gardens of Constantinople. Because they were exotic, hardy, and brilliantly colored, the handsome spring blooms quickly gained wide popularity with nobles and wealthy landowners in Italy, Germany, and France, but most of all in Holland.

By the 1620s tulip culture had become a mania—tulipomania, as historians have called it. Tulip prices had been rising steadily for half a century, and there was tremendous confidence that the boom market would continue indefinitely. The bourgeoisie and even the peasants began to acquire tulips at fantastic prices, not out of a love for flowers, but in hopes of making a fortune in the flourishing, bulbous economy.

In 1623 a Paris collector refused to sell ten prized bulbs for 12,000 francs ($30,000). Not long afterwards, 120 tulip bulbs auctioned off for the benefit of an orphanage in the Netherlands brought 90,000 florins or roughly the equivalent of 10,800 sheep in the economy of that age.

Tulipomania was at its maddest in 1637, when Tulip Exchanges were established in Amsterdam, Rotterdam, Harlaam, Leyden, and other cities throughout Europe. Trading was vigorous. Speculators invested heavily in tulip futures and followed the rise and fall of the daily tulip quotations as avidly as today's brokers watch the fluctuations of the Dow Jones averages.

Farmers abandoned food crops and devoted their attention to the cultivation and hybridization of the red, yellow, and lavender blossoms. Among the most valuable were the *Admiral Van der Eyck, Childer*, and *Viceroy* varieties, and a single *Semper Augustus* bulb could go for as much as 2,000 florins—the equivalent of eighty fat swine.

Then, late in 1637, the inevitable crash occurred with effects as dismal and far-reaching as Black Friday on the New York Stock Exchange. In a matter of days even the magnificent *Admiral Liefken* tulips fell to about one-twelfth their previous value. Ruined investors jumped out of windmills to their deaths; the poor were reduced to eating the bulbs they had purchased with their life savings. Fearing total financial chaos and the collapse of all credit, the Dutch government stepped in and declared a moratorium on the tulip trade and cancelled all tulip debts.

**Worst Job:** Much as Alan Lefler, of Des Moines, Iowa, dreaded being asked at parties what he did for a living, his job itself was vastly more unpalatable. Lefler spent forty hours a week burning the carcasses of unwanted dogs and cats for the Scott County Humane Society.

The job made him ill, caused him to vomit and shiver, and produced alternating fits of insomnia and nightmares. Finally Lefler quit and appealed to the Iowa Employment Security Commission for unemployment benefits, claiming that the $10,600-a-year job required "constant stoking, tending, poking and prodding of the burning carcasses, suffering the stench and odor, and actually seeing the flames consume the body."

To be sure, any number of factors can make a job unappealing: its sheer difficulty, the hazards involved, the repellent nature of the work, or its spirit-chilling dullness. In a report for *U.S. News and World Report*, a New Jersey manpower consultant, Roy Walters, produced a list of the ten most boring jobs. Leading the list was assembly-line work, and in second place was "elevator operator in a push-button elevator."

**Worst Job Title:** Thirty women, hired in 1974 by a Canadian construction company to fasten clusters of steel rods to a crane, organized to protest being designated as "hookers."

**Worst Landlord:** How sharper than a serpent's tooth it is to have a thankless landlord: *Moneysworth* magazine reported that a Chicago landlord evicted his mother because she could not meet the rent and refused to move.

Circuit judge Edwin C. Hatfield, who presided over the internecine dispute in renters' court, said, "It was pathetic. Because of taxes and upkeep costs the man felt he just had to collect the rent on the apartment his mother occupied."

In all fairness to the son, however, we should add that after giving his mother the gate, he dutifully invited her to move in with him. But, Judge Hatfield noted, "she detested his wife and refused." In the end, the judge felt he had no choice but to sign the eviction order, giving the betrayed parent fifteen days to vacate the premises.

**Worst Promotion Device:** The United States Consumer Product Safety Commission recently paid some $1,700 for 80,000 promotional buttons with the slogan, "Think Toy Safety." Ironically, the buttons themselves were more of a danger than any toy ever concocted by the most socially irresponsible toy manufacturer. The metal tags had sharp, unrounded edges and metal tab fasteners that broke off easily and were a sure bet to be swallowed by orally aggressive children. Worst yet, the buttons were coated with lead paint. Much chagrined, the Commission recalled the buttons, with an eye to recycling them—as weapons of war, perhaps?— or just scuttling the lot.

**Worst Real Estate Project:** History's worst defense system—the Maginot Line—is now being broken into lots and sold as sites for hotels, summer bungalows, and tourist havens.

Built by the French as a barricade against German invasions in 1940, the Maginot Line, extending nearly 200 miles from Belfort, France, to the Belgian border, crumbled quickly, and France fell to the Nazis soon thereafter. Now a German real estate firm has purchased the line and all its battlements outright. To date the land parcels moving the fastest are those with subterranean bunkers, which can be easily converted to resort hotels. Asking price is forty-seven dollars per bunker, an undisputed bargain since they cost as much as $1.2 million to build.

**Worst Steel-Driving Man:** The Transcontinental Railroad was completed on May 10, 1869, when the Union Pacific linked up with the Central Pacific just outside Promontory, Utah. On that momentous occasion, as everyone learns in grammar school, representatives of the two great railroad companies met to drive the Golden Spike. But the history books usually neglect to tell the whole story.

Leland Stanford, president of the Central Pacific, had the honor of taking the first whack at the spike. He gripped the handle firmly, raised the fifteen-pound sledge hammer above his head, brought it down with a mighty stroke—and missed completely. The crowd was solemn as Stanford passed the hammer to Thomas C. Durant, vice president of the Union Pacific. Durant also swung and missed, perhaps out of politeness. The job of driving the spike was left to the professionals.

**Most Unusual Accident Insurance:** Waterbed accident insurance is now available from the Maryland Casualty Company. For an annual premium of fifteen dollars, policyholders can insure their floors and ceilings against the ravages of leaky, volatile, or otherwise aberrant waterbeds up to $100,000 in damages.

**Most Unusual Advertising Medium:** Cows grazing in the English countryside near the London-Brighton railroad line wear coats carrying advertisements for bourbon, razor blades, and toothpaste. It's the work of a London-based ad agency.

**Most Unusual Baby-Sitter:** If summer vacation is coming up and you're not keen on sending the kids off to camp, here's an exciting alternative: *you* go off to camp—or the Spanish Riviera—and leave the kids at home. University Home Services, located in University Park, Pennsylvania, offers a "Rent-a-Parent" service to vacationing parents for a $24-a-day fee. In your absence the surrogate couple will move into your home and care for your children, clean the house, and keep the crabgrass cut.

**Most Unusual Business Card:** Police in Canada recently designed a wallet-sized card to be carried by business executives explaining what to do in case they are kidnapped.

**Most Unusual Contractual Clause:** In the interests of both his personal safety and his employer's investment, Johnny Roventini, the four-foot-tall midget who appeared as a bellhop in countless Philip Morris cigarette commercials, was forbidden by the terms of his contract with the tobacco company from riding the New York City subways during rush hours.

**Most Unusual Convention:** Britt, Iowa, is the perennial site of the National Hobo Convention. The event attracts hoboes from all over the

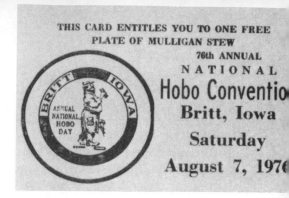

THIS CARD ENTITLES YOU TO ONE FREE
PLATE OF MULLIGAN STEW
76th ANNUAL
N A T I O N A L
Hobo Conventio
Britt, Iowa
Saturday
August 7, 1976

Ticket to the Annual Hobo Convention

country—as few as a dozen during good times, as many as fifty in bad years.

Actually, the convention dates back to 1900 when activist hoboes organized a mass-meeting of their own in Britt; it was an excuse to get together, tell lies, cuss, share some cheap wine, and talk over common problems encountered while riding the rails. The local Chamber of Commerce invited the hoboes back in 1933, and every year since then, as the honored guests of the town. Predictably, a carnival has been staged around them, featuring a Mulligan stew dinner and an election to choose the Queen and King of Hoboes.

Some eight thousand tourists congregate to sample the stew and ride the ferris wheel. But there are also authentic hoboes in attendance—unshaven men with names like Steamtrain Maury, Lord Open Road (elected king in 1973 and 1974), and Slow Motion Shorty. Railroad guards look the other way for a few days as the early morning freight pulls into town and discharges its passengers. And the people of Britt stake every hobo to a $7.50 per diem allowance and provide a cozy cell in the local jail to stay in free of charge.

**Most Unusual Income Tax Payment:** In 1973 an irate taxpayer from Oregon paid his federal income taxes with a plaster-of-paris check weighing several pounds.

**Most Unusual Insurance Policy:** When a teen-age Italian girl announced in 1971 that she was going off to work as a waitress in Germany, her family, fearing her morals might be corrupted, decided to insure her virginity. After negotiating with several firms, they took out a $1,400 policy with the Italo-Peruvian Insurance Company in Rome. Premiums were set at a modest $1.75 per month. Italo-Peruvian has discreetly refused to reveal whether the family ever collected.

Incidentally, concerned with his professional image, Flamenco dancer José Greco once took out a policy through Lloyd's of London against his pants splitting during a performance.

**Most Unusual Laundered Money:** A surprising note: in pre-Watergate times United States government officials laundered their own money without sending it to Mexico. During the Wilson Administration the Treasury Department tried cutting corners by drycleaning soiled currency rather than burning it and printing new bills. The experiment ended during World War I when shortages of wood pulp made it necessary to print money on a cheaper grade of paper that could not withstand vigorous cleaning.

When the Great War ended, the government considered returning to its pressing-and-cleaning system, but the Secret Service, entrusted with the responsibility of preventing counterfeiting, complained that genuine paper money, once laundered, was impossible to distinguish from funny money. Since then, no money has been laundered.

**Most Unusual Nonprofit Organization:** A topless/bottomless nightclub in Chicago earned special tax breaks recently by claiming to be a nonprofit organization. However, its charter was revoked when Illinois Attorney General William Scott learned that the club had been charging its guests $35 for soft drinks.

**Most Unusual Occupational Hazard:** You've heard of athlete's foot. Would you believe historian's lung?

There is such an ailment—a bronchial infection marked by shortness of breath, wheezing, and overall debilitation, generally brought on by excessive exposure to old books. In a report in *Science Digest*, Wilfred Spencer, a British librarian, described his own symptoms—the first ever recorded: "I spent eight hours a week moving old books around, rearranging them, and withdrawing them. I was right in the middle of a pretty horrific concentration of moldy documents. I became increasingly breathless and my general health became progressively worse." While Spencer's symptoms baffled physicians at first, matters were cleared up when he recalled that the pages of some of the dustier tomes he had been handling were festooned with tiny fungi—virus-infected fungi, it turned out. Now warnings have been issued to the British Libraries' Association and the Society of Archivists.

If you are, in fact, a historian, and considering a job change because excessive reading may be hazardous to your health, don't try meat packing. Scientists at the University of Oregon Health Science Center have identified yet another highly unusual occupational hazard—meat packer's asthma. It's a broadly defined syndrome of wheezing, coughing, and nasal congestion caused by inhaling fumes from the heated plastic wrapping in which supermarket meats are packed.

There are also unexpected risks in the fine arts and physics. Medical historians now theorize that the haunted visions depicted in Goya's late paintings were the result of delusions brought on by lead poisoning. Goya mixed his own heavily leaded paints. Likewise, professors J. R. M. Seitz of Harvard and Jerome Y. Lettvin of MIT have suggested that Isaac Newton's palsy, paranoia, and decline in productivity at the age of fifty-four were caused by chronic mercury poisoning. In his optical experiments, Newton made extensive use of mercury.

One final note in this morbid vein: A California professor, John H. Winslow, speculates that Charles Darwin's poor health and deep despondency were the result of daily applications of arsenic used to treat his eczema.

**Most Unusual Pay Cut:** Sam "Mr. Clean" Silverstein, a self-declared independent candidate for president, suggests taking United States congressmen off salary and paying them instead "on a straight commission basis."

**Most Unusual Tax Exemption:** A man operating a fully franchised temple of love out of his home in Rochdale, England, where women came for advice on sex problems, applied for a tax exemption on his property. He claimed that his house was a place of worship.

**Most Unusual Union Demand:** Gold miners in Suva, Fiji, not content with a midday lunch hour, are now clamoring for a thirty-minute "sex break," as well. According to a representative of the mine workers, "as it now stands, the men are so exhausted by the end of the working day that they are unable to fulfill their husbandly obligations to their wives. A half-hour recess just after lunch, when they are rested and their sexual powers and inclinations are at their peak, is essential." The spokesman added that the demand is being made on behalf of married union members only.

(Unmarried sailors in the Greek navy are similarly excluded from the benefits of a regulation stipulating that if a married sailor dies while engaged in sex during shore leave, his family is entitled to receive a pension.)

**Most Unusual Union Member:** A two-hundred twenty-five-pound African lion was recruited by picketing automobile mechanics in Detroit as an attention-grabber. According to *The Wall Street Journal*, the lion was named an honorary Teamster for his efforts.

# Goods and Services

**Best Automobile:** Joseph H. Wherry, a former editor of *Motor Trend*, has stated that the Type 41 Bugatti is "probably the world's most elegant and technically perfect car." Only six hand-assembled specimens were ever manufactured, the last one completed in 1939, making the Type 41 the rarest and most expensive of collectors' models.

Ettore Bugatti decided to build the Type 41 in 1927 because of a cocktail-party conversation he had with an outspoken Englishwoman. "Mr. Bugatti," the woman said, "you undoubtedly make the world's fastest automobiles, but I'm afraid the Rolls Royce is still the finest." Deeply hurt, Bugatti went back to his shop and immediately began work on the plans for his masterpiece.

The Type 41 was the epitome of engineering excellence. Under the seven-foot-long hood was a 12.7 liter eight-cylinder engine capable of generating 300 horsepower. The car would accelerate to 95 mph in second gear, and in third she hit 125 without so much as a shudder. The pistons sang grand opera. Furthermore, the Type 41 offered high-styling, incomparable luxury, and a long, sleek 170-inch wheel base.

Dubbed the Royale, every Type 41 was custom-made and totally guaranteed for the lifetime of the original owner. Ettore screened prospective buyers himself, paying special attention to their pedigrees; he sold his Royale only to bona fide kings and princes—no mere dukes or millionaires need apply. The sticker price was $55,000.

A Type 41 convertible is on display at the Henry Ford Museum in Greenfield, Michigan.

**Best Bed:** The McDonald's Corporation, which at last count had sold over twelve billion burgers, has installed a seven hundred-gallon hamburger-shaped waterbed in the "brainstorming chamber" of their Oak Brook, Illinois, headquarters. Executives are encouraged to take time

The 1930 Bugatti "Royale"

out from their busy schedules to lounge on the "burger bed" and dream up new concepts in fast foods.

**Best Clock:** As his own personal tribute to America's centennial observances, clockmaker Felix Meier of Detroit labored ten years, beginning in 1866, on the clock to end all clocks. When completed, it stood eighteen feet high, weighed two tons, and recorded the time of thirteen cities, along with the day, month, year, season, zodiac sign, and the revolution of the planets of the solar system.

Even more impressive was the manner in which the hours were chimed. In the words of one contemporary observer, a mechanical George Washington "slowly rises from the chair (beneath the canopy) . . . extending his right hand, presenting the Declaration of Independence. The door on the left is opened . . . admitting all the presidents, including President Hayes. . . . Passing in file before Washington, they face and raise their hands as they approach him, and walking naturally across the platform, disappear through the opposite door. . . . Washington retires into his chair, and all is quiet save the measured tick of the huge pendulum. . . ."

Bicentennial fireplug

**Best Comfort Facilities:** A co-ed public restroom for dogs—and, presumably, other quadrupeds as well—was installed recently in San Francisco's Golden Gate Park. Modeled after the Dutch "Hondentoilet," the facility is a five-foot-square sandpit enclosed by an eighteen-inch-high retaining wall. Park gardeners clean it kitty-litter-style every evening. (In Warren, Rhode Island, these days, where the doggie commode has not yet been introduced, canines can relieve themselves on fire hydrants repainted to look like American Revolutionary soldiers. The left-handed honor is the work of the Warren Bicentennial Commission.)

And while California was experimenting with canine comfort stations, New York City's Environmental Protection Administration had joined forces with the Sanitation, Police, and Health departments in a two-month campaign to teach dog owners "how to train their dogs to defecate in sewers." The plan, unfortunately, did not work, and ultimately the entire effort fell victim to the massive budget cuts forced on the city by economic pressures.

The encouragement of fastidiousness among animals, incidentally, was carried to elephantine lengths at the Portland, Oregon, Zoo, where a shower stall designed specially for elephants was introduced. A car wash

Elephants' shower stall at the
Portland Zoo

in its former life, the shower is a big hit with the pachyderms, who are
being trained to turn it on and off themselves.

**Best Keepsake:** After a three-day bout with cholera, five-year old Max
Hoffman of Wisconsin died. The year was 1865.

Max was buried in the village cemetery, but that night his mother's
sleep was troubled by visions of her son still breathing and trying to claw
his way out of the coffin. In the middle of the night she woke up screaming and told her husband of the nightmare, insisting that they dress and
go at once to the grave to rescue the child. Mr. Hoffman consoled his
wife, telling her that her vision was the product of grief and nerves. The
two went back to sleep.

The following night Mrs. Hoffman had the same dream, and this time
she *insisted* that the boy was still alive. Reluctantly, her husband took
shovels and a couple of neighbors and went to exhume the body. With
the coffin before them, they pried open the cover and found the boy
lying on his side--although he had been buried on his back, in the conventional manner. He appeared lifeless, but Hoffman lifted the body
from the box and took it home to be examined by the family physician.

The doctor found a weak pulse, and began massaging the boy's heart and trying to revive him with sips of brandy. After an hour, little Max opened his eyes, and his pulse grew more distinct. Remarkably, he was on his feet within a few days, and a week later was leading the life of a normally active five-year-old.

Max Hoffman lived into his eighties. To his dying day the possession he cherished most dearly was the pair of brass handles he had unscrewed from his coffin.

**Best Pay Telephone:** The pay phone near the ticket counter at the Greyhound Bus Terminal in downtown Chicago is, according to Bell System researchers, the most heavily used in the United States, averaging 270 calls a day. Most pay phones average about eighteen.

---

**Worst Automobile:** How did the automobile industry's most egregious flop acquire a name that rhymes with pretzel? It was the result of a massive marketing research campaign. Ford executives left no stone unturned in their efforts to select the ideal monicker for their new entry into the mid-size car field. They even entered into a lengthy correspondence with the poet Marianne Moore. "We should like this name . . . to convey through association or other conjuration some visceral feeling of elegance, fleetness, advanced features and design," the research director explained. And who knows how successful the new automobile would have been had Ford adopted Bullet Cloisonné . . . Utopian Turtletop . . . Pastelogram . . . Mongoose Civique . . . Andante con Moto . . . or one of Miss Moore's other imaginative suggestions. But when the chairman of the board looked over the list of finalists, he disregarded the offerings of the poets, and he ignored the conclusions of the man-in-the-street interviews (who favored the name "Corsair"). "I don't like any of them," he said. Then looking over the roster of 18,000 discarded ideas, his eyes fell on the euphonious Edsel— there as a concession to the Ford family's vanity. "Let's call it that," he decided, and the die was cast.

A consumerist might nominate the unsafe-at-any-speed Corvair for honors as the worst car, but from the industry's point of view the Corvair was a success, until Ralph Nader spoiled it; the Edsel, which lost an estimated $350 million, was the ultimate disaster. Not that the Edsel was a well-engineered car; it wasn't. A company spokesman admitted that in the first model year (1958) no more than half of the Edsels manufactured actually performed properly. A car tested by the Consumer

The 1958 Edsel

Union was not atypical: It had the wrong axle ratio and the power steering pump leaked . . . an expansion plug in the cooling system blew, and the rear axle gears produced horrible, grinding sounds . . . the heater heated even when it was turned off.

Americans were ready for the transition to small cars, and Detroit gave us another overpowered, push-button, gas-guzzling giant. The horizontal fins were monstrous; the front grill, which resembled a sucked lemon, was a kitsch classic. *Time* called it "the wrong car for the wrong market at the wrong time." *Business Week* called it "a nightmare." By the time ads began to proclaim "The Edsel is a success—It's a new idea—It's a you idea," the car was already a laughingstock. When, after two years, two months, and fifteen days, production on the Edsel assembly line was mercifully halted, only 109,466 had been sold, many of those to Ford dealers, executives, and advertising men.

Only 2,864 Edsels were built in the 1960 model year, making it a genuine collector's item. And although it seems a little like joining a fan club for the Chicago Fire (WFL), proud Edsel admirers have now banned together to form the Edsel Owners of America. The organization, based in West Liberty, Illinois, boasts some 1,600 members. The Chairman of Governors is Edsel Henry Ford of California, no relation to the motor company Fords. They sponsor an annual meet where diehard owners socialize and swap information about where to find spare parts.

**Worst Cigar:** To discourage visitors from helping themselves to handfuls of his expensive panatelas, Thomas Edison once ordered several boxes of custom-made stogies filled with cabbage leaves. However, when the rank-smelling cigars were delivered to the inventor's laboratory at Menlo Park, New Jersey, his secretary sent them on to his home, where Edison's wife packed them in a trunk that he planned to take with him on a business trip to the West Coast. Consequently, he wound up smoking them himself.

**Worst Fire Extinguisher:** A few hours after West German Chancellor Willy Brandt had laid a wreath at the Tomb of the Unknown Soldier, in Paris, an unidentified thirty-two-year-old Algerian extinguished the Tomb's eternal flame by urinating on it. Police who arrested the unauthorized voider said that while certifiably unstable, he had apparently not intended the act as a comment on Chancellor Brandt's visit.

**Worst Fuel:** Cows burp a lot, but until recently, no one paid much attention. Now researchers at the Texas Department of Highways in Fort Worth are sitting up and taking notice. Each year the bovine population of the United States burps some fifty million tons of valuable hydrocarbons into the atmosphere. If they could only be captured and efficiently channeled, say the researchers, the accumulated burps of ten average cows could keep a small house adequately, if indiscreetly, heated and its stove operating for a year.

**Worst Knife:** A ten-foot long jackknife weighing twenty-seven pounds was built by Bill Farley of Phoenix, Arizona. The knife took him fifteen years to build, has four blades, and is totally useless.

**Worst Purse:** A Detroit inventor has created a woman's handbag made to fall apart when grabbed suddenly. Rationale: a thief will disappear rather than risk being caught while scooping up the spilled contents.

**Worst Shortage:** In the midst of bona fide shortages of fuel oil, copper, firewood, and fertilizer in 1973, millions of Americans began stockpiling toilet paper under the illusion that supplies of the cherished tissue were rapidly dwindling. The scare had started when a congressman noted casually that certain government agencies were having difficulty getting supplies of toilet paper. His innocent remarks made grist for a few Johnny Carson routines, and within weeks, toilet paper shelves in supermarkets were emptied by panicking hoarders. However, according to a public information officer of the Scott Paper Company in Philadelphia, "There is no shortage, nor do we envision any shortage in the next two years."

However, there *was* a real scare when the manufacturers of vitreous china, the stuff of which toilets are made, struck for ten days in 1974.

**Worst Silver:** The very term "German silver" is a lie: there is no silver in German silver. It consists instead of copper, zinc, and nickel.

**Worst Swimming Pool Accessory:** A plastics firm is marketing an inflatable, life-size pool toy of Brian Jones, deceased member of The Rolling Stones, that floats facedown in the water, simulating the guitarist's suicide.

**Worst Telephone System:** Despite reports to the contrary, it is still possible to put through a telephone call in Great Britain these days. It may take some concentrated effort, a half-dozen tries, and cooperative atmospheric condiditions, but it can be done.

Not that it's always worth the try. According to *Which,* the British consumer magazine, costs of operating the telephone system have increased dramatically "whereas the reliability of the service hasn't improved. About one in ten calls still go wrong." Skyrocketing costs and dwindling efficiency, says *Which,* have conspired to make Britain's telephone system among the worst in the world. And the *Daily Mail* of London has observed that the British Post Office, which operates the nation's telephones, has broken all records for fiscal misfortune. In 1975 alone, the newspaper said, the post office lost $722.6 million. That works out to twelve dollars a minute.

---

**Most Unusual Doll:** Women's groups in Connecticut, Pennsylvania, New York, and Massachusetts have called on Mattel Toys, Inc., to stop manufacturing and advertising a girl doll that matures when its arm is twisted.

The "Growing Up Skipper" doll becomes one-quarter-inch taller and develops breasts and an hourglass waistline when its arm is cranked around. The Connecticut Feminist Committees for Media Reform have charged that Skipper is a "grotesque caricature of the female body that invites ridicule" and "caters to psychotic preoccupation with instant culture and the instant sex object." A spokesperson for Mattel retorted that girls love Skipper and accept her for what she is—"two dolls in one." Despite the protests, sales have been good since the doll was introduced in the spring of 1975.

Skipper is not the first doll to receive criticism for being too sexy. A boy doll named Le Petit Frère was withdrawn from over fifty stores throughout the country in 1967 when parents complained that it was an obscene toy. The model for the cuddly moppet was a Renaissance cherub painted by Verrocchio, Leonardo da Vinci's master. A French import distributed in the United States by Creative Playthings, Le Petit Frère boasts that which no boy doll has ever had before, the genitals of a four-month-old male.

An Ohio housewife led the opposition to anatomical honesty; the committee she formed sent thousands of letters to clergymen, politicians, and department store managers expressing moral outrage. Le Petit Frère is now difficult to obtain in retail outlets, at least over the counter. But he has sold well through the mails, even though he's not shipped in a plain brown paper diaper.

**Most Unusual Door-to-Door Salespersons:** Several pharmaceutical manufacturers in Japan have come up with the sexual revolution's answer to the Fuller brush man—the door-to-door condom peddler. According to *Forbes* magazine, most of the salespersons are ex-midwives who hawk their rubbery wares during normal working hours, when they can make their pitch to housewives.

Condoms are for sale, along with other birth control devices, at the world's only known contraceptive boutique, The Rubber Tree, in Seattle, Washington. The store is operated on a non-profit basis by the Zero Population Growth Organization.

**Most Unusual Floor Covering:** The Democrats of Fairfax County, Virginia, raised money in 1975 by selling one-and-a-half-inch squares of the carpeting from the Democratic Party's national headquarters in the Watergate complex. The swatches, which sold for $7.50 each, were mounted on a wooden plaque and festooned with a plastic ladybug. Included in the package was an affidavit affirming that this was, in fact, the carpet trod upon by the Watergate burglars.

**Most Unusual Garbage Pick-up:** In 1975, a twenty-seven-year-old reporter for *The National Enquirer* talked his way out of an arrest after being seized and questioned by police for taking five bags of Henry Kissinger's garbage.

The reporter, Jay Gourley, took the garbage, stored in heavy-duty plastic bags, from the sidewalk in front of Kissinger's home in Georgetown, Maryland. The unauthorized trash pick-up caused Kissinger's wife, Nancy, "grave anguish," according to a State Department official, and Kissinger himself was "revolted" by what he considered "a violation of the privacy of his house."

But was it theft? Police officers and Secret Service agents moved in on Gourley and questioned him for two and a half hours before he convinced them that garbage once discarded is in the public domain.

Needless to say, Gourley spent additional hours sorting out the trash, but came up with little of real news value. He did determine that the Kissingers occasionally throw away *The New York Times* unread, smoke Marlboro cigarettes, drink Coca-Cola in cans, and use store-bought patent medicines. The *Enquirer* also claimed that the garbage contained "hundreds of Secret Service documents."

To be sure, nosing through garbage is not uncommon among hard-nosed information gatherers. According to the *Enquirer,* the FBI itself has sent its operatives rummaging through the trash of private citizens for years. Said one ex-agent, "It's a standard FBI method of investigating anyone they have under surveillance. The FBI even uses it to check on other governmental agencies."

**Most Unusual Jewel:** In eighteenth-century Europe, sugar was such a rare and highly prized commodity that it was included in a list of jewels and precious gems presented as wedding gifts in 1736 to Maria Theresa, the future Queen of Hungary and Bohemia.

**Most Unusual Linen Closet:** The high cost of dying got you down? Then buy now and die later, says the Rocky Mountain Casket Company, of Whitefish, Montana. In 1975 the company's sturdy pine coffins were priced at only $125 each, prompting one official of the firm to urge customers to buy while prices were still low. "The casket can be used as a wine rack or a linen closet until the buyer's time has come," he said.

**Most Unusual Mail Drop:** When the crew members of the German tanker *Hong Kong* learned that they would be steaming past Honolulu without docking, they devised an ingenious way to post their letters: they packed them in an empty oil drum, attached the drum to a wooden buoy, and tossed it overboard. Several hours later the drum was spotted by the crew of a United States Customs patrol boat, who picked up the mysterious capsule and opened it. Inside they found not only the letters but twenty-five dollars in cash, a carton of cigarettes, and a bottle of whiskey to cover postage and handling. The letters were in the mail that afternoon.

**Most Unusual Mail-Order Service:** Having lost a leg in World War II, Jack Norenberg was naturally resentful at having to pay for two shoes when he could use only one. Assuming, and rightly so, that fellow amputees were similarly indignant, Norenberg established a mail-order shoe exchange out of his home in Grand Prairie, Texas. Amputees are invited to send him their useless shoes, in exchange for which Norenberg will send them shoes for the opposite foot. The service is free, but swappers must foot postage costs. The Amputee Shoe and Glove Exchange, operated out of College Station, Texas, works on a similar basis.

Amputee Clarence Foltz, of Clinton, Iowa, has contrived a less pragmatic use for the closetful of unwearable left-footed shoes he has accumulated over the years. "There had been a lot of petty thefts in the neighborhood," he says, "when I thought of a way to get back. I put those shoes out on my porch about six P.M. and before I went to bed they were gone. I reckon someone got a little mad when they got home."

**Most Unusual Paper Airplane:** An airplane made from Passover matzos was entered in the annual Paper Airplane Flying Classic at the University of California in 1973.

**Most Unusual Six-Pack:** Nineteen seventy-six was the year of the Great Bicentennial Semen Sale. For a limited time only, the Midwest Breeders' Cooperative, of Shawano, Wisconsin, offered its customers seven quarts of top-quality bull ejaculate for the price of six. What more appropriate way to honor our Founding Fathers?

**Most Unusual Toilet Seat:** Standing on a toilet seat was considered a breach of social etiquette a century ago, and thus U.S. Patent #90,218 was granted in 1869 to the inventor of a specially designed seat impossible to stand on. The seat had a square, rather than oval, frame, consisting of four wooden rollers, each mounted on its own axle. Sitting comfortably on the seat was no problem, but should the user succumb to the urge to stand on it, the rollers would spin under his feet and throw him to the floor.

# Food

---

**Best Appetite:** When "Diamond Jim" Brady died in April 1917, a post-mortem examination revealed that his stomach was six times the size of a normal man's. As Albert Stevens Crockett observed, "One would be willing to match his shade against the most valiant trencherman of all times." He was a gourmet and gourmand without peer.

At a typical breakfast, Brady devoured vast quantities of hominy, eggs, cornbread, muffins, flapjacks, chops, fried potatoes, and beefsteak, washing it all down with a gallon of fresh orange juice. Generally, he paused for a morning snack at 11:30—two or three dozen clams or Lynnhaven oysters. (Shellfish were Brady's particular passion, and the Maryland dealers always saved their choicest specimens for him, bivalves measuring up to six inches in length.) Not long afterwards, the ravenous gentleman sat down to luncheon, the first serious meal of the day. Another serving of shellfish comprised the first course, followed by two or three deviled crabs, a brace of boiled lobsters, a joint of beef, and an enormous salad. For desert he ate several pieces of homemade pie. And, of course, there was more orange juice.

Here we remind the reader that this is an *average* day at the table, not some gross effort to set a record for gluttony. Brady ate in this grand, omnivorous fashion day-in and day-out. Often he was accompanied by Lillian Russell, the famous actress who tipped the scales at well over 200 pounds; she was Brady's sometime lover and the only person who could match him course for course. When the check arrived, Brady was never afraid to look at the total; his personal collection of dinner jewelry alone was worth well over $2 million. He made his immense fortune as a railroad equipment salesman, financier, and speculator.

Afternoon tea was the occasion for another platter of seafood, accompanied by two or three bottles of lemon soda. Strangely enough, although he indulged every other human appetite to the fullest, Brady

"Diamond Jim" Brady

never drank wine or hard liquor. The highlight of any day was dinner. Brady's favorite restaurant was Charles Rector's at Broadway and Forty-fourth Street in Manhattan. Needless to say, he was always welcome there; Rector once said, "Diamond Jim was the best twenty-five customers we had." The first items on the menu were two or three dozens oysters, six crabs, and two bowls of green turtle soup. Then in sumptuous procession came six or seven lobsters, two canvasback ducks, a double portion of terrapin, sirloin steak, vegetables, and for dessert a platter of French pastries. To top it all off, he singlehandedly wolfed down two pounds of chocolate candy.

Once, Diamond Jim revealed the secret of his fantastic feeding technique: "Whenever I sit down to a meal, I always make a point to leave just four inches between my stummick and the edge of the table. And then, when I can feel 'em rubbin' together pretty hard, I know I've had enough."

**Best Beer Can:** A featured entry in the next edition of the comprehensive *Encyclopedia of Beer Cans* (there really is such a volume) will certainly be the disposable aluminum Amana Beer container. From the point of view of beer-can collectors, thousands of whom belong to the Beer Can Collectors of America based in St. Louis, Amana may be the true king of beers. Generally, beer cans are stamped out by the tens of millions, but production of Amana Beer was stopped after just 40,800 cans had been stocked on grocery shelves. The courts ordered a halt to all brewing when the Amana Society, the corporate remnants of an early American utopian community, slapped Gemeindebrau, Inc. with a lawsuit claiming trademark infringement. The relative scarcity of Amana Beer has driven the retail price up from $1.89 to $6.00 a six-pack, and some collectors predict that if production is permanently curtailed the price could go as high as $25 per can or more—empty.

Previously, we selected Labatt's, a Canadian lager, as the *ne plus ultra* of beers. We stand by that selection, but also recognize our obligation to present significant opposing viewpoints. Therefore, we mention that Ernest Hemingway, a great writer with a great thirst, always held that Ballantine Ale was the brewer's finest achievement.

One final note: We won't vouch for the contents, but the *cans* in which "Porn Beer" is packaged are an ogler's delight, adorned with photographs of nude women and erotic captions. The beer is manufactured in Copenhagen by Granges Breweries, who say that sales have been astronomical.

**Best Beverage:** According to the Boston *Globe*, a team of scientists has found that, "the fruit of the vine not only helps the body absorb more nutrients from food but that moderate amounts consumed with meals help to promote weight loss." The researchers are now hard at work trying to ascertain which of the four hundred chemical components of wine acts as the reducing aid.

Among wines, connoisseurs have consistently acknowledged Chateau Rothschild as the most prestigious of labels and some vintages have fetched incredible prices. The Park Bernet Galleries in New York City sold a 1929 jeroboam of Chateau Mouton Rothschild in 1972 for $9,200; that works out to roughly $300 a glass.

Coffee is the only drink that bears the Vatican's seal of approval. When coffee was introduced to Europe in the sixteenth century it was condemned by conservative clergymen as a pagan drink, "the wine of Islam." Its stimulating effects, they believed, proved that the beverage must be bewitched. But Pope Clement VIII, a prodigious coffee drinker himself, dispelled clerical resistance in 1592 when he issued an edict officially recognizing coffee as a Christian drink.

**Best Candy Bar:** You can have a bust of your head done in chocolate—milk, semisweet, Mr. Goodbar, or any other variety of your choosing—by Kron Choclatiers of New York. The cost is $350, but for lesser amounts you can have other parts of your anatomy thus enshrined. A chocolate finger, for example, costs only fifty dollars.

**Best Carrots:** Carrots needn't taste like damp twigs or look like the gnarled fingers of toothless old ladies. Dr. Larry R. Baker, a Michigan State University horticulturist, has crossbred tame and wild Afghanistan carrots and come up with an improbably appealing hybrid that, he claims, "is as sweet as candy." Variously called Spartan Fancy, Spartan Delite, and Spartan Bonus, the juicy new carrots are straight, rather than tapered, eight inches in length, and as much as an inch and a half thick. According to an article in *The National Observer*, they are just chock-full of vitamin A (good for night vision, if you'll recall from your grade-school days) and other important nutrients.

**Best Cookie:** In an *Esquire* magazine article entitled "Quick Before It Crumbles," architect Paul Goldberger has provided the first authoritative criticism of cookies from a structural standpoint. Ideally, of course, cookies—like skyscrapers—should adhere to Frank Lloyd Wright's maxim that "Form follows function." And the simple, tasteful, unassuming Lorna Doone does just that; it is the Parthenon of the cookie maker's art. As Goldberger observes, "It is a superb example of the ordinary made extraordinary."

The most dreadfully designed cookie is the Oatmeal Peanut Sandwich for which Goldberger has nothing but disdain: "Oatmeal Peanut Sandwich is not pretentiously modern but rather eager to prove its ordinariness, its lack of real design, and in so zealous a way that it ends up looking far dowdier than a really ordinary cookie like your basic gingersnap. The OPS is frumpy, like a plump matron in a flower-print dress, or an old piece of linoleum."

**Best Cucumbers:** To encourage federal subsidies for "inflation gardens," Massachusetts congressman James A. Burke distributed seeds for burpless cucumbers in 1975.

Speaking of burps, Americans drink more soda pop than any other beverage, downing an average of 34.8 gallons per capita annually. Coffee comes in a close second, at 34.7 gallons, and milk is third in popularity, with 25 gallons consumed per person.

**Best Diet Soft Drink:** With the possible exceptions of thermal underwear and low sodium cheddar cheese, the greatest technological advance of this century is unquestionably the development of noncaloric soft drinks. Don't repeat to us their varied evils—we already *know* that low-calorie fizzy water causes gas, ulcers, and insomnia, that it fills the body's byways with nefarious toxins and effluents masked as sweeteners, that as a beverage it is utterly lacking in grace, dignity, or nutritional value. All the same, diet soda is indispensable to the continued existence of Western civilization as we know it.

The reason is simple: one can drink it in gross immoderation—one can drink it till the stomach walls rupture or pour it in one's ear, or even *bathe* in it—without gaining an ounce. (For once the advertisements don't lie.) Diet soda provides a vital source of nourishment—even if it's nourishment in a purely emotional sense—in a world plagued by the twin evils of obesity and gluttony.

Unfortunately, few diet sodas are distinguishable in taste from rancid Crisco or battery acid. The best of them, however, is Tab. It's hardly delicious, but it is palatable and thirst-quenching as well. Drink enough of it over a sufficiently long timespan and the aftertaste either disappears, or at least you become desensitized to it; in any event, you ultimately cannot tell the difference between it and Coca-Cola.

Not long ago, *New York* magazine brought together seven self-proclaimed diet-cola experts and asked them to sample and rate fifteen different—and unidentified—commercially marketed diet colas. All fifteen were weighed in the balance and swished around in the mouth and found wanting. But the best, or at least the most tolerable, was judged to be Diet Pepsi in cans, followed by Diet Rite Cola in the bottle. Tab in cans placed third, and bottled Tab, than which there is no better, finished in eighth place. What can we say? *Chacun à son goût.*

**Best Foods:** The emperor Ch'eng T'ang ordered his chief minister, I-Yin, to prepare an inventory of the most flavorful foods available in all of China. I-Yin's selections, compiled in the year 1500 B.C., represents one of the earliest known surveys of "the best."

"Of meat dishes," I-Yin wrote, "the best are orangutan lips . . . the tails of young swallows . . . and the choice parts of yak and elephant. The finest fish are the turbot of Lake Tung-t'ing and the sardines of the Eastern Sea. The tastiest vegetables are the duckweed of the K'un-lun Mountains and the flowers of the Tree of Long Life . . . the parsley of Yang-hua, the cress of Yün-meng, the leeks of Chü-ch'ii, and a plant that grows in Chin-yüan called 'earth blossom.' The best spices are Yang-p'u ginger, Choo-yao cinnamon, Yüeh-lo mushrooms, sauce made from bonito and sturgeon, and salt from Ta-hsia. Lichens from Han-shang are best for bringing out the finest flavor." If the local A & P is out of any of these ingredients, ask the manager to order them.

From a nutritional standpoint, outdoorsman Bradford Angier would argue with the choice of orangutan lips as the best meat. "Animal proteins," Angier says, "are desirable in direct ratio with their chemical similarity to the eating organism." Ergo, "for the fullest and easiest assimiliation of flesh materials, human meat can hardly be equalled."

Of course, there are those who are left cold by even the most delicately seasoned, lovingly prepared *Homme rôti avec patates.* In Texas and other southwestern states, chili con carne is considered the best of all possible foods, and has acquired a cult following, much like Coors beer and Baskin-Robbins ice cream. At Terlingua, Texas, not long ago, a pint of prize-winning chili sold for $260. Says the 1974 winner of the Annual World Chili Cook-off, held for the past nine years in that dessicated little ghost town, "Chili is an aphrodisiac. It makes enemies friends and friends lovers." Other partisans of the fiery dish claim it can cure anything from head colds to ingrown toenails.

The cook-off, interestingly, has been dominated by women of late, although it was originally closed to women less than one hundred years old. A 1975 competitor, Suzie "Mother Gonzo" Watson, was the hands-down winner with a unique concoction that was seasoned, or so she claimed, with fluids secreted by human pineal glands (located in the brain). One runnerup used Japanese mustard in her entry; another added farkleberries. In any event, said one participant, "Great chili can't be made. It's born."

But in general, most connossieurs are agreed that a good bowl of chili needs these basic ingredients: ground meat, garlic, onions, Mexican cornmeal, chili peppers, and tomato sauce. Beans are verboten. To add them would be considered an unjustifiable adulteration.

**Best Fruit:** If popularity counts for anything, the best fruit is the banana. According to the United States Department of Agriculture, Americans eat more bananas than any other fruit, consuming an average of 18.7 pounds per person in 1974, against 15.7 pounds of apples and 14.8 pounds of oranges. What would Freud have said?

**Best Kitchen:** The great kitchen of the Cistercian monastery in Alcobaça, Portugal, was built to accommodate the Alcoa River, which flows through it, providing a bountiful supply of fresh fish every day of the year.

**Best Milk:** Every year Americans drink about 133 quarts of milk and cream per capita. Unfortunately, although milk is indeed nature's finest food, cows' milk is a comparatively poor source of nutrition. We'd do much better to drink four glasses of porpoise milk each day; it's almost

Seal milk, the most nutritious of all

50 percent fat, far richer than the milk available in the supermarket. And Future Farmers of America and young 4-H Club members should also consider setting up rabbit dairies; milk from a good milch rabbit has three times the protein of Borden's. But the best beverage of all is seal milk (not to be confused with Sealtest) which contains 12 percent protein and 54 percent fat. By way of comparison, milk from a Guernsey cow consists of a meager 3.42 percent protein and 3.66 percent fat.

Human milk (1.2 percent protein, 3.8 percent fat) is practically the least nutritious milk produced by any mammal. It ranks just below the she-ass and the zebu in quality.

**Best Mushroom Farm:** The world's largest mushroom farm, the Butler County Mushroom Farm, in Winfield, Pennsylvania, is a perpetual frenzy of subterranean activity that is most reminiscent of the New York subway system. The farm, employing nearly five hundred workers, occupies an abandoned limestone mine containing fifteen miles of underground passageways. Out of it comes seven thousand tons of mushrooms a year.

**Best Mushrooms:** Want to add a special kick to your next Caesar's salad? Throw in a handful of *Amanita muscaria*—the granddaddy of hallucinogenic mushrooms. Known more familiarly as "Fly Agaric," this crimson-topped fungus has been a favorite for centuries among vege-heads all over the world. Hindu mystics partook of it in ancient times, and bored Siberians still use it today to weather the long, gloomy, winter nights. It was the Siberians who discovered that the mind-expanding properties of the *urine* they excreted after eating *Amanita mus-*

*caria* surpassed those of the mushroom itself. In fact, years ago the Siberians would often make a ritual of sharing their drug-rich urine with each other.

While the *Amanita muscaria* is classified as a nonpoisonous mushroom, eating it in immoderate amounts can be dangerous and even fatal. In Washington, D.C., in 1897, an Italian count mistook a bowlful of them for their tamer cousins and ate them in one sitting. He died soon thereafter.

**Best Poultry:** Ortolans are a variety of Old World bunting highly prized as a table delicacy. Their meat is exquisitely sweet and delicate because the tiny birds eat nothing but ripe berries. Ortolans are best when roasted, dipped in butter sauce, and swallowed whole—head, bones, and all. The novelist and gourmet chef Alexander Dumas advises in his famed cookbook that ortolans be asphyxiated in a strong vinegar; "it is a violent death that improves their flesh."

**Best Reason to Avoid Second Helpings:** Obesity can make lovemaking more laborious than enjoyable. But here is particularly chilling news for the overweight: a pair of rhinoceri at London's Whipsnade Zoo died recently during an aborted attempt at copulation, he of a heart attack, she of spinal injuries. Each weighed over two tons.

**Best Snacks:** If you've got the munchies, the most healthful foods to snack on are granola and milk, almonds, peaches, peanuts, and cashews, according to the Center for Science in the Public Interest, a consumer interest group.

**Best Steak:** According to Cleophus Griffin of the New York Explorers' Club, "Bison is better than beef. . . . Best roast I ever cooked." And though Stewart Udall diplomatically stopped short of calling it tastier than a Hereford, the former Secretary of the Interior has said that buffalo steak is "more succulent by far than the steak of a longhorn steer."

When the buffalo herds roamed freely, a good hunter armed with a Winchester rifle could bring in over one thousand hides a year. The meat, millions of pounds of it, was left to rot on the prairies. The only part of the buffalo that a frontiersman would deign to eat was the tongue, which was considered a great delicacy. Back in 1900 there were fewer than thirty-head of buffalo left in the entire country. They have made an impressive comeback and now there are nearly twenty thousand in protected herds. Moreover, for about twice the price of beef, buffalo meat is again available. The adventurous can sample pan-sautéed buffalo steak at Pittari's restaurant in New Orleans or sup on buffalo stew at Tommy's Joint in San Francisco.

Incidentally, the world's least-expensive beefsteaks are served in Montevideo, Uruguay; a sixteen-ounce sirloin, broiled to your taste, costs about one dollar in a good restaurant. Unfortunately, it is likely to be tough, as Latin nations generally do not age their meat. Beef should be aged about two weeks at temperatures between 34 and 58 degrees Fahrenheit, giving the muscles, tight with rigor mortis, time to relax.

**Best Way to Drink Champagne:** Russell C. Erb, a professor of organic chemistry and author of *The Common Scents of Smell,* maintains that the best way to drink champagne may be from the slipper of a beautiful woman, as romantics have long insisted. This is not mere fetishism on Dr. Erb's part, but a considered scientific opinion. "Actually the drink is improved for a very logical reason," he says. "The leather of the slipper is nitrogenous, which accentuates the flavor and aroma of the beverage."

**Best Wurst:** At the Chicago World's Fair of 1893, Anton Feuchtwanger, a Bavarian sausage salesman, was having difficulty distributing his fried bratwurst. The price of serving the sausages on plates with silverware was prohibitively high, so for a while the vendor tried issuing each customer a pair of protective gloves. This accessory enabled hungry fairgoers to hold the red-hot sausages in their hands without burning their fingers, but it was expensive to launder all those gloves and too many people walked off without returning them, which seriously cut into his profits.

Then Feuchtwanger came up with the inspiration of a lifetime. He wrapped his wurst in a long roll. Customers loved the new snack—the first hotdog.

---

**Worst Appetizer:** No matter how daring our palates, there are just some things few of us will eat or even politely sample, and dogs, lizard skins, and termites are three of them. But a growing band of protein-at-any-price nutritionists are offering to the world a sumptuously prepared spread of just such delicacies and others equally improbable, claiming them to be a fertile source of body-building protein. Perhaps. Who cares?

Termites strike us about the worst (and about the most boring, if you will ignore the pun). U.S. Department of Agriculture entomologist Philip Callahan says that an expertly grilled termite contains 36 percent fat and 45 percent protein, and that he can "vouch personally for the value of boiled woodboring beetle larvae as food. I lived on them for five days."

Roy Snelling, an entomologist at the Los Angeles Museum of Natural History, is equally enthusiastic about insects as food. "Beef," he offers, "has about sixteen percent protein, but termites and grasshoppers fried in their own juices"—*fried in˙ their own juices!*—"have about sixty to sixty-five percent protein."

If protein is all that important to you, Snelling advises against purchasing canned termites since the oils in which they're packed tend to go rancid. Better to catch your own, he believes, and feed them on corn meal to make them fat and juicy. When you're ready to fry up a batch, scald them to death in boiling water, then heat in a skillet in a bit of vegetable oil over a low flame for about twenty minutes.

**Worst Between-Meal Treats:** The Center for Science in the Public Interest (see "Food," *Worst Food*) singles out M & M's, Cracker Jacks, Hostess Sno-Balls, Three Musketeers, and Chuckles as the worst snacks. They're mostly sugar, have no redeeming nutritional value, and are largely a waste of jaw movement and digestive juices.

**Worst Breakfast:** Ulysses S. Grant's favorite breakfast was a cucumber drenched in vinegar. (Which somehow brings to mind Alice Longworth Roosevelt's acidic characterization of Calvin Coolidge: "He was weaned on a pickle.")

Henry Kissinger prefers blander fare than gherkins. His breakfast includes a serving of egg whites—dyed yellow to make them look like yolks.

**Worst Butcher:** Meat was scarce and prohibitively expensive in prewar Berlin, but an enterprising butcher named Karl Denke was able to sell high-quality smoked pork at improbably low prices. Denke's customers, though baffled by his modest rates, asked no questions.

However, had they chewed their food more reflectively, they would have tasted something decidedly unporklike. When Denke became embroiled in a loud argument with a neighbor, local police came round to check, and uncovered several barrels of freshly smoked human flesh, along with a boxful of bones and a healthy supply of human lard—all distilled from the carcasses of Denke's thirty murder victims. They also discovered a ledger book—with the date of each slaying—and the weight of the victim—recorded in the butcher's neat hand.

**Worst Cake:** Christie's, the respected London auction house, sold an uneaten portion of Queen Victoria's wedding cake (c. 1841) to an Australian, Lieutenant Colonel Keith Carey, for $154, in 1974.

Also on our dessert menu: edible biscuits made from processed human excrement were noted in the *Times* of London recently. One British scientist who tried them observed that "the result, when feelings of revulsion have been overcome, is not unpalatable, since the wastes are cleansed, sterilized, and cooked thoroughly. However," he cautioned, "I don't suggest anyone try it except in famine."

**Worst Chewing Gum:** *Playboy* magazine noted this public service sign on a men's room condom dispenser: "Don't buy this gum. It tastes like rubber."

**Worst Coffee:** Just how bad can a cup of coffee be? One Long Island, New York, refreshment vendor sold a cup reputedly so infernal that he was handcuffed and hauled before a magistrate who screamed insults at him and threatened to revoke his license. That's pretty bad.

On the evening of April 30, 1975, William M. Perry, a judge, asked the deputy sheriff to purchase two cups of coffee from a mobile refreshment stand parked outside the courthouse. The judge tasted the coffee when it was set before him and found it wanting. The deputy returned to the refreshment stand, handcuffed the vendor, Thomas Zarcone, and told him he was taking him to the judge's chambers "to see about the coffee because it was terrible."

It was in his chambers that Judge Perry screamed at Zarcone and accused him of selling watered-down coffee. He released the vendor after extracting a promise to improve his product, but hauled him into his chambers two hours later for a second reminder. Zarcone was so outraged by the ordeal—being dragged through the courthouse lobby in full view of regular customers could only hurt his business, he said—that he filed a $5 million damage suit against Perry in federal court.

**Worst Cook:** Mary Mollon. This buxom blond Irishwoman first attracted the attention of the culinary world in 1897 while working for a family in Mamaroneck, New York. Mary served generous portions, the entrees were subtly and inventively seasoned, her pie crusts were delicate and flaky—on that score her employer had no complaints. The only problem was that, after she had been in the kitchen just ten days, the master and the missus, the servants and the children—everyone except Mary—came down with typhoid fever. And as soon as the illness broke out, the new cook disappeared in the middle of the night. She was the infamous Typhoid Mary.

For ten years Mary Mollon moved from job to job, working in private homes and restaurants in Maine, Massachusetts, and New York, and everywhere she went, typhoid invariably broke out within a week or two. At least fifty-three cases of fever—many of them fatal—were definitely traced to her cooking. And there were probably hundreds of additional victims who were never identified.

Mary was an unfortunate victim herself, a carrier who continuously discharged deadly germs; she could not be cured, and yet she never suffered from the symptoms of the disease. Unhappily, Mary was also a maniac, who either never understood that she was virulently infectious or, according to some reports, took a perverse delight in serving up feculent dishes. When George Soper, a New York City health official, first confronted her with evidence that she was a carrier, she attacked him with a carving fork; Soper fled in terror. When, after a merry chase, she was finally apprehended, it took five policemen to subdue her.

Civil libertarians debated whether Mary could legally be detained, since she had committed no crime for which she could be prosecuted. State legislatures hastily passed "Typhoid Mary laws" to ensure that she could never cook up another Irish stew within their jurisdiction. Overnight Mary Mollon became an international celebrity. In Britain, *Punch* devoted an issue to poems inspired by her notorious cooking. And fame brought her a suitor, a twenty-eight-year-old mental patient; they were wed in 1909.

Finally, Mary was released from the state hospital on the condition that she never be involved again in the preparation of food. Soon after she disappeared once more. For months she kept one step ahead of health officials and, under an alias, took jobs in a Broadway restaurant, a Long Island hotel, and a fashionable sanitorium. She was ultimately located when typhoid broke out in Sloane Maternity Hospital. As one magistrate described it, Mary was discovered in the kitchen, "spreading germs among mothers and babies and doctors and nurses like a destroying angel."

Arrested for the last time in March 1915, Mary Mollon's cooking days were over. The rest of her life was spent in confinement reading and rereading Charles Dickens' novels. At her funeral on November 12, 1938, the nine mourners in attendance refused to divulge their names.

**Worst Cucumber:** Strictly speaking, sea cucumbers are *not* cucumbers. For one thing, they're inedible and, for another, they *move*. Sea cucumbers are actually tough-skinned, tentacled echinoderms that prowl about the ocean's floor, looking for all the world like ambulatory cucumbers, but lacking all of the social graces and innate *politesse* of their edible cousins.

The most obnoxious of the sea cucumber's habits is its relentless vomiting. When threatened by a predator, a sea cucumber will retch up its insides, practically turning itself inside out like an old glove, and spewing forth a poison that is frequently fatal to the attacker.

Zoologists have known for years of the sea cucumber's—or holothurian's—propensity for defensive vomiting, but the toxic properties weren't discovered until the early 1950s, when Dr. Ross F. Nigrelli, of the New York Zoological Society, noticed that the creature's upchucked innards could kill. To explore the matter further, Dr. Nigrelli took a one-ounce sample of the toxin and placed it in a tank holding several fish and 750 gallons of water. The fish died within 30 minutes.

While scientists were quick to name the new poison—they called it holothurin—South Seas fishermen have used it to kill fish for centuries. Now biochemists have found it to be a potent nerve poison and thus, possibly, an effective anesthetic as well.

**Worst Cuisine:** During the siege of Paris in December 1871, the Prussian army was intercepting all food shipments to the city. To stave off starvation the government was forced to take drastic steps. Firing squads were ordered to execute all the animals in the Paris Zoo—the apes, ostriches, lions, camels, and bears, even the beloved elephants Castor and Pollux. Elephant meat commanded the highest prices, and Paris butchers reportedly sold slices of elephant trunk for as much as forty francs a pound. But even in adversity the French insisted on seasoning their meats with rich sauces. In Joseph Trager's *Foodbook* we read that at least one restaurant was serving elephant trunk in béarnaise sauce.

Under normal circumstances, however, French cuisine—along with Chinese—is widely recognized as the best in the world. Only the fiery curries of India could compete in the same cooking class.

There is considerably more competition among the worst. We might, for instance, select the vile sausages and overcooked kraut of Germany as the culinary rock bottom. And we share the aversion of Voltaire who observed that "the British have a hundred religions and only one sauce." Moreover, at the risk of appearing provincial, we could not stomach the everyday fare of African pygmies: ants, caterpillars, dried and roasted monkey, boiled elephant's foot, crocodile meat, beetles, grasshoppers, and lizards.

But perhaps the most unappealing victuals of all were prepared in the American pioneer kitchens of the early nineteenth century. In his history of the United States, Henry Adams recounts the nausea of a visiting French gourmet, Constantin François Chasseboeuf, the Comte de Volney: "I will venture to say that if a prize were proposed for the scheme of a regimen most calculated to injure the stomach, the teeth, and the health in general, no better could be invented than that of the Americans. In the morning at breakfast they deluge their stomach with a quart of hot water, impregnated with tea, or so slightly with coffee that it is mere colored water; and they swallow, almost without chewing, hot bread, half-baked, toast soaked in butter, cheese of the fattest kind, slices of salt or hung beef, ham, etc., all which are nearly insoluble. At dinner they have boiled pastes under the name of puddings, and the fattest are esteemed the most delicious; all their sauces, even for roast beef, are melted butter; their turnips and potatoes swim in hog's lard, butter, or fat; under the name of pie or pumpkin, their pastry is nothing but a greasy paste, never sufficiently baked. To digest these viscous substances, they take tea almost instantly after dinner, making it so strong that it is absolutely bitter to the taste, in which state it affects the nerves so powerfully that even the English find it brings on a more obstinate restlessness than coffee. Supper again introduces salt meats or oysters. As Chastellux says, the whole day passes in heaping indigestions on one another; and to give tone to the poor, relaxed, and wearied stomach, they drink Madeira, rum, French brandy, gin, or malt spirits which complete the ruin of the nervous system."

**Worst Dessert:** According to Agence France-Presse, a man in Gummersbach, West Germany, was stabbed to death by his enraged and fastidious wife when she found him wiping his hands on the sheets after eating strawberries in bed.

And a man in Hamilton, Scotland, was hospitalized with frozen tonsils after devouring fifty scoops of ice cream in sixteen minutes in an ice-cream eating contest.

**Worst Dietary Supplement:** In an experiment designed to prove that "DDT is harmless," pest control executive Robert Loibl and his wife Louise gulped down a ten-miligram capsule of dichloro-diphenyltrichlorothane with their breakfast coffee every morning for six months. The dosage of poison consumed by the North Hollywood, California, couple was three hundred times the average daily intake. And, in all, they ingested as much DDT as individuals eating dusted produce for eighty-three years. Blood tests and urinalysis conducted by U.S. Government physicians showed "nothing out of the ordinary." And Loibl insisted, "We feel better than we used to. In fact, I think my appetite has increased since I began taking DDT."

**Worst Drunkard:** When an ill-tempered two-hundred-fifty-pound Hell's Angel ties one on, he can be dangerous and unruly, but with all due respect an intemperate biker is tame compared to a pie-eyed elephant.

Drunken elephants are a mammoth problem in South Africa's Kruger National Park. It seems that pachyderms are particularly fond of the sweet fruits of the marula tree (*Sclerocarya birrea*) which thrives within the park's boundaries. After a feast of marula fruit, an elephant becomes enormously thirsty and wanders off to the nearest stream to fill up on gallons of water. Intestinal fermentation then converts the fruit sugars to alcohol and leaves the animals thoroughly shellacked. You can hear a drunken elephant from miles away; it trumpets like a warped Al Hirt record. Furthermore, a crapulous elephant loses all its inhibitions; it stampedes, galumphs, staggers, and finally collapses into a stupor. Park rangers are concerned about the property damage the animals cause on their rampages and the possibility that the elephants will injure themselves.

Another intoxicated member of the animal kingdom is the cuddly koala bear of Australia. Through their television commercials, Qantas Airlines has made the vacant, confused, slightly out-of-it facial expression of the koala familiar to every American. But what the commercials do not tell us is that the koala's blank stare and slow-motion reactions are the product of a mind-altering drug found in the eucalyptus leaves on which the bears feed exclusively. In its natural form, eucalyptus has no effect on human beings, but it leaves the koala completely stoned.

**Worst Flavor:** For a pair of Rhode Island researchers, putting the finger on the world's worst flavor was literally a question of life and death. Since it isn't uncommon for young children to pick peeling paint chips off the wall and eat them like Raisinettes, along with plaster, putty, and other readily available toxic substances, psychologist Trygg Engen and teacher Florence E. Gasparian figured it would make sense to find out what flavor turns kids off most and use it to keep them away from household poisons. To that end, they rounded up 102 children between the ages of three and six, and had them sample and rate a variety of flavored sweets. To a child, they selected not creamed spinach, liver, or Tang—but *peppermint*—as rock-bottom worst.

Interestingly, adults tested in the same way found horehound, a flavor akin to that of Diet Moxie (see *Felton & Fowler I*, page 225) the most repellent. "This indicates the potential hazards of predicting children's preferences by adult norms," said the testers.

**Worst Hamburgers:** A New Orleans research organization says that cottonburgers—ersatz hamburgers made from cotton rather than meat—"may be a potential solution to the world's food problems." At the Southern Regional Research Center, scientists have developed a method of extracting the protein from cottonseed hulls and mixing it into food as a valuable nutritional supplement. In powdered form, they say, the extract can be dissolved in fruit juices or baked into pastries and meats—or it can be eaten in the form of texturized patties. The very idea of eating cottonburgers gives a whole new meaning to the term flannelmouth.

**Worst Hors D'Oeuvres:** In a fit of before-dinner passion, Mrs. Stoyan Pandov, of Bulgaria, affectionately bit her husband on the ear. He went into shock and was rushed to a hospital where he died of blood poisoning.

**Worst Meat:** For the ultimate in synthetic dining, Armour Food Service Systems is now supplying cost-conscious restaurant owners with Sir Broil, "the low-cost answer to the high cost of steak." Sir Broil is actually steak-sized patties of beef leavings, held together with a heady dose of marginally edible adhesives, texturizers, preservatives, and assorted crud, and imprinted with authentic-looking grill marks. An advertisement tells restaurateurs that Sir Broil "is hard to tell from a strip steak and you can serve it at a menu price that will build traffic while it builds your profits." Distressing to think that some yahoos will insist on ruining it by drowning it in ketchup.

**Worst Seafood Dinner:** Recently, eight men, charged with fraud and menacing the public health, were jailed for a year in Palermo, Sicily. Their crime: thawing out commercially packaged frozen fish and selling it as freshly caught. Worse yet, processed sewage is emptied into the sea quite close to where they did their thawing.

**Worst Snack:** President Zachary Taylor spent the afternoon of July 4, 1850 listening to two hours of tedious speechmaking by Senator Samuel A. Foote of Maine. It was a sizzling summer's day in Washington; the flies were buzzing in the open sewers; and the President was reported to have perspired splendidly. On returning to the White House, Taylor devoured an amazing quantity of chilled cucumbers and ripe cherries, washed down with "copious draughts" of iced milk.

Within hours the President was doubled up with stomach cramps; that evening he began to retch. The White House physicians were called in. They diagnosed the case as *cholera morbus,* now known as acute gastroenteritis, and drugged him with ipecac, opium, and quinine in forty-grain doses. A phlebotomist was summoned from Baltimore to apply leeches and blister him with a hot iron. After four days of bleeding, branding, and the most outrageous quackery money could buy, the old general was dead. And the country was in the well-manicured hands of (who else?) Millard Fillmore. (See also "Health and Death," *Worst Cure.*)

**Worst Source of Protein:** Your morning newspaper is just chock-full of cellulose, which is a juicy source of carbohydrates, as any home economics student knows. While carbohydrates in excess are of questionable food value, Dr. Keith H. Steinkraus of the New York Agricultural Experiment Station, in Geneva, New York, points out that a thousand pounds of those carbohydrates, if fermented properly, can be transmogrified into 12,000 pounds of body-building protein. At present, it is soybeans, used more and more frequently as a substitute for meat, that are the world's greatest protein crop. But properly processed newsprint, he says, will produce triple the protein yield of soybeans.

If that sounds unappetizing, there *is* another possible use for that pile of old *Herald Tribunes* gathering dust in your basement. Scientists at the United States Army's Natick Laboratories in Massachusetts have successfully derived pancake syrup as a by-product of a new process for converting cellulose from newspapers into ink. Thus far, the thick, sweet topping is too expensive to compete with Log Cabin or Aunt Jemima's because of the complicated filtration procedure required to separate the deadly poisonous ink from the syrup. But the future is ripe with possibilities. Possible ad slogan of tomorrow: "In Philadelphia, nearly everyone eats the *Inquirer.*"

**Worst Sundae:** In San Francisco, a man protested the proliferation of curbside dog-droppings by wandering the streets and garnishing every pile he saw with whipped cream and maraschino cherries. "I want to bring some sort of attention to this goddam mess," he said.

**Worst Tea:** The "tea" made by boiling a well-worn shoe was considered an effective if unappetizing cure for lumbago in some parts of the midwest in the 1800s.

**Worst Toast:** The Vikings staged gala victory celebrations at which they drank draughts of their enemies' blood out of vessels fashioned from human skulls. The toast "Skol!" may be derived from this custom.

**Worst Wurst:** First hot *dogs*, and now . . . zoologists at Cardiff University in Wales are studying the possibility of producing high-protein sausages from rats.

---

**Most Unusual Barbecue:** A passenger train in Cordoba, Argentina, was derailed recently when it struck and killed a cow lazing about on the tracks. No one was injured, apart from the cow, but the appetites of the seven hundred passengers were apparently whetted by the mishap. While waiting for a repair crew to arrive and set the train on its way again, the passengers dug a barbecue pit, roasted the cow over a large fire, and devoured it with gusto.

**Most Unusual Cherry Pie:** Every July fourth, the residents of George, Washington, honor their namesake by whipping up a 1,200-pound cherry pie made from 150 pounds of flour, 72 pounds of shortening, 100 gallons of cherries, 200 pounds of sugar, two cups of almond extract, a cup and a half of red food dye, and 75 cups of tapioca, all baked in a special brick oven at 400 degrees for 19 hours.

Despite the magnificence of its pastries, George, Washington, founded a few years ago by a wealthy shoe salesman, has fallen on hard times recently; the town has been put up for sale, at an asking price of $2 million. At one point a consortium of Arab investors was seriously considering the purchase, but the deal fell through, much to the relief of many of the townspeople. Said one local, "Somehow it just wouldn't be right, them Arabs owning George, Washington."

**Most Unusual Deep Freeze.** Australia has so much meat on its hands that it is considering stockpiling its surplus in the Antarctic and then drawing upon the supply as needed—or when world meat prices climb higher.

**Most Unusual Fish:** One of the most highly prized dishes in Japanese cuisine is raw fugu fish; its firm texture and exotic salty flavor make it a national favorite. The only drawback is that fugu flesh contains a fast-acting, deadly poison, 150,000 times more potent than curare.

A prickly fish without scales, the fugu is a variety of puffer that thrives in shallow coastal waters. When hooked or frightened, like all puffers, it inhales large quantities of air and water and swells up to three times its normal size. Although much of the fugu is perfectly safe to eat, seafood lovers long ago discovered that the dorsal flesh, viscera, roe, and skin contain fatal quantities of tetrodotoxin. In Japan, only specially licensed restaurants are permitted to serve the fugu, and then only when the fish has been prepared by chefs who have gone through an intensive course in the subtleties of fugu anatomy. Despite these regulations and precautions, hundreds of Japanese die of fugu poisoning every year.

The best of the best is the raw fugu liver, considered by gourmets to be the greatest delicacy the ocean has to offer. But carving the liver is so tricky that the government has completely outlawed it from the menus of commercial establishments. Still, for those with a keen appetite for danger, the fugu liver can be obtained in a few private clubs, frequented by the very rich. As part of a gala fifty-seventh birthday celebration in 1975, Mitsugoro Bando, a leading Japanese kabuki actor, went to a posh geisha club, and in response to a challenge from his friends, ordered a raw fugu liver. He picked up the delicious organ with his chopsticks, took a few confident bites, and died within five minutes.

**Most Unusual Fruit:** *Dioscoreophyllum cumminsii* berries have yet to capture the palate of the American people, principally because they are three thousand times sweeter than sugar. The small red fruits grow in clusters in West Africa and their extract has been suggested as a possible alternative to both artificial sweeteners and Julie Eisenhower.

**Most Unusual Mushroom:** A golfer in search of an errant golfball in Melbourne, Australia, discovered a toadstool weighing twenty-two pounds.

**Most Unusual Pizza:** Ambitious chefs at a restaurant in Little Rock,

Arkansas, produced a pizza eight feet in diameter using 150 pounds of dough, 25 gallons of sauce, 75 pounds of pepperoni, and 200 pounds of grated cheese. To date it's the largest pizza ever.

**Most Unusual Pudding:** H.M.S. *Cardiff,* a Welsh freighter laden to the portholes with a twin cargo of lumber and tapioca powder, was about to dock at Cardiff in 1974 when the lumber caught fire. The crew brought the blaze under control and kept it confined to one hold by wetting down the wood, but an overzealous shore patrol turned their hoses on the wood and drowned the fire with thousands of gallons of unneeded water from dockside pumps.

The water eventually seeped into the holds where the tapioca was stored, turning the powder into a watery gruel which was then cooked by the heat from the blazing timber. At this point, the crew had to deal with an ever-swelling ocean of syrupy tapioca pudding that threatened, as it grew larger, to burst the ship's hull. Finally, the shore patrol brought in a fleet of five hundred dump trucks to relieve the *Cardiff* of what was estimated to be several million gallons of cooked tapioca.

**Most Unusual Restaurant:** On some evenings there is music at Juanita's in Fetter's Springs, California—a blowsy woman sings "Roll Me Over in the Clover," "Barnacle Bill the Sailor," and other Cole Porter favorites. And back in the late sixties, diners were entertained and embarrassed by the antics of four spider monkeys who used to cavort and swing from the chandeliers; now they are caged by order of the Public Health Department. Still, Juanita's remains far-and-away the most outrageous restaurant in the nation.

Juanita's bedroom-office is dominated by an enormous brass bed, with Christmas tree ornaments, bric-a-brac, china dolls, old magazines, and the restaurant books scattered everywhere. The main dining room is decorated in what a New York *Times* reviewer called "Grand Rapids Grotesque." There are Chinese gongs, chamber pots, cuspidors, dentists' chairs, roll-top desks, palm trees, and baby scales—all arranged like an obstacle course among the tables. Customers eat by the light of kerosene lamps, while brilliant green parrots wing by their heads. Stuffed alligators and iguanas lurk behind the curtains.

Behind the bar hangs a singularly tasteless painting entitled "Day Dreams," depicting corpulent nymphs hovering above the San Francisco waterfront. At the front desk, afterdinner mints are served from a disinfected bedpan, bouquets of peacock feathers spring up everywhere, and a decapitated mannequin in a pink dancehall gown lounges seductively by the cash register. On the porch and grazing in the front yard is a menagerie worthy of the San Diego Zoo. There are goats, geese, and chickens (Juanita often carries a pet chicken under her arm as she circulates from table to table), cats, dogs, snakes, and lizards.

And the food, surprisingly, is not bad at all. A wide menu is served buffet style, and the specialty of the house, roast ribs of beef, is moderately priced at about ten dollars. But don't ask for a doggy bag if you can't finish it all. A roll of aluminum foil is provided so customers can wrap their own leftovers.

**Most Unusual Wurst:** Swiss Colony, a gourmet food shop in Monroe, Wisconsin, sells thirty-foot sausages. They weigh four and a half pounds and cost $14.95 each.

# Life-Styles

**Best Cause for Celebration:** When Greek mathematicians first proved that the square root of two is not a rational number they celebrated by sacrificing one hundred oxen.

**Best Club:** Ever since the Jockey Club was founded in 1834, membership has been "the ultimate stamp of French social approval." It is almost certainly the world's most exclusive club, the only other contender being the Royal Yacht Squadron at Cowes, England. In 1905 the Jockey Club listed among its dues-paying members the monarchs of England, Belgium, Holland, Denmark, and Serbia. Current American members (there are roughly twenty of them) include C. Douglas Dillon, the man whose signature is on all those dollar bills, and David K. C. Bruce, former United States Ambassador to the Court of Saint James.

There are no secret handshakes, no funny hats, and no kinky initiation rites, but if you are interested in joining, you can stop by the clubhouse at 2 Rue Rabelais in Paris. Even to be blackballed is considered a high honor.

**Best Proof That Texans Are Not Like the Rest of Us:** Jim "Silver Dollar" West of Houston, who died in 1958, owned thirty cars, lived in a $500,000 castle, packed a pair of .45 caliber pistols, and always wore a diamond encrusted Texas Ranger badge. When dining out at a fancy restaurant, West brought a tub of butter, churned from the cream of his own cows, to spread on his biscuits. If the service was good, he tipped the waitress with a pile of eighty silver dollars.

**Best Things in Life:** To simulate the effects of prolonged confinement on board a spacecraft, the National Aeronautics and Space Administration isolated a number of volunteers in "Tektite," an underwater living chamber. After spending up to ninety days in close quarters, eating nothing but dried and reconstituted foods, the aquanauts made out lists of the activities and creature comforts they missed the most. Ranked one, two, and three were family contact, sex, and creative work, respectively. Fourth was milk and ice cream. Fresh fruits and vegetables finished fifth, while alcohol was seventh and tobacco was fourteenth.

**Best Women:** Respondents in a flagrantly sexist twelve-nation Gallup poll ranked Italian women as the world's most desirable. The women of Spain finished second, followed closely by Sweden and France, while American beauties finished a dowdy fifth.

Italian men, of course, are notorious for their uninhibited appreciation of feminine pulchritude, and for generations women walking alone in Rome and Naples have been subjected to pats and pinches of the most personal kind. Crowded buses have always been especially hazardous; an attractive woman often runs the risk of sustaining a volley of intimate assaults before finding her way to a seat. But now, at least in Sicily, Italian women are beginning to organize to defend their modesty and to put an end to posterior bruises. The women of Catania, in the shadow of Mount Etna, have forced the municipal bus company to provide separate vehicles for men and women.

---

**Worst Club:** Zama, Inc., is an organization of wealthy Californians who are convinced that the earth's destruction, whether by nuclear holocaust or natural disaster, is just around the corner, but that by taking precautions and working together, they can survive. New members are expected to pay a fee of $12,000 upon joining Zama, and annual dues of $300. Most members own guns and keep a permanent supply of freeze-dried and dehydrated foods. And, since secrecy is essential to survival, visitors are absolutely forbidden at Zama headquarters, whose very location is a jealously guarded secret. In fact, Zama leaders take great pains to let prospective members know that the road leading to the club's headquarters, wherever it is, can be dynamited easily, so that its members may insulate themselves from outside attacks.

The Atomic Energy Society of Great Britain, in direct contrast to the California group, believes that nuclear power is the most benevolent force in the universe. It is time that scientists ended their short-sighted policy of atomic containment, the AES asserts, and released the barrage of alpha, beta, and gamma rays currently imprisoned in bombs. Free-floating radiation could work miracles, they say; we would get used to it in no time. "If we can use it to ripen all the corn people need," declares AES director Mrs. Ronald Copeland, "then we can banish war."

Another offbeat fellowship was the twentieth-century British group known as The Society for the Prevention of People Being Buried Alive, whose members took their shared phobia quite seriously. The now extinct SPPBBA devoted much of its energies towards perfecting antiburial devices, including a set of electric bells that would alert bystanders to the presence of a prematurely interred body. Approaching the problem from another angle, society members spoke darkly of a coffin equipped with poison gas capsules that would be punctured when the nails were driven in, insuring that the individual thus interred go into the ground quite dead.

**Worst Courtship Ritual:** In his book *Rats, Lice and History*, Hans Zinsser tells of an Austrian anthropologist named Weizl who while living among the natives of northern Siberia, was frequently badgered by giggling young virgins who appeared at his door and pelted him with freshly killed lice. According to Zinsser, Weizl learned that among the northern Siberians, lice-throwing was the traditional manner for a woman to express her love for a man and indicate that she was available for marriage.

**Worst Memento:** As historian Lesley Blanch has quipped, Russia is a country "where nothing succeeds like excess."

A certain Mrs. Hamilton was the favorite mistress of Peter the Great, one of the most successful and excessive of czars. But despite her wit and beautiful features, Peter showed her no mercy when he discovered that she had been unfaithful. He had her beheaded immediately. Still, the czar had a soft spot in his heart for Mrs. Hamilton; he would never forget her. He ordered that the severed head be pickled in alcohol and displayed in the royal bedroom as a trophy of love, and as a warning for future lovers to remain true.

**Worst Mixer:** William John Cavendish Bentinck Scott (1800–1879), the fifth Duke of Cavendish, may have been the shyest person who ever lived. For a short while he occupied his inherited seat in the House of Lords, but soon found he was too timid to participate in the debates. So at a young age he retired to his estate and devoted all his energies to the cultivation of the most beautiful greenhouses in England. Unmarried and socially awkward, he withdrew further and further into himself.

Eventually, the Duke shut himself off in one corner of his mansion, Welbeck Abbey. He refused to receive visitors and would not even face his own servants. All communications to and from the butler and maids passed through a message box outside his door. And when Sir William went for his evening walk in the garden, the servants were instructed to stay out of sight or to avert their eyes; those who failed to do so were punished by being forced to skate on the Duke's private skating rink until they were exhausted.

To further guarantee his seclusion, Sir William hired unemployed miners to bore a tunnel from Welbeck Abbey to the town of Worksop, one and a half miles away. On his rare trips to London, the Duke would go down to his basement, climb into his shuttered coach, and ride through the subterranean passageway to the Worksop train station, where his coach was mounted on a flatcar. When the train arrived in London, a coachman and a team of horses were waiting to drive him to his place of business. In this fashion he was able to travel from Welbeck Abbey to London and back without seeing a single human face.

Later Sir William burrowed additional tunnels to his greenhouses and other outbuildings, eliminating those embarrassing encounters with servants on his evening walks. He also designed an underground dining room where he ate all of his meals. The cook sent dinner down to the basement on a dumb waiter, and the butler transferred the silver serving dishes to the cars of a model railroad train which delivered the meal, piping hot, to the duke's table without disturbing his privacy.

Since World War II, Welbeck Abbey has been a training center for British army cadets.

**Worst Way to Start the Day:** Antonio Lama of Naples, Italy, awoke one fine summer's morning in 1975 to find his wife Amalia removing his nose with a pair of scissors. "She was jealous," he explained to hospital surgeons who stitched up the wound.

Worse yet, a similarly angered housewife in Thailand woke her slumbering spouse by scissoring off his penis and spitefully tossing it out the window, where a duck picked it up in its mouth and waddled away with it, according to the Bangkok *Post*.

Jealousy inspired Vital da Silva to cut off his wife's ears with a twelve-inch stiletto when he spotted her flirting with another person in a bar in Maceió, Brazil, in 1975. He then tossed them idly on the floor and walked out of the bar.

**Most Unusual Adoption:** Can a twenty-six-year-old computer programer find happiness as her younger brother's daughter? (Please don't ask us to repeat that. Chances are you heard right the first time.)

When twenty-three-year-old Air Force Sergeant David Erwin was notified that he was to be relocated to Japan, his immediate concern was the care and upbringing of his two preschool children whose custody he had been granted upon his recent divorce. Erwin had been helped in caring for the kids by his twenty-six-year-old sister, Sharon Strickland, who now offered to go to Japan with her brother and continue to look after the children. It seemed an ideal arrangement on the face of it, but a hitch developed: Air Force regulations prohibited anyone but legal dependents from accompanying a serviceman overseas. Erwin, however, sidestepped that obstacle by going to court and petitioning to adopt his sister. While Texas District Court Judge Don Lane called the adoption case "the strangest on record," he granted Erwin's petition, noting that "Mr. Erwin's 'real children' will benefit best from this arrangement."

In a related case in Sacramento, California, fifty-four-year-old Guillaume Armondreaux adopted his forty-four-year-old friend Eugene Christian Cremers.

"We've known each other quite a while," Mr. Armondreaux told the Associated Press. "One day Gene said he would like to be my brother. I said that would be fine with me and I got to looking into the legal side of things and found I could adopt him as a son but not as a brother. So we went ahead with that."

**Most Unusual Black Sheep of the Family:** Motorcycle stuntman Evel Knievel is the cousin of John Knievel, Director of Public Affairs for the Federal Highway Traffic Safety Administration. John calls Evel "a bad example."

**Most Unusual Duel:** When Monsieurs Lenfant and Mellant quarrelled over a game of billiards in 1834 both men insisted on immediate satisfaction. After drawing lots to see who should fire first, Mellant seized the red billiard ball and hurled it at his opponent's forehead. The ball struck Lenfant squarely between the eyes, killing him instantly.

While there have been no recorded billiard balls duels in the United States, dueling is very much a New as well as Old World custom. The first duel in North America took place in 1621 at Plymouth Colony when two Pilgrim Fathers maimed each other with daggers. They were sentenced to lie with their heads and feet bound together for twenty-four hours without food and water. From that time on, Americans clashed regularly on the field of honor for the next 250 years.

The most trivial of disputes could provoke a challenge. For example, when John Randolph, the swashbuckling congressman from Virginia, was enrolled at Williams College, he fought and wounded a fellow student over the pronunciation of a word. Another strange encounter took place in St. Louis on August 27, 1831, when Spencer Pettis, a congressman from Missouri, met Major Thomas Biddle, U.S.A., to settle an argument over the Bank of the United States. The two men aimed and fired at each other from the astoundingly short range of five feet out of consideration for Biddle's extreme nearsightedness. Both were mortally wounded.

To prevent further depletion of its numbers, Congress outlawed dueling soon after Representative William Graves of Kentucky shot and killed Representative John Cilley of Maine in 1938, but legislation could hardly stop gentlemen from defending their honor frequently and violently. Perhaps one of the most celebrated American duelists was Cassius Marcellus Clay, a cousin of Henry Clay and a Kentuckian who remained loyal to the Union throughout the Civil War, thereby inviting countless challenges. Clay had a reputation of being able to sever a string three out of five times from a distance of ten paces. But even a great marskman can get the jitters. In his first duel, Clay and his opponent each fired three times; when none of the shots drew blood, the contestants shook hands and declared their quarrel resolved. Asked how he could possibly have missed three times, Clay said, "That damned string never had no pistol in his hand."

**Most Unusual Encounter in the Class War:** Fauchon in Paris, France, is perhaps the world's foremost epicurean store. The late Duke of Windsor kept an account there; Aristotle Onassis was mad about Fauchon cheeses. But when a cadre of Maoist revolutionaries burst in one morning in May 1970, the proprietor knew immediately that they were not regular customers.

The vanguard of the working class had come to liberate the petit fours. Disguised with red kerchiefs over their faces and armed with makeshift nightsticks, the Maoists forced the staff to the back of the store and began helping themselves. They appropriated quart jars of caviar and tubs of foie gras. They filled laundry bags with magnums of fine pear brandy and vintage champagne. But when the intruders went beyond the bounds of decency and began pocketing Périgord truffles, the proprietor let out an anguished scream. The staff took heart and fought back for privilege and *haut cuisine*, driving the Maoists from the shop with a hail of canned sturgeon and vichyssoise.

The next day in the slums of Ivry-sur-Seine and Nanterre, the raiders distributed their booty of foie gras truffé, pâté en croute, and marrons glacés to the people.

**Most Unusual Hermit:** The eighteenth-century British eccentric Charles Hamilton apparently considered it a mark of prestige to have a hermit living in his garden, and offered handsome wages for the service, including a stipend of seven hundred pounds and such valuable perks as an hourglass, a hairshirt, and a Bible. In return, the hired hermit was expected to live in an artificial cave, not speak, and leave hair, nails, and beard untrimmed. The one hermit Hamilton was able to lure into the position nearly went mad with boredom after six weeks, however, and quit.

A countryman of Hamilton's in Lancashire had better luck, maintaining a hermit in a cave for nearly four years, but only on the condition that the hermit be supplied with books, bathtub, and an organ.

# Fashion and Grooming

**Best Bra:** The modern bra was invented in 1902 by a Frenchman, Charles R. Debevoise. The word brassiere is a blatant euphemism, by the way; it means "arm protector." And the French are no more frank in these matters; they call the garment *le soutien gorge*—"the throat support."

The most elaborate, ostentatious, and expensive brassiere—and therefore by some standards the best—was created by fashion designer Elsa Peretti. Made of 18-karat gold mesh, the halter is worn over the bare breasts, complemented with a shirt, open to the waist. You can pick yours up at Tiffany's for about four thousand dollars.

Another notable brassiere was invented by Frederick Mellinger, the foremost designer of lacy, lewd nightwear known as "passion fashion." Mellinger had patented the first inflatable bra. The advertisements invite you to "Blow yourself up to your favorite size."

**Best Clothes:** The U.S. Agriculture Department interviewed over two thousand mothers with children under fourteen to determine whether they preferred iron or no-iron fabrics. The findings were released in a 113-page report entitled "Mothers' Attitudes Toward Cotton and Other Fibers in Children's Lightweight Clothing." Surprise! Mothers overwhelmingly replied that no-iron clothing is the best. Since taxpayers paid $113,147 for this revelation, we thought you would like to know.

**Best Dressed:** Mustafa Kemal Ataturk was determined to make Turkey the best-dressed nation on earth. As President of the Turkish republic from 1923 to 1938, he sought to wrench his nation out of the traditional Oriental mold and nestle it in the bosom of Western culture. In a passionate speech before the National Assembly, Kemal said, "We shall wear shoes and boots; we shall wear trousers, shirts, waist-coats, collars, neckties; we'll have a headcovering with a brim, more precisely, we'll have a hat. We shall wear redingotes, jackets, dinner jackets, and tail coats." And he added the warning, "Only idiots would hesitate to do so."

A few dozen dissenters, loyal to the old style, refused to exchange their fezzes for fedoras; they were hanged. The rest of the people got the message, and by 1925, Kemal's proclamation had created in Istanbul the worst hat shortage on record. But, overall, dress-reform went well— far better than the earlier attempts by Napoleon and Peter the Great to legislate national fashions.

As for the best-dressed individuals, you cannot rely on the highly touted rankings of *The Women's Wear Daily* and other publications; they are a far better barometer of the political and social climate than of the current state of fashion. For example, Lady Bird Johnson, a tasteful but unimaginative dresser, was regularly included on the various "ten best-dressed" lists during her husband's administration, but as soon as Lyndon cleaned out his desk in January 1968, she dropped off the charts. Or consider Richard Nixon. He was no clothes horse, and since his resignation he has not received any offers to take up a modeling career. Still, he showed up on many of the best-dressed lists in the company of Henry Kissinger (who would never be appointed Secretary of Threads).

In our judgment, the two best-dressed individuals of our time are Jacqueline Kennedy Onassis and the late Duke of Windsor. The Duke was incomparably dashing in tails, and Mrs. Onassis has had a greater influence on popular fashion than any woman since Marie Antoinette. The pillbox hat and miniskirt gained wide public acceptance because she wore them. And certainly few women have done more to support the Paris couturiers; Aristotle Onassis reportedly gave her an annual allowance of between $250,000 and $500,000 to spend on clothes alone.

**Best Ear:** A prize of $1,000 went to Mrs. Lloyd Borne of Binghamton, New York, in the Koss Corporation's first annual "Most Beautiful Ear" contest. Koss, manufacturers of stereophonic earphones, ran the contest in 1975 as a promotional stunt. Instructions for entering: "Merely press an inkpad to the ear. Then press the ear to a postcard. Then mail the postcard to us."

**Best Figure:** There is a spirited polka that begins with the lyrics "I don't want her/You can have her/She's too fat for me." But the slim American (and Polish-American) ideal is by no means the universal standard of

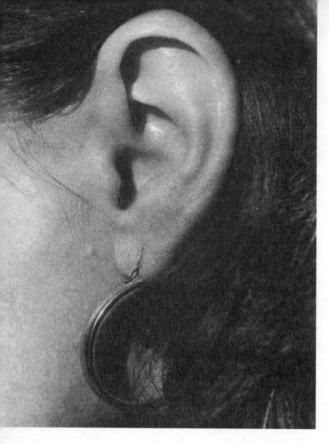

The winning entry in the "Most Beautiful Ear" contest

beauty. In many cultures men despise skinny women and love their wives in direct proportion to their pulchritudinous poundage.

The Efik tribe of southern Nigeria used to seclude every girl of marriageable age in the *m-bobi* or fattening hut. Depending on the affluence of her family, the bride-to-be might remain in the fattening hut anywhere from six months to two years. L. W. G. Malcolm has described life in the *m-bobi* for the British anthropological journal *Man:* "During the fattening process she is compelled to eat vast quantities of fat-producing foods, including pounded yams cooked in palm oil. She is not allowed to exert herself in any way and on no account must she perspire." At the end of her seclusion, the girl attends (what else?) a feast in her honor and receives an assortment of gifts including a dead chicken, which she wears around her neck on her wedding day.

And there are even more extreme cases: An eighteenth-century king of the Karagwe tribe of Central Africa liked his wives so obese that they could not walk, but "could only grovel on the floor like seals." To keep

Danish astronomer Tycho Brahe

themselves pleasingly plump, the women continuously sipped milk from hollow gourds.

**Best Hairdresser:** Empress Catherine the Great of Russia (1729–1796) kept her personal hairdresser imprisoned in an iron cage for three years to protect the secrets of the royal coiffure. And Catherine was not the only one who insisted on such confidentiality; the Countess Saltikov also kept her stylist in a cage to make damned certain that "only her hairdresser knew for sure."

**Best Nose:** While studying at the University of Rostock, the Danish astronomer Tycho Brahe (1546–1601) fought a duel in which his nose was sliced off with a sword. Tycho commissioned a jeweler to make him a brilliant new nose of gold and silver which he wore for the rest of his life. The man with the golden nose is remembered for his precise observations of the heavens which paved the way for the discoveries of Kepler and Newton. The largest crater on the moon was named in his honor. Tycho also dabbled in astrology; he once forecast the exact date of Sulei-

Dwight D. Eisenhower's five-star pajamas

man the Magnificent's death, only to discover that Suleiman was already dead.

**Best Pajamas:** For many years Dwight Eisenhower wore a pair of red pajamas with five golden stars emblazoned on the lapels. They are now on display at the Division of Political History of the Smithsonian Institution.

**Best-Scrubbed Nation:** Great Britain's population is the cleanest of any nation in Europe, according to a study by the Swiss Union of Soap and Detergent Manufacturers. In 1974, the average per capita consumption of soap throughout the British Isles was 40 ounces. Switzerland was runnerup in the Great European Soap-Box Derby with 37 ounces of soap per person, followed by Germany with 34, Sweden with 33, France with 22.6, and the Netherlands with 22.2.

Personal hygiene, of course, can be carried just so far. Dr. Barry Keverne, an anatomy professor at Cambridge University, cautions that really vigorous scrubbing under a long, luxurious shower may wash away more than mere dirt; you might see the very odors that trigger the brain's sexual responses go down the drain.

**Best Sternutophile:** Margaret Thompson, a wealthy English gentlewoman, had a passionate fondness for sneezing. When she died in 1776, her will directed that she should be buried in a coffin packed with snuff. She named the six most prodigious snuff takers in London to be her pallbearers, and they were instructed to wear snuff-colored suits and beaver hats as they carried her remains to the cemetery. Six maidens preceded the cortege, inserting snuff into their own nostrils, distributing quantities of fine Scottish snuff to onlookers every twenty yards, and scattering snuff to the four winds like flower petals. The minister, for his services and continued prayers, was bequeathed one pound of snuff.

A list of other fervent snuff takers should include Dolly Madison, Marie Antoinette, Alexander Pope, and Samuel Johnson. A serious sniffer stores his supply of pulverized tobacco in a weasand—a container made from a cow's esophagus. And, if you are thinking about taking up the habit, experience has shown that white snuff is the best because it does not leave stains in your handkerchief, although some purists complain that it lacks the kick of the original brown variety.

**Best Tattoo:** King Harold, slain at Hastings, was identified by a tattoo across his chest reading "Edith and England." Lady Randolph Churchill always wore a wide gold bracelet to conceal the tattoo of a snake devour ing its own tail which encircled her left wrist. Czar Nicholas II, kings George V and Edward VII, and Queen Olga of Greece are among the other notables who have sported indelible works of art.

George Constantine, however, was undoubtedly the most elaborately tattooed man ever seen in America or Europe. Every square inch of his skin—even his eyelids, ear canals, and privates—was etched with swirling rococo designs in brilliant reds and blues. In all, Constantine was decorated with a total of 338 separate motifs: monkeys, leopards, crocodiles, lizards, eagles, flowers, storks, fruits, peacocks, salamanders, brawny men, naked women, and many, many more. P. T. Barnum paid him one thousand dollars a week to tour the United States.

One problem that has always plagued tattoo wearers is how to get rid of an unwanted design, such as an old girlfriend's name. Now a dermatologist at the University of Cincinnati has developed a method of eradicating old tattoos with a laser beam. The colored dye particles absorb the laser heat and are vaporized and obliterated almost painlessly.

---

**Worst Cosmetic:** Preparation H, the granddaddy of hemorrhoid ointments, is now being used as a facial cream by a growing number of women throughout the United States. Reports from the cosmetic grapevine indicate that small dabs of the viscous gonk will mask wrinkles and give the complexion a youthfully radiant look. One Beverly Hills woman told *Newsweek* magazine that she saves the ointment for chic gatherings, "when I want to look extra special." A New York druggist told of selling out her entire stock in one day soon after the craze hit the East Coast. "Everybody left with one lipstick and one tube of Preparation H," she said. "Nobody with hemorrhoids could buy it because everybody with wrinkles had grabbed it up."

Nonetheless, whatever its immediate positive effects, Preparation H users would do well to remember which end is up. Says one New York dermatologist, "Women could become sensitized to it after not much use. The skin could redden, burn, scale, and blister after a week of use."

**Worst Cure for Baldness:** Scientists have known for years that one method of halting hair loss in men is castration.

**Worst Fashion Craze:** Breast piercing was a popular fashion in England during the Gay Nineties. Women pierced their nipples and inserted gold and silver rings or jeweled pins. This immodest style is currently undergoing a revival among a sect of topless female sun worshipers on the French Riviera.

The maddest fashion of the nineteenth century was the brief-lived mono-bosom style; hideous undergarments forced the breasts together to make it appear that women were endowed with a single, massive, perfectly centered protruberance.

**Worst Hair:** Remember Dean Stockwell in *The Boy with Green Hair?* Well, green hair is no mere cinematographic sleight-of-hand: cases of green hair growing on real people have actually been recorded. At Framingham (Massachusetts) State College, professors Joseph Goodman and Robert Cooper reported an epidemic of green hair, especially among blonde co-eds. The reason for the color change, they said, was large quantities of copper in the town's water supply. Dr. Lawrence C. Parish of the University of Pennsylvania Medical School also noted that years ago the hair of copper workers in the mines of Pennsylvania and West Virginia frequently turned green.

**Worst Hair-Style:** *Coiffure à la victime* was all the rage during the Reign of Terror. Fashionable young women in England and France bobbed their hair and shaved the napes of their necks, in imitation of Marie Antoinette and the other victims of French Revolutionary justice who went to the guillotine. For an added touch of drama, some women wore blood-red ribbons around their necks.

**Worst Perfume:** This may give Catherine Deneuve a few sleepless nights but honor compels us to tell you anyway: Chanel No. 5 is made from pussycat sweat.

Jacques Leal, chairman of Chanel Ltd., told an interviewer recently that a principal ingredient of Chanel No. 5 is "the sweat of [an] Abyssinian civet cat," collected according to ancient tradition: "They put the cat's head into a sort of torture chamber," he explained, "whip it, the cat gets mad, and gives off a glandular secretion." While Mr. Leal later insisted that his remarks had been misinterpreted, cat fanciers everywhere were up in arms. In New York, the Society for Animal Rights suggested a mass boycott of Chanel's products, and *Cat Fancy* magazine urged its readers to write letters of protest to the company.

**Worst Shoes:** Along with spike heels, platform shoes are unquestionably the most hazardous and impractical footwear ever designed. A woman atop platforms runs about the same risk of serious leg or ankle injury as a skier about to descend a treacherous downhill slope. (There is an apocryphal tale of a woman who committed suicide by jumping off her platforms.)

Platform shoes in sixteenth-century Venice

The folly of platforms is by no means restricted to modern times. Venetian women of the Renaissance wore "chopines"—high pedestals—attached to the soles of their shoes. Chopines originated with courtesans, as did many other fashions, but they soon caught on with all the women of elevated society. Year by year chopines increased steadily in size until many women were walking around on stilts twenty inches high. It was quite precarious.

An English visitor to Venice found the style amusing. "All their Gentlewomen, and most of their wives and widows that are of any wealth, are assisted and supported either by men or women when they walk abroad, to the end they may not fall," he observed. Venetian men apparently thought the platforms were sexy, not because they liked their women tall, but because they liked their women unstable. It increased the likelihood that a gentleman would be called upon to offer a helping hand or a steadying embrace to a teetering lady. Chopines had one practical asset, too: they lifted a woman's feet and skirts high above the filth of the streets and open sewers. Nonetheless, in the sixteenth century, the doge of Venice condemned platforms as "frivolous, ridiculous instruments" and banned their manufacture, sale, or use.

In the United States, the Shaker religious communities of the nine-

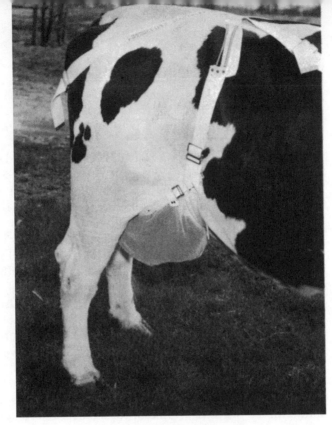

Cow brassieres
in sizes up to 108

teenth century produced highly idealistic, though ill-fitting shoes. One of the commandments of Shaker life maintained that "it is contrary to order to have right and left shoes," and their cobblers obediently ignored the obvious asymmetry of the human foot.

---

**Most Unusual Bathtub Ring:** Incredible as it may seem, thirty centuries of scientific progress have not improved the bathtub ring. Israeli archaeologists not long ago unearthed a three-thousand-year-old bathtub from the ancient Mycenaean palace at Pylos in Greece. When they trained infrared rays on the relic, they found a three-thousand-year-old ring as well. Invisible to the unaided eye, the ring, consisting of decomposed body oils, dead bacteria, and assorted organic detritus, reflected more infrared radiation than the unsoiled part of the tub.

**Most Unusual Bra:** Brassieres for cows? The Franksville Specialty Company, of Conover, Wisconsin, manufactures them and claims they're big sellers. Utilitarian rather than aesthetic, the bras keep the cows from tripping over their own udders. All sizes are available up to 108.

**Most Unusual Cause of Baldness:** Will eating fried chicken make your hair fall out? Quite possibly. The latest scientific findings point towards cholesterol as a principal cause of baldness among men.

**Most Unusual Coat:** In his memoirs Hieronymus Cardanus (1501–1576) comments on the standards of personal hygiene in the sixteenth century: "The men as well as the women are crawling with fleas and lice, and the odour from their armpits, feet, and mouths is quite terrible." One popular remedy for infestation was the "flea coat"—an outer garment made of thick fur designed to attract vermin away from the skin and hair of the wearer. A typical flea coat was a cape lined with wolf's fur, worn for a few minutes before going to bed to divest oneself of bothersome insects.

Some authorities believe that lapdogs were specially bred to decoy fleas, ticks, and lice away from their masters and mistresses. (Others, including Rabbi Dr. R. Brasch, author of *How Did Sex Begin?*, insist that lapdogs first were used by ladies at the Polish court of Boleslav the Bold to defend their chastity while their husbands were away fighting the Russian wars.)

**Most Unusual Deodorant:** A breakthrough in masculine deodorant sprays will be the most significant technological development of the next twenty-five years, according to Dr. Jib Fowles, chairman of the Committee on Studies of the Future. The spray will have no ozone-destroying fluorocarbons, says Dr. Fowles, and will smell "vaguely athletic, perhaps like a new baseball glove."

**Most Unusual Diapers:** A city ordinance passed in Charleston, South Carolina, in 1975, required horse owners there to diaper their animals. The law predictably met with opposition from the five horse-and-buggy operators in the old section of town, who considered it an unconscionable subversion of equine dignity.

Ultimately, the groundswell of opposition forced the city into a compromise: rather than diaper their horses, the drivers would use two-way radios to call for an emergency cleanup vehicle whenever needed.

**Most Unusual Figure:** The death of the French actress Anna Held is one of the great unsolved mysteries of Hollywood. Miss Held, as old-timers will remember, was the one-time wife of Flo Ziegfeld and was once the defendant in a celebrated lawsuit. A dairy company accused the starlet of refusing to pay sixty-four dollars for four hundred gallons of milk delivered to her hotel suite. Miss Held, who habitually bathed in milk to keep her complexion fresh and rosy, contended that the delivery was sour. The matter was eventually settled out of court.

Anna Held

Miss Held's principal claim to fame, however, was the most dramatic hourglass figure ever to appear on stage or screen. When she passed away suddenly in 1918, her doctors officially maintained that the cause of death was myeloma. But after an in-depth investigation, reporters revealed that the proud actress had been experimenting with crash diets and had actually had her lower ribs surgically removed to preserve her incredible eighteen-inch waistline at age forty-five. The newspaper reports claimed that Anna ultimately died of internal injuries caused by tight lacing of her corset.

**Most Unusual Fire Hazard:** A properly teased Afro, says Dr. Bruce Zawacki of the University of South California, contains hundreds of tiny air pockets that make the entire head of hair a lethal firetrap.

**Most Unusual Pants:** Eldridge Cleaver, the former Minister of Information for the Black Panther Party, has designed a revolutionary new line of men's pants. The tight-fitting slacks, called Cleavers, are provided with a pouch or "appurtenance" into which the wearer fits his sexual organ; presumably one must also wear altered underwear—or none at all. "There are some beautiful materials out for women's pants but men can't wear those," Cleaver notes. "They can in my designs since there is no mistaking they are men's pants." The radical designer believes the sexual honesty of his pants will reverse the unisex trend in fashion, will diminish neuroses and inhibitions, and consequently will lead to a decline in the violence of society.

Cleaver's "new exhibitionism" harks back to the days of the codpiece. First introduced in the late Gothic period, this remarkable accessory started out as a simple leather case and gradually became a spectacular ornament of display made of brightly colored silk. At the same time, the codpiece grew larger and larger until, as R. Broby-Johansen says in *Body and Clothes,* "it achieved its most provoking proportion in 1560"—about the size of a small melon. Most men, however, were not that amply endowed and many used the extra room to store small change, a handkerchief, or bon-bons. Bernard Rudofsky, author of *The Unfashionable Human Body,* claims "a musical version of the codpiece was once the vogue in South Burma." The Peguans, he says, wore golden and silver bells hanging from their virile members and made a delicate tinkling sound as they walked through the streets. Rudofsky believes that the codpiece died out not because the male genitals are unattractive, but "rather they seem too unsubstantial to warrant display."

Mr. Cleaver should be pleased to hear that help is on the way. An article in *Vogue* magazine recently described a program of silicone injections for men.

**Most Unusual Perspiration:** Hippopotamuses exude red sweat when hot, excited, or in pain.

**Most Unusual Soap:** During the days of the Roman empire, when bath soap was both primitive and scarce, wealthy ladies often washed themselves with a sugary mixture consisting of twenty pounds of crushed strawberries and two pounds of raspberries.

**Most Unusual Underwear:** Architect Buckminster Fuller says a good way to stay warm on underheated airplanes—one he's tried himself—is to stuff newspapers under your clothes.

**Most Unusual Wedding Gown:** Lady Madonna, a chain of boutiques dealing exclusively in apparel for mothers-to-be, now sells a full line of maternity wedding gowns for expectant brides. Price: $1,500.

# Travel and Places

**Best Caveat for Americans in Paris:** In Paris, muncipal law permits a taxi driver to bar you from his car if he thinks you will leave an offensive odor behind you.

**Best Guide Book:** An invaluable aid when traveling abroad is *The Insult Dictionary*, subtitled "How to be abusive in five languages." There are well-chosen words in this book for every aggravating situation. For a reckless taxi driver in Berlin: *"Ihre Fahrgäste benötigen wohl eine Sonder-Unfallversicherung?"* (Do you make your passengers take out special accident insurance?) On the crowded Metro in Paris: *"Pouah! Ça pue les doigts de pieds!"* (Phew! Whose socks are those?) At that "two-star" hotel in Florence: *"Rimane mai nessuno qui piú di una notte?"* (Does anyone ever stay more than one night?) Or on a date in Barcelona: *"Guarde sus pezuñas para otra ocasión."* (Keep your filthy paws to yourself.).

   *The Insult Dictionary*, available from Wolfe Publishing Ltd., London, contains seven hundred entries, all insolent but clean. For expert advice on saltier language we recommend an article in *Horizon* magazine by Charles Berlitz. If you are groping for an interjection in Leningrad, Berlitz suggests a heartfelt *"huy morzhevyi"* (You walrus member!). Or for a shiftless clerk on the Trans-Siberian Railroad, you might try *"b'yez-pasportnik"* (meaning passportless person), a strong Russian equivalent for "lazy lout."

   *"Too-tze"* is the most potent obscenity in Peking. Literally translated it means turtle, which sounds innocuous enough unless you are familiar with the old Chinese legends concerning the turtle's incestuous proclivities. More direct, but in the same spirit, is the Spanish curse *"tu madre"* or the intensive form *"chinga tu madre."* While in France, the favorite

affront is to point your index finger at your temple, twist it abruptly, and snarl *"connard!"* or simply *"con!"* (an indelicate term for the female organ).

As vile as they may be, such expressions are tame compared to the epithets one hears on the streets in Mexico City. Radio personality Barry Farber tells us that there is a Mexican obscenity so offensive and so familiar that cab drivers merely have to beep its distinctive rhythm on their horns to make fellow motorists fly into a rage. Similarly, you do not need to know a word of Greek to hold your own in Athens. Just give them the old *"mountza."* Turn your palm face out and shove it energetically toward your antagonist. Berlitz claims this gesture is guaranteed to provoke a fight or at least a "double *mountza*" in return.

**Best Means of Transportation:** One method for judging the efficiency of various modes of transportation is to compare the energy consumed in moving a given distance as a function of the weight moved. Using this formula, physicist S. S. Wilson, writing in *Scientific American,* found that "an unaided walking man does fairly well (consuming about .75 calories per gram per kilometer) but he is not as efficient as a horse, a salmon, or a jet transport."

But give a man a bicycle, an ordinary three-speed Raleigh, and he becomes a highly efficient traveling machine. "With the aid of a bicycle . . . the man's energy consumption for a given distance is reduced to about one-fifth (roughly .15 calories per gram per kilometer)." With stout-hearted pedalling, a biker can travel three, four, or even five times faster than he can walk. Moreover, "the cyclist improves his efficiency rating to number one among moving creatures and machines," Wilson found.

One hundred years ago the bicycle entered into direct competition with the trains—and lost. During the 1870s, a Mr. M. Lawson began construction of a nationwide railroad network for quadracycles. Lawson founded a company called Cyclorail, Inc., to manufacture specially designed four-wheeled pedal vehicles; the wheels locked into grooves in the bikeway's wooden rails, making spills and derailments impossible.

The Cyclorail motto was, "A true gentleman needs no motor other than himself." As this was before the invention of the pneumatic tire, the bikeway promised the most comfortable ride available—much smoother than a horse, a buggy, or the two-wheeled "bone-shaker" could provide on the unpaved roads of the day. And riding the bikeway would be far less expensive than booking passage on the new locomotive-powered trains. Lawson raised enough capital to begin laying track in New Jersey. He also built service areas along his right-of-way, where a weary cyclist could spend the night and have his quadracycle repaired. But the scheme soon collapsed. Long-distance pedalling, however, efficient as it might have been, did not appeal to most speed-loving Americans.

**Best Taxi Drivers:** *"Best* taxi drivers?"* you say to yourself. *"As if there were *good* ones."* Well, there *are* good taxi drivers—in some places, anyway—and in spite of what George Custer might have said had he lived in the twentieth century instead of the nineteenth, they're not just the dead ones, either.

Some are in Minneapolis, a few work in Seattle, and there are about a half-dozen scattered throughout the nation east of the Mississippi. However, the world's most competent, courteous, honest taxi drivers are in London, England.

Some 15,000 licensed taxi operators work in London, and that number represents but a fraction of all who would aspire to the trade if only they could hack it. Many can't. A recent study in *The New York Times* noted that no fewer than half the 1,500 men who apply each year for a cabdriver's license there wash out before they have completed the battery of police examinations and rigorous studying of routes and techniques that qualify them.

Unlike so many of their myopic brethren in Rome and New York, London drivers are literate, well mannered, and willing to keep their political views under their hats. They also rarely get lost and are ruthlessly honest. Not so long ago, writes New York *Times* London correspondent Bernard Weinraub, a London newspaper reporter masquerading as a foreign tourist spent a day hailing taxis and found that "in eleven out of twelve cases taxi drivers took the correct route and fare."

**Best Toll Booth Attendant:** Wondering about those massive tie-ups on the Pennsylvania Turnpike? A woman working there as a toll collector was dismissed from her job for having sexual intercourse with a truck driver while she was on duty. (The actual charge was "Conduct unbecoming an employee.") She was ultimately rehired, largely due to pressure from the Teamsters Union.

**Best Way to Get a Seat on the Subway:** The best way to get a seat on a crowded bus or subway is to ask for it. That was the finding of fifteen graduate psychology students from the City University of New York. The landmark study, initiated by Dr. Stanley Milgram, determined that when students approached dour, dyspeptic commuters and said, "Excuse me. I'd like to sit down. Could I have your seat?" approximately 49 percent of those asked promptly yielded their places.

Not surprisingly, sex was a significant variable in the results. When women students asked to sit down, 66.7 percent of the male riders got up, but only 34.7 percent of the female passengers gave away their seats. Furthermore, only 30 percent of the female passengers would give their seats to men. The best tactic is apparently a simple direct request. When, as an additional variable, the students offered a reason for wanting a seat, such as "May I sit down so I can read my book?" their overall success rate declined to 37.2 percent. "When the asker gives no reason, it appears that people supply their own reasons," Dr. Milgram explained. "They tend to think the asker is not feeling well, or that he must have some good, unspoken reason of his own."

**Worst Air in the World:** The world's worst air pollution is in Seoul, South Korea, according to a report issued by the Asian Foundation, in San Francisco. In a one-kilometer-square section of Seoul's Youngdongpo industrial district, for example, over thirty tons of dust particles fell in a single month. Seoul's pollution, says the report, is largely the product of thousands of antiquated buses vomiting diesel exhaust fumes into the air every day.

**Worst Airport:** The competition, frighteningly, is tough. One possibility is Washington National Airport. "It has one runway that is 6,870 feet long, only 370 feet longer than minimum standards allow," says Brian Power-Waters, a commercial airline pilot with nineteen years' experience behind him. "This is sufficient in good weather, but on a wet strip it could easily put you in the river. The airport should be made into a park."

Nevertheless, Power-Waters is reluctant to pin "world's worst" honors on National. He notes that New York City's La Guardia Airport, for example, has two runways that are barely 7,000 feet long and end at the water's edge. "Were it not for a dike and a series of pumps," he writes in an article in *Harper's*, "La Guardia at times would be under water." Indeed, for the death wishers among us, there is no better way to cap a vacation or business trip than to zoom in low towards La Guardia over the forbidding waters of Jamaica Bay. It is only at the last possible moment that the runway appears, just a second or two before the plane actually touches down. Until it does, passengers are treated to the thrill of watching the water rise at them and the events of their lives pass before their eyes. Says pilot Power-Waters, "Buildings obstruct the traffic controllers' view of the airport, and the airport is without a full complement of controllers. . . . La Guardia should be no more than an airport for light planes."

Chicago's Midway Airport, kid sister to O'Hare International, is also relatively unsafe. But the International Federation of Airline Pilots singles out Los Angeles International as the nation's worst. The reason is that LA International is located near residential areas, mandating that pilots land to the east and take off to the west between midnight and 6:30 A.M., in order to keep noise to a minimum. While this hamstringing of navigational mobility protects the eardrums and sanity of local residents, it makes piloting an airplane unduly hazardous.

**Worst Cruise:** When 103 vacationers paid for a "Cruise to Nowhere," aboard the pleasure ship *World Discoverer*, they had no idea that that was precisely what they would be getting for their money.

A few miles out of Norfolk, Virginia, the embarkation point, the ship ran into a thick fog and then had generator trouble. It finally had to be towed back to port.

**Worst Museum:** Not long ago, a Reuters reporter, armed with a notebook and a strong stomach, became the first Western journalist to visit the "House of Bones of Our Ping Ting Shan Compatriots," a museum of war atrocities in Fushun, China. Some three thousand men, women, and children, comprising the total population of Ping Ting Shan village, were machine-gunned to death and their bodies unceremoniously dumped in a mass grave by Japanese soldiers in 1932. A stark-looking L-shaped building was later built around the grave by Chinese locals to commemorate the massacre. As Reuters noted, "except for a narrow walkway around the edge, the entire floor area is littered with skeletons, shreds of clothing and bullet-riddled gasoline cans." Poking up through the wreckage are descriptive captions such as "Pregnant Woman," "Baby Wrapped in Charred Cloth," and "Sabre Wound in Skull." Parking is free. No gift shop.

**Worst News for Italophiles:** In 1975, Italy had to *import* over 1,500 tons of pasta—mostly from Greece.

**Worst Subway:** After stepping off the IRT at rush hour, the French Prefect of Transportation Maurice Doublet commented, "If they brought New York's subway to Paris, I assure you there would be a revolution." Like Monsieur Doublet, most visitors to the city are appalled at how noisy, crowded, filthy, obsolete, and dangerous the New York trains really are. And with the recent financial crisis, the fares and crime rate have gone up while the service has deteriorated even further. Outrageous graffiti covers every square inch of the trains and stations like a multicolored infectious rash, and even the calligraphy seems to be declining in quality. Though you would hardly know it, the Transit Authority spends $500,000 a year just trying to eradicate the spray-painted names and obscenities; one official noted, "We are always looking for new solvents."

Carolyn Jabs has enumerated some of the best stops to miss in an article in *The Great Escape*, a book on travel and exotic places. The 125th Street IRT station, she says, "is in danger of collapse, passengers in danger of mugging," while in the 110th Street IND station, "Sawdust and water grace the tunnel." For our fare however, the Grand Concourse in the Bronx is the most dismal and depressing platform in the universe of public transport. And before moving on to a brief discussion of the Rolls Royces of mass transit, it is only fair to warn the reader that the Philadelphia subway is not exactly the Disneyland monorail either.

In contrast, the subway systems of Montreal, San Francisco, and Moscow are dazzlingly clean, quiet, and efficient, and the Budapest underground, built at the turn of the century, is a quaint antique rich with atmosphere. But the best ride in the world for one franc is still Monsieur Doublet's own Paris Metro; the best stop is the Louvre where there are glass cases displaying Egyptian statuary and Greek vases right alongside the gum machines.

**Worst Tour:** If you are crazy about liquid- and solid-waste disposal, you will find the guided tour of the Paris sewers utterly enthralling. Parisians are justifiably proud of having the finest system in Europe, and, indeed, the vast maze of pipes, sumps, and subterranean tunnels is considered one of the great achievements of civil engineering. But that does not make it a nice place to visit, and you would not want to live there. About all you can say in favor of this excursion is that the echoes are nice, and the sights, sounds, and smells will linger with you for days.

The Michelin Green Guide to Paris, which ranks all the major tourist attractions, gives the sewers no stars out of a possible four.

**Worst Tourist Attractions:** Some years ago veteran travel writer Joseph Wechsberg published an article called "What Not to See in Europe." Tourists would do well to heed his worldly wise advice. Heading Wechsberg's comprehensive list of "don't sees" were two highly touted German attractions, the Oktoberfest in Munich and Hitler's Eagle's Nest, high atop Mount Kehlstein near Berchtesgaden.

The fabled Oktoberfest, which begins a bit prematurely in late September, is one of the largest and most commercialized of European festivals. Every year over 700,000 weenies of every description are devoured and washed down with 3,300,000 quarts of German beer. Wechsberg accurately characterizes the event as "an exhaustive study in noise and vulgarity, beer and belching."

The Eagle's Nest was Hitler's private Alpine retreat. To get there you take the special Bundes-Post bus from Berchtesgaden up a winding, hair-raising mountain roadway to a point 450 feet from the summit; from there you ride the rest of the way on a brass-plated elevator that lifts you through a shaft of solid rock to the "tea room." But don't bother. Despite the beautiful view from the top, the trip is not worth the effort. The comforts are second-rate and the chalet is swarming with tourists, more than a few of whom are nostalgic for the days when the master of the house vacationed there with Eva Braun. Quoth Wechsberg: It is "highly discommended."

Wechsberg also comes down hard on such major attractions as Rome's Palazzo Venezia ("when something goes wrong in Italy, it's a beaut") and Warsaw's Palace of Culture. Other great places to miss include "the 3-Os," overdone, overcrowded, and overpriced resorts like Capri, Cannes, and St. Tropez, and "the 3-Ds," the dull, dreary, depressing industrial cities of Birmingham, Lille, Frankfurt, Salonika, and the Hague.

Despite rising prices, Europe is still the number one tourist Mecca, but New Guinea is also bidding for it's share of the tourist dollar.

Tribal leaders from central New Guinea convened in Port Moresby recently to try to convince the people running the Mount Hagen Show, a popular cultural festival, of the tourist appeal of cannibalism.

The profit-oriented tribesmen offered to eat human flesh at the show, arguing that it would be a great crowd-pleaser. Rather than hunt down fresh victuals, they agreed to dine on a body supplied by a local hospital. The show's organizers declined the offer. Very politely.

**Worst Town:** Until a few years ago, Eckley, Pennsylvania (population 200), was just another mining town, no more drab or depressed than hundreds of other communities in the Appalachian Mountains. But everything changed when Hollywood discovered Eckley.

Paramount Studios was searching for a location to shoot *The Molly Maguires*, a movie about radical Irish coal miners in the 1870s. Eckley was selected over a number of other candidates, thanks to its authentic, sooty, nineteenth-century ambience. Paramount invested $500,000 to pry off aluminum siding, remove wires and electric signs, and reconvert the asphalt main street to a swampy dirt road. The transformation was enough to make one gasp for breath; in no time Eckley began to look like the tuberculosis and black lung capital of the world—a grim reminder of how wretched conditions in the old company towns really were.

After the filming was completed, Paramount was preparing to restore the town to its original, 1970s splendor, when a banker from nearby Hazleton, Pennsylvania, came up with an idea. He persuaded the townspeople and the movie company to leave the grimy sets in place. The banker then arranged to purchase the entire town for $100,000 and turned it over to the state to operate as a museum of coal-mining life. Tourists can now visit Eckley (from 9 to 5 daily except holidays), talk to the retired miners about their hazardous work, and experience for one fleeting moment the worst that the industrial revolution has to offer.

**Worst Traffic Hazard:** The tiny sheikdom of Abu Dhabi earns $30 million a day in oil revenues, and the affluent Abu Dhabians are using their newfound wealth to buy automobiles—thousands of them. Although new car registrations are increasing at a rate of 1,200 per month, traffic jams are not yet a problem, nor are speeding and tailgating. The worst traffic hazards in Abu Dhabi are camels.

In that desert country camels are naturally camouflaged and blend right into the landscape. Drivers, especially if they have had a drink or two too many, are prone to crash into slow-moving dromedaries with disastrous results. Consequently, the government is sponsoring a massive campaign to outfit the humps of Abu Dhabi's six thousand camels with high-visibility, day-glow orange safety jackets.

**Worst United States City:** Was Mayor Ed Hanna of Utica, New York, merely joshing when he advised his constituents to leave the town and never come back "because it's a lousy place to live"? *We* assumed that he was in dead earnest and accordingly rated Utica "Worst United States City" in *Felton & Fowler I.*

And perhaps it *is* the worst. But in November 1975, Mayor Hanna won reelection and, with it, more time to initiate and push through the plans and projects that may well improve this depressed and depressing upstate New York community. In his first year in office, Hanna cut his own salary from $20,000 to $1, dropped 300 workers from the municipal payroll (there were only 900 to begin with), produced a budget surplus of $337,000, and lowered real estate taxes for the first time since 1947.

He also had the door to his office removed from its hinges and took to answering his own phone, both acts aimed at making himself "the People's Mayor" he claims to be.

It might be fair, then, to leave the industrious Mayor Hanna to his good works, looking in on him in a few years to see if he has succeeded in whipping wheezy, arthritic Utica into bristling good health. Perhaps we'll be surprised.

Besides, if we shine the proctologist's probe too strongly on Utica we may well blind ourselves to such urban hemorrhoids as Detroit, Newark, or Philadelphia.

In 1975, Arthur Lewis, associate editor of *Fortune* magazine, set out to identify "the worst American city" in an article of the same title in *Harper's*. Limiting his inquiry to the nation's fifty most populous cities—that lets Utica off the hook immediately—Lewis based his ratings on seven criteria: crime, health, affluence, housing, education/professional achievement, atmosphere, and amenities. Newark, New Jersey, for example, is the nation's most crime-ridden city (our assessment of Compton, California, in *Felton & Fowler I* notwithstanding), although there are more forcible rapes committed in Washington, D.C. than anywhere else. The city with the worst *air* is New York. The worst place to be sick is—again—Newark.

Lewis took his twenty-four tables of statistics and distilled from it all a single statistical abstract that made Newark the absolute worst city in the country. "The city of Newark stands without serious challenge as the worst of all," he writes. "It ranked among the worst five cities in no fewer than nineteen of the twenty-four categories, and it was dead last in nine of them. . . . Newark is a city that desperately needs help."

---

**Most Unusual Cruise:** It was the policy of many municipalities in fifteenth-century Germany to gather together the insane and imprison them on riverboats. These floating insane asylums were known as *Narrenschiffs* or ships of fools. In *Madness and Civilization*, Michel Foucault explains that the *Narrenschiffs* served a dual purpose. First, of course, "To hand a madman over to sailors was to be permanently sure he would not be prowling beneath the city walls." And secondly, it was thought at the time that the insane had literally lost their souls, and thus the ships of fools were pilgrimage boats carrying "cargoes of madmen in search of their reason: some went down the Rhineland rivers toward Belgium and Ghent; others sailed up the Rhine toward the Jura and Bensançon."

Brain collection at Cornell University

**Most Unusual Exhibit:** After nearly fifty years in cold storage, the fabulous brain collection of Dr. Burt Green Wilder was put on public display at Cornell University in 1973.

Brains were Dr. Wilder's passion. As a professor of animal biology, he devoted his life to investigating the correlations between brain size and intelligence. His findings were monumentally inconclusive, but all was not in vain; over the years he assembled in airtight glass jars the largest, most prestigious gallery of brains the world has ever seen.

Dr. Wilder acquired brains from idiots, brains from paupers, and brains from executed criminals. He even had some success in persuading "learned people" to bequeath their brains to him for study. Each new addition was carefully weighed, measured, labeled, classified, and preserved in formaldehyde. It was a big job—too big for one man alone—and so Dr. Wilder founded the Cornell Brain Association to which he willed his own brain upon his death in 1925.

Regrettably, the brain trust was relegated to a basement after Wilder passed on. When the brains were rediscovered in 1973, only 122 had survived the decades of neglect; the rest had to be thrown away. The recent Cornell exhibit featured fourteen of the most celebrated specimens. Visitors were fascinated by Edward Howard Ruloff's massive four-pound cerebrum, by far the largest in the collection. Ruloff was executed for murder in 1871. Helen Hamilton Gardener's brain also attracted favorable comment. Ms. Gardener (1853–1925) was a prominent feminist and women's suffrage leader, who in 1888 attacked a U.S.

A historic site—America's first commercial broiler house

Surgeon General's report that claimed the brains of men and women are structurally different. She left her own brain to the Association "to help provide superior female brains for future research." Also on display were the thoughtful donations of poets, professors, physicians, and one curiously labeled "an erotic German."

Eager to contribute? Sorry, the Cornell Brain Association is no longer accepting new organs. But if any individual or institution would like to begin its own collection, we refer you to the step-by-step surgical guidelines found in Dr. Wilder's handy pamphlet, *How to Make a Brain Bequest*. (See also "Health and Death," *Worst Brains*.)

**Most Unusual Historic Site:** A chicken coop in Georgetown, Delaware, has been officially listed in the National Register of Historic Places. A commemorative plaque was installed during a brief ceremony in the fall of 1974. And federal regulations now protect the coop from being razed to make way for a new superhighway or shopping center.

The coop was nailed together in 1923 by Mrs. Wilmer Steele, the mother of the American broiler industry. And now her first coop has been restored to its original condition by the Delmarva Poultry Industry Association.

**Most Unusual Hotel (Economy):** For the troglodyte tourist, there are two good hotels in the town of Matmata, Tunisia, both of them subterranean. As a matter of fact, all five thousand inhabitants of old Matmata live underground in a cluster of man-made pits and tunnels. Originally, the caves served as protection. In that flat open desert region of Tunisia an ordinary village of brick buildings constructed aboveground is hopelessly conspicuous. Invading armies could sight it from miles away. But by hiding their town ten to forty feet underground, the Matmatans ensured that their enemies could never locate them. Later they also discovered that the excavations provided a cool, naturally air-conditioned retreat from the blazing African sun.

The two hotels in town are Marhala and the Sidi Driss. At either one you can enjoy dinner, a comfortable bed, and a Continental breakfast for about four dollars per person. The floors are compacted dirt, but they are hard, smooth, and polished by centuries of use. Space is at a premium, and you may find yourself with as many as five roommates. If you stay on the second floor, you will have to shinny up a rope ladder to your quarters. Otherwise the accommodations are very similar to the Sheraton.

The Marhala has over forty rooms and one hundred and fifty beds, with all the modern conveniences. Hot and cold running water is provided along with showers, electric lighting, and flush toilets. There is a cavernous cocktail lounge where the whiskey bottles rest on shelves cut out of the solid stone walls, and where you will be entertained by local snake charmers and belly dancers. Make your reservations through Transtours Tunisie. American Express cards are accepted.

There is, by the way, an underground mansion just north of Fresno, California. It was the life's work of Baldasare Forestiere, a Sicilian immigrant who learned to dig while working on the construction of the Boston subway system. Using only a pick, a shovel, and a wheelbarrow, Forestiere mined himself a subterranean home of one hundred rooms. He tirelessly bored parlors, patios, passageways, and a solarium open to the sun, where he raised citrus trees and a vegetable garden. At his death in 1941, he was hard at work on an enormous underground ballroom. The catacombs are now a museum known as Forestiere's Underground Gardens.

**Most Unusual Hotel (Luxury):** Hotel living is a luxury inaccessible to all but the very wealthy or the very discerning. At least it was, until the recent grand opening of the Kennelworth, a luxury hotel on New York City's posh Upper East Side, where rooms on the American plan rent for as little as nine dollars a day. One catch, however: the hotel is open to dogs and cats only.

"This is a one-of-a-kind facility," says owner Les Wiener, an ex-actor who spent $250,000 making the Kennelworth worthy of such biped-oriented counterparts as the Plaza in New York or the Gritti in Venice. "It answers a realistic need for pet owners who are loath to leave animals in the traditional kennel atmosphere." The 116-room hotel is equipped with a unisex beauty salon, modern kitchen, and airport limousine service. Guests and their owners can choose from among three room sizes and four color schemes—in spite of the fact that dogs and cats are notoriously color blind—and every room is steam-cleaned daily and furnished with piped-in music and a window with a view.

"Our main care is to keep the animals happy," says Wiener. Toward that end, he has hired a staff of ten—among them a dietician, a portrait artist, domestic help, and workers to comfort homesick animals and walk them four times a day on the indoor village green around which the circular hotel is built.

And the food? The Kennelworth kitchen offers an enticing menu of simple but wholesome dishes, including dog biscuits and beef stew. For those guests with more demanding palates, take-out service is available from the nearby Animal Gourmet, the world's most unusual restaurant (see *Felton & Fowler I*, page 231).

**Most Unusual Island:** The briefest-lived piece of real estate on record was Kovachi Island located just off Guadalcanal in the South Pacific. With little warning, an underwater volcano coughed up a lava mountain, which rose to a height of thirty feet. The new *terra incognita* was reported by a number of passing ships, but by the time investigating teams and cartographers arrived at the scene, Kovachi had collapsed and sunk eight feet below the ocean.

Another geological disappointment occurred in December of 1967, when the blue Pacific near the Tonga Islands turned a sickly green and yellow. The water boiled furiously; a 6,000-foot column of smoke and steam belched into the air. By December 11, a half-mile-long island had formed on the site. Metis Shoal, as it was named, grew steadily until it was a full four miles long. Then suddenly, like Atlantis, it disappeared beneath the waves forever.

Finally, an unnamed island, believed to be a chunk of Brazil, was sighted by a U.S. Navy vessel in the Caribbean on July 4, 1969. It measured about fifteen yards in diameter with ten or twelve palm trees growing on it. Located just south of Cuba, the island was drifting in a westerly direction at about 2.5 knots per hour. Later it was reported missing, believed sunk.

**Most Unusual Package Tour:** Tokyo Ryoko, a Japanese travel agency, has put together a $480 six-day package tour to nearby Taiwan which, it claims, has been a howling success among both Japanese and American tourists. The tour price includes hotels, sightseeing, and high-quality dental care at one of Taiwan's clinics, where prices average a fifth of what they are in Japan and the United States.

**Most Unusual Regularly Scheduled Airline Flight:** Loganair, a Scottish airline, operates the world's shortest regularly scheduled flight—a thrice-weekly shuttle from Papa Westray to Westray in the Orkney Islands. The trip takes two minutes normally, eighty seconds or less with a tailwind.

"The flight's a godsend to folks in these parts," says John Scott, the owner of Westray Airport. "Only a few hundred people live on Papa Westray and they have to come to Westray to see doctors or shop." Sea passage between the neighboring North Sea islands is a chancy affair at best, and the reliability of the flights has made them such a big hit that the twin-engine eight-seater is often booked a full week in advance. One-way fare is $10.35, but that's without movies, drinks, or meals. "There's just no time," says pilot Andy Alsop. "By the time the passengers have their seatbelts fastened they're halfway there."

**Most Unusual Street:** Spook Hill, in Lake Wales, Florida, is an unusual name for a most unusual street. Apparently no one has heard of the law of gravity there because it is blithely disobeyed every day of the year, to the frequent amusement of both tourists and natives. When the parking brake is released, a car parked in neutral will roll mysteriously uphill, as will ball bearings, tennis balls, and Florida grapefruit dropped experimentally on the ground. Even water flows uphill on Spook Hill. Or so it seems.

"We've had all kinds of people trying to figure it out," says the City Manager of Lake Wales, Carl Cheatham. "Engineers come out here with tripods and levels measuring the slope of the ground and go away shaking their heads. It's an optical illusion, of course, but exactly how it works I'll never tell. I won't be the one to destroy the mystery of the hill."

**Most Unusual Travel Book:** *An Historical and Geographical Description of Formosa* by George Psalamanazar contained some pretty sensational revelations, including the assertion that Formosans annually sacrifice eighteen thousand babies to their bloodthirsty gods on New Year's Day. This widely popular work, published in 1704, also claimed that Formosans ate nothing but raw meat, poisonous snakes being the preferred fare.

The manners and customs described in the book seemed laughable and outlandish, but English readers accepted them as authentic. After all, this was the account of a genuine Formosan aborigine, George Psalamanazar, who had been converted to Christianity by Chaplain William

Innes of the English army. Indeed, Oxford University had appointed Psalamanazar to its faculty as a special instructor in Formosan language and culture, and the Anglican Church had commissioned him to translate the Old and New Testaments into his strange native tongue.

From lecture platforms all over England, Psalamanazar captivated audiences with vivid descriptions of his homeland, only recently discovered by Western explorers. He told them about the severities of Formosan law. ("Whosoever shall strike the King, Intendant, or Governor shall be hanged by his feet till he dies, having four dogs fastened to his body to tear it to pieces," warned one grisly statute.) He pleased classicists by revealing that Greek was taught in every Formosan school. And he added color to his lectures with a short discourse in Formosan, which had a sound and grammar like no other language known to linguists. (Man is translated as *banajo;* woman is *bajane;* and so on.)

Psalamanazar's fatal mistake was to claim that Formosans live underground during the hot months of the year. At a question-and-answer session in 1706, a skeptical Dr. Edmund Halley, the astronomer who gave his name to the comet, asked how long the sun shone down the chimney on an average day. The Formosan's answers were wildly incorrect as Halley proved using simple mathematics and his knowledge of latitude. Psalamanazar was revealed as a fraud. He was not a Formosan; he had never been to Formosa; he had never been outside of Europe. The gibberish he spoke and the stories he told were all complete fabrications.

Later, Psalamanazar, whose real name is lost in history, reformed and became a respected journalist and essayist. After his death in 1763 and the subsequent publication of his memoirs, Samuel Johnson called him "the best man I ever knew."

# Architecture

---

**Best Bricks:** Bricks made from compressed cow dung have been developed by research scientists at the University of California at Los Angeles. A spokesman for the UCLA labs says the bricks are "elegant, cheap, and as strong as ordinary bricks at half the weight." Suggested trade names include "KauHaus" and "MooBrick."

**Best House of Cards:** A five-and-a-half-foot, twenty-eight story house of cards was built in 1974 by Dave Novikoff and Ted Michon, students at the California Institute of Technology.

In building the house, the two men brought all their engineering and mathematical expertise to bear, but even then it was no piece of cake. "We discovered very quickly that careful alignment of each story was necessary for any structure above fifteen stories or so," said Michon. To achieve that alignment they used plumb lines and carpenters' levels to make the building platform perfectly horizontal. And they recorded the entire project on videotape so that they were able to watch their earlier failures collapse in slow-motion and see where they went wrong.

After completing the twenty-eighth story of their house, Novikoff and Michon took photographs. Then they hubristically tried to add a twenty-ninth story. They were on their way when the entire structure shivered and collapsed. Two hundred twenty-four cards were involved. No injuries were reported.

---

**Worst Pyramid:** The ruthless Mongol warrior Tamerlane was known for leaving behind a macabre calling card at the site of a conquest: a huge pyramid built from the skulls of people killed by his soldiers. At Delhi there was. such a pyramid consisting of 100,000 skulls; at Isfahan was one with 70,000. And in Sebsewar, Persia, Tamerlane once playfully interred 2,000 men, women, and children within a tomb of brick and stone.

**Worst Time Capsule:** There is a time capsule built into the Washington Monument, somewhere, but to date no one has been able to find it. The capsule, lined with zinc and stocked with a representative assortment of documents and artifacts, was enclosed in the twelve-and-a-half ton marble cornerstone that was laid on July 4, 1848. Over twenty thousand spectators were on hand for the ceremony; however, once construction began no one took the trouble to remember where the cornerstone had been placed.

But the cornerstone was not the only part of the monument to disappear. On the night of March 6, 1854, a band of anti-Catholic partisans stole onto the construction site and escaped with a valuable chunk of Roman marble that had been donated to the project by Pope Pius IX. It, too, was never found.

**Most Unusual Architect:** There is a plaque on Ferdinand Cheval's Palais Idéal that reads, "If there is anyone more obstinate than I, let him fall to work." Each day for thirty-four years Cheval, a diligent postman, walked eighteen miles through the Drôme countryside of southern France delivering the mail and collecting colorful stones. After the deliveries were completed, he would work late into the night on his magnificent obsession—an ornate, hand-carved palace. It was an edifice too small to be of any practical use, except perhaps as a residence for elves, but Cheval labored over it for 65,000 hours. He mixed the mortar and sculpted every pillar and portico singlehandedly.

Cheval had no training whatsoever in art or architecture, but he insisted that his castle represented "the rebirth of all ancient architectures in primitive times." Every style and every architectural influence can be seen somewhere among the amazing assembly of tombs, grottoes, turrets, and caryatids. The architect Corbusier has praised this wild and uninhabitable structure, and the poet André Breton claimed the obscure postman as a spiritual ancestor of surrealism.

Measuring twenty-six yards long, fourteen yards wide, and twelve yards high, the Palais Idéal is built on a scale too small for even a child to enter. It is flamboyant, florid, and dreamy like the jungle temples of Angkor Wat and, like an exotic sand castle, it is a monument to pure self-expression.

The Bank of Vernal, Utah

The Palais Idéal was completed in 1902 and Cheval died soon thereafter. He had hoped to be buried near his masterpiece, but the Church refused the necessary permission. On Cheval's tombstone is inscribed an epitaph he composed himself: "The child arrives in this life with hands full of the future. If he knows how to use it, he will leave them full of remembrances."

**Most Unusual Bank:** Writer Roy Bongartz points out that the Bank of Vernal, in Vernal, Utah, is the only bank in the world built from bricks sent through the mail. In 1919 the people of Vernal discovered that it would cost less to mail the bricks from Salt Lake City, seven to a package, then to have them shipped commercially.

**Most Unusual Engineering Feat:** When the Army Corps of Engineers took over construction of the Washington Monument in 1880, they were faced with a seemingly unsolvable problem: since there had been no work done on the project in twenty-five years, the ropes and scaffolding leading to the top had rotted with age. If additional bricks and mortar were to be hauled to the top, the ropes would have to be replaced, but no one had any idea how to get the *ropes* to the top either. The project seemed stymied even before it had begun.

Then, a brainstorm. Inside the 156-foot-high hollow shaft, a wire was tied to the leg of a pigeon. A gun was fired and the frightened bird flew skyward, emerging from the top, where it was killed with a blast from a second gun. The pigeon fell to the gound, still tied to the wire, which the engineers then used to haul up heavier cables and, ultimately, the scaffolding needed to complete the job.

**Most Unusual Floor:** The floors of the outer rooms of Nijo Castle, in Kyoto, Japan, squeak loudly when trod upon, and the squeaks bear an uncanny resemblance to the song of the nightingale. No mere structural quirk, the squeaks were designed into the floor as a warning system for the shogun, who lived at the castle in continual fear of would-be assassins.